TIME AND DIFFERENCE IN RABBINIC JUDAISM

TIME AND DIFFERENCE IN
Rabbinic Judaism

Sarit Kattan Gribetz

PRINCETON UNIVERSITY PRESS
PRINCETON & OXFORD

Copyright © 2020 by Princeton University Press

Requests for permission to reproduce material from this work
should be sent to permissions@press.princeton.edu

Published by Princeton University Press
41 William Street, Princeton, New Jersey 08540
99 Banbury Road, Oxford OX2 6JX

press.princeton.edu

All Rights Reserved

First paperback printing, 2022
Paperback ISBN 9780691242095

The Library of Congress has cataloged the cloth edition of this book as follows:

Names: Kattan Gribetz, Sarit, author.
Title: Time and difference in rabbinic Judaism / Sarit Kattan Gribetz.
Description: Princeton : Princeton University Press, [2020] | Includes
    bibliographical references and index.
Identifiers: LCCN 2020033753 (print) | LCCN 2020033754 (ebook) | ISBN
    9780691192857 (hardback) | ISBN 9780691209807 (ebook)
Subjects: LCSH: Time in rabbinical literature. | Rabbinical
    literature—History and criticism.
Classification: LCC BM496.9.T47 K38 2020 (print) | LCC BM496.9.T47
    (ebook) | DDC 296.1—dc23
LC record available at https://lccn.loc.gov/2020033753
LC ebook record available at https://lccn.loc.gov/2020033754

British Library Cataloging-in-Publication Data is available

Editorial: Fred Appel & Jenny Tan
Production Editorial: Ali Parrington
Cover Design: Layla Mac Rory
Production: Erin Suydam
Publicity: Kate Hensley & Kathryn Stevens

Cover art: Jacqueline Nicholls, *Brachot 2* (2012)

This book has been composed in Miller

For Jonathan, Daniela, Sophie, and Max

CONTENTS

Prologue · ix

INTRODUCTION
1

CHAPTER 1
Rabbinic and Roman Time
35

CHAPTER 2
Jewish and Christian Time
92

CHAPTER 3
Men's and Women's Time
135

CHAPTER 4
Human and Divine Time
188

CONCLUSION:
Temporal Legacies: What Difference
Does Time Make?
228

Acknowledgments · 251
Notes · 257
Bibliography · 323
Index · 383
Figure Credits · 391

PROLOGUE

I RECENTLY DEVOTED A DAY to renewing my passports. Early in the morning, I took the subway to midtown Manhattan for my appointment at the Swiss Consulate. It was important for me to arrive on time; otherwise I would have missed the twenty-minute slot I had scheduled months in advance. When I entered the pristine and peacefully quiet office, a clerk greeted me by name and helped me immediately. The appointment lasted precisely twenty minutes, and I was told that the passport would be delivered to my home in exactly two weeks' time. The machine used to generate passport photos and other biometric data looked as though it belonged to the distant future. I barely had time to notice the state-of-the-art design of the space, the modern paintings on the walls, and the beautiful views before I headed out.

My next stop was the Israeli Consulate, two blocks away. I hadn't made an appointment because there are no appointments to be made; one can arrive at any time during their working hours, whenever one pleases. After I passed through numerous rounds of security and x-ray machines, I entered the office, which was already filled with dozens of people, some standing and many others sitting in the waiting area. Before I had time to take a number, I heard a young man yelling at the clerk behind the counter: "The passport will only be mailed in three weeks? The website says that passports are returned in two weeks, and now I came for nothing, as my trip is two and a half weeks away. *Bizbazt et ha-zman sheli!* You've wasted my time!" While I waited and waited in the chaotic room—televisions blaring, families chatting boisterously—for my number to be called, I noticed that the place had not been renovated in years. Photographs from archaeological excavations hung from the walls.

The contrast between the Swiss and Israeli consulates could not be more pronounced, but I am especially amused by their different attitudes to time: appointments in advance versus spontaneous walk-ins; instant service versus long waits; certain versus uncertain time frames; uncompromising punctuality versus temporal flexibility.

These differences don't surprise me, though. I find myself in these consulates precisely because I grew up with a Swiss mother and an Iraqi Israeli father. Competing conceptions of time and temporal rhythms were a part of my childhood. I vividly remember two oft-repeated patterns. The first unfolded whenever we took a family vacation. My mother, who has an internal Swiss clock, was ready to leave for the airport hours before our scheduled departure and grew increasingly nervous that we would not arrive at the check-in desk a full three hours in advance of take-off time, as the airline recommended. My father, for whom punctuality is not particularly important, would slowly finish packing his suitcase and find other excuses to stall so that he would not have to wait unnecessarily at the gate. This would occasionally result in a missed flight, but a missed flight was usually not the end of the world because there would be another flight headed to the same destination soon enough, and my father had patience to wait for it. My second memory is from extended family gatherings, when my Swiss relatives arrived at the exact time listed on the invitation, while my Iraqi Israeli aunts and uncles interpreted the start time as a suggestion, anytime after which they were welcome to show up. The former left at the end of the meal or event, even if they had no plans to go elsewhere thereafter, as the norms of politeness dictated; the latter preferred to stay indefinitely, as the host brought out additional rounds of desserts, nuts, and fruit, and everyone continued to enjoy one another's company, as the norms of politeness dictated.

These temporal cultures exist simultaneously in the present—neither is more "advanced" or "modern," nor more "primitive" or "backward," neither superior to the other. They are both contemporary. They are simply different, and they exist today for a complex set of interwoven cultural, political, economic, social, and historical reasons.[1] Both cultures, along with their attitudes to time, are beloved to me, and I am a product of both. Within every society, various time frames and attitudes to time operate simultaneously, and they all continually intersect, not only in my family but also on a global level, mutually affecting one another.

The study that follows explores the ways in which hourly, daily, weekly, and annual times unite groups and communities as well as form distinctions between them, and how temporal rhythms change over time. Time, I argue, can create or reinforce difference, and it can also elide difference. Moreover, such a process can be variously motivated: the formulation of daily schedules and annual calendars, for example, can be consciously conceived. But the process can also be less deliberate, an unintended consequence of other activities and traditions.

I have a third passport, too. I am reminded of this on the subway ride back from the consulates as I pass the post office in the Bronx where I recently renewed my American passport. It is my experience of time here, in the United States, that has most significantly informed my interest in time as a marker of difference. Adhering to two conflicting calendars has struck me as one of the most disorienting aspects of observant Jewish life in America. Observing the Sabbath, and thus being unavailable to work (or drive, and much else) on Saturdays, kept me from pursuing acting professionally and fencing competitively when I was younger. In college, and now as a university professor, I regularly face the challenge of Jewish holidays overlapping with class meetings, rather than the luxury of my vacations corresponding with my festivals. Being an observant Jewish American entails a constant negotiation between two—or more—temporal rhythms, ones that are rarely aligned. The same is true, for example, for an observant Muslim American. In these cases, again, time accentuates difference.

In this book, I argue not only that time establishes difference but also that it can obscure or diminish difference. One of my favorite artifacts from life in New York City is the annual "Alternate Side Parking Suspension Calendar" that the city distributes to its residents. The calendar contains a list of religious holidays when the city suspends its parking rules (in place to allow street sweepers to tidy up the roads) so that those celebrating any of the holidays on the list need not be bothered to move their cars. I do not know the politics behind the creation of these lists, how some holidays—such as Eid Al-Fitr, the Asian Lunar New Year, Ash Wednesday, Orthodox Good Friday, Diwali, the Feast of the Assumption of Mary, Martin Luther King Jr. Day, and Yom Kippur—are included and others are not, nor when new ones were added and others removed. Regardless, the printed calendar that hangs on our fridge has assembled a remarkably diverse set of religious and civic festivals, lining them up alongside one another and, in the process, eliding their differences. From the perspective of sanitation workers, parking enforcers, and car owners, they are all regarded equally as days on which some members of the city have more sacred tasks to fulfill than moving their cars. This is particularly striking on years when two or more holidays fall on the same day. The calendar also alerts residents to the sacred days of their neighbors, coworkers, and friends, of which they might otherwise not have been aware—but from which they likewise benefit, for they, too, are exempt from moving their cars during these holidays, even if they do not observe them. In this seemingly mundane document—"junk mail," as it were—the city's parking calendar has actually synchronized the various holidays and created a rhythm of time that bridges, rather than accentuates, the religious and cultural differences of its city's residents. It is through this idiosyncratic parking calendar that the city is able both to communicate its commitment to pluralism and to cultivate respect for others and acceptance of the diverse religious and cultural traditions of those who live within its city limits.

The stakes for determining time remain high. I lived in Jerusalem as I worked on this book. One of the aspects of this year abroad that I most appreciated was experiencing the temporal rhythms of a different civic calendar. I felt a sense of belonging when shops closed early on Friday afternoons (I realized, of course, that others felt alienated by these same temporal rhythms, that did not acknowledge Christmas or the start of a new year on January 1 or a secular lifestyle, which is precisely the point). Living in a context that recognized—and indeed was organized around—the same calendar and weekly schedule that I observed highlighted for me what it means to temporally "fit in" and accentuated for me, when I returned to the United States, the challenges of being a temporal "outsider."

Nonetheless, experiences in Jerusalem reminded me that other dimensions of difference can be constructed even among those who share a calendar. On a research tour of the Jewish quarter of Jerusalem's Old City that included a visit to the Hurva Synagogue, only the men in our group were permitted to enter the main sanctuary. The women were told that, as it was "time for prayer [*sha'at tefillah*]," we were forbidden from viewing the sanctuary from within. We would need to climb a narrow winding staircase to the women's balcony for a glimpse at the space. I looked at my watch in bewilderment: it was 10 a.m., long past the time for the morning recitation of the Shema according to traditional rabbinic law.[2] "The time for prayer," I realized, was being treated as a fluid temporal category, invoked whenever the men within the sanctuary pleased, for they could begin spontaneously praying as soon as a woman pried the door open. In the Hurva Synagogue, the time for prayer functioned as much as a way of differentiating women from men—and thereby limiting women's access to the sacred space and their participation in the practices of prayer and worship that occurred within it—as a fixed period of time during which prayer was mandated and recited. Time and difference, in this case as in numerous other instances from ancient sources that I analyze in the pages that follow, have always been, and remain, intimately intertwined. The one constitutes the other.

Back in New York, I taught an undergraduate course about time and value. During one particularly illuminating discussion with my students, I asked each of them to articulate what it meant for them to be "punctual." Their answers varied; there were just as many answers as students in the room. As we listened to one another, we learned that for some students being punctual meant being early, while for others showing up before the end of an event constituted punctuality. I shared with students the idea of "Jewish Time" (which simply means "late"), and they introduced me to "Dominican Time," "CPT," and "Gay Standard Time."[3] We realized together not only that conceptions and practices of time are culturally specific, relative, and local but also that time can deliberately be used, individually and communally, to assert and celebrate ethnic, racial, religious, or gendered difference. The legislation and use of time can oppress others. It can likewise be harnessed as a form of resistance.

Many contemporary traditions and conceptions of time and difference have roots in antiquity: in calendar reforms, in conceptions of punctuality and power, in the formation of rituals and of religions, in debates about the value of time and how best to spend it. This book focuses on one segment of this ancient history—the experiences and writings of late antique Jews, and specifically those preserved in the corpus of rabbinic literature—to illuminate the ways in which time operated, in antiquity as it does today, to generate, construct, crystallize, articulate, blur, and dismantle various kinds of difference. It studies some of the rhythms of time that animated the rabbinic world of late antiquity, the temporal footprints that the rabbis left behind in their writings, and the lasting impact that they had on those who have continued to grapple with the legacies of these times and differences.[4]

TIME AND DIFFERENCE IN RABBINIC JUDAISM

INTRODUCTION

THE FOUNDATIONAL DOCUMENT of rabbinic Judaism, the Mishnah, opens with a question about time: מאמתי, "from what time?" A person must declare devotion to God each morning and evening; the question is: *when*? Rabbinic literature is replete with concerns about time and the triangular relationship between people, God, and the hour.

These concerns about time were timely in the early centuries CE, when rabbinic Judaism emerged and flourished. In a period of Jewish theological creativity and ritual innovation, in the context of the Roman Empire and its imperial calendar, and in competition with developing Christian times, how did the rabbis of late antiquity conceive of the temporal rhythms of Jewish life? This book examines how, in this complex cultural context, rabbinic texts from the first six centuries CE constructed imperial, communal, individual, and divine rhythms of time through the practices that they mandated and the stories that they told.

Though time may appear to be natural and universal, based on elements such as the rising sun, the phases of the moon, or the seasons, time is, in fact, culturally constructed and communally specific. Temporal institutions can cultivate shared notions of time along with shared communal identities, but they can also differentiate those who mark their time in certain ways from those who mark their time differently. Time—as it is constructed, interpreted, and enacted—thus creates both shared worlds and different worlds, and through measurements and manners of conceptualizing and organizing time, different groups intertwine with each other in multiple ways. Mapping rabbinic timescapes, as this book does, demonstrates the central role that time played in how rabbis attempted to construct Jewish identity, subjectivity, and theology—indeed, how they constructed their worlds—during this formative period in the history of Judaism.

The overarching argument of this book is that the rabbis used time-keeping and discourses about time to construct crucial social, political, and theological difference. The book demonstrates, through close analysis of rabbinic texts, that as the rabbis fashioned Jewish life and theology in the Roman and Sasanian worlds, they articulated conceptions and structures of time that promoted and reinforced new configurations of difference in multiple realms. It explores four such realms: imperial, communal, gender, and theological cosmology.

Rabbinic texts constructed imperial difference by distinguishing rabbinic time from Roman time; communal difference by separating Jewish time from Christian time; gendered difference by dividing men's time from women's time; and theological difference by contrasting the time of those who dwelled on earth from the time of those in the heavenly sphere, including God and the angels. The four chapters that constitute this book analyze rabbinic texts that employ time to negotiate difference in each of these realms.

The book further contends that the processes through which various forms of difference are constructed in rabbinic sources, be they, for example, differences between men and women or between Jews and Christians, cannot fully be understood without also considering the constructions, discourses, and practices of time that undergird them. That is because time—its conception and its organization—serves as a powerful mechanism through which to enact difference and forge identity. Uncovering the specific ways in which conceptions of time and practices of time-keeping were used practically and discursively by rabbinic authorities actively to forge multiple types of inter- and intracommunal difference reveals the central role that constructions of time play in processes of differentiation within rabbinic texts. The book's primary intervention in the fields of rabbinics, ancient Judaism, and the study of religion in late antiquity is to identify the temporal dimensions that facilitated the construction of difference in the rabbinic corpus. The history of difference and the processes through which difference is forged, in rabbinic sources as in other corpora and cultures, are more fully comprehended when the role of time is both acknowledged and investigated. That conceptions of time and practices of time-keeping are often assumed to be natural or self-evident (or indeed to be objective) because they so frequently rely on natural or bodily phenomena (whether the rotation of the sun or the aging of a body) masks the fact that conceptions of time and practices of time-keeping are just as constructed as difference itself. It is the task of this book to investigate how time was used in rabbinic sources to construct the differences—between rabbis and Romans, Jews and Christians, men and women, humans and the divine—that the texts, and often their readers, take for granted.

This introductory chapter is structured in three parts. Part I introduces the underlying theoretical framework of the book by reflecting upon the categories of "time" and "difference" and the interrelationship between the two. Both time and difference are examined conceptually, informed by previous scholarship as well as the peculiarities of rabbinic sources, with an eye toward distilling what is particularly illuminating about probing the intersection of the two. Part II seeks to transport the reader back in time to the first and early second centuries CE, in order temporally to situate the rabbinic texts analyzed in the subsequent chapters. Three interrelated cultural and political dimensions of the rabbis' late antique world are discussed. Rather than set within a conventional historical contextualization, however, the story is told as a history of time, highlighting specifically temporal aspects of the Jewish, Greco-Roman, and Christian contexts in which the rabbinic movement emerged and developed. Part III outlines the book's organizational structure, methodological orientation, and indebtedness to previous scholarship. The chapter concludes with a note about the terminology used in the book. Just as we cannot experience the world outside of time, so too we cannot escape the limits of language—leaving us to seek words that make adequate sense of the world and of time.

Part I: Time and Difference

WHAT IS TIME?

The question "What is time?" has preoccupied history's most sophisticated minds. More than two millennia of effort, however, has failed to yield a clear answer to this seemingly simple problem. Consider Augustine's iconic puzzlement as he groped for the proper language to articulate ideas about time: "What, then, is time? There can be no quick and easy answer, for it is no simple matter even to understand what it is, let alone find words to explain it."[1] Maimonides expressed similar exasperation about the notion of time, explaining that "the analysis of the concept of time has presented difficulties to most thinkers, so much so that they became bewildered as to whether it had any real existence or not."[2] Virginia Woolf, too, thematized the mysteriousness of time when she wrote, in 1928, that "time, unfortunately, though it makes animals and vegetables bloom and fade with amazing punctuality, has no such simple effect upon the mind of man. The mind of man, moreover, works with equal strangeness upon the body of time. An hour, once it lodges in the queer element of the human spirit, may be stretched to fifty or a hundred times its clock length; on the other hand, an hour may be accurately represented on the timepiece of the mind by one second. This extraordinary discrepancy between time on the clock and time in the mind is less known than it should be and deserves fuller investigation."[3]

Despite difficulties articulating notions of time, this vexing topic has endlessly fascinated scholars from antiquity to the present.[4] Naturally, each scholar's approach is informed by her particular methodological and disciplinary angle of inquiry: physical, metaphysical, phenomenological, biological, sociological, historical, religious, narrative, psychoanalytic. Philosophers, theologians, and scientists have contemplated whether time actually *is* (is time real? is it an illusion?), *what* time is (is it a precondition of being? a part of experience? a sense?), and *how* time functions (does it flow? is it relative?).[5] Such questions have generated an extensive debate the outcome of which remains (necessarily, perhaps) inconclusive.

Sociologists, anthropologists, historians, and scholars of religion have largely set aside questions about the absolute nature of time, instead choosing to interrogate time as it is conceived and comprehended, and how it functions, within particular societies. Such scholars have sought to understand how cultures and religious traditions conceptualize time, how these conceptions manifest themselves in the ways communities structure and narrate their times (rhythms of daily life, calendars, the recording of history and chronology, and so on), and what they reveal about the values and views of these cultures.[6] Precisely because assumptions about time seem so natural and intuitive, it is easy to forget that these, too, are cultural products that merit contextual and historical investigation. Asking fundamental questions about how people in periods and places far removed from ours made sense of time can lead to surprising insights about their lives.

This book follows the latter approach, aiming to understand how a particular group of people (the ancient rabbis), as their ideas were preserved in a particular set of texts (rabbinic literature), conceptualized time and coped with the need to organize and signify it, and how their structuring of time constructed new identities, subjectivities, and forms of difference. Rabbinic sources devote much interpretive energy to outlining the precise timing of daily, weekly, and annual practices; many rabbinic texts can be regarded as elaborate deliberations about how a member of the rabbinic community might best organize and use their time in accordance with rabbinic values. Speculation about cosmic origins, memories of mythical pasts, constructions of chronologies and histories, and anticipation of a redemptive future also feature on the rabbis' agenda, alongside the nitty-gritty details of determining hours and setting calendars.[7] Such concerns animated the rabbis and provide a broader temporal and historical context for understanding rabbinic attitudes to daily time. The study that follows therefore navigates between the conceptual and the practical, the symbolic and the quotidian, weaving together the history of daily life, social history, cultural studies, religious studies, and rabbinics.[8]

Not long ago, some scholars of the Hebrew Bible and ancient Israel held that the limited temporal range of biblical Hebrew grammar and its tenses and the absence, in biblical texts, of philosophical discourses on the nature of time similar to those found in Greek and Roman philosophy signal that biblical sources—and thus ancient Israelites and later Jews—lacked chronological and temporal sophistication.[9] In response to this claim, the historian Arnaldo Momigliano passionately insisted on the opposite: ancient Jewish texts indicate that ancient Jews conceived of time and temporality in ways no less complex and compelling than their Greek counterparts.[10] Biblical sources, he acknowledged, are often more concerned with structuring quotidian time than in philosophizing about time in the abstract. "Biblical writers speak about time in the concrete way which would have been understandable to the ordinary Greek man, for whom there was a time of day in which the agora was full," he quipped.[11] Meditations about the abstract category of time might not have been central features of rabbinic texts either, but their absence does not mean that rabbis did not hold sophisticated opinions about time.[12] Indeed, they did.

This book is most interested precisely in the fashioning and conceptualization of time for Momigliano's "ordinary Greek man" on his way to the agora as well as the Roman woman going to the forum or the nearby church, her Jewish neighbor making his way to synagogue for evening prayers before the time for the recitation of the Shema has passed, and this neighbor's wife who, at the same time, walks in a similar direction to immerse herself in the ritual bath.[13] How did their conceptions and experiences of time shape their respective identities and senses of self? When did the temporal rhythms of the daily lives of Jews and non-Jews and of men and women overlap? When did they diverge? And how did time play a role in the differentiation and synchronization of these people and their communities?

Rabbinic sources, written by a limited number of elite men in intellectual and scholastic contexts, do not provide decisive answers to these questions. Scholarship has emphasized just how little is known about how authoritative the rabbis were in the early centuries of the Common Era, how many Jews actually followed rabbinic laws, and how closely those who did complied with the many details outlined in rabbinic sources.[14] The rabbinic corpus, however, does constitute a fascinating set of texts—an elaborate discourse—that reveals how these rabbis imagined, and hoped to shape, the times and identities of these subjects in relation to one another.[15] This book, therefore, examines how the late antique rabbis whose ideas were preserved within the rabbinic corpus conceived of and constructed the rhythms of daily time, irrespective of whether their compositions describe a social "reality." The book focuses on the timescapes that emerge in rabbinic texts and the possible social effects that this rabbinic system might have had on those who read their texts, heard their sermons, or abided by their prescriptions, either in late antiquity or in subsequent periods, when rabbinic tradition proved more authoritative and more widely studied, scrutinized, and observed.[16]

DEFINING DIFFERENCE

Difference, as a concept, operates on multiple levels in this study. *Time and Difference in Rabbinic Judaism* argues that the conceptualization and organization of time were mechanisms the late antique rabbis employed to construct various forms of difference and, occasionally, the mechanism through which they also unsettled such difference. Moreover, new conceptions and structures of time articulated in rabbinic texts promoted new configurations of difference. As with "time," the concept of "difference," too, has a long history in linguistics, philosophy, and critical theory (Derrida's *différance* captures the temporality of difference itself: always simultaneously distinct and deferred).[17] As Jonathan Z. Smith has written: "Difference is rarely something simply to be noted; it is, most often, something in which one has a stake. Above all, it is a political matter."[18] Along these lines, difference throughout this study is construed not as simple fact but as continually constructed through oral and written discourses and the circumstances that condition such discourses.[19]

Of particular interest are rabbinic texts that concern competing time frames and how these time frames constructed and reinforced multiple dimensions of difference—imperial, communal, gendered, and theological. That is, when sources insist that rabbis and Romans, Jews and Christians, men and women, humans and God, function within different time frames, how do rabbinic sources reify these very dimensions of difference? For example, how do they construct gendered difference through maintaining that men and women operate in differing timescapes? In part, rabbinic texts cultivated gendered difference by differentiating men's and women's times; similarly, these texts shaped rabbinic-Roman difference by distinguishing between rabbinic and Roman time. Excluding women from men's time or banning rabbinic participation in Roman time, in turn, contributed to the construction of the difference that is assumed in these very distinctions. Additionally, various dimensions of difference also intersect, such that, for example, women's and men's times not only create gendered difference but can simultaneously reinforce ethnic, class, status, and other differences as well.

Time, so fundamental to human experience, plays a unique, if underappreciated, role in processes of differentiation. Émile Durkheim noted that "we can conceive of time only by differentiating between discrete moments."[20] Natural phenomena such as the movement of the heavenly bodies, the tides, animal migrations, and plant cycles serve as points of reference for marking distinctions in time. Institutions as mundane as annual calendars, the unit of the week, rituals that mark the start and end of each day, and the portioning out of hours divide time and differentiate between years, months, weeks, days, and hours. On the one hand, then, communities cultivate the category of time through the differentiation of time into identifiable units. On the other hand, while calendars and schedules differentiate between moments of time, they are also mechanisms through which communities synchronize multiple types of time onto a single grid. Paul Ricœur, Jack Halberstam, and Carolyn Dinshaw, among others, remind us of the existence of many different dimensions of time: cosmic time, mythic time, historical time, lived time, narrative time, queer time.[21] Calendars, for example, not only *differentiate* between days and months; they also *merge* the imagined universal "cosmic" time of the world and the "historical" time cultivated by a community with the personal "lived" time of the individual.[22] The very same calendars, schedules, and rituals that distinguish between different units of time thus synchronize various dimensions of time into a unified system.

Additionally, temporal institutions such as annual calendars, weekly schedules, and daily rituals at once create commonality between people and differentiate those people from others. Shared time frames have long been recognized as mechanisms that foster group cohesion and community.[23] But when calendars apply to particular people and not to others, when certain rituals are mandated for some but not all members of a community, or when narratives are told from one perspective rather than another, they also cultivate different conceptions of time and temporality that, in turn, construct communal difference.[24] Distinct communities can maintain competing calendars and festivals, and groups and individuals within a single community can interact with time in different ways, even when they look to the same temporal markers or use similar technologies of time-keeping to anchor their days, nights, weeks, months, and years.[25] Eviatar Zerubavel writes: "One of the most effective ways to accentuate social contrasts is to establish a calendrical contrast. Schedules and calendars are intimately linked to group formation, and a temporal pattern that is unique to a group often contributes to the establishment of social boundaries that distinguish as well as actually separate group members from 'outsiders.'"[26] These different temporal rhythms and conceptions in turn reinforce other dimensions of difference. Marking time is thus itself a practice of synchronization and differentiation—both between moments and between subjects and communities. Instances of temporal transgression, when they occur, simultaneously accentuate and upset those differences.

Rabbinic sources affirm the multiplicity of time. Tractate *Rosh Hashanah*, devoted to the New Year and the rabbinic calendar, begins with an explanation not of a single moment in time but of four: "There are four New Years: on the first of Nissan is the New Year for Kings and Festivals; on the first of Elul is the New Year for the Tithe of Cattle . . . ; on the first of Tishre is the New Year for Years, Sabbaticals, Jubilees, and planting vegetables; and the first of Shevat is the New Year for Trees."[27] The Mishnah introduces its section on the rabbinic calendar with an acknowledgment that annual time does not have one absolute beginning on a single date on the calendar. Rather, various months each mark new temporal beginnings of different sorts.[28]

Other rabbinic sources recognize that distinctions in time-reckoning differentiate Jews from others. The Mekhilta de-Rabbi Ishmael states that a solar eclipse is a bad omen for gentiles and a lunar eclipse is a bad omen for Israel because gentiles reckon time by the sun and Israel reckons time by the moon.[29] Genesis Rabbah further identifies the lunar calendar with the descendants of Jacob and the solar calendar with the descendants of Esau.[30] A theological dimension is added to the Mekhilta's description of Israel's calendrical system. By observing the moon every month, the Israelites regularly "lift up their eyes to their father in heaven."[31] The lunar calendar is thus presented as a mechanism for differentiation not only because it is distinct from the solar calendar but also because its rituals connect Israel more directly to its God. Moreover, the Mekhilta distinguishes between competing chronological systems. The midrash notes that biblical sources usually "count according to their own era" when they date events in reference to the Exodus or the temple's construction or destruction (as they do in Numbers 1:1, 33:38; 1 Kings 6:1, 9:10; Ezekiel

40:1) but that they also occasionally "count according to the era of others" when they date events relative to the start of foreign rulers (as they do in Hagai 1:15).[32] The midrash dramatically argues that relying on the times and histories of others rather than on "their own era" diverts Israel's devotion away from God and eventually leads them to subjugation and oppression under the very authorities upon whose times they rely.[33]

These rabbinic passages, as well as others across the rabbinic corpus, depict the coexistence and tension of multiple times and time frames. They even explicitly acknowledge that different groups of people divide time differently and that doing so differentiates them one from the other. Regarding the organization of time as a mechanism for the construction of identity, subjectivity, and difference suggests that time, in these rabbinic texts, was not only (or necessarily) a dimension through which individuals and communities pass but also (or rather) a dynamic force—a powerful if intangible tool that was harnessed and even manipulated to effect certain results.[34]

Part II: Contextualizing Rabbinic Times

The classical rabbinic era encompasses, roughly, the period between the formation of the earliest rabbinic source, the Mishnah, in the second and early third centuries CE, and the redaction of the Babylonian Talmud, dated variably to the fifth or sixth century CE. Many additional rabbinic sources were composed throughout this period, as well as thereafter. There are a number of ways to contextualize these sources historically: with reference to previous and contemporaneous events; in light of internal developments in Israelite and Jewish history; in relation to the Roman and Sasanian empires in which the texts were composed; and in conjunction with other religious communities who lived alongside, sometimes in harmony and sometimes in tension with, rabbinic communities in those empires (these contexts, interrelated and mutually constitutive as they are, are themselves not easily distinguishable). Historical contextualization in these multiple realms informs the textual analyses throughout this book. The section that follows, in contrast, provides select glimpses into the temporal worlds of the first and second centuries in order to situate the emergence of rabbinic Judaism and rabbinic engagement with temporal phenomena within a context of shifting conceptions of time and practices of time-keeping. Rather than a comprehensive pre-history, it aims to set the scene.

THE DESTRUCTION OF THE TEMPLE AS A TEMPORAL TRAUMA

The second Jewish temple stood in Jerusalem from 515 BCE, when the region was controlled by the Persian Empire, until 70 CE, when it was destroyed by

Roman forces. Sources from this period as well as modern scholarship about it often conceive of the temple as a center of gravity, anchoring Jewish cultic and intellectual life. The temple is portrayed, in such contexts, as a *spatial* center—a monumental building, a place of cultic worship, a site of pilgrimage—whose destruction left a spatial void as the war dispersed and fragmented the Jewish community in Jerusalem to other regions of Palestine, to Rome, and beyond.[35] But the temple can also be conceived as a *temporal* center and its destruction as a temporal trauma. After all, the temple's destruction and the broader political and theological shifts of the late first and early second centuries CE disrupted the way in which time was conceived, anticipated, and experienced. This is one of several contexts in which rabbinic conceptualizations and organizations of time can fruitfully be placed.

For the several hundred years when the temple operated, its daily sacrifices and associated cultic practices, along with priestly night watches, marked and divided day and nighttime hours. Weekly or biweekly schedules of priestly tasks enforced somewhat longer cycles of liturgical time, and annually recurring festivals punctuated the year with agricultural, biblical, and historical celebrations and an influx of worshippers to Jerusalem.[36] All of these rhythms variably shaped time for the priests who worked within the temple, their families who ate from their sacrifices and offerings, and the residents of the city, whose lives were necessarily affected by its scents, its sounds, and the congestion that it caused at certain times of the day, month, and year, even as these times affected distinct populations differently.

The temple's rhythms—real and imagined—also informed time for those unable to smell the smoke of its sacrificed animals, hear its trumpet's pre-Sabbath call, and witness the entourage of palm and myrtle on the festival of Sukkot. Biblical texts such as the book of Ezekiel and the Priestly and Holiness Codes constructed a world that anchored itself according to tabernacle/temple times even in the absence of a physical temple.[37] Many in the diaspora sent annual monetary contributions to help sustain the temple, and they were invested in the idea and practice of pilgrimage at particular times of year.[38] To cite another example, from the Second Temple period: one of the central ways through which those who lived about thirty kilometers east, in the Judean desert commune at Qumran, differentiated themselves from those who remained in Jerusalem was through their solar calendar, which conflicted with the temple's lunisolar calendar.[39] In their view, the solar calendar was the correct one, and they thought that it ought to be used in the temple. Thus, the members of this community consciously aligned their temporal daily and weekly schedules to this ideal temple calendar, even as they deliberately replaced sacrifices with prayers and developed new liturgical practices to punctuate those times.[40] The Songs of the Sabbath Sacrifice marked Sabbath times, for instance, through liturgical song instead of animal sacrifices.[41] The book of Jubilees, over two dozen manuscripts of which were found buried in the caves adjacent to Qumran, extolls the virtues of the sun for its calendrical and chronological time-keeping abilities, drawing a sharp contrast to texts such as Ben Sira, which emphasizes the moon's function as a temporal marker.[42] This conflict of times most dramatically appears in Pesher Habakkuk, in which the temple's high priest, identified as the Wicked Priest, is described as visiting the community's Teacher of Righteousness when he was celebrating the Day of Atonement, specifically to disrupt his worship because, according to the Jerusalem temple's calendar, the festival was set for a different day.[43] Even while at odds with the calendar of the Jerusalem temple, those in the Qumran community imagined themselves to be maintaining the temple's accurate times (which, they argued, the corrupt authorities in Jerusalem had gotten wrong), to remain in sync with the times of the heavenly temple and its ministering angels, and to capture eternity through their daily practices.[44] The Psalms Scroll, for example, claims that David composed 364 songs, one for each day of the year, corresponding to the daily temple offerings; 52 songs for the weekly Sabbath offerings; and 30 songs mirroring the temple's new moon and festival offerings, linking the community's solar calendar with the temple's sacrificial schedule.[45] The sect also maintained a schedule of 24 priestly courses that James VanderKam writes "raises intriguing questions about why a group that was physically and ideologically separated from the current temple cult took the trouble to align the periods when the priestly courses would be on duty with other entities in their calendars . . . the act of coordinating the periods of service for the priestly divisions with the movements of the heavenly luminaries has a deep theological meaning."[46] Steven Fraade adds that such calendrical and liturgical texts from Qumran "convey[ed] the idea that the life of the community *as a whole* was in rhythmic concordance not only with the divinely created and serving celestial rotations, dominated by the sun, but also the cultic cycle of priestly service, which could be understood to function both humanly and angelically in the absence of a legitimate physical temple."[47] For those at Qumran who did not have a physical temple, as presumably also for others in the broader region, the temple's temporal rhythms of sacrifice and festivals nonetheless served as a powerful conceptual template for their own times of prayer and purity.

Even farther from Jerusalem, in communities that did not develop in opposition to the temple priesthood but that were at a significant geographical remove from it, the temple's times nonetheless anchored some of their own conceptions of time. The first-century philosopher Philo of Alexandria, who only visited Jerusalem in middle age, aligned the temple and its times with other biblical and non-biblical temporal rhythms in his meditation about daily, weekly, seasonal, and annual time. In *The Special Laws*, Philo presents a "festival manual" that lists ten festivals, their origins, and the practices associated with each one.[48] The list begins with a festival that Philo calls "every day" and then proceeds to discuss the Sabbath, the day of the new moon, three festivals related to Passover, Pentecost, the Trumpet Feast, the Fast, and the Feast of Tabernacles. Philo's description of the festivals universalizes their meaning; he incorporates agricultural and historical dimensions of the festivals with Stoic and Platonic philosophical ideas.[49] Nonetheless, Philo refers to a biblical list of sacrifices from Numbers 28–29 as the grounding source for his explanation of these Jewish festivals.[50] The most surprising festival on Philo's list is the first, which he titles "every day [ἡμέρα πᾶσα]." Though there is no such festival mentioned in the biblical book of Numbers or elsewhere in ancient Jewish sources, Philo interpreted the description of the morning and evening *tamid* offerings and the *minha* offerings brought each day in the tabernacle (and later in the temple), mentioned in Numbers 28:1–8, as one reason for treating each day as a festival. Though Philo's reliance on the Septuagint's Greek caused him to misunderstand the biblical text, he creatively structured his philosophy of daily time in part around the assumed regularity of the sacrificial rituals of the temple.[51] The imagined rhythms of daily sacrifices became a scriptural hook on which to hang his call to dedicate each day to meaningful philosophical contemplation.

Even though there were multiple rhythms of time throughout the Second Temple period, many of which were not connected to the temple, temporal ties to the cultic center ran deep and wide. Thus, the temple's destruction—and the war that led to its destruction and to tremendous loss of life, property, and hope in and beyond Jerusalem—caused temporal crises on a number of levels. While, as Mira Balberg argues, for many Jews the temple, even as it still stood, had already functioned as a concept rather than a physical place of worship (and they thus could continue to relate to such a temple regardless of whether it still stood), the physical temple's destruction demanded contemplation about the role of the temple in contemporary life and the theological significance of its destruction, even for those far away. For example, the apocalyptic text 4 Ezra, written in the 80s or 90s CE, presents an urgent theological reflection about temporal uncertainty. Ezra, the text's protagonist, suffers from insomnia as he mourns the loss of the temple and contemplates unanswerable questions about the nature of the universe and his fate in the approaching future.[52] According to Hindy Najman, 4 Ezra was written at a moment in which time seemed to stand still for its author, and the narrative attempts, through reimagining the past, to "unfreeze the present and recover the future."[53] One of the recurring themes of the narrative is Ezra's desire to know precisely when redemption will transpire and how soon the "end of time" will arrive.[54] An angel explains to Ezra, however, that, just as a pregnant woman cannot predict with certainty the day and hour of the onset of labor and birth, he cannot know in advance the timing of redemption.[55] While Ezra's main concern is the eschaton, he anticipates the end so desperately in part because his present time—the daily markings of time associated with the temple and his lost city and with regular life as he used to live it—has been upended. Ezra thus becomes a protagonist suspended in time (both quotidian and existential), grasping for signs and markers that might anchor his sense of timelessness. Because he no longer has them, he, too, finds himself in a temporal void—in a liminal time(lessness), a "time of zwischen" similar to the days before the onset of a woman's labor.[56] The text begins with Ezra struggling to fall asleep in the wake of the temple's destruction—his schedule, as his era, is no longer ordered.

The first-century historian Josephus's *Jewish Wars* and *Antiquities of the Jews* represent examples of post-destruction works in a historiographical vein. The first provides a detailed chronological account of the revolt against Rome and the city's destruction, and the second contextualizes the revolt and destruction in a longer account of Jewish history, starting at the beginning of time. Notably, Josephus not only vividly recounts the contours of the temple and the war; he also records the precise times—including the hours—when temple rituals were performed and when key battles transpired, preserving these important times in detail in his writings.[57] Both works seek to document and come to terms not only with the political and theological consequences of the temple's destruction and the war that caused it but also with the temporal and historical uncertainties that the post-destruction era presented, in light of the recent past.

The phenomenon of temporal reordering after the destruction of Jerusalem can be comparatively contextualized among other periods of historical disruption that precipitated new configurations and conceptions of time. One of the longest-lasting innovations of the Seleucid Empire was its invention of an abstract, continual, linear dating system (the idea of which is still used today), conceived precisely at a moment of dramatic territorial and imperial reconfigurations and projected back by its innovators to the empire's founding.[58] In the years following the French Revolution, the National Convention introduced a new calendar to replace the Gregorian calendar. New names were given for the new months; a decimal clock divided French days into ten hours of 100 minutes each; and the calculation of years began on the day when the Republic had been declared, thereby establishing a new chronological system.[59] The revolution signaled a new era, and part of the process of differentiating this period from what preceded it was the imposition of new conceptions of calendars, clocks, and chronologies (though they did not last long, in this case). In the midst of World War II, Emperor Hirohito decided to host massive celebrations commemorating the twenty-sixth centennial of the founding of the Empire of Japan.[60] Rather than inventing a new chronological system, as the Seleucids and the French had done, Emperor Hirohito revived an ancient—and mythological—chronological system in order to reshape Japanese national identity at a period of war. Again, a departure in time-keeping during a moment of crisis was used to signal and shape the uniqueness of the moment. Industrialization, capitalism, globalization, and technological and scientific innovations such as the railway, telegram, and telephone in the nineteenth and twentieth centuries also marred the fabric of social and economic life in Europe, the Americas, the Middle East, and beyond. In these periods, too, fierce debates accompanied the adoption of mechanical clocks, standardized clock time, and national mean times, again promoted as attempts to align the time with the times, even as "countertempos" developed in response and resistance.[61] In the Roman context, to which this introduction will return, reforms to the Roman calendar—including standardizing intercalary days, renaming months, and adding festivals—followed the military and political turmoil of Julius Caesar's wars. Fittingly, the year preceding these reforms was referred to as *ultimus annus confusionis*, the final year of confusion; though this phrase technically refers to the confusion of an unpredictable calendar, it might as well also have applied to the broader disorientation that Caesar's brash decisions had caused for Rome in the years preceding his calendrical reforms. Caesar's standardization of the calendar and the resulting predictability of time were attempts, in part, both to signal a new era and to impose temporal stability at an unstable time of transition.

The destruction of Jerusalem and its temple and the broader historical context in which that destruction transpired might be considered another such moment—a crisis of time following political and theological upheaval—for ancient Jewish communities.[62] For if the temple was a temporal center, whether in a literal or a conceptual sense or both, then the temple's physical destruction left a practical and philosophical temporal void. In the absence of sacrificial and cultic practices, how should Jews structure daily and annual time? Which temple-oriented time-markers and timely rituals could or should be maintained, and which ones needed to be reconceived? How ought Jews relate to the competing calendars and schedules of those who had destroyed their temple as well as to the organizations of time of the various other communities among whom they lived? What might God be doing with so much free time now that temple worship no longer punctuated the divine schedule? Those who regarded the temple's destruction as a catastrophe needed (among many other things) to reimagine how time was demarcated and deployed on a daily basis and to give new meaning to their hours, days, weeks, and years—as well as to the times in which they lived.[63]

RECONCEIVING TIME IN THE RABBINIC ERA

Despite the temple's physical destruction, it never disappeared from Jewish, and especially rabbinic, consciousness. Rabbinic sources, composed in the period following Jerusalem's destruction and, moreover, after hope for the physical temple's rebuilding and Jewish sovereignty in Palestine vanished in subsequent decades, engaged with the loss of the physical temple and its accompanying times. For the rabbis, though, the temple still existed on a conceptual plain, even in the absence of a physical structure, and it continued to anchor time. Rabbinic texts thus provide a lens through which to understand how this group of thinkers wrestled with the confusion of living in a new era and how they configured their time in this complex context.

Rabbinic texts capture contrasting dimensions of the rupture as well as the continuity between the rabbis' times and those prior to theirs, and rabbinic sources, multivocal as they are, variably attempt both to bridge and to widen temporal gaps. Whether we understand the rabbinic movement as beginning in the late first century CE, the years following the Bar Kokhba revolt in the 130s, or closer to the redaction of the Mishnah in the early decades of the second century, the destruction of the Jerusalem temple tends to play a key role in the periodization of this history, both as rabbinic texts imagine the origin of the rabbinic movement and as modern critical scholars understand it. Mishnah *Rosh Hashanah*, for example, draws a distinction between the period when the temple stood and the era that followed it by using the phrase "since the destruction of the temple" to describe how rituals were observed when the temple still stood and to differentiate these practices from how they could later be practiced in the absence of a temple.[64] This deliberate periodization is part of the process of rabbinic self-fashioning, in which rabbinic ritual reforms projected rabbinic authority as a replacement of previous forms of communal power, while also paying homage to the temple and preserving its memory.[65] Mishnah *Hullin* 5:1 likewise mentions that a law applies both "when the Temple existed and when the Temple did not exist," emphasizing the role of the temple in constructing a temporal distinction between the periods of "then" (when the Temple stood) and "now" (when it no longer stands). Such passages within the earliest rabbinic composition suggest that there was life before and after the temple's destruction and that these early rabbis, whose laws and other exegetical and narrative compositions are preserved in the Mishnah, thought of themselves as living in a new era, distinct from the Second Temple period. In these new times, they articulated the need to rethink their practices.

Mishnah *Rosh Hashanah* stresses the urgency of spatial and temporal reconfigurations: "Originally [בראשונה], the palm frond was carried in the temple for seven [days], and in [the rest of] the land one day; since the destruction of the temple, Rabban Yohanan ben Zakkai ordained that the palm frond should be carried [in the land] seven [days], in memory of the temple."[66] Subsequent reforms are also introduced with the term "originally" (בראשונה) to refer to practices from the Second Temple period that were adapted after the temple's destruction.[67] This particular reform not only marks two distinct historical periods but also assumes that temporal distinctions between Jerusalem and the rest of the land collapse after the destruction. It explains that prior to the temple's destruction the palm frond was used on all seven days of the festival of Sukkot in Jerusalem but only on the first day outside of the city, while after the temple's destruction, it is carried on all seven days of the festival, anywhere in the land. In this new era, space and time have shifted, and rabbinic rituals reflect such changes. Significantly, however, this rabbinic reform does not discard temple practices and times. Rather, the temple's rituals are expanded to new spaces and thus the temple's temporal rhythms continue to be observed far beyond Jerusalem. Even as the physical temple no longer stood, a conceptual temple still dictated time. We notice here negotiation between preserving earlier temporal rhythms from the temple period and changing them to suit contemporary times. These altered rhythms of time simultaneously evoked memories of the temple and temple time frames, through what Eve-Marie Becker terms "ritual memory," and emphasized temporal continuity, but they also showed the rabbinic era as distinct from that which preceded it by adapting the temple's ritual times to different geographical regions.[68] Such negotiation stimulates forms of ritual reinvention that themselves embody the temporal tension between past and present. These ongoing rituals also served to perpetuate the memory of the temple, and perhaps to keep it standing, conceptually if not physically. Moreover, we see that periodization itself was forged through new practices and conceptions of time.

In contrast to these temporal conceptions, other rabbinic passages make no distinction between the pre- and post-destruction eras and presume, instead, a seemingly unremarkable continuity through time, blurring the boundaries between past, present, and future.[69] Substantial parts of the Mishnah and other early rabbinic texts thus simultaneously imagine a world in which the temple has never been destroyed, and they elaborate upon and innovate forms of piety associated with the temple. For example, when rabbinic texts address the ritual and spatial details of the temple and its sacrifices, to which one of six mishnaic orders is dedicated, or purity practices, to which a second order is devoted, the discussions unfold as though the temple were still standing, in the present tense, fashioning these matters as ones of great contemporary concern, rather than simply of antiquarian or theoretical interest.[70] This phenomenon can be observed in the opening lines of the Mishnah, which proclaim that the evening Shema can be recited at the time "when the priests enter to eat their *terumah* offering."[71] Here, the Mishnah uses a time-marker related to the now-destroyed temple to explain when a rabbinic practice—performed long after the temple's destruction—ought to be performed.[72] In this text, it is as though the temple in Jerusalem still stands and dictates when people ought to begin reciting the Shema each evening.[73] Other tractates recount temple rituals as contemporary practices.[74]

Yet other passages skip over the temple entirely or altogether ignore its significance, such as when Mishnah *Avot* details its chain of transmission, omitting any mention of priests and linking the periods of Moses, Joshua, and the elders with the early generations of rabbinic thinkers without a hint of worry about the temple—its presence or its absence—or its priestly leaders.[75]

Early rabbinic sources also reconceive of present time somewhat differently from the way that many Jews in the period preceding them and contemporaneous with them did. The late Second Temple period as well as the decades following the temple's destruction were fraught with messianic anticipation, apocalyptic thinking, and eschatological expectations. Josephus reports that several figures presented themselves as ushering in a new era, and texts such as the War Scroll from Qumran simulated what an end-time battle might entail.[76] Those who followed Jesus likewise awaited the coming Kingdom of God. Paul proclaimed that "the appointed time has grown short [ὁ καιρὸς συνεσταλμένος ἐστίν]" and urged the Corinthians to live as though present circumstances were temporary, "for the form of this world is passing away [παράγει γὰρ τὸ σχῆμα τοῦ κόσμου τούτου]."[77] To the Thessalonians, worried that their temporal expectations for an imminent end were not being met, Paul encouraged: "Now concerning the times and the seasons . . . the day of the Lord will come like a thief in the night."[78] The Gospels, written later in the century, depict Jesus as the messiah who, in Lynne Bahr's words, "continually asserts that the hour is unknown."[79] The protagonist of 4 Ezra, too, waits in eager suspense for the eschaton, which he believes to be imminent, even—or especially—after Jerusalem has been defeated. Rabbinic sources depict (albeit negatively) some rabbinic figures, most notably Rabbi Akiva, as fervent supporters of Bar Kokhba, who sought not only to rebuild the temple but also to bring about the final redemption.[80]

The earliest strata of rabbinic texts, in contrast, tend to shy away from such speculation of cosmological origins as well as of cataclysmic end times, proscribing study of "what is ahead and what is behind."[81] After Bar Kokhba's failed messianic attempt, anticipating an imminent redemption was politically dangerous and theologically futile. Even though rabbinic sources do not altogether abandon hope for a final redemption, several rabbinic calculations of the end continually postpone redemption to later dates or indefinitely push redemption well off into the distant, virtually unimaginable future rather than expecting it at any moment.[82] Some passages express skepticism about such redemptive times and defiantly insist instead on life in the enduring present: Avot de-Rabbi Natan instructs a person who hears that the messiah has come while he is planting a tree to "go and plant the sapling, and then go to greet the messiah."[83] This passage, as others in the rabbinic corpus, urges care for the next generation and the natural environment rather than relying on an imminent end of this world. Apocalyptic and cosmogonic themes receive sustained attention mainly in later rabbinic texts, most notably the Babylonian Talmud, post-classical midrashim such as Pirqe de-Rabbi Eliezer, and in non-rabbinic compositions such as Sefer Zerubavel, expressing, often at times of renewed persecutions or large-scale geopolitical conflicts, "a sense of living in an epoch on the verge of the messianic era," in Rachel Adelman's words.[84]

Rabbinic sources likewise reconceive of the historical past and do not produce historiographical writings with the same enthusiasm nor in the same generic forms that some earlier biblical and Second Temple sources did.[85] While the rabbis certainly had a historical sense of past time and robustly engage with the past, they often deliberately played with the temporality of history, creatively blurred past and future, and chose to put their legal and hermeneutic energies elsewhere.[86] Such rabbis thus avoided both dwelling on a past of painful memories and harping on an imagined redemptive future that they did not believe would imminently end time as they knew it. They concentrated their temporal energies, instead, on present time, which seemed to them would continue in its current state indefinitely. It made sense, in this context, to establish a calendrical system that was sustainable in the long term (at first an observed calendar, and eventually a fixed and calculated calendar), delineating the days and months ahead with regularity, uniformity, and predictability.[87]

This is all to say that many, though certainly not all, discussions preserved in rabbinic sources direct their gaze toward present time—on daily life, its hourly schedules and its annual calendar, and the quotidian, if sacred, activities therein—rather than on the beginning or end of time, or on the historical past as such.[88] The rabbinic phrase "this time" (הזמן הזה), employed to refer to contemporary times, captures this temporal focus well.[89] Even discussions of temple rituals, sacrifices, and purity practices unfold in the present tense, as matters of daily concern. This temporal orientation can be understood, in part, in the context of the disintegration of the physical temple and its established times. Turning to present daily time had become a more urgent concern and perhaps also a more comforting task. It was certainly a practical necessity. Though rabbinic timescapes did not emerge suddenly as a result of destruction, the persistent absence of a physical temple and its accompanying times—and yet its prominent place in rabbinic memory of the templed past and of its continued conceptual presence in the present—played a role in the development of new conceptions of both daily and cosmic time within the rabbinic corpus that continued to change throughout the rabbinic period and that, in their crystallized forms, were applied by Jews to their lives in periods thereafter.

ROMAN TIME

The Jewish revolt and the subsequent destruction of Jerusalem also exacerbated tensions and precipitated new relations with the Roman Empire. Seth Schwartz writes that "the failure of the Jewish revolt against Rome brought about a comprehensive transformation of life in Palestine: the old political system was replaced by direct Roman rule, the Roman army became a permanent presence, the size of the population and the ratio of Jews to pagans changed."[90] After 70 CE, the Roman Empire annexed Palestine as an imperial province, named it Provincia Judaea, and appointed a governor of ex-praetorian rank (and soon thereafter ex-consuls, who were direct imperial appointees). The Army's Tenth Legion Frentesis remained in Jerusalem after the revolt, a second legion was soon permanently encamped in the province as well, and detachments were situated elsewhere in the region.[91] These troops posed problems for the local population, but they also spent their disposable income in nearby communities, built elaborate road systems, and settled in the region after discharge.[92] Jews were forced to redirect their temple contributions to the temple of Jupiter Capitolinus, and some voluntarily adopted Roman or provincial law for certain aspects of their lives.[93] Many Jews embraced these new forms of Roman political, economic, social, and cultural life, while others sought to distance themselves from them.[94] All Jews, though, needed to contend with changing notions of Romanness in this and subsequent centuries, even as Roman authorities continued to permit them, for the most part, to practice Judaism freely.[95]

One of the ways in which such Romanness must have been regularly encountered, both before and after 70 CE, was through calendrical time. According to Denis Feeney, Rome was "a society that [was] deeply invested in the semiotics and regulation of time. . . . At any period of Roman history one enters, the organization of time will be found to be integral to the way the Romans presented to themselves their religion, their past, and their identity as a culture."[96] Indeed, Rome was obsessed with time: calendars, parapegmata, water clocks, horologia, sundials, and depictions of time all constituted a grand visual presence not only in public temples but also in private dining rooms and other domestic spaces and eventually in scrolls and codices owned by individuals, both in Rome and in the provinces.[97] James Ker has highlighted how the Roman nundinal cycle likewise articulated core Roman values through the empire's temporal rhythms, especially as the seven-day week gained traction in the region.[98] By the late fourth and fifth centuries, Jewish synagogues, along with Christian churches, throughout the Galilee and beyond featured elaborate zodiac mosaics that depicted the months and seasons with local Greco-Roman imagery.[99] The sun god Sol Invictus/Helios riding a chariot along with an image of the moon and stars usually sat at the center of these mosaic floors, drawing attention to solar and lunar astronomical and temporal rhythms. These synagogue mosaics often also placed the zodiac, including its pagan imagery, alongside illustrations of the temple and ritual objects related to daily sacrifices and annual festivals as well as images of the biblical past, such as the story of the binding of Isaac.[100] The combinations of these images—Helios, the zodiac signs and names, personified seasons, temple objects, and biblical narratives—depicted biblical and temple times in dialogue with Roman temporal rhythms.

In the preceding centuries, too, Roman time informed renewed rabbinic interest in notions of time. The first century was precisely the period of calendrical and temporal reform in Rome. In 46 BCE, Julius Caesar reformed the Roman calendar, and in 8 BCE Augustus corrected its intercalary system. In the Augustan age and the early imperial period, this revised Roman calendar made its way to the far reaches of the empire and its provinces.[101] Feeney suggests that the calendar, especially after Caesar's reform, "progressively redefined the meaning of what living as a Roman now meant, capitalizing on the *fasti*'s age-old function as a vehicle for representing Roman ideology and identity."[102] The Roman calendar "itself continued to be a distinctive marker of Romanness . . . a context for apprehending and exploring Roman identity."[103] Ovid's moving—as well as deeply ambivalent—*Fasti* of 8 CE contended with these reforms, which restructured Roman time, standardized the calendar, and imposed an imperial character on a much-revered republican institution. As Roman control and presence in the region of Palestine grew, both in the first century BCE and especially after the destruction of the temple in Jerusalem in the following century, those in Palestine were increasingly affected by the new calendar and the consciousness of time that it evoked.[104] Emmanuel Friedheim has suggested that rabbis might first have encountered the Roman calendar and its festivals through the Roman legions whose daily lives were bound to its rhythms and rituals in the late first and second centuries CE.[105] Sacha Stern, for his part, has proposed that the rabbis' own calendrical reforms—their tendency toward standardizing and fixing the Jewish lunar-solar calendar—can be understood, at least in part, in relation to the Julian calendar's fixedness.[106] These rabbinic calendrical changes were initiated in the early centuries CE but continued into the fourth century and thereafter in broader Roman contexts of continued empire-wide calendrical shifts.

Other time-keeping practices became connected with imperial ideology and Romanness in this period as well. The twelve-hour division of the day did not originate in Rome:[107] it developed in Egypt over the course of the second millennium BCE, where it remained in continual use in the millennium thereafter.[108] This hourly scheme made its way to other parts of the Greek-speaking world in the late Classical, Hellenistic, and Ptolemaic periods.[109] The practice of dividing the day into twelve hours and the technology that allowed people to do so were slowly incorporated into limited Roman contexts during the third or second century BCE, probably through contact with Egypt and Greece.[110] Pliny the Elder notes that the first public clock in Rome hailed from Catania in Sicily, where it was acquired during the First Punic War as booty; it was placed in the forum Romanum.[111] Julius Caesar and Cicero both mention hours in their writings.[112] Hours were wholeheartedly adopted and popularized by Augustus, who is said to have erected an *horarium*, an hourly clock, in the Campus Martius.[113] Such an ostentatious display of hourly time signaled imperial power and was used, as well, by the Roman military.[114] Suetonius highlights Augustus's punctuality by mentioning that the emperor recorded the exact hour of day or night in each letter he sent.[115] Pliny remarks that all nations agree in the use of hours even though the Romans were quite late in adopting them.[116] By the end of the first century and through the second and third centuries, hours began to be used more widely throughout the Roman Empire, including in rabbinic sources, which are the earliest Hebrew and Jewish Aramaic sources to employ the term "hour" (שעה) to refer to the twelve units of time that make up a day or night.[117] The appearance of hours in such rabbinic texts was neither inevitable nor obvious: this trend, too, demonstrates the impact that technologies of time-keeping within the Roman Empire (even those that did not originate in Rome) had on the temporal rhythms of the diverse populations that lived within the empire's boundaries.

The Roman Empire's larger preoccupation with time—manifested in its chronologies, calendars, and clocks—thus offers a critical context for the story of rabbinic conceptions of time in antiquity. Rabbinic reevaluations of their own time as well as their negotiation of the times of others, however, must also be understood as participating in these broader Roman imperial trends, into which the Jews of Palestine entered as their region became, itself, increasingly Roman following Rome's destruction of Jerusalem. For them, setting the time was bound up with what it meant to be a rabbinic Jew living in a Roman empire.[118]

THE EMERGENCE OF CHRISTIAN TIMES

Rabbinic reconfigurations of time forced rabbis not only to reenvision Jewish ritual life without a temple and to negotiate their position as minorities within an empire that had destroyed that temple but also to forge their distinctiveness vis-à-vis competing minority communities. In the later first through third century CE, communities of Jesus followers flourished in the Galilee, where the rabbis soon founded the centers of their communities as well, and in many other regions of Asia Minor, Greece, and Rome.[119] For some followers of Christ, the temple's destruction fulfilled Jesus' prediction that the temple would fall and played a role in the parting of the ways between Jews and those who would soon be called, and call themselves, Christians.[120] The rejection of Sabbath observance, the setting of their own festival dates, and, eventually, the establishment of an alternative Lord's Day were all integral to their differentiation as well.

This process of deliberate differentiation between Jewish and Christian communities is clearly articulated in medieval manuscripts of Toledot Yeshu, in a passage that Daniel Stökl Ben Ezra has dated to late antiquity.[121] In a section of the text known as the anti-Acts, the apostle Paul (alias Elijah), serving as a double agent for the rabbis, is sent to forge unmistakable and irreversible distinctions between Jews who follow Jesus and those who do not—that is, to insist that followers of Christ truly sever their ties to Judaism and become full-fledged Christians.¹²² One of the primary ways that Paul effects this differentiation is through time. Thus, Paul reports to the Jesus-followers that Jesus himself instructed them to celebrate a new set of festivals:

> Everybody in my possession shall desecrate the Sabbath that already the Holy One, blessed be He, hated and keep the First Day [Sunday] instead, since on this day the Holy One, blessed be He, enlightened his world; and for [the days of] Passover, which Israel keeps, make them into the festival of the Resurrection, since on this [day] he rose from his tomb; and for Shavuot, Ascension, as this is the day on which he ascended to heaven; and for Rosh Hashanah the Passing Away / Invention of the Cross, and for the Great Feast [Yom Kippur] the Circumcision, and for Hanukkah, Kalends.¹²³

This narrative explains that Jewish followers of Christ *became* Christians through marking Sundays instead of Sabbaths, Easter instead of Passover, Ascension (or Pentecost) instead of Shavuot, and so on. Time and its marking through festivals, the passage suggests, were not incidental to the parting of the ways, nor a result of the separation of Christians from Jews. Time served as a primary mechanism through which difference was formed and differentiation accomplished.¹²⁴

One need not turn to a satirical polemic compiled in the medieval period, however, to observe how central time became in the gradual differentiation between Jewish and Christian communities, as well as the ways in which Jewish and Christian authorities employed time to articulate communal difference even when communal affiliations and identities remained fluid on the ground. Already the historical Paul, years before the temple's destruction, showed his appreciation of this mechanism when he reprimanded the Galatians: "You are observing special days, and months, and seasons, and years. I am afraid that my work for you may have been wasted!"¹²⁵ In this epistle, Paul accuses the Galatians of following the wrong calendar and celebrating the wrong festivals. Despite two millennia of interpretation, it remains a matter of scholarly debate whether Paul thought that the Galatians ought to use a Jewish or Roman calendar and celebrate Jewish or Roman festivals.¹²⁶ Either way, for Paul, much was at stake concerning the Galatians' adherence to correct times.

In the late first century, the Didache instructed its readers: "let not your fasts be with the hypocrites," who fast on Mondays and Thursdays.¹²⁷ Instead, the Didache mandated its adherents to fast on Wednesdays and Fridays. Here again, the days of worship served to distinguish true believers from hypocrites.¹²⁸ The Didascalia Apostolorum, a treatise contemporaneous with the rabbinic Mishnah, outlines detailed instructions for how followers of Christ should behave on Sabbaths and Sundays and states how doing so would distinguish them from other Jews.¹²⁹ A century later, John Chrysostom vigorously warned his congregants against participating in the Jewish Day of Atonement, articulating his opposition to marking Jewish time in a sermon:

> There are many in our ranks who say they think as we do. Yet some of these are going to watch the festivals and others will join the Jews in keeping their feasts and observing their fasts. I wish to drive their perverse custom from the Church right now.... But now that the Jewish festivals are close by and at the very door, if I should fail to cure those who are sick with the Judaizing disease, I am afraid that, because of their ill-suited association and deep ignorance, some Christians may partake in the Jews' transgressions; once they have done so, I fear my homilies on these transgressions will be in vain.[130]

For Chrysostom, preventing his congregants from celebrating Jewish festivals and fasts was a timely problem. As the fall festival season approached, he experienced the predicament of overlapping times with such urgency that he left aside all other matters. One aspect of being a true Christian, Chrysostom insists, is to adhere to Christian times, not Jewish ones.[131] Christian bishops and councils also devoted much effort to ensuring, through formal ecclesiastical channels, that the dating of Easter and Pentecost no longer relied on the Jewish calendar nor intersected with the Jewish festivals of Passover and Shavuot.[132] The Nicaean Synodal Letter to Alexandria emphasizes this point, noting that the agreement about Easter's date was significant because it guaranteed "that all our brethren in the East who, until now, have kept this festival when the Jews did" are able to celebrate it, instead, on the date that the Western Christians did.[133] Commenting on this temporal split, the fifth-century church historian Socrates Scholasticus remarks that the new Easter date signaled the transition "when Judaism was changed into Christianity."[134] Other festivals, such as the fall celebrations of Rosh Hashanah, Yom Kippur, and Sukkot, were likewise reconfigured in early Christian communities; Jewish festival celebrations also participated in forging difference between Jews and Christians, as on Purim.[135] These processes of temporal differentiation became so pressing precisely because, at first, these groups shared the same calendar and observed the same Sabbath.[136] Time was on the minds of Christians as they defined themselves vis-à-vis Jews. Christian concerns about proper times thus constitute a crucial context for understanding the other side of this differentiation, namely, how rabbis, too, contemplated time as they defined themselves vis-à-vis their neighbors.

Part III: Differentiating Rabbinic Timescapes

The empire in which the rabbis lived was adapting to a new Roman calendar and temporal system. A growing Christian minority made up of a constellation of communities (not all of whom agreed with one another about the

Christian calendar) was also differentiating itself from other Jews through marking its time separately—and independently—from them. The times and temporality imposed on Jewish institutional and ritual life by the temple and its schedules lay in ruins. And who knew, the rabbis wondered, what occupied God's time; these circumstances suggested that perhaps God had taken some time off. Much was thus at stake in how rabbis conceptualized and structured time for those within their communities. Multiple processes of time-marking enabled those who composed rabbinic sources to construct their unique identities within the Roman Empire (and eventually within the Christian Roman Empire), distinguish themselves from other communities within that empire, differentiate various groups from one another within their communities, and mediate a temporal relationship between themselves and their God.

Many rabbinic tractates—including *Avodah Zarah*, *Berakhot*, and *Niddah*, analyzed in this book alongside additional rabbinic sources—begin with elaborate discussions of time and use the category of time as a primary lens through which to construct and articulate rabbinic practices and beliefs. In the United States, students are taught as early as grade school to ask the fundamental questions of "who, what, when, where, and why?" of any given text or idea (a tradition that can be traced back to the Carolingian period, and which itself relies on ancient Roman rhetorical techniques).[137] The redactor(s) of the Mishnah often began with the question of *"when?"*[138] Just as tractate *Berakhot* begins with a series of questions about the timing of the Shema prayer, tractate *Avodah Zarah* opens with an elaborate debate about when Jews were obligated to separate from their Roman neighbors, and the first passage in tractate *Niddah* refers to the period of a woman's impurity as "her time" (שעתה) while establishing the contours of the times of menstruation. Tractate *Shabbat*, itself devoted to detailing the rituals and prohibitions of the central temporal institution of the Sabbath, not only begins with questions about time but also is the first tractate of the order of *Moed*—literally "Appointed Time." Other rabbinic texts about the Sabbath likewise theorize about what makes the time of the Sabbath sacred (קדוש, literally "separated" or "differentiated").[139] First and foremost, then, these rabbinic tractates and texts are concerned with answering questions about time. *When* must one refrain from engaging with those who worship other gods? *When*, how, and why must one sanctify the Sabbath day? *When* each day can one begin blessing God and how else can one mark one's time in devotion to God? *When* is one's body ritually impure and in need of purification? These debates about time unfold in their earliest forms in the Mishnah and then further develop in ways that show their centrality to the project of communal definition and differentiation in the Palestinian and Babylonian Talmuds as well as in other rabbinic compositions, including halakhic and aggadic midrashim.

In the past two decades, the topic of time has garnered increasing attention from scholars of ancient Judaism, rabbinic literature, and Jewish Studies.[140]

Several studies, including a number by Sacha Stern, have interrogated the rabbinic calendar—how it functioned, the processes through which it became fixed, and its reception and adaptation by later communities—while calendrical and other time-related astronomical and eschatological texts among the Dead Sea Scrolls have been examined by James VanderKam, Devorah Dimant, Jonathan Ben-Dov, and Eshbal Ratzon, among many others.[141] In addition to Stern, James Barr, Gershon Brin, Shamma Friedman, Avraham Yoskovich, and others have traced the origin, meaning, and evolution of specific units of time and duration, times of day, and time-markers (e.g., מועד, זמן, יום, שעה, רגע, הנץ החמה, קורת הגבר, עולם, and so on) across the biblical, Second Temple, and rabbinic corpora.[142] Rabbinic notions of history and memory have been reexamined by Isaiah Gafni, Margarete Schlüter, Amram Tropper, Meir Ben Shahar, Naftali Cohn, Nathan Schumer, and others engaging with the work of Yosef Hayim Yerushalmi's *Zakhor*.[143] Alongside a tradition of exploring the theme of temporality in studies of rabbinic midrash, exemplified, for example, in the early work of Isaac Heinemann and Jonah Fraenkel and the more recent work of Rachel Adelman and Rivka Ulmer, other scholars, such as Sergey Dolgopolski and Moulie Vidas, have considered how notions of transmission through time shaped the formation of talmudic traditions and genres.[144] Max Strassfeld has productively introduced notions of queer temporality into the study of the Talmud.[145]

Most recently, Lynn Kaye, in her book *Time in the Babylonian Talmud*, has outlined uniquely rabbinic temporalities, exploring concepts such as "simultaneity," "fixity," "permanence," "retroactivity," "tradition," and "memory," as they are developed and theorized in legal, narrative, and midrashic sources.[146] Kaye demonstrates that talmudic sources, far from lacking a time dimension (as has sometimes been argued), navigated between natural and imagined times, constructing imagined temporalities in order to overcome legal and narrative challenges posed by the ordering of natural time. Both times coexist simultaneously, on different temporal "registers." Rabbinic sources thus ought to serve, according to Kaye, as resources for challenging contemporary taken-for-granted notions of time, especially the idea that time is exclusively linear and progressive, precisely because of how philosophically and conceptually complex rabbinic engagement with time and temporality actually is.

Scholars of later periods, including Elisheva Carlebach, Elisheva Baumgarten, Philipp Nothaft, and Justine Isserles, have dealt with the development of the Jewish calendar and Jews' engagement with other calendars, especially the Christian calendars used in medieval and early modern Europe.[147] These studies have also contemplated how media, including print culture and other material dimensions of time-keeping, impacted Jewish calendrical practices in calendrically diverse contexts. Literary and philosophical notions of time and temporality in medieval and modern Jewish texts and contexts, moreover, have been studied by Tamar Rudavsky and Elliot Wolfson.[148] David Zvi Kalman has examined the impact of changing technologies of hourly time-keeping on the development of halakhah.[149] Additionally, recent scholarship in rabbinics has outlined the construction, in the rabbinic period, of new notions of rabbinic identity, subjectivity, and difference.[150]

This book draws from these earlier studies while homing in on the regulation of everyday time as it is conceived and mandated in rabbinic texts. It demonstrates the central role that rabbinic ritual, narrative, and conceptual reconfigurations of time played in facilitating the development of rabbinic notions of imperial, communal, gendered, and theological difference. The focus specifically on time as a mechanism for the creation of varieties of difference aims to contribute both to the study of rabbinic literature and to the fields of religious studies, Jewish studies, and time studies more broadly defined.

The analysis in this book assumes that the rabbinic corpus contains polyphonic ideas about time and timing rather than a unified and singular "conception of time," an idea emphatically articulated as well by Sylvie Anne Goldberg in *La Clepsydre*.[151] It mines ancient sources for the temporal complexities and contradictions that rabbinic discussions bring forth, within each rabbinic composition as well as between sources from various periods of rabbinic history. It also argues, though, that among this multiplicity, some general trends about time and difference emerge, however messily, from these rabbinic compositions.

The chapters of this book are structured around units of time, social realms, discourses of difference, and rabbinic genres. The first chapter addresses rabbinic-Roman difference through examining annual time in the context of Roman imperialism; the second chapter focuses on Jewish-Christian difference through analyzing weekly time in the context of intercommunal relations; the third chapter centers on gendered difference through a study of daily time within communal boundaries; and the fourth chapter dwells on divine-human difference through a consideration of hourly time within theological discourse. Thus, the chapters shift from annual to weekly, daily, and hourly cycles, and they turn to increasingly constricted social domains, proceeding from the broadest context of the Roman Empire, to intercommunal relations between Jews and Christians (members of parallel yet competing communities within a broader imperial context), to gendered time within rabbinic communities, and then, expanding outward again, to the intersection of human and divine spheres.[152] The choice to devote each chapter to a particular temporal cycle—annual, weekly, daily, hourly—is not meant to suggest that rabbis only constructed imperial difference on an annual basis, Christian difference on a weekly basis, gendered difference on a daily basis, and theological difference on an hourly basis. Rather, this editorial choice is intended to spotlight the variety and diversity of strategies used within rabbinic texts to order a wide range of different temporal durations, each chapter demonstrating a unique time frame.

Nevertheless, the unit of the day remains central throughout this study: the first chapter examines discourses about the significance of certain days of the year; the second chapter studies the status of certain days of the week; the third chapter investigates practices that mark the beginnings and ends of each day; and the fourth chapter analyzes the subdivision of days into hours and other units. The first two chapters deal with special or sacred types of days, those differentiated from other times; the second two chapters address quotidian time and more regular, seemingly mundane temporal rhythms of the day, on earth as well as in heaven. At its core, then, the book is about the construction of difference in daily life, through various scales of time-keeping from the annual to the hourly.

Each chapter begins with an examination of rabbinic sources from the second and third centuries (known as "tannaitic" literature) and then proceeds, in its second half, to an analysis of narrative materials from later rabbinic compositions from the fourth, fifth, and sixth centuries (known as "amoraic" and "post-amoraic" literature). The chapters engage with texts from both Palestine and Babylonia, though the focus remains largely on Palestinian sources. The rabbinic material from the Babylonian Talmud is essential to the book's argument even though it was composed and redacted beyond the borders of the Roman Empire and indeed in a different historical, cultural, and political context than rabbinic texts composed in the region of Palestine. Juxtaposing the Palestinian and Babylonian sources often brings into sharper relief what is distinctive about the Palestinian materials and how they approach time in ways that are different from how Babylonian sources approach the same or similar questions about time. At times, highlighting how the Babylonian Talmud interprets earlier traditions also proves generative. Moreover, following how ideas from Palestinian sources were received and adapted in Babylonia demonstrates how Palestinian ideas changed when they were applied and appropriated in new contexts.

CHAPTER OUTLINE

The first chapter explores the differentiation and synchronization of rabbinic and Roman time by examining rabbinic attitudes toward the Roman calendar and its annual festivals. Mishnah *Avodah Zarah* begins with a list of Roman festivals and prohibitions against participating even in the non-cultic commercial activities that surrounded them. Ironically, by trying so deliberately not to observe the Roman calendar and by formulating laws intended to limit interactions between Romans and Jews on certain calendar days, the rabbis of the Mishnah actually integrated the rhythms of the Roman calendar into their own daily lives, embedding Roman temporal sensibilities into the Jewish calendar. However, the Roman calendar became integrated into the Jewish calendar not only through the formulation of rabbinic laws intended to limit interactions between Romans and Jews on certain calendar days but also through the Judaization of the Roman calendar in the rabbinic imagination. The rabbis explicitly ban economic interaction and deride social engagement between gentiles and Jews. Yet, in the Palestinian and Babylonian Talmuds, the origin and history of Roman festivals are presented as Jewish or biblical at their core. In one story, about the festival Kratesis, the geological, mythical, and historical origins of the city of Rome are traced to the idolatrous sins committed by a series of Israelite kings. In another story about this same festival, the Romans are said to draw on the power of the Torah and their alliance with the Jews in order to defeat their Greek rivals. Similarly, both Talmuds attribute the festival of the Kalends of January to the biblical Adam. In the Babylonian Talmud, Adam establishes this festival "for the sake of heaven" but the passage concludes that the festival was later corrupted by the Romans and made into an idolatrous celebration. Through these later rabbinic eyes, the Roman year was punctuated with days that had Jewish stories—and indeed a long Jewish past—attached to them, even as they maintained a cautious distance from them. As Fritz Graf has argued, the Roman calendar mapped Roman history onto an annual cycle.[153] Rabbinic prohibitions against and stories about Roman festivals had a similar function, mapping a rabbinic anti-imperial narrative of Jewish history onto the Roman imperial year. These sources illuminate just how integral past and present Roman time was for the rabbis—a grave threat from which the rabbis sought to protect and distance their community, and so pervasive in the rabbis' environment that they sought to Judaize the Roman calendar.

Chapter 2 turns to rabbinic discussions of the Sabbath in light of Roman pagan critiques of and competing Christian claims to a weekly sacred day and other weekly worship practices. The first half of the chapter analyzes a section of Mekhilta de-Rabbi Ishmael that contains an extended exegetical discussion about the Sabbath. This midrash offers passionate engagement with ideas that were popular in Second Temple and early Christian debates about Sabbath observance. The second half of the chapter analyzes a series of rabbinic stories that explore the sanctity of the Sabbath, found in fifth-century rabbinic sources compiled after Sunday became an imperially sanctioned day of rest and worship. It appears that rabbis proactively promoted the Sabbath as a day with distinct qualities that were inherent to it and persuaded Jews of this dimension of the Sabbath precisely because they worried that Jews might be drawn to other weekly temporal rhythms or that they could be susceptible to Roman Christian and non-Christian disparagement of the Sabbath and might therefore stop observing the Sabbath altogether. In each narrative, rabbinic outsiders confirm the constitutional singularity of the Sabbath day. In one story, an emperor visits a rabbi for a Sabbath meal and concludes that food on the

Sabbath is more delicious than dishes prepared on any other day of the week. The narrative explains that the food is delectable thanks to the Sabbath's special qualities, which cannot be accessed by those who do not observe the day properly. In another story, a governor questions a rabbi about the qualities of the Sabbath, and the two figures engage in a long discussion that culminates in the official conjuring up his dead Roman father to verify the sanctity of the day. Although these stories are quite humorous, they are not told for purposes of entertainment. They appear in the later stratum of Palestinian rabbinic literature composed at the height of the Christianization of the Roman Empire, during the period when Sunday was added to the imperial calendar in an official legal capacity. The narratives address specific critiques of the Jewish Sabbath that are known to us from non-Christian Greek and Latin polemics as well as contemporaneous Christian polemics against Jews and Judaism, all of which were prevalent within the lands of the Roman Empire. They can be understood as rabbinic attempts to make the Jewish Sabbath more attractive to other Jews, who may have been inclined to view the Sabbath as a temporal burden and even an embarrassment. Here, again, rabbinic insistence on the Sabbath's essential sanctity and therefore the importance of its proper observance asserted Jewish difference vis-à-vis not only alternative Roman pagan time but also Christian rhythms of weekly time in a period in which these Christian times were becoming more deeply embedded into a Roman imperial framework and had become increasingly dominant.

Chapter 3 tracks the construction of a gendered temporality by examining a set of daily rituals mandated in rabbinic sources, some of which applied to men and others that were only required of women. The chapter begins with the first ritual discussed in rabbinic sources, the recitation of the Shema prayer. Timing became an essential component of the Shema's recitation (in contradistinction to the biblical passage on which this rabbinic practice is based), and thus the tractate includes numerous debates about ritual time. One's time, it is suggested, ought to be marked first and foremost by this regularized declaration of devotion to God each morning and evening. Another feature of the rabbinic Shema is that only men became obligated in its recitation. According to the Mishnah, women are exempt from the fulfillment of this particular ritual as well as from the entire category of rituals that are labeled "positive time-bound commandments." Women, in other words, are kept apart from the central devotional prayer that marks important moments of temporal transition during each rabbinic day, as well as from other rituals that similarly construct time for the individual and the community. Rabbinic texts do not regard women as completely disconnected from time-boundedness, however. While women are excluded from positive time-bound commandments, an entire set of rituals related to the laws of menstrual purity applies *only* to women and constructs a woman's time in ways that were markedly different from the time of men. The second half of this chapter follows the development of the laws of bodily purity from biblical texts, which provide extensive instructions concerning both men and women, to rabbinic texts, which focus far greater attention on laws related to the menstruant woman. By the end of the classical rabbinic period, the web of menstrual purity laws functioned in ways that are remarkably different from the laws of purity that pertain to men, especially with regard to time. One of the defining features of women's time, in contrast to men's time, is the alternation between times of purity and impurity. This feature emerges already in tannaitic sources but is especially striking in the Babylonian Talmud. These alternating times were dictated by the state of a woman's body as well as the associated daily practices of bodily examination, which women were required to perform at the same times at which men were required to recite the Shema. It is not incidental that positive time-bound commandments are based on external time-markers such as the celestial bodies and are designed to orient men's time toward God while the menstrual purity laws, in contrast, rely on the internal rhythms of a woman's body and orient women's times toward their bodies, their husbands, and other objects that could be contaminated at times of impurity. When men and women are mandated to perform different rituals that structure their days in unique ways, their conceptions of time can radically differ as well. What it meant to be a halakhically observant rabbinic man or woman, then, was defined by distinct embodied rituals and experiences of time.[154]

Chapter 4 explores the day and its hourly subdivisions as rabbinic sources imagine God and humans to operate within the same units of time. The first three chapters detail annual, weekly, and daily rhythms of time in human realms and analyze the various ways in which people were instructed to use their time to worship God and observe God's commandments. The fourth chapter, in contrast, concentrates on rabbinic sources that wonder whether God keeps time, and if so, whether God keeps the same time as humans and how God's time is used in service of them. In texts from across the rabbinic corpus, God's divinity is contingent, in part, on time. As this chapter demonstrates, the unit of the hour became especially associated with God's time. God keeps to an hourly schedule during the day, has an active nightlife, and engages in tasks that sustain earthly life. Often, in these texts, God spends time performing activities in which humans engage as well, for example studying Torah, wearing phylacteries, and matchmaking, but God also performs tasks that are exclusively divine, such as judging the world's creatures and worshipping with the angels. These aspects of God's temporality thus simultaneously differentiate God in the heavenly sphere from those in the earthly realm and draw similarities between the time of those in heaven and on earth. The end of the chapter returns to the historical events that frame the beginning of this book. In the Babylonian Talmud, one of the most surprising aspects of God's time is how much of it God spends mourning the temple's destruction. Just as Ezra, in 4 Ezra, suffers from insomnia as he struggles to comprehend the tragedy of the destruction, God, as portrayed in the Babylonian Talmud, awakens to mark the nightly watches with pained cries of despair that the temple no longer stands. The fall of Jerusalem thus not only radically alters the human time frames that rabbinic sources attempt to reconfigure through revised rituals and laws. The destruction is also understood, in these later rabbinic sources, to cause a crisis of time for God, whose subsequent (post-destruction) times, too, needed readjustment. These sources about God's time highlight what the rabbis regarded as unique to human and divine time as well as how they imagined these two timescapes to intersect. They reinforce how important conceptualizing and dividing time was for the rabbinic enterprise not only in distinguishing men from women, Jews from Christians, and rabbis from Romans but also in distinguishing people from God and articulating what it meant, temporally and existentially, to be human or divine.

These processes of definition and differentiation did not end with the redaction of the Talmuds or the composition of later midrashim. Even as these temporal developments in classical rabbinic sources were tentative and gradual—and some of their social effects unintentional—many of the temporal practices became normative in the medieval period, establishing rhythms of time for later Jewish communities. Rabbinic discussions might have begun as legal and exegetical debates among the intellectual elites of the tannaitic and amoraic periods. Once the Babylonian Talmud gained semi-canonical status and dictated Jewish life more broadly in the subsequent centuries, however, its laws were often more widely mandated, enforced, and practiced even as they continued to evolve in new historical and cultural settings.[155] Medieval and modern legal literature and treatises devote much hermeneutical energy to interpreting prohibitions against participating in the forbidden times of those among whom Jews lived, marking the Sabbath, determining times for prayer, explicating the category of time-bound commandments, and further detailing the rhythms and rituals of bodily impurity and of God's time. In other words, the *conceptions* of daily time in the classical rabbinic sources that are at the heart of this study did, sooner or later, directly impact many aspects of Jewish *experiences* of time and influence the rhythm of daily life—to this day. The conclusion outlines how select groups of later Jews adopted and adapted (and, at times, ignored) these rabbinic concerns about time to their present circumstances and the lasting legacy of these time frames and the differences they constructed on the history of Judaism and Jewish life in the *longue durée*.

A NOTE ON TERMINOLOGY

The terms used to identify and distinguish between groups of people are constructs, not merely descriptions. Nor are they stable categories but rather ever-evolving, contingent, and complicated. Whom one includes under a particular label or how one categorizes texts is rarely simple or obvious; labeling functions deliberately or inadvertently to include and exclude certain people or groups of people—to forge similarity or difference. Labeling or categorizing is thus often a matter of contestation. This is as true today as it was in earlier times and places: one need only think of the politics surrounding contemporary questions about who counts as a "Jew" to understand the constructed nature of categories as well as the real and wide-ranging stakes and consequences of labeling and categorizing. This fact poses challenges for deciding which terms to employ, especially when writing about the process through which such identities, subjectivities, and differences were forged over the course of centuries. Here, I explain the terms I use in this book and the rationale behind my choices.

Scholars have stressed just how little we know about ancient Jewish life, given that our primary sources are texts that were produced by rabbis who were not necessarily representative of Jews more broadly. Thus, in my analysis, I generally refer to "rabbinic" texts and to "rabbis" as agents but to the target of their interests and prescriptions as "Jews" and the "Jewish" calendar, as the rabbis' ambitions (if not their actual authority or influence) extended beyond their own limited circles to the entirety of the Jewish community, as they defined it.

When I use the noun "Roman(s)," it is in recognition of the shifting and diverse populations that this term encompassed from the first through the fifth century CE and cognizant of the evolving dimensions that notions of "Romanness" underwent during this period.[156] In the first century CE, few people in the region of Palestine were Roman citizens and most lived under local provincial law, while in the second century, many elites were Roman by virtue of individual citizenship grants and such status projected their superiority over non-Romans. By the second decade of the third century, virtually all free men in Palestine and the eastern provinces had been granted Roman citizenship through the Antonine Constitutions and were governed by Roman law.[157] That is, by the time of the Mishnah's redaction, the rabbis were Roman citizens—they *were* Roman. Hayim Lapin writes that the rabbis of Palestine are "best understood as shaping their texts and their religious, social, and political stances as Roman provincials."[158] Living in provincial Palestine, rabbis participated in the life of the empire and even their seemingly insular writings reflect the degree to which they were integrated and embedded within the empire. At the same time, rabbinic engagement with the Roman Empire and with Roman institutions and narratives was complicated.[159] Even though the rabbis living within the Roman Empire were Roman citizens, they actively asserted distinctions between rabbinic Jewish culture and practices and Roman imperial culture and practices. This book illuminates the intricate relationship that rabbis had with Romanness by examining the ways in which they confronted one aspect of Roman culture: its calendar. I therefore use, when appropriate, the adjectives "rabbinic" and "Roman" to capture such distinctions, for example, when writing of "rabbinic time" and "Roman (imperial) time."[160] It is a central claim of this book that rabbinic sources themselves participated in the very process of differentiation between rabbis and other Romans precisely in a period when the rabbis were Roman.

Occasionally, I employ the more controversial term "pagan" as shorthand for non-Jewish and non-Christian Romans from whose cultic practices the rabbis sought to distance themselves, despite the term's negative connotations and historical anachronism.[161] I do so to capture the charged distinctions the rabbis tried to create between themselves and these others rather than to describe these populations in a historical way. They would certainly not have called themselves "pagans" nor their worship "pagan," nor would they have identified as a unified group. When appropriate, I use the rabbis' own, equally derogatory, term "gentiles" (*goyim*) or "idolaters" (literally "worshippers of foreign worship") for these same reasons.[162] My use of these terms deliberately conveys the rabbinic conflation of these distinct populations into a single undifferentiated unit, as well as the disparaging meaning associated with them in rabbinic sources.

Similarly, scholars have conceptualized the distinction, constructed over time, between Jews and Christians and between Judaism and Christianity, as well as their continued intersections and overlaps. Some scholars present Christianity as the offspring of Judaism and speak of the birth of Christianity out of Judaism.[163] Others view the development of rabbinic Judaism and Christianity through the familial metaphor of siblings descended from an earlier form of parental Israelite religion or Judaism.[164] A third approach invokes the metaphor of paths and describes a "parting of the ways" between groups (made of yet more subgroups) that had earlier been a single entity or traveled on a single road, with insistence that in important respects the "ways never parted" or never fully parted.[165] A fourth, related, approach conceptualizes the continued development of Judaism and Christianity in constant conversation with one another.[166] Most recently, attention has been placed on Jewish-Christian difference by highlighting theological and rhetorical dimensions of similarity upon which such difference is constructed.[167] With regard to terminology, it has been demonstrated that texts from the first several centuries CE employ the term "Christian" but that the meaning of this term shifted, including and excluding various groups in accordance with the particular context of its use.[168] The terms "Jew," "Judaean," "Jewish," and "Judaism" have similarly fraught histories.[169] Even after the crystallization of the categories "Jewish" and "Christian," however, people applied them differently and crossed between them.

In this book, I use the terms "Jews," "Christians," "Jesus- or Christ-followers," "Jewish-Christians," and so on advisedly. In general, I aim to avoid anachronism, preferring to use the labels and categories employed by the subjects of this book either to identify themselves or to identify others. For instance, I choose not to label a text as "Christian" simply because it later came to be included in the Christian New Testament canon, though when writing about a text that was later regarded as belonging to those who by then regarded themselves as "Christians" (e.g., the Gospels or the Letters of Paul), I note this as well if discussing the text in the later context. If the text was written by a late antique follower of Christ who would not have recognized the category of "Christian," I label the text and its author as "Christ-following." If the author was a follower of Christ and also regarded himself as a Jew (to the extent that we can ascertain), I label the author as "a Christ-following Jew" or a "Jewish follower of Christ." For later authors who insisted on firmer distinctions between "Christian" and "Jew," for example, bishops, I label them according to their preferred identity labels. This principle of preferring the labels with which authors identified themselves is often challenging to apply, given that authors do not always tell us their preferred labels. My approach to this challenge is conservative; I often use more cumbersome labels so as to avoid imposing anachronistic terms on texts or authors. Sometimes, though, for the sake of readability, I use less precise language and offer clarification in the notes. I trust that readers will keep in mind that all of these terms were never self-evident or absolute categories (nor necessarily mutually exclusive ones) but rather unstable and constructed.

Likewise, the binary categories "men" and "women" do not map onto nor account for the diversity of types of bodies and sexual/gendered identities in antiquity or in the present. These categories also often conflate sex and gender, usually referring to those born biologically female as women and biologically male as men while excluding other types of men and women and effacing altogether those born biologically between or beyond male and female, with gendered identities that do not fit into either of these imagined groups.[170] Rabbinic sources themselves acknowledge and make visible such gendered diversity when they discuss matters related to the categories of *tumtum, androgynous, saris, aylonit*, and so forth.[171] Indeed, rabbinic discussions are often most interested in the areas between the binaries rather than in the binaries themselves.[172] Yet rabbinic texts also often subsume these additional gendered groups, for practical ritual and legal purposes, within the broader categories of men and women (e.g., in laws of menstrual purity or circumcision), simultaneously reinforcing a gendered binary while also unsettling it. In this study, I use the categories "men" and "women" as inclusively as possible, denoting whomever rabbinic sources would have included within them and leaving their meaning deliberately open-ended.

In all these terminological choices, I do not intend to unnecessarily impose binary oppositions (rabbinic/Roman, Jewish/Christian, male/female, human/divine) upon the past but rather to recognize how such difference was constructed and developed over the course of the rabbinic period within rabbinic sources, as well as to identify instances in which such distinctions were challenged and binaries complicated. Throughout, I demonstrate the role that time and temporality played in these messy processes of differentiation and synchronization.

CHAPTER ONE

Rabbinic and Roman Time

JEWS ACROSS THE ANCIENT MEDITERRANEAN often mediated between their own calendar and imperially sanctioned ones.[1] An early third-century Greek inscription carved onto the long side of a limestone sarcophagus found in the southeastern necropolis of Hierapolis in Asia Minor left the following instructions: with the interest of the 350 denaria that Publius Aelius Glykon Zeuzianos Aelianus bequeathed, he requested that the purple-dyers guild celebrate Passover and the carpet-weavers guild celebrate Kalends and Pentecost at his family tomb each year following his death.[2] This inscription constructed an annual festival calendar that marked both Jewish and Roman time, leaving no trace of conflict in so doing.[3]

Another postmortem example of the synchronization between the Roman and Jewish calendars appears on a Jewish fourth-century funerary inscription from Catania in Sicily, erected in memory of Lasia Erine. The inscription, dedicated by the deceased's husband, Aurelius Samuel, and written in a combination of Hebrew and Latin, records the dates of Lasia's death according to the Julian calendar and its consular year.[4] Yet the inscription also includes the lunar day, which functioned to align the Jewish festival calendar with the Roman solar calendar.[5] Both the Roman and the Jewish calendars were important enough to this couple that referencing just one of them did not suffice to commemorate the wife's date of death.

Throughout late antiquity, rabbis in Palestine attempted to separate Jewish temporal rhythms from those of the Roman Empire. As these inscriptions vividly reveal, however, this was a distinction that not all Jews were willing to make. This chapter analyzes rabbinic texts about the Roman calendar and its annual festivals in order to understand how rabbis conceived of their relationship to the empire and its temporal rhythms—the rhythms of the Roman year in the present as well as those of Rome's historical past.[6]

At the most practical level, calendars function as instruments of social, economic, religious, and political organization and control through dividing and ordering annual time.[7] The Mishnah's attempts to differentiate Jews from other Romans and from the rituals of the empire by mandating that Jews separate from Roman temporal rhythms is one example of how calendars are used to regulate time and difference in a given community. Because calendars incorporate festivals that mark important moments from a community's past within the framework of the present, calendars also map past time onto present time.[8] Thus, in addition to their other practical functions, calendars make the past meaningful to those in the present through the rhythms of the year.[9] For example, the rabbinic calendar reenacted a rabbinic narrative of the Jewish past and its central tenets in the present through its set of annual festivals and commemorative days.[10] The Roman calendar similarly served to convey a Roman narrative of Rome's collective past and ideology to contemporary Romans through its annual festival celebrations.[11] The present chapter explores the impact of the Roman calendar and its version of Roman history on the rabbinic year and corresponding rabbinic conceptions of the Roman past.

This chapter advances three interrelated arguments. The first addresses the differentiation and synchronization of rabbinic and Roman present time. A primary strategy the rabbis used to construct difference between Jews and other Romans was to insist that Jews separate themselves from the time frames of their neighbors and maintain their own times. The rabbinic tractate *Avodah Zarah*, devoted to regulating interactions between Jews and gentiles, begins by addressing the times of year when Jews were forbidden from interacting with others.[12] The Mishnah and Tosefta even provide specific lists of Roman festivals during which Jews were prohibited from engaging in business transactions with their gentile neighbors. Such separation had a paradoxical and counterintuitive effect, however. In order to abstain from interactions with gentiles during their festival times, Jews were required to keep track of the Roman annual calendar and to manage the intersections between the Roman calendar and the lives of Jews. The Roman year was punctuated, according to these rabbinic laws, by days when Jews were required to change their behavior and mark themselves as different from those who celebrated the empire's annual festivals. Thus, even though the rabbis urged scrupulous avoidance of every aspect of Roman festivals and their related activities, abstaining or participating similarly mapped the Roman festival calendar onto the rabbinic year and, as a result, merged Roman with rabbinic time. The very mechanism of time through which the rabbis sought to forge difference worked to solidify an intimate interconnection between them and the empire.

A century and a half prior to the Mishnah's redaction, the Roman philosopher Seneca the Younger captured this complexity of synchronization and differentiation in his reflections on the festival of the Saturnalia. In a letter to Lucilius concerning the celebration of the festival, he writes: "Should we make no alteration in our daily habits, or should we take off our togas . . . and have dinner parties with a note of festivity about them, to avoid giving the impression that we disagree with the ways of those around us? If . . . you had to give a decision in the matter, you would say that we should be neither altogether like nor altogether unlike the festive-hatted crowd. But perhaps this is the very season when we should be keeping the soul under strict control, making it unique in abstaining from pleasure just when the crowds are all bent on pleasure."[13] In this passage, Seneca ponders the various ways of differentiating himself from those who celebrate the Saturnalia. He notes that he could ignore the festival altogether or halfheartedly imitate the celebrations to fit in. Alternatively, he could actively choose to abstain from participation in it. Regardless of which option Seneca ultimately prefers, it is in this season, he writes, that he wishes to mark his difference through his use of time. In a move remarkably resonant with the rabbis of the Mishnah, Seneca suggests altering his behavior so as to distance himself from this Roman festival, and in this very act he becomes bound closer to it.

The chapter's second argument addresses rabbinic conceptions of the Roman past as they are projected onto the Roman calendar year. In their elaborations of the Mishnah's list of Roman festivals, the Palestinian and Babylonian Talmuds provide detailed etiologies for each of these festivals. By inserting biblical and other Jewish motifs into their interpretations of the Roman past, they suggest that it is Jews, not Romans, who have formed the heart of Roman history. These etiologies construct rabbinic versions of Roman history: they present the Jews as integral to the origins of Roman festivals and indeed to the foundation and history of Rome itself. They deliberately connect the history of Israel and the history of Rome, curiously inserting themselves into the past of others by reinterpreting the festivals that populated those people's annual calendar.[14] Imagining Jews as defining actors in these etiologies merged Jewish and Roman history and projected this hybrid historical time onto the Roman annual calendar. The Roman calendar was thus inscribed, by the rabbis, with Jewish meaning.

Such rabbinic stories about Roman festivals functioned primarily as "counter-histories" or "competitive historiography," practices of storytelling aimed at forging difference.[15] The Palestinian and Babylonian Talmuds present the Jewish role in Roman history in two distinct ways. The sentiment of the deeply anti-imperial Palestinian Talmud is that Roman festivals originated with Israelite sin, divine hatred of Rome's ancestors, and other biblically inflected themes of rivalry and oppression. The set of stories thus functions to undermine the greatness of the Roman past as well as to stimulate Jews to act according to rabbinic halakhah, maintain their distance and difference from the empire, and stop short of living comfortably as Romans in Roman society and adopting its temporal rhythms. The Babylonian Talmud, by contrast, which was redacted beyond the borders of the Roman Empire and in a period in which Rome's imperial power had significantly diminished, conveys more positive pride in the role of Jews and Judaism in the early success of Rome. The narratives evoke an idealized golden age of collaboration and mutual partnership between the Jews and the Roman Empire. They reclaim the importance of Jewish political and ritual power in Rome's early imperial history while still critiquing the empire's later treatment of Jews, especially the empire's destruction of the temple and the oppression of Jews in the centuries thereafter. Despite these divergences, the Roman festal days identified in the earlier tannaitic texts become, through the talmudic stories about these festivals, intertwined with the history of the Jews who are beckoned, in these same rabbinic texts, to abstain from the celebration of these days. Through constructing these etiologies, both Talmuds inscribe rabbinic Jewish narratives of the Roman past onto the imperial Roman year.

The third argument that the chapter advances is that rabbinic engagements with Roman time—both rabbinic rules about abstaining from commercial transactions during Roman festival times and subversive tellings of imperial narratives about the Roman past that such festivals sought to promote—represent specifically temporal modes of imperial resistance. Even as rabbis synchronized their time with the time of the empire, they also found ways of cultivating countertempos, to adapt a phrase from On Barak's study of temporality in colonial Egypt.[16] Through these countertempos, rabbinic Jews resisted the times of those who governed them, insisting instead on the superiority of their own times and their own historical perspectives. The ways in which rabbinic communities imagined the Roman annual calendar and its festivals shaped their own collective rhythms in the present as well as their understanding of the past that those rhythms sought to capture, constructing rabbinic-Roman difference in both temporal realms.

The Roman Calendar in the Mishnah

TIMES OF RESTRICTED EXCHANGE

The Mishnah's tractate *Avodah Zarah* sets forth in great detail how to observe the biblical prohibition of idolatry in a Roman context. The rabbinic commitment to avoid practicing idolatry was intimately connected to broader questions of day-to-day interactions as well as communal boundaries between Jews and those among whom they lived. At issue was both how not to violate biblical laws regarding idolatry in a narrow sense and how more expansively to cultivate Jewish identity and difference while making life livable within an empire and an economy that was considered by the rabbis to be both idolatrous and oppressive.[17] The laws and narratives throughout the tractate, in the Mishnah as well as in the corresponding Tosefta and the two Talmuds, seek to define those boundaries and determine how they might be maintained and, indeed, when they could be blurred or crossed. In these negotiations, the matter of time was central.

The Mishnah's redactor chose to open the tractate on idolatry by presenting the times when Jews were not allowed to interact with gentiles and with prohibitions related to festival observance. Notably, the redactor could have discussed, instead, other related matters, such as prohibitions on entering idolatrous spaces or the ingestion of certain foods related to idolatry. In making this editorial choice, the redactor highlighted the great cultural and religious importance of the Roman calendar and its rhythms for those living in the Roman Empire, as well as the centrality of time in rabbinic attempts to differentiate themselves from that empire.[18]

> On the three days preceding the festivals of the gentiles, it is forbidden to transact business with them, to lend articles to them or borrow from them, to lend money to them or to borrow money from them, to repay a debt or receive payment from them . . . Rabbi Ishmael says, Three [days] before them and three [days] after them it is prohibited. And sages say, Before their festivals it is prohibited, but after their festivals it is permitted.[19]

These opening lines of the tractate do not explicitly prohibit direct participation in Roman festivals. Indeed, the tractate presupposes that such participation is forbidden and assumes that its audience already knows that this is the case (whether or not they would have in fact abstained from such participation).[20] The Mishnah does not even acknowledge the possibility of direct participation in Roman festival celebration, pretending that the separation of Jews from others is much more established than it actually was. Instead, the rabbis of the Mishnah ban certain practices that brought Jews into business encounters with gentiles in the days leading up to Roman festivals (and, according to the opinion of Rabbi Ishmael, also in the days that followed them), and they prohibit any actions that might lead to indirect and even inadvertent worship of pagan gods during such festival times.[21] The specific actions that the Mishnah prohibits in the days preceding a Roman festival entail various types of business interactions between Jews and gentiles: buying and selling, lending and borrowing, and repaying loans.

Significantly, though, the tractate does not distinguish between direct and indirect, or intentional or unintentional, idolatrous worship. Idolatrous worship entails the performance or participation in cultic rituals as well as actions that contribute to someone else's cultic worship. That is, the Mishnah regards these two forms of participation as categorically similar. For example, selling an animal to someone in the days leading up to a festival is prohibited because participating in such commercial transactions was considered to be part of festival practice (a topic discussed below) and also because if the person who purchased the animal sacrificed it for an idolatrous ritual in an upcoming festival, the seller is considered to have contributed to and thus participated in the idolatrous worship even though that person did not intend to contribute

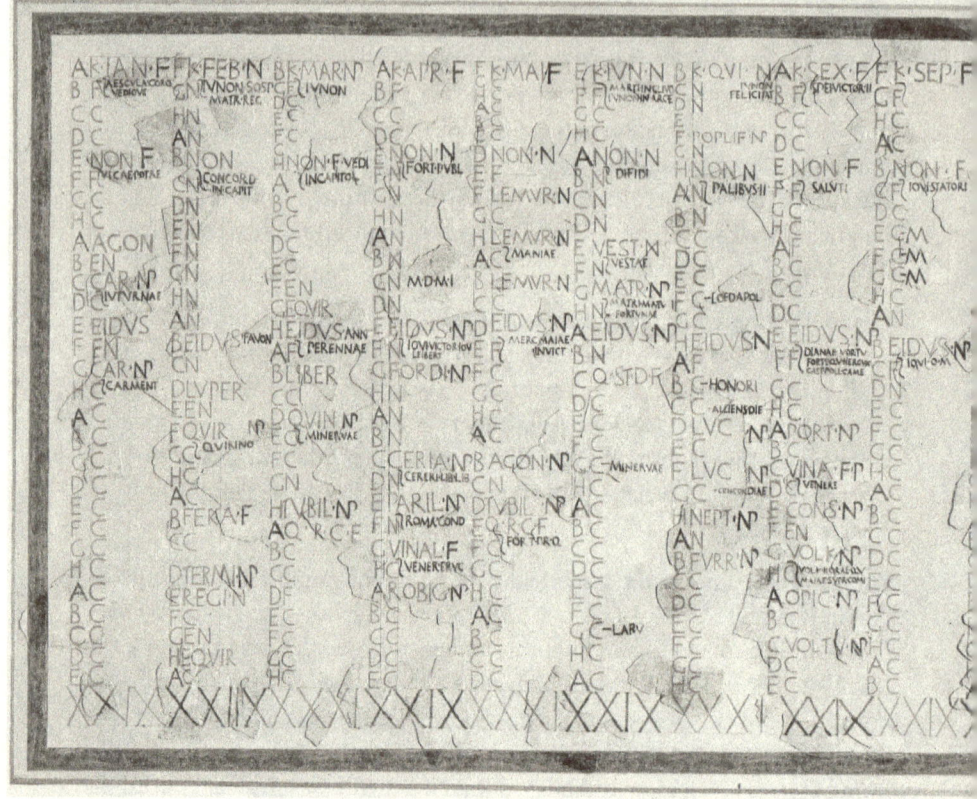

FIGURE 1. Reconstruction of a first century BCE Roman republican calendar, Fasti Antiates Maiores.

to such worship. The Mishnah assumes that contributing materially to idolatrous worship through business transactions, even if such contribution is indirect and/or unintentional, constitutes participation in that idolatrous worship.

The Mishnah approaches the obligation to avoid idolatrous practice specifically through setting limits on commercial interactions between Jews and gentiles before and after festivals.[22] Numerous examples illustrate that commerce was an integral part of Roman festivals and played a central role in their celebration. It should be no surprise, then, that the rabbis ban commercial exchange in a tractate that centers on idolatrous worship and pagan festal days. Commerce in the days leading up to a festival was part and parcel of the way in which such times were observed.

One of the primary purposes of the Roman calendar, from its earliest attestations in the republican period as well as during the imperial period, was to align market days with festal days and to alert Roman citizens of these up-

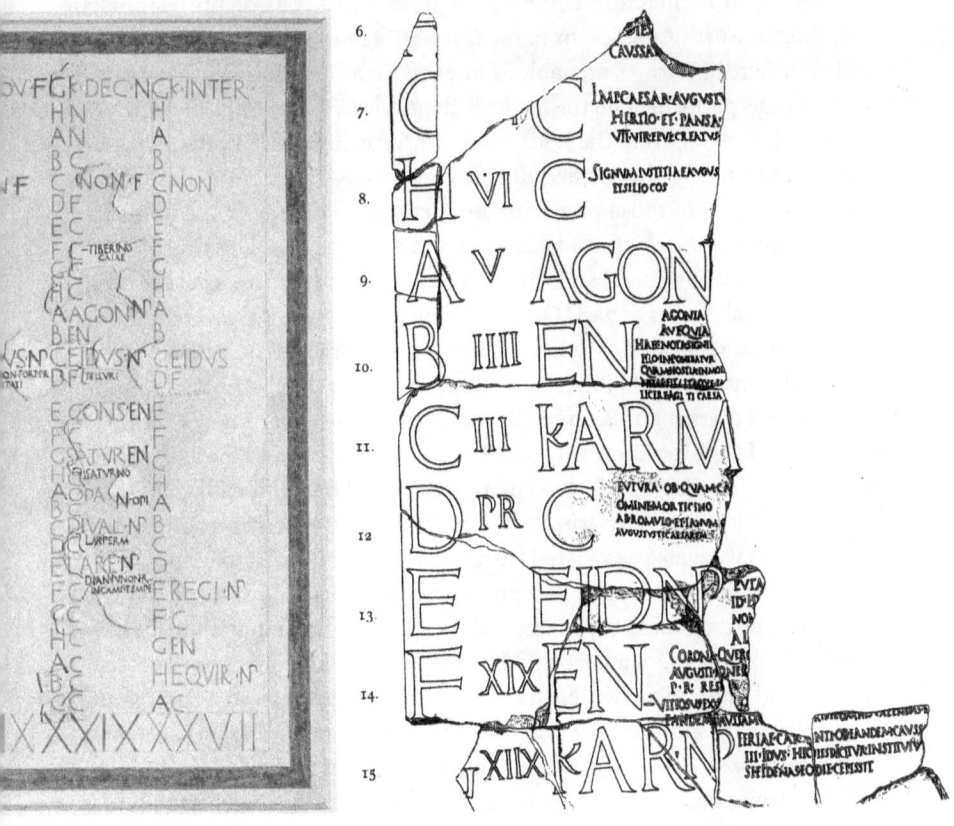

FIGURE 2. January 6–15 section of an early imperial calendar, Fasti Praenestini.

coming times.[23] As a material document, the Roman calendar visually depicts this interrelatedness of commerce and festival worship. Standard Roman calendars of this period record the nundinal cycle of market days for each month (the *nundinae*) alongside the festal days in adjacent parallel columns.[24] The impression one is left with when looking at such a document is how inseparable the rhythms of the market were from the rhythms of cultic worship. Concerning the Roman republican calendar, Michels notes that "because the Romans never separated religion from civic affairs, we shall find that a study of the state calendar leads into many areas of Roman life which at first sight seem to have little to do with religion, such as civil law, electoral and legislative assemblies, even market days. The rites of the state cult combine with all these affairs to make up what is truly a civil calendar, because it represents the life of a citizen, a *civis Romanus*, in all its phases."[25]

Indeed, an important part of celebrating a festival throughout the Roman world entailed engaging in commerce in the days that led up to the festival. An analogy could be made to contemporary pre-Christmas or pre-Hanukkah shopping in North America, or to the Christmas markets in Germany, France, and elsewhere in Europe, arguably as integral to the celebration of the festivals as the rituals performed on the festivals themselves.[26] The English word "fair" is derived, after all, from the Latin word for festival, *feria*.[27] In Roman antiquity, market activity intensified during these times to accommodate the increased demand of those preparing for festivities.[28] Many of the items that tractate *Avodah Zarah* forbids Jews to sell to gentiles at any time, such as frankincense, white cocks, and various types of dates, were items used specifically in festival celebrations.[29] Other rabbinic sources also suggest that Roman festivals were associated with local and regional markets. The Palestinian Talmud mentions that Rabbi Zeira sent Rabbi Bebai to purchase yarn "from the *Saturnalia* [market] of Beshan [Scythopolis]," which was known for its big fairs around festival times.[30] The text also describes Rabbi Hiyya ben Abbah requesting sandals from a festival market at Tyre.[31] In addition to commercial preparations such as purchasing supplies, food, and livestock, certain financial transactions were also associated with named days of the Roman month. For example, the first day of each Roman month, the Kalends, was a day on which one repaid interest and fixed loans, and the middle of the month, the Ides, was the day for paying rent and debts.[32] It is precisely because of how integral commercial and financial activities were to the celebration of annual festivals and the marking of significant days each month that the rabbis banned such business interactions in the days leading up to Roman festivals.

The strong link between commercial activities and the celebration of festivals also appears in documentary sources. In a letter from Fayyum, in Roman North Africa (today's Faiyum, Egypt), dated to 103 CE, Lucius Bellenus Gemellus wrote to his son, Sabinus, detailing the preparations that were necessary for two upcoming festivals: "send ten cocks from the market for the Saturnalia, and for Gemella's birthday feast [γενέσια] send some delicacies and ... an artaba of wheaten bread."[33] In this letter, the celebration of the Saturnalia and Gemella's birthday—two of the same festivals listed in the Mishnah—is marked by purchasing birds and food at the market. Another letter, dated to the first or early second century, was sent from an enslaved man named Severus to another enslaved man, Candidus, in the region of Vindolanda (in today's northern England) requesting that he purchase donkeys and radishes for the Saturnalia.[34] Several other letters from the third century, found at Oxyrhynchus in Middle Egypt, discuss the purchase and shipment of wheat, lentils, honey, wool, and clothing in preparation for festivals as well.[35] Dio of Prusa, in his speech to Apamea Celaenea, mentions that before festivals "those who have goods to sell get the highest price and there is no lack of work in the city."[36]

The interrelation between commerce and festival celebration extended beyond the bounds of daily life, spilling into literature and philosophy. In Ovid's

Fasti, Janus, the god of January, discusses the Kalends of January: "I entrusted this newborn time to business, lest the year's start enervate the whole, every man gives a taste of his occupation and offers some proof of his normal work."[37] The Roman New Year, also mentioned in the Mishnah's list of Roman festivals, is characterized by Ovid as a day of commerce that foreshadowed the year's financial success. Seneca, in his letter about the Saturnalia, describes the preparations that preceded the festival: "It is the month of December, and yet the whole city is in a sweat! . . . Everywhere there echoes the noise of preparations on a massive scale. It all suggests that the Saturnalia festivals are different from the ordinary working day, when the difference is really non-existent—so much so in fact that the man who said that December used to be a month but is now a year was, in my opinion, not far wide of the mark!"[38]

The Mishnah defines what it means to "contribute" to idolatrous worship expansively to include tangible material effects as well as affective dimensions of financial interactions. The group of financial prohibitions enumerated in the first half of the *mishnah* presents the prohibitions as attempts to limit financial participation in the acquisition or sale of materials used in idolatrous worship or in the exchange of money that would ultimately be used (or that had been previously used) to purchase idolatrous materials. The second half of the *mishnah*, however, records a dispute between Rabbi Judah and the sages that suggests not only that in their prohibitions rabbis had in mind material contributions to idolatrous practice but also that they worried about financial transactions that bring joy to gentiles and thus would likewise result in, or themselves constitute, idolatrous worship.

> Rabbi Judah says, One may accept repayment from them, because he [the gentile] is [thereby] distressed. They said to him, Even though he is distressed now, he will be happy about it later.[39]

Rabbi Judah posits that while Jews are prohibited from repaying a loan to a gentile, they are permitted to accept repayment of a loan from a gentile during the three days preceding a festival. According to Rabbi Judah's logic, Jews are not allowed to repay a loan shortly before a gentile's festival because Rabbi Judah assumes that a gentile who receives a loan repayment in the days before celebrating a festival might direct his gratitude and joy for his good fortune to his gods through the idolatrous rituals of the festivals. This outcome would mean that the loan repayment constituted indirect idolatry. Rabbi Judah argues that while a Jew is not permitted to repay a loan, a Jew may accept repayment of a loan from a gentile because repaying a loan would depress the gentile, giving him no extra reason to worship his deities. The collectivity of rabbis takes a more stringent approach, banning loan repayment both to and from a gentile. Acceptance of loan repayment, in this line of thinking, is prohibited because even though the gentile might immediately regret parting with his money, he would surely be glad to have paid off his debt in the long run, and such happiness might, again, lead to some future form of idolatrous worship on his part. This disagreement between Rabbi Judah and the sages is predicated on a shared understanding that the affective consequences of financial transactions with gentiles are just as real and problematic as the material consequences of such financial transactions and that both violate the prohibition against contributing to idolatrous worship. It also alludes to a connection between cultic festival celebration and joy. Causing gentiles emotional states of joy, it is posited by both opinions, violates the prohibition against idolatry either because a person is more likely to engage in cultic rituals of thanksgiving as a result of that joy and therefore such interactions must be avoided or because joy in this context is itself synonymous with idolatrous practice (and thus the passage would read "even though it is distressing to him now, he will *worship idolatrously* later"). The financial prohibitions in the Mishnah thus seek both to limit direct and indirect *material* contributions to idolatry and to curb direct and indirect *affective* contributions to or participation in idolatrous worship.

By delineating such specific prohibitions, the Mishnah does more than limit Jewish participation in idolatrous activity and separate Jewish and Roman festival days; it also implicitly permits forms and times of interaction that are not explicitly banned. For example, if business between Jews and gentiles is prohibited during the three days prior to a pagan festival, then trading on all other days is implicitly permissible.[40] The rabbis balance prohibitions against idolatry and pagan practice, on the one hand, with the necessity to design a framework of Jewish law and a set of times that allow for the coexistence of Jews and gentiles in a single society, on the other. This rabbinic strategy responds to those who believed that absolutely no interaction with gentiles (conceived collectively as idolaters) and idolatry was permitted as well as to those who thought that all interaction with gentiles and idolatry was permitted. Mediating deftly between the extremes of this wide spectrum, these rabbinic rules allow sufficient interaction to afford participation in Roman society but circumscribe the interactions enough that they maintain difference.

THE MISHNAH'S LIST OF ROMAN FESTIVALS

Having established that business transactions are forbidden in the days preceding idolatrous festivals, the Mishnah specifies the particular festivals to which such restrictions applied. The comprehensive list that follows indicates a broad knowledge of the Roman calendar and resembles other lists of Roman festivals found in contemporaneous military, literary, and legal sources from across the empire. What emerges from the Mishnah's text is a concise Roman calendar—or, more accurately, a *feriale*, a list of festivals—that includes many different types of festivals. This was a calendar that, according to rabbinic law, Jews were required to follow in order to avoid Roman festival times.

These are the festivals of the gentiles: Kalends, Saturnalia, Kratesis, and the day of Genousia of kings, [and] the day of birth and the day of death. These are the words of Rabbi Meir. And the sages say, Every death [ritual] that includes burning is [considered] idolatrous, and when there is no burning, there is no idolatry.[41]

The Mishnah's list of Roman festivals begins with the most widely celebrated public festivals, the Kalends of January and the Saturnalia; proceeds to imperial festivals associated with the eastward expansion of the empire as well as the emperor cult; and concludes with feasts and festivals held by individuals, including coming-of-age rituals and celebrations of thanksgiving.[42] The ordering of these festivals is categorical rather than calendrical. Instead of following the cycle of the Roman year from January through December, the Mishnah organizes the festivals by type. It also distinguishes between public and private festivals.[43] This distinction echoes the categories of *feriae publicae*, utilized in Roman sources to denote public festivals such as the Kalends of January and the Saturnalia, and *feriae singulorum*, which commemorated important days and celebrations in the lives of individuals.[44] The most stringent restrictions concern commercial exchange before public festivals, with more lenient standards applying to private celebrations (in these latter cases, the prohibition applies "only to that day and that particular person").

Comparable lists of Roman festivals appear elsewhere in Roman sources, both those contemporaneous with the Mishnah and also later texts. Tertullian marks a similar set of festivals—including public festivals, most prominently the Kalends of January and the Saturnalia; emperor cult festivals; and private feasts—in his instructions for Christians about how to avoid idolatry and stop participating in the festivals of the empire while remaining on good terms with imperial authorities.[45] He divides the festivals into precisely the same categories and order as the Mishnah, though he does not always give the same instructions as the Mishnah (for example, while he bans public festivals, he is more lenient about certain aspects of imperial and private festivals). A *feriale* from Dura-Europos from the first quarter of the third century CE, discovered in the room of a temple complex of an auxiliary Roman military base, lists festival days with their associated prescribed offerings. This list includes ordinary public festivals such as the Kalends of January and the Saturnalia; imperial occasions such as the *dies imperii* of Trajan, Antoninus, Aurelius and Verus, Septimus Severus and Caracalla; and military celebrations, namely, the day of *honesta missio* and the two *rosaliae signorum*.[46] These are the very kinds of public and imperial festivals that the Mishnah includes in its list, though it prohibits rather than encourages or requires participation in them. Later lists of Roman festivals also appear in an edict of Theodosius I from 389 and Macrobius's fifth-century treatise *Saturnalia*.[47] In both these texts, too, Roman festivals are listed categorically, and the organization resembles that of the Mishnah. The Theodosian rescript lists agricultural seasons, traditional Roman festivals, Easter, and days associated with the emperors. Macrobius begins with four kinds of public festivals (fixed, movable, commanded, and held every ninth day); includes festivals associated with specific clans; and ends with festivals for individuals. Each of these lists preserves a somewhat different assembly of festivals based on its specific function. Juxtaposing the Mishnah's list alongside these other festival lists, it is easy to see how similar they all are with respect to content and style.

Extant Roman calendars from the mishnaic period contain dozens of festivals, both those that date back to the republican era and those introduced in the imperial period.[48] The Mishnah does not include all of these Roman festivals but rather only a small portion of them. What is the significance of the Mishnah's particular selection? As discussed later in the chapter, the tannaim deliberately chose to include the Roman festivals that enjoyed particular popularity in the eastern part of the empire, that promoted imperial ideologies, and that were associated with both cultic worship and civic celebrations.

The first two festivals, the Kalends of January and the Saturnalia, are the oldest public festivals on the Mishnah's list and are often associated with one another.[49] Both date back to the Roman Republic but continued to be observed during the imperial era and even thereafter.[50] These festivals, which numbered among the most widely celebrated festivals in the empire, represent the beginning and end of the Roman year.[51] The Kalends of January, the Roman New Year, began on January 1. The festival celebrated Janus, the deity of entry and exit, as Janus faces both backward to the past and forward to the future. In addition to offering sacrifices, consuls assumed office on that day and took the auspices. Vows were made for the success of the emperor and the empire, and after three days of celebrations, the festival culminated with games given by the newly appointed consuls.[52] The Saturnalia was celebrated in mid-December and marked the upcoming end of the Roman year.[53] Celebrations began on December 17 with sacrifices to the deity Saturn at the Temple of Saturn. The carnivalesque festival, which featured the reversal of social hierarchies, often included a feast at which masters served those whom they enslaved or ate alongside them, in addition to other practices such as dice games, drinking, and intellectual conversations. The Kalends of January began as a one-day festival but by the third century was celebrated over the course of several days; the Saturnalia, too, extended over several days.[54]

The next festivals on the Mishnah's list include Kratesis, Genousia, and the imperial anniversaries of births and deaths. These festivals originated during the imperial period in veneration of the emperors and members of the imperial family.[55] One of the major shifts between the republican and imperial calendars of Rome was the imposition of festivals related to the emperor cult onto a calendar filled previously with primarily ancient agricultural and cultural festal days that harked back to the city's founding and early development.[56] The insertion into the Julian calendar of festivals related to the imperial cult, such as the day of the emperor's accession (*natales imperii*) or the emperor's birthday (*dies natalis*), promoted imperial aims through religious rituals and wove the emperor and his family into the daily lives of those who relied on the Roman calendar. Such festivals, according to Simon Price, cultivated a "perception of the permanence and stability of the Roman empire. . . . Indeed time itself was changed by the imperial cult."[57] It was this layered calendar, replete with festivals associated with the emperor cult, that made its way to the Galilee and with which the rabbis of the Mishnah had to contend. Festivals related to the imperial cult were likely first celebrated in the region of Palestine at the imperial temples built by Herod in Caesarea Maritima, Samaria, and Banias; further popularized by the local Roman army legions stationed throughout the region; and later observed at the temple of Jupiter Capitolinus in Aelia Capitolina and at other monuments erected throughout the region of Palestine in the second and third centuries.[58]

Scholars have remained uncertain about the festival named "Kratesis," suggesting either that it commemorated the empire's expansion in the eastern territories under Augustus or that it marked the day of the current emperor's accession to the throne (or both).[59] The name of the festival, based on the Greek word κράτησις, "power" and "dominion," evokes notions of military strength, conquest, and political sovereignty.[60] The term "Kratesis" was used in Egyptian documentary sources to refer to the formal start of Augustus's rule over Egypt on 1 August 30 BCE (8 Mesore in the traditional Egyptian calendar), when Augustus captured Alexandria.[61] In these documents, the "kratesis era" (*kaisaros kratesis theou huiou*—"dominion of Caesar, the son of a god") refers to the beginning of the years of Augustus's rule in Egypt. The Roman historian Dio Cassius, who lived at the time of the Mishnah's redaction, mentions that the day of Alexandria's conquest was indeed declared a *dies festus*: "The day on which Alexandria had been captured they declared a lucky day, and directed that in future years it should be taken by the inhabitants of that city as the starting-point in their reckoning of time."[62] The Mishnah might have had this festival, celebrated on the first of August, in mind when it lists Kratesis. Macrobius, too, lists several victories and milestones related to Augustus that were associated with the month of August, including Augustus's entering the consulship, three triumphal processions, the end of the civil wars, and, most notably, "in this month Egypt was brought under the power (*potestas*) of the Roman people."[63] Both Talmuds, redacted in subsequent centuries, suggest that the festival name Kratesis was eventually conflated with a variety of festival days dedicated to commemorating moments of the empire's eastward expansion as well as the accession of the current emperor to the throne. Thus, in time, Kratesis came to be understood in rabbinic sources as an imperial festival associated with the empire's military strength and victory even as it was applied to different historical events and calendrical dates.

The Mishnah's forbidden festival list continues with other imperial festivals, including anniversaries, birthdays, and commemorations of deaths associated with various emperors and their families.[64] Genousia probably refers to the ruling emperor's birthday, and perhaps also to other important anniversaries such as the emperor's accession to the throne or the date on which an emperor visited a particular city.[65] The Mishnah's phrase "days of birth," in contrast, likely refers to the celebration of the birthdays of the emperor's wife and other family members. Augustus's birthday, for example, was celebrated on September 23, the same day as the festival of Apollo.[66] In Mytilene, Augustus's birthday was celebrated each month, and the sitting emperor's birthday was commemorated annually as well.[67] The town of Gortyn celebrated Rome's *dies natalis* along with Marcus Aurelius's accession and the birthdays of three of his family members.[68] The birthdays of emperors and imperial family members were also celebrated in Ephesus and Gytheum.[69] In addition to birthdays, the designation *dies natalis* was used for other anniversaries, dedications of temples, and the deaths of martyrs.[70] The Mishnah's reference to "days of death" might have referred specifically to the marking of the death of certain imperial figures, especially those who died young or tragically, or to certain funeral or burial practices that involved cultic rituals (hence the mishnaic debate about whether all "days of death" ought to be avoided or only those that involved "burning").[71]

The public festivals listed in the Mishnah would have been alluring for Jews at least in part because of their civic dimension. By this period in the late second and early third centuries, many residents of the Roman Empire regarded Kalends, Saturnalia, and festivals related to the emperors as occasions for civic celebration rather than as exclusively or primarily cultic in practice and meaning.[72] They often featured well-attended public activities such as games, races, theatrical performances, and other spectacles, of which rabbinic texts are aware.[73] Fritz Graf suggests that the Kalends of January was included in the Mishnah's list, for example, specifically because people viewed the festival as a sign of "the unity and stability of the empire, to tie it together by a ritual shared by all inhabitants of the empire, from Britain, Spain and Africa to Anatolia, Syria and Egypt."[74] Peter Brown writes that the Kalends came to represent "a neutral public culture" in which "men of different *religiones* could collaborate to maintain a Roman world restored to order."[75] Our sources attest that many Jews across the Roman Empire participated in public festivals alongside Christians and other Romans. Roman festivals that included cultic worship but that lacked a civic dimension, however, might not have been as enticing to Jews, such that the rabbis did not feel the need to proactively dissuade their followers from celebrating them.

While civic festivals can unite members of different communities in common celebration, such times can have the opposite effect, too. Oftentimes, they facilitate highly charged assertions of identity.[76] Indeed, the very definition and character of such festivals were being contested throughout the period when the Mishnah was composed and edited, precisely because not everyone was pleased with how widespread their observance had become. Origen, in a treatise written in Caesarea shortly after the Mishnah's redaction, admits that most Christians of his era regard these public Roman festivals as civic celebrations in which they could participate.[77] He insists, however, that because such festivals are the invention of human beings and are not directed toward the Christian God, they constitute false worship and Christians must not participate in them. The rabbis of the Mishnah, some of whom lived in Caesarea and others of whom were not far away in Sepphoris and Tiberias, faced a similar situation in which Jews of this region regarded public festivals as primarily civic celebrations and thus assumed that they were permitted to participate. These rabbis, similar to their Christian bishop counterparts, thus sought to put an end to such assumptions.

It was once Jews began to feel more comfortable partaking in the empire's festivals and balancing their own religious commitments with their sense of belonging within their broader social and political world that the rabbis of the Mishnah chose to assert their own authority over Jewish practices more vehemently. The need to insist on difference emerged, that is, precisely when the rabbis feared that rabbinic and Roman difference was beginning to disintegrate. Similar to Tertullian and Origen, the rabbis found it necessary to argue that these festivals were not merely civic but, in fact, idolatrous in order to limit their congregants' participation in them (this, itself, was a political act of definition). By defining these specific festivals as idolatrous affairs rather than civic events, and mandating that their congregants mark their times differently, these figures of authority sought to create a wedge between the ways that Jews, Christians, and Roman pagans related to them—and to each other.

PRIVATE FESTIVALS IN THE MISHNAH

The Mishnah's insistence that its rabbinic adherents vigilantly avoid Roman times was predicated upon, and also cultivated, deep familiarity with the Roman calendar, its festivals, and its annual temporal rhythms—as is patent from the Mishnah's own list. The final group of festivals found in the Mishnah includes personal celebrations observed by individuals on their own initiative: rites of passage, moments of thanksgiving, and familial feasts.

> The day on which [a gentile] shaves off his beard and lock of hair; the day on which he returned from the sea; the day on which he was released from prison; [and a gentile who made a banquet for his son]:

[commerce] is not prohibited except on that day and with that particular person.[78]

By prohibiting commercial interactions with gentiles not only before well-known public festivals but also preceding private ones, the mishnaic laws in tractate *Avodah Zarah* required rabbinic Jews to keep track of both public and private rhythms of time—that is, of the times of the empire as well as of its imperial subjects.

The celebration of personal birthdays, in addition to imperial birthdays, was a Roman tradition, without Greek or other precedent.[79] Individual Romans celebrated their birthdays and the birthdays of family members and friends with sacrifices to one's Genius or Juno, fire on domestic altars, incense, ritual cakes, wine, garlands of flowers, and white robes.[80] The birthday poem (*genethliacon*), too, was a Roman genre popular enough to last three centuries after the Augustan period.[81] Censorinus's *De die natalie*, a birthday book about birthdays, was composed for the author's patron in the 320s. Beryl Rawson writes: "By celebrating the anniversary of their birthday every year, Romans marked the passage of time. They gave thanks for the past year and prayed for divine protection for the coming year."[82] Denis Feeney notes that after Caesar's reforms, an anniversary was "not just [a] recurrence of a day but [a] recurrence of a day after an identical interval every year"; indeed, time is regularized as one regards the same date from year to year as *idem dies*, the same day, and is then able to count year-units from the day of birth.[83] On one's birthday, an individual "gave thanks for having had 'many happy returns'" and "prayed for many more."[84] In addition to marking birthdays, Romans eagerly commemorated other life stages as well.[85] The most significant moments were birth, coming-of-age (for boys), and death, which were all marked by taxes or financial offerings given at temples along with social gatherings and other festivities.[86]

The Mishnah specifically mentions rituals that involve shaving one's beard or hair. Dio Cassius recalls Nero's Juvenalia, an elaborate beard-shaving celebration that included performances, choruses, and quadrennial games.[87] Individual beard-shaving celebrations would have been more low-key but festive nonetheless. Such ceremonies listed in the Mishnah might refer to a shaving ceremony performed by enslaved people who had been manumitted as well as freedmen who were released from captivity before they donned the brimless conical hat, the *pilleus*.[88] The practice could also refer to a ritual that marked the transition from a period of mourning, when one's hair was visibly disheveled, back to regular life.[89]

Rituals of travel, especially vows and votives offered upon disembarking from a sea voyage, were common too.[90] Prayers and offerings of devotion were dedicated to *lares compitales* at crossroads, *lares viales* and *lares semitales* on the roads, and *lares permarini* on the seas.[91] The compital shrines in particular became more widespread and geographically scattered during the imperial age, when Augustus and emperors after him transformed them into monuments to honor the emperor within neighborhood contexts in addition to marking spaces of transition.[92] Steven Muir writes about the importance of the divinity Janus as well: "Janus was the Roman god of the doorway and gate. Like a door, he looked outward to the road and inward to the home. . . . It was thought that he controlled the beginnings of an enterprise, so his protection was evoked at the commencement of a journey."[93] Marble and terracotta votive offerings were made to Redicolus, the god of return.[94] Fifty bronze plaques from a shrine of Jupiter Poeninus contain vows of travelers for a safe journey across the Alps.[95] Additional divinatory practices could be performed at the start of journeys and as navigational tools, and thanksgiving rituals marked travelers' safe return from sea.

The final private festivals listed in the Mishnah are banquets hosted by fathers in honor of their sons.[96] Here the mishnaic text might refer to coming-of-age rituals for young men, in which boys donned the *toga virilis* for the first time.[97] These celebrations included extended family and other community members. The ceremonies consisted of offerings to household gods, a public procession through the forum or other public spaces to display a boy's transition to manhood, and sacrifices in the temple. The celebration ended with the distribution of food and money to those present.

From the mishnaic point of view, Roman and rabbinic time were imagined to be intricately interwoven. Some prohibitions, such as forbidding business transactions with those who recently returned from travel or marked a birthday, presuppose a high degree of familiarity with the lives and schedules of celebrants. In other words, the more extreme the mandated separation, as detailed in the rabbinic text, the more intimate the relations and rhythms are assumed to have been and the more entwined their times would have become.

Roman Festivals in the Palestinian and Babylonian Talmuds

The Mishnah's prohibitions regarding Roman festivals did not remain a static tradition. Rabbinic engagement with these laws flourished in the centuries after the Mishnah's redaction, and these subsequent rabbinic traditions were eventually preserved within the Palestinian and Babylonian Talmuds. Over the course of these same centuries, the Roman festival calendar underwent significant changes. Questions about the official status of these festivals as well as their observance continued to be a source of tension and discussion well into the fifth century and thereafter. Multiple processes of imperial legislation and Christianization transformed how various individuals and communities within the Roman Empire, including rabbinic figures, related to the celebration of Roman festivals. It is in this complicated context that the discussion of Roman festivals in the two Talmuds is best understood.

Amoraic rabbinic interpreters of the Mishnah wrestled with a number of different challenges. First, they sought to understand and to further define the Mishnah's prohibitions. Second, they attempted to update the Mishnah's laws to fit contemporary life and its ever-evolving calendrical cycle. Third, they added new narrative dimensions to the Mishnah's list of prohibited Roman festivals, explaining their origins and positioning rabbinic interpretation of Israel's history vis-à-vis the Roman past.

The legal trajectories of these later rabbinic texts sometimes took a different course than the narrative ones. In their clarification, interpretation, and development of the Mishnah's festival prohibitions, the Palestinian and Babylonian Talmuds often advance more permissive regulations than the Mishnah and Tosefta. For example, the Palestinian Talmud records a debate between Rav and Rabbi Yohanan about how broadly the Mishnah's commercial limitations ought to extend. Rav suggests that absolutely no business can be conducted on the Kalends, while Rabbi Yohanan limits such interactions to those who actually celebrate the festival. In this way, Rabbi Yohanan raises the possibility that the Mishnah's ban on commercial exchange surrounding Roman festivals is too expansive and could be curtailed. Both Talmuds also significantly reduce the time during which the ban on engaging in commercial activity is effective in the Diaspora, though the Babylonian Talmud is more stringent in some cases.[98] The Mishnah dictates that all Jews abstain from business with gentiles three days prior to a festival (and, according to another opinion, also three days thereafter), while the Tosefta and the two Talmuds restrict trade to the day preceding the festival or the day of the festival itself for those living in Babylonia.[99] Scholars have explained that these shifts were likely motivated by a combination of exegetical, hermeneutical, generic, and cultural-historical concerns on the part of later rabbis. Among the various factors, some of these revisions to mishnaic laws indicate that the more extreme forms of separation envisioned by the rabbis of the Mishnah were no longer reasonable or practicable expectations, both because the festivals themselves included fewer cultic dimensions and because Jews were more comfortable participating in them. The Talmudim are also more concerned with the practical application of these laws rather than with imagining ideal circumstances in which these laws function, as the Mishnah often does.

While the later legal sources tend toward moderation, the later narrative traditions point in a different direction. The Palestinian Talmud describes the festivals themselves in biting polemical terms, a sentiment also found in contemporaneous Christian sermons that argue against Christian participation in Roman festivals. Even as rabbinic authorities in Palestine felt a need to temper the extent of the Mishnah's prohibitions, these narratives reveal the use of rabbinic polemical strategies to minimize participation in Roman time. The Babylonian Talmud, for its part, despite its inclusion of some halakhic stringencies absent from the Palestinian Talmud, often frames its discussions of these same festivals in somewhat more conciliatory terms, again for a combination of internal and external factors.

In trying to make sense of the rabbinic legal and narrative approaches to Roman festivals, it is important to bear in mind that these festivals remained part of the calendar even after the Christianization of the empire. Over the course of the fourth century, Christian emperors played an important role in the simultaneous Christianization of the empire and the continued celebration of traditional Roman festivals. In the mid-fourth century, Constantine declared Sunday to be a day on which legal and urban business halted, officially incorporating a weekly Christian festival into the Roman calendar.[100] Nevertheless, Constantine and several subsequent Christian emperors promoted the celebration of traditional Roman festivals, even as they eliminated their associated cultic rituals, especially sacrifices, in order to facilitate the continued civic involvement of the empire's religiously diverse, and increasingly Christian, inhabitants.[101] This imperial hybridization of time is vividly depicted in Philocalus's codex calendar of 354, which included both a traditional Roman calendar with its nundinal cycles and Roman festival days, alongside the Christian seven-day week and Christian festivals.[102] Despite the gradual adoption of Christianity by many of the empire's inhabitants, several major Roman festivals actually increased in popularity.[103] By the late fourth century, for example, the Kalends of January had moved far beyond the confines of the city of Rome and was celebrated throughout the empire.[104] The Saturnalia and various festivals associated with the emperor cult continued to flourish as well.[105] Through these imperial adjustments, Roman and Christian time became ever more enmeshed.

A more radical shift occurred toward the end of the fourth century, as a result of an imperial edict issued by Emperor Theodosius I in the summer of 389. Fearing for the functioning of the state, with the abundance of feasts and festivals on the Roman calendar causing the courts to be endlessly out of session, the emperor issued an imperial rescript that dramatically altered the empire's official festival calendar. This new calendar limited the courts' closure to two months of summer, the Kalends of January, the foundation days of Rome (April 21) and Constantinople (May 11), the period of Easter, Sundays, and the birthdays and anniversaries of a few emperors.[106] Gesturing toward the empire's Roman past, the order also signaled its decidedly Christian character: its calendar and its annual temporal rhythms included only the most popular pre-Christian Roman festivals alongside a growing number of Christian feasts.[107] Later laws from the decades after Theodosius's rescript added other Christian festivals to the list, instituted prohibitions concerning work on those days, and more explicitly excluded the festivals the empire considered pagan.[108] By 438, the Theodosian Code ensured that these laws applied across the empire.

Theodosius's rescript failed to please almost anyone. Non-Christian Romans such as Libanius were furious that so many older Roman festivals had been eliminated.[109] The move had effectively purged the Roman calendar of most of its traditional pagan times.[110] Christian bishops, for their part, were dismayed that the emperor had retained non-Christian Roman festivals they considered to be idolatrous. Before and after the rescript, Christian bishops and Palestinian rabbis voiced increasing animosity toward these Roman festivals, especially in light of their growing popularity and their continued imperial sanctioning. Graf has suggested that a spate of anti-pagan sermons in the late fourth and early fifth centuries might be understood as a specific reaction to Theodosius's retention of the Kalends in the official Roman annual calendar.[111] In Antioch, for example, John Chrysostom denounced the various rituals performed on the Kalends, including special decorations, lamps, libations, night choruses, gift exchanges, and omens.[112] He urged Christians to stay home rather than participate in these celebrations. In their place, he offered spiritualizing alternatives for his Christian congregants, as did Asterius, bishop of Amasea, in the year 400 CE.[113] On the Kalends of January in 404 CE, Augustine of Hippo similarly stood before a congregation in Carthage numbering as many as two thousand people and encouraged the audience to refrain from celebrating the Roman New Year and participating in the time of the pagans.[114] Instead, he exhorted, they ought to sanctify time in a Christian manner.[115] Augustine made his point in a dramatic manner, speaking for three full hours and thereby preventing the congregants from joining in the Kalends celebrations just outside the church.[116]

It was within this profoundly shifting temporal context that the Palestinian Talmud was collated and redacted. Similar trajectories can be traced in the Palestinian Talmud's laws and narratives about Roman festivals. The Palestinian Talmud, for example, draws a distinction between the Kalends of January and the Saturnalia. The text states plainly that the Saturnalia is off-limits for everyone. Unlike the discussion surrounding the Kalends, there is no debate about whether commercial prohibitions apply to all gentiles or only those actively participating in the festivities. Perhaps this is so because the festival—with its drinking, gambling, cultic activities, and general debauchery—was not regarded as a civic festival but was, by the late fourth century, more narrowly considered a pagan celebration through and through.[117] This development parallels the omission of the Saturnalia from Theodosius's rescript and the relative lack of engagement with the festival by later Christian bishops. It might also explain Macrobius's choice in the early decades of the fifth century, not long after the Palestinian Talmud's redaction, to use the Saturnalia as the calendrical backdrop for his treatise on the Roman calendar and the promotion of a deliberately pagan Roman culture.[118] At a time of imperial transformation, Macrobius chose a quintessentially Roman festival—one that was spurned even by the Christian emperors in their official Roman calendars—for the setting of his meditation on an old world that was slipping away. As the Roman Empire was deciding how to integrate elements of this pre-Christian calendar into its relatively new status as a Christian empire, Jews struggled with similar questions.

TALMUDIC STORIES ABOUT THE ORIGINS OF ROMAN FESTIVALS

The Palestinian and Babylonian Talmuds expand on Mishnah *Avodah Zarah* with etiologies of the Roman festivals. Several of these narratives reflect on Rome's origins and tell rabbinic versions of early Roman history. This history was the subject of important literature during the early years of the empire and became associated with Roman imperial ideology. The rabbinic stories about that ancient history are best regarded as part of this broader Roman engagement with the Roman past.

The Roman historian Livy's *Ab urbe condita* opens with the story of Rome's origins. Livy recounts Aeneas fleeing Troy and founding Lavinium in Latium; the birth of Romulus and Remus to Rhea Silvia, a Vestal virgin; Romulus's murder of his twin brother and his subsequent founding of Rome on the Palatine Hill; and the institution of the city's laws and governing structures.[119] This account includes the appointment of Numa as the next king of Rome, the consecration of the Temple of Janus and Rome's priestly offices, and Numa's calendrical reforms.[120] In telling these origin stories, Livy seeks to demonstrate Rome's greatness. He writes in his prologue that his recollections of Rome's past are "a source of satisfaction to celebrate, to the best of my ability, the history of the greatest nation on earth."[121] The Roman poet Ovid, too, wrote of Roman origins. Rather than composing a chronological prose history starting in the distant past and proceeding to more recent times, though, Ovid anchored moments of early Roman history to dates in the annually recurring Roman year.[122] Ovid's work on the Roman calendar, the *Fasti*, is organized by month and day. Each date commemorates a different moment in the founding and development of Rome. Ovid's *Fasti* begins, for example, with an ode to Janus, after whom the month of January is named.[123] The month of March commemorates the god Mars, his rape of Rhea Silvia, and her conception of Romulus and Remus, "her belly plumped with celestial weight."[124] The festival of the Parilia took place in April and commemorated the day of Rome's foundation as a city.[125] By mapping Roman history onto the festival calendar, Ovid highlighted how Romans were expected to experience and encounter Roman history on an annual cycle. He concludes his account of this day by invoking Rome's origins and its subsequently unparalleled power: "A city rises (who could then have believed it?), to set its victor's foot upon the earth."[126]

Livy and Ovid were not the only Romans who wrote about the origins of the empire in which they lived. In the early years of the fifth century, Macrobius authored his *Saturnalia*, a multivolume work on Roman history, myth, language, and culture. Macrobius begins his explorations of the formation of Roman identity and history with a winding overview of the Roman calendar, its origins and development, and the significance of its days, months, and annual festivals. In his etiologies for the Saturnalia, Macrobius recounts tales of the gods Janus and Saturn prior to the founding of the city of Rome, as well as the city's evolving sacred topography, filled as it was with temples and shrines that gestured toward the annual calendar and its cycles.[127] The remainder of the book provides the most detailed account from antiquity of all aspects of the Roman calendar—when days began and ended, the structure of the calendar, processes of intercalation, and so on. This discussion, a late antique attempt to preserve a sense of traditional Roman identity, also records Roman history through the cycle of the year.

Just as Ovid and Macrobius embedded their histories of Rome into a calendrical framework, the rabbis in the Palestinian and Babylonian Talmuds told their own version of Roman history as they glossed the Mishnah's list of Roman festivals. And, much like these authors, the rabbis used such stories to construct and cultivate their own identities—as Romans and as rabbis. One of the most fascinating dimensions of these stories is their merging of Roman history and rabbinic Israelite history. In the rabbinic texts, the Roman New Year in January was founded not—as Ovid and Macrobius suggest—by the Roman king Numa but rather by the biblical figure Adam, who observed the sun as an astronomer. The festival marking Rome's expansion into eastern territories not only commemorates Rome's great military strength but also recalls the sins of Israelite kings, whose idolatrous practices, as mentioned earlier, are presented as the true causes for Rome's founding, or alternatively celebrates the Roman-Jewish alliance and the role of the Torah in Rome's victories against its enemies.

In her work on the etiologies of festivals, Mary Beard argues that ancient Roman authors layered multiple meanings on a single festival day.[128] In the case of the festival of the Parilia, for example, Ovid, Dionysius of Halicarnassus, and Plutarch couple agricultural and historical etiologies about the foundation of Rome. Beard highlights the variety of explanations provided for this single festival. She claims that the ongoing generation and accumulation of interpretations afforded the festival its relevance. This allowed the festival to be understood anew in various contexts, even when older etiologies became irrelevant to new generations. Rather than settling on a simple interpretation, the constellation of religious, historical, civic, and natural explanations imbued Roman festivals with a rich significance and allowed different demographic groups to relate to the festival in ways that were most appropriate to them. In much the same way, biblical and rabbinic sources offer agricultural, mythological, and historical reasons for festivals such as Passover and Pentecost.

The etiologies of the Roman festivals presented in rabbinic sources participate in this same Roman phenomenon: the rabbis reimagined the origins of the empire's festivals in ways that were relevant to their communities. In his prologue, Livy explains that "the special and salutary benefit of the study of history is to behold evidence of every sort of behavior set forth on a splendid memorial; from it you may select for yourself and for your country what to emulate, from it, what to avoid, whether basely begun or basely concluded."[129] The rabbinic stories function in a similar fashion. They offer their ancient Jewish audiences a version of history meant to suggest how, as rabbinic Jews, they ought to act and the behaviors they should avoid as they live in a Roman world (in the case of the Palestinian Talmud) or reflect on the Roman Empire (in the case of the Babylonian Talmud).

There is an element in these rabbinic etiologies, however, that fundamentally differentiates them from other Roman ones. The stories told in the Palestinian and Babylonian Talmuds constitute what James C. Scott has called a "hidden transcript."[130] Thus, while they appear to participate in the Roman practice, they undermine Roman imperial claims by replacing Romans with Jews. "The public transcript," Scott writes of public discourse, "is unlikely to tell the whole story about power relations," as it usually aligns with the wishes and views of the dominant class.[131] The other part of the story, the opinions of the subordinate class, is not completely absent, though. The careful reader can discern it (1) within the public transcript; (2) more explicitly and fully in a hidden transcript that takes place "offstage," "beyond direct observation by powerholders"; and (3) in discourse that mediates between the public and hidden transcripts and manifests itself in ironic or veiled modes of expression such as rumors, gossip, folktales, jokes, songs, rituals, codes, and euphemisms.[132] The rabbinic stories of Roman festivals and their biblical origins can be taken to exemplify these various modes of discourse, texts that bring to light alternative perspectives, those of the rabbis, within a Roman imperial context that the authors of these texts often interpreted as hostile or threatening.[133] All of rabbinic literature produced within the Roman Empire fits into Scott's various registers, but these particular rabbinic stories about Roman festivals and their histories are especially subversive and specific in their engagement with the empire's public transcript. So, while these rabbinic stories participate in a Roman project, they simultaneously resist it by telling Roman history through a rabbinic lens. To adapt Paul Kosmin's formulation, they were Roman in derivation and anti-Roman by consequence.[134]

Through telling stories about Roman festivals, rabbis made a place for themselves in Roman history and within the Roman calendar, opposing Roman imperialism while participating in Roman discourses about the empire's origins. Indeed, they hardly acknowledge any Roman role in Israel's history, while emphasizing Israel's role in Roman history; they present Israel as influential but not influenced. These rabbinic narratives thus articulate a unique Roman-rabbinic identity, which claims that Jews were instrumental in Rome's founding yet nevertheless bemoans rather than celebrates Rome's power. Unpacking several examples of such etiologies will expose the variety of ways in which different rabbinic voices sought to impose Jewish anti-imperial themes onto the Roman calendar and the version of the Roman historical past it sought annually to commemorate.

IDOLATROUS FESTIVALS: TESTIMONIES OR CALAMITIES?

Before revealing the origins of each Roman festival, both Talmuds include a discussion about the spelling of the term *eideihem*, which the Mishnah uses to refer to Roman festivals.[135] By the time of this debate, the rabbis were no longer sure which term was used in tannaitic traditions; *eid* spelled with an alef and *eid* spelled with an ayin would have been pronounced indistinguishably in the Roman Galilean dialects of both Hebrew and Aramaic. The Palestinian Talmud's interest in identifying the biblical passages and etymologies that lie behind the rabbinic term for "festivals" corresponds with the subsequent etiologies it provides for specific Roman festivals, which are also primarily concerned with how the etymologies of the festival names belie their origins and meaning. According to a tradition transmitted by Rav, the term *eid* is spelled with an ayin, while according to a tradition transmitted by Shmuel, the term *eid* is spelled with an alef. The Palestinian Talmud presents the divergence in spelling as a result of two distinct traditions that each rely on distinct biblical proof texts. Those who spell the word with an ayin, such as Rav, are alluding to Isaiah 43:9: "Let all the nations gather together, and let the peoples assemble; who among them declared this, and foretold to us the former things? Let them bring their witnesses [עדיהם] to justify them, and let them hear and say, 'It is true.'"[136] In this biblical verse, the term *eid* is used to refer to the "testimonies" that the nations of the world will bring as "witnesses" during the time of the ingathering of nations. The gentiles' festivals, according to this midrashic reading, function as testimonies of their (false) beliefs.

Those, however, who use an alef in their spelling of the term *eideihem*, such as Shmuel, rely instead on Deuteronomy 32:35: "Vengeance is Mine, and recompense, for the time when their foot shall slip; because the day of their calamity is at hand [כי קרוב יום אידם], their doom comes swiftly."[137] This verse employs the term *eid* to mean "calamity" and refers to the day of calamity that will befall the nations during the end times.[138] With this spelling, the term implies that gentile festivals are themselves calamities and signs of disaster.

While the Palestinian Talmud places this debate about the spelling and meaning of this term at the start of its section about Roman festivals, the Babylonian Talmud records the same spelling debate between Rav and Shmuel at the beginning of the entire tractate, thus using it to frame the entire subsequent analysis of idolatry rather than only that of the Roman festivals. The Babylonian Talmud also adds a more robust theological dimension to the debate about the term's spelling. The text proposes that Shmuel preferred the spelling that used an alef because its meaning, "calamity," highlights the calamitous nature of idolatry. Rav's spelling, which uses an ayin, is justified by explaining, in contrast, that the (false) "testimony" of gentiles leads to calamity. Yet another anonymous opinion about this verse suggests that "testimony" does not refer to the testimony of *gentiles* but rather to the testimonies of *Israel*, whose good deeds will bear testimony for them in the World to Come and will convince gentiles to admit the truth of Israel's beliefs and renounce their own. The text then offers a second proof text from Isaiah 44:9 further to support Rav's spelling. Finally, the Babylonian Talmud elaborates upon this opening debate with a homiletic narrative that builds upon the reference to Isaiah 43:9. In this narrative, the nations of the world, led by Rome, try to gain admission to the World to Come during eschatological times, but God finds their testimonies inadequate and, in the end, rewards Israel while rebuking and mocking the nations.[139] Though the story begins with Rome, it subsequently divides the world's population into two groups: Israel on the one hand and all the other nations on the other.[140] It is not specifically Roman-Jewish difference with which the story is interested but rather Jewish-gentile difference more broadly construed. The Babylonian Talmud's discussion of the two terms contains the same biblical proof texts as the Palestinian Talmud but it takes a more thematic and theological approach to the terms, in line with the Babylonian Talmud's overall approach to the origins and meanings of the other festivals in the remainder of the tractate, which focuses less on the etymological significance, as does the Palestinian Talmud, and more on their theological dimensions. These distinctions between the Palestinian and Babylonian Talmuds' approach to the etiology of the category of Roman festivals align with the distinctions they make in their explanations of specific Roman festivals as well.

KALENDS AND SATURNALIA

The Palestinian Talmud provides two etiologies for the Kalends of January, each of which offers an alternative etymology for the festival's name. The first etiology is attributed to Rav and the second is credited to Rabbi Yohanan. According to Rav, Kalends was established by the biblical Adam in the weeks following the world's creation:

Kalends: the first man established [this festival]. Because the night was getting longer, he said: Woe is me! Perhaps concerning whom it is written: "He shall strike at your head, and you shall strike at their heel" (Genesis 3:15)—perhaps he is going to come to bite me? And I say: "Surely darkness will strike me" (Ps 139:11). Because the days began to grow longer, he said: Kalends [קלנדס], [meaning] καλον *dies* [how beautiful is the day].[141]

This etiology seeks to explain the seasonal significance of the Kalends of January, which takes place a few days after the winter solstice and is therefore the first sign that the winter darkness is beginning to abate. In this story, we meet Adam sometime between the summer and winter solstices, when the days get increasingly shorter. The daily reduction of light and the accompanying expansion of the dark night frighten him. He worries that the encroaching darkness is part of his payback for sinning in Eden.

Adam's logic stems from a midrash. He connects God's curse in Genesis 3:15, "he will *strike* [ישופך] your head, and you will *strike* [תשופנו] his heel," with a phrase from Psalm 139:11 that uses the same verb, to strike: "surely the darkness shall *strike* me [ישופני], and the light about me shall be night."[142] Rather than reading Genesis 3:15 literally, that the serpent will strike Adam and Eve, the biblical figure links it with Psalm 139:11 and interprets it to mean that *God* will strike specifically with darkness. That is, Adam fears that he is experiencing God's punishing strikes of darkness as the light around him turns to night. But then everything changes. The days begin to lengthen, and Adam learns that his sin was not the cause of the increased darkness. He gains a fuller understanding of the verse from Psalm 139, which he had originally understood as a premonition that God would strike him with darkness, by considering the remainder of the verse: "If I say, 'Surely the darkness shall cover me, and the light around me becomes night,' even the darkness is not dark to you; the night is as bright as the day, for darkness is as light to you."[143] Adam comes to realize that "even the darkness is not too dark" and that the night eventually "shines as the day." The clever linguistic play accounts for both Adam's initial fears and the resolution of those fears.

Relieved and elated, Adam exclaims: "Kalends!" The rabbinic story explains that this expression is a combination of the Greek word καλον, beautiful, and the Latin word *dies*, day, meaning that Adam remarked "how beautiful is the day!"[144] The Kalends of January does not take place immediately following the winter solstice but a few days thereafter, enough time for Adam to have seen that the daylight hours were increasing.[145] The story that Rav tells thus transforms the Kalends from a festival that is Roman to its core to one whose protagonist is the Hebrew Bible's first human being at the beginning of history.[146] Ovid also calls the Kalends of January a "good day" when he writes that "now must good words be spoken on a good day" (*nun dicenda bona sunt bona verba die*) and explains that it is appropriate for the new year to begin in January because "midwinter is the beginning of the new sun and the end of the old one," also alluding to the winter solstice as a good time to restart the annual cycle.[147] Moreover, one of the rabbinic Hebrew terms for a festival is *yom tov*, literally translated as "good day," and thus Rav's etiology might also suggest that Adam declared the day a *yom tov*, literally a "good day," but that he expressed himself in Greek and Latin, "καλον *dies!*"[148]

Rav's etiology only makes sense if the world's creation is dated to the period between the summer and winter solstices, when the days get shorter. That is, if the world and Adam were created in early fall, shortly after the summer solstice, then throughout the first weeks of his life Adam would have experienced the daylight hours decreasing each day. As he reached mid-December, the days were at their shortest and Adam would have started feeling desperate because of the darkness. In the days immediately following the winter solstice, Adam would have noticed the daylight hours increasing for the first time, and on the first day of January he would have finally been confident enough in his observations to make his declarations about the increased daylight, thereby naming the day "Kalends."

Not all rabbis agreed, however, with Rav's calendrical placement of the world's creation in the fall and thus with Rav's explanation of the origins of the Kalends. Some rabbis maintained that the world was created in the month of Nissan, in the spring, when the hours of sunlight increase each day. Had the world been created in the early spring, as these rabbis suggested, rather than in the fall, the chronology underpinning the story about Adam would not make astronomical sense. Rabbi Yohanan therefore offers a second account of the festival of Kalends that does not depend on placing the world's creation in the fall. Through an alternative etymology, Rabbi Yohanan attributes the origins of the Roman New Year not to Adam but to a moment of military victory in Roman history when the Romans engaged in battle with their Egyptian enemies:

> Rabbi Yohanan did not hold the same opinion [as that of Rav], but rather [suggested the following origin of Kalends]: the kingdom of Egypt and the kingdom of Rome were at war with one another. They said [to each other]: How long are we going to kill one another in battle? Come and let us make a rule that whichever kingdom will say to its chief general: Fall on your sword [and kill yourself], and [whose general] will listen to that command—[that kingdom] will seize the power [over both of us] first! The Egyptian [general] did not listen to them. The Roman [general] was a certain old man with the name Januarius. He had twelve sons. They said to him: If you will listen to them [and fall on your sword], we shall make your sons commanders, prefects, and generals. So he listened to them [and took his own life]. That is why

they call it קלנדס יינובריס [*kalendas yanubris* = Lat. *calendae Ianuarii*]! On the next day they mourned for him, [it was a] black day [אימירא מילני].[149]

According to Rabbi Yohanan's story, the Kalends of January commemorates the death of a Roman general named Januarius, in a battle against the Egyptians.[150] This Januarius sacrificed his own life for the greater good of the kingdom of Rome.

Similar to Rav's etiology about Adam, the story told by Rabbi Yohanan carries possible biblical resonance and thus connects biblical history with Roman history. The only biographical information given about Januarius is that he is the father of twelve sons. This detail alludes to the twelve altars dedicated to the god Janus in Rome, as well as to the twelve officials appointed by Numa, who, according to the sixth-century antiquarian John Lydos, represent the twelve months.[151] Reading this narrative in the context of the other stories about Roman festivals in this section of the Palestinian Talmud, it seems likely that mention of Januarius's sons was meant to bring to mind the biblical patriarch Jacob, who also fathered twelve sons—who in turn became the tribes of Israel.[152] The eponymous patriarch of Rome's army, responsible for Rome's success in subsequent generations, is thereby put into parallel with the eponymous patriarch of Israel, who likewise was responsible for Israel's continued existence in subsequent generations.

Rabbi Yohanan's explanation relies on an etymology of the words *Kalendae Ianuarii*. The festival derives its name from Januarius's self-sacrifice, which occurred on the first day (the Kalends) of the Roman month January. The text references the Latin *calendae* ("the first day of the month," itself derived from the Latin *calare*, to declare the new month or to call out) and the army general's name, *Januarius*.[153] When his sons mourn their father's death, they call out (*calendae*) his name (*Ianuarii*). More literally, they name the Kalends of January—the Kalendae of January—in their father's memory.[154]

This story alludes to both calendrical and historical themes related to Rome's ascent to power that were embedded into the Roman calendar. By this time, January 1 was the day when consuls began their duties, as well as the start of the military season.[155] Januarius's story fits into this context, given that he is promised commanders, prefects, and generals as a reward for his self-sacrifice. It is appropriate for the consuls to begin their responsibilities on the anniversary of the death of the general who made their rule possible.

The text also refers to the day following the Kalends as a "black day" (אימירא מילני). The term is derived from the Greek words μέλαινα (black) and ἡμέρα (day), which is the literal Greek equivalent of the Latin *dies ater*, a "black day."[156] Such "black days" (*dies atri*) occurred frequently in the Roman calendar and were considered times of bad omen, particularly for military activity, because they often commemorated days on which the Roman army had been defeated in battle.[157] Notably, Philocalus's calendar of 354 marks the second day of January not as a *dies ater* but as a *dies aegyptiacus*, an alternative way of noting days of bad omen and ill health, which appears on various dates in the calendar (this particular term dates to the fourth century).[158] If the day following the Kalends of January was known more broadly in the fourth and following centuries as a *dies aegyptiacus*, it might explain further why the Palestinian Talmud's story features a battle of Rome against Egypt as the reason behind the date's significance. In this etiology, the rabbis' familiarity with the Roman calendar is revealed, for indeed Roman calendars mark January 2 as a *dies ater* and associated it, in some cases, specifically with Egypt. Although the overall rabbinic story does not portray Rome in a negative light, this negative ending might have been intended to indicate that, even in victory, Roman rule was followed by an ominous day.[159]

The Palestinian Talmud presents two alternatives for the origins of the Kalends of January.[160] Either the festival originated with Adam's declaration of joy, following the winter solstice when the days brightened again, or it memorializes the declaration of sorrow upon the death of a Roman general. Both of these accounts are most convincingly understood polemically. According to Rav, Adam, a biblical figure, was responsible for the institution of the festival of the Kalends as a beautiful day, or a *yom tov* (a festival), long before the establishment of the city of Rome. This explanation seems to be a polemical move, even as the Romans might have been flattered that some rabbis believed the festival to have such ancient origins. According to Rabbi Yohanan, the beginning of Rome's dominion is marked by death and is therefore followed by an ominous day a *dies ater*. The two stories present the reader with two distinct approaches to the festival. The Kalends of January commemorates the natural renewal of the year (not inherently Roman) and by association the festival's mythological origins (Adam is a mythological figure for the rabbis). At the same time, the day commemorates a moment in Roman military history (and is thus Roman to its core). In the context of the passage in the Palestinian Talmud, the stories might even have been harmonized by its ancient readers: the festival was first established by Adam as he observed the natural rhythms of the sun, and then again by the sons of the Roman general Januarius after the Roman victory over the Egyptians. In both etiologies, the Kalends of January has biblical resonances, imparting to the first day of the Roman year biblical overtones.

Similar to the Palestinian Talmud's first etiology for the Kalends of January, the etiology that the Palestinian Talmud provides for the festival of the Saturnalia is both etymological and exegetical. First, it links the Latin festival name to a biblical passage about Esau, and second, it links the biblical figure Esau to the Roman Empire and its army. An anonymous statement proposes that the name "Saturnalia" stems from the phrase "hidden hatred" (שנאה טמונה). This phrase alludes to Esau's hatred of Jacob in Genesis 27:41: "Now Esau hated

[וישטם עשו] Jacob because of the blessing with which his father had blessed him, and Esau said to himself: 'The days of mourning for my father are approaching; then I will kill my brother Jacob.'"[161] In the biblical narrative, Jacob has tricked Esau into selling him his birthright. Esau has, as a result, lost his status as Isaac's firstborn son and thus also the coveted blessing of his father. The talmudic text interprets "hidden hatred" to mean that Esau "hates, takes vengeance, and is vindictive [שונא נוקם ונוטר]."[162] While this interpretation is rather enigmatic in the Palestinian Talmud, it is linked to a midrash on Genesis 27:41 that appears more fully in Genesis Rabbah.[163] There, the phrase "Esau hated" (וישטם עשו) is interpreted by Rabbi Eleazar bar Yose as a reference to Esau's loathing of his brother Jacob and his resolve to kill him once their father has passed way: Esau "hated, took vengeance, and was vindictive toward him [Jacob] so that to this day we speak of the centurion of Rome."[164] This midrash links Esau to Rome, a connection also made in the Palestinian Talmud: "In Rome they cry out against Esau's centurion."[165]

In addition to presenting Esau as Rome's biblical ancestor, these passages also associate him specifically with the Roman army. When the rabbinic texts mention Esau as foreshadowing Rome's centurion, they refer to a subunit (*centuria*) of a Roman army legion, the commander of which was called a *centurion*. The midrash thus likens Esau to a Roman army commander, implying that Rome's army—the very entity responsible for the destruction of the temple in Jerusalem—acted in line with a biblical passage that describes Esau's desire to destroy Jacob. The festival of the Saturnalia is thus associated not only with Esau and Rome but with the Roman Empire's military aggression toward the Jews, which resulted in their temple's destruction. In this way, the Palestinian Talmud's etiology of the Saturnalia, like the etiology of Kratesis, functions as a pointed polemic against the Roman Empire and its festivals. It references the rivalry between Esau and Jacob, and then associates the biblical figure of Esau with Rome and specifically with the Roman army, responsible for the destruction of the temple. The biblical rivalry between the brothers is thereby projected onto the antagonistic relationship between Rome and Israel.[166]

The biblical passage cited by the Palestinian Talmud to explain the etymology and etiology of the Saturnalia specifically references the moment in the narrative in which Esau's and Jacob's fates are reversed. Born first, Esau sells his birthright to Jacob, and thus Jacob becomes the eldest son in place of his brother. Jacob, in place of Esau, is blessed by his father, Isaac. Esau then vows to kill his brother once their father dies. Earlier in this narrative, God explains Rebecca's complicated twin pregnancy to her: "Two nations are in your womb, and two peoples born of you shall be divided; the one shall be stronger than the other, the elder shall serve the younger."[167] This reversal of fates, in which the younger and weaker brother supersedes the older and stronger brother, evokes the main theme of the carnivalesque Saturnalia celebrations, which entailed a temporary reversal of social hierarchies and roles. While Saturnalia celebrations varied across regions and periods, one of the most ancient and central features of the festival was a feast in which enslaved people were treated to an elaborate meal and ate as their masters usually did (in some contexts, masters and the people whom they enslaved reclined together, elsewhere the masters served those whom they enslaved, and elsewhere still masters celebrated with their own feast in a different room).[168] Freeborn men wore unique clothing, including the *synthesis*, in place of their *togas*, and they wore the *pilleus*, a hat usually worn by freedmen, a sartorial gesture to the festival's theme of reversals, however temporary they were.[169] The author of this passage taps into these features of the Roman Saturnalia when referencing the inverted power dynamics of the biblical twin brothers.[170] By doing so, the story also alludes to the disempowered position of the Jews, Jacob's descendants, as a minority in the Roman Empire, Esau's heirs, and their wish for a more permanent reversal of fates. The author conjures the resentment that must have characterized the experiences of those who only tasted the privileges of freedom during the festival days of the Saturnalia and who, when the festival ended, returned to their life of subservience and enslavement.[171] While, for powerful people, the festival served as a day for releasing social tensions and recalibrating hierarchies (and perhaps for alleviating guilt), for the generally disenfranchised, the festival was likely more painful than empowering.[172] Once again, the Palestinian Talmud turns to biblical figures, themes, and verses to explain the biblical origins of the Roman festival.

The Babylonian Talmud provides a single combined etiology for Kalends and Saturnalia.[173] Though the text of the Babylonian Talmud attributes this etiology to a tannaitic source, it draws on the same tradition used by Rav in the Palestinian Talmud's etiology for the Kalends of January:

> When the first man Adam saw that the days were getting shorter, he said: Woe is me. Perhaps because I sinned, the world is dark on my behalf, and is reverting to chaos [תהו ובהו], and this is the death that has been decreed upon me. He sat for eight days, fasting. Because the winter solstice transpired, he saw the day getting longer. He said: it is the way of the world. He got up and made eight days of festival [ימים טובים]. The following year, he made both sets of days festivals. He [Adam] established them as such for the sake of heaven, while they established them for the sake of idol worship.[174]

As in the Palestinian Talmud, the Babylonian Talmud imposes a biblical sense onto the Roman calendar by attributing the Kalends' origins to Adam.

This etiology does not include the etymology and the exegetical midrash that are so central to the narrative told in the Palestinian Talmud. Instead, in the Babylonian Talmud's more narrative-driven story, Adam performed rituals preceding and following the winter solstice, which in turn established the festivals of Saturnalia and Kalends for all subsequent years. Notably, these variations reflect broader cultural and literary differences between the two Talmuds.

The redactors of the Babylonian Talmud might not have been sufficiently fluent in Greek or Latin to appreciate the pun preserved in the Palestinian Talmud, and so they dispensed with it. Moreover, biblical midrash, especially such intricate interpretations that build upon the juxtaposition of two verses with similar vocabularies found in the Palestinian Talmud's etiology, is a particular Palestinian technique ubiquitous in midrash from the region but not as common in Babylonian sources. The story that the Babylonian Talmud offers is more reminiscent of the latter's overall literary aggadic style.[175] Such differences between the Palestinian and Babylonian Talmuds' accounts of the Kalends can thus be understood in light of differing linguistic, hermeneutical, cultural, and literary contexts.

The rabbinic text is rather exacting in its dating of the festivals: Adam creates two eight-day festivals, the first corresponding to the Saturnalia and the second corresponding to the Kalends. In its introduction to the etiology, the Babylonian Talmud inaccurately explains that the Saturnalia is celebrated for eight days before the winter solstice and that Kalends is celebrated for eight days after the solstice (though both festivals were multiday affairs in this period, neither extended to a full eight days).[176] Moshe Benovitz has suggested that the Babylonian Talmud imports its understanding of Hanukkah, an eight-day festival, and imposes it onto its conceptualization of Saturnalia and Kalends.[177] This conflation occurs in part because both sets of festivals were considered, at this time, winter solstice festivals in addition to their other associations, and perhaps the rabbinic text even suggests that Hanukkah was more ancient than the wintertime Roman festivals that were celebrated at similar times during the season. The text's rendering of the name "Saturnalia" in Hebrew (which appears as סטרנורא and סטרנריא in the manuscripts and can be split into two words, סטר-נורא, meaning "concealing the fire or light") plays with its association with the winter solstice, as the Saturnalia was celebrated precisely in the days leading up to the solstice, when the days are shortest.[178] In fact, the same wording is used in the story about Saturnalia and Kalends as is used in the Babylonian Talmud's discussion of Hanukkah—"the next year, they declared these days ... to be festivals."[179] Thus, what was an etiology for the Roman festival of the Kalends of January in the Palestinian Talmud is, in the Babylonian Talmud, understood independently of its Roman origins and seen instead through the light of a Jewish festival, Hanukkah—a festival, moreover, that had become prominent specifically in Jewish Babylonia (and that had, for at least a couple of centuries, been abandoned or downplayed in the region of Palestine).[180]

It is possible that the celebration of the winter solstice, in both Rome and the region of Babylonia, then part of the Sasanian Empire, provides background for understanding how this story about Adam was interpreted by the rabbis of Babylonia and why this version specifically, as opposed to its various parallels, appears in the Babylonian Talmud. In the story that appears in the

Babylonian Talmud, Adam's observation of the sun—first the increasing darkness and then the increasing light—becomes an even more central feature of the story. Believing that he has sinned, he assumes that the world is reverting to chaos, to a time before the creation of light, when darkness hovered upon the abyss. Adam's appeals to God and the rituals he performs might evoke more ancient Babylonian practices related to the times of the solstices as well, attested, for example, in sources that describe rituals at Esagil, the "day temple" associated with the sun god Marduk, "when the days have become short ... to lengthen the days."[181] The ideas of sin and evil are also associated in Zoroastrian texts specifically with the period surrounding the winter solstice, when darkness appears most powerfully, and rabbinic readers in Sasanian Babylonia might have read this story about Adam with these ideas in mind.[182]

In the Babylonian Talmud's etiological account, Adam both invents Saturnalia and Kalends and celebrates the festivals long before the Romans. The last line of the story insists that the legitimate godly celebration of these festivals by Adam predates the Roman celebrations: "he [Adam] established them as such for the sake of heaven, while they established them for the sake of idol worship." This ending emphasizes that Adam did not celebrate for pagan reasons, as others do, but that he held feasts in order to thank and serve the true God. Nonetheless, Adam is depicted as playing an active part in the festivals, establishing them long before the Romans corrupted these same days of celebration with their cultic worship. The story suggests that a time is created during which those who practice "for the sake of heaven" celebrate at precisely the same time as those who practice "for the sake of idolatry," synchronizing seemingly irreconcilable values within a single day on the Roman calendar. Again—and in this case quite literally—Roman and rabbinic times are conceived as simultaneously constructing mutuality as well as difference.

The editorial passages that follow the etiologies about Adam in both the Palestinian and Babylonian Talmuds connect the story of the Roman calendar and the Roman New Year with the Jewish calendar and the Jewish New Year. As discussed earlier, the Talmuds explain that the story about Adam declaring the Kalends of January only works with the rabbinic opinion that places the creation of the world in the month of Tishre, in the fall. The Palestinian Talmud explains that Rav indeed dated the world's creation to the fall; in other rabbinic traditions, the school of Rav interprets the blows of the shofar on Rosh Hashanah to be a declaration of the world's creation. This observation thus notes that, according to Rav, the world's creation on the Jewish New Year in the fall (Rosh Hashanah) was intimately connected with and eventually led Adam to declare the Roman New Year's festival in the winter (Kalends). In this etiology for Kalends, the Jewish New Year and the Roman New Year are synchronized—although they do not take place on the same day of the year, they are linked through stories about Adam, the season of creation, and the winter solstice.

KRATESIS

The Palestinian Talmud offers two different explanations for the origins of Kratesis. The first view suggests that the festival commemorates one of Rome's victories over its enemies ("the day on which the Romans seized power"). The Talmud clarifies that the festival cannot commemorate Rome's initial victory, which was already associated by Rabbi Yohanan with the Kalends of January (when the Roman general Januarius defeated the Egyptian army). Rather, the festival marks the second time that Rome seized power, when Augustus conquered Egypt in 30 BCE. This explanation aligns well with the *kratesis caesaris* associated with the date of Augustus's victory in Egypt attested in documentary sources from the region, a date that commemorates Rome's further expansion into the east rather than earlier moments of victory.[183]

The second etiology offered by the Palestinian Talmud connects the Roman festival with the foundation of the city of Rome itself.[184] As with the Palestinian Talmud's etiologies for the Kalends and the Saturnalia, this explanation, attributed to Rabbi Levi, relies on in-depth knowledge of Roman myth and history as well as the Roman calendar. Its emphasis, moreover, on connecting pre-Roman history to Roman history and on producing a unified historical narrative of Rome's past also fits with broader intellectual trends of the Roman fourth century and, to quote Clifford Ando about a contemporaneous Latin text, claims "what had been a domain of merely mythological speculation . . . instead as a domain of historical knowledge, with all of the political implications that this act entails."[185]

In Rabbi Levi's story, the geological formation, urban development, and political organization of Rome are attributed to the idolatrous sins of Israelite kings rather than to the great actions of the earliest Roman leaders and kings. The festival of Kratesis is thus reimagined: it is no longer a day that points to the military victories and expansion of the Roman Empire eastward as a *Roman* affair but one that represents the *Jewish* sin of idolatry and its far-reaching political consequences of empowering the Jews' Roman oppressors at formative moments of Rome's earliest beginnings. In marking a day on the Roman calendar with Jewish misfortune, this rabbinic story served as a strong warning against both idolatrous practice and acculturation into Roman society.[186] Moreover, it is perhaps the clearest case of the biblical past being inscribed by the talmudic rabbis onto the annual cycle of the Roman calendar.

The story told in the name of Rabbi Levi is partially based on an earlier rabbinic tradition about Rome's origins.[187] The Palestinian Talmud's version, however, develops the narrative into a full account of the city's founding, and it is the only source to connect the narrative with a Roman festival day.

> It is the day on which Solomon married into [the family of] Pharaoh Necho, king of Egypt. On that day [the angel] Michael descended and

thrust a reed into the sea, and pulled up muddy alluvium [שלעטוט], and it grew to a large thicket of reeds [חורש], and this was the great city of Rome. On the day on which Jeroboam erected the two golden calves, Remus and Romulus came and built two huts in the city of Rome. On the day on which Elijah disappeared, a king was appointed in Rome: "There was no king, in Edom a deputy was king" (1 Kings 22:48).[188]

It is with Solomon, the Israelite king remembered for his construction feats, wisdom, many marriages, and idolatrous lapses, that the story begins. This text argues that the same king who famously built the first temple and delivered a passionate dedication address at its consecration is also responsible, because of his sins, for sowing the seeds of the destruction of the second temple many centuries later.

Solomon's marriage to a foreign princess is said to have provoked the angel Michael to throw a reed into the sea, causing the geographical territory of Israel's archenemy, Rome, to arise out of it. This portrayal of Solomon develops a theme that is already present in the biblical passages about him, in which his marriages cause him to pursue idolatrous practices. In 1 Kings 3:1–4, the description of his marriage to Pharaoh's daughter is coupled with an account of the continued illegitimate sacrifices that Israel brought at the open shrines prior to the building of the temple. Solomon's marriages are again linked with his idolatrous sins in 1 Kings 11:1–10.[189] Highlighting Solomon's marriages with foreign women accentuates a related theme as well: these marital alliances blur the boundaries between Jews and gentiles. While such marriages might not have been particularly problematic in the biblical context, were it not for associated lapses into idolatry, rabbinic sources present such unions as much more so.[190] It is therefore both Solomon's pining after the gods of his wives and their idolatrous tendencies, along with the practice of intermarriage, that the rabbinic text finds disturbing. Because of these two interrelated sins, Solomon is held responsible for the emergence of the geographical area that would later become the city of Rome, the center of an idolatrous empire that came to rule over the Jews.

Rabbi Levi's passage could be understood as related to the myth of Aeneas. In the rabbinic passage, Solomon's marriage to Pharaoh's daughter precipitated the very earliest step in the founding of Rome; in the myth of Aeneas, Aeneas's marriage to King Latinus's daughter is also central to Rome's founding. Turning to Virgil's take on the story, Aeneas flees the coasts of Troy during the Trojan war, crosses the Mediterranean, and eventually reaches the shores of Italy: "much buffeted by sea and land by violence from above . . . and much enduring in war also, till he should build a city and bring his gods to Latium; whence came the Latin race, the lords of Alba, and the lofty walls of Rome."[191] Similar to the story that Rabbi Levi tells about Solomon and the founding of the territory of Rome from alluvial waters, Virgil foregrounds the leading role that water plays in the earliest origins of Rome. Another important part of Virgil's story about Aeneas is his marriage to Lavinia, the daughter of King Latinus.[192] Following Aeneas's victory over Turnus, who battles him for Lavinia's hand in marriage, Aeneas and the Trojans settle the land. Evander shows Aeneas the area that will eventually become Rome and the river that will eventually be named the Tiber.[193] In another rendition of this foundation myth, Livy, too, presents this alliance through marriage as a watershed event in the earliest moments of Rome's history: "Aeneas became a guest in the house of Latinus; there the latter, in the presence of his household gods, added a domestic treaty to the public one, by giving his daughter in marriage to Aeneas. This event removed any doubt in the minds of the Trojans that they had brought their wanderings to an end at last in a permanent and settled habitation."[194] In the Palestinian Talmud's narrative, the Israelites had their own warrior, Solomon. His sinful marriage mirrors Aeneas's fateful marriage. In Latin sources, Aeneas's marriage secured the beginnings of Rome; as the Palestinian Talmud portrays the city's history, it was Solomon's marriage that effected this development. Moreover, Aeneas does not establish the city of Rome but rather settles the region of Lavinium, from which Remus and Romulus are said to have descended, in line with Rabbi Levi's portrayal of Solomon's marriage as the first step in the origins of Rome, followed later by the births of Remus and Romulus, who erect huts and establish a city-community. Aeneas founds Lavinium, the center of the Latin league, as a port city along the shore, near the mouth of the Numicus and Tiber rivers in the wetlands of the Pontine Marshes. Thus, Solomon's marriage alliance and the angel Michael's creation of the region of Rome out of alluvial waters correspond to Aeneas's marriage to Lavinia and the founding of Lavinium from the marshy region south of Rome.

The talmudic representation of the founding of Rome from watery origins echoes the images and stories that Romans told about their city's history but deploys them to undermine Roman mythology. Vividly depicting the geological formation of the city of Rome with an image of the angel Michael sticking a reed into the sea inverts the popular symbol of the Tiber, which appears frequently in narratives and depictions of Rome's origins.[195] The Tiber and the reed crown are commonly associated with Rome's origins in texts, statues, and coins. One coin from 71 CE, for example, captures the centrality of water in a particularly evocative image: Roma sits on a rock beside the seven hills of Rome alongside the she-wolf and twins of the city's founding, while the river Tiber, depicted as a traditional bearded figure, holds a reed.[196] In a second coin minted that same year, Roma is pictured seated on seven hills, with Remus and Romulus suckling from the she-wolf's breasts on one side and the Tiber River on the other.[197] A third coin, issued by Antoninus Pius, presents the Tiber "as an old man, half-draped and crowned with reeds, reclining either on an urn, from which water flows, or on a rock; he holds a reed in his left

FIGURE 3. Sestertius issued by Antoninus Pius between 140 and 144 CE, with a personified Tiber River holding a reed in water.

hand while the right rests on the prow of a ship."[198] Significantly, rabbis in Roman Palestine would have encountered just this type of iconography in their daily lives.[199]

In such numismatic depictions, the personified Tiber grasps a reed as though he is about to insert it into the water, just as the angel Michael does in the rabbinic midrash. The reed, celebrated in Roman mythology and iconography, becomes a negative element in the Talmud's account, and the biblical angel Michael replaces the mythologized Tiber. The positive association between water and Rome was widespread in antiquity.[200] The name "Rome," itself, might derive from the Etruscan word for "river" (*rumon*).[201] This rabbinic reference to the angel Michael in place of the Tiber may best be understood as an evocative example of Scott's "hidden transcript," an inversion of imperial ideology that gives voice to a different—subversive— rabbinic narrative.

The text describes the angel Michael placing a reed into the sea and pulling out of it a sediment of mud or muddy alluvium (שלעטוט = שלע טוט).[202] From this substance grew a large thicket of reeds, for which the text uses the word חורש, a term associated specifically with the use of reeds for construction.[203] The text has a geological phenomenon in mind in which alluvial deposits accumulate in a watery area, preventing water from running through it and eventually creating an area of land for settlement. Parts of Rome were indeed built above thick alluvial deposits,[204] and Livy incorporates these geological details in his *History of Rome* when he writes about a "floating cradle . . . left by the retreating water on dry land."[205] The rabbinic author behind the story in the Palestinian Talmud accesses these geological understandings and their multivalent cultural associations about urban development upon alluvial deposits.

The idea that the geographical origins of Rome are rooted in Israelite sin might also function on an additional polemical register. In contrast to Jerusalem, which was regarded as the focal point of God's actions during the world's creation, the foundation of Rome is here portrayed as an afterthought and a mere punishment for the Jews' improper behavior, not as the eternal expansive city and empire it claimed to be.[206] This is a Judeocentric understanding of Roman history. The geographical origins of the great city of Rome, in other words, are not as ancient and illustrious as Jerusalem's but rather of more recent origins. Moreover, whereas Jerusalem is sometimes characterized as the geographical location under which the watery depth (תהום) of creation is kept at bay by the city's powerful spiritual or divine presence, in this story, Rome is associated with a reed placed in the sea and the alluvial deposits left behind by unruly, chaotic waters, an image at odds with the positive functions that water plays in Roman myths of the city's origins.[207]

The passage in the Palestinian Talmud continues with Jeroboam's sin of idolatry. As king of Israel, Jeroboam erected two golden calves.[208] Jeroboam was motivated to set up these calves at Bethel and Dan as alternative pilgrimage sites to keep his people away from Jerusalem, the region of his rival, King Rehoboam of Judah.[209] Jeroboam built places of worship in his own territories that were considered idolatrous, appointed priests who were not Levites to preside over them, and established his own festival to be celebrated at these two idolatrous shrines. The final passages of 1 Kings 13 read: "Even after this event Jeroboam did not turn from his evil way.... This matter became a sin to the house of Jeroboam, so as to cut it off and to destroy it from the face of the earth."[210]

The rabbinic passage couples this biblical episode with the mythological story of Rome's settlement by the twin founders of the city of Rome, Remus and Romulus, thus creating a parallel between Jeroboam's two golden calves and the two founders of Rome. The twin brothers erect two huts: this moment of mythological founding is associated with the beginning of Roman society, which developed once the geological parameters of Rome had been established. The popular tale of the birth of Remus and Romulus and consequent establishment of the city of Rome is presented by authors such as Livy, Plutarch, and numerous others as the mythical origins of the empire.[211] It was also a narrative widely depicted on Roman coins, monuments, wall art, and floor mosaics from the republican era through the medieval period, including in the province of Palestine.[212] Coins minted under Trebonianus Gallus (251–253 CE) from the city of Neapolis depicted a suckling she-wolf with the twins, as did coins from Aelia Capitolina, Caesarea, and Sebaste.[213] Joseph Geiger has suggested that the two huts mentioned in this rabbinic story specifically refer to two temples, tombs, or pyramids imagined, in the early fourth century, to have

FIGURE 4. Sestertius issued by Vespasian in 71 CE, with a she-wolf suckling twins alongside the Tiber River.

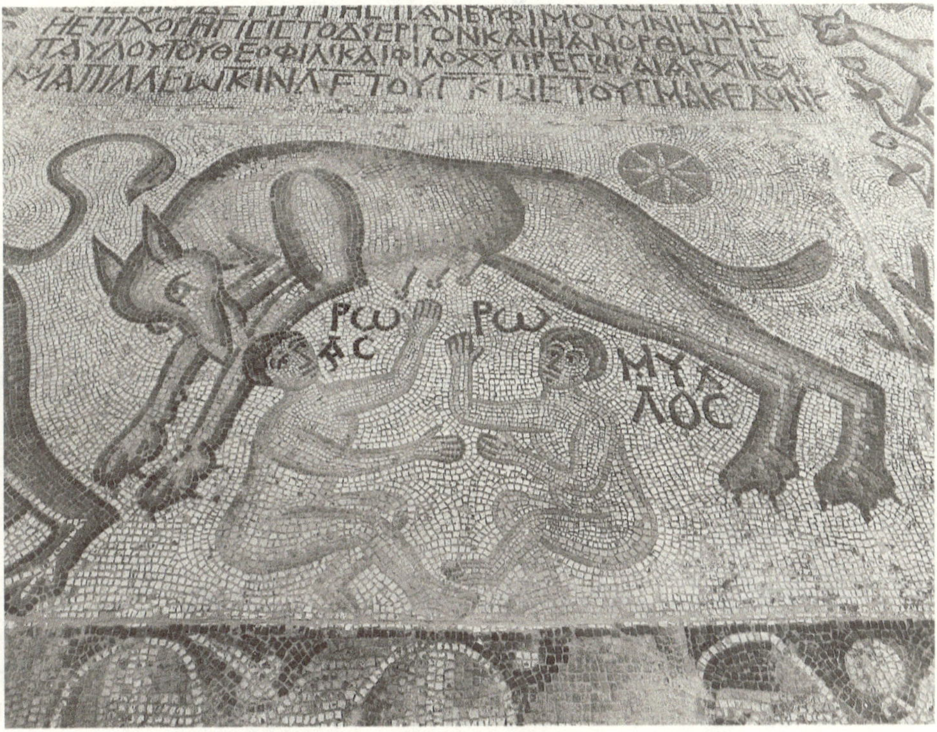

FIGURE 5. A floor mosaic depicting a she-wolf suckling Remus and Romulus from Frikya, in Syria.

been built by Remus and Romulus (though they were likely built or rebuilt in the early fourth century): the Pyramid of Cestius in the Aventine and the Pyramid of Romulus near the Mausoleum of Hadrian in Rome.[214] If so, this rabbinic text discloses the degree to which some rabbis were aware of Roman architecture and the urban landscape. As Solomon's sins caused the *geological* formation of the territory that became Rome, Jeroboam's idolatry through the building of two shrines in the land of Israel caused the *mythical* and *architectural* founding of the city of Rome by the twin brothers.

The third part of the etiology of Kratesis portrays the end of Elijah's life and argues that his disappearance in a whirlwind mirrored the final step of Rome's foundation, in which a Roman king is appointed. In 1 Kings 18:20–40, the biblical text portrays the prophet Elijah as actively combatting the idolatrous practices of the Israelites and their kings. Elijah gathers the Israelites outside the city to denounce idolatry and sacrifice to the true God. The prophet's disappearance thus symbolizes the conclusion of an active attempt to root out this idolatry. The end of Elijah's life is narrated in 2 Kings 2. Immediately preceding this chapter, in 2 Kings 1:17–18, the text recounts the death of King Ahaziah. Then, in 2 Kings 2, a chariot and horses of fire appear, and Elijah ascends to heaven in a whirlwind: "As they continued walking and talking, a chariot of fire and horses of fire separated the two of them, and Elijah ascended in a whirlwind into heaven."[215] This dramatic event is followed by Elijah's protégé Elisha's mourning for his mentor. When the sons of the prophets in Jericho realize what has happened to Elijah, they appoint Elisha to replace him as Israel's prophet, and a new king is appointed as well.

In referencing the appointment of a Roman king as a consequence of Elijah's departure, the Palestinian Talmud likely refers to Numa Pompilius, the second king of Rome.[216] Numa is associated in Roman sources with the *historical* founding of the city of Rome, and the pairing of Elijah's death with Numa's rise is a sophisticated and nuanced exegetical move. Plutarch's *Life of Numa* narrates the end of Romulus's life in strikingly similar terms to the passage in 2 Kings 2. The rabbis artfully evoke this story in their narrative about Kratesis:

> For thirty-seven years, now, Rome had been built and Romulus had been its king; and on the fifth of the month of July, which day they now call the Capratine Nones, Romulus was offering a public sacrifice outside the city at the so-called Goat's Marsh, in the presence of the senate and most of the people. Suddenly there was a great commotion in the air, and a cloud descended upon the earth bringing with it blasts of wind and rain. The throng of common folk were terrified and fled in all directions, but Romulus disappeared, and was never found again either alive or dead.[217]

In the midst of sacrificing among the senators and people, Romulus is taken in a cloud to the heavens, where he is eventually made into a god. As in the case of Elijah, the text remains ambiguous about the circumstances of Romulus's disappearance: Does he die in his ascent, or is he taken alive, never to reappear on earth?

It was this very event that led to the appointment of a new king in Rome. According to Plutarch, Romulus's ascent terrified the people of Rome, and it took some time before they accepted Numa, who is said to have been born "by some divine felicity" on the day that Rome was founded by Romulus, the twenty-first of April. In light of this serendipitous birth, however, it was decided that Numa would make an ideal king. In Livy's account, too, Romulus's disappearance in a cloud is presented as an event about the need to fill the vacant royal seat: "A violent thunderstorm suddenly arose and enveloped the king in so dense a cloud that he was quite invisible to the assembly. From that hour Romulus was no longer seen on earth. When the fears of the Roman youth were allayed by the return of bright, calm sunshine after such fearful weather, they saw that the royal seat was vacant [*ubi vacuam sedem regiam vidit*]."[218]

The midrash in the Palestinian Talmud thus parallels Elijah's sacrifices, ascent, and disappearance into the heavens with Romulus's, the very event that led to the appointment of Numa as king of Rome. Here, again, the story demonstrates the rabbis' intricate alignment of biblical history with Roman history. Perhaps not coincidentally, Romulus and Numa were the two Roman figures credited by Plutarch, Macrobius, and others with the establishment of the Roman calendar, and here they appear in a rabbinic story about one of the festivals on this same calendar.[219]

The proof text provided in the rabbinic story (1 Kings 22:48) refers to the failure of Jehoshaphat, who reigned as king of Judah during part of Elijah's lifetime, to dismantle the idolatrous shrines set up by previous kings. According to the rabbinic narrative, the idolatry stemming from Israel's and Judah's kings, which Elijah attempted to curtail during his lifetime but which nonetheless resumed after his departure, was the direct cause of the appointment of a king in Rome who would be even more destructive to Israel than the previous idolatrous Israelite kings had been.[220] The rabbinic reading of this passage (ומלך אין, באדום נצב מלך) renders the text as follows: "there was no king, in Edom a deputy was king," rather than the traditional Masoretic interpretation (ומלך אין באדום, נצב מלך) that translates as "there was no king in Edom, a deputy was king." This reading allows for the interpretation that a lack of Israelite leadership after Elijah's departure coincided with and caused the installment of a king in Edom. This proof text, moreover, implicitly links the biblical text's Edom to Rome, an association also developed in the etiology of Saturnalia.[221]

FIGURE 6. Depiction of Elijah's sacrifice on a fresco from the synagogue at Dura Europos.

This story in the Palestinian Talmud presents Solomon, Jeroboam, and the entire Israelite nation—in their adoption of idolatrous ways of life and integration into their idolatrous surroundings—as responsible for the rise of Rome. With each sin of idolatry that these Israelites committed, they allowed their Roman enemy to gain still greater power and, ultimately, to conquer and oppress them. Here, the Jews are held morally culpable not only for their own sins and those of their ancestors but also for the sins of Rome.[222] Rome's fate is tied to that of Israel: Israel's archenemy Rome, in this story, ascended at each step as a direct consequence of Israel's idolatrous mistakes. While the narrative in the Palestinian Talmud condemns Israel for bringing about the founding of Rome, it also legitimizes the Roman Empire; Roman rule is portrayed as a divine punishment for Jewish missteps. Through this rereading, the biblical past is mapped onto Roman time as the Roman festal day identified in the earlier tannaitic text becomes intertwined with the history of the Jews. The message of the story is clear: participating in idolatrous practices and intermingling with idolatrous neighbors led directly to Rome's founding, assumption of power, and oppression of the Jews; in order to overcome their enemies,

Israel must reverse its actions and avoid idolatry and, in particular, the pagan festivals that commemorate the geographic and symbolic foundation and expansion of this pagan world. Recall that Rabbi Levi insists that this day on the Roman calendar became a festival because of the idolatrous practices of a series of Israelite kings. The only appropriate way for Jews to mark such a day is to abstain from any form of idolatrous practice or commercial participation that would mark it as a day of celebration.

The three parts of this rabbinic story about Kratesis blame Israel's leaders' iniquities for the geological, mythical, and historical origins of Rome. Peter Schäfer notes: "This is an abbreviated version of the early history of Rome told from the Rabbinic point of view ... Rome's physical foundation (a sandbank with a thicket of reeds), its mythical foundation and the beginning of its civilization (Romulus and Remus), and finally the founding of Rome's kingship."[223] Rome rises as Israel falls, a direct result of Israel's idolatrous sins. This tripartite explanation for Rome's founding also appears in Roman sources, making the structure of this rabbinic passage all the more intriguing. Livy, for example, brings together the three stages outlined and undermined so clearly in the rabbinic narrative: the geological foundation upon deposits left by receding water (*Ab urbe condita* 1.4), the founding of the city by Remus and Romulus (*Ab urbe condita* 1.6–7), and the appointment of Rome's first king, Numa, after Romulus's disappearance in a whirlwind (*Ab urbe condita* 1.16). Thus, this rabbinic text can be read as a polemical or subversive parallel to the myth of Roman origins that Livy, too, preserves in his writings.

Rabbinic figures could gain access to such stories in many places: at the marketplace, in the bathhouse, on the streets and in city centers, and in conversations with others. The empire, after all, took great pains to disseminate its imperial propaganda to those within its territories, specifically to reach those who were not familiar with these myths. Regardless of how these rabbinic authors learned about the myths, though, it is clear that they knew them well enough not only to refer to them but also to build upon and to undermine them in intricate ways.

Though stories about Roman origins were told during the late Republic, they were retold in new ways and with renewed vigor during the Augustan age and thereafter.[224] Virgil, Livy, and Ovid, for example, all turned to stories about Rome's beginnings precisely at a time when Rome underwent drastic changes, transitioning from a republic to an empire. These stories celebrated— and also critiqued—Rome's founding and its long, illustrious history in the contemporary moment of the imperial present.[225] Augustus himself actively promoted his persona as Rome's refounder, deliberately evoking the memories of Aeneas, Romulus, and Numa. When he constructed the Augustan Forum, he placed statues of Aeneas and Romulus in the central apses of the Temple of Mars the Avenger.[226] Down one side of the Forum, Augustus erected statues of his ancestors, including a series of figures who descended from Aeneas. A

FIGURE 7. Coin depicting Augustus and Numa Pompilius, dated 16–15 BCE.

large statue of himself in a chariot stood at the very center of the Forum. According to Alison Cooley, "The portico advanced the claim that the Julian family, through Aeneas, could be seen as the ultimate founders of Rome—a claim which also underlay Virgil's *Aeneid*, and represented Augustus as completing the full circle of history, resuming his fated role as refounder of Rome."[227] In 16–15 BCE, Augustus minted a series of coins with his portrait on one side and Numa's on the other, boldly asserting continuity between the two.[228] Numa Pompilius, Rome's second king, had refused initial offers to rule Rome, as Augustus had done as well. He also became associated with divinities and was himself deified, similar to Augustus. And just as, in the distant past, Numa had revolutionized Roman society with his political, legal, and religious reforms—not least his radical calendrical reforms—Augustus, too, undertook wide-ranging reforms to transform Roman society.

The Palestinian Talmud explains that the festival of Kratesis commemorated either Augustus's conquest of Egypt and his general expansion into eastern territories or the accession to the throne of subsequent emperors who followed in Augustus's imperial footsteps. Rabbi Levi's story connects the Roman festival associated with Augustus's conquest of Egypt and the east to the very figures and narratives that Augustus himself promoted in the wake of this important conquest. The Palestinian Talmud's etiology thus fits these broader discursive trends that linked Augustus's military expansion, political innovations, and calendrical reforms with Roman origins and, specifically, with Aeneas, Romulus, and Numa. The story is told through a comparison between Israelite and Roman kings—the same Roman kings that took center stage in Augustan propaganda. Augustus's imperial propaganda seems, then, to have worked wonders: the rabbis of the third and fourth centuries CE associated his military feats and the imperial age that followed with these earlier stories and myths about Roman origins. Indeed, these imperial origin narratives continued to be advanced in Roman Palestine throughout the rabbinic period. This

FIGURE 8. Wall painting fragment from Royal Room at Herodium. Nautical scene featuring ships in battle, dated c. 20–15 BCE.

was especially the case in the second and third centuries, in the context of the founding and refounding of colonial and other imperial cities such as Aelia Capitolina, Neapolis, and Caesarea.[229] By recounting the founding of Rome and alluding to the figures of Aeneas, Romulus, and Numa, the Palestinian Talmud participates in this trend that associated Augustus's imperial feats with Rome's origins. In this context, rabbinic efforts to undermine these imperial motifs and tell their own versions can be understood as part of ongoing, and persistently timely, attempts to promote imperial agendas through stories of Roman origin.

Similar to the Palestinian Talmud, the Babylonian Talmud offers a number of explanations for the festival of Kratesis. Rav Judah, citing Samuel, provides a brief historical explanation for the origins of the festival, describing Kratesis as "the day on which Rome extended her dominion."[230] The text then preserves a debate about whether earlier sources refer to one festival (Kratesis *as* the day on which Rome extended her dominion) or two festivals (Kratesis *and* the day on which Rome extended her dominion).[231] A comment attributed to Rabbi Joseph attempts to resolve the disagreement by identifying two historical moments of Roman expansion: the defeat of Antiochus III and the Seleucids during the Greco-Roman war in the late 190s and early 180s BCE ("in the days of the Greeks") and Augustus's victory over Cleopatra in 30 BCE ("in the days of

Cleopatra the Queen").[232] According to Rabbi Joseph, therefore, it remains possible for Kratesis to be a festival that commemorates Rome's initial expansion in the east in the second century BCE and for there to be another festival in celebration of a second expansion during the reign of Augustus a hundred and fifty years later.

A tradition attributed to Rav Dimi, a late fourth-century Babylonian rabbi, then offers a narrative about Rome's defeat of Greece during Rome's initial foray into eastern territories.[233] It is a strange story in which Jews play a surprisingly important role:

> The Romans fought against the Greeks in thirty two battles and could not prevail against them until the Romans made an alliance with the Israelites. And these were the conditions made with them: if kings are chosen from among us, the prefects should be chosen from your midst, and if the kings are chosen from among you, prefects shall come from our midst. Then the Romans sent word to the Greeks as follows: until now we have been fighting [עבדינן קרבא], and now let us turn to justice [עבדינן בדינא]: a pearl and a precious stone, which shall form a setting for which? They sent the reply: The pearl for the precious stone. And a precious stone and an onyx [which shall form a setting to the other]? The precious stone for the onyx. An onyx and the Book of Torah? The onyx for the Book of Torah. They [the Romans] sent word [to the Greeks]: Israel is with us and the Book of the Torah is with us, for Israel is with us. Thereupon they [the Greeks] gave in.[234]

According to Rav Dimi, the Romans were capable of defeating the Greeks only because they had the Jews and the Torah on their side. The Romans first make an alliance with the Jews, and then the Romans convince their Greek enemy to surrender by informing them that they possess the most precious object, the Torah. That is, once the Romans and Greeks cease from military activities and resort to settling their confrontation through diplomatic channels, the Romans make the case that now that they have the Jews on their side, the Greeks should surrender to them. This is the proper order of the universe, the Romans imply, as the world's most precious belonging is allied with the Romans. Not only do the Romans admit that their victory depends on the Torah; the Greeks, too, recognize the value of Rome's Jewish alliance and immediately capitulate.[235]

This rabbinic text seems to know of the alliance between the Jews and the Romans, also recorded in 1 Maccabees and Josephus.[236] By connecting this historical alliance to Rome's ultimate victory in the rendition offered by the rabbinic text, and by identifying the Jews as the source of the festival of Kratesis, the passage insists that this festival's appearance on the Roman calendar necessarily also alludes to the Jews—and even acknowledges and celebrates their most precious possession, the Torah. This victory is also a less complicated one for Jews: Romans and Jews were allied, and their shared enemy was Antiochus, as opposed to Rome's later victory, which gradually led to reduced Jewish sovereignty, increased Jewish-Roman hostilities, and eventually the destruction of the temple. The text emplaces the Jews in the story of Rome's expansion even though that empire eventually abandoned its treaty with the Jews and began mistreating them, as the passage subsequently explains. The pericope in the Babylonian Talmud then uses this narrative as the beginning of a longer discussion about Roman-Jewish relations as well as about the messianic future. These stories are no longer told because of their particular focus on specifically Roman history, as is the case in the Palestinian Talmud; rather, they are preserved as stories about foreign empires more generally and embedded within an expansive soteriological narrative oriented toward a final redemptive future.

In this story, the Jews share their Torah with the Romans via a political alliance. Through its recognition of the power of God's Torah, Rome prevails over its foreign enemies and safeguards its Jewish allies. The Torah preserves the Jewish community during Rome's ascent to regional dominance, rather than Jewish sin condemning them as an oppressed minority within that empire. Whereas the etiological account for Kratesis in the Palestinian Talmud *blames* the Jews and their idolatrous sins for the original founding of Rome, the Babylonian Talmud's etiology for this same festival *credits* the Jews and their promotion of the Torah for the success of the Roman Empire.

GENOUSIA

In the Palestinian Talmud, the festival of the Genousia (the emperor's birthday festivities) is paralleled with Pharaoh's birthday feast.[237] Pharaoh's birthday is the only such celebration mentioned in biblical sources.[238] This account casts the contemporary Roman leader in the shadow of an ancient enemy of Israel, a biblical character who epitomizes the enslavement of Israel and the denial of God.[239] In this case, again, the Palestinian Talmud evokes a biblical archenemy in reference to Rome and its sacred days. The Genousia is thus framed, similar to Kratesis, as an anti-festival. As the Jews celebrate their liberation from Egypt and Pharaoh's defeat on the Jewish festival of Passover, the text implies, they ought to abstain from a festival that celebrates the birthday of those who, like Pharaoh, oppress Jews.

The Babylonian Talmud, by contrast, does not associate the Genousia with Pharaoh but rather provides a more general explanation of the festival. For Rav Judah, "it is the day on which the king ascends" to the throne.[240] According to a second opinion, the Genousia refers to the emperor's birthday. The text then launches into a series of stories highlighting the friendship between the Roman emperor Antoninus and Rabbi.[241] In each vignette, Rabbi solves a problem or provides advice to the emperor about his leadership. One story involves a tunnel that led directly from the emperor's house to the home of the rabbi. In these stories, just as in the Babylonian Talmud's account of Kratesis, influential Jews work behind the scenes, as allies of the emperors, to influence Roman governance and curry favor on behalf of their own communities.[242]

ROMAN FESTIVALS BETWEEN THE PALESTINIAN AND BABYLONIAN TALMUDS

The rabbinic authors of the narratives in the Palestinian Talmud were familiar with many aspects of Roman culture. They discuss Roman festivals, myths, and etymologies in sophisticated and specific ways, even if not all of their information is accurate or attested in extant Roman sources. The Palestinian Talmud's etiologies, for example, are anchored in etymological explanations that use Greek and Latin words and motifs found in Roman literature. This feature of such etiologies corresponds well with other Greek and Latin texts about Roman festivals, which mine the etymological roots of a festival's name to uncover the origins of or reason for the festival and which often provide a range of overlapping natural, mythological, and historical explanations.[243] Additionally, the etiological accounts in the Palestinian Talmud engage in intricate biblical exegesis, often reading two biblical verses together based on a shared word found in both verses, typical of Palestinian midrash.[244]

The overarching sentiment of the Palestinian Talmud's stories is deeply anti-imperial. Thus, the etiology of Saturnalia evokes Esau, a vilified biblical figure; in the account of Genousia, the Roman emperor is compared with Pharaoh, the Bible's ultimate oppressor; and regarding Kratesis, Rome's foundations are attributed to the sins of Israelite kings and the Jews are blamed for their own oppression. The narrative of Rome's past that is projected, through these stories, onto the Roman calendar emphatically portrays the Roman Empire, its foundations, and its history in negative polemical terms. In contrast to the ways in which etiologies are often evoked in late antique Mediterranean contexts, these accounts do not seek to build bridges of commonality. Rather, they insist on severing links to Rome through pious practice for the sake of Jewish continuity. Intended as warnings to Jews to break their ties by not indulging in idolatrous practices, the stories delineate the devastating consequences of retaining such connections. Such stories thus function both to undermine the greatness of the Roman past and to caution Jews to act according to rabbinic halakhah, to maintain their distance and difference from the empire, and not to become too comfortable living as Romans in Roman society and adopting its temporal rhythms. The Palestinian Talmud's etiologies for Kalends are highly ambiguous, but one of them insists on the association of the festival with a day of bad omen; they remind us that rabbinic voices were themselves diverse, preserved a variety of perspectives on the Roman Empire, and struggled with their relationship to Rome and its history.

When Palestinian traditions about Roman festivals were adapted in Babylonian sources, they were applied in new ways for novel ends, a familiar process when stories travel between different cultural spheres. The Babylonian Talmud, for example, omits the etymologies and biblical exegeses that feature so prominently in the Palestinian Talmud.[245] Its stories also appear to be less aware of the specificities of Roman festivals. Adapting a line from the Palestinian Talmud, one passage states that Kalends and Saturnalia were eight-day festivals; the passage prefers to understand these Roman festivals in light of the eight-day festival of Hanukkah, a more important festival in Babylonia than it was in Palestine, rather than on their own terms as Roman festivals. Other narratives also overlook or omit the Palestinian Talmud's punchlines (e.g., that the festival of the Kalends derives from the verb "to call") and subversions of Roman culture (e.g., evoking Esau and Jacob's reversal of fortunes in a discussion of the Saturnalia). The story about Kratesis rejects the opinion that this festival celebrated Augustus's victory in Egypt—though this was likely the original festival to which the Mishnah refers—and understands it, instead, as a festival commemorating Rome's earlier victory over the Greeks in the second century BCE. Babylonian sources thus use Palestinian traditions for their own purposes, even if they sometimes misrepresent details from the Roman cultural context. Perhaps doing so was a deliberate choice on the part of Babylonian rabbis, or perhaps it reveals a lack of cultural literacy regarding Roman traditions (cultural references that would have made most sense to rabbis living in a Roman cultural context)—or both. Moreover, the Babylonian Talmud often opts to tell stories in its signature aggadic mode rather than in the midrashic fashion more typical of Palestinian sources.[246]

The Palestinian and Babylonian Talmuds share a common sense of the interconnectedness of Jews and Romans. Yet, the essence of this interconnectedness differs in the two corpuses. In contrast to the Palestinian Talmud's anti-imperial perspective, the Babylonian Talmud recounts its Roman festival etiologies from a competing, and generally more positive, perspective, conveying pride in the role of Jews and Judaism in the success of Rome. Correspondingly, the Roman festivals and their origins are attributed in the Babylonian Talmud to Adam as the first celebrant of the Kalends and the Saturnalia and to the political alliance between Jews and Rome in the case of Kratesis. In reference to the Genousia, the text evokes the imperial-rabbinic friendship of Antoninus and Rabbi. They reclaim the importance of Jewish political and ritual power in Rome's early imperial history while simultaneously critiquing the empire's later treatment of Jews. The Babylonian Talmud almost pines for a lost golden age in which Jews were respected in the expanding Roman Empire and mourns the far inferior period that followed it, marked as it was by oppression and destruction.[247]

As in the Palestinian Talmud, the laws articulated in the Babylonian Talmud are unwavering in their prohibition of participation in the Roman festivals and their related commercial activities. But in the realm of history and memory, the authors of the narratives about Roman festivals in the Babylonian Talmud are more comfortable laying Jewish claim to their origins. By inscribing positive moments of the Jewish past onto a Roman calendar day, these stories enmesh Jewish and Roman time in a way that is markedly different from that in the Palestinian Talmud. This discrepancy might result from chronological shifts and different geographical settings: rabbis in Roman and later Christian Roman Palestine felt more threatened by their neighbors and their rites than those in Babylonia. The Palestinian Talmud was written within the Roman Empire, at a time when Jews regarded the empire as dangerously persecutory. In contrast, the Babylonian Talmud was redacted beyond the Roman Empire, not only in a different empire but also at a later time when the Roman calendar had been stripped of most of its traditional Roman festivals and cultic practices and when many peoples, including the Gauls who had been conquered by Rome and had long perceived the Romans as enemies, were claiming Romanness for themselves.

Reading the Babylonian Talmud's etiologies in a diasporic context further explains its unique celebration of the Jews, their Torah, and their impact on Roman expansion.[248] The Babylonian Talmud's retelling of Rome's victory over the Greeks in its explanation of the origins of Kratesis, for example, resembles Philo's depiction of Augustus's military victories and especially his admiration of Augustus. Maren Niehoff has observed that Philo does not complain about Augustus, as might have been expected, but rather lauds the emperor's virtue, character, moderation in governance, imperial beneficence, and amiable relationship with the Jews.[249] Moreover, Philo spotlights Augustus's adoption of Jewish customs, almost portraying them as a conversion.[250] In the Babylonian Talmud, too, the Romans affirm the Torah as central to their success in battle. This is the case even though, as has been argued by Katell Berthelot, Philo was critical of other aspects of Rome and viewed the Jews as superior and ultimately triumphant over the Roman Empire—as is the Babylonian Talmud generally more negative and often hostile concerning the Roman Empire in other contexts.[251] Such tales of origin that place Jews at the center of Roman history—crediting the biblical Adam with establishing the Kalends of January and the Saturnalia, portraying the Torah as Rome's secret weapon, and depicting the friendship between the Roman emperor and a prominent rabbi—also share the predilection of Artapanus's writings on Abraham, Joseph, and Moses, in which these biblical figures are credited with inventing astrology, boats, weapons, philosophy, and other important cultural contributions valued by those far beyond their Israelite or Jewish communities.[252] Moses is even responsible, in Artapanus's account, for strengthening the Egyptian regime.[253] Artapanus, a Jew living in Egypt in the second century BCE, attempted to present the Jewish past in a way that not only was palatable in the Diaspora but also elevated the contribution of the Jews to the society in which they lived, a form of "competitive historiography."²⁵⁴ Rather than stressing the tensions between Jews and Romans, as the etiologies in the Palestinian Talmud do, those in the Babylonian Talmud tend to highlight the positive impact and influence of Jews on Roman culture and its temporal landscape (without ignoring nor forgiving the violence and destruction of the later Romans).²⁵⁵ In this way, the stories in the Babylonian Talmud engage in a discourse that had different effects on the temporal synchronization of Roman festivals with Jewish history than those that emerged from a Palestinian context.

On Which Day Are Both Jews and Gentiles Happy?

In the fifth-century Palestinian midrash Genesis Rabbah, a story is told about a gentile who approaches Rabbi Joshua ben Karha. "We have festivals [מועדות] and you have festivals," the man tells the rabbi.²⁵⁶ The phrasing of this statement stresses the contrast between Roman pagans and rabbinic Jews: these two different groups of people follow their own annual calendar with a distinct set of festivals. Their times, according to this statement, are mutually exclusive. Moreover, the festivals each group celebrates define their difference. The contrast between rabbinic and Roman festivals that the gentile draws reinforces the difference that the Mishnah's laws so forcefully attempt to create by prohibiting Jews from participating in any aspect of Roman festivals—"we have our festivals, and they have their festivals, and never the twain shall meet," the Mishnah implies.

"At the time [בשעה] when you are happy, we are not happy, and at the time when we are happy, you are not happy," the man continues. (In a parallel found in Deuteronomy Rabbah, the idolater is even more specific: "We have Kalends, Saturnalia, and Kratesis, and you have Passover, Pentecost, and Tabernacles.")²⁵⁷ In contrast to the first line, which presents rabbinic and Roman festivals as absolutely distinct, this second statement acknowledges that rabbinic and Roman times were also intimately linked. At times when rabbis joyfully celebrated, Romans were unhappy and did not celebrate, and when Romans joyfully celebrated, rabbis were unhappy and did not celebrate.²⁵⁸ This aspect of the intersection between rabbinic and Roman time also emerges in the Mishnah, which required Jews to keep track of the Roman calendar in order to know when to avoid the markets and abstain from celebrations—that is, to know when Romans were happy so that they could make efforts *not* to be happy at those very same times. Rabbinic and Roman times were thus not only different, they were also at odds with one another. Furthermore, they mutually—if inversely—affected one another. This complicated entanglement of Jews in Roman time is most fully observed in the Palestinian and Babylonian Talmuds' etiologies of Roman festivals, in which the Jews and the Torah play central roles.

The reader of this midrashic narrative, however, has a surprise in store for her. The narrative ends with the gentile earnestly inquiring of the rabbi: "On which day are we and you both happy?" The genre of the story—a dialogue—complements its theme. The Roman pagan and the Jewish rabbi encounter one another, they speak with each other, they even try to find a time to rejoice together. Whereas the Mishnah's prohibitions were recorded as a set of rules designed to limit interaction with others and construct absolute boundaries between them, and the Talmuds invent etiologies to polemicize against others, here the text's form gestures toward mutuality and shared time. (Though the very exceptionality of the few days in which the rabbi and gentile celebrate together might also suggest a carnivalesque or ironic valence.) This dialogue, though constructed as a conversation, was written by rabbis and reflects the rabbinic struggle with the reality of living in a non-Jewish society, with gentile neighbors whose times were dictated by a different set of sacred days.[259] On the one hand, the rabbinic author of this fictive dialogue reinforces the division between Jews and their neighbors; on the other, the author imagines there to be a time of mutual joy.

The conciliatory tone of this narrative in Genesis Rabbah is quite different from the polemical sentiment expressed in the etiological narratives about specific Roman festivals collected in the Talmuds. This tone fits with Genesis Rabbah's overall rhetorical strategy, which is generally more accommodating and tends to encourage Jews to practice rabbinic Judaism rather than arguing against Rome and the empire. The midrash tries to present a strong case for the superiority of rabbinic Judaism over Roman and/or Christian alternatives, often even presenting aspects of Judaism as better versions of them (this aspect of the midrash is discussed at greater length in the next chapter).[260] Nonetheless, rather than shunning his interlocutor, the rabbi assures him that there is indeed a shared time of joy and celebration: "The day on which the rain falls!" Rabbinic Jews and Roman pagans might use different calendars and mark distinct festival days, but, living in the arid province of Palestine, they could all celebrate when it rained. Between the lines of this story, one glimpses the tension between the shared rhythms of the natural world and the culturally specific markers and divisions that are overlaid upon them through calendars and festivals, and of the rabbinic awareness of this dynamic. The complicated temporal universe through which the rabbis navigated in the early centuries CE and how rabbis used time to construct difference and resist empire as well as to diminish difference and dismantle boundaries also shine through here. Reading this story alongside the passages from the Mishnah and the Talmuds analyzed in this chapter underscores that the rabbinic corpus itself preserves a range of diverse perspectives about the relationship between rabbinic and Roman time, as indeed between rabbis and Romans, and how the two might best be negotiated.

If this story in Genesis Rabbah seeks to imagine a time of common joy, a story in Lamentations Rabbah addresses the challenges (and even potential impossibility) of finding such a time of shared celebration.[261] The midrash narrates that Trajan's wife gave birth on the ninth of Av, the day on which Jews mourn the destruction of Jerusalem. This calendrical asynchrony implies that the day of imperial joy was a day of Jewish sadness. This occurrence was no mere coincidence, however, but rather providential, the story implies, because the day that same imperial baby dies happens to be the Jewish holiday of Hanukkah, a day on which Jews publicly display lights of celebration to express their thanksgiving to God for past miracles. The Jews debate whether they should proceed with their Hanukkah celebrations given this imperial tragedy, possibly facing the repercussions of not participating in collective imperial mourning. On that day, the Jews decide to light the Hanukkah flames—a ritual that marks a past triumph of Judaism over idolatry—rather than mourning with the Romans. Their asynchronous behavior angers Trajan's wife and leads her to request the persecution of the Jews. In this story, Jews and Roman simply mark time independently, but the accidental collision of their differing times is interpreted by imperial officials as hostile and the Jews are punished accordingly. Lamentations Rabbah, a generally more fiercely anti-Roman midrash, seems to suggest in this story that Jewish time and Rome time are not merely distinct but fundamentally opposed in a cosmic sense.

Conclusions

Roman calendrical reform, initiated by Julius Caesar and completed by Augustus, marked an important development in Rome's transition from republic to empire. With Roman territories extending farther than ever and encompassing so many people, a more organized and accurate calendar could ensure that everyone's time was synchronized despite geographical distance and cultural difference.[262] An imperial calendar represented a strategy for incorporating the provinces into the empire more fully without imposing too heavily on its subjects. The celebration of Roman festivals played a central role in this imperial project as well, as the empire designed these festivals to cultivate civic community, belonging, and loyalty, especially among those at the empire's periphery. While Roman principles of governance encouraged those in its territories to continue following their own religious rites and civil laws, the standardization of the calendar and the celebration of its festivals laid the foundations for unifying the empire's territories and populations through time. Even as communities were urged to continue worshipping their own ancestral gods and adjudicating according to their local legal systems, they were nonetheless required to contend with the empire's calendar, its festivals, and the imperial ideology that they projected. This did not mean that local communities were not allowed to maintain their own calendars and festivals—indeed, they were, and many did, as the rabbinic case demonstrates. But such communities were now also required to synchronize their own times with the empire's calendrical rhythms. The Roman calendar thus became a vehicle for Rome's imperial project as well as a symbol of it.

For the rabbis of late antiquity, Roman imperialism, especially after the destruction of the temple in Jerusalem and the continued Romanization of the province of Palestine, constituted a direct contradiction to the biblical promise of Jewish sovereignty in the land of Israel. Living under Roman imperial rule also meant, more practically, that the rabbis could not fulfill the biblical command to eradicate idolatry from that land. Instead, they were governed by what they considered to be an idolatrous empire and surrounded by idolatrous practices. Tractate *Avodah Zarah* lays out an elaborate set of laws for dealing with this situation in practical—and temporal—terms. Biblical injunctions against idolatrous practices do not focus particularly on idolatrous festivals, whereas the earliest rabbinic sources emphasize a need specifically to separate from pagan sacred times.[263] This new stress on time, and keeping separate times, is a distinct product of the Mishnah's Roman environment: because the Roman calendar was a central symbol of Roman identity and its festivals were so influential in the cultivation of its empire, abstention from Roman festivals became an important form of resistance for the rabbis. This context might also explain why the Mishnah does not list any number of other local pagan festivals or ritual calendars, such as the celebrations at Mamre, but instead chose to include only Roman festivals. Rather than being of practical concern, this was an ideological choice of asserting rabbinic identity and authority in the face of Roman imperialism and its temporal cycles.

Rabbinic texts about Roman festivals offer unique perspectives on how the Roman Empire disseminated its ideas and imperial ideologies through its annual calendar and how one particular minority in the eastern reaches of that empire contended with this cultural project.[264] Throughout their writings, the rabbis challenge Roman culture and imperial rule by mandating separation from imperial temporal rhythms. Most essentially, the rabbis insist on maintaining their own annual calendar and festival cycle. But they also formulated their rules about idolatrous practices in ways that would minimize the impact of idolatrous Roman festivals and the Roman calendar upon them. These rabbinic rules, designed to accentuate rabbinic-Roman difference, wound up necessitating an intimate knowledge of the annual Roman calendar and unceasing attention to its times.

Rabbinic sources are most concerned with differentiating between the times of Jews and other Romans in the present—that is, during particular festival times throughout the year. In their elaborations of the Mishnah's list of Roman festivals in the two Talmuds, however, later rabbis also devoted energy to reinterpreting the Roman past that is enacted in and through the

Roman calendar. The Palestinian and Babylonian Talmuds infuse biblical and Jewish resonances into their explanation of Roman festival origins, including Kalends, Saturnalia, Kratesis, and Genousia. In these rabbinic etiologies, Roman festivals are no longer about the Roman gods Janus and Saturn, nor about consuls or emperors, but mainly about biblical figures—Adam, Jacob and Esau, Pharaoh, Solomon, Jeroboam, and Elijah, or about the supreme power of the Torah. Indeed, the series of etiologies overlays a series of narratives modeled on biblical stories from Genesis (Adam, Jacob, Esau) through Exodus (Pharaoh) to the books of the Prophets (Solomon, Jeroboam, and Elijah) onto Roman history. Just as Ovid recounts Roman history, and especially Roman origins, through his musings on the months and days in his *Fasti*, these rabbis told their own versions of Roman origins and history through their stories about Roman festival days.

The literary practice of inserting biblical and rabbinic themes into Roman history, as these rabbinic etiologies of Roman festivals do, functioned simultaneously as a form of acceptance of Roman domination and a resistance to it.[265] Ando writes that "the internal stability of the empire relied not on Roman power alone, but on a slowly realized consensus regarding Rome's right to maintain social order and to establish a normative political culture."[266] This consensus was cultivated, in part, as the empire's provincials "began to conceive for themselves a role as participants in rather than subjects of Roman imperial power."[267] It was also promoted by the belief that Roman rule was divinely sanctioned. Ando elaborates:

> Many around the Mediterranean regarded Roman success in war as evidence that their own gods had sanctioned Roman conquest. Similarly, there is abundant evidence that populations around the empire, particularly in the Greek East, recognized and appreciated the political and economic stability with which the imperial government endowed daily life. . . . We must therefore separate provincials' occasional reactions to particular impositions or individuals from their acknowledgment that the imperial government had the right, indeed, the responsibility, to maintain its normative order.[268]

Indeed, the rabbis whose narratives about Roman festivals are compiled within the Talmuds began to see themselves and their own history within the Roman calendar—and thus within the empire and its history. Were a rabbi to glance at a Roman calendar, he would encounter a list of festal days that resonated with Jewish historical significance: festivals that were instituted by biblical characters, established as a divine response to the sins of Israelite kings, or that commemorated political alliances between the Romans and the Jews and that highlighted the military-political efficacy of the Torah. To invoke Ricœur, these rabbinic stories present the Roman calendar as a document that encapsulates within it a historical time that is not exclusively Roman but also Jewish.

Moreover, such rabbinic narratives of the Roman past depict Roman imperial rule as divinely sanctioned.[269]

This merged history, however, was not narrated to celebrate the empire but rather to polemicize against it.[270] It undermined Roman history and Roman power by attributing Rome's origins, rise to power, and continued success to the powers of Jews, the Torah, and the Jewish God—either through positive alliances or as a result of divine punishment. Many of these rabbinic stories impose an anti-imperial historical narrative onto the Roman year, while some also look back more nostalgically at pre-imperial moments of the Roman past that were kinder to Jews, itself a critique of contemporary Roman imperialism. Even as these stories integrated the Jewish past into the Roman past, they were designed to keep Jews away from idolatry and at a remove from their Roman neighbors. The intended effect was the cultivation of a rabbinic identity that was conceived as differentiated from and contrary to Roman identity.

The rabbinic year, then, was a combination of the Jewish calendar and the Roman calendar, superimposed onto one another. The rabbis mandated that, on an annual basis, the rabbinic festivals be closely observed in all of their detail and that the Roman festivals, in all of their detail, be just as carefully avoided. In addition, these two calendars, as the rabbis perceived them, told two simultaneous and sometimes conflicting historical narratives. The Jewish calendar, with its festivals of Passover, Shavuot, and Sukkot, memorialized a positive view of Jewish history and Jewish devotion to God. Its festival cycle told a narrative about God's redemption of the People of Israel in the past and their continued chosenness as recipients of the Torah in the present. The Roman calendar, in contrast, told a narrative, according to the Palestinian Talmud, of the rise to power of one of Israel's oppressors and Israel's sinful role in bringing about their own oppression. According to the Babylonian Talmud, the Roman calendar encapsulated a narrative about the agency and power of the Jews in the formation of one of the world's great empires. To be clear, the extensive laws, rituals, and liturgical practices required in the observance of the rabbinic calendar and its festivals occupy numerous rabbinic tractates, whereas the call to abstain from the Roman calendar and its festivals appears only in the context of rabbinic laws pertaining to the abstention of idolatrous practice; rabbinic texts clearly emphasize the observance of rabbinic festivals over the course of the rabbinic year while downplaying the Roman calendar and its festivals. This distinction notwithstanding, rabbis, and rabbinic Jews, were required to navigate between these two timescapes on both a day-to-day and a seasonal basis—as they were expected to experience the present, and also as the past was continually inscribed in new ways onto that present.

There remains a somewhat puzzling element to these rabbinic laws about Roman festivals and narratives devoted to their origins in rabbinic sources. While the Mishnah's concern with Roman festivals seems to stem from a geographical and cultural context in which such festivals were likely the most popular ones observed in Roman Palestine, the religious and political landscape had changed dramatically by the time of the redaction of the Palestinian and Babylonian Talmuds as well as the amoraic midrashim. By the end of the fourth century, pagan festivals were still observed in the region, but rabbis must have also been concerned about the growing and increasingly influential Christian communities (and eventually a Christian Roman Empire), which presented their own set of competing festivals and calendrical configurations that were at odds with, and often in direct opposition to, Jewish times of celebration.[271] Likewise, in the Babylonian context, Roman festivals were hardly a practical issue, while Zoroastrian and other festivals celebrated by those in the Sasanian Empire might have been attractive for Jews. The next chapter addresses rabbinic grappling with Christian times and the construction of Jewish-Christian difference both before and after the Roman Empire's Christianization, while the book's conclusion returns to the question of Zoroastrian and other festivals.

CHAPTER TWO

Jewish and Christian Time

"THE DAY OF THE SABBATH . . . [is] good."[1] These words of Greek graffiti were found on a piece of broken clay tile dating to the fourth or fifth century CE near the ancient theater at Taormina in Sicily. Epigraphists debate whether the central image, etched between the words "the day of the Sabbath" and "good," worn and fragmentary as it now is, depicts a menorah or a cross.[2] Modern scholarly uncertainty about the symbol that accompanies a declaration praising the Sabbath serves as an apt introduction to the subject of this chapter, which explores the weekly Sabbath as a contested time between Jews and Christians.

The previous chapter argued that one of the ways rabbis differentiated themselves from other Romans was by deliberately distinguishing their time from the time of the empire in which they lived. They did so through maintaining their own calendar and mandating separation from the rhythms of the Roman calendar. Jews also divided their time into weekly units of seven days, which further differentiated them from other Romans, whose time was typically divided not into seven-day weeks but into nundinal cycles of eight days, and who regarded these nundinal cycles as an integral part of their Roman identity and culture (though a planetary seven-day week was incorporated as well, as will be discussed).[3] In addition to the seven-day week, the Sabbath as a weekly day of rest was regarded as a uniquely Jewish temporal practice, one championed in Jewish sources as separating Jews from other nations while often derided within Greek and Latin writings as evidence of Jewish idleness or repugnance, in contrast to Roman industriousness and time well spent, even as the empire officially tolerated and sometimes even encouraged its observance by Jews.[4] Pagan Romans who observed a weekly day of rest were chastised for acting like Jews and thus confusing communal temporal boundaries.[5]

Communities of Christ-followers, in continuity with ancient Jewish timekeeping practices, likewise used a seven-day week as a way of organizing time.[6]

Sacha Stern notes, for example, that in a cemetery at Zoar, all Christian tombstones use the Julian solar calendar and all Jewish tombstones use the Jewish lunar calendar, but both use the same seven days of the week.[7] This posed a problem for rabbinic Jews and Christ-followers: even though their seven-day unit of weekly time (as well as their basic festival calendar) differentiated them from other residents of the Roman Empire in which they lived, it did not differentiate their communities from one another. Such communal difference was forged, in part, through demarcating distinct weekly sacred days for each of these two groups. Various Christian bishops and authors throughout late antiquity deployed a range of critiques of the Jewish Sabbath, asserting, for example, that the obligation to observe the Sabbath was a sign of Jewish sinfulness and supersession, that biblical passages about the Sabbath referred to an eschatological era rather than a day of the week, and that Jews marked the Sabbath in inappropriately carnal ways. In addition, many advocated the celebration of the Lord's Day on Sunday instead of the Sabbath on Saturday. They often also repurposed Greek and Latin critiques of the Sabbath for their own polemical ends.[8] The rabbis thus found themselves in a peculiar situation, in which early Christian communities, and later also the Christian Roman Empire, promoted an organization of time that was based, at least in part, on their own weekly system but that eventually elevated a different day as the week's sacred focal point. Complicating matters further, this system of time encompassed some shared understandings of the purpose of that day, such as rest, and some differing dimensions, such as Christ's resurrection, that cast Jewish observance of the Sabbath in disparaging terms.

This chapter argues that rabbinic texts struggled with these developments in weekly time, especially the status of the weekly Sabbath, and that some rabbinic laws, exegeses, and narratives about Sabbath practice sought to construct and amplify communal difference not only between Jews and Roman pagans but also between Jews and Christians, both in the Roman Empire and beyond it. It is worth mentioning that the chapter does not claim that rabbinic texts about the Sabbath *only* considered competing Christian developments; indeed, rabbinic texts about the Sabbath usually addressed internal rabbinic matters of practice or exegesis, and on occasion they also asserted Jewish temporal distinctiveness vis-à-vis non-Christian Romans, who found the Jewish weekly day of rest a harmful or pointless institution. Rather, the chapter contends that developing Christian practices and rhetoric regarding the Jewish Sabbath added unique dimensions to anti-Sabbath critiques found in non-Christian Greek and Latin sources and that some rabbinic texts not only defended Sabbath observance in light of anti-Sabbath polemics found within such non-Christian sources but also took into account critiques of the Sabbath that had become increasingly popular in specifically Christian theological contexts.[9] In addition to countering the opinions of vocal Roman non-Christian authors who regarded a day of rest as a waste of time or indicative of Jewish foreignness, rabbinic emphasis on Israel's obligation to continue observing the Sabbath for eternity, the divine status of the Sabbath, and the praiseworthiness of the material dimensions of the day's observance, such as feasting, stands in contrast to the position of those, in Jewish-Christian and Christian communities, who argued that the Sabbath represented a superseded covenant between God and Israel, that the Sabbath ought to be celebrated spiritually rather than materially, or that a different day of the week had replaced it. In total, the rabbinic texts about the Sabbath analyzed in this chapter seek to justify and valorize rabbinic Sabbath observance in light of competing Jewish attitudes, existing Roman "pagan" criticism, and emerging Christian anti-Jewish polemics (often simultaneously). They use weekly Sabbath observance, both practically and discursively, to forge difference.

The first half of this chapter focuses on the portrayal of the Sabbath in Mekhilta de-Rabbi Ishmael, a third-century midrash on the book of Exodus. The midrash begins with an extended analysis about when Sabbath observance ought to be violated, a topic that was of concern in a diverse set of second temple texts, including the Damascus Document and the Synoptic Gospels. Following its discussion about this particular aspect of Sabbath law, the Mekhilta presents the Sabbath primarily as a day that distinguishes Israel, in the sense of separating Jews from other nations as well as marking them as holier than they. The midrash insists that the Sabbath will never be abolished—and in fact that it will be kept throughout the generations, forever, even during the eschatological age. Moreover, the midrash categorizes Sabbath observance as one of a few select practices (including circumcision, Torah study, and the maintenance of purity) essential to Jewish communal identity. Finally, the midrash argues that divine authority, rather than human authority, ordains the time of the Sabbath. This section of the Mekhilta seems to tackle competing ideas about the Sabbath that circulated among followers of Christ throughout the region of Palestine and the Mediterranean in the period before and during the Mekhilta's composition, in sources such as the letter to the Hebrews and the Epistle of Barnabas, as well as in texts composed contemporaneously with the Mekhilta, such as the writings of Justin Martyr, the Didache, and the Didascalia Apostolorum. These texts illuminate the Mekhilta's interpretive decisions, which cannot easily be explained without them. That is, when read in its third-century context, the Mekhilta engages in a debate that was no longer exclusively intra-Jewish or Jewish-Roman but that had spilled over into a debate between Jews and Christians as well.

The second half of the chapter turns to midrashic and aggadic texts preserved in rabbinic texts from the later fourth and fifth centuries, redacted within a Christian empire that boasted a far larger percentage of Christians than in previous centuries. Rabbinic communities in Palestine in these centuries encountered a temporal landscape in which Christians widely celebrated the Lord's Day on the day following the Sabbath (some also celebrated the

Jewish Sabbath, while the majority had rejected its celebration), the Roman Empire had legally adopted Christian organizations of weekly time along with a Christian weekly day of rest on Sunday, and Christian ecclesiastical authorities launched even harsher critiques against the Jewish Sabbath. Similar to earlier rabbinic texts, these later texts emphasize that the Sabbath symbolizes Israel's continued chosenness by God and ought to be observed for eternity. Additionally, however, these texts also seek to show that the Jewish Sabbath, celebrated on Saturday rather than Sunday, was a holy day and that specific Jewish Sabbath practices properly honored the day. These later rabbinic sources thus devote significant attention to proving that the Sabbath is inherently—that is, naturally and cosmologically—different from all other days of the week. They also defend the material dimensions of Sabbath observance, addressing both restrictions regarding the type of foods that could be consumed and the centrality of feasting to the day's celebrations. Surprisingly, they present the Sabbath as a day whose sacredness and observance are legitimized through imperial channels. These new ways of depicting the Sabbath in fifth-century rabbinic compositions could have developed, at least in part, in view of the institution of Sunday as a competing sacred day in the Christian Roman Empire's calendar, sanctioned by the emperor and widely practiced by the empire's increasingly Christian population, as well as in light of increasingly dominant Christian theological critiques of the Jewish Sabbath as unnecessarily restrictive while also inappropriately carnal.

In addition to participating in intra-Jewish discourse about the Sabbath, the rabbinic texts analyzed in this chapter simultaneously confront critiques of the Jewish Sabbath found in both Roman pagan and Christian theological polemics.[10] That they engage with issues raised by such external sources does not mean, however, that rabbinic texts directly addressed Christian or non-Christian audiences. Quite the opposite. It is clear that the rabbis did not compose their works for external audiences. Even when their narratives respond to critiques from outsiders, they speak to an internal audience of Jews, urging them—through either encouragement or cautioning—to remain (or become) pious Sabbath observers regardless of the harsh words against the Sabbath that they might have heard.[11] Rabbinic midrashim about the Sabbath were designed to boost Jewish confidence in Sabbath observance in light of the aforementioned animadversions.[12] The rabbinic texts examined in what follows, then, represent instances of internal and indirect rabbinic engagement with others: counterpolemics, apologetics, alternative exegeses, and conceptual reframings formed in the context of external polemics against Jewish practice as well as competing practices by others, but directed inwardly. That is not to say that rabbinic ideas did not find their way beyond their intended Jewish audiences: Jews who heard such exegeses or stories in sermons might have used them as talking points in response to challenges from their neighbors, or retold them as folktales to friends within and beyond their communities.[13] As far as the evidence suggests, however, the intended audience of these narratives was a Jewish, if not an exclusively rabbinic, one.

Jewish rabbis, Christian bishops, and Roman elites faced similar legal, political, social, and cultural challenges in negotiating the conception and organization of time in their communities and the empire. Traces of these debates are preserved in their respective legal corpora as well as in sermons, homilies, and commentary literature, composed in the context of this changing temporal landscape and written to persuade each of their specific audiences of particular dimensions of their ideas or resistance to them. The chapter's final argument, then, is that even though rabbinic sources do not explicitly name Christian practices and polemics in their discussions of the Sabbath, these competing practices and polemics were part of the web of ideas and circumstances that shaped how some rabbinic texts narrated and legislated weekly time and how they conceived and framed Jewish Sabbath observance.[14] While rabbinic passages did not necessarily respond directly to specific Christian texts, such ideas, as they are now preserved in Christian sources, could have informed and even motivated rabbinic Sabbath discourse, just as Jewish ideas impacted Christian discourse.[15] Nor did the rabbis grapple unidirectionally with Christian and non-Christian critiques. Rather, they developed their ideas about the Sabbath and weekly time—as about so many other issues—in tandem, in conversation, and in conflict with the various groups that comprised the complicated and dynamic context of the Roman Empire. This might already be the case in tannaitic texts, composed in the second and third centuries CE, and is even more likely in amoraic and post-amoraic compositions, composed in the fourth and fifth centuries. Ancient Jewish texts suggest that the Sabbath was designed to differentiate Jews from others and, in the rabbinic period, to differentiate Jews not only from gentiles writ large but also specifically from Christians.

Jewish-Christian Difference in Rabbinic Sources

Scholars disagree about the extent to which rabbinic sources engage with Christianity.[16] Some posit wide-ranging if subtle engagement with Christian ideas throughout the rabbinic corpus, including in tannaitic texts from as early as the third century. Martha Himmelfarb, Marc Hirshman, Israel Yuval, and Ishay Rosen-Zvi, for example, have noted select instances in the Mekhilta de-Rabbi Ishmael and other tannaitic texts in which interpretations of biblical passages or idioms correspond to or contest popular readings of these same biblical texts or idioms found in contemporaneous Christ-following or Christian compositions.[17] Burton Visotzky, Maren Niehoff, Adam Gregerman, David Brezis, Hanan Mazeh, and others have argued that rabbinic midrashim from the amoraic period are best understood in relation to theological and exegetical positions found in the writings of Origen, Eusebius, and other Christian authors.[18] Peter Schäfer, Richard Kalmin, and Michal Bar-Asher

Siegal have noted the pervasive concern with Christianity in the Babylonian Talmud, both in the context of biblical exegesis and in narratives about Jesus.[19]

These studies suggest that rabbinic texts often home in on biblical passages that were central to Christian anti-Jewish texts, offering alternative readings that are most robustly understood within a cultural milieu in which these very texts and their meanings were contested.[20] Hirshman argues that such overlaps in rabbinic and patristic texts attest to intense exegetical debates between Jewish and Christian scholars over the course of late antiquity. He notes that "one of the chief arguments adduced by Christians was that Jews had not understood the Bible properly" and suggests that it was in part for this reason that Jewish-Christian tensions often manifested themselves in the specific context of biblical exegesis.[21] Additionally, according to Hirshman, "the need of both religions to define themselves, vis-à-vis the competitor as well as vis-à-vis the external pagan threat, gave special impetus to the creation of written and oral collections of their sacred teachings."[22] Hirshman thus focuses not only on the substantive disagreements between Jewish and Christian biblical interpreters but also on the distinct literary and generic styles of rabbinic midrashim and patristic exegesis.[23] He ultimately argues that "neither Judaism nor Christianity ... attempted to hide the views of their rivals. Instead, they contested them, and their controversies have been preserved in the Midrash, the Talmuds, as well as in many Christian works.... Only when biblical exegesis is considered within a broader literary context will the rabbis' beliefs, as well as those of their opponents, emerge clearly."[24]

Other scholars do not detect in rabbinic texts significant engagement with Christianity, citing the paucity of explicit references to Christian ideas, especially in the earliest rabbinic texts.[25] If rabbinic sources had been concerned with Christians or with Christianity, in this line of thinking, they would have dealt with them more directly. Martin Goodman claims, for example, that "the silence of the rabbis reflects not a reaction but a lack of interest," though even he acknowledges that "there is clear evidence not of debate or confrontation but of the gradual permeation of Christian assumptions into the lives of Jews."[26] For his part, Menahem Kister presents overlaps between New Testament writings and rabbinic texts as proof of the antiquity of rabbinic traditions, contending that certain passages in the New Testament (in Kister's case, passages in the letters of Paul) build upon ancient Jewish traditions that have been incorporated into rabbinic texts (rather than that rabbinic texts engage with ideas from the New Testament, even though rabbinic texts were composed after those in the New Testament).[27] Adiel Schremer cautions against assuming that all references to Rome and the Roman Empire in later rabbinic sources are implicitly about Christians or a Christian empire.[28] He notes that the Christianization of the empire was a slow and uneven process and that significant portions of the empire's inhabitants remained non-Christian long after Constantine's conversion.[29] For Schremer, then, one need not assume that Christianity was of much concern to the rabbis even in such later periods. And Mira Balberg has conveyed misgivings about framing rabbinic ideas as having developed in conversation or conflict with external pressures, including Christian ones, because it minimizes the creative power of the rabbis themselves, whose innovations ought not always be presented as reactive.[30]

This chapter joins this scholarly debate. On the one hand, the textual analyses that follow heed Schremer's advice not to assume, from the outset, that rabbinic texts about the Sabbath necessarily engaged with Christian ideas simply because they were composed in contexts in which Christian communities flourished.[31] In fact, the initial hypothesis of the research on this chapter was that rabbinic sources focused internally and, to the extent that they were indeed reactive, they reacted to Roman "pagan" polemics against the Sabbath. On the other hand, the chapter argues, following Hirshman, that some rabbinic texts about the Sabbath are most fully understood when they are analyzed in the context of ideas and tropes that were widespread not only in Greco-Roman but also in specifically Christian texts of these same periods—that is, in the context of a world in which Christian texts and ideas (including many directly on the topic of the Sabbath) circulated widely.

Though Christians represented a small percentage of the population within the Roman Empire in the second and third centuries, they represented a far larger percentage in the region of Palestine, where the majority of rabbinic sources were composed. The size of the Christian population rose steadily in the fourth, fifth, and sixth centuries such that, according to a recent reassessment by Bart Ehrman, half of the Roman Empire was Christian by 400 CE.[32] In addition, just because Christians were a minority does not mean that their practices or theologies would not have concerned the rabbis. (Population size does not necessarily indicate the influence or perceived influence of a particular group of people.)[33] This is especially true during the period in which the Roman Empire transformed into a Christian Empire. It therefore seems reasonable to investigate whether the rabbis of the Galilee—living as they did in the very same towns and villages as growing Christian communities—encountered and responded to an increasingly popular and extensive set of traditions produced by those who presented themselves as replacing Israel. That rabbinic texts might engage with ideas prominent in their cultural context, moreover, does not diminish assessments of the creativity or integrity with which they developed such traditions.

This chapter's methodology draws upon Rosen-Zvi's work on the influence of Paul in rabbinic sources. "Instead of focusing on shared themes and trying to locate their origins," Rosen-Zvi shows "how and when matters discussed in rabbinic texts became *problems* in need of solutions.... Looking for 'problematization' means that we ask not just when a theme appears for the first time but when it first appears *as a problem*, an issue that needs resolving."[34]

Similarly, the analysis that follows demonstrates that the Mekhilta and Genesis Rabbah both raise exegetical questions and offer theological arguments that can best be understood in relation to specific problems raised in texts that originated in communities of Christ-followers composed before as well as contemporaneously with the compilations of these two rabbinic texts. The authors of both midrashim, in their distinct historical contexts, seem to wrestle with the meaning of biblical references to the Sabbath in light of competing Christian interpretations, and they offer novel readings that resolve new exegetical and theological problems first proposed in such Christian sources. While this chapter's conclusion might not apply to all rabbinic texts on all matters, regarding certain dimensions of the Sabbath, rabbinic traditions display an awareness of Christian theological argumentation and a willingness to engage with it.

Historical Contextualization

Before turning to rabbinic sources, some introductory words of historical contextualization, both Roman and Christian, are necessary to set the scene. For the most part, the Roman Empire encouraged those within its territories to continue observing their "ancestral rites."[35] For Jews, such rites included practicing the Sabbath in whatever way they were accustomed to doing.[36] Josephus catalogues several documents in which various Roman prefects and proconsuls, including Augustus, assured Jews that they were permitted to abstain from work and travel on the Sabbath, even if such Sabbath observance prevented them from contributing military service to the empire.[37] Philo, too, describes Augustus's respect for the worship of the Sabbath in Jewish synagogues and mentions a case when an exception was made for Jews during grain distribution so that they could observe the Sabbath and collect their grain the following day.[38] Only for a brief period following the Bar Kokhba revolt in the mid-second century CE were such allowances temporarily withdrawn.[39]

Notwithstanding official Roman tolerance of the observance of "ancestral rites" found in edicts and imperial documents, there was no shortage of rhetorical attacks against the Jews and their Sabbath. Greek and Latin literary and satirical sources preserve many of these polemics. These sources demonstrate the extent to which Greeks and Romans regarded the Sabbath in negative, vulgar terms, as a feature of the Jews' foreignness, disease, and revulsion.[40] Agatharchides of Cnidus, Apion, Seneca the Younger, Persius, Tacitus, Juvenal, Martial, Plutarch, Dio Cassius, and Rutilius Namatianus all mock the Sabbath or express skepticism about its observance.[41] Apion, for example, explains that the Israelites developed tumors of the groin on the seventh day of their journey out of Egypt as the etiology (and etymology) for Sabbath rest; Tacitus ends his discussion of the Jewish Sabbath by stating that "the Jews are extremely loyal toward one another, and are always ready to show compassion, but toward every other people they feel . . . only hatred and enmity"; Persius describes the fear of those who encounter Jews celebrating the Sabbath: "you silently twitch your lips, turning pale."[42]

Given such caustic claims, it is not surprising that early Jewish sources present the Sabbath in apologetic terms. Aristobulus, in a fragment that deals with the Sabbath, connects universalistic themes such as light and wisdom to the Jewish Sabbath, emphasizing that the number seven not only is holy for Jews but also figures prominently in the writings of Homer and Hesiod.[43] Philo, too, was quick to defend the Sabbath in light of claims that Jews are slothful. He argued that the observance of the Sabbath is its own type of labor—the laboring of the soul—rather than an abstention from work, and moreover that giving the body a break not only allows time for the soul to be exercised but also renews the body for more efficient laboring during the rest of the week.[44]

Extant non-Christian Greek and Latin sources that contain anti-Sabbath polemics date as early as the third century BCE and persist through late antiquity, into and past the fifth century CE. The overwhelming majority of evidence, however, dates to the first and early second centuries CE. Whether this fact is due to the randomness with which sources from antiquity survive in the historical record or due to trends in the popularity and pervasiveness of such polemics at different chronological periods cannot be known, but the evidence is suggestive.[45] Christian sources—including those of Justin Martyr, Eusebius of Caesarea, Aphrahat, John Chrysostom, and Augustine of Hippo, as well as many others, both from the eastern and western reaches of the Roman Empire and indeed also beyond its boundaries—incorporate ideas found in non-Christian Greek and Latin sources into their own specifically Christian anti-Jewish polemics. Seneca's anti-Sabbath polemic serves as a paradigmatic example. In the first century CE, Seneca apparently railed against Sabbath rest because he viewed it as an utter waste of time. His polemical writings about the Sabbath, however, do not survive except in Augustine of Hippo's early fifth-century work *City of God*, which quotes Seneca's text.[46] It is noteworthy, too, that such later Christian authors did not simply regurgitate existing Roman anti-Sabbath polemics; they appropriated them for particular rhetorical ends and specifically Christian theological arguments.[47] This is all to say that (non-Christian) Greek and Latin anti-Sabbath polemics themselves influenced how certain rabbinic ideas about the Sabbath developed but also that such non-Christian critiques of the Sabbath must likewise be seen in the context of their appropriation by Christians, who used them to polemicize against Jews and Judaism in ways that were both similar to and different from their use by others in the Roman Empire. It is to such Christian discourses about the Sabbath that this historical overview now turns.

Discussions about the Sabbath and the structuring of weekly time featured centrally in the construction of early communities of Christ-followers of the first, second, and third centuries. Their attitudes toward the Sabbath and the structure of their week, however, were as variable as the communities themselves.[48] Some texts called for followers of Christ to continue observing the Sabbath.[49] Others critiqued Sabbath observance for its unreasonable rigidity; for being a practice no longer required; or for altogether misinterpreting scripture's original command to rest on the seventh day.[50] Others advocated for the Sabbath to be marked as a day of fasting and mourning, in commemoration of Jesus' death and crucifixion, or a day that should be observed spiritually rather than as a day of feasting and celebration, as it was in many Jewish communities.[51] Some began observing an *additional* sacred day on Sunday, the day after the Sabbath, while others considered Sunday an *alternative* weekly sacred day (with its own set of practices).[52] Christians eventually preferred calling Sunday "the Lord's Day."[53] Many communities gathered on the Lord's Day for reading, worship, and breaking bread in order to commemorate Christ's resurrection.[54] Eviatar Zerubavel writes that the "choice of Sunday as a [sacred] day other than Saturday was at least as significant, from a sociological standpoint, as their association of that day with the Resurrection!"[55] In the fourth century, Christian authorities, perhaps following Constantine's lead, reconceived of the Lord's Day as a day of rest, modeled on the Sabbath.[56] Despite such variations among different communities, already at quite an early date the observance of the Sabbath on Saturday as a joyous day of rest celebrated with festive meals was associated, at least in Christian literary and homiletical sources, with Jewish communities and was regarded as a marker of Jewishness, while the gathering of communities on the Lord's Day (i.e., Sunday, the day following the Jewish Sabbath) usually signaled that a community and its members were Christian. Those who attended both communities' services or observed both days as sacred caused a confusion of boundaries that confounded and frustrated those intent on setting clear and permanent communal borders. John Chrysostom aggressively warned his congregants, for example, against attending the local synagogue on Saturdays and church on Sundays.[57]

Once Emperor Constantine began the process of Christianizing the Roman Empire in the first half of the fourth century CE, the temporal landscape that marked Jewish-Christian difference changed significantly. Two pieces of Constantinian legislation from 321 CE survive, one in the Justinian Code and the other in the Theodosian Code. Each of them indicates the official adoption of the seven-day week and the declaration of Sunday as a day of rest, which adopted Sabbath rest rules for Sunday for the first time. According to the Justinian Code, certain types of labor were prohibited on Sunday, though agricultural work remained permitted:

> Let all judges, the people of cities, and those employed in all trades, remain quiet on the Holy Day of Sunday. Persons residing in the country, however, can freely and lawfully proceed with the cultivation of the

fields, as it frequently happens that the sowing of grain or the planting of vines cannot be deferred to a more suitable day, and by making concessions to Heaven the advantage of the time may be lost.[58]

The Theodosian Code's law adds additional exceptions to the types of activities that may be performed on Sunday, including the emancipation and manumission of enslaved people:

> Just as it appears to us most unseemly that the Day of the Sun [Sunday], which is celebrated on account of its own veneration, should be occupied with legal altercations and with noxious controversies of the litigation of contending parties, so it is pleasant and fitting that those acts which are especially desired shall be accomplished on that day. Therefore, all men shall have the right to emancipate and manumit on this festive day, and the legal formalities thereof are not forbidden.[59]

Though the compilation of the Theodosian and Justinian codes postdates the Constantinian era, a documentary papyrus from 2 October 325 CE, written just over four years after Constantine's edict was issued, references Constantine's Sunday law, suggesting that the law already affected those as far as Egypt not long after it was initially issued.[60]

Scholars debate whether Constantine intended to elevate Sunday because it was the Day of Sol, in veneration of the sun deity Sol and perhaps also of Mithras, or the Lord's Day, a reference to Christ.[61] Such a distinction was itself blurry in the early fourth century. Concerning this issue, Goodman states: "Constantine's notorious adherence to the sun-god after his conversion to Christianity is best understood as his identification of the sun-god with the Highest God worshipped by Christians."[62] Michele Salzman, for her part, suggests that perhaps Constantine was deliberately "playing both sides of the fence."[63] The earliest literary sources that recount Constantine's law already present it as an effort to Christianize the empire, so regardless of Constantine's original intent, it was promoted by others in that light.[64] In his *Life of Constantine*, composed in the 330s CE in Caesarea, Eusebius praises Emperor Constantine's establishment of the Lord's Day as a day of worship:

> He also decreed that the truly sovereign and really first day, the day of the Lord and Savior, should be considered a regular day of prayer. . . . He therefore decreed that all those under the Roman government should rest on the days named after the Savior, and similarly that they should honor the days of the Sabbath, in memory, I suppose, of the things recorded as done by the universal Savior on those days. The Day of Salvation, then, which also bears the names of Light Day and Sun Day, he taught all the military to revere devoutly. To those who shared the divinely given faith he allowed free time to attend unhindered the church of God, on the assumption that with all impediment removed

they would join in prayers. To those who did not yet share in the divine Word he gave order in a second decree that every Lord's Day they should march out on an open space just outside the city, and that there at a signal they should all together offer up to God.... Such were the things he decreed should be done by the military regiments every Sunday, and such were the words he taught them to recite in their prayers to God.[65]

Eusebius frames Constantine's Sunday legislation as one of the primary and most public ways through which Constantine (wittingly or not) effected the empire's Christianization.

Subsequent Christian emperors followed Constantine's lead.[66] Later in the fourth century, Theodosius I referred to Sunday specifically as the "Lord's Day" and announced that it would be one of the days on which law courts were required to close throughout the Roman Empire.[67] By the mid-fifth century, these and other laws related to the Lord's Day were consolidated within the Theodosian Code.[68] These laws prohibited tax collectors from suing Christians on Sundays, debtors from collecting private and public debt, and city officials from hosting spectacles.[69] Between 321 and 429 CE, Roman law thus underwent a fundamental—and quite radical—shift in how it legislated time. These changes occurred in conjunction with legislation that introduced other Christian festivals into the imperial calendar, limited the number of traditional Roman non-Christian festivals that would officially be celebrated in the empire, and restricted activities considered idolatrous, such as sacrifices and public spectacles, on the festival days that continued to be celebrated.[70] The gradual incorporation of the Christian Lord's Day into the Roman imperial calendar, like other calendrical reforms, signaled the new, and specifically Christian, character of the empire. Banning certain forms of labor on Sunday had become a way of temporally Christianizing an empire that had previously organized its time in different ways.

In contrast to the status of Sunday as a sacred day of rest, however, the adoption of the seven-day weekly cycle within the Roman Empire did not only or even primarily occur by imperial edict. Salzman has demonstrated that the transition within the Roman Empire from a nundinal cycle of eight days to a seven-day week occurred gradually in the centuries before as well as during the fourth century, and that it was as much the cumulative result of organic developments in time-keeping in previous centuries as it was the outcome of imperial legislation.[71] In addition to the Jewish seven-day week, already a central feature in the Hebrew Bible's cosmogony and observed by contemporaneous Jews, another seven-day week, widely attested in Roman sources, had developed in the ancient Mediterranean as well.[72] Individuals throughout the Roman Empire slowly adopted this system, based on the tracking of the seven visible planets across the sky, following Julius Caesar's conquest of Egypt, in the same period when Jews and their cultural practices,

FIGURES 9. Saturday (left) and Sunday (right) in Philocalus's codex calendar of 354 CE.

with their unique time frames, also became more integrated into the empire.[73] Ancient sources often conflated the two weekly systems, and eventually they made no distinction between them; authors such as Frontinus, Tacitus, Dio Cassius, and Juvenal regularly interchange "Sabbath" and "Saturday," for example, and some Christian sources used "Sunday" and the "Lord's Day" reciprocally as well.[74] By the beginning of the third century CE, Dio Cassius wrote that the seven-day week was popular even among Romans, who themselves already regarded it as an "ancestral tradition."[75] Thus, the adoption of the seven-day week into Roman imperial time was not exclusively the result of imperial legislation. Rather, it was the culmination of a long and complicated process among a diverse set of Roman (Christian and non-Christian) individuals and communities. The incorporation of Saturday and Sunday as unique days within the seven-day week, in contrast, was particular to Jewish and Christian communities prior to Constantine, and it was only over the course of the fourth century that Sunday came to be marked within the empire as an official day of rest, mirroring the Jewish Sabbath and developing Christian practices.[76] These two interrelated shifts in popular and imperial time-keeping thus overlapped with the gradual Christianization of the empire's communities and contributed to its further Christianization in an official capacity through imperial legal channels. Communal developments worked in tandem with imperial legislation to solidify this momentous temporal rearrangement. And still, the nundinal cycle did not completely disappear: the nundinal cycle's division of time into eight-day units persisted alongside the seven-day cycle in calendars and parapegmata into and past the fourth century, as Philocalus's codex calendar of 354 demonstrates.[77] As the empire's population increasingly Christianized, the seven-day week, with its weekly sacred day, dominated and eventually replaced other units of time, including both the Roman nundinal cycle and the Egyptian decade.

The Sabbath as Temporal Differentiator in Exodus and Jubilees

In order to isolate the unique features of early rabbinic portrayals of the Sabbath, it is instructive to analyze select biblical texts at the heart of rabbinic interpretations as well as to consider pre-rabbinic interpretations of those biblical passages. The idea that Sabbath observance creates difference between God's people and others is not, per se, a rabbinic innovation: it already appears as a dominant theme in biblical and Second Temple texts. In Exodus 31, for example, God commands Moses to tell the Israelites to observe the Sabbath as follows:

> You shall keep my Sabbaths, for this is a sign between me and you throughout your generations, given in order that you may know that I, the Lord, sanctify you. You shall keep the Sabbath, because it is holy for you; everyone who profanes it shall be put to death; whoever does any work on it shall be cut off from among the people. Six days shall work be done, but the seventh day is a sabbath of solemn rest, holy to the Lord; whoever does any work on the Sabbath day shall be put to death. Therefore, the Israelites shall keep the Sabbath, observing the Sabbath throughout their generations, as a perpetual covenant. It is a sign forever between me and the People of Israel that in six days the Lord made heaven and earth, and on the seventh day he rested, and was refreshed.[78]

This passage presents the Sabbath as a day that, through its observance, separates Israel from others: it sanctifies them, symbolizes their ongoing unique covenant with God, and reminds them of God's creation of the world (and thus affirms God as the creator of that world). The passage also notes that violating the Sabbath carries with it a death penalty, stressing the importance of Sabbath observance. Other biblical passages emphasize that the Sabbath commemorates the Israelite exodus from Egypt, enumerate some specific Sabbath prohibitions such as not kindling fires or collecting manna, and mandate that householders ensure that everyone in their households, including children, people they have enslaved, and livestock, can spend the day abstaining from work.[79] The command to observe the Sabbath is also included among the ten commandments, elevating its importance further as one of only a select number of laws revealed directly by God to Moses and the Israelites at Sinai.[80]

The Sabbath features prominently, as well, in the creation narrative found in the book of Jubilees. This text frames the entire world's creation in light of God's heavenly observance of the seventh day and depicts the Sabbath as the ultimate symbol of Israel's chosenness by the divine from the very beginning of time.[81] The angels, who observe the Sabbath together with God in the heavens, explain that, according to God, the Sabbath separates Jews from other people and allows God to sanctify them: "I will separate unto Myself a people from among all the peoples, and these shall keep the Sabbath day, and I will sanctify them unto Myself as My people, and will bless them; as I have sanctified the Sabbath day and sanctify [it] unto Myself, even so will I bless them, and they shall be My people and I will be their God."[82] This passage presents the Sabbath not only as a sign of the ongoing covenant between God and Israel but as an institution mandated by God to mark Israel's separateness from others and to bless them.[83] The narrative deliberately links the distinctiveness of Jacob's offspring with the abstention from work on the Sabbath: "And I have chosen the seed of Jacob from amongst all that I have seen, and have written him down as My first-born son, and have sanctified him unto Myself for ever and ever; and I will teach them the Sabbath day, that they may keep the Sabbath."[84]

The bulk of the book of Jubilees further reframes the narratives of Genesis and the first half of Exodus in temporal terms, linking Israel's linear history and periodization with sabbatical cycles of different lengths.[85] The Sabbath plays a dominant role throughout. The text proposes a chronological division of historical time into weeks of years (that is, periods of seven years) and jubilees (that is, 49 years, seven cycles of seven years), starting with the world's creation and extending into later events. Jubilees divides the calendrical year, too, into 52 equal weeks of seven days, with the Sabbath thus punctuating and framing the annual cycle in a symmetrical way. The text returns to the topic of the Sabbath again in its closing section: "And thus He created therein a sign in accordance with which they should keep the Sabbath with us [the angels] on the seventh day, to eat and to drink, and to bless Him who has created all things as He has blessed and sanctified unto Himself a peculiar people above all peoples, and that they should keep Sabbath together with us."[86] In the book of Jubilees, Sabbath observance distinguishes Jews from other communities and also forges a temporal bond between Israel and the angelic realm, which celebrate the Sabbath in synchrony.

Scholars have interpreted Jubilees' Sabbath rhetoric, like other dimensions of the composition, in light of attempts by its author, sometime in the second century CE, to deal with questions of Jewish-gentile difference. According to Himmelfarb, for example, Jubilees seeks to critique the integration of gentiles into Israel during the period of Hasmonean rule.[87] Those who date the text to an earlier period, prior to the Maccabean revolt, interpret Jubilees' emphasis on time and difference as contending with other matters of intercommunal boundaries, such as intermarriage.[88] In either historical context, scholars understand Jubilees' emphasis on the Sabbath as extending the biblical framing of the Sabbath as a sign that separates Israel and other nations and as adapting it to contemporary concerns.[89] In other intra-Jewish disputes of the late Second Temple period, too, Sabbath practice became the topic of intense debate, to which rabbinic sources indeed allude.[90]

The Sabbath and the Lord's Day, the Sabbath as the Lord's Day

The Mekhilta de-Rabbi Ishmael, in its exegesis of passages related to the Sabbath, also emphasizes that the Sabbath serves as a sign of Israel's covenant with God and as a temporal practice that separates Jews from others, a theme that it develops in consonance with traditions such as those found in Exodus 31 and the book of Jubilees. Strikingly, however, some of the specific ways in which the Mekhilta expands its interpretations of the Sabbath in Exodus 31 can be explained most compellingly not as straightforward readings of the biblical text or as continuous with prior Second Temple readings but rather as proposing interpretations of biblical phrases that engaged with matters central to biblical interpretations and theological arguments articulated in texts that circulated widely among Christians in the third century, when the Mekhilta was redacted. These texts include the Synoptic Gospels, the Letter to the Hebrews, and the Epistle of Barnabas, as well as Jewish-Christian and Christian writings produced contemporaneously with the Mekhilta, such as the Didascalia Apostolorum and the writings of Justin Martyr. As the analysis that follows proposes, the first section of Mekhilta *Shabbata* can be contextualized within broader intracommunal debates from the Second Temple period, even as the Mekhilta's text resonates most closely with gospel traditions about Sabbath observance. Yet, midrashic interpretations in the subsequent sections of Mekhilta *Shabbata* do not find expression in earlier Second Temple texts. Rather, in these sections, the Mekhilta resolves exegetical problems that are raised by competing Christian readings of the same biblical passage.

"THE SABBATH IS GIVEN TO YOU BUT YOU ARE NOT SURRENDERED TO THE SABBATH"

The end of the Second Temple period and the early rabbinic period saw vigorous debate about whether one is permitted to violate the Sabbath for the sake of a competing value; this debate spanned several communities, including at Qumran, among the Synoptic Gospel writers, and in rabbinic sources. The Mekhilta begins its section on the Sabbath with a long discussion about this topic, situating the midrash within a cross-communal conversation concerned about the limits of Sabbath observance.[91]

The phrase "Verily, you shall keep my Sabbaths [אך את שבתתי תשמרו]" from Exodus 31:13 prompts the Mekhilta to wonder how this Sabbath command differs from the command recorded in Exodus 20:9, which notes that "you shall not do any work [לא תעשה כל מלאכה]." The Mekhilta explains that while Exodus 20:9 prohibits all activities that directly constitute work, Exodus 31:13, because its wording is somewhat more vague, refers to a prohibition against doing any activities that detract from the day's restfulness, even if such activities do not strictly constitute work.[92] This midrash thus establishes that observing the Sabbath entails abstaining from activities both that constitute work and that detract from the day's restfulness, and it identifies the two biblical passages that correspond to each of these prohibitions.

The Mekhilta then seeks to identify the biblical verse or legal principle that underpins a different rule, namely that, in a situation in which violating a Sabbath law will result in saving the life of a human being (פיקוח נפש), that Sabbath law must be violated. The Mekhilta does not ask *whether* a Sabbath prohibition can be violated on the Sabbath in such a circumstance—it takes for granted that doing so constitutes rabbinic law. Rather, it wonders which biblical verse or legal principle underpins this rule. This is a typical type of question in halakhic midrashim, which seek to connect rabbinic rules to particular biblical verses and to highlight, through biblical exegesis, the biblical sources of rabbinic law.[93]

As recorded in the Mekhilta, the answer to the question—which biblical verse mandates the violation of Sabbath prohibitions in order to save a life?—is contested. A lively debate then ensues between different rabbinic authorities about the correct biblical source. In total, the Mekhilta offers six different proofs for this single rule.[94] Rabbi Ishmael, with whose opinion the Mekhilta begins, cites Exodus 22:1-2 to shed light on the exegetical question. According to this verse, one is not accountable for murder if one kills a burglar who enters one's home under the cover of night, as one is considered to have acted in self-defense. Rabbi Ishmael reasons that, if one is permitted to kill someone to potentially save a life, one should certainly be permitted to violate the Sabbath to actually save a life. In contrast to Rabbi Ishmael, who cites a biblical passage, Rabbi Eleazar ben Azariah and Rabbi Akiva suggest distinct legal principles for the rule that saving a life overrides Sabbath laws. Rabbi Eleazar ben Azariah derives the rule from the laws of circumcision. According to these laws, one may perform a male circumcision on the Sabbath if an infant's eighth day of life—the day prescribed for circumcision—falls on the Sabbath, even though circumcision involves acts that normally are prohibited on the Sabbath.[95] Rabbi Eleazar ben Azariah reasons that whereas circumcision concerns only a single body part, saving a life concerns many body parts and therefore ought to be permissible on the Sabbath even if it requires actions generally prohibited on the Sabbath. Further supporting the Mekhilta's original claim, Rabbi Akiva argues that saving a life should supersede the Sabbath on the grounds that, according to biblical law, punishing a murder supersedes the laws associated with the Temple service, whose importance, in turn, according to other biblical texts, supersedes the Sabbath. The final three figures in the midrash offer alternative exegeses of passages from Exodus 31. Rabbi Yose the Galilean explains that the word "verily [אך]" at the beginning of the command "Verily, you shall keep my Sabbaths" plays a crucial role, indicating that there are two types of Sabbaths: Sabbaths on which one must rest, and Sabbaths on which one must not rest (for instance, when one ought to save a life). Thus, the seemingly superfluous word "verily" serves as the biblical proof text for the rule regarding saving a life on the Sabbath. Rabbi Shimon ben Menasiah contends, in contrast, that the following verse, Exodus 31:14, provides the strongest proof text: "You shall keep the Sabbath, because it is holy for you."[96] Rabbi Shimon ben Menasiah explains that this verse means that "the Sabbath is given to you but you are not surrendered to the Sabbath."[97] In other words, the Sabbath is an institution created for people ("it is holy *for you*"), and therefore one must violate the Sabbath in order to save a person. Finally, Rabbi Nathan cites yet another subsequent verse, Exodus 31:16, which commands the Israelites to keep the Sabbath "throughout their generations." Rabbi Nathan deduces the permissibility of violating a single Sabbath for the sake of saving a life because that single violation will then permit the saved person to observe many subsequent Sabbaths—and presumably also for many generations to come.

Introducing the Mekhilta's chapter on the Sabbath with a discussion of biblical proof texts regarding when the Sabbath must be violated may seem odd.[98] The discussion appears less strange, however, when it is contextualized among overlapping debates about Sabbath observance in Jewish communities from the Second Temple period. In his analysis of this passage in the Mekhilta, Aharon Shemesh writes: "The amount of discussion [in the Mekhilta] is itself telling and is typical of Tannaitic literature regarding laws that stand at the center of the debate between the Tannaim and the tradition of the priestly Sadducean/sectarian law."[99] According to Shemesh, the Mekhilta's extended focus on the question of saving a life on the Sabbath indicates that different groups of Jews in the later Second Temple period hotly disputed the matter at hand; ancient sources confirm Shemesh's observation. Second Temple texts— including 1 Maccabees, the book of Jubilees, Pesher Habakkuk, the Damascus Document, and the Gospels (all sources that predate the Mekhilta's redaction)—question whether one might violate the Sabbath for the well-being of others (whether to save the life of an individual, for instance following an accident, or to save the lives of groups of people, for instance during times of war).[100] Some Jews, such as the authors of the Dead Sea Scrolls documents 4Q256 and 4Q265, opposed the position presented in the Mekhilta, arguing that it was not permitted to violate the Sabbath even for the sake of saving a life or that only limited means could be used, while other texts argued for more lenient positions.[101] That the Mekhilta preserves opinions also attested in these earlier sources suggests that the Mekhilta's traditions on this topic are not rabbinic innovations but preservations of more ancient positions.

Jews who were followers of Jesus—yet another group of Second Temple Jews—also partook in these conversations. The Gospels portray Jesus himself as addressing questions of when and on what biblical basis Sabbath laws must be violated for the sake of people's health and well-being. A number of stories about Jesus healing on the Sabbath include justifications that appear, as well, in the Mekhilta.[102] John 7:21–24 specifically mentions the permissibility of circumcision on the Sabbath as an explanation for Jesus' healing on the Sabbath, and the topic of saving a life appears as Jesus's words in Mark 3:4: "Is it lawful to do good or to do harm on the Sabbath, to save life or to kill?"[103] In addition, all three Synoptic Gospels feature a story (with variations) in which Jesus and the Pharisees disagree about whether violating the Sabbath in order to feed Jesus' hungry disciples constitutes proper Sabbath observance. The Gospel of Mark presents the episode as follows:

> One Sabbath he was going through the grain fields; and as they made their way his disciples began to pluck heads of grain. The Pharisees said to him, "Look, why are they doing what is not lawful on the Sabbath?" And he said to them, "Have you never read what David did when he and his companions were hungry and in need of food? He entered the house of God, when Abiathar was high priest, and ate the bread of the Presence, which it is not lawful for any but the priests to eat, and he gave some to his companions." Then he said to them, "The Sabbath was made for humankind, and not humankind for the Sabbath; so the Son of Man is lord even of the Sabbath."[104]

When the Pharisees confront Jesus about plucking grains on the Sabbath, which the Pharisees in the story regard as a violation of Sabbath laws, Jesus offers them two different exegetical explanations as justifications for his actions.[105] First, he references the biblical story of David in 1 Samuel 21:1–6, in which David comes to the temple and asks for five loaves of bread for his men. When the priest explains that he only has consecrated showbreads from the temple, which were to be eaten by priests in a state of purity, David convinces the priest to hand over the loaves on the condition that the men who eat them do so in a state of purity. Though David does not violate the Sabbath, he violates other laws related to the temple and temple purity in order to feed his hungry men. By invoking this narrative, Jesus implicitly draws a parallel between himself and David, who, according to other gospel traditions, was his ancestor.[106] The narrative connects David's violation of temple norms and Jesus' violation of Sabbath norms, justifying the latter by way of the example of the former.[107] As in the Mekhilta, though, a single proof for justifying Jesus'

Sabbath-violating actions does not satisfy the gospel author; in addition to providing a biblical proof text, he also offers a logical explanation: "The Sabbath was made for humankind, and not humankind for the Sabbath."[108] In contrast to 4Q265, and more closely aligned with the Mekhilta, the Synoptic Gospels promote a somewhat more lenient approach to circumstances that call for the violation of Sabbath laws (though they do not call for the abolishment of Sabbath observance or of Mosaic law more generally, staying well within the scope of Jewish internal debates about Sabbath observance).[109]

Scholars have noted the similarities between the gospel story and the Mekhilta, both of which provide meditations about when and why Sabbath laws can legitimately be violated.[110] The Mekhilta and the gospel story, along with John 7:21–24 and Mark 3:4, argue that the Sabbath can be violated at times when people's well-being is at stake (though the texts differ regarding what precisely "people's well-being" entails). They offer multiple explanations, based on different types of reasoning, for the rule. Most strikingly, both sets of texts agree with the sentiment that "the Sabbath was made for humankind" and thus that certain circumstances necessitate violating the Sabbath for the sake of a person. These shared idioms attest to fundamental commonalities in their approaches to and traditions about Sabbath observance.[111]

The congruence of these texts has several implications. The Mekhilta positions itself between the views expressed in the Dead Sea Scrolls and those advocated in the Synoptic Gospels. On the one hand, the Mekhilta does not universally ban Sabbath violation (as some texts among the Dead Sea Scrolls seem to do). On the other hand, it does not permit Sabbath violation for non-life-threatening purposes (as Jesus does in the gospel traditions about healing and feeding on the Sabbath). Rather, the Mekhilta argues that the Sabbath may be violated, but only in the extreme circumstance when a life must be saved. By staking out a "middle way" on questions of Sabbath observance, and drawing on similar idioms, the Mekhilta advances a position distinct from, but not opposed to, that found in the Gospels and other Second Temple sources. The similarities between the texts, in this case, do not necessarily suggest that the Mekhilta polemicizes against gospel traditions or contemporary applications of those traditions. The Mekhilta could just as likely preserve a debate and legal positions from the Second Temple period, continuing to engage in the same debate and drawing upon the same traditions concerning Sabbath observance that the Gospels preserve as well.

"A SIGN BETWEEN ME AND YOU, BUT NOT BETWEEN ME AND THE NATIONS OF THE WORLD"

Unlike its opening section, which takes up a question of common interest, other sections of the Mekhilta provide rabbinic perspectives on central points of contention concerning the Sabbath that were at the heart of disagreements among diverse sets of ancient Jewish and Christian communities. The Mekhilta asserts that the Sabbath distinguishes Israel from other nations, and sanctifies Israel, emphasizing that those beyond Israel cannot claim the same sort of relationship with God. Thus, for example, immediately following the discussion of saving a life on the Sabbath, the Mekhilta turns to the next phrase in Exodus 31:13: "this is a sign between me and you." The midrash explains that the Sabbath serves as a sign between God and Israel, "but not between Me and the nations of the world."[112] Here, the Sabbath represents a positive marker of the close bond between God and Israel.[113]

Insisting that the Sabbath is a sign of the relationship between God and Israel, and moreover that this bond created through Sabbath observance is limited to Israel, addresses a problem raised in some communities of Christ-followers about what Jewish Sabbath observance symbolized. In the third-century Mediterranean context, this claim would have countered the contentions of Christ-followers who viewed Sabbath observance as a sign of Israel's continued sin. In his mid-second-century polemical text *Dialogue with Trypho*, for example, Justin Martyr cites Ezekiel 20:19–26 and alludes to Exodus 31:13 to argue that the Sabbath was a sign of sin and that those who follow Christ rather than the Sabbath would receive God's inheritance instead of Israel:

> As I stated before, it was by reason of your sins and the sins of your fathers that, among other precepts, God imposed upon you the observance of the Sabbath as a sign ... those who have persecuted Christ in the past and still do, and do not repent, shall not inherit anything on the holy mountain, unless they repent. Whereas the gentiles who believe in Christ and are sorry for their sins shall receive the inheritance, along with the patriarchs, the prophets, and every just descendant of Jacob, even though they neither practice circumcision nor observe the Sabbath and feasts. They shall undoubtedly share in the holy inheritance of God.[114]

Regarding Justin Martyr's polemics against the Sabbath, Gregerman writes:

> There are many commandments that he [Justin] agrees with and that go unmentioned in his disputes with Trypho precisely because both Jews and Christians accept them. It is the few commandments that function as markers of Jewish identity, separating Jews from non-Jews, which dominate the *Dial.* and explain [Justin's] reprobation of the Law. He repeatedly singles out commandments such as circumcision, ritual washing, restrictions on food, and Sabbath observance, and maintains that they are now abrogated, at least in the literal sense.... The rituals most associated with Jews are what Justin finds threatening, for he strongly opposes those which, if observed, may serve to divide the Christian community.[115]

According to Justin in the passage cited above, God commanded Israel to observe the Sabbath as a way of atoning for their sins.[116] Current followers of Christ, in contrast, do not need to observe the Sabbath because they are not sinful, just as the patriarchs who lived before Moses gave the Torah to Israel did not observe the Sabbath. Justin emphasizes that those who practice the Sabbath now are sinners, in contrast to those who do not observe the Sabbath but believe in Christ, who will be saved. Belief in Christ, rather than Sabbath observance, leads to receiving God's inheritance.

For the Mekhilta, in contrast, the Sabbath serves as a sign of Israel's holiness rather than its sinfulness, it binds God and Israel to one another, and other nations are excluded from this exclusive relationship with God. The matter at hand concerns the nature of the relationship between Israel and God. While Justin suggests that God punishes Israel by necessitating Sabbath observance, the Mekhilta presents the Sabbath as an invitation to Israel to join God in a unique holy relationship. Such a framing both neutralizes the claim that the Sabbath is a sign of sin and makes Sabbath observance more attractive to rabbinic adherents.

"THE SABBATH WILL NEVER BE ABOLISHED IN ISRAEL"

The Mekhilta also counters claims that the coming of Christ rendered Sabbath observance obsolete. In his *Dialogue with Trypho*, Justin Martyr declares: "if circumcision was not required before the time of Abraham, and if there was no need of Sabbaths, festivals, and sacrifices before Moses, they are not needed now, when, in accordance with the will of God, Jesus Christ, his Son, has been born of the Virgin Mary, a descendant of Abraham."[117] Justin argues that, just as those before Abraham were not circumcised and those before Moses did not observe the Sabbath and festivals (because the law had not yet been given to Moses), now such practices likewise need not be observed. Along similar lines, Tertullian, too, writes extensively about the Sabbath as a temporary institution.[118]

The Mekhilta proclaims precisely the opposite: that Israel will keep the Sabbath forever and that such observance preserves Israel. In its interpretation of the phrase "throughout their generations," the Mekhilta states explicitly that "this law will be practiced for generations."[119] Later, about the phrase "it is a sign forever," the Mekhilta explains further: "This tells that the Sabbath will never be abolished [בטלה] in Israel. And so you find that anything to which the Israelites devoted themselves has been preserved among them. And anything to which the Israelites were not devoted has not been preserved by them. Thus the Sabbath, circumcision, the study of the Torah, and ritual immersion, to which they were devoted have been preserved, while the temple, civil courts, Sabbaticals, Jubilees, to which Israel was not devoted have thus not been preserved."[120] The Sabbath's applicability to all generations was taken for granted in Second Temple texts; the Mekhilta, faced with claims that such biblical commandments no longer applied, seeks to prove that very applicability.

"THE SABBATH POSSESSES A HOLINESS LIKE THAT OF THE FUTURE WORLD"

The Mekhilta seems further to confront contemporaneous contentions voiced by followers of Christ in its insistence that the weekly Sabbath offers a taste of—but is distinct from—the World to Come. Such texts interpreted biblical references to the Sabbath as referring to the eschatological age, the World to Come, and the kingdom of heaven rather than to the seventh day of each week. In its reading of Genesis 2:2, the Letter to the Hebrews suggests, for example, that God's Sabbath rest refers to an eternal rest achieved by those who follow Christ:

> Therefore, since the promise of entering his rest still stands, let us be careful that none of you be found to have fallen short of it. . . . Now we who have believed enter that rest. . . . For somewhere he has spoken about the seventh day in these words: "On the seventh day God rested from all his works" (Genesis 2:2). And again, in the passage above he says, "They shall never enter my rest" (Psalm 95:11). Therefore, since it still remains for some to enter that rest, and since those who formerly had the good news proclaimed to them did not go in because of their disobedience, God again set a certain day, calling it "Today."[121]

The Didascalia Apostolorum similarly explains that the Sabbath was originally established to model what the final resting of the world will entail: the Sabbath "has been set as a type for the times, even as many other things have been set for a type. The Sabbath therefore is a type of the [final] rest, signifying the seventh thousand [years]."[122] The Epistle of Barnabas likewise interprets God's rest at the end of six days not as six days but as six eras of one thousand years each:

> Give heed, children, what this means: "He ended in six days" (Genesis 2:2). He means this, that in six thousand years the Lord shall bring all things to an end; for the day with Him signifies a thousand years; and this He himself bears witness, saying, "Behold, the day of the Lord shall be as a thousand years" (2 Peter 3:8). Therefore, children, in six days, that is in six thousand years, everything shall come to an end. "And He rested on the seventh day" (Genesis 2:2). This He means, when His Son shall come, and shall abolish the time of the Lawless One, and shall judge the ungodly, and shall change the sun and the moon and the stars, then shall he truly rest on the seventh day. Yea and furthermore He says, "Thou shalt hallow it with pure hands and with a pure heart" (see Psalm 24:4). If therefore a man is able now to hallow the day which God hal-

lowed, though he be pure in heart, we have gone utterly astray.... Finally He says to them, "Your new moons and your Sabbaths I cannot away with" (Isaiah 1:13). You see what is His meaning; it is not your present Sabbaths that are acceptable, but the Sabbath which I have made, in which, when I have set all things at rest, I will make the beginning of the eighth day which is the beginning of another world.[123]

According to this text, the world will exist for six thousand years, at the end of which God will bring about a period of a thousand years of Sabbath rest, considered the final seventh "day." Observing a weekly Sabbath, the Epistle of Barnabas argues, misreads scripture. Origen similarly writes in a homily that "the true Sabbath on which God will 'rest from all his works' will be the future age.... On this Sabbath God may grant to us as well the celebration of a feast day with him and rejoicing in these festivities with his holy angels."[124] The idea that God's Sabbath refers to an eschatological age became standard in Christian theology.

In stark contrast to these texts, the Mekhilta argues that even though the whole World to Come might in fact be characterized as one long Sabbath day, the weekly Sabbath, when it is properly observed, is itself a taste of the World to Come.[125] While interpreting the verse "That I am the Lord who sanctifies you," the Mekhilta comments: "for the future world, like the holiness of the Sabbath in this world. We thus learn that [the Sabbath possesses] a holiness like that of the World to Come [מעין קדושת העולם הבא]. As it says, 'A Psalm; a song of the Sabbath day' (Psalm 92:1), [referring] to a world that is fully Sabbath [לעולם שכולו שבת]."[126] The Mekhilta's linkage between the Sabbath and the World to Come does not draw on earlier traditions but rather advances an innovative interpretation about the Sabbath's relationship to the eschatological future World to Come, a connection that Christian texts make quite frequently. That is, Second Temple sources consistently interpret biblical references to the Sabbath as indicating the seventh day of the week. Once new interpretations proposed that biblical references to the Sabbath might not indicate observance of a sacred day but rather a sacred era projected into the future, this alternate interpretation seems to have posed a problem that the Mekhilta seeks to resolve. The Mekhilta's explanation, however, not only counters competing interpretations that diminish the necessity of Sabbath observance; it also promotes weekly Sabbath observance as an unparalleled opportunity to experience the holiness of the future world each week in the present one.[127]

"THE SABBATH IS IN THE CHARGE OF GOD"

Finally, the Mekhilta presents a position that seems to critique the declaration of a new holy day. Interpreting the phrase "But on the seventh day is a Sabbath of solemn rest holy to the Lord" (Exodus 31:15), it explains that God, rather than the rabbinic court, sanctifies the Sabbath day. Here, the Mekhilta contrasts Exodus 31:15 with Leviticus 23:4, which commands the Israelites to proclaim certain festivals and which rabbinic sources understand as referring to the observation of the moon and the declaration of new months. Some people, it says, might assume that just as rabbinic authorities declare new moons and thereby determine the dates of annual festivals, they might also have the authority to declare which day is the Sabbath. The Mekhilta thus clarifies that while Leviticus 23:4 refers to rabbinic pronouncements of festivals, Exodus 31:15 teaches that the Sabbath can be established only by God:

> One might think that just as the holiness of the festival depends on the *bet din* [rabbinic court], so also does the holiness of the Sabbath depend on the *bet din*. Therefore it says: "but on the seventh day is a Sabbath of solemn rest holy to the Lord," meaning that the Sabbath is in the charge of God [who fixes the day], and it does not depend on the *bet din*.[128]

Here, the Mekhilta picks up on an essential difference between the units of the month and the week. While the lunar months (and thus the festivals that are observed according to the lunar months) are determined through observation of nature (the phases of the moon), the weekly cycle of seven days (and thus the Sabbath, the seventh day of that cycle) is entirely independent of the natural world.[129] There is nothing to observe that would help determine the day of the Sabbath. As the Mekhilta presents it, the timing of festivals is dependent on human observation of nature, but the timing of the Sabbath is ultimately up to God because it is beyond human reckoning, control, or manipulation.

By referring to the Sabbath as a day ordained only by God, the Mekhilta presents a position that is similar yet stands in contrast to the emergence of a new sacred day within communities of Christ-followers, a day moreover that was called the "Lord's Day" but that was not celebrated on the Jewish Sabbath. Ignatius, in his Letter to the Magnesians, contrasts the Sabbath with the Lord's Day. He expresses the wish that "those who lived in old ways came to newness of hope, no longer keeping Sabbath, but living in accordance with the Lord's Day."[130] The Didache commands that on the Lord's Day the community ought to gather together, break bread, confess transgressions, and offer thanksgiving.[131] Though Justin Martyr calls the day Sunday (rather than the Lord's Day), he describes the day as follows:

> Sunday is the day on which we all hold our common assembly, because it is the first day on which God, having wrought a change in the darkness and matter, made the world; and Jesus Christ our Savior on the same day rose from the dead.[132]

For Justin, the Lord's Day commemorates both the first day of creation and Jesus' resurrection. The day thus references the beginning of two eras (creation and resurrection) as well as two dimensions of God (God as creator of the world as well as the resurrected Christ). Arguing that God established the Sabbath at the end of the week of creation and that the day of the Sabbath cannot be altered by human authorities, in contrast to festivals, allows the Mekhilta to insist that the Jewish Sabbath, not the Lord's Day, is the day chosen by God and the day that honors the true God who created the world.[133]

THE SABBATH IN THE MEKHILTA

The Mekhilta claims that Sabbath observance not only distinguishes Jews from others but also signals their chosenness; that the Sabbath will be kept eternally; that it is connected to the World to Come but not replaced by it; and that it is divinely ordained. The midrash, whether deliberately or not, distinguishes rabbinic Jews from followers of Christ, some of whom regarded Jewish Sabbath observance as a sign of Israel's sinfulness and rejected it, read the biblical references to Sabbath rest as allusions to divine eschatological rest, and held that the day of the Sabbath was superseded by the Lord's Day. The Mekhilta can be viewed as a rabbinic attempt to convince rabbinic Jews to regard the Sabbath as a unique opportunity to establish a relationship with God in a context in which competing communities were both arguing about Jewish Sabbath practices and promoting the ultimate sacrality of different days of the week.

It appears that the Mekhilta (surprisingly, because of its early date) struggles with ideas firmly based in second- and third-century anti-Jewish Christian theological works, though it is difficult to definitively conclude whether it is responding directly to such claims or was more generally the product of a cultural context in which such Sabbath discourse operated. The resonances between it and the texts discussed above can be explained in numerous ways. One might be inclined to suggest that the Mekhilta's biblical exegeses are internal (rabbinic) readings of scripture and thus that similarities between rabbinic and early Christian interpretations of these verses stem from limited interpretive possibilities rather than evidence of interaction or a shared cultural context. Yet the rabbis, particularly those whose exegeses are preserved in the Mekhilta, were daring—even audacious—readers of texts; the straightforward meaning of a word or phrase rarely hinders them from preferring a less intuitive reading. Some scholars have suggested that the Mekhilta preserves ancient pre-rabbinic traditions and disputes about the Sabbath from the late Second Temple period, traditions that were likewise carried forward by communities of Christ-followers (and that they thus have a common earlier history but little or no relation in the rabbinic present).[134] Indeed, some of the Mekhilta's exegeses—including its discussion about saving a life—do appear to engage vibrant debates about Sabbath observance that transpired among first-century Jewish groups, including both the community that produced the Dead Sea Scrolls and the Jesus movement, to which several texts from that period attest. However, even though the Mekhilta preserves traditions that engage halakhic disputes from the Second Temple period, some of its readings of Exodus 31 are innovative, and they seem to deal with exegetical and theological problems introduced specifically in texts produced by followers of Christ who argued against Sabbath observance. The Mekhilta proposes solutions to these new problems that frame the Sabbath as a practice that was not only still required and relevant but also a sign of the unique relationship between God and Israel, which ought to continue being cultivated by present-day Jews. Even, however, if the crafting of the Mekhilta itself bore no relation to contemporaneous discourse among Christ-followers, later rabbis studied and transmitted the Mekhilta's traditions. In this way, the Mekhilta's framing of the Sabbath indeed played a role in shaping later rabbinic discourse about the Sabbath as Christian apologists continued to argue that the Sabbath was a sign of Jewish sinfulness and that its observance should be altered or abolished.

The Jewish Sabbath in a Christian Empire

The second half of this chapter identifies a number of persisting, amplified, and new attitudes toward the Sabbath in amoraic and post-amoraic rabbinic sources that can be contextualized within the cultural milieu of the fourth and fifth centuries. Some rabbinic sources advocate particular types of Sabbath observance, going to great lengths to justify both the law of abstaining from cooking and the custom of serving lavish festive meals. By stressing that material dimensions are central to the celebration of the Sabbath, these rabbinic texts subvert Christian polemics that deemed such Jewish Sabbath practices to be dangerous detractions that diminished its spiritual worship. Other rabbinic sources engage in discussions about whether Jews celebrated the correct sacred day by addressing the natural and supernatural elements that prove the sacredness of the Sabbath day. The popularization of a competing sacred day on the Christian calendar, with its accompanying set of imperial laws and prohibitions, might thus have been met by rabbinic insistence that a different day was actually the weekly sacred day. Finally, these rabbinic texts consider the question of who has the authority to declare facts about the nature of time and legislate the sacredness of time. Perhaps counterintuitively, these rabbinic sources feature Roman officials as ultimately affirming the holiness of the Jewish Sabbath and confirming that Jews celebrate the sacred day on the correct day of the week and in praiseworthy ways. They engage with specific themes in their discussions of the Sabbath that were prominent in fourth- and fifth-century Christian and non-Christian Roman texts, polemics that drew upon older traditions of Sabbath critiques but employed them in new ways. The analysis that follows offers a discursive context in which best to understand these texts.

THE EMPEROR TASTES AND SMELLS SABBATH FOOD

The first of the rabbinic narratives to be analyzed in this section, which appears in different versions in Genesis Rabbah and the Babylonian Talmud, insists on the deliciousness of Sabbath food. Though the story is, at first glance, a playful meditation on the idea that the Sabbath contains a special quality that makes it different from all other days of the week, the story also participates in a more culturally and theologically specific debate between Jews, Christians, and other Romans about what constitutes appropriate Sabbath observance.

Genesis Rabbah devotes a full chapter to discussing the nature of the Sabbath. The chapter, anchored around Genesis 2:3, asks what the biblical passage means when it states that "God blessed the seventh day and made it holy."[135] It wonders whether there is something essentially different, blessed, and sacred about the Sabbath day, and if so, what that might be. The text contains an abundance of stories, dialogues, exegeses, and sayings about the various specific ways in which God blessed and hallowed the Sabbath, as well as about how people who worship the Sabbath can properly bless and hallow the day through their practices.

One answer, attributed to Rabbi Ishmael, claims that God "blessed it [the Sabbath] with manna":

> He blessed it with manna and hallowed it with manna. He blessed it with manna, for every day of the week one *omer* [per person] descended, but on the eve of the Sabbath two *omers*. And He hallowed it through manna, that the manna did not descend on the Sabbath at all.[136]

This interpretation ponders the difference between God's "blessing" of the Sabbath (ויברך) and God's "hallowing" of the Sabbath (ויקדש). In midrashic hermeneutics, these two verbs, used in the same biblical verse (Genesis 2:3), cannot mean the same thing, and so the rabbis deliberated how to understand each of them. According to Rabbi Ishmael, the double portion of manna that arrived on Friday (in preparation of the Sabbath) constituted God's "blessing" of the Sabbath. The fact that manna did not descend on the Sabbath day, in contrast, constituted God's "hallowing" of the Sabbath. The practice of collecting two pieces of *manna* in the desert in advance of the Sabbath is one of the few practical Sabbath observances recorded in the Hebrew Bible.[137] This midrash, which reads Genesis 2:3 in light of Exodus 16:4–30's description of the desert manna, establishes that God blesses and sanctifies the Sabbath through food practices: both God's bestowal of a double portion on Fridays and God's refraining from providing manna on the Sabbath. God provides extra, preprepared food on Fridays, which the Israelites collect in advance and then eat on the Sabbath, while at the same time God does not provide (and the Israelites do not collect) new food on the Sabbath. In the rabbinic midrash, this doubled act of food distribution and food abstention signals God's sanctification of the day. Indeed, food—its planting and harvesting, sale and acquisition, preparation and consumption—played a central role throughout the laws, customs, and debates about the Sabbath, from the very earliest discussions of Sabbath observance in biblical sources through texts from the Second Temple and rabbinic periods.[138] This midrash, too, describes God as using food as a mechanism for Sabbath sanctification.

Genesis Rabbah proposes several additional ways in which God "blessed" and "hallowed" the Sabbath, but one of the recurring themes in the chapter is the role of food in both divine and human sanctification of this day. One midrash suggests that God blessed the Sabbath with especially delicious food, even though it was prepared prior to the Sabbath, and then offers a narrative that features an encounter between the Roman emperor Antoninus and Rabbi Judah the Patriarch that illustrates this point.[139] Far from being a historical account, the story uses the figure of Antoninus—likely a reference to Emperor Antoninus Pius—to laud the culinary delights of the Sabbath, made delicious, despite the lack of freshness, because God has blessed the day's foods:[140]

> "[God] blessed [the Sabbath]" (Genesis 2:3): with tasty dishes. Rabbi made a meal for Antoninus on the Sabbath. He [Rabbi] set out cold dishes before him [Antoninus]; he ate them and found them delicious. [On another occasion] he [Rabbi] made a meal for him [Antoninus] during the week. He [Rabbi] set out hot dishes before him. He [Antoninus] said to him [Rabbi]: "Those others I enjoyed more than these." He [Rabbi] replied, "These lack a certain spice." "Does then the royal pantry lack anything?" he [Antoninus] exclaimed. He [Rabbi] responded, "They lack the Sabbath; do you indeed possess the Sabbath?"[141]

In this story, an emperor drops by a rabbi's house for a visit.[142] As it is the Sabbath, the rabbi cannot cook fresh food for his honored guest and instead serves him a cold repast.[143] The emperor is so taken by the food that he returns a few days later for another meal. Because this second visit does not occur on the Sabbath, the rabbi is able to prepare a freshly cooked feast for him. Much to the emperor's surprise, the quality of this second meal disappoints him, and he informs his rabbinical host that he preferred the cold Sabbath food to the hot weekday meal. In response, the rabbi explains that the first meal contained a special ingredient or flavor, the Sabbath. The emperor cannot replicate the dish because the royal pantry lacks this spice—it is only found in the kitchens of Sabbath observers. Here, the midrash employs a pun, as the word שבת refers both to an herb used for seasoning (dill) and to the seventh day of the week (the Sabbath), though the word is vocalized differently.[144] The rabbi's response could be understood to mean that the emperor's pantry lacks the specific spice used in the dish, but the rabbi actually means that the emperor cannot replicate the dish's delicious taste because he does not observe the Sabbath. From a literary perspective, this is an exquisite tale. Rendering it even more remarkable is that earlier Jewish sources that mention festive meals as part of Sabbath worship, such as the book of Jubilees and Josephus's autobiography, do not discuss the Sabbath as a day of especially tasty food.[145]

A clue to the impetus for this focus and innovation may lie in the tale's historical, cultural, and theological context. One of the recurring critiques of the Sabbath in contemporaneous sources is that the Jewish prohibition against cooking on the Sabbath resulted in cold or even revolting food. In fact, this critique appears most prominently in fourth- and fifth-century sources. In the second half of the fourth century in the region of Syria, the author known as Pseudo-Ignatius revised and expanded a letter by the first-century bishop Ignatius, inserting the injunction that Christians ought to "observe the Sabbath spiritually, by rejoicing in meditation on laws and not in the release of the body, by marveling at the creative work of God, not by eating day-old food, drinking lukewarm beverages, walking measured distances, and rejoicing in dancing and senseless clapping."[146] The Jews, Pseudo-Ignatius claims, eat and drink thusly because, according to Jewish law, Sabbath food needs to be prepared before the beginning of the Sabbath on Friday evening.[147] Joining Pseudo-Ignatius in such remarks, the fifth-century author of the *Brevis Expositio in Vergilii Georgica* mentions the cold food that is consumed by Jews on the Sabbath: "It has been sufficiently known that the star of Saturn is cold, and therefore the food among the Jews on the day of Saturn is cold."[148] Comments on the quality of Sabbath food could be related to the common (mis)conception in antiquity that Jews fasted on the Sabbath (the prohibition against purchasing and cooking food on the Sabbath might have contributed to the belief that Jews fast on that day, or, alternatively, abstaining from freshly cooked food might have been considered a form of fasting, i.e., a form of abstention, as the term is employed in Christian contexts).[149] The "coldness" of the Sabbath—not only of the food but of the day itself (because of the prohibition against kindling fire in Exodus 35:3)—featured frequently in other non-Jewish descriptions of the Sabbath as well. An early reference, for example, appears in the work of the second-century Meleager, who playfully writes that "love burns hot even on cold Sabbaths," and in Rutilius Namatianus's poetry from the fifth century, which compares the Jews unfavorably to the Sabbath: "chill Sabbaths are after their own heart yet their heart is chillier than their creed."[150] The story about Rabbi and Antoninus in Genesis Rabbah answers these critiques by portraying no less than the Roman emperor as recognizing both the excellence of Sabbath food and its divine source. In this rabbinic narrative, then, Christian, Roman "pagan," and rabbinic ideas, traditions, and stereotypes might engage in an implicit conversation.

The Babylonian Talmud preserves a parallel narrative in the form of a dialogue between an anonymous emperor and Rabbi Yehoshua ben Hananiah, another important early rabbi. Though at least one of the characters differs from those who appear in the passage from Genesis Rabbah, the narrative is clearly an alternative version of the same story.[151] In the Babylonian Talmud, this story no longer functions within an exegesis of a biblical passage, as in Genesis Rabbah. Rather, a legal discussion about permitted and prohibited Sabbath activities related to food becomes the impetus for a theological meditation on the importance of Sabbath food. The narrative section begins by outlining the anticipated rewards one receives for partaking in three meals on the Sabbath: "He who observes three meals on the Sabbath is saved from three evils: the travails of the messiah, the retribution of Gehena, and the wars of Gog and Magog."[152] A series of narratives follows, including this one about the quality of Sabbath food:

> The emperor said to Rabbi Yehoshua ben Hananiah, "Why does this Sabbath dish have such a fragrant aroma?" "We have a certain spice," replied he, "called the Sabbath, which we put into it, and that gives it a fragrant aroma." "Give us some of it," he requested. "For one who keeps the Sabbath," he [Rabbi Yehoshua ben Hananiah] replied, "it is efficacious, but to one who does not keep the Sabbath it is not efficacious."[153]

In the Babylonian version of this story, the emperor is surprised not by the food's good *taste* despite its cold temperature but by the pleasant *smell* of the rabbi's food.[154] The rabbi does not prepare food especially for the emperor (or so it seems), as in Genesis Rabbah; the emperor simply happens to notice its appealing aroma. The emperor inquires as to its ingredients, and even demands to know the seasoning used for it, but the rabbi responds that the seasoning works only for those who observe the Sabbath. The aroma teases the emperor, who, as someone who does not observe the Sabbath, cannot himself produce such sweet-smelling fare.

This story, too, may be understood in the context of contemporaneous polemics. In addition to sources that comment on the taste of Sabbath food, another tradition associates the Sabbath with a putrid smell. A particularly colorful passage appears in Martial's *Epigrammata*, in which Martial likens "the breath of fasting Sabbatarian women" to other stenches, including "the raw vapors of sulphur springs, the putrid reek of a sea-water freshpond, a stale he-goat in the midst of his amours."[155] Portraying a Roman emperor as stunned by the fragrant smell of Sabbath food, rather than the stench of Sabbath fasting, this rabbinic story could serve as an apt rebuttal of similar rumors that Jews fasted on the Sabbath, if they circulated in later periods.[156] In all cases, they render the Jewish Sabbath appealing to Jews, whom rabbinic texts encourage to observe the Sabbath festively.

Genesis Rabbah and the Babylonian Talmud are not the first sources that connect an emperor's food habits to the food consumed by Jews on the Sabbath. In commenting on Augustus's light eating habits (he apparently preferred sparing quantities of coarse bread, small fish, moist cheese, and second-crop figs to elaborate meals), Suetonius quotes from a letter penned by Augustus to Tiberius that claims that "not even a Jew, my dear Tiberius, fasts so scrupulously on his Sabbaths as I have today; for it was not until after the first hour of the night that I ate two mouthfuls of bread in the bath."[157] Suetonius reports that Augustus himself boasted about his meager diet by comparing it to that of the Jews on their Sabbath; the rabbinic narratives discussed above, in contrast, boast about the succulence of Sabbath food by referring to the emperor's praise of it.

Other stories in the same sections of Genesis Rabbah and the Babylonian Talmud describe the rewards that rebound to individuals who honor the Sabbath with special foods, stressing that food can be a vehicle for the sanctification of a special day. In one rabbinic narrative from Genesis Rabbah, a Jewish butcher from Laodicea, a town in Asia Minor, hosts a rabbi on the Sabbath.[158] This man prepared such a generous spread that the table contained all of God's edible creations on it—presumably fruits and vegetables, fish, poultry, and meats. The rabbi asks his host how he became so wealthy, and he responds that his riches resulted directly from his observance of the Sabbath. Whenever he came across an especially good animal, he would save it for the Sabbath, as a way of sanctifying the day. As a reward for observing the Sabbath in such an unstinting manner, God blessed him unstintingly with wealth—so much so that he can host such lavish feasts as the one the rabbi was attending. Similarly, in a story in the Babylonian Talmud, a man named Joseph goes to extreme lengths to honor the Sabbath, purchasing fish for the Sabbath every week.[159] His reward for honoring the Sabbath with delicious foods—even those he could not always afford—was to discover a precious stone within a fish. Joseph ends up becoming a wealthy man with roomfuls of gold coins, able to continue honoring the Sabbath with fine delicacies.

Brezis has noted that rabbinic insistence that material practices are essential to the proper observance of the Sabbath and worship of God contrasts with Christian polemics that disparaged Jewish Sabbath practice as being carnal rather than spiritual.[160] For example, John Chrysostom notes, in his critique of the Jewish Sabbath, that "the Jews, having been set free from the concerns of daily life, did not turn their attention to spiritual matters, that is, to sobriety, self-control, and the hearing of the divine words, but they did the opposite, feasting, becoming drunk, bursting [with food], luxuriating."[161] Augustine makes similar claims about Jewish Sabbath observance in his instructions to Christians: "Observe the Sabbath: not carnally, not with delicacies of the Jews, who misuse their leisure for wickedness. It would be better if they were to dig the whole day rather than to dance the whole day."[162] In sharp contrast to this portrayal of the ideal abstemious Sabbath, several Sabbath narratives in Genesis Rabbah and the Babylonian Talmud argue that respect for the Sabbath ought also to be expressed specifically through the preparation of fine food and that God rewards such practices with resources for even more festival meals to come.

The notion that Jews consume only simple uncooked foods or nothing at all on the Sabbath, found throughout ancient sources about Jews, alongside specifically Christian anti-Jewish polemical portrayals of Jews as entirely carnal beings, resulted in the depiction of Sabbath food, and thus of Jews, as at once inappropriately ascetic and disgustingly carnal. At a time when Christians wrote about how Jews celebrated the Sabbath through food consumption rather than spiritual exercises, and when both Roman pagans and Christians argued that Jewish Sabbath food was unappealing, these stories about an emperor dining with a rabbi and the rewards for preparing lavish Sabbath meals served a clear purpose. In the stories, the Sabbath was an inherently holy day upon which special food, which appropriately honored its sacrality, was consumed. God blesses the Sabbath week after week through the day's delicious food, and Jews properly bless God each week through the purchase, preparation, and consumption of food before and on the Sabbath.

"WHY DOES THIS DAY DIFFER FROM OTHER DAYS?"

This same chapter of Genesis Rabbah tells yet another story about an imagined encounter between a Roman imperial official and a rabbi, in which, again, they dialogue about the sanctity and significance of the Sabbath. This story, too, can be interpreted as arguing against anti-Sabbath polemics found in both Christian and non-Christian Greco-Roman sources. In this tale, Tinneus Rufus, the Roman governor of Jerusalem, approaches the famed Rabbi Akiva with deep skepticism about the unique qualities of the Sabbath day:

> The wicked Tinneus Rufus asked Rabbi Akiva, saying to him: "Why does this day [the Sabbath] differ from other days?"
> He [Rabbi Akiva] said: "Why does one man differ from other men?"
> He [Tinneus Rufus] said: "What did I ask you and what did you answer me?"
> He [Rabbi Akiva] said: "You asked me why does the Sabbath differ from all other days? and I answered you, Why does Rufus differ from other men?"
> He [Tinneus Rufus] said to him: "Because the emperor desired to honor him."
> "Then this day, too, the Holy One wished to honor."
> "How can you prove it to me?"
> He [Rabbi Akiva] said: "The river Sambatyon will prove it, for it carries stones the whole week but on the Sabbath it rests."
> He [Tinneus Rufus] said: "You are evading the question."
> He [Rabbi Akiva] said: "Then he who raises a necromantic apparition

will prove it, for every day [the dead] rise but on the Sabbath [the dead] do not rise."¹⁶³
- He [Tinneus Rufus] went and performed a test with his father. Every day he rose [from the dead], but on the Sabbath he did not rise. After the Sabbath, he brought him up [again].
- He [Tinneus Rufus] said: "Father, have you become a Jew after death, that you rose during the whole week but you did not rise on the Sabbath?"
- He [Tinneus Rufus's father] said to him: "Anyone who does not keep the Sabbath among you of his own free will keeps it here in spite of himself."
- He [Tinneus Rufus] said: "And what work do have you there?"
- He [Tinneus Rufus's father] said: "All the days of the week we undergo judgment,¹⁶⁴ but on the Sabbath we rest."
- He [Tinneus Rufus] returned to Rabbi Akiva and said to him: "If it is as you say that the Holy One, blessed be He, honors the Sabbath, then He should not stir up winds or cause the rain to fall on that day."
- He [Rabbi Akiva] said to him: "Woe to that man! It is like one who carries [objects] four cubits."¹⁶⁵

The governor begins this dialogue by questioning the singularity of the Sabbath.¹⁶⁶ He fails to understand why the Sabbath day differs, in any fundamental way, from the other days of the week. In response, Rabbi Akiva offers a comparison: just as the emperor singled out Tinneus Rufus to serve as governor, so too God chose to elevate the Sabbath above all other days of the week. It is a matter of honor to be chosen by an authority, the rabbi explains. As God chose the Sabbath in order to honor it, the emperor chose the governor in order to honor him. In likening the emperor to God, the text draws on a widespread trope of the ruler's divinity.¹⁶⁷

Thus far in the dialogue, God's particular choice of the Sabbath has been explained. The essential difference of the Sabbath day from all the others, however, remains an open question. Tinneus Rufus, hence, further asks Rabbi Akiva to account for this characterization. Three explanations concerning the operation of nature on the Sabbath day follow. A famous river, the Sambatyon, says Rabbi Akiva, ceases to flow on the Sabbath in order to give the water and the rocks it moves a break from work.¹⁶⁸ The governor remains unconvinced and accuses the rabbi of evasion. Rabbi Akiva then challenges him with a task: to conjure someone up from the dead on the Sabbath, which the rabbi suggests is impossible. Tinneus Rufus discovers that, although he succeeds in bringing up his deceased father every day of the week aside from the Sabbath, he is unable to conjure him on the Sabbath. The general's father explains that even those who do not observe the Sabbath in this world are forced to do so after their death. That is, even though, as a pagan, Tinneus Rufus's father did not cease from activity on the Sabbath during his lifetime, in the next world he does indeed observe the day of rest because judgment (or torture) ceases on the Sabbath.[169] The Sabbath, then, is embedded in both this world and the next.[170]

Yet, Tinneus Rufus is still skeptical. If the Sabbath is embedded within nature, why does God continue to direct the winds and the rain on the seventh day, when God is supposed to be resting? The governor has scored a powerful point here, as the winds and rain are elements of the natural world that do *not* rest on the Sabbath. Rabbi Akiva, in turn, acknowledges that these particular natural processes continue even on the Sabbath but draws on rabbinic Sabbath laws to explain why this apparent exception does not disprove that the Sabbath is a unique day with extraordinary features: weather-related activities should not be considered work for God because, relative to God's enormity, the entire world is less than four cubits in size. Thus, God can "carry" elements, including wind and rain, without transgressing the prohibition against carrying and transferring objects from one domain to another on the Sabbath.[171]

As with the narrative discussed in the previous section, this story can be understood most fully when it is read as engaging in the Sabbath polemics of the later Roman Empire.[172] The story aligns with "Christian" and "Roman" ideas but provides a positive valence instead of a negative one. Indeed, it may be understood as countering Roman stories that cast the periodic drying up of rivers in negative terms. Rabbi Akiva claims that the Sambatyon stops flowing on the Sabbath. This curious detail harkens back to old Roman lore. The earliest mention of it appears in Pliny the Elder's *Natural History*, which explains that a certain set of famous springs dry up on occasion: "Each one dries up for periods of twelve, occasionally of twenty days, without the slightest trace of water, although there is an abundant spring near them that never dries up."[173] Pliny follows his description of this phenomenon with a reference to a stream in Judaea: "In Judaea is a stream that dries up every Sabbath."[174] Thus, the rabbi responds to the governor's challenge with a legend that is familiar to him from his very own Roman tradition.[175] Crucially, for Pliny, it is a sign of bad luck—a bad omen—for the water to cease flowing: "It is an evil portent if those wishing to look at [the famous springs] find them not flowing."[176] In presenting the phenomenon as holy rather than ominous, Rabbi Akiva successfully defends the cosmic significance of the Sabbath.

The participation of a non-Jew in Sabbath observance in Genesis Rabbah also may be understood in a context in which Christian and non-Christian Romans continued to attend synagogue services on the Sabbath even though Sunday was now officially recognized as a sacred day by the empire.[177] John Chrysostom famously berated those among his congregants who betrayed Christianity by observing the Jewish Sabbath and going to the Jewish synagogue precisely in the decades before scholars date the redaction of Genesis Rabbah.[178] Similarly, in the early fifth-century work *City of God*, Augustine cites the first-century laments of Seneca regarding Romans resting on the Sabbath: "Besides criticizing the superstitions of 'civil' theology, Seneca attacks the rites of the Jews, and the Sabbath in particular."[179] The Roman philosopher not only upbraids the Jews for wasting time by abstaining from work on the Sabbath; he has no kind words for those who have adopted the Jewish rhythms of the week and the Sabbath out of pure laziness: "At least they [the Jews] know the origins of their ceremonies: the greater part of our people have no idea of the reason for the things they do."[180] Thus, he suggests that while the Jews rest in imitation of their God and in light of their beliefs, pagan Sabbath worshippers do so because they want a day "off" and that they are, moreover, equally ignorant about their own practices.[181] It is worthwhile mentioning that it is a Christian fifth-century source that preserves this critique of the Sabbath, which it attributes to Seneca, a first-century Roman.[182]

In the course of the story, Tinneus Rufus learns that his father celebrates the Sabbath in the underworld. In depicting a non-Jewish Sabbath observer, Genesis Rabbah might allude to such contemporary practices of Romans (Christian and pagan) observing the Jewish Sabbath mentioned by Chrysostom and Seneca while turning them into demonstrations of the divine status of the Sabbath, spinning shared knowledge in a way that glorifies Jewish customs. Rabbi Akiva not only evokes a Roman legend about the natural world to prove the blessedness of the Sabbath day; he also suggests that the governor discover the Sabbath's singular status through experimental means. Despite his best efforts to discredit the Sabbath day, however, the Roman governor learns that the underworld, too, is bound by its strictures.[183] The story ends with an ironic twist—as much as imperial officials struggle with the Sabbath, they cannot contain its observance by those who are not Jewish; and even those who deride the idea of Sabbath rest and refuse to celebrate it in this world will be obliged to observe Sabbath rhythms in the World to Come. And, indeed, the governor's father implicitly encourages his son to observe the Sabbath in the present world so that he is spared the tortures of the next.

The governor's final objection—that wind and rain continue on the Sabbath—probably refers to a widespread trope in Christian anti-Sabbath polemics.[184] The governor declares that "if it is as you say that the Holy One, blessed be He, honors the Sabbath, then He should not stir up winds or cause the rain to fall on that day."[185] The Didascalia Apostolorum elaborates on a contemporaneous argument:

> If God willed that we should be idle one day for six ... God Himself also [would have remained idle] with all His creatures. But now all the governance of the world is carried on ever continually, and the spheres do not cease even for a moment from their course, but at God's command [their universal and perpetual motion proceeds]. For if He would say: "You shall be idle, and your son and your servant and your animal"

(Exodus 20:10; Deuteronomy 5:14), how does He work, causing to generate, making [the winds blow], and fostering and nourishing us His creatures? On the Sabbath day He causes [the winds] to blow, and [the waters] to flow, and [thus] works.[186]

The Didascalia Apostolorum cites biblical verses that command heads of households to allow everyone whose time they control, including those whom they have enslaved, to abstain from work on the Sabbath. The biblical command to "rest on the seventh day," the text argues, must not be taken as a call to abstain from work on every seventh day, the Didascalia Apostolorum suggests, because God and God's servants, such as the natural elements, do not literally cease working on the Sabbath. Justin Martyr makes a similar argument when he writes "Is it not evident to you that the elements do not refrain from work, and that they do not observe the Sabbaths?" to prove that followers of Christ need not observe the Sabbath.[187] Origen, too, argues along the same lines: after citing Genesis 2:2, Origen writes that "for we see God always working, and there is no Sabbath on which God does not work, on which he does not 'bring forth his sun on the evil and on the good and send rain on the just and on the unjust' (Matthew 5:45); on which he does not 'bring forth hay on the hills, and grass for the benefit of men' (Psalm 104:14); on which he does not 'strike and heal' (Isaiah 19:22) . . . God does not rest from His management of the world.'"[188] In the rabbinic narrative, Rabbi Akiva counters such claims with reasoning taken straight from the playbook of Jewish law.[189]

In the context of an empire in which Jews may have doubted the wisdom of a weekly day of rest, in which a different day of the week from the Jewish Sabbath was declared a day of rest, and in which the means of observing that new sacred day were not the same as those required of Jewish Sabbath observance, this Genesis Rabbah story argues that the Sabbath is an inherently sacred day and that its special status is inscribed in the cosmos. Moreover, the narrative presents observance of the Sabbath as an important marker of Jewishness, a widespread trope in Greek, Roman, and Christian sources. Thus, Tinneus Rufus's response upon realizing that his father observes the Sabbath in the underworld is to blurt out: "have you become a Jew after death?"

THE SABBATH IN PALESTINIAN AND BABYLONIAN RABBINIC NARRATIVES

Reading these passages in the cultural and theological context of a Christianizing fifth century sheds light on what the authors of these stories might have imagined the purpose of their midrashic project to be. By way of clever stories, dialogues, and sayings, the rabbinic narratives discussed in this chapter defend the Sabbath against a range of prejudices that were popular in contemporaneous Christian and non-Christian Greek and Roman literature. The Roman emperor affirms the excellence of Sabbath food and drink (they are, in fact, more delicious than any food produced by the imperial chefs or found in the imperial pantries). Other Roman government officials, try as they might, cannot escape Sabbath observance because the sacredness of the Sabbath is all-pervasive, in this world and also the next. Some of the ideas against which the rabbinic stories argue are articulated most cogently in late antique Christian sources, such as Pseudo-Ignatius's *Letter to the Magnesians* and the Didascalia Apostolorum, while others appear as long-standing common tropes in both Christian and non-Christian texts. This is not surprising, given that, in the fourth and fifth centuries, the Jewish Sabbath was an especially heated topic of debate.

Imperial figures of authority feature in both of these stories, and they are the ones who end up validating the singularity of the Sabbath. The first story makes the Roman emperor an unwitting admirer of the Sabbath. Antoninus, as he is depicted in Genesis Rabbah, was not a Christian, but the sitting Roman emperor during the composition of Genesis Rabbah would have been Christian—and might well have been issuing legislation promoting the Christian Lord's Day and regarding the Jewish Sabbath with increasing suspicion. The blurring of the emperor's identity suits a story that engages with tropes common in both Roman "pagan" and Christian anti-Sabbath polemics. The counterpolemic functions in this complex context, in which an attack against a Roman emperor within a rabbinic narrative could serve as a rebuttal to ideas articulated in both Christian and "pagan" sources.[190] For example, whether the emperor is imagined to be Christian or pagan, the emperor's affirmation of the Sabbath undermines both Christian and non-Christian Sabbath polemics. Alternatively, imagined specifically as a pagan, the emperor could also be seen as siding with the Jewish Sabbath against the Christian Lord's Day. In any of these configurations, the precise identity of the emperor or other imperial official is not nearly as important as the fact that a figure with imperial authority lends credence to the status of the Jewish Sabbath.

It is understandable that Palestinian rabbis, living in the Roman Empire, would have felt moved to compose stories about the Sabbath in response to Greco-Roman and Christian traditions against the Sabbath. Rabbinic redactors incorporated stories that originated in a Palestinian context into the Babylonian Talmud as well, perhaps because Babylonian rabbis were familiar with Christian anti-Sabbath polemics, either from their own milieu or from the region of the Roman Empire (and thus they used such stories to respond to these polemics, much as their Palestinian counterparts did).[191] After all, discussions about the Sabbath and the Lord's Day appear in Syriac sources, including in the Didache, the Didascalia Apostolorum, and in the exegeses and sermons of Ephrem and Aphrahat, which were produced in the very region in which the Babylonian rabbinic communities existed.[192] Though the Sasanian Empire was officially Zoroastrian, many Christian communities inhabited the region as well. Additional sources from the region also present the celebration of the Sabbath with festive meals as a disparaging marker of Jewishness. The

Syriac *History of the Slave of Christ*, set in Sinjar, depicts a Jewish father forcing his son, who had converted to Christianity, to join the family's lavish Sabbath meal.[193] Refusing to participate, the lad announces his Christian faith to the assembled guests. In the narrative, the youth's rejection of Judaism is validated through his refusal to participate in his family's Sabbath feast. He explains: "Had you known the things that have happened, perhaps you would not urge me to eat with you. For, until now, a veil has been set on the face of Moses, the establisher of the law."[194] The story equates partaking of the Sabbath meal with observing the entire law of Moses. Stories about the greatness of Sabbath food, such as those the Babylonian Talmud recounts, function as counternarratives to precisely such Christian conversion narratives that circulated contemporaneously. Alternatively, the Babylonian rabbis might not have been directly familiar with such polemics, but the traditions and stories they inherited from Palestine nevertheless had embedded the polemical responses within them. In this case, even though echoes of the polemics persist in passages in the Babylonian Talmud (and can be detected by modern scholars), they might not have been recognized as such by Babylonian rabbis or the redactors of the Babylonian Talmud and were included in the Talmud for other reasons, perhaps as general tales about the benefits of the Sabbath or for internal legal, literary, or social purposes. The stories, after all, make compelling cases for Sabbath observance. It is difficult to conclude which of these scenarios is most likely from the passages themselves.

Finally, that both stories appear in the form of a dialogue between a rabbi and a Roman official is likewise significant. Though these passages do not represent historical accounts of actual encounters and conversations, they do participate in a different kind of a "dialogue" with others. The "outsider" characters do not simply stand in as projections of internal rabbinic anxieties, as is common in rabbinic literature, but rather embody in these narratives prejudices, stereotyped judgments, and theological arguments actually held by those for whom the figure speaks, in this case a segment of the Roman pagan and Christian literate, literary, and ruling elite.[195] In addition, these sentiments might have been held by those beyond the elite, as they were incorporated into Roman satires and Christian sermons, heard by diverse portions of these populations.

The Sabbath between Jews and Samaritans

Sabbath observance was often invoked as a marker of Jewish-gentile difference. One may wonder if rabbinic Sabbath discourse engages Jewish-Samaritan difference as well. This question takes on particular significance because whereas rabbinic, patristic, and other Greco-Roman texts refer to weekly Sabbath observance as a marker of Jewishness, Jews and Samaritans, at least during the rabbinic period, both seem to have been regarded as groups of people who observed the same weekly Sabbath and who anchored their Sabbath observance on the same set of biblical passages. Many rabbinic sources discuss the status of Samaritans at length, but they rarely invoke the day of the Sabbath or Sabbath observance to differentiate between Jews and Samaritans. Quite to the contrary, in fact: rabbinic passages usually portray Jews and Samaritans as people who share the Sabbath, and thus rabbinic texts turn to other matters when they wish to highlight Jewish-Samaritan difference.[196]

One of the rabbinic passages that discusses Jewish and Samaritan Sabbath observance does so to highlight Jewish-Samaritan similarity. The third chapter of Mishnah *Nedarim*, devoted to the language of vows, contains a brief but illuminating discussion of the Sabbath in relation to Jews and Samaritans. Mishnah *Nedarim* 3:10 notes that if one vows not to benefit from "those who keep the Sabbath [שובתי שבת]," one's vow would prohibit deriving benefit from Israelites and Samaritans, because both are considered people who observe the Sabbath. The label "those who keep the Sabbath" thus includes both Jews and Samaritans; Sabbath observance literally cannot be the means by which to differentiate between them. The Sabbath is not the only practice that Jews and Samaritans share (and that thus cannot serve to distinguish them). The Mishnah adds that a vow not to benefit from "those who eat garlic" similarly prohibits benefiting from both Israelites and Samaritans, presumably because both groups of people were considered "people who eat garlic."

That is not to say that rabbinic texts do not distinguish between Jews and Samaritans at all. References to Samaritans in rabbinic sources frequently highlight difference, and the question of whether Samaritans count as Jews or gentiles often lies at the heart of such rabbinic discussions.[197] The continuation of the same passage in Mishnah *Nedarim* stresses one such distinguishing feature: making pilgrimage to Jerusalem. A vow not to benefit from "those who go up to Jerusalem" prohibits benefit from Israelites, who make pilgrimage to their holy city of Jerusalem, but permits benefit from Samaritans, whose sacred site of worship and pilgrimage is Mount Gerizim near Nablus.[198] This short mishnaic passage exemplifies how complicated the intersection of Jewish-Samaritan identities was regarded as being, especially in tannaitic sources: Jews and Samaritans shared a sacred time but had different sacred places.

Discussion about Samaritan-Jewish difference in Mishnah *Nedarim* precedes a section about Jewish-gentile difference, constructing the category of Samaritans as distinct in some ways from Israel but also not part of the category of gentiles.[199] The minor tractate *Kutim* uses the fraught and blurry boundary between Jews and Samaritans to frame the entire tractate: "The ways of Samaritans sometimes resemble gentiles and sometimes resemble Israel, but in the majority [they resemble] Israel."[200] A disagreement between two rabbinic figures in the Tosefta, too, highlights the ambiguity of the status of Samaritans in rabbinic sources: "The Samaritan is like a non-Jew, the words of Rabbi. Rabban Simeon ben Gamaliel says, a Samaritan is a Jew in all respects."[201] Rabbinic passages about Samaritans frequently grapple precisely with questions of whether Samaritans are Jews or non-Jews, for example in matters involving marriage, witnesses, conversion, purity practices, tithing, wine, and sacrificed meat. Some rabbinic texts focus discussion about Jewish-Samaritan similarity and difference on calendrical matters, including the declaration of new months and the dates of festivals. Mishnah and Tosefta *Rosh Hashanah* 2:2 explain that rabbis changed their practices of new moon declaration (they originally sent signals via fire torches from city to city) because similar Samaritan practices led to confusion between rabbinic and Samaritan communities, who could not differentiate between the two communities' torches and thus did not know whether the fire they saw in the distance signaled a new Samaritan or rabbinic month.[202] Tosefta *Pesahim* 2:1–3 discusses whether Samaritan leaven can be consumed after Passover, noting that the answer depends on the synchrony of Samaritan and rabbinic Passover dates in any given year.[203] The Babylonian Talmud discusses whether one may rent one's bathhouse to gentiles and Samaritans.[204] Concluding that it is forbidden to rent to gentiles, as they violate the Sabbath and festivals, the text then deliberates whether it is similarly forbidden to rent to Samaritans, given that they do observe the Sabbath and festivals. The debate thus hinges on the question of whether Samaritans observe the same practices on the intermediate festival days as rabbinic Jews—if they do, then renting the bathhouse would be permitted; if they do not, it would be forbidden. According to Lawrence Schiffman, who has used these sources to trace the trajectory of Jewish-Samaritan difference, the earliest stata of tannaitic sources view Samaritans as Jews (though usually of an inferior status), while later tannaitic and amoraic sources increasingly treat Samaritans as non-Jews.[205]

Rabbinic sources are not the only ones to categorize Jews and Samaritans together as Sabbath observers. Origen, too, notes that some Jews (by which Origen seems to mean rabbinic Jews) limit their movement on the Sabbath to 2,000 cubits, while others, such as Dositheus the Samaritan, remain in their places for the duration of the Sabbath.[206] Jews, Origen claims, interpret Exodus 16:29 ("let none of you go out from his place on the seventh day") in one of two ways, either that "not going out from one's place" indicates a travel limit (an interpretation indeed found in rabbinic sources) or that one must stay in the very same position the entire Sabbath (an idea Origen attributes to a particular Samaritan man).[207] Notably, Origen considers both these practices, as well as the biblical exegeses upon which they are based, Jewish; he does not use diversity in Sabbath observance among Jews and Samaritans to indicate communal difference. For Origen, as for Mishnah *Nedarim*, both Jews and Samaritans are "Sabbath observers," despite differences in how they might observe the Sabbath (which could easily have been used to construct them as two different groups, a path not pursued in either text).

Origen does, however, use Sabbath observance to construct difference between Jews (a category that, for Origen, includes Samaritans) and Christians, a group that he presents as no longer observing the Sabbath as Jews do. *De Principiis*, a treatise devoted to refuting various Jewish interpretations of scripture in favor of Origen's own, Christian, readings, contains a telling example. Origen explains that Christians ought not to observe the Sabbath as Jews deem necessary, as a seventh day of rest, feasting, and forms of abstinence, but rather according to Christian interpretation, in light of the Sabbath as an eschatological era rather than a day of the week—the very critiques against which rabbinic sources contend.

Rabbinic Sabbath discourse regarding Samaritans serves as an important test case, because this discourse does not attempt to construct difference from all "others." Rabbinic sources are not concerned, for example, with identifying differences in Sabbath observance between Jews and Samaritans; despite some discrepancies in particular practices, the Mishnah presents both communities as Sabbath observant. Rather, rabbis designed Sabbath discourse, as it appears in the sources analyzed in this chapter, more specifically to engage with Christian and pagan critiques of the Jewish Sabbath—critiques that, in some cases, were directed as much against Samaritans as against other Jews, as Origen's text indicates—and thus to forge Jewish-Christian and Jewish-pagan difference. Perhaps Samaritans found themselves dealing with the very anti-Sabbath rhetoric that prompted some rabbis to frame the Sabbath in the ways examined above.[208]

Conclusions

In late antiquity, the terms "Jewish," "Christian," and "Roman" never denoted static identities or affiliations. Rather, they indicated diverse types of (overlapping) communities and identities, with fluid and contested boundaries. It is worth noting, though, that, within the shifting borders of the Roman Empire, the boundaries and relationships between "Jews," "Christians," and other "Romans" operated quite differently at the beginning and end of the classical rabbinic period; the situation also differed in the Sasanian Empire and other regions beyond the Roman Empire. In the second and third centuries, Jews, Christians, and Jewish-Christians constituted (often persecuted) minority communities within a pagan Roman Empire, even as Christian communities grew in number and significance throughout this period. In contrast, in the fourth century, and even more so in the fifth and sixth, Jews and non-Christian pagan Romans constituted (often persecuted) minority communities within a Christian Roman Empire.[209] Christians were no longer members of a disenfranchised minority but rather those wielding imperial power, while Roman pagans (even elites) often found themselves in more marginalized positions. These dynamics of power are well illustrated by—and indeed were enacted by and expressed through—the empire's shifting ways of structuring time, including its gradual and ultimately official adoption of the seven-day week and the Lord's Day, as well as the texts composed and circulated in these centuries.

Polemics, apologetics, and derogatory statements about the Jewish sacred day of rest circulated in the Greco-Roman world in Greek and Latin from at least the second century BCE to the fifth and sixth centuries CE and beyond. While they took various forms, many of the standard tropes persisted over an exceptionally long period of time, appearing in a diverse set of sources from a large geographical and chronological spread. Such discourses about the Sabbath were thus part of an ongoing process through several centuries that, in different contexts, included Greek, Roman, pagan, rabbinic, Christian, and other voices. The rabbinic sources analyzed in this chapter participated in this multivocal dynamic conversation.

Shaye J. D. Cohen identified a number of patristic sources that criticize the Jews' carnal observance of the Sabbath—indulging in food and drink, dancing, and clapping.[210] He demonstrates that these themes of eating and rejoicing appear often in rabbinic discussions of the Sabbath and are not simply Christian projections of biblical sins onto contemporaneous Jews. Such critiques, instead, reflect actual rabbinic Sabbath practices and serve as external patristic evidence for the ways in which the Jewish Sabbath was observed. If, in certain cases, ancient Christian critiques of the Sabbath illuminate rabbinic Sabbath practices from the period, in other instances such criticisms help explain not only rabbinic Sabbath practice but also rabbinic Sabbath discourse. In the face of widespread and enduring anti-Sabbath polemics from both Christians and non-Christians within and beyond the border of the Roman Empire, some rabbinic exegeses and narratives offer counterpolemics aimed primarily at encouraging Jews to observe the Sabbath despite negative attitudes toward such observance.

Not all rabbinic stories about the Sabbath have a counterpolemical focus. Rabbinic texts scrutinize each and every particular detail of the Sabbath, and generally these writings deal with internal—and highly practical—matters of halakhah, which were not subject to external critique. As such, the passages in the Mekhilta, Genesis Rabbah, and the Babylonian Talmud that use weekly Sabbath observance to construct Jewish communal difference are especially noteworthy. They focalize the Sabbath's abiding status as the day on which Israel reaffirms its covenant with God, in a world in which Sabbath observance was often scorned and derided. This rabbinic choice reflects the central role the Sabbath played not only in establishing the rhythms of the week but also in constructing Jewish-Roman and Jewish-Christian difference.

CHAPTER THREE

Men's and Women's Time

THE ROMAN CALENDAR AND ITS annual festivals played an important part in the construction of imperial and counterimperial time in rabbinic sources, and resonances of Second Temple and contemporaneous Roman and Christian attitudes toward Sabbath and Sunday observance impacted rabbinic discourses about marking weekly time as well. This chapter shifts away from exploring time between empire and community as well as between communities to analyzing attempts to organize time and difference for particular constituencies—primarily those of different genders, and more broadly also members of various social classes, including enslaved people, commoners, and the poor, and those of various of age groups, including children, postmenopausal women, and so on—within rabbinic communities. It likewise transitions from constructions and conceptions of intercommunal identification and identity to constructions and conceptions of intracommunal selves and subjects. Specifically, the chapter focalizes the development of a gendered temporality within rabbinic sources and on the formation of gendered subjectivity and difference that emerged alongside and intertwined with it.

At the heart of this chapter stand two practices, both of which entail daily rituals. The first is the evening and morning recitation of the Shema prayer, a declaration of devotion to God and commitment to fulfill God's commandments and teach them to one's children. This ritual is presented, in rabbinic sources, as one in which men are obligated but from which women are explicitly excluded. The second practice is the expansive set of rituals related to the maintenance of menstrual purity, in which women are obligated to count their days of purity and impurity as they kept track of the status of their bodies and which are presented in rabbinic sources as occupying a good deal of women's time, constructing their days around the rhythms of their menstrual cycles. In addition, within this set of menstrual purity practices, rabbinic sources further mandate that women perform bodily examinations of blood each morning and evening, a ritual in which women were obligated but which men were explicitly banned from practicing. These rituals of Shema and Niddah were designed to mark daily time, but they did so in explicitly gendered ways. What sort of temporality did each of these rituals (and the many rules about their observance that rabbinic sources detail) deliberately attempt to or inadvertently cultivate, and did these rituals, given their gendered dimensions, cultivate specifically gendered temporalities and subjectivities?

This chapter advances three arguments. First, it identifies a series of rabbinic ritual innovations related to daily markings of time. Close analysis of Mishnah *Berakhot*'s rules regarding the recitation of the Shema and tractate *Niddah*'s discussion of menstrual purity laws demonstrates that rabbinic sources develop both practices as ones that mark daily time. While these two rabbinic sets of rituals refer to biblical passages as their ostensible origins, the rabbinic texts transform previous practices into daily rituals, and ones that were, moreover, designed to function as rituals that marked transitions between day and night. Deuteronomy 6 and 11, the passages that serve as the biblical basis for the rabbinic Shema prayer, suggest a call to constantly express one's devotion to God. Rabbinic sources reinterpret these passages differently, as mandating daily ritualized recitations of the biblical verses at the start of each evening and morning. Likewise, the menstrual purity laws of Leviticus 15 ostensibly dictate monthly time and other units of time, such as seven-day periods, but rabbinic laws impose additional practices that transform the biblical concern for maintaining purity writ large into a daily concern that entailed, in addition, a ritual performed, similar to the Shema, each evening and morning. These two sets of rituals (Shema and Niddah), as they are reconceived in tannaitic rabbinic texts, mark, on a daily basis, the temporal transition between days as well as from day to night and from night to day.[1]

Second, the chapter argues that these two sets of daily rituals—the Shema and its associated practices, on the one hand, and the expansive set of bodily purity practices of which menstrual purity is a part, on the other—became gendered in the rabbinic period. This process, in turn, cultivated different gendered temporalities. The recitation of the Shema and the maintenance of bodily purity are based on biblical injunctions that apparently applied to everyone. That is, the obligation to declare one's devotion to God and transmit God's commandments to one's children, as outlined in biblical sources, is incumbent upon all of Israel. In rabbinic sources, however, the recitation of the Shema becomes primarily a men's practice. Though women are permitted to recite the Shema, they are explicitly excluded from the obligation to do so. The Shema is eventually also included within the rabbinic category of "positive time-bound commandments" from which women are likewise exempt. Within these new rabbinic ritual parameters, then, the Shema came to be construed as a man's practice. Similarly, bodily purity laws applied to all adults in biblical sources, and, in Second Temple and rabbinic literature, everyone was obligated to observe them. Still, even as the broader category of bodily purity laws applied to both men and women in rabbinic sources, purity concerns and daily rituals associated with bodily purity primarily came to construct women's daily time. This occurs in part because rabbinic sources downplay men's impurity while simultaneously elaborating women's purity practices. Menstrual purity is of cardinal importance for women in rabbinic discourse; for men, bodily impurity is just one among many obligations. Consider, for example, that rabbinic sources extend the duration of women's impurity while decreasing the overall time of men's impurity. Or the fact that the daily morning and evening practices that became central to women's observance of bodily purity laws in rabbinic sources were not developed for men. Indeed, men were actively discouraged and even banned from conducting bodily examinations as a daily ritual. Such developments transformed bodily purity itself into a woman's daily concern. Strikingly, the Palestinian and Babylonian Talmuds contain long and detailed tractates devoted to Niddah but no tractate whatsoever dedicated to male bodily impurity, even though the Mishnah contains tractates of roughly equal length and content for both male and female impurity. The prohibition against coitus during the period of a woman's menstruation, moreover, remained a central component of sexual relations between husbands and wives, and thus menstrual purity laws were observed long after concerns for other types of ritual purity became less important in the absence of a temple cult. The gendering of such rituals required men and women to orient their daily time in different ways. These differing rabbinic rules regarding Shema and Niddah produced a gendered temporality distinct from that found in earlier periods. The chapter argues that this process of gendering daily rituals began in tannaitic sources (in the Mishnah, Tosefta, and midreshei halakhah) and reached fuller development in amoraic and post-amoraic sources, especially the Babylonian Talmud.

These sets of rituals were not performed by, nor did they impact, only men or only women but rather became gendered in rabbinic law.[2] Women were permitted to recite the Shema, and they also performed some of the rituals included within the rabbinic category of positive time-bound commandments, either because there were exemptions to the rules that necessitated their participation or because some women observed rituals without being obligated to do so. Moreover, women were obligated alongside men in daily prayers, which also established rhythms of daily liturgical worship.[3] Likewise, men were obligated to observe their own set of rituals related to bodily purity in addition to being implicated in their wives' cycles of purity and impurity. For example, men and women were equally affected by laws related to corpse impurity and food impurity. There was, therefore, overlap in the performance of these sets of rituals by men and women as well as additional rituals in which all members of the community were obligated. But while many prayers and purity rituals seemingly applied to everyone and constructed daily rhythms of time for those who observed them, key aspects of these rituals became gendered. It is worthwhile highlighting further that rabbinic sources rhetorically associate the Shema and positive time-bound rituals more strongly with men while excluding from this temporal category rituals surrounding the maintenance of purity, including menstrual purity laws. Rabbinic sources also exclude men from the daily rituals of maintaining purity that they obligate women to observe. In this way, the temporal frameworks established by these two sets of practices became increasingly, though not absolutely, gendered. They were both structured around marking days and transitions of days, but men and women were obligated to mark these shared times in different ways.

Moreover, while rabbinic sources require both men and women to perform rituals that are temporally dependent, another major distinction bears mention. Rhetorically, only the rituals performed by men are labeled as bound by time in rabbinic sources, while these same sources exclude women from those rituals on the very premise that they are time-bound. It is not clear why rabbinic sources do not understand menstrual purity laws also as positive time-bound commandments, but the rhetorical dimension seems central to the creation of differing temporalities for men and women in rabbinic sources and the temporal value each is afforded. Some apologetic literature on women's roles in Judaism understands women's exemption from positive time-bound commandments and their obligation in menstrual purity in light of women's biological rhythms or their obligations to parental or familial rhythms.[4] Taking a different tack, however, this chapter leaves aside the notion that women's exemption from positive time-bound commandments was a deliberate move made by the rabbis *because* women's biology already connected them to temporal rhythms that were ritualized through the laws of Niddah and therefore they did not need the additional set of positive time-bound commandments in which men were obligated; the ancient sources do not contain evidence that the rabbis viewed these sets of rituals as parallel or causal. Rather, the chapter argues that a possible *effect* of these gendered sets of commandments was the bifurcation of time for men and women, as well as the association of men's and women's bodies with different types of time.

Rabbinic practices of Shema and Niddah present an intriguing case of the mapping of social and cultural structures of time onto biological rhythms of time.[5] The Mishnah reads the biblical passage upon which the Shema is based as referring to circadian rhythms—the times of sleeping and rising. Niddah practices are anchored around a woman's cyclical menstrual cycles and, thereafter, also on sleeping and waking. These biological daily and monthly rhythms of people's bodies are given meaning, and thus ritual significance, by the sociological and discursive rhythms to which they become attached. The rabbinic rituals, in turn, affect how biological rhythms are regarded, blurring the dichotomy between natural and constructed bodies and times, as well as between the times of the sun as they are embedded in the cosmos and as they manifest themselves in living bodies.[6]

In rabbinic sources, Shema and Niddah practices are both conceived as embodied rituals. The recitation of the Shema is a bodily practice as much as it is an oral declaration (and the utterance of the Shema itself is an embodied practice), as Elizabeth Shanks Alexander and Rachel Neis have shown.[7] There are rules about how to treat one's body and body parts during the ritual as well as exemptions based on the status of one's body—for instance if one finds oneself unclothed, or on one's wedding night. The practices of Niddah not only are based on a woman's state of menstrual purity and bodily cycles but also involve physical examinations, the sighting of blood, and immersion in a ritual bath. They ultimately dictate bodily and sexual relations between men and women as well as a woman's relationship both to other people and to objects. Though the etymology of the term *niddah* is uncertain, it might derive from the root *ndh*, evoking "separation" (of blood from a woman's body or of the woman from others), or from the root *ndd*, "to be distant." Both suggested etymologies highlight the physical dimension of separation from cultic contexts as well as people and objects in the domestic sphere due to menstrual impurity, though never communal ostracism or expulsion.[8] The place and orientation of one's body are quite different in each of these practices, however. In the case of the Shema, the primary time-markers for determining the proper time span for its recitation are external, related to the sun and other heavenly bodies. The amount of sunlight is considered in order to determine precisely when the evening and morning Shema ought to be recited. That is, even though the biblical verse upon which the Shema ritual relies mentions bodily rhythms—"when you lie down and when you rise"—the timing of the Shema is in fact not determined directly by a person's sleeping and rising but rather by the setting and rising of the sun, which is used as an external "clock" or referent, which stands in for the more abstract and individually variable times of rising and sleeping. Additionally, the most important bodily orientation in the ritual of the Shema's recitation is the turning of one's heart to God. The primary time-markers for determining a woman's state of menstrual (im)purity, in contrast, are internal, stemming from the detection or lack thereof of blood from a woman's uterus. Moreover, a woman is obligated to examine her body when she wakes up each morning and before she retires to bed each evening. That is, the times of her daily examinations are dictated by the rhythms of her body's rising and sleeping patterns and her body's menstrual cycle rather than by external markers such as the amount of sunlight visible at a particular time of day (though other bodily examinations are determined, as with the Shema, also by external time-markers). Finally, the most important body part for the practice of maintaining menstrual purity is a woman's uterus, not her heart. Both sets of bodily rituals thus mark morning and evening, but the rabbinic rules that dictate the determination of time for performing them, and the body parts and bodily positions these rituals entail, differ significantly in the cases of men and women.

Rabbinic sources also impose a hierarchy upon these men's and women's rituals. The Shema is presented as a declaration of love of God and the fulfillment of the most important biblical commandment. It affirms a relationship with God and commitment to love God, embody God's Torah, and transmit God's commandments to one's descendants. Its recitation also functions as a sign of one's full membership in the rabbinic community. In contrast to earlier rabbinic and non-rabbinic sources about menstrual purity, menstruation is presented by amoraic rabbis as a punishment for Eve's sin and as an ongoing reminder to women of their sinfulness and inferiority. These later sources also present menstrual purity rituals as uniquely feminine forms of piety. These two aspects of Niddah are not mutually exclusive but rather mutually reinforcing: the more associated menstruation became with sin, the more vigilance toward maintaining bodily purity was construed as a sign and performance of piety. The rituals associated with maintaining women's bodily purity and their exclusion from the set of positive time-bound commandments, moreover, mark women's liminal status as secondary members of the rabbinic community, people who are only obligated in a portion of the Torah's commandments. In these later rabbinic sources, a clear hierarchy emerges: men mark mornings and evenings in ways that highlight their communal status and relationship to God, while women mark their days in ways that reinforce their inferior status and sinfulness.

Building upon these insights, the chapter's third argument suggests that these rabbinic rituals did not construct gendered time only by dictating how men and women ought to conduct themselves at different moments of their days and months: they also constructed new types of gendered bodies and gendered selves. The Shema became a ritual the timing of which was determined by the heavenly bodies—the sun and stars, and various other time-markers that were dependent upon the amount of sunlight or the position of the celestial bodies. These are external time-markers. Furthermore, the Shema was construed as a daily practice that directed a man's body, heart, and self toward God. Finally, the Shema, explicitly connected to teaching one's children, is a ritual that is oriented toward the future. Rabbinic Niddah laws, in contrast, are predicated on the temporal rhythms of a woman's body—her menstrual cycle and the presence or absence of blood that flowed from within her, as well as the time of her waking and sleeping when she was required to check her body for blood. These are all internal time-markers. Additionally, the daily rituals associated with menstrual impurity regulated a woman's relationship to her husband as well as other bodies and objects for fear that she might profane those things that ought to remain pure. In contrast to the future-oriented Shema, rabbinic discussions of menstrual impurity are predominantly concerned with the past rather than the future: one of the main challenges posed in rabbinic texts, but that is altogether absent in the biblical sources upon which they are based, is the problem of retroactive impurity and how long into the past (after the time when a woman sights blood) should she and everything with which she came into physical contact be considered impure. Niddah is thus reoriented in rabbinic sources toward the past both by focusing on retroactive impurity and, in later sources, by connecting it to Eve's sin and its ongoing impact on subsequent generations of women, who cannot escape its effects on their bodies.[9] Men's time was determined by the heavenly bodies and defined men's relationships to God and to the future, while women's time was determined by their own bloody bodies, required serious retrospection, and defined their relationships to their husbands and surrounding objects—and only indirectly to God.

The comparison between the Shema and Niddah daily practices is not one that rabbinic sources make explicitly. The texts do not present them as parallel practices but rather treat them in different tractates and as separate practices, though they do occasionally reflect on the challenge that bodily impurity poses to the recitation of the Shema. Each practice—Shema and Niddah—is discussed in detail in a tractate largely devoted to it, though in different ways and with differing emphases. Scholars, however, can step back and see how these seemingly unrelated practices were simultaneously developed in rabbinic sources. Even though they appear in different tractates, these tractates are brought together within the very same rabbinic compilation, the Mishnah. They are also engaged with and interpreted in a number of compositions based upon and in conversation with the Mishnah (namely, the Tosefta, halakhic midrashim, and the two Talmuds). These diverse rabbinic laws and practices had a cumulative effect, as the rabbinic corpus itself mandates that its adherents observe all of its many rituals and rules. The Shema and Niddah practices are thus part of a shared ritual and legal system, and the rabbinic passages that detail the guidelines for their observance participate in a shared, if evolving, discourse that constitutes that system. Moreover, explicit contrast between men's and women's time is a feature of rabbinic texts, given that women are excluded from the category of commandments labeled "positive time-bound commandments." Even if all this were not the case, however, contemporary scholarly boundaries for historical inquiry ought not to exclusively be set at the ideological boundaries of the objects of their study. On the contrary, expanding the boundaries of inquiry—for example, by comparing two rabbinic practices that rabbinic texts did not think to compare nor perhaps even thought comparable—might uncover some of the ideologies or assumptions that undergird rabbinic discourse, about which rabbinic sources do not necessarily explicitly reflect. Labeling rituals that men must perform as "time-bound" and dismissing women's rituals as unrelated or not bound to time, for example, is itself an ideological position, normative rather than descriptive.

This is not to say that rabbinic texts are concerned equally with outlining and regulating men's and women's time. The rabbinic corpus was conceived by and for a particular group of men, and its system of laws and rituals is primarily oriented around such rabbinic men. The corpus also explicitly and deliberately excludes women in a number of ways: the texts do not address women nor assume female subjects but rather address men and assume male subjects, even when discussing matters related to women; women are excluded from entire categories of rituals within the rabbinic system, categories that themselves were created to exclude them; and women were interpreted out, starting in the earlier rabbinic sources, of the command to study, legislate, and transmit this rabbinic tradition, which is presented in those very sources as the seminal rabbinic practice, one that is central to rabbinic identity. In other words, women were not included in the development of the rabbinic legal and ritual corpus, nor imagined to be a part of its continued study and transmission, though they were nonetheless bound to its laws and norms. Drawing comparisons between constructions of men's and women's time in rabbinic sources, then, should not be taken to imply that rabbinic sources were equally concerned with developing daily rhythms for men and women, nor that they devote equivalent space or detail to each. Rather, the far greater emphasis that rabbinic sources place on men's time and the development of men's subjectivity through daily rituals (clear, to cite just a single example, from the prominent place that the recitation of the Shema has at the very start of the rabbinic corpus and the detailed elaboration of every aspect of this ritual) and the relatively scant concern with women's time and rituals (which are often figured in relation to men, and treated in less detail in rabbinic texts, as is evidenced in the limited attention these texts devote to the mechanics of daily bodily examinations) ought also to be understood as part of the construction of gendered time and indeed of gendered difference within the rabbinic corpus. These rabbinic texts, in the emphasis they place on men's time, construct a gendered temporality that not only constructs different times for men and women but that values men's time as it devalues that of women.

Finally, it bears mention that the concept of "ritual," employed throughout this chapter, is not a category or term used in rabbinic texts but rather one that contemporary scholars apply to rabbinic texts in order better to understand them.[10] In her survey of the integration of ritual studies into the field of rabbinics, Mira Balberg discusses various recently proposed definitions of the category "ritual." As "a cultural artifact, ritual is usually considered to be a form of *script*: a formula that is enacted in communal settings in particular circumstances so as to fill certain social and religious functions."[11] As "a mode of behavior," emphasis shifts "to the performative and embodied aspects of ritual activity" and "to the process of turning ordinary activities such as eating, washing, speaking, walking, and so on into rituals, and thus speaks of *ritualization* rather than of rituals."[12] Ritualization, to quote Catherine Bell, is "a way of acting that differentiates some acts from others."[13] Balberg further suggests that "what distinguishes rituals from other actions is that when one performs a ritual, one does not attempt to achieve anything except for the successful completion of the ritual itself: ritual is thus a completely self-referential activity."[14] This chapter uses the term "ritual" to describe practices mandated by rabbinic sources to be carried out according to a script and/or for specific purposes. Moreover, an expansive view of "ritual," following Bell, encompasses the intermeshing of thought and action. It captures the interwoven discursive and embodied performative dimensions of prescribed activities and gestures toward the ever-present dynamics of power and authority in a way that the term "practice" does not as readily do (though the terms "practice" and "ritual practice" are also employed in this chapter with reference to the Shema and Niddah).[15] Thus, as it is used in this chapter, "ritual" applies both to the recitation of the Shema and to practices related to menstrual impurity, including daily bodily examinations, even though the precise parameters for the recitation of the Shema are more elaborately described in rabbinic texts than are some aspects of the observance of the laws of Niddah. The fact that rabbinic sources discuss one ritual at more length and in greater detail than the other does not mean that one ought to be characterized as a ritual and the other not, nor that the two are incomparable. Rather, it points to the lopsided interests that rabbinic texts exhibit toward men's and women's rituals writ large—a lopsidedness that contemporary scholarship need not replicate.[16]

Despite these caveats, rabbinic sources actively and deliberately constructed, developed, and mandated both men's and women's time. Moreover, rabbinic texts created a new system of gendered time that their texts mask as natural, ancient, and self-evident.[17] Two sets of times—at once competing and intertwined—were thus produced. But the effects were greater still. These rituals and the temporalities they promoted also functioned as important mechanisms through which rabbis constructed gendered difference itself.[18] Part of what it meant to be a rabbinic man was to recite the Shema mornings and evenings, and part of what it meant to be a rabbinic woman was to perform the practices associated with maintaining menstrual purity. On Barak captures this complexity inherent in the cultivation of gendered and classed temporality in his study of masculine and feminine time in early twentieth-century Egypt:

> But only complicating and destabilizing such abstract schedules would be merely pointing out the obvious, that reality is inherently messier than the modes of its simplification into workable and livable categories. Therefore, the next and more significant analytical step must be retracing the logic animating these evidently fragile instances of purification, examining how time was gendered, classed, and politicized in ways that reduced it, simplified it, and made it possible to keep. In other words, it is important yet insufficient to collapse binary oppositions between task-oriented feminine time and masculine clock-time, or between natural and social time. In addition, one has to also do exactly the opposite: to trace how these fragile contrasts were created,

stabilized, and maintained ... the mechanisms that assigned different temporalities to different actors, pushing men, women, and their servants to occupy different temporalities, while simultaneously binding them together to the same time system.[19]

This chapter uncovers the specific mechanisms through which the rabbis of late antiquity drew on biblical traditions in order to invent new sets of daily rituals, gender them, and then present them as merely reflecting the natural temporal rhythms of human and heavenly bodies.

The Shema as a Rabbinic Daily Ritual

The very first ritual discussed in rabbinic sources is the daily recitation of several biblical passages known as the Shema.[20] This prayer, which consists of three sections of scripture (Deuteronomy 6:4–9, 11:13–21; Numbers 15:37–41), begins with a declaration that "the Lord is our God, the Lord is one!" and proclaims the commandment to love God and fulfill God's laws.[21] The recitation of the Shema was regarded as such an important component of rabbinic practice and identity that the entire Mishnah starts with a detailed discussion of its ritual enactment.[22] It begins, moreover, with the requirement that it be recited each morning and evening—that is, by highlighting the importance of the ritual's timing to its performance. The Mishnah fashions the ritual of the Shema recitation as an ancient biblical practice. It also takes for granted that its audience is so familiar with the ritual of the Shema that it does not even define it; rather, the tractate begins by outlining when the Shema ought to be recited each evening and morning.

Yet there is strong evidence that the daily obligation to recite the Shema was a rabbinic ritual innovation.[23] Early rabbis either popularized an existing Second Temple ritual performed primarily by priests in the temple or even created a practice of reciting these biblical passages that had not previously existed in the precise form that rabbinic texts mandate. By turning a biblical verse about the constancy of devotion to the divine into a central liturgical ritual that was performed by members of the rabbinic community at the start and end of every day, the Mishnah institutionalized this daily practice and the rhythms of time it cultivated.

The rabbinic Shema has its roots in a short biblical phrase found within Deuteronomy 6:4–9 and a parallel set of verses in Deuteronomy 11:13–21. These biblical passages from which the rabbinic Shema is derived were already interpreted in some Second Temple period texts as indicating habits or practices of morning and evening, an interpretation that is assumed by and expanded upon in the Mishnah and other tannaitic sources. Examining Deuteronomy 6:7 and Second Temple interpretations of this verse in comparison with early rabbinic instructions for the recitation of the Shema highlights both the aspects of continuity with previous traditions and the innovative dimensions of the rabbinic interpretation of this biblical command.

Deuteronomy 6:4–9 reads:

> Hear, O Israel! The Lord is our God, the Lord is One. You shall love the Lord your God with all your heart and with all your soul and with all your might. Take to heart these instructions with which I charge you this day. Impress them upon your children, and recite them when you stay at home and when you are away, when you lie down and when you get up. Bind them as a sign on your hand and let them serve as a symbol on your forehead; inscribe them on the doorposts of your house and on your gates.[24]

This biblical passage obligates its readers to (1) devote themselves to God ("love the Lord your God"); (2) constantly remind themselves of the commandments and speak them ("take to heart, recite them"); (3) educate their children in them ("impress them upon your children"); and (4) surround themselves with physical reminders of God and God's commandments ("bind them as a sign on your hand and let them serve as a symbol on your forehead; inscribe them on the doorposts of your house and on your gates").

Exegesis of these verses transformed the biblical injunction to "love the Lord your God with all your heart and with all your soul and with all your might" (Deuteronomy 6:5) into a set of clearly defined rituals that express one's love of God. The phrase "bind them as a sign on your hand . . . [and] between your eyes" became instructions for the practice of binding phylacteries to one's arm and head. "Inscribe them on the doorposts . . . [and] gates" was practiced by affixing mezuzot, parchment with scripture, on one's doorpost as protective and declaratory amulets. Both these practices—donning phylacteries and affixing mezuzot—were already practiced during Second Temple times.[25] The phrase "impress [these instructions] upon your children [lit. sons]" became a call, within the rabbinic corpus, to teach Torah to one's sons. Finally, the phrase "recite [these instructions] . . . when you lie down and when you get up" was similarly interpreted by rabbinic scholars in literalized fashion, as instructions to its adherents literally to recite the very words of this biblical pericope on a daily basis, at the time of sleeping and waking. These passages are embedded within a covenantal chapter of Deuteronomy that exhorts its readers to follow and serve God in overarching terms, rather than within a section that lists laws or rituals. Nonetheless, they were interpreted at various historical moments as dictating specific ritual practices.

The temporal language of Deuteronomy 6:7 ("when you stay at home and when you are away, when you lie down and when you get up") was intended, within the literary context of the biblical passage, to stress constancy and permanence: one should love God and remember and repeat the commandments at all times and under all circumstances. The phrases "when you stay at home," "when you are away," "when you lie down," and "when you get up" serve as merisms, a type of synecdoche in which totality is expressed by contrasting parts of the whole.[26] By referring to the opposite spaces of home and the road (that is, being home and not being home) as well as the contrasting times of retiring to bed and arising from sleep (that is, being awake and being asleep), the verse implies that the act of repeating God's commandments should be practiced at all places and at all moments—that is, continuously or permanently, all the time and everywhere, without cease. Emphasizing that these practices ought to be done "with all your heart and with all your soul and with all your might" similarly mandates that people ought to do so with their full being—with every part of themselves (heart, soul, might, however defined).

Some ancient interpreters of this biblical verse retained the Hebrew Bible's meristic meaning and understood Deuteronomy 6:7 as a call for constant devotion to God. A passage from Proverbs, for example, evokes this reading: "My child, keep your father's commandments, and do not forsake your mother's teaching. Bind them upon your heart *always* [תמיד]; tie them around your neck. When you walk, they will lead you; when you lie down, they will watch over you; and when you awake, they will talk to you."[27] Apparently interpreting Deuteronomy 6, Proverbs makes clear that the requirement applied "always" or "at all times."[28] The author of the Community Rule, a text from the Dead Sea Scrolls, alludes to Deuteronomy 6 as well: "As soon as I stretch out my hand or my foot, I will bless His name; as soon as [I] go out or come in, to sit down or rise up, and while I recline on my couch, I will cry out to Him."[29] Here, the practice of prayer is described in poetic terms. The entire section stresses the obligation to praise God and pray to God at all times, at the turning of years, seasons, months, and days. The text emphasizes that "I shall bless Him for [His] great marvels and shall meditate on His power and shall rely on His compassion the whole day."[30] Deuteronomy's superordinate model of constant thanksgiving and remembrance is thus maintained.[31]

Philo of Alexandria also articulates an abstract reading of Deuteronomy 6. According to him, the biblical passage refers to the daily contemplation of justice. Philo describes what it means to commit oneself to justice by embodying it: placing the law in one's heart, fastening it on one's head, and wearing it between one's eyes; acting according to one's ideas of justice; and teaching justice to others once one has internalized it oneself.[32] He then writes that a person must "teach the principles of justice [προδιδασκέτω δὴ τὰ δίκαια] to kinfolk and friends and all the young people at home and in the street, both when they go to their beds and when they arise, so that in every posture and every motion, in every place both private and public, not only when they are awake but when they are asleep, they may be gladdened by visions of the just."[33] Hence, Philo invokes the idea that love of God must be taught to one's children, and he emphasizes the constancy of such instruction and devotion. One must ensure that justice is taught at *all* moments—when one is sitting at home, walking about, lying down, and rising up. Even though other texts preserved in the Dead Sea Scrolls and the writings of Philo include references to morning and evening prayers, none of them base the obligation of daily prayer on these biblical verses from Deuteronomy 6.[34]

Other Second Temple Jews, in contrast, understand the phrase "recite [these instructions] ... when you lie down and when you get up" as a command to express devotion to God at specific moments of each day, either literally at the time when one lies down to sleep and rises from bed or more generally during the times of morning and evening. In these texts, the commandment to love God and recite "these words" *always* is actualized ritually by doing so at the beginning and end of each day. Rather than *constantly*, at all times, the commandment is fulfilled *regularly*, twice each day, and moreover at the two moments of daily transition.[35] In these interpretations, the Bible's meristic language is literalized.[36] A hermeneutic move allows the regularity of the ritual performance to stand in place of the constancy of such performance.

The earliest non-biblical source that refers to Deuteronomy 6 is the second century BCE Letter of Aristeas. This text describes an act of meditating on God's works of creation: "He also commands that 'on going to bed and rising' men should meditate on the works [κατασκευῆς] of God, observing not only in word but in understanding the movement and impression which they have when they go to sleep, and waking too, how divine and incomprehensible the change from one of these states to the other is."[37] "Meditat[ing] on the works of God [μελετᾶν τὰς τοῦ θεοῦ κατασκευάς]" ought to be practiced, according to this text, specifically when one lies down to sleep and rises.[38] The subject of the meditation described was most likely God's creation of the world or of humans.[39] The text plays with the idea that the body's creation and daily re-creation at the moment of waking serves as a type of microcosm of the entire world's initial creation and its continual re-creation each morning when the sun begins to shine upon it. Focusing on the miracle of sleeping and waking—literally, the change of consciousness from entering the different states of sleeping and waking—provides an opportunity to marvel at God's ability to rejuvenate a person by giving renewed life at the moment of waking and to re-create the cosmos each morning. Though the author of the Letter of Aristeas does not mention a specific recitation of biblical verses as a part of this meditative practice, as the rabbinic Shema entails, for this author the times of waking and retiring to sleep ought to be marked by the contemplation of God's initial creation of day and night as well as God's daily (re-)creation of people through sleeping and waking.

In *Antiquities*, Josephus frames the obligation in Deuteronomy 6:7 as a commandment to commemorate the deliverance out of Egypt twice daily. This is the first text that definitively presents the practice as being performed at two distinct moments each day rather than continuously: "Twice each day, both at the beginning and when the time comes for turning to sleep, bear witness to

God for the gifts that He granted them when they were delivered from the land of the Egyptians, since gratitude is proper by nature: it is given in return for those things that have already occurred and as a stimulus for what will be."[40] Josephus explains that God is commemorated at the beginning and end of each day specifically because God bestowed gifts—here, Josephus may be referring to the daily manna—on the Israelites each morning and evening.[41] Remembering these gifts of sustenance not only serves as a form of daily thanksgiving, it also functions as a daily request for God's ongoing sustenance.[42] As Josephus interprets the biblical passage, the timing of the ritual is integrally linked to its function of praising God for bestowing benefaction at specific times of the day.

While the Letter of Aristeas and Josephus both interpret Deuteronomy 6:7 as indicating contemplation of God's miraculous acts mornings and evenings, the practices they depict are rather remote from what eventually became the recitation of the Shema as it is described in rabbinic sources. The only source that explicitly mentions the Shema as a ritualized recitation of a set of biblical passages during the Second Temple period is Mishnah *Tamid*, which lists the Shema and its blessings as part of temple worship: "They said a blessing, pronounced the Ten Commandments, the Shema, 'And it shall come to pass if you shall hearken,' and 'And the Lord spoke to Moses.' They blessed the people with three blessings: 'True and sure,' the Avodah, and the Priestly Blessing."[43] This reference to the recitation of the Shema by priests in the temple can be understood in two different ways. Either the recitation of the Shema was indeed a ritual performed by priests in the temple during the later Second Temple period, which the rabbis expanded into a broader post-temple practice after the temple's destruction, or this rabbinic passage anachronistically reimagines temple worship through the lens of the later rabbinic liturgical practice of the recitation of the Shema. Given that the list of prayers and blessings in the tractate differs from what the Mishnah prescribes for its current-day readers (and that the Decalogue has indeed been preserved in liturgical fragments from the Second Temple period), it seems plausible that, by the end of the Second Temple period, the Shema passages were recited by priests in the temple as part of temple worship.[44] Those beyond the temple, in contrast, likely did not understand their obligation in Deuteronomy 6:7 in the same terms, as the Letter of Aristeas, the Community Rule, and the writings of Philo and Josephus indicate. The rabbinic obligation to recite the Shema daily expanded this temple liturgy, which had been limited to priests, to all men—though not to women.

Between the temple's destruction in the first century and the redaction of the Mishnah in the early third century CE, the diversity of practices associated with Deuteronomy 6:7 in the Second Temple period—within the context of the temple as well as beyond it in Qumran, Alexandria, and lay communities in Palestine—was replaced by the standardization of the Shema ritual within the rabbinic corpus. By then, the biblical commandment was presented in the Mishnah as a mandate for all members of the rabbinic community to recite the biblical passage each morning and evening rather than as a call for constant contemplation of God or a daily prayer of thanksgiving. The Mishnah's choice to foreground the practice of the Shema recitation at the start of tractate *Berakhot* and its "always-already" tone represent key parts of this process of the ritual's standardization during the rabbinic period.

The Shema's Timing

In rabbinic sources, the Shema's recitation became a marker of the transition between day and night. Each evening and each morning, the Shema's recitation signaled the temporal shift from light to darkness and then again from darkness to light. The decision to begin the rabbinic corpus with rules about this particular ritual, and to introduce the ritual with an elaborate delineation of the proper times for its performance, conveys to the Mishnah's adherents that one's daily time—especially the start of a new day each evening, and the beginning of one's waking hours each morning—ought to be marked first and foremost by this ritualized declaration of devotion to God. The Mishnah begins, just as each night and day ought, with the Shema.

Determining the precise timing of the Shema's recitation was so central to the rabbinic ritual precisely because the ritual was about how to mark the official start of each new day in the evening and the effective start of each new day in the morning. Reciting the Shema at these two key moments of the day was a ritualized way of committing to God *at all times*. That timing was of primary concern for the rabbis' conceptualization of the recitation of the Shema is made abundantly clear at the very outset of the Mishnah. Much of the tractate's first chapter is devoted to outlining the exact times the Shema may be recited for one's ritual obligations to be fulfilled. Even though the rabbinic Shema builds on previous hermeneutical traditions, the role of the Shema's timing as well as the specific times that are mandated differ considerably from earlier traditions. First, the timing of the rabbinic Shema is ultimately based on (external) astronomical time-markers rather than on the (internal) biological events of sleeping and waking. Second, the timing is so vital to the rabbinic ritual that the recitation of biblical passages only constitutes the Shema ritual when the ritual is performed at its proper time.

The opening discussion of the Shema in Mishnah *Berakhot* begins by outlining the start and end times for the evening and morning recitations:

> From what time may one recite the Shema in the evening [ערבים]? From the hour when the priests enter to eat their *terumah* offering, until the end of the first watch, [these are] the words of Rabbi Eliezer. And the sages say, Until midnight. Rabban Gamliel says, Until the rise

of dawn. . . . From what time may one recite the Shema in the morning [שחרים]? From when one can distinguish between [the colors] blue and white. Rabbi Eliezer says, Between blue and green. [And one must complete it] until sunrise. Rabbi Joshua says, Until the third hour, for it is the practice of royalty [lit. sons of kings] to rise at the third hour.[45]

While some earlier sources also interpreted "when you lie down" and "when you rise" in Deuteronomy 6:7 as times of day, the Mishnah explains explicitly, for the first time, the underlying mechanics of the exegesis: "when you lie down and when you rise" means "at the hour when people [normally] lie down [at night] and at the hour when people [normally] rise [in the mornings]."[46] The Mishnah interprets "when you lie down and when you rise" not to indicate the moment when any given individual goes to sleep or wakes up but rather the times of evening and morning when it is typical for people to go to sleep and arise. "Sleeping" and "rising" are thus abstracted to indicate particular astronomical times of day. This interpretation of the verse is not taken for granted in the Mishnah, however. The House of Shammai argues that the phrases "when you lie down" and "when you rise up" also indicate the positions of one's body during recitation rather than exclusively as instructions for the times of day when the Shema ought to be recited.[47] According to the House of Shammai, one should physically recline in the evenings ("when you lie down") and deliberately stand in the morning (upon rising). This opinion is ultimately rejected by the Mishnah's redactor, in favor of the exclusively temporal interpretation offered by the House of Hillel.

The exegetical basis for the ritual's timing also appears in Sifre Deuteronomy:

> "When you lie down" could be interpreted to mean even as [the act of] lying down in the middle of the day [rather than reciting the Shema in the evening], therefore scripture adds "And when you rise." [This latter phrase, however,] could be interpreted as [the act of] standing in the middle of the night, therefore scripture adds "and when you stay at home and when you go on your way." The Torah speaks according to the ways of the world.[48]

This midrash explains that the words "when you lie down" and "when you rise" do not prescribe proper bodily positions for the recitation of the Shema (lying down and standing) but rather times of day (morning and evening). The Bible's figurative language is explained away as simply a manner of speaking.

According to the opening passage in Mishnah *Berakhot*, each evening and morning a person is obligated to consider any number of time-markers in order to determine whether the time for the recitation of the Shema has arrived or passed. The evening Shema may be recited any time starting from when the priests would have returned in the evening to eat the *terumah* offering (after their daily purification) until either the end of the first nightly watch, midnight, or dawn.[49] The morning Shema may be recited when there is enough light to distinguish between two colors (though there is debate about which colors: blue and white, or blue and green) until sunrise or the third hour of the day. Tosefta *Berakhot* and Sifre Zuta on Deuteronomy also provide lists of times for the evening and morning Shema.[50] Some of the time-markers correspond with the Mishnah, while others add alternative times and time-markers. For example, the Tosefta records that the evening Shema should be recited around the time when people return home to eat their evening meal or at the time when priests would have been allowed to eat their *terumah* offering (these times appear to be different, as they are presented as two opposing time-markers in the text, the former attributed to Rabbi Meir and the latter to the sages). In the mornings, there must be enough light for someone to recognize another person's face from a particular distance. Sifre Zuta recounts a disagreement between the House of Shammai, which mandates that a person can recite the evening Shema from the time when the priests are purified to eat their *terumah* offering, and the House of Hillel, which argues, in contrast, that one may only recite the Shema when it gets dark (that is, later than the time of the priests' purification).[51] Sifre Zuta also replaces the Mishnah's "dawn" with "the time of the crowing of the cock," though these two different time-markers seem to refer to the same time.[52] The midrash suggests that the latest time for the recitation of the morning Shema is sunrise (הנץ החמה), in contrast to the Mishnah, which places it considerably later, at the third hour of the morning.

In all of these texts, the answers regarding the timing of the evening Shema's recitation are arranged in order from the most limited time frame to the most flexible. The times for the start of the morning Shema's recitation, by contrast, begin with the most lenient opinions and end with the most stringent. A variety of time-markers are employed: the division of time into abstract units (e.g., hours, watches) and the marking of time based on natural processes (the amount of sunlight, the darkening of the evening) and human activities (the time when certain people return home from the field or the temple). Some of the time-markers relate to the temple; others rely on celestial changes.[53] Notably, all of these time-markers are external: they are not based on the bodily processes of physically going to sleep in the evenings or awaking in the morning but on external referents. Also, they all ultimately relate to the position of the sun during the day or the stars during the night, either directly or indirectly. That is, even time-markers related to the schedules of priests or laypeople (e.g., "the time when the priests return to eat the *terumah* offering"), the habits of animals (e.g., the "time of the crowing of the cock"), or the abilities of human eyes to see certain things (e.g., recognizing a person's face or distinguishing the subtlety between two similar colors) are all based on the amount of sunlight from dusk to dawn and the position of the stars during the night.[54]

The timing of the Shema was regarded by the rabbis of the Mishnah not only as important for the performance of this ritual but as essential to it: the recitation of the biblical verses is only considered the Shema ritual when it occurs at the proper time. When the same biblical verses are recited at other times of day, the recitation is considered to be a different activity. After detailing the latest possible time for the morning Shema recitation (which, according to Rabbi Joshua, is the third hour of the day), the Mishnah declares that: "One who recites thereafter [later than the third hour] has not transgressed, [but should be considered] as one who recites from the Torah [הקורא מכאן ואילך לא הפסיד כאדם שהוא קורא בתורה]."[55] This *mishnah* posits that when the Shema verses are recited within certain temporal parameters, the recitation is considered a liturgical ritual, but when they are recited after the proper time, the act of reciting the words of the Shema is an act of reading or studying Torah. The recitation fulfills a commandment whenever it is performed, but the particular commandment fulfilled depends on the time of its performance. According to this ruling, the act of reading the Shema has a different significance and ritual identity depending on whether it is done before or after the third hour. Before that hour, it is the recitation of the Shema; after, it is the recitation of Torah, itself a virtuous activity but categorically different from the Shema. Proper timing defines the significance or efficacy of the act of reciting these words. Delineating the precise time of recitation, as the Mishnah and other tannaitic sources do, therefore becomes crucially important because the ritual's proper timing is constitutive of the fulfillment of the commandment.[56]

In the rabbinic schema, it is rare for the timing of an act to constitute its essence. More typically, commandments that have set times must be performed during a particular time period or they fulfill no religious duty.[57] The Mishnah states, for example, the "governing principle" that "a matter that is commanded [to be done] by day is valid [when it is done] all day, and a matter that is commanded [to be done] by night is valid [when it is done] all night."[58] There is no mention, in this rule, that if such an act is done outside of the correct temporal parameters it is considered a different pious activity. Sacrifices, for example, are only efficacious if they are performed at their correct times, and one cannot offer sacrifices at other times.[59] In the Mishnah's discussion of the Passover sacrifice, only an animal slaughtered after midday is considered fit to serve as a Passover offering.[60] If this same animal is slaughtered earlier in the day, it cannot be used for the purpose of the offering; it is an invalid Passover offering because it was not slaughtered at the proper time. This is in marked contrast to the case of the Shema prayer, which, uniquely, is considered *the recitation of the Shema* when it is recited at a specific time and a categorically different (though still ritually significant) act when it is performed too early or too late.[61]

Men's Time: The Shema and Time-Bound Commandments

The requirement of the Shema's daily recitation structured rabbinic time in particular ways and sought to instill certain values. Reciting the Shema constituted a verbal declaration of faith in God and a daily renewal of one's commitment to fulfilling God's commandments.[62] In the Mishnah, the recitation of the Shema is compared to the acceptance of "the kingdom of heaven" and "yoke of the commandments."[63] Its accompanying blessings also serve as daily reminders of the exodus from Egypt.[64] The ritual is only fulfilled, according to the Mishnah, if one turns one's heart toward God, which entails orienting both one's interior thoughts and more physically one's body and internal organs toward the divine.[65] This rule conveys the idea that one needs to commit with one's full self—body, thoughts, and speech (which are interrelated and mutually constitutive in the sources)—to affirming God. Given the Mishnah's framing of the Shema as an acceptance of "the kingdom of heaven," the recitation of the Shema might have also constituted a polemical declaration of one's acceptance of the kingdom of heaven above any other kingdom, including that of Rome, and one's continued commitment to God's commandments above any other laws or declarations.[66] Mishnah *Tamid*, redacted more than a century after the temple's destruction, mentions that priests in the temple recited the Shema daily. Although this text cannot uncritically be treated as a historical source, it provides perspective on how the mishnaic rabbis regarded the recitation of the Shema as an ancient temple ritual that continued to be practiced long after the temple's destruction and that captured, in some sense, the temple's daily rhythms.[67] Finally, the recitation of the Shema also became a way for lay Israelites to participate in the highly valued rabbinic practice of Torah study and to cultivate an identity of belonging within the rabbinic community.[68] The Shema ritual thus effectively punctuated ritual practitioners' time by affirming their dedication to God and their membership in the rabbinic community at key moments each day.

In an arresting story in the Mishnah, Rabban Gamliel is said to have recited the Shema on the first night of his marriage, a time when men are typically exempt from reciting the Shema for fear that they might not have sufficient concentration before consummating their marriage.[69] When his students inquire into his choice to recite the Shema, Rabban Gamliel answers that he could not possibly shirk the kingdom of heaven even for a single hour. This story highlights in a playful manner both the importance of the Shema and how its recitation functions as a way of marking oneself as a pious member of the rabbinic community and in relationship with God. It also juxtaposes Rabban Gamliel's dual loyalties—to his wife and to God/Torah—and notes that, even on his wedding night, Rabban Gamliel chose to mark his time with the Shema rather than devote his time and attention to his wife.[70] Notably, the story stands in contrast to the first narrative of the tractate, in which Rabban Gamliel rules that his sons can recite the evening Shema until dawn if they forgot to recite it earlier.

The recitation of the Shema each morning and evening is thus presented as a centerpiece of what it means to be a rabbinic Jew—more so, even, than the obligation to pray daily, which is also discussed in tractate *Berakhot*.[71] Specifically, however, the Mishnah presents the Shema ritual as a centerpiece of what it means to be a rabbinic man, for it excludes women from the obligation. After discussing the Shema's proper timing, the Mishnah's focus shifts to other elements of the prayer's composition and the practice of its recitation, including a clause that exempts certain people from the very obligation of reciting the Shema. That is, after foregrounding the Shema in the most prominent place, at the beginning of the entire corpus, and highlighting the daily ritual's importance for cultivating a commitment to God, the commandments, and the rabbinic community, the text reveals that the ritual is actually intended to serve such a purpose only for certain people—free adult men. Women, along with enslaved people and children, were not obligated in its daily recitation. The Mishnah explicitly states that "women, slaves, and minors are exempt from the recitation of the Shema."[72]

The daily recitation of the Shema itself seems to have been a rabbinic innovation; the exclusion of women, enslaved people, and children from this ritual was another aspect made explicit for the first time by the rabbis. No source from the Second Temple period mentions that women did not participate in the fulfillment of the commandment in Deuteronomy 6 to "recite [these instructions]" or that they were not obligated in it, as rabbinic sources explicitly do. It is certainly possible that, in these patriarchal ancient contexts, only men were implicitly assumed to be obligated in such rituals, but this need not be the default assumption. In fact, Josephus might suggest that women were included in this ritual remembering. In *Antiquities*, Josephus first notes the act of remembrance on the sabbatical year in the temple in Jerusalem. There, he explains that all members of the community participated in the rituals ("let the high priest . . . recite the laws to the whole assembly"), as the biblical *haqhel* command enumerated in Deuteronomy 21:11–12 dictated. Josephus explicates further: "and let neither woman nor child be excluded from this audience, nor those who are enslaved either; for it is good that these laws should be engraved in their souls."[73] Josephus stresses that women, children, and enslaved people partook in the public recitation rituals that he describes. He continues in this same passage to write that everyone was obligated to engage in commemoration on a daily basis, implying, perhaps, that, like the sabbatical remembrance, women, children, and enslaved people were also obligated in the daily ritual anchored in Deuteronomy 6. Whether or not Josephus meant that women in particular were obligated, he does not explicitly exclude them. Other sources, including the Letter of Aristeas, make no mention of gendered distinctions in the context of Deuteronomy 6 either.[74] In contrast, the rabbinic ritual of the daily Shema recitation became explicitly gendered.

The Mishnah offers no reason for the exemption of women, children, and enslaved people from the Shema ritual. It is simply conveyed as an additional instruction. However, Sifre Zuta, in its midrashic commentary on Deuteronomy 6:7, provides an exegetical explanation that justifies, through a scriptural proof text, the exclusion of women from this requirement.[75] The midrash addresses the first half of the verse, about teaching one's children Torah, and extends it to the Shema. It interprets the biblical phrase "impress them upon your children [לבניך]," which presumably included all children, in its scriptural context to mean only *sons*, excluding daughters, because of the plural male construction. Sifre Zuta states: "'Impress them on your children [lit. sons].' Rabbi Judah says, to your sons and your sons' sons, but not to your daughters."[76] Thus, according to this exegesis, the command to teach one's children Torah as well as the related obligation of reciting the Shema, which appears in the same biblical verse, apply only to sons—that is, men—and not to women. Alexander explains that rabbinic sources exclude women from the recitation of the Shema on categorical grounds: "the rabbis exempt women from the Shema and tefillin because they know from elsewhere that women are exempt from Torah study," and rabbinic texts regard the recitation of the Shema as a form of Torah study.[77] The exclusion of women from studying Torah, donning phylacteries, and reciting the Shema is interrelated: all of these practices are about how to incorporate Torah into one's daily time; they are rituals aimed at renewing one's covenant with God and cultivating a particular relationship with God through recitation, embodiment, and text study.

The association of the Shema with the study of Torah, through Deuteronomy 6:7, has additional implications for understanding the gendered dimension of these intertwined obligations. Rabbinic sources present the practice of Torah study as the ultimate rabbinic definer of masculinity, as the activity that should occupy all of a rabbinic man's time, and as a safeguard against wasting time with women (or children) or succumbing to sexual temptations.[78] Torah is thereby constructed as the worthy object of affection, over and against one's wife, with the concomitant familial and marital obligations that a wife represents.[79] Whereas rabbinic sources encourage men to spend their time engaging in the study of Torah in part to protect themselves from inappropriate sexual desire, rabbinic sources warn that teaching women Torah can lead such learned women to sexual impropriety.[80] The same act of Torah study that, for a man, presents the most worthy use of time and protects him from temptation, for a woman leads her directly to it. Rabbinic men are encouraged not to "waste time" by doing anything *other* than Torah study, and they are also warned by these same sources not to speak too much to women because engaging with them is a waste of men's time: "anyone who speaks at length to a woman . . . causes evil upon himself, wastes time that could be spent studying Torah, and ends up inheriting [a place in] Gehinom."⁸¹ (MS Kaufmann qualifies this statement with reference to a *niddah*: "anyone who speaks at length to a woman *who is a menstruant*...," a particularly evocative gloss given the subject of this chapter.) This is not to say that rabbinic women did not study Torah or that all rabbinic opinions agreed that only men were obligated or permitted to study Torah but rather that this opinion that gendered Torah study as men's work consistently appears in rabbinic texts, from the Mishnah through the Babylonian Talmud, where it is found in its most developed form. In summary, there are serious implications for women from the fact that rabbinic sources present the morning and evening recitation of the Shema as an instantiation and expansion of the daily, habitual, and even continuous study of Torah. Women's exemption from these obligations further solidifies the idea that the study of Torah constituted men's work that ought to occupy men's time. These rabbinic sources simultaneously regard women as a deep and existential challenge, the epitome of the opposite of Torah study—the sources of men's time wasted or ill spent.

By the later rabbinic period, the Shema prayer is also categorized among the group of rituals that are labeled "positive time-bound commandments," from which women are exempt.⁸² It is the rabbis of the Mishnah who, for the first time, categorize commandments according to their relationship to time.⁸³ Tractate *Qiddushin* of the Mishnah introduces two sets of categories to define commandments: positive versus negative, and time-bound versus non-time-bound. According to this formulation, all commandments are either positive (requiring action, e.g., reciting a blessing) or negative (requiring the abstention from action, e.g., refraining from murder), and either time-bound (pertaining to a particular time of day, week, or year, e.g., laws pertaining to waving the *lulov* on the festival of Sukkot) or non-time-bound (applicable all of the time, or when a particular circumstance presents itself, e.g., honoring one's parents). The Mishnah explains:

> Every positive commandment that is timebound, men are obligated and women are exempt. And every positive commandment that is not timebound, men and women are [both] obligated. For every negative commandment, whether it is timebound or not timebound, men and women are [both] obligated.⁸⁴

The list begins with the group of commandments (positive, time-bound) that apply only to men and from which women are exempt, and then details the other three groups, each of which is followed by a statement about its common applicability to both men and women.

Contemporary scholars debate whether or not these categories were conceived in order to create distinctions based on gender, or if existing categories were harnessed for this purpose.⁸⁵ According to some scholars, women's inferior social and religious status (or simply societal customs and practices) might stand behind rabbinic interest in exempting them from this particular set of positive time-bound commandments.[86] Other scholars have speculated that the Mishnah proposed this rule in order to define, independent of social reality, women as partial members of the rabbinic community by excluding them from the most public and important rabbinic rituals.[87] Yet others have located the origins of the category and the exclusion of women from it with more neutral exegetical developments, or with the exemption of women from the obligation to devote their time to Torah study, from which the Shema ultimately derives.[88]

Whatever the initial intention of the rabbis who formulated this categorization may have been, the way that the Mishnah introduces and explains the four groups of commandments leaves a strong impression of conscious classification. Gender and its relationship to time is the driving force of the categorization of commandments that the passage proposes.[89] The Mishnah either invents or utilizes a categorization of commandments based on time specifically to draw distinctions between men's and women's practices.

Women's exclusion from the category of positive time-bound commandments might be explained by the fact that the rabbinic authors of this rule assumed that rabbinic women did not have control over their time and therefore could not be required to perform particular rituals at predetermined times of day. The best evidence for this assumption about women's relationship to time is, in fact, the Mishnah's discussion of women's exemption from the recitation of the Shema. Mishnah *Berakhot* 3:3 exempts women, alongside enslaved people and children, from the Shema's recitation. One of the commonalities between these categories of people is that their time is not their own. Moreover, they cannot honestly declare their acceptance of "the kingdom of heaven" precisely because they must accept the dominion of others.[90] Only fully free people—that is, free men—can be obligated to perform rituals that require them to be temporally available to God at all times.[91]

Women's exemption from the category of positive time-bound commandments itself provides a glimpse into the way in which rabbinic texts construct the relationship between time and gender. Regardless of how these categories came to be, the texts conceive of women's relationship to time—indeed women's temporality—as distinct from that of men. Either their conception of men's and women's differing relationship to time dictated their differing ritual obligations, or their differing conceptions of men and women's ritual obligations constructed their time as distinct. These two alternatives are ultimately inseparable already in the tannaitic sources as well as in subsequent rabbinic texts, in which men and women are assumed to operate according to different times and their difference is conveyed through their distinct obligations to time-bound commandments. If women's time was not already viewed as distinct from men's time, the rabbinic exemption of women from positive time-bound commandments constructed men's and women's time as distinct.

Other rabbinic texts likewise distinguish between men's and women's relationships to time, time-keeping, and punctuality. For example, in a passage analyzed by Lynn Kaye, Rabbi Yose resolves a conflict between two contradictory mishnaic rules about time by insisting that men are zealous about punctuality while women are temporally lax.[92] It is for this reason that male witnesses are expected to be precise about the exact hour of an event they witness when they provide testimony about it in court. In contrast, rabbis add an extra hour of "buffer time" when they set the final time for eating leavened bread on Passover Eve because they assume that women, who are the ones primarily responsible for removing leaven from their homes, will not be punctual about this task given that "women are lazy."[93] Here, again, rabbinic laws distinguish between men and women based on their perceptions of men's and women's differing attitudes toward, and practices of, time and punctuality.

The long-term effect of this system of categorization was the legitimization of women's exclusion from the obligation to fulfill positive time-bound commandments (most of which are ritual and liturgical practices), which entailed social, ritual, and temporal consequences, both intended and unintended. Positive time-bound commandments mark sacredness in time. Just as the recitation of the Shema transforms the moments of marking the start of the day in the evening and the arousal from sleep in the morning into times that affirm belief in and devotion to God, many rituals in the category of positive time-bound commandments mark time in similar ways. The principle of excluding women from time-bound commandments was not simply a description of religio-sociological reality in prescriptive terms. It was a radical—and radically new—position.

The requirement to recite the morning and evening Shema, which was intimately linked to the time of its performance, contains the features of a positive time-bound commandment. Palestinian tannaitic and amoraic sources do not include the Shema in lists of positive time-bound commandments.[94] The Babylonian Talmud, however, explicitly places the Shema in this category and thereby presents the recitation of the Shema as a ritual obligation from which women are categorically exempt, arguing explicitly that the Shema is a time-bound positive commandment from which women are exempt (calling this a "simple matter").[95] Whereas in tannaitic sources women are excluded specifically from the Shema as well as from the entire category of positive time-bound commandments, in the Babylonian amoraic sources their exclusion from the Shema is cast in particularly temporal terms as they are exempt explicitly *because* the ritual is one that is bound by, and marks, time in ways that have by then been limited primarily to men.

In the rhetoric of rabbinic sources, time and ritual are linked in terms of gendered difference in multiple ways. Women are exempt from the daily recitation of the Shema as well as from the entire category of positive time-bound commandments. Eventually, the Shema becomes included within this latter category. In the absence of positive time-bound commandments, women, who are excluded from observing such rituals because of their gender, are not bound by this type of ritual time as defined by this group of observances, even when certain exceptions to the rule are made. While men mark time through rituals that are bound by time, women seemingly do not; while men are encouraged not to waste their time with activities other than Torah study, of which the Shema is a part, women are regarded as potential wastes of men's time. This process unfolds in rabbinic sources as rituals explicitly associated with the demarcation of time become gendered: men's time is defined by the daily recitation of the Shema as well as by positive time-bound commandments such as phylacteries and festival-related rituals such as *lulav* and *sukkah*, in addition to the obligation to devote the most time possible to the study of Torah.[96] Women's time, in contrast, is not defined by these same rituals, nor by the obligation to spend time studying Torah.

A passage from the Babylonian Talmud sheds light on the sustained conceptual impact of the exclusion of women from this group of time-bound commandments beyond the tannaitic period. In a series of attempts to define the identity of the *'am ha-aretz*, a category employed in rabbinic sources to refer to the uneducated masses, whom the rabbis scorn for their lack of piety and knowledge, the Babylonian Talmud states: "Our Rabbis taught: Who is an *'am ha-aretz*? Anyone who does not recite the Shema evening and morning."[97] The passage continues by suggesting other practices as well, the negligence of which distinguishes rabbinic Jews and *amei ha-aretz*: donning phylacteries, wearing fringes, affixing a *mezuzah*, and studying Torah. All of these practices are encompassed within the text of the Shema prayer. An alternative opinion within the pericope also mentions unrelated practices, which women were also obligated to perform, such as tithing. Nonetheless, according to at least one rabbinic opinion, one of the rituals (the Shema) that distinguishes a righteous from a non-righteous individual and a member of the rabbinic community from one who is not a member of the rabbinic community is a ritual from which all women are exempt.[98] All women, so the logic of this passage goes, must thus be identified alongside *'amei ha-aretz*, neither full members of the rabbinic community.[99]

Women were excluded from the Shema and the category of positive time-bound commandments, but they were nonetheless obligated, already in the Mishnah and through the Babylonian Talmud, in daily prayer. This meant that even though women were not obligated to recite the Shema each morning and evening, they had other avenues for communicating with the divine and expressing their piety through prayer on a daily basis. The times for these prayers are explicitly connected in the Mishnah to the times of the temple sacrifices (the morning prayer could be recited until noon because the morning *tamid* could be offered until the same time; the afternoon prayer could be recited until evening because the afternoon *tamid* could be offered until evening; the evening prayer had less defined times).[100] These times for prayer divided the day into segments during which a particular prayer could be recited—e.g., the morning prayer was recited during the first half of the day, the afternoon prayer was recited during the second half of the day, and the evening prayer was recited at night. Such prayers nurtured regularized liturgical practices, recited throughout the day. Daily prayers were not conceived of, nor did they function as, however, rituals to begin and end each day, as was the Shema. Temporally, therefore, these two practices—Shema and Tefillah—served two distinct functions, and women were only obligated in the latter.

Menstrual Impurity as "Her Time"

In an instance of conceptual parallelism, Mishnah *Berakhot* begins by delineating men's times for the recitation of the Shema, and the mishnaic tractate on menstrual purity, *Niddah*, begins with a set of guidelines for determining the times of a woman's menstrual impurity. The opening lines of this tractate refer to the period of a woman's impurity simply as "her time," or more literally "her hour" (שעתה).[101] These sources reveal a set of purity rituals that applies primarily to women and that was designed to construct a woman's time in ways that were markedly different from the time of men.[102] Rhetorically, these two tractates begin in strikingly similar ways, with detailed discussions about proper ritual timing, emphasizing the centrality of timing to the fulfillment of both sets of practices. Just as men were obligated by rabbinic law to recite the Shema each evening and morning and to observe other daily and monthly rituals, women were likewise obligated to perform a set of rituals that marked their mornings, evenings, days, and other times throughout their months. While men and women shared many times of prayer and purity, these particular rituals were designed to frame their days in distinctly different ways, constructing a gendered temporality.

Leviticus 11–15 and Numbers 19 contain series of instructions concerning ritual impurity associated with food, childbirth, skin eruptions, eruptions in houses and fabrics, genital discharges, and contact with corpses.[103] Bodily purity laws are outlined in Leviticus 15. Men's and women's bodily impurity results from regular and irregular genital flows, including menstruation. The biblical passages about bodily purity are parsed and elaborated upon in two rabbinic tractates as well as in other rabbinic compositions: tractate *Niddah* addresses female impurity and tractate *Zavim* addresses male impurity.[104] These biblical and rabbinic laws regarding bodily impurity cover both men and women. Indeed, concern for maintaining purity was of utmost importance for men and women in the Mishnah and in other tannaitic sources, long after the destruction of the temple, even though practices of purity as they are construed in biblical sources were primarily relevant in relation to the temple cult and precinct.[105]

One important aspect of these purity laws was the alternation between times of purity and impurity that these laws engendered. As Adriana Destro has observed, "from a phenomenological point of view, throughout Leviticus impurity appears as something not discernible, elusive and inexorably hidden to everybody, even to the unclean person.... It is made accessible and decipherable exclusively through the idiom of time, and by the mechanism of temporal cycles. In its general construction, the book of Leviticus seems to convey the idea that for human beings detecting impurity means detecting or structuring times."[106] In the biblical chapters about purity, a central subject of delineation is the duration of impurity.[107] Various forms of impurity last different amounts of time. Biblical law generally employs the period of seven days or sets of seven days as the period of time that a person or object is impure. For example, if someone is afflicted with a skin eruption, a priest declares that person impure for sets of seven days (the number of sets depends on the progression and type of eruption).[108] A house plagued with eruptions is shut up for seven days. Someone who comes into contact with a dead body, which was also considered to transmit impurity, is impure for seven days.[109] A man with a normal genital emission (the emission of semen during coitus or nocturnal emission) is impure until evening. A man with other forms of discharge, which the biblical passage considers to be abnormal genital flows, remains impure for an additional seven days after the cessation of the flow. A woman with a normal menstrual flow is impure for a total of seven days, from the start of her menstrual bleeding. A woman with an irregular flow (uterine blood at times other than during menstruation) counts seven days after the flow ends.[110] A woman who has given birth is impure for seven days after the birth of a son and then continues "in the blood of purification" for thirty-three days; a woman who gives birth to a daughter is impure for fourteen days and continues "in the blood of purification" for sixty-six days.[111] Objects and people who come into physical contact with men or women in a state of impurity are themselves impure until evening. Waiting—that is, letting time pass—was part of the process of purification at least as early as the biblical sources in which they are codified. In certain situations, waiting the prescribed amount of time is sufficient for ridding oneself of impurity. In most cases, some ritual is needed to mark the transition from impurity to purity, including immersion in water, laundering clothing, or bringing a sacrifice.[112]

Despite the similarities between men's and women's purity laws, however, there are crucial differences in how the biblical text approaches the temporal dimension of women's bodily impurity in contrast to men's bodily impurity and in the language that the text uses to describe the time of impurity for men and women. For men, impurity arises because of an emission—regardless of the time of the emission. The particular type of emission determines the length of time of impurity, but the type of emission is defined by non-temporal qualities (e.g., a normal emission occurs because of sexual activity and an abnormal flow occurs because of a disease). Ágnes Vetö suggests that these two types of male genital emissions are defined in Leviticus 15 "in terms of their definition and defilement properties: they seem to be categorized by two different taxonomies. One of these taxonomies focuses upon the manner in which each emission is exuded and its concomitant impurity level. The other taxonomy involved the ability (or lack of ability) of each emission to facilitate procreation."[113] For women, though, the type of emission, and whether it is considered a normal or abnormal flow, is defined by the flow's timing. The biblical text labels the time during which it is "natural" to experience menstrual flows as a woman's "time of impurity [עת נדתה]" and designates a flow that occurs when it is "unnatural" to experience a flow as occurring "not in the time of impurity [בלא עת נדתה]."[114] The "time of impurity" is not an externally defined period of time but an occurrence relative to the woman's menstrual cycle. When a woman menstruates, she is considered to have a normal flow, and when she bleeds at a time other than during her menstruation, she is considered to have an abnormal flow. That is, the two types of female impurities are defined by the different times of their appearance rather than by the manner or emission of procreative properties, as they are for men. Moreover, men's impurity is conceived as a result of an event regardless of time whereas women's impurity is largely defined by the time at which the bleeding occurred. Women's impurity in the Bible is temporally determined; hence, the exceptional language of "the *time* of impurity."[115] The time of menstrual impurity is, even semantically in these sources, represented as a different kind of time, a period that is distinct from the periods in which a woman is not in a state of menstrual impurity. Relatedly, Tirzah Meacham has observed that, already according to biblical laws of purity, women would have spent significantly more time impure than men had they followed these laws: "it seems that both sets of rules [for men and women] were motivated by the same concern for seed pollution rather than by a motive to restrict female sexuality or to exclude women from society. However, if we add to a woman's menstrual impurity of seven days the impurity that she contracts from male seed pollution during sexual conduct ... the woman's ritually pure time is greatly limited."[116] Female impurity's dependence on and shaping of a temporal framework thus distinguishes it from male impurity already in Leviticus 15, in which only women's impurity is defined, semantically and practically, by the cyclical time of her body. For men, impurity was occasional and unpredictable, and hence characterized as normal or abnormal based on the reason for emission or flow, rather than its timing.

Rabbinic texts recognize and extend these temporal aspects found in the biblical passages when they created a complex system of laws to determine the onset and duration of male and female impurity. The timing of emissions and flows as well as the duration of male impurity are dominant themes in Mishnah and Tosefta *Zavim*. Mishnah *Zavim* begins with a discussion between the Houses of Hillel and Shammai about how to deal with a flow of unclear type (either a normal emission or abnormal male genital flow that occurs only a single time) and how long someone in such a circumstance remains in a state of impurity.[117] The tractate then discusses the duration of impurity and rituals for purification for more severe forms of impurity (those who experience two flows in two days or three flows in three days, or any combination of flows on several consecutive days). Experiencing genital flows on consecutive days alters the severity of male impurity and thus the duration of impurity and the rituals of purification. One of the tractate's concerns is to establish how much chronological continuity between occurrences of flux is needed for the flow to be considered a multiday one rather than several disconnected short-term flows.[118] The discussion centers around determining which type of flow a man has (determined by how many flows over the course of how many days) and subsequently how long that man remains impure. The remainder of the tractate focuses on how to determine the causes of genital flows in order to establish what type of flow has occurred and how long impurity lasts.[119]

The Mishnah's discussion of female impurity in tractate *Niddah* also revolves around questions of time. Whereas in the Bible a woman's own body determines when to expect her menstrual flow, the rabbis of the Mishnah fix this period across all women. In this new rabbinic system, formulated in tannaitic sources, time is divided for women into a period of time (seven days) when a woman, were she to bleed, would be considered a *niddah*, and a second period of time (the eleven days following the cessation of a menstrual flow) when a woman, were she to bleed, would be considered a *zavah*.[120] In addition, a woman is in a presumptive state of purity at certain times of the month and in a presumptive state of impurity at others.[121] According to this rabbinic innovation, the "time of her impurity" (עת נדתה) becomes a fixed standard period, and women count their days of purity and impurity in twenty-four-hour blocks of time (לעת מעת). This new conceptualization gives rise to a whole set of additional practices geared toward women's detection of their flows to determine their status of purity.

A single example from the opening chapter of the mishnaic tractate *Niddah* illustrates the centrality of timing to the rabbinic discussions of the laws and rituals surrounding women's maintenance of menstrual purity.[122] The biblical commandment concerning menstrual purity states: "When a woman has a discharge of blood that is her regular discharge from her body, she shall be in her impurity for seven days, and whoever touches her shall be impure until the evening."[123] An unasked question lies behind the tractate's opening passage in the Mishnah: from when (that is, from what point in time) does a woman consider herself to be in a state of impurity? Leviticus assumes that the process of determining the onset of impurity is self-evident to its audience, but to rabbinic interpreters it is no longer so.[124] This is especially the case because rabbinic sources assume that menstrual impurity commences as soon as a woman begins menstruating, even before menstrual blood is visible outside her body.¹²⁵ Three possibilities are proposed to the Mishnah's implied question. Shammai, the first and most lenient opinion, suggests that women are impure from the time at which they discover a flow of blood. Hillel offers a more stringent ruling: women are deemed impure retroactively, from the last time they performed an internal examination to determine their state of purity. For Hillel, it is not sufficient for a woman to consider herself impure from the moment she sees that she is bleeding, for no doubt she did not begin bleeding right then. Instead, Hillel rules that a woman must assume that she could have become impure at any point in time *after* she last examined herself and found that she was still in a state of purity, even if this means retroactively determining that she has been impure for "many days."¹²⁶ The sages, as a collective, propose a compromise: a woman is impure retroactively, either by a unit of twenty-four hours before the discovery of blood or from the last time she examined herself—whichever one is less time. According to this third opinion, a woman is deemed retroactively impure by at most one day, but even less time if she examined herself and found herself in a state of purity more recently. The Tosefta produces yet a fourth opinion about when a woman ought to deem herself impure: in contrast to the Mishnah's position of compromise in which the default is the shorter amount of retroactive time, the Tosefta explains with a series of concrete examples that the *longer* period of elapsed time is counted as part of a woman's time of impurity.¹²⁷ Even if a woman has checked herself, she still must consider herself impure for a full twenty-four-hour period, and if her last self-examination occurred more than twenty-four hours earlier, she is impure from her last examination. The Mishnah's compromise advocates that a woman can be retroactively impure for *at most* twenty-four hours, while the Tosefta explains that she must be retroactively impure for *at least* twenty-four hours.

This discussion about the onset of women's menstrual cycles applies to the generic category of women. There are additional individualized factors in the determination of the onset of female impurity. If a woman has a fixed menstrual cycle (that is, if she can accurately predict when she will become impure because of the regularity of her periods or the predictive nature of the preceding symptoms), she is deemed impure from the discovery of a flow of blood (again, דייה שעתה) and not retroactively as with other women, according to the Mishnah.¹²⁸ The Mishnah enumerates the symptoms used for prediction: yawns, sneezes, abdominal pain, discharges, shuddering, and similar phenomena.¹²⁹ A woman who can accurately identify a specific symptom as a sign of her oncoming menstruation three times can consider the symptom to be a reliable predictor of when she will begin menstruating in the future as well and thus does not need to take the precaution of deeming herself impure prior to the sight of blood.¹³⁰ The Mishnah and Tosefta both agree that virgins, pregnant women, nursing mothers, and postmenopausal women fit into the category of women with regular cycles, all of whom are deemed impure from the moment of discovery and not prior (not because these women have regular cycles but because they do not typically menstruate at all).[131] The Mishnah thus distinguishes between two classes of women, those who have regular (predictable) menstrual cycles and those whose menstrual cycles are erratic, and then legislates different strategies for determining the onset of impurity for each of these categories. The Tosefta adds a debate about the laws regarding those with ambiguous gender identities, including the *tumtum* and *androgynous*: one rabbi suggests that such people consider themselves impure only from the moment of discovery and not retroactively, while another rabbi declares that the rules are identical to those of women.[132] Mishnah *Zavim* similarly promotes the rule that for a *saris*, *tumtum*, and *androgynous*, the stringencies that apply in the case of a man and the stringencies that apply in the case of a woman both apply.[133]

Menstruation and this complex web of rabbinic laws designed to regulate women's bodily impurity would have structured women's time into cycles of impure and pure days. Women were expected to keep track of both their bodies and their days. Indeed, they were asked to count their days in order to synchronize their bodies and their time and to be hypervigilant about such timekeeping. The number of days in each cycle differs in rabbinic sources as the laws of menstrual purity changed. In tannaitic sources, women needed to keep track of their seven days of menstrual impurity followed by eleven days of potential *zivah*, totaling eighteen-day cycles; in the Babylonian Talmud, seven clean days were added to the end of the period of menstrual impurity. A woman who bleeds for a day or two outside the time of her menstrual flow is considered, in the Mishnah and Tosefta, to be "a woman who watches one day for one day."[134] According to rabbinic sources, however, *all* women effectively needed to pay attention to their body's status of purity day by day. Menstrual purity writ large—and in ways that were quite different from male bodily impurity—was thus constructed, in rabbinic sources, as a daily concern for women.

Niddah as a Rabbinic Daily Ritual

Rabbinic sources about menstrual purity required women to count their days and keep track of their bodies' times on a daily basis. In addition, the Mishnah added the practice of self-examinations of women's bodies each morning and evening, further distinguishing menstrual purity from other forms of bodily purity.[135] Because women could retroactively become impure, it was important to develop a system for limiting the amount of time between the start of the flow and its detection. If women checked their bodies regularly, then retroactive impurity and its implications could be limited. This new ritual, never mentioned in biblical and Second Temple period texts, is introduced at the end of the first chapter of tractate *Niddah* in the Mishnah and extends into the beginning of the second chapter: all women must perform internal physical examinations each morning and evening to make sure that impurity is discovered within a relatively brief time frame, as well as at other times, such as preceding sexual intercourse or, in the case of priestly women, before eating the *terumah* offering (one rabbinic opinion also mandates a check after consuming the *terumah* offering).[136] The institution of morning and evening internal bodily examinations and other frequent examinations throughout the day further transformed the daily aspects of menstrual purity rituals. According to the Mishnah, women used "test rags [עידים]" in their examinations at the time of intercourse, and if a drop of blood was discovered on this piece of cloth, they would be deemed unclean; it is unclear if such cloths were used only in the context of sexual encounter or if they were also used for examinations at other times of day.[137] Daily examinations were required of both women whose menstruation was predictable and those with unpredictable flows. The practice of checking one's body at the start and end of each day is further explicated in *b. Niddah* 4b, which explains that the morning examination is to verify the purity of food prepared the previous night and the evening examination is to verify the purity of food prepared the previous day. The only women exempted were those menstruating or those bleeding after childbirth, because in these two cases, there is no presumption that the woman is not bleeding.

How important were these daily examinations in rabbinic sources? Michael Rosenberg has noted that a reference to them appears in the very opening discussion of tractate *Niddah*, when Hillel and Shammai debate the time of the onset of impurity: "Shammai says: no woman has retroactive impurity; Hillel says: from examination to examination."[138] A longer discussion about these examinations, placed at the end of the discussion of the timing of Niddah in the first chapter of the tractate, suggests that they were proposed as a solution to the practical problem of retroactive impurity, which the rabbis themselves invented and introduce at the beginning of that same chapter. In order for a woman to be retroactively impure for only a short period of time, she needed to examine her body for menstrual impurity each morning and evening. Once she did so, the longest unit of time she would be retroactively impure would be a day or a night (shorter than a full-day unit, had she not checked herself). The daily exams, therefore, are a solution to a rabbinic rule about menstrual impurity. This solution might have originated in the rabbinic setting of the study house or, alternatively, as a practice initiated by women to mitigate the rabbinic laws of retroactive impurity.[139] Tannaitic sources devote only limited energy to the intricacies of these examinations. Perhaps this was the case because they assumed the method of these examinations to be self-evident, or because they found them to be beyond the scope of the corpus given that women initiated and performed them and that rabbinic sources imagine a rabbinic male audience rather than an audience of the women who were expected to perform these examinations. Nevertheless, rabbinic sources that outline women's daily morning and evening examinations imagine this daily practice as framing the start and end of a woman's day. Moreover, for the women who intended to follow these prescriptions, the fact that they are discussed in only a handful of passages in rabbinic sources would in no way have lessened their importance.

In amoraic and post-amoraic sources, the practice of daily examinations is further fleshed out. The Palestinian and Babylonian Talmuds discuss the circumstances during which these daily examinations ought to be performed, suggesting that they were construed as important daily practices, the intricacies of which needed to be explained for various circumstances.[140] Certain changes are implemented in these later sources. For example, women are no longer obligated, as they were in the Mishnah, to examine themselves before sexual intercourse (the rabbis deem this practice too prohibitive and declare women to be in a state of presumptive purity for their husbands), but they are still required to perform examinations each morning and evening.[141] Shai Secunda has argued that the Palestinian Talmud exhibits stringency in its upholding of these examinations, while the Babylonian Talmud tends to limit their applicability.[142] Still, the practice is regarded as so important that women's examinations are characterized according to most rabbinic figures in the Babylonian Talmud as related to ordinances from the Torah (even though they clearly originate with the tannaitic rabbis) and therefore necessary (at least in theory).[143] Even if they were not practiced by contemporary women, discussion about them occupied rabbinic attention.

Whereas rabbinic sources promote concern for male and female bodily purity, regular daily self-examination was a practice promoted for women and actively discouraged for men. The Mishnah declares that "every hand that performs multiple examinations—in women it is praised, and in men it should be severed."[144] While women are commanded to examine their bodies each morning and evening to detect the slightest hint of impurity, men are specifically commanded *not* to do so. The Mishnah does not provide a reason for this differentiated obligation, though later sources do.[145] The obligation of women to check themselves daily marked mornings and evenings, only for women, as times to assess their status of (im)purity. That is, even though both men and women were obligated to be vigilant about maintaining purity, the requirement that women perform daily self-examinations further transformed women's maintenance of purity into a daily habit, while the ban on men's self-examination prevented men's purity from becoming a daily ritual.[146]

There is one exception: men with continual abnormal genital discharges (*zavim*) were obligated to examine themselves in the same ways and at the same times as women.[147] Remarkably, the Mishnah characterizes these men in feminized terms, reinforcing the notion that such examination practices defined women's time in contrast to men's time.¹⁴⁸ Thus, Balberg has argued, men with abnormal flows in many cases become associated with women as a category:¹⁴⁹

> Several rabbinic sources suggest that the *zab* is not just a man comparable to women, but in certain ways a man who has *turned into a woman*. The rabbis make clear that men with genital discharge must adopt life habits that are normally prescribed only for women (both pure and impure): that is, they must constantly scrutinize and examine their bodies in the same way that women do ... the man with genital discharge is not only physically comparable to a woman, but also performs the same actions as a woman, as if taking on a feminine way of life.¹⁵⁰

As in Greek medical literature, according to rabbinic texts the continual flow of seed stripped away a key component of masculinity and feminized the subject; because their masculinity was in question and their flows resembled the uncontrollable and ongoing flows associated with women, men with such flows were treated like women for matters of bodily impurity, and women's laws of purity were applied to them as well.¹⁵¹ Checking one's body at regular daily intervals was considered a woman's activity even though the practice was performed by some men—or, more precisely, these men adopted women's practices because their bodies were acting like women's bodies. Constant attention to bodily impurity was categorized as women's work.

Structurally and experientially, the mandate to check oneself daily, at the beginning and end of each day, meant that rabbinic sources orchestrated a gendered schedule. The times for these two rituals were not entirely identical. The Mishnah legislates that bodily examinations should be performed in the mornings (שחרית) and at twilight (בין השמשות)—that is, when there is enough sunlight at or after dawn, and at twilight when there is still sufficient sunlight at the end of the day before nightfall to be able to detect a stain of blood.¹⁵² The Mishnah legislates that the Shema ought to be recited at night (ערבים) and in the mornings (שחרים)—when the sun has begun to set, at or after dusk, and then again when the sun has begun to rise, at or after dawn.¹⁵³ The Shema's timing bases itself on the biblical language to recite "these words ... when you lie down and when you get up," the time when a person generally retires to bed in the evening and wakes up in the morning.

The term used to indicate "morning" in the context of daily examinations in Mishnah *Niddah* corresponds to the term used for the morning recitation of the Shema in Mishnah *Berakhot*. The term שחר derives from a root that means "to break through" (as in, when the sun breaks through) but is used in rabbinic sources as a general designation for morning.¹⁵⁴ The terms שחרית, שחרין, and שחרים are all used interchangeably in manuscripts of rabbinic texts to refer to the morning.¹⁵⁵ In Mishnah *Berakhot*, the exact time frame for "morning" is debated and delineated with other time-markers (discussed above), whereas Mishnah *Niddah* does not further delineate the definition of morning, perhaps assuming that such a time was known or that this time period had already been defined elsewhere in the Mishnah. The times for the morning recitation of the Shema and for the morning bodily examination seem to be the same. In the evening, however, women were required, according to Mishnah *Niddah*, to check themselves at a period usually translated as twilight (בין השמשות), a span of time that receives much interpretation in rabbinic sources but generally indicates the period between the end of the day and the beginning of evening (with sufficient natural light to spot menstrual blood).[156] בין השמשות is literally translated as "between the suns," likely meaning between the time of one day and the next day, that is, once the sun has begun to set but when it is not yet night. Regardless of when exactly twilight (בין השמשות) occurs according to rabbinic sources, this time is generally earlier (and briefer) than the time of evening (ערבים), when the Mishnah requires the recitation of the Shema.[157] The term ערב means "sunset" or "evening," and the terms ערבים, ערבין, and ערבית indicate "evening time" in rabbinic sources. Mishnah *Berakhot* and also other tannaitic sources offer a range of time-markers for determining and denoting the time of evening (e.g., when the priests return home, discussed above), indicating that the precise parameters of this time were also understood in a variety of different ways by various rabbinic authorities, some of whom permitted the recitation of the Shema at dusk and others only later in the evening. The argument of this chapter, however, is not that these rituals were meant to take place at precisely the same times of day, such that men and women were imagined simultaneously to perform different rituals at the exact same time. Rather, it suggests that gendered daily rituals, including those to be performed twice daily, cultivated gendered senses of time.[158] The fact that men and women were obligated to perform different rituals at the same time of morning, and different rituals during different portions of twilight/evening, underscores how time was used to construct an elaborate web of gendered similarity and difference.

The Palestinian and Babylonian Talmuds further conflate the timing of these two rituals. In its discussion of the times of day when a woman performs her examinations, a comment in the Palestinian Talmud in the name of Rabbi Yose ben Rabbi Bun states that "these two examinations are the counterpart to the two times that the day changes."[159] Even though evening-time examinations ought to take place at "twilight," they were conceptualized, at least in this passage, as occurring at the transition moments of the day, similar to the timing of the Shema, which was likewise recited at the transitions between days—when the sun rises and sets. The language also evokes the *tamid* offering and times of daily prayers.[160] Moreover, the Babylonian Talmud does not use the Mishnah's time-markers for bodily examinations (שחרית and בין השמשות) but rather uses its own time-markers (שחרית and ערבית), which are identical to those that the Babylonian Talmud uses for the timing of the Shema's recitation in tractate *Berakhot* (ערבין and שחרית): "Rav Judah said in the name of Shmuel: the sages decreed that the daughters of Israel should check themselves in the mornings and evenings [שחרית וערבית], in the morning to determine the status of purity [of food] during the night, and in the evening to determine the status of purity [of food] during the day."[161] This passage in particular establishes a close rhetorical and linguistic parallel between men's and women's temporal cycles (even if the rituals did not actually occur simultaneously, if they were observed at all). There are pragmatic considerations for the practice of daily bodily examinations: marital relations at night and the potential of coming into contact with impurity throughout the day. The exemption and effective exclusion of women from the Shema and from time-bound obligations, however, seem to be undermined in these time-constructed and time-constructing requirements that were focused on women's bodies and their status of impurity. Ironically, then, through the insistence that women examine themselves each morning and evening, the rabbis constructed women's time on the model of men's time (or they scheduled women's and men's time synchronically, through two rabbinic innovations for how women and men ought to mark their times and their bodies).

Rabbinic sources also downplay other daily aspects of men's rituals of purity. The Tosefta, for example, opposes the practice of daily morning immersion by men.[162] In its view, men who immerse each morning are sectarians whose practices deliberately subvert rabbinic halakhah. The Palestinian Talmud also seeks to discourage daily immersion by men when it states: "Rabbi Hanina passed by the gates of public baths before dawn and said: What are those who immerse at dawn [טובלי שחרית] doing here? They should go and study Mishnah. In the morning he said: Whoever has work, let him go and do it."[163] While earlier in the same pericope the text speaks approvingly of immersion after coitus, it does so on the basis of personal hygiene and decency (so as to maintain boundaries between coitus and other activities) rather than for fear of bodily impurity. This passage, in contrast, juxtaposes a daily morning ritual of bodily immersion, which it deems unnecessary, with time spent studying rabbinic traditions. Daily bodily checks are constructed as pious uses of time for women, while daily immersions are presented as a waste of time for men, who should be spending their time studying Torah rather than needlessly if vigilantly ensuring bodily purity. The same types of daily practices related to establishing bodily purity thus mark women as pious practitioners of rabbinic law and simultaneously mark men as wasting their time. These final examples again demonstrate the broader trend of diminishing the importance of daily rituals of purity for men in favor of practices related to the commandment in Deuteronomy 6 to "teach your children and recite" the words of scripture—namely, Shema and Torah study. For women in the rabbinic system, attention to purity through daily rituals of examination structured their days in a way that came to be regarded as uniquely feminine, while they were deliberately excluded from marking their time with ritual recitations of the Shema and the study of Torah.[164]

Menstrual Purity as a Practice of Women's Piety

In amoraic and post-amoraic sources, the matter of maintaining menstrual purity became more strongly associated with notions of women's piety and impiety.[165] Rabbinic sources from this later period suggest that menstruation is a punishment for Eve's sin and a reminder of women's essential inferiority. In addition, the laws of women's bodily purity and impurity became more stringent, most noticeably in the increased attention women were expected to pay to their status of purity as well as to the amount of time that they remained impure following menstruation. Sources suggest that women themselves extended the duration of impurity because they saw maintaining purity to be a form of piety and they wanted to be extra cautious about maintaining proper purity. These two trends are by no means necessarily contradictory ways of thinking about the gendering of purity and the development of menstrual purity practices. In fact, they can even be mutually reinforcing. One response to the idea that menstruation is a consequence of women's sin and inferiority is regarding menstrual purity practices as uniquely feminine forms of piety.[166]

Amoraic midrashim as well as the Babylonian Talmud promoted the idea that women are obligated in menstrual purity laws because of Eve's sin. Genesis Rabbah explains, for example:

> Why was [woman] given the commandment of Niddah? Because she spilled Adam's blood, therefore the commandment of Niddah was given to her. Why was she given the precept of Hallah? He said to them, because she corrupted Adam, who was the *hallah* of the world, therefore the commandment of Hallah was given to her. And why was she given the commandment of [kindling] Sabbath lights? He said to them, because she extinguished Adam's soul, therefore she was given the commandment of [kindling] Sabbath lights.[167]

In this passage, the three paradigmatic women's rituals, listed in Mishnah *Shabbat*, are presented not as privileges but as punishments. This sentiment corresponds well to the mishnaic passage that states that women who do not observe these three rituals die in childbirth.[168] A parallel tradition in Avot de-Rabbi Natan explains further that "the commandments of menstrual purity were given to her [that is, to Eve and subsequently to all women] so that the blood she spilled might be atoned for."[169] The Babylonian Talmud, too, incorporates a tradition that Eve was punished with ten curses, including two drops of blood—the blood of menstruation and the blood of virginity.[170]

While these traditions connect menstrual impurity with women's sinful nature, vigilance about adhering to menstrual purity laws and rituals is framed, in these same sources, as a form of women's piety. Frequent checking of one's body for blood, for example, is valorized, characterized in the Palestinian Talmud as a practice performed by "modest women."[171] A story is recounted about a servant who worked in the household of Rabban Gamliel.[172] She examined herself constantly throughout the day, after lifting each jug of wine. At first, the narrative presents her frequent checking as absurd. But as the story unfolds, it is clear that her actions are actually meant to be understood as pious. By the end of the story, her constant checking saves all of Rabban Gamliel's wine from becoming impure. This story promotes continual checking and always knowing one's status of (im)purity. It aptly highlights the sense of piety associated in amoraic sources with vigilant checking.

While the Palestinian Talmud emphasizes women's piety through valorizing continuous attention to menstrual impurity, the Babylonian Talmud expresses women's piety through explaining that women themselves increased the total duration of impurity. The impulse to extend the time of impurity as a way of stressing the increased piety of a community or of its individual members appears in earlier texts about bodily purity, including the Dead Sea Scrolls.[173] Whereas those sources increased the stringency of both male and female impurity, however, rabbinic sources tend to reduce the duration of men's impurity while prolonging the duration of women's impurity. As the Babylonian Talmud presents these developments, adherence to purity laws and being hypervigilant about them thus became a way for women to fashion themselves as pious. The longer one waited to become pure—the larger buffer one set to ensure purity—the more pious one could fashion oneself to be.

Tannaitic sources present the duration of impurity as a fairly straightforward issue, presumably because Leviticus 15 so clearly delineates these rules: a woman is impure for the duration of a normal (that is, menstrual) flow, and a woman is impure for an additional seven days after the cessation of her flow when she experiences an abnormal flow.[174] The Babylonian Talmud records a peculiar popular practice that arose among women to wait an additional seven days after the conclusion of menstruation before immersing in a ritual bath and entering into a state of purity.[175] Rather than waiting a total of seven days from the onset of her menstruation (the practice recorded in Leviticus and elaborated upon in Palestinian rabbinic sources), this new custom nearly doubled the time during which a woman was considered impure by conflating the categories of *niddah* and *zavah*.[176] In effect, every menstruant (*niddah*) is treated as a woman with an abnormal discharge (*zavah*) and thus must wait "seven clean days" after the end of her flow before immersing herself in a ritual bath. A statement in the Babylonian Talmud proclaims: "Now the rabbis have made all *niddot* into doubtful *zavot*."[177] This shifting time frame reflects new stringencies on women's menstrual impurity while presenting the prolonging of periods of impurity as an expression of piety, whether imposed on women by rabbinic authorities or developed and advocated by women themselves.[178] The tractate also debates whether the obligation of waiting seven clean days is a law (הלכה) or custom (מנהג), suggesting that the status of the practice remained a matter of dispute until quite late in the rabbinic period.[179]

Yaakov Elman and Shai Secunda have suggested that the custom of waiting an additional seven so-called "clean days" was introduced as rabbinic menstrual purity laws developed in Zoroastrian and Mandean contexts that were extremely concerned with maintaining menstrual purity.[180] Perhaps rabbinic authorities or Jewish women found themselves to be in competition with their neighbors over whose purity practices were most pious. The *Vidēvdād*, for example, discusses the practice of sitting in a menstrual hut (the *daštānistān*) after the conclusion of menstruation. The Young Avestan text reads: "If a woman sees blood when three nights have passed for her she should sit in a quiet place until four nights have passed her. If a woman sees blood when four nights have passed for her she should sit in a quiet place until five nights have passed for her," and so on, through a total of nine nights.[181] The reasoning behind this extra day tacked on to the end of the period of impurity in the Zoroastrian text is the same as that articulated in rabbinic sources: to ensure that a woman is truly in a state of purity and no longer bleeding. According to Elman, when women who adhered to rabbinic practices noticed that Zoroastrian women waited an extra day after their menstruation before emerging from their state of impurity, these Jewish women took upon themselves an even more stringent practice of waiting a full week to make sure, beyond a doubt, that they were no longer in a state of impurity. While many elements of these two practices differ, the principle of prolonging the time of impurity for the sake of establishing a woman's purity with more certainty underpins both systems.[182]

Elman's analysis hinges on a peculiar turn of phrase in the Talmud's discussion of this custom: "the daughters of Israel were those who were stringent on themselves that even if they see a drop of blood as [small as] a mustard seed they sit seven clean [days before purification]."[183] The Babylonian Talmud's choice of language, that "the daughters of Israel were stringent on themselves" rather than a more typical talmudic appeal to legal precedent or an attribution to a rabbinic figure, along with the reference to the measurement of a "mustard seed" (not a standard rabbinic measurement but one that appears in other sources), might suggest a popular origin for this practice of adding extra days to the end of a woman's time of menstrual impurity.[184] The line could be understood as women themselves taking on this extra practice, or the trope could be an apologetic way of framing an imposition of rabbinic stringency upon women. If Elman's and Secunda's suggestions are correct, that Jewish women or rabbinic authorities altered their practices based on what they observed their Zoroastrian counterparts to be doing, it is a fascinating example in which women's piety is represented by a willingness to reconfigure their times of purity and impurity by extending the duration of their impurity.

There are also instances in which rabbis try to be more lenient about menstrual purity. For example, in its elaboration on the Mishnah's discussion concerning the onset of impurity, the Babylonian Talmud seeks to explain why Shammai and Hillel have opposite opinions about retroactive impurity, the former rejecting the idea and the latter endorsing it to its most extreme. Shammai, it is written, assumes that a woman's default status is one of purity, and therefore she can assume that she is in a state of purity until she discovers that she is not. Hillel, on the other hand, cannot accept this position because a woman's impurity stems from her body (that is, it is internal), and thus, according to Hillel, a woman cannot rely on the accuracy of her usual status. The text continues, after an elaborate discussion in which it seeks to clarify the two opinions, by engaging in a debate about Shammai's and Hillel's positions on retroactive impurity. The discussion transforms the debate in the earlier sources from a legal ruling about impurity to one about procreation, hinting at the consideration of possible social implications of these two different approaches.[185] According to some opinions, Shammai's reason for rejecting retroactive impurity is fear that "[the obligation of] being fruitful and multiplying will be annulled"—that is, Shammai limits the amount of time a woman must consider herself impure and by implication maximizes the time when she is pure and available to be sexually intimate with her husband.[186] In this answer, Shammai's ruling is interpreted as taking into consideration the possibility that the more time a woman is impure, the less likely it is for her to become pregnant (and hence it is desirable to minimize the time of a woman's impurity for reproductive reasons). Shammai is concerned about the practical implications of these laws of menstrual impurity, which deem a woman impure and thus unable to engage in sexual activity with her husband for the duration of her period of impurity. Hillel, in his stringency, explains that he is choosing one value (levitical purity) over another (marital relations). The debate is complex, but it highlights how the Babylonian redactors imagined their predecessors relating to women's time and the debate this topic sparked over the necessity to take women's experiences into account in the determination of rabbinic law.

Bodily Impurity as Women's Time

Rabbinic texts build upon biblical purity laws and also radically extend the complex system of laws created to determine the onset and duration of menstrual impurity. These rules, as they evolved through the rabbinic period, heightened the temporal aspects of this set of ritual practices for women through introducing retroactivity at its start, extending the duration at its end, instituting daily rituals of examination, and so on. The alternation between states of purity and impurity was characterized as a habitual concern. Through these and other dimensions of menstrual purity laws, one important dimension of women's daily time was constructed around the status of their bodies. Even though rabbinic sources mandate that men and women maintain bodily purity, the analysis above demonstrates that amoraic and post-amoraic sources tended to downplay male impurity while ruling increasingly stringently on matters of menstrual impurity—on a daily basis, through the practice of daily bodily examination and the need constantly to count pure and impure days to remain on the correct schedule, as well as over the course of the month, through extending the duration of menstrual purity.[187] At the same time, rabbinic texts, especially those from the amoraic period, consistently minimize the temporal aspects of male impurity. While the laws of purity and impurity for men and women are presented in almost complete parallel in biblical texts and thus might have affected men's and women's experiences of the alternation of times in similar ways, in rabbinic sources female menstrual practices became more stringent while male purity practices were regarded more leniently. While the Mishnah and Tosefta include tractates on male and female bodily impurity as well as many other tractates in the order of *Purities*, the Palestinian and Babylonian Talmuds only contain the tractate of *Niddah*. As a result of these shifts within these later rabbinic texts, the bodily status of impurity and the structuring of time according to times of purity and impurity became more associated overall with women than men. By the end of the classical rabbinic period, it was specifically women's temporality that was characterized by the alternation between periods of purity and impurity.

Judith Hauptman has demonstrated that rabbinic law gradually transformed the seemingly gender-equal laws of ritual purity and impurity found in biblical sources into laws that primarily focused on the impurity of women.[188] She writes:

> First, the rules of immersion for the *niddah*, and the ban on sex with her, remained in force throughout the rabbinic period, whereas the rules for the *zav, zavah*, and ejaculant disappeared over time. Second, both Talmuds have Gemara on Mishnah Niddah (although the Yerushalmi's Gemara ends at the end of chapter 3), but neither has Gemara on Zavim, or any other tractate in the Order of Purities. An even more marked difference between the two tractates is that Niddah, in the Mishnah, Tosefta, Bavli, and Yerushalmi, is filled with halakhic anecdotes, whereas Mishnah and Tosefta Zavim contain none at all. The asymmetry of material again leads to the conclusion that Niddah was a set of rules that many people lived by in the rabbinic period, whereas Zavim, and most other topics of Seder Tohorot, after the destruction of the Second Temple, were no longer relevant to their lives.[189]

Balberg identifies additional gendered distinctions embedded within mishnaic purity laws. For example, even though both men and women are required to be diligent about bodily impurity within the Mishnah, the rules surrounding women's menstrual and parturient impurity are complex, are not always intuitive to the women observing these laws, and often benefited from consultation with rabbinic authorities, while the laws of male impurity were more straightforward; women are considered to have less self-control and thus to be less mindful about practices of purity than men, and thus purity laws must be adjusted to account for a heightened level of doubt.[190] Secunda shows, as well, how practices of segregating menstruating women from their husbands are absent in early rabbinic texts and appear only in amoraic and later rabbinic sources, highlighting the increasingly stringent rabbinic approach to menstrual impurity.[191] Other scholars have also noted that in their attempts to maintain male purity, the rabbis significantly limit or perhaps even practically annul male abnormal impurity by constructing so many caveats and exemptions to their laws that few men would actually fit into the category, while these same rabbis extend the restrictions regarding abnormal bleeding to all women, even those with normal menstrual flows.[192] On this very trend, Yair Furstenberg writes: "Taken together, the two rabbinic innovations transformed the biblical *zab* into a theoretical male defined in feminine terms while only women were the actual imparters of this severe impurity."[193] In Mishnah *Zavim*, a statement attributed to Rabbi Akiva explicitly acknowledges the deliberate erasure of the category of male abnormal flows: "Rabbi Akiva says, [Even] if he ate any food, good or bad, or drank any drink [he is not a *zav*]. They said to him, [If so,] there are no longer any *zavim*! He [Akiva] responded, It is not your responsibility [to worry that there be] *zavim*!"[194]

Hauptman proposes two possible reasons for the maintenance of the menstrual purity laws while other forms of bodily purity fell out of practice. First, the ban on sexual relations with a menstruant and the characterization of such an act as sinful independent of its purity-defiling nature made the laws relevant even after the need for other forms of ritual impurity became largely obsolete.[195] While Leviticus 15:24 only characterizes sexual relations with a menstruant as defiling (as in the case of sexual relations with men during their periods of impurity), other passages, such as Leviticus 18:19 and 20:18, characterize sexual intercourse with a menstruating woman as a sin, for which the punishment (in Leviticus 20) is *karet*, a severe form of divine retribution often understood as premature death or similar tragedies.[196] Second, Hauptman suggests that the cultural context of the ancient Near East promoted the idea that menstrual blood ought to be feared and reviled, in contrast to other forms of bodily purity, which were not.

In her work on levitical purity, Mary Douglas emphasizes the importance of tracing shifts in conceptions of purity as an avenue for understanding the symbolic significance of purity to the social order. She writes:

No one knows how old are the ideas of purity and impurity in any non-literate culture: to members they must seem timeless and unchanging. But there is every reason to believe that they are sensitive to change. The same impulse to impose order which brings them into existence can be supposed to be continually modifying or enriching them.[197]

The rabbis inherited biblical laws, but, in their modification of them, reveal their own interests, values, and priorities. That the rabbis expanded the opportunities for female impurity while limiting the possibility of male impurity speaks to the rabbis' perceptions of purity and gender. As a result of this gendered disparity in rabbinic texts concerned with purity, women's daily time as the rabbis constructed it was regulated by matters of purity and impurity while such concerns became more marginal for rabbinic men, except insofar as they related to their wives' status of purity.

Gendered Temporality

The marking of men's time through the obligation of reciting the Shema and observing the entire set of positive time-bound commandments, from which women were exempt, and the creation of an alternative women's time through increased emphasis on women's adherence to an array of menstrual purity laws was the result of a series of rabbinic innovations that began in the tannaitic period and that came into fuller rhetorical effect in amoraic and post-amoraic sources, especially in the Babylonian Talmud. The frequency, duration, and applicability of women's impurity increased in rabbinic sources, while men's impurity diminished. This trend already appears in the Mishnah, where purity is presented as a lopsided concern for men and women. In amoraic rabbinic sources, laws of bodily purity continue to be deemphasized for men while the constellation of menstrual purity laws, designed especially for women, gain increasing importance as forms of women's religiosity and piety.[198] The opposite can be said about the Shema. While the biblical passage mandates a commitment on behalf of all of Israel, the Mishnah reframes it as a ritual for free men—and, in later sources, categorically excludes women from it. It is also the rabbis of the Mishnah who, for the first time, categorize commandments according to their relationship to time and then exclude women from the obligation of performing so-called positive time-bound commandments. In Alexander's words: "Insofar as the mishnaic rule indicates that men and women engage the commandments differently and insofar as observance of commandments is a central form of religious devotion to Judaism, the rule constructs men and women as different kinds of religious actors."[199] In both Talmuds, the distinction between men's and women's time becomes more crystallized. Men are defined by their adherence to the Shema while women's exclusion from the Shema and time-bound commandments is more emphatically expressed. Women's piety becomes ever more defined by their adherence to menstrual purity while men's impurity is no longer addressed in a tractate of its own. An increasingly gendered ritual system conceived of time as gendered and of gender as having explicitly temporal dimensions.[200]

Rabbinic sources remark on the intersection of bodily impurity and the Shema. Mishnah *Berakhot*, for example, asks about whether a man with a seminal emission is permitted to recite the Shema. There, the Mishnah concludes that such a man must meditate upon the Shema "in his heart" but not out loud and without reciting the blessings that precede and follow the Shema.[201] Similarly, the Mishnah explains that if a man went to immerse in a ritual bath and was able to emerge from the bath and clothe himself before the time for the recitation of the Shema had passed, he is permitted to finish the process of immersing and dressing before reciting the Shema. If, however, emerging from his immersion and getting dressed would take so much time that he would miss the opportunity to recite the Shema, then he is required to remain in the water and recite the Shema while the water covers his body. Tosefta *Berakhot* addresses such questions as well.[202] These sources present male bodily impurity as a potential complication for the daily recitation of the Shema. The texts offer, however, creative solutions in order to permit men who are ritually impure or in the process of purifying themselves to recite the Shema, even in non-ideal circumstances. Such sources suggest that the recitation of the Shema is so important that even bodily impurity ought not to exempt men from this practice.

One way of articulating or signaling one's values is through devoting one's time to particular tasks. Making the time each day to recite the Shema or consider one's status of bodily purity—that is, integrating such practices into one's daily schedule—is an expression of one's values (or a function of one's coercion within a system that operates with such values). Many twenty-first-century Americans, for example, begin and end their days with brushing their teeth. As mundane as this practice might seem, it is an expression of values: the value one places on oral hygiene and health, care for one's body and mouth, and dental aesthetics.[203] The same is true for the recitation of biblical verses or the wiping of one's vaginal area for traces of blood. These are all practices that are not nearly as time-consuming (they only take a few minutes to perform) as they are thought- and body-consuming. Mandating their practice is a way of cultivating among adherents a sense of obligation and commitment to God's laws, as well as to their gendered implications.

The rabbis did not necessarily *intentionally* create two distinct systems of time for men and women. Though the rabbis, as early as the Mishnah, deliberately exclude women from a large set of rituals and simultaneously minimize the practical and ritual effects of male impurity, it is not clear that they did so in order to differentiate men's and women's *time*. Instead, a series of individual and presumably uncoordinated legal and exegetical decisions, often concerned with matters of gender but not necessarily related directly to the gendering of time, created a system in which men and women operated within different temporal orders. Thus it is perhaps most accurate to consider the results of these many laws as the potential social and communal *effects*, intended or not, rather than as the deliberate fashioning of ritual laws for the specific purpose of creating a gendered temporal system. Regardless of the intentionality behind each of these laws, however, by the end of the rabbinic period the sources depict men's and women's time as punctuated by a unique set of rituals that oriented their time in drastically different ways. These rituals also embed men's and women's experiences of time with different significance, and a hierarchy definitively emerges: men mark mornings and evenings in ways that signal their membership within the rabbinic community and their relationship to God, while women mark their mornings and evenings in ways that highlight their inferior status and collective presumed sinfulness. Not only did rabbinic institutions and rituals, then, structure time—they also gendered it.

One of the features of the Shema, the category of time-bound commandments, and the bodily purity laws for men and women as they are developed in rabbinic sources is the linkage of men's and women's bodies to their experiences of temporality. Women who observed rabbinic law turned inward, into their bodies, to mark time.[204] Their bodies' rhythms and the structures imposed on them determined their times of purity and impurity and, by extension, the way they conducted themselves at different times of the month and the day. This inward orientation is very different from the bodily orientation of the recitation of the Shema and, in turn, the larger category of time-bound commandments, in which men turn toward the celestial bodies and other external signs to mark the appropriate times for rituals and prayers. Rituals that marked men's time oriented the subject toward God, for the purpose of establishing a relationship with the divine (the Shema prayer required turning one's heart to God), while rituals that marked women's time functioned to turn the subject's attention inward, toward the body, for the purpose of establishing the purity status of objects and people that have come in physical contact with that woman.[205] While earlier sources present both sets of rituals as constitutive of men's and women's experiences and observances, rabbinic sources create a division in which men are most strongly associated with one form of temporality cultivated by a set of liturgical rituals while women become associated with another form of temporality related to the daily tasks of maintaining purity. This bifurcation resulted in gender-differentiated time(s).

Structuring the day around maintaining menstrual purity or asserting one's dedication to God through reciting the Shema became gendered temporal practices in rabbinic texts. Such practices cultivated conceptions not only of the day and of the body, however, but also of the self. Balberg has suggested that rabbinic laws of purity are oriented to the self and are predicated on intentionality and other aspects of the interiority of a person that require self-reflection in ways that biblical laws of purity do not.[206] She writes: "Questions of subjectivity and consciousness profoundly shape the rabbinic discourse on the emergence, discernment, and management of impurity, and on the pursuit of purity" in ways that distinguish it from the biblical discourse of purity.[207] The same observation also applies to other rabbinic rituals, for example the Shema, which is also recomposed (to use Balberg's terminology) in rabbinic sources as a practice of orienting one's body and one's intentions to the divine and to future generations.[208] The Shema was figured as a recitation practice that was determined by its timing as well as the intention of the practitioner and his bodily state and orientation.

It stands to reason that if rabbinic practices of purity as well as other rituals such as the Shema were oriented around the human body and the self as a conscious introspective being, then differences in the legislation of those rituals for men and women both assume and construct gendered notions of these ritual selves. Selves are not only assumed in the rabbinic texts but also cultivated through the practices that the texts mandate as well as through the discourses of the texts. If so, the observation that rabbinic texts mandate different rituals of prayer and purity for men and women indicates not only that these sources presuppose that selves are gendered but also that they sought to cultivate gendered notions of the self through the daily rituals that they mandated.

Gender, Class, Status, and Ethnicity

This chapter's focus on gendered temporality may be considered an extended inquiry into one dimension of several intersecting intracommunal differences—including ethnicity, class, status, and age—that rabbinic texts construct through their legislation of daily time.[209] The Mishnah does not only exclude women, for example, from the recitation of the Shema. Just as women do not mark their time by turning their hearts toward God, neither do enslaved people and children. The Palestinian Talmud is explicit in its explanation: those who are enslaved cannot declare their full acceptance of the kingdom of heaven because they have human masters.[210] They cannot devote their time to this daily task because someone else controls their time. Also in its discussion of the Shema, the Mishnah extends the time of the morning Shema until the third hour, for "it is the way of kings to rise at the third hour."[211] The temporal parameters of the Shema are broadened not only to accommodate the time of early risers (presumably those required to work in fields and markets) but also to include the morning hours of those—presumably wealthy, elite, and aristocratic members of society—with the privilege to wake up late.

According to the Mishnah's rules, all free men are permitted to recite the Shema until the third hour, but the rhetoric that the Mishnah uses indicates that its composers or redactors were well aware of how class and status impacted the structuring of time.

The Babylonian Talmud's analysis of the Shema's timing, in fact, delves into the topic of class and status at length. The text records an extended debate about whether the "time of priests" (who return home in the evenings to eat their *terumah* offering) is the same as the "time of the poor" (who come home to eat bread with salt) or identical to the "time of the people" (who return to eat their meal on Sabbath eve).[212] The discussion revolves around whether each of these temporal designations describes the same moment (that is, all people eat their evening meal at the same time, and that is the time when people can begin reciting the Shema), or if indeed different types of people not only mark time differently but also mark different times (and thus there are different opinions about when the recitation of the Shema can begin each evening). The Babylonian Talmud concludes that the priests, the poor, and the people observing the Sabbath indeed eat their evening meals at different times. This talmudic discussion acknowledges the social and economic dimensions of difference that underlie these distinct time-markers: the poor return home earliest to eat their meal before dark, for they cannot afford burning oil; priests return home at dusk after completing their temple duties; and on the Sabbath people attend synagogue and eat their meals after sundown by candlelight. Here, the evening begins at different times for different social classes, and at the heart of the halakhic discussion is the time at which the Shema must be recited given this social asynchrony.

A similar discussion appears in another tractate of the Babylonian Talmud. Yoma 37b explains that the golden chandelier that Queen Helena of Adiabene donated to the temple served as a time-piece: "at the time when the sun rose, sparks emanated from it, and everyone would know that the time for the recitation of the Shema had arrived." The text notes that the reflection of the sun on the chandelier could not possibly indicate the time for the recitation of the Shema for everyone. Those who rise for the priestly watches and those who rise for the lay watch both do not recite the Shema at the time that everyone else does so, the former reciting it earlier and the latter later than usual. For whom, then, do the rays of the sun reflecting off of the chandelier indicate the proper time for the Shema's recitation? Abaye explains that Helena's chandelier benefited the rest of the people of Jerusalem, who could use it as a clock for the Shema.

Regarding menstrual purity, too, rabbinic sources use time to construct classed, ethnic, and sectarian difference. While all women were required to check their bodies each morning and evening, women of the priestly class were also required to examine their bodies before and after eating the *terumah* offering.²¹³ Their time, as a result, was punctuated by concerns over purity more frequently than it was for women of the Levite and Israelite castes. Furthermore, the Mishnah constructs difference between Samaritan, Sadducean, and Israelite women by regarding some of them as perpetually impure—from the moment of their birth—and others as impure only at times when they are physically menstruating.²¹⁴ Mishnah *Niddah* 4:1 explains that "the daughters of Samaritans are [impure as] menstruants from their cradle." The "daughters of Sadducees" are similarly considered impure like Samaritans if they conduct themselves according to Sadducean practice but pure like Israelites if they follow Israelite practices. Gentiles are considered impure "as *zavim*" at all times, similar to the permanent status of niddah impurity of Samaritan women.²¹⁵

Charlotte Fonrobert has demonstrated that it was not only rabbinic sources that sought to create ethnic and communal differentiation through the temporal dimension of menstrual purity. The Didascalia Apostolorum and other early Christian texts likewise construct communal difference by insisting that women should no longer observe menstrual purity practices.²¹⁶ The polemic against the practice of menstrual purity is framed as a dispute over the essence of time and the body's relationship to time, arguing that the separation of time into distinct periods of purity and impurity is incoherent for those who have been baptized: "And again, let them tell us, in what days and in what hours they keep themselves from prayer and from receiving the Eucharist, or from reading the Scriptures—let them tell us whether they are void of the Holy Spirit."²¹⁷ Could it be, the author asks, that there are times during which certain people lack the Holy Spirit? This is impossible, "for through baptism they receive the Holy Spirit, who is ever with those that work righteousness, and does not depart from them by reason of natural issues and the intercourse of marriage, but is ever and always with those who possess Him, and keeps them."²¹⁸ In this text, dividing women's time into states of purity and impurity becomes a marker of difference; abandoning the division of time based on purity becomes essential for full acceptance into the Didascalia's community.

Several other passages from across the rabbinic corpus indicate that rabbis were well aware that not everyone had the same schedule and that one's financial means, class status, and other related factors affected the daily schedule of different segments of their communities. Mishnah *Ketubbot*, for example, discusses a scenario in which a married man vows not to have sexual intercourse with his wife. Coitus, however, is part of a man's marital obligations to his wife. The Mishnah therefore attempts to determine for how long a man is allowed to uphold his vow of celibacy. The School of Shammai suggests that a man may keep his vow for two weeks, while the School of Hillel counters that the man may only keep his vow for one week. The anonymous editorial voice of the Mishnah proposes a more nuanced answer, in which the amount of time a man may remain celibate depends on his profession. Rabbinic sages may abstain from sexual activity for thirty days as they engage in Torah study. Laborers, in contrast, may only abstain for a single week. The difference between these times seems to indicate the Mishnah's higher estimation of the work of Torah scholars to that of laborers: sages engage in more important work, and therefore they can pursue it for longer without the need to stop to fulfill their marital obligations. The Mishnah, citing an opinion of Rabbi Eliezer, then proceeds to offer an even more detailed schedule of men's marital obligations based on the profession of the men in question: unemployed people must fulfill their marital duties every day; laborers must do so twice each week; donkey riders ought to do so once per week; camel drivers once every thirty days; and sailors once every six months. The logic behind this arrangement is based on the availability of each of these professionals. Those who are unemployed have much free time, and so there is not a single day when they are unavailable for their wives, whereas agricultural laborers work hard but remain close to home, and therefore they are required to have intercourse with their wives twice per week. Donkey riders, camel riders, and sailors all work at varying distances from home, and so their obligations are relative to the distances they typically travel. In this passage, as in the texts regarding the Shema, the Mishnah deliberately distinguished between people based on their relationship to time, and it uses time to distinguish between those with various professions.

Other passages in the Mishnah further develop the idea that time ought to be structured and observed differently based on financial or professional status. When discussing laws about providing poor people with access to produce, the Mishnah mandates that three times a day—in the early mornings, at noon, and in the afternoons—landowners provide poor people with access to a corner of the field for them to harvest.[219] There are times of day, that is, for poor people to be in the fields. Rabban Gamaliel and Rabbi Akiva disagree about whether these outlined times are meant minimally or maximally. Regardless, the Mishnah explicitly states that, in the context of the field, there are times of day when the poor should have access.

In its discussion of Passover, the Mishnah proposes that "in a place where the [local] custom is to work on Passover eve until noon, that is what they do; in a place where the [local] custom is not [to work], they do not."[220] It elaborates that if a person from one place (with one custom) goes to another place (with another custom), the restrictions of both that person's place of origin and destination apply. Later in the same chapter, the Mishnah explains that, for example, those in the region of Judea work on Passover eve, while those in the Galilee do not.[221] After a full discussion of the importance of geographical place and belonging to customs about permissible work times, the Mishnah shares an opinion it attributes to the sages: three types of professionals are permitted to work on Passover eve, presumably even if in their region work is generally prohibited on that day.[222] Those professionals include tailors, hairdressers, and those who launder clothing. An additional type of professional, the shoemaker, is added to the list in a comment attributed to Rabbi Yose bar Judah. One may guess the reason for these exceptions to the rule—perhaps these are the professionals who help others prepare their bodies and attire for the festival. What is noteworthy in the context of this discussion is the Mishnah's acknowledgment that people of different professional status (in addition to different local custom) ought to observe pre-festival times distinctly, some resting or preparing for the festival and others working, because of either financial need or communal service.

Furthermore, the Mishnah emphasizes the local dimensions of time in its discussion of the treatment of day laborers in *Baba Metsia* 7:1: "He who hired workers and tells them to begin early and stay late—in a place where the [local] custom is not to begin early and stay late, he is not allowed to compel them [to begin early and stay late]." According to this passage, employers do not have exclusive privilege to set work schedules; local temporal customs override the preferences of employers regarding start and end times of their workdays (as well as regarding other aspects, such as the food they are fed, as the text continues to elaborate). The Babylonian Talmud's discussion of this mishnaic rule dwells on additional facets of the intersection between local culture, class, and status. A statement attributed to Resh Lakish states that "a worker is on his own time when he begins work, and on his master's time upon his exit."[223] The Babylonian Talmud objects to Resh Lakish's statement because it seems to contradict the Mishnah: how can workers' times be determined according to Resh Lakish's rule when the Mishnah so clearly posits local culture as the determinant of daily start and end times? Maybe, the text suggests, Resh Lakish was referring to a new city (i.e., with no local culture already established). The text counters this possible resolution with an additional objection: even if the city was newly established, what about the local culture of the places from which the workers originated—shouldn't these temporal cultures determine their schedules? The Babylonian Talmud forcefully rejects this resolution with a single but powerful word: בנקוטאי—they are "gathered from different places." As they come from different places, none of their individual times are synchronized.

This same section of the Babylonian Talmud recounts a story about how the same hour is experienced differently—and reveals different things about a person's class, status, and identity.[224] In this narrative, Rabbi Eleazar ben Rabbi Simeon meets a government official whose job it is to arrest thieves. The rabbi wonders how this official distinguishes between thieves and innocent people. The official explains that his strategy is based on timing: thieves prefer the night (and so those out and about at night are assumed to be thieves, the text intimates). Upon hearing this, Rabbi Eleazar worries that such a strategy might result in the unjust capture of an innocent person. While the official acknowledges the possibility of this outcome, he states that his hands are tied—he is operating according to the king's order. The rabbi then offers the official an alternative strategy: "Go into a tavern at the fourth hour of the day. If you see a man dozing off with a cup of wine in his hand, ask what he is. If he is a learned man, he has risen early to pursue his studies; if he is a day laborer, he must have been up early to do his work; if his work is of the kind that is done at night, he might have been rolling thin metal. If he is none of these, he is a thief, arrest him."[225] This story rests on the idea that scholars, day laborers, and night-shift workers experience "four o'clock" in very different ways. It even uses this idea to suggest a form of criminal justice reform.

Mealtimes are also a matter of discussion in the Babylonian Talmud. Tractate *Pesahim* catalogues the differing times when people of various professions eat their morning meals: gladiators in the first hour, thieves in the second, heirs in the third, workers in the fourth, sages in the fifth, and everyone else in the sixth.[226] Another rabbinic opinion in the same pericope posits that all people eat in the fourth hour but that workers wait until the fifth hour and sages until the sixth. Tractate *Shabbat* offers a slightly different timetable and adds that thieves eat early in the morning because they are hungry after working all night.[227] Notably, the temporal distinctions in these lists are based on stereotypes about professions, economic class, and social status. Sages eat at their own time, as they are on a special schedule.

In Mishnah *Berakhot*, we learn that the most pious rabbis do not share the time of ordinary others. Even though rabbinic law exempts bridegrooms from reciting the Shema for several days after their wedding (if they have not yet consummated their marriage), the Mishnah explains that Rabban Gamliel recited the Shema on the first night of his marriage. When his students ask him why he violated his own legal ruling, he answers that it was not possible for him to suspend the acceptance of the kingdom of heaven for even "one hour."[228] For Rabban Gamliel in this story, the temporal dimension of piety is wholly evident.

Conclusions

Christina Schües, in addressing the feminist phenomenology of time, writes: "*The* gender, *the* woman, and *the* man are concepts that are as senseless as saying *the* time. Thus, for both we might pose the same kind of question: How does time show itself? How does gender show itself? And: how does gender show itself in relation to time? And how does time show itself in relation to gender? Thus, temporality is gendered, and gendering is temporal."[229] This chapter has presented an argument precisely along these lines, suggesting that rabbinic sources constructed gender through time and, simultaneously, that these same sources constructed time through gender. The textual analysis in this chapter has attempted to show the specific, and often local, dynamics involved in rabbinic genderings of time as they adapted and transformed rituals laws from biblical and Second Temple texts for their own rabbinic ends.

Starting with its opening statement, the Mishnah not only inquires about time but also draws a conceptual link between the ritual of the recitation of the Shema and priestly practices of purity. As Chaim Saiman observes, the first time-marker used in the Mishnah to define when the evening Shema ought to be recited—when the priests enter to eat their *terumah* offering—functions "as a hyperlink that takes us from the familiar laws of the Shema to the obscure laws of ritual purity," in this case to the laws of priestly purity associated with the consumption of consecrated food.[230] In the Mishnah's discussion of women's daily bodily examinations for menstrual purity laws, too, one finds a reference to the *terumah* offering. The Mishnah obligates those who eat the *terumah* offering to check their bodies to determine purity status not only each morning and evening but also before consuming this consecrated food.[231] The recitation of the Shema and the maintenance of bodily purity, seemingly separate practices, are thus intertextually and conceptually linked already in the earliest rabbinic source. They are connected, moreover, specifically through time and timing. The construction of a gendered daily temporal framework based on the gendered observance of these daily practices in rabbinic texts is not purely a modern scholarly juxtaposition or imposition but also embedded, if subtly, in ancient rabbinic discourses about daily rituals, time, and gender.

Both practices, moreover, relate back to the temple and its times. One of the original motivations of the laws of bodily purity was maintaining a status of purity in relation to the temple precinct and cult as well as to the *terumah* offerings given to priests and their families, which needed to be eaten in a state of purity. This care for purity remained even after the temple's destruction. A central feature of the recitation of the Shema was preserving temple liturgy and maintaining the temple's liturgical rhythms. Valérie Rhein argues that the positive time-bound rituals from which women were exempted all relate to temple worship and that women's exemption from them sought to create a gendered hierarchy in place of a priestly hierarchy during the rabbinic period.[232] The timing of women's daily bodily examinations also gestures toward the timing of the *tamid* sacrifice.[233] Requiring men and women to observe these practices in the particular configurations in which they are outlined in rabbinic sources thus also functioned as a way of relating contemporary daily actions to past times, and in particular to the times and practices of the temple and its cult.

This chapter has focused on the temporal unit of the day, including on rituals associated with the start and end of each day. Festivals celebrated annually and sacred days observed weekly punctuate longer temporal cycles: years and weeks. Sabbaths and festivals are conceived as days of special significance that stand apart from quotidian time. Indeed, such days deliberately depart from quotidian time and create a different type of time—set apart, separated, different. The daily rituals at the heart of this chapter, in contrast, were designed by the rabbis to cultivate regular daily rhythms, what Eviatar Zerubavel calls "sociotemporal order"—that is, to mold and construct regular, daily, even predictable quotidian time.[234] And they cultivated difference, too, through the temporal rhythms and rituals of "every day."[235] Just as with annual calendars and weekly cycles, in the realm of quotidian time, as well, rabbinic rituals and schedules constructed difference between men and women; children and adults; enslaved, freed, and free people; rural and urban dwellers; priests and non-priests; poor and wealthy; and members of various ethnic groups.

The role of the body in these daily rituals—indeed, the construction of gendered bodies in the construction of quotidian time—makes perfect sense. In his explanation of Henri Lefebvre's work, Stuart Elden writes: "in the collision of natural biological and social timescales, the rhythms of our bodies and society, the analysis of rhythms provides a privileged insight into the question of everyday life."[236] Rabbinic sources sought to synchronize a set of embodied daily rituals with the natural rhythms of the sun's daily rise and set, the biological circadian rhythms of individuals, and the imagined rhythms of a templed past. They did so differently for men and women, and through their ritual rules they constructed not only time but also gendered difference.

CHAPTER FOUR

Human and Divine Time

RABBINIC CONSTRUCTIONS of annual, weekly, and daily time had an important impact on human activities. The previous chapters explored how rabbinic texts forged difference between various groups of people—rabbis and Romans, Jews and Christians, men and women, as well as those of differing ethnicities, classes, and status—through rabbinic legislations of time. This chapter turns to another realm: rabbinic ideas about God's time. It investigates the construction and deconstruction of human-divine difference by analyzing rabbinic texts that engage with the notion of God's hours and other precise time-units that subdivide the day.[1] Rabbinic reflections on the similarities and differences between human and divine time provide a lens into their understanding of what distinguished human beings from God as well as the role that time could play in bridging the gap between heaven and earth. The rabbinic narratives at the heart of this chapter engage with the same topics, and several of them come from the same rabbinic tractates and pericopes as those explored in the preceding chapters: rabbinic discussions of idolatrous worship; the Sabbath and festivals; and the recitation of the Shema and observance of time-bound commandments by men and simultaneous times marked by women and children. That is because depictions of God's time, as they appear in rabbinic sources, are integral to, rather than separate from, discussions of human rhythms of time.

In their book *The Daily Life of the Greek Gods*, Giulia Sissa and Marcel Detienne reflect upon the questions that Cicero, Lucian, Seneca, and other ancient authors and philosophers asked about their gods:

> What do they do? or, more to the point, "Do they do anything at all?" For, as Cicero remarks, much is said about what they look like and the places where they live, and about their houses and the exploits of their lives, but the question that above all underlies any difference of opinion as to their nature is whether or not they do nothing, meddle in nothing,

abstain from all concern and all cares.... Whatever would one do with carefree and passive gods of leisure?... the question of their *activity* was the touchstone for their presence in the world.[2]

How gods organize and use their time is a question with serious implications. The topic interested the rabbis for the same reasons it occupied others in the ancient world: rabbis sought to understand how their God relates to human beings and the world they inhabit, how their God's actions impinge upon human existence, and whether their God's existence matters for those who dwell on earth. Imagining how God's time is divided and what God does during each hour of each day and night also allowed the rabbis to confront the question of what distinguishes divine from human, as well as to differentiate themselves from those around them who held different theological perspectives on these very topics.

The question of whether God exists in time, and how divine time relates to human time, animated the theological work of many ancient thinkers. Philo of Alexandria, for example, argued in his treatise on the creation of the world that, in contrast to people and all other creations, God exists out of time and that this timeless aspect of the divine differentiates the divine from the human.[3] According to Philo, time was created simultaneously with the material creation; that is, time did not preexist matter. God is thus presented as both eternal and atemporal, while the created world, including all of its inhabitants, is temporally bound. In this account, Philo argues not only that God is atemporal but that to be divine is to be eternal and atemporal—that these are constitutive features of divinity. Being bound by time, in contrast, is a defining feature of what it means to be materially created by God.[4] Time, then, distinguishes—and even defines the difference—between divine and human. A few centuries later, Augustine, drawing on a set of philosophical assumptions and exegetical concerns overlapping those of Philo, made a similar argument: God is uncreated and therefore eternal, while all creations by definition change and are thus temporally bound.[5] According to Augustine, people experience and perceive the world temporally, with a sense of duration and distinctions between past, present, and future (though for Augustine time is still only "a dimension of the mind"),[6] while God cannot change and thus exists in an all-encompassing eternal present.[7] As with Philo, Augustine's meditation about divine-human difference is predicated on divine eternity and human temporality.

In contrast, in rabbinic texts, both humans and God exist in time—and indeed in the same time.[8] People, right along with God, reckon time according to the same seven-day week, daily hours, nightly watches, midnight, and other subdivisions of the day. God also uses time to engage in activities with which humans occupy themselves. In rabbinic sources, time thus functions to connect humans and God within a shared temporal system. But time also functions to distinguish between humans and God in rabbinic texts. For while rabbinic sources present God as existing in time, they also suggest that God has a different relationship to time than humans do. God has days, nights, and hours, but God's time never ends, God has control over time (e.g., over how much time created beings are given to live), and God is temporally exacting in ways that humans cannot be. In addition, God engages in some daily activities that are exclusively divine. In total, then, humans and God operate within the same temporal system, and they even overlap in their schedules and in some of their daily tasks, but they also have different time-keeping abilities and activities. This temporal tension captures an underlying theological tension present throughout rabbinic texts that discuss God. In such sources, God is at once part of this world, involved in its daily rhythms, and spends much time caring for all of the world's creations on a daily and even hourly basis. Importantly, rabbinic sources do not portray God as spending time caring only for humans or for the People of Israel; God spends time each day caring for all creatures on earth, even as God spends additional time ensuring human flourishing, and devotes parts of each day to cultivating a reciprocal relationship specifically with the People of Israel. God is also available "upon request," as it were, to spontaneously respond to human actions—God's rigid schedule notwithstanding. Despite God's constant care for creation, however, God simultaneously stands temporally apart from the created world and is sometimes glaringly absent from intervention in timely human affairs. As a result, these rabbinic sources imagine a God whom humans might wish to emulate but, ultimately, one whom they cannot fully resemble or completely understand. Imagining human and divine time thus becomes an avenue through which rabbinic sources articulate ideas about human-divine similarity and difference.

This chapter analyzes exegetical and narrative texts from the rabbinic corpus that reflect on the following questions: (1) how does God divide time? (2) how does God spend time? (3) how does human time relate to these divine time-keeping practices? These topics are interrelated, because descriptions of God's daily and hourly schedule are often utilized in the sources to highlight what God values and what, in turn, humans ought to value; when God is depicted as spending some or all hours of the day on a particular task, time is used rhetorically to emphasize the importance of that particular divine activity. What God *does*, that is, is frequently interrelated with *when* and *for how long* God does it. Meditations about God's hourly schedule, habitual activities, and daily rituals thus become narrative tools for thinking through God's actions and habits and how they impact the created world and its inhabitants.

The rabbinic narratives analyzed in what follows address several topics. The first set describes how God spent each hour of the sixth day of the world's creation. The second set of sources depicts what God has been doing with all of time since the world's creation. The third set of narratives provides hour-by-hour schedules of God's day. Additional narratives reflect on emotions or tasks that God experiences or undertakes for brief periods of time each day, or highlight that God uses time in ways that human beings cannot. Yet other passages address God's nighttime hours, God's nocturnal activities, and how God divides the night. Some of these narratives thus provide answers about the totality of God's daily time or about fleeting moments of God's day, while others divide up God's days into hourly units and describe God's different daily activities during each of these discrete blocks of time. Finally, some of these rabbinic narratives wonder how God's daily activities have changed since or have been affected by the temple's destruction.

Many passages about God's daily schedule appear in several parallel versions across multiple rabbinic compositions, all from the amoraic period or later, in texts from the regions of both Palestine and Babylonia.[9] They circulated for hundreds of years and were incorporated into rabbinic texts that span several centuries. This textual multiplicity indicates that they were widespread and popular narratives, told and retold in various iterations in oral and written form (the manuscripts of each of these stories contain significant variants as well, which might further indicate their fluid form even in later periods). The narratives appear in exegetical, polemical, ritual, and mystical contexts both within and beyond the classical rabbinic corpus. Notably, several of the traditions about God's time appear in specifically homiletical and liturgical literary contexts: in homiletical midrashim, targumim (Aramaic translations of the Hebrew Bible used during synagogue worship), liturgical poems, and even in rare homiletical sections of the Babylonian Talmud. That is, the literary form, variety, and context of these narratives about God's daily schedule suggest not only that they circulated widely but also that they could have been preached in synagogues or other communal settings and incorporated into Sabbath, festival, and life-cycle worship, rituals, and celebrations rather than being confined to the more exclusive, esoteric, and limited discourses of rabbinic study houses and scholastic environments.[10] It is often argued that rabbinic texts were not particularly interested in theological questions—that they discuss God mainly incidentally and that theology is rarely the center of the conversation.[11] Even if theological questions were not at the heart of the rabbinic project, they seem to have been at the nexus of the rabbinic project and popular piety. Perhaps surprisingly, these rabbinic stories about God's schedule are precisely the types of rabbinic traditions that those beyond the narrow confines of rabbinic circles might have encountered.

The rhetorical force and function of these narratives about God's daily time, therefore, ought to be understood not only as internal rabbinic discussion but also as part of broader communal discourses about God, humans, and the times that they shared. It is worth mentioning, for example, that if such rabbinic stories were preached, poetry recited, and biblical translations chanted in synagogues in Sepphoris, Hamat Tiberias, Bet Alpha, Huqoq, or

FIGURE 10. Helios depicted at the center of the zodiac mosaic in the Hamat Tiberias synagogue, dated to the second half of the fourth century CE.

elsewhere in the Galilee in the later fourth, fifth, or sixth century, they would have been heard by congregants sitting or standing alongside elaborate mosaics adorning the floors of their synagogues. Many of these mosaics featured ornate circular zodiacs at the very center of the synagogue, which visually incorporated annual, seasonal, monthly, and even hourly time into synagogue experiences. The twelve segments of the zodiac represented the year's twelve months and the cyclical passage of years.[12] Female personifications of the four seasons adorned the corners of the zodiacs, signaling the passing of the four seasons. At the center of each zodiac stood a depiction of Helios, the sun god. Though those at the synagogues might have identified this figure simply as their God (rather than as an image of the sun god), iconographically the mosaics unmistakably feature images of the Greco-Roman sun god Helios as he was typically represented in contemporaneous art from this region; congregants were thus prompted by such zodiacs to associate the God worshipped at the synagogue with the sun.[13] Beyond marking the solar year and the passing of the four seasons, the sun played a key role in the determination of daytime hours as well. Hours, as they were conceived and calculated in the ancient Mediterranean in this period, were subdivisions of the day based on the position of the sun. The observation of the sun's path across the heavens, with or without the use of a sundial, thus determined daily hours.[14] Moreover, Helios

FIGURE 11. Zodiac mosaic from the early fifth century CE synagogue at Sepphoris, with the sun and moon depicted at center.

is often accompanied in these mosaics by the moon and stars, visual elements that gesture toward both the lunar months and the nighttime hours, which were determined by observing the path of the constellations across the dark skies. Thus, the relationship between God and annual, monthly, daily, and hourly time was prominently depicted in the very spaces where such homilies and liturgies about God's time would have been recited and performed. The anthropomorphism of God's daily schedule and the human activities therein, as constructed in rabbinic texts, diminishes in turn the surprise retroactively experienced by contemporary scholars in viewing such artistic anthropomorphic depictions of God on synagogue floor mosaics.[15] Stories about God's daily schedule that emphasize that God spends each hour of the day and night deeply concerned about and invested in the created world and human well-being were visually complemented by the depiction of God as the sun, alongside the moon and stars, at the center of such sacred spaces.[16] God was literally present in the synagogue, front and center for all to see—at all hours of the day, when the sun was shining, and throughout the night, when the stars glistened.

The rabbinic narratives about God's time analyzed in this chapter also demonstrate how the unit of hourly time in particular came to be most associated with the divine. Hours were conceived as integral to God's creation of humanity as well as to God's subsequent involvement in human history. The division of the day into twelve hours was a relatively recent division of time in the region of Palestine in the early centuries CE, originating millennia earlier in Egypt but popularized in the Levant by the Roman Empire, and it remained relatively rare in the Sasanian Empire. Hours are less frequently attested in rabbinic sources from the earlier tannaitic period than they are in texts from the later amoraic period, and even in later sources three-hour divisions of the day, which segmented the day into quarters, were more common than distinctions between each hour of the day, presumably because distinguishing between individual hours is challenging without sophisticated time-keeping devices and expert knowledge. Determining precise hours remained a practice, therefore, largely limited to those with access to sundials and similar devices, which were expensive and therefore uncommon even in public locations. This is true even of portable sundials, which often functioned more as status symbols than as precise hourly time-keepers, though such extant sundials and related inscriptions on stone, metal, and wax tablets do suggest that hours were increasingly used even by non-elites and those in rural contexts within the Roman Empire for matters such as burials, court appearances, and sharing resources and spaces.[17] The history of hourly time-keeping might therefore explain why stories about God's hourly time appear primarily in amoraic sources, when hours were a more mainstream division of time. Stories that impose hours onto biblical creation narratives or conceptions of the divine create the sense that time has always been ordered as it is "now," according to hours, even though those divisions of time were radically new and relatively limited in daily life. In addition, associating the unit of the hour with God's time functions particularly effectively in a context when hourly time-keeping was still most commonly an elite practice available to those with the technology, resources, and status accurately to distinguish between hours. That God's day was so easily divided into hours signaled God's privilege and power.

Lynn Kaye's study demonstrates that rabbinic texts portray God as perfectly punctual, with the exceptional ability to distinguish between even the smallest units of time and to respond immediately to (and even simultaneously with) human action.[18] Human beings, in contrast, are presented in these same rabbinic sources as being more constrained in their time-telling abilities, barely able to approximate hourly time, and equipped only to react in temporally delayed fashion to the deeds of others. What distinguishes humans from God in the sources that Kaye analyzes is their differing abilities to determine time precisely and to act at precise times. A couple of brief examples illustrate well this temporal distinction between God and people. The Mekhilta de-Rabbi Ishmael, for instance, asks why Exodus 12:29 specifies that God came to smite the firstborn Egyptians precisely at midnight (בחצי הלילה) rather than around midnight (כחצת הלילה, used in other verses depicting this same event).[19] The midrash seeks to resolve this exegetical curiosity with a rhetorical question: "is it possible for a human being to fix the time of midnight? None but the Creator can divide the night exactly.... The one who knows its hours and its fractions, he divided [the night]."[20] Playing with the word for midnight—in Hebrew, literally "at the middle of the night"—and the exacting preposition that the verse uses ("at" rather than "around" midnight), the midrash explains that God can divide the night exactly into two, and thus God acted at exactly midnight. Only God can act with such precise timing, the midrash insists, and therefore the plague of the firstborns was not merely a feat of might but also a feat of time. Genesis Rabbah, too, identifies God as the most precise timekeeper.[21] The midrash notes the seeming contradiction in Genesis 2:2, which declares both that "God finished [creating the world] on the seventh day" and that God "rested on the seventh day."[22] The midrash wonders: How can the passage state that God both finished creation and rested on the seventh day? By way of explanation, the midrash comments that God is so precise with time that God was able to continue creating the world right until the Sabbath began and then stopped creating just as the Sabbath started. This temporal precision, the tradition adds again, is a feature exclusively of the divine. In contrast to God, who can start observing the Sabbath at the very moment when it begins, people must begin observing the Sabbath well before the official start of the Sabbath day in order to create a temporal buffer and be sure that they are not inadvertently violating the Sabbath.[23] Whereas Philo interpreted the creation narrative in Genesis in order to maintain God's eternality and atemporality, Genesis Rabbah's interpretation of this same creation narrative insists on God's extreme temporal precision and hypertemporality. This text also highlights how the rabbinic notion that, unlike humans, God is an accurate time-teller is applied to ritual and devotional practices such as determining when to begin the Sabbath rather than only to exegetical contexts concerned with harmonizing seemingly contradictory biblical passages or homiletical or liturgical texts engaged more directly with theological questions.[24] As Kaye shows, other areas of rabbinic legislation, such as determining the legitimacy of witness testimony, also often allow for temporal approximation and even mandate temporal precautions to counteract human limitations regarding time-reckoning, contrasting people's temporal imprecision with the exactness of

God's.[25] Part of what makes God divine is the very ability to be punctual beyond human capabilities.

The rabbinic narratives about God's daily schedule and nightlife analyzed below also construct and deconstruct human-divine difference through imagining God's time. As demonstrated by both the texts studied by Kaye and those analyzed in this chapter, it is precisely the units that subdivide the day (watches, hours, and fleeting moments) that are regarded by rabbinic authors as most conducive for exploring the differences and similarities between divine and human time.

The Hours of Creation

A rabbinic narrative, told in different versions in Leviticus Rabbah, Pesiqta de-Rav Kahana, the Babylonian Talmud, and Pirqe de-Rabbi Eliezer, describes each hour of the sixth day of the world's creation. Leviticus Rabbah describes the hour-by-hour schedule of that day as follows (the parallel narrative in Pesiqta de-Rav Kahana is very similar):

> In the first hour, the idea [of creating a person] occurred [to God], in the second [God] took counsel with the Ministering Angels, in the third He kneaded his dust, in the fourth He shaped him, in the fifth He made him into a lifeless body, in the sixth He breathed a soul into him, in the seventh He stood him on his feet, in the eighth He brought him into the Garden of Eden, in the ninth he was commanded [against eating of the fruit of the tree of knowledge], in the tenth he transgressed, in the eleventh he was judged, in the twelfth he was pardoned.[26]

This narrative conceives of a world in which God and people share hourly, annual, cosmic, and historical time. On a narrative level, the hourly division of time breaks down the day into a series of divinely ordered activities, much like a storyboard, comic strip, or published schedule. The audience of such a story is meant to understand the various steps that were involved in the creation of the first human over the course of the twelve hours of a single day.

According to the midrash, God's acts of creation—the various steps involved in the creation of Adam, and then Adam's first few hours of life—have a timetable. In the first two hours, God contemplates the creation of humans, initially alone and then in consultation with the angels. This second-hour meeting with the angels alludes to other midrashim in which God consults the angels in an extended process of discernment about whether the creation of people would be beneficial.[27] In most of these midrashim, the angels advise God against creating people, but God ignores their advice and creates the first human anyway, an apparent one-upmanship on the part of the rabbis, who assert human superiority over the heavenly angels. In the next four hours, God slowly and carefully creates Adam's body and finally endows him with a soul. The creation and role of Eve are not mentioned in this text, nor does Eve appear in the parallel narrative in Pesiqta de-Rav Kahana. The first half of this midrash could be read as an extended exegetical interpretation of Genesis 1:26–27, focusing both on the plural language of God's creation of the first human ("let *us* make ...," which the midrash reads as an allusion to God's consultation with the angels) and then on the creation of an androgynous first human being ("and God created the person [אדם] in his image, in the image of God He created him, male and female he created them"), which could account for why the rabbinic midrash only mentions the creation of Adam and not of Eve.[28] Then the midrash outlines the remaining six hours of the day: God helps Adam stand, brings him to the Garden of Eden, commands Adam to follow certain prohibitions, watches as Adam sins, judges Adam, and ultimately forgives him, which draws on the narrative in Genesis 2–3. The entirety of a human life, from pre-birth through final judgment, occurs on the sixth day of creation.

One interesting feature of this narrative is that God is the subject in the first nine hours: God thinks about creating Adam, consults with the heavenly angels, creates Adam, places Adam in the Garden of Eden, and then commands Adam not to eat from the fruit of the tree of knowledge. Then the narrative shifts subjects so that Adam's activities are the focus of the remaining three hours: Adam transgresses, is judged, and is finally pardoned by God.

In the literary context of Leviticus Rabbah, this narrative appears as part of an interpretation of Leviticus 23:24, a verse about the festival of Rosh Hashanah. This verse details God's command to the People of Israel that they celebrate a festival with trumpet blasts: "In the seventh month, on the first day of the month, you shall observe a day of complete rest, a holy convocation commemorated with trumpet blasts."[29] While this festival, celebrated on the first day of the month of Tishre, does not have a proper name in biblical sources, it is called Rosh Hashanah in rabbinic sources. Rosh Hashanah is the start of the rabbinic calendar year.[30] This midrash teaches that Rosh Hashanah is not only the start of the calendar year but also marks the anniversary of God's creation of the first human being, and that it came to be associated as well with God's annual judgment of each living human being, even though neither of these dimensions of the festival is mentioned in biblical sources. In Pesiqta de-Rav Kahana, this midrash is embedded within a homily for Rosh Hashanah, indicating that this midrash not only explains the significance of the festival's date but could have been shared as part of synagogue services with worshippers on the festival itself.[31]

The midrash at hand adduces a prayer recited on Rosh Hashanah to explain how it is possible that God created Adam on this festival. According to this prayer, God begins creating the world on the 25th day of the month of

Elul, and therefore the sixth day of creation falls on the first day of the seventh month of Tishre.[32] Rosh Hashanah thus annually commemorates the creation of human beings on the sixth day of creation. The midrash then connects the idea that Rosh Hashanah commemorates the creation of human beings with another rabbinic tradition, namely that Rosh Hashanah is the day on which the deeds of nations and individuals are remembered and judged by God and their fate determined for the entire year ahead. Building upon these two aspects of the festival—its association both with the creation of humanity and with God's annual judgment of humanity—the midrash outlines the events of that fateful day as they occurred hour by hour: Adam was created, then sinned, was judged, and was finally forgiven. The midrash casts Rosh Hashanah as a festival on which both the creation of humanity is celebrated and the fate of humanity is established through annual judgment. Leviticus Rabbah and Pesiqta de-Rav Kahana further connect the narrative of Adam's creation with the festival of Rosh Hashanah as it was celebrated by contemporary Jews when, after explaining that God pardons Adam for his sin in the twelfth hour of the day, they state: "The Holy One, blessed be He, said to him: Adam, this is a sign for your children. Just as you came into My presence for judgment on this day and you went forth free, so too in the future your children will come into My presence for judgment on this day and go forth free. When? 'In the seventh month, in the first day of the month.'"[33]

In these two midrashic versions, God and Adam are connected through hourly time: God's actions at each hour slowly form Adam from a mere idea into a body with a soul. Then, once Adam is fully formed, Adam's transgression and God's forgiveness also unfold over the course of hours. This monumental twelve-hour day is commemorated, year after year, when Jews celebrate Rosh Hashanah as the day of the creation of the first human life as well as the day on which God judges the lives of all living human beings. The midrash implies that God and humans are intertwined from the very first hours of the creation of the first human being, extending to the annual festival of Rosh Hashanah, the day on which this midrash would have been preached as part of a holiday homily.[34] Importantly, this midrash also reimagines the sixth day of creation as a day during which God was solely occupied with the creation of Adam. In the biblical account of the sixth day of creation in Genesis 1:24–31, God first creates a series of animals and recognizes them as good creations before deciding to make a human being as well. It is also on the sixth day that God realizes that the first human needs a mate and creates Eve. This midrash makes no mention of animals or women. The focus rests exclusively on Adam's creation. All of God's time that day, as the midrash chooses to remember it, is devoted to the origins and care of humanity (or of men, depending on whether one chooses to read Adam as representative of the first man or the first human being).

A composition by the seventh-century liturgical poet Yannai also mentions the hours of the sixth day of creation, in this case not to comment on the process of God's creation of Adam but to mark the onset of the Sabbath.[35] The poet was probably familiar with the rabbinic tradition about the twelve hours of the sixth day of creation and incorporates this time frame into his poem:

> And also on the sixth day You created the human first,
> and like one of the divine beings he seemed,
> but he sinned . . . and to judgment he was brought in terror
> and in the twelfth [hour], at the setting of the sun,
> the Sabbath approached [and alleviated his guilt]
> and his sentence was determined: to work the land
> and "a hymn: a song for the Sabbath day" (Psalm 92:1)—
> and also "to give thanks" (Psalm 92:2) to the Artist
> whose works were thus perfected.[36]

Though this poem does not provide a full twelve-hour timetable, the division of the day into twelve hours is clear, and the twelfth hour, just as the Sabbath begins, is marked by God's judgment of Adam, God's subsequent forgiveness, and humanity's enduring grappling with the consequences of the day's events— to work, to celebrate, and to praise God. This poem, a *qedushta* for Genesis 1:1, recalls the creation of the world and would have been recited on the Sabbath morning when that portion of scripture was communally chanted in the synagogue or on other days when the creation of the world would have been evoked.[37] The connection to the Sabbath at the end of the sixth day within the poem makes good sense for the temporal context of the poem's performance, the Sabbath day. The poem frames the story so that the onset of the Sabbath each week—rather than once a year on the New Year—becomes a time when God forgives human sins.

Not all versions of this story contain the same set of hourly activities. Leviticus Rabbah and Pesiqta de-Rav Kahana preserve one form of the narrative, whereas the Babylonian Talmud and Pirqe de-Rabbi Eliezer contain a similar but notably distinct version of the same tradition. The former midrashic tradition is associated with the festival of Rosh Hashanah and a set of verses from Genesis, Leviticus, and Psalms. It uses the unit of hours to demonstrate the close relationship Adam enjoys with God and the latter's continual presence in the life of each human being, ensuring their welfare even when they sin. It also maps the story of human creation and human-divine partnership onto the start of the rabbinic calendar year and its New Year festival. The latter midrashic tradition is associated in the Babylonian Talmud with a broader set of rabbinic narratives about the creation of the world and of Adam and Eve. It is anchored in a different set of verses from the Genesis creation narrative, and it functions primarily as an explanation for why Adam and Eve were exiled from the Garden of Eden so quickly, mere hours after their creation. It emphasizes the irreversible damage that human sin caused to the human-divine relationship, rather than highlighting the restorative dimensions of human repentance and divine forgiveness that the other version of the narrative did so powerfully.

While human sin features prominently in the description of the sixth day of creation in all versions of this midrash, the hourly activities as well as the human-divine relationship established through these hours differ significantly in the Babylonian Talmud's version of this narrative (and in a very similar version in Pirqe de-Rabbi Eliezer and other later midrashim), which outlines the sixth day of creation as follows:

> The day consisted of twelve hours. In the first hour, his [Adam's] dust was gathered. In the second, it was made into a shapeless mass. In the third, his limbs were shaped. In the fourth, a soul was infused into him. In the fifth, he stood on his feet. In the sixth, he gave names [to the animals]. In the seventh, Eve became his mate. In the eighth, they ascended to bed as two and descended as four. In the ninth, he was commanded not to eat of the tree. In the tenth, he sinned. In the eleventh, he was judged. In the twelfth, he was expelled [from Eden] and departed.[38]

In this version Adam, rather than God, is the subject of the story throughout all twelve hours. The story presents God as a passive actor during the creation story, while the focus remains on Adam. For example, the text explains that in the first hour Adam's dust was gathered, rather than stating, as Leviticus Rabbah and Pesiqta de-Rav Kahana do, that God gathered Adam's dust. So while this source is, ostensibly, about how God spent the sixth day of creation, the story in its iteration in the Babylonian Talmud does not present God's timetable but rather a timetable of how man was created by God. A certain distance to God is assumed through this narrative choice, though God's actions are all still implied and described.

The second difference in this version of God's sixth day of creation is God's hourly tasks. Whereas the first few hours of God's formation of Adam resemble the hours in the schedule provided by the other midrashim, the Babylonian Talmud expands Adam's social orbit in the subsequent hours of the day. During the sixth hour, Adam names the animals. In the seventh, he finds his mate, Eve. In the eighth, Adam and Eve conceive two children together. That is, Adam interacts with animals, finds a spouse, and bears children, all aspects of the creation story that are not included in the versions of this midrash found in Leviticus Rabbah and Pesiqta de-Rav Kahana. The Babylonian Talmud seems to have the second creation narrative, found in Genesis 2, more centrally in mind as it reconstructs the hours of God's day to include animals, Eve, and their children, rather than focusing more narrowly on the first creation narrative in Genesis 1, which does not mention Eve.

Most importantly, the Babylonian Talmud's narrative does not end with God's forgiveness of Adam's sins. Rather, it ends on a darker and more pessimistic note, with Adam's permanent exile from the Garden of Eden and a disappointed, betrayed deity. Whereas the Palestinian midrashic versions use God's hours on the sixth day of creation to establish a positive, reciprocal, and even intimate relationship between Adam and God (through thick and thin), this Babylonian version and other versions based upon it use the story to establish difference between creator and creation, ending with Adam's dramatic exit from God's sacred garden after a sin that cannot be undone. The theological difference is highlighted not only temporally but also spatially, as Adam leaves the Garden of Eden and the distance between human and divine permanently and irreversibly increases.

These rabbinic narratives resonate with other retellings of Adam and Eve's creation, for example that found in the Syriac *Cave of Treasures*, which likewise plots the events of the sixth day of creation over the course of twelve hours.[39] In the first three hours of the day, God creates the first man and woman. The text explains that, "on the sixth day, which is the eve of the Sabbath, at the first hour of the day," when all of the angels were quiet, God declared that they should create a person in the image of God.[40] God then takes a grain of dust, a drop of water, a puff of air from the wind, and a bit of fire for warmth and, in the divine hand, forms Adam. Upon witnessing Adam's creation, Satan is horrified, jealous of the attention bestowed upon Adam, and separates from God; in the second hour, God banishes Satan from heaven. In the third hour, God creates Eve, much to Adam's delight. At the end of the third hour, God commands Adam not to eat from the forbidden food and welcomes the couple into Paradise. Adam and Eve, clothed in glory and luminosity, spend the following three hours enjoying Paradise. At midday (precisely at noon, the end of the sixth hour), they sin. The first couple thus spends three subsequent hours in a state of disgrace. At the ninth hour, God expels them from Paradise and they spend the remaining three hours of that sixth day of creation exiled. The story ends with a summary: "At the third hour of the day Adam and Eve ascended into Paradise, and for three hours they enjoyed the good things thereof; for three hours they were in shame and disgrace, and at the ninth hour their expulsion from Paradise took place."[41]

The text not only provides an hour-by-hour account of the sixth day of creation but also deliberately parallels the hours of the sixth day of creation with the twelve hours of the day of Jesus' crucifixion.[42] This theme is introduced early in the text, in a section about Adam's death. Adam passed precisely "at the ninth hour, on the day of the Eve of the Sabbath. At the same house in which the Son of Man delivered up his soul to His Father on the Cross, did our father Adam deliver up his soul to Him that fashioned him and he departed from this world."⁴³ The connection between the creation of Adam and the crucifixion of Christ appears most explicitly in the text's extended description of the passion, which retells the hourly schedule of the sixth day of creation alongside the hourly schedule of Christ's crucifixion. In the first hour, when God had fashioned Adam out of dust, Christ received spittle from the sons of Adam. In the second hour, when the animals came to Adam to be named, the Jews gathered together to plot against Christ. "At the third hour of Friday a crown of glory was placed on the head of Adam, and at the third hour of Friday the crown of thorns was placed on the head of Christ."⁴⁴ Just as Adam spent three hours in Paradise, Christ endured three hours of beatings in the Judgment Hall. At the sixth hour, when Eve ascended to the tree and gave Adam the fruit of death, Christ ascended the Cross, the Tree of Life, and the crowd offered Christ vinegar. Adam and Christ both spent three hours naked under the tree. The text then elaborates further on the parallels: "On Friday Adam and Eve sinned, and on Friday their sin was remitted; on Friday Adam and Eve died, and on Friday they came alive; on Friday death reigned over them, and on Friday they were freed from dominions," and so the long list continues.⁴⁵ The passage then describes how, in the ninth hour, Adam descends from Paradise to the depths of the earth, just as Christ descends from the Cross into the dust of the earth. The message of the text is clear: "that Christ was like unto Adam in everything."⁴⁶

The *Cave of Treasures* narrative can be read as Christ's hourly unmaking of creation time in lieu of salvation time. Whereas in the rabbinic narratives Adam is created, sins, and is redeemed (or is exiled from Paradise, depending on the particular tradition) over the course of the twelve hours on the sixth day of creation, in this text Christ, conceived as the Second Adam, suffers through all twelve hours of the day of his crucifixion in order to redeem Adam's sin. Strikingly, both events (Adam's creation and Jesus' crucifixion) are set on Fridays. The rabbinic traditions about Adam's creation found in Leviticus Rabbah and Pesiqta de-Rav Kahana could even be interpreted as arguing that there is no need for a Second Adam who redeems the sins of the First Adam—the first (and only) Adam was created, sinned, and forgiven within the twelve hours of the sixth day of creation. That redemption from sin, moreover, recurs annually on the festival of Rosh Hashanah (and, according to Yannai's piyyut, also weekly, every Friday in the final hour before the Sabbath begins) obviates the need for a later redemption by Christ.⁴⁷ The traditions in the Babylonian Talmud and Pirqe de-Rabbi Eliezer align more closely with the narrative of the *Cave of Treasures* in that both stories end with Adam and Eve's sin and expulsion. Their differences notwithstanding, these various stories all employ the cosmic and hourly time of the sixth day of creation—the day on which God spent the hours creating humanity—to reflect on the intimate yet fraught connection between divine and human, heavenly and earthly.

God's Time since Creation

The tendency to juxtapose human and divine time is true as well of accounts that imagine what God does with the seemingly infinite free time after the work of creation has been completed. Leviticus Rabbah portrays an exchange between Matrona and Rabbi Yose in which a skeptical Matrona tries to figure out what keeps God so busy during the many hours of each day:

> Matrona asked Rabbi Yose ben Halafta, saying: For how many days did the Holy One, blessed be He, create His world? He said to her: For six days, as it says "For six days God created the heavens and earth..." (Exodus 31:17). She said to him: And since then [or: from that hour until now],[48] what does God sit and do? He said to her: "He sits and creates matches, so-and-so's daughter to so-and-so, so-and-so's wife to so-and-so, so-and-so's wealth to so-and-so." She said to him: How many slaves and maidservants do I have, and easily within a single hour [בשעה אחת][49] I could match them up! He said to her: If it is easy in your eyes, it is as difficult for God as splitting the Sea of Reeds, as it says "God makes the solitary dwell in a house..." (Psalms 68:7). Rabbi Yose ben Halafta went to his home. What did [Matrona] do? She sent for and brought a thousand slaves and a thousand maidservants and she stood them in rows. She said to them: so-and-so will go with so-and-so, and so-and-so will go with so-and-so. In the morning, they came to her, this one's head disheveled (as in mourning), this one's eyes blinded, this one's arm broken, this one's leg broken. One said: I do not want this one, and another said: I do not want this one. She sent for [the rabbi] and said: Good is your Torah, beautiful and praiseworthy. He said to her: I did not tell you this, rather I said that if it is simple in your eyes it is as difficult for God as the splitting of the Sea of Reeds, as it says, "God makes the solitary to dwell in a house, He brings out the prisoners into prosperity..." (Psalms 68:7).[50]

After learning that God created the world in six days, Matrona wonders what God has been doing in all of the hours since the final day of creation. Rabbi Yose explains that God acts as a matchmaker, matching marriage partners based on family status, wealth, and other considerations, and making all sorts of other matches for the sake of social order. Matrona is dubious about God's time management. She remarks: "How many slaves and maidservants do I have, and easily within a single hour I could match them up!" Matrona's reference to hours at this point in the narrative indicates either a relatively short duration that is still long enough to complete a task (as it does in Rabban Gamliel's declaration that he would not allow even a single hour to pass without declaring his devotion to God in *m. Berakhot* 2:5, discussed in the previous chapter) or a seasonal hour, meaning a twelfth of the day. Either way, in her remark, Matrona equates the entirety of God's time (all of the hours since the world's creation, as Matrona states earlier in the story) to a single hour of her own time. To prove her case, Matrona matches up the many men and women she has enslaved with one another (the lightness with which Matrona treats the intimate needs of those she has enslaved in this narrative is troubling, and yet the power and status differential between the characters is central to the dynamics of this story). She does this task hastily, in the course of a short afternoon, perhaps even in a single hour as she had predicted, and sends them off with their new partners for the evening. In the morning, all of the couples she had created return in a severe state of marital disharmony: bruised, unhappy, and traumatized.

The narrative describes God as spending all of divine time matchmaking in heaven. The narrative might function exegetically, picking up on Genesis 2:18–21, which explains God's reasoning for creating Eve as a partner for Adam: "Then the Lord God said: 'It is not good that the man should be alone; I will make him a helper as his partner . . . but for the man there was not found a helper as his partner. So the Lord God caused a deep sleep.'"[51] All other creatures have pairs, God notes, and Adam should have one too. God as creator, that is, already functions as a matchmaker (and, indeed, matchmaking is God's final act of creation), and so it makes sense, according to the midrash's logic, that God continues in this role after the creation of the world. Other midrashim and targumim develop the theme of God as matchmaker more specifically. Genesis Rabbah 18:1, for instance, describes God adorning Eve as a bride before presenting her to Adam. Numerous sources depict God braiding the first woman's hair on the sixth day of creation, before introducing her to Adam.[52] In Genesis Rabbah 18:4, God's creation of a first wife does not work out and thus God creates a second wife, Eve, in her place. These traditions emphasize that finding an appropriate spouse takes considerable amounts of time and effort and that God is committed to this task. In the rabbinic interpretation developed in the dialogue between Matrona and Rabbi Yose, God initiates the matching of pairs among animals and eventually between Adam and Eve during the week of creation (and specifically on the sixth day of creation). Thereafter, in the time following the world's creation, God is imagined to continue this work of producing pairs by playing the permanent daily—even hourly—role of heavenly matchmaker for each and every human couple, and perhaps not only for humans but for all beings and things that require pairing. In the midrash, after all, God not only matches couples but is also responsible for other types of matches, ordering the entire cosmos and ensuring its equilibrium.

This story might also function polemically. The failed figure, Matrona, is an obvious foil to the wildly successful deity. This rabbinic dialogue could be engaging with ideas about creationism in Greco-Roman philosophical thought.⁵³ Matrona, who represents the view that the world no longer requires a deity after the world's initial creation, is controverted because her shortcomings as a matchmaker show that the universe cannot continue to exist in harmony without the direct, ongoing intervention of God during each hour of each day. The central debate here is one about the beginning of time and the eternity of the universe, and God's place within it. From the perspective of this rabbinic story, God not only still exists actively in the world, God also exists within time, on a daily and hourly basis, and God is busy with the tasks involved in maintaining cosmic harmony. Indeed, the task at hand exemplifies God's keeping order: God ordered the world during the process of creation, which entailed creating pairs of both animals and humans, and now God needs to keep it ordered by continuing the work of human matchmaking.⁵⁴ It is an exact science, like telling exact time. It is also a way of perpetuating creation through the generation of generations, because couples are often assumed in rabbinic sources to have children (though this is an idealized view of the world, as in reality couples often cannot).⁵⁵ Such matchmaking, that is, presents God as laboring in an unceasing hourly creation, necessary for the world to continue to exist.

There is an additional twist in this narrative. God's time is spent creating the conditions for human relationships—marriage, business partnerships, and so on. This narrative is preceded by an exegesis of Proverbs 19:14, "Property and riches are bequeathed by fathers, but an efficient wife comes from the Lord." This scriptural passage explains that wealth is inherited from one's father but that a wife is provided by God. Thus, this passage provides a biblical underpinning for the portrayal of God as ultimately responsible for finding a good spouse. This exegetical context frames the story as one about God's role in the marriage process as well as in the related process of wealth inheritance. Understood from this perspective, perhaps the story also engages with Christian privileging of abstinence and asceticism as the highest form of piety.⁵⁶ In some contemporary Christian texts, the metaphorical system for describing the choice of an ascetic life is that of marriage: to be a virgin is not to remain unmarried but to be "married to Christ"; a virgin becomes Christ's "bride"; and in some sources there is even mention of a wedding chamber.⁵⁷ In his correspondence to the Emperor Constantius II in the mid-fourth century, the Patriarch Athanasius of Alexandria goes so far as to suggest not only that through a state of virginity Christians achieve angelic holiness on earth but also that attaining such stature proves the truth of Christian claims over those of Jews and heretics: "Accordingly such as have attained this virtue, the Catholic Church has been accustomed to call the brides of Christ. And the heathen who see them express their admiration of them as the temples of the Christ. For indeed this holy and heavenly profession is nowhere established, but only among us Christians, and it is a very strong argument that with us is to be found the genuine and true religion."⁵⁸ To be clear, marriage itself was not portrayed as illicit or negative by Paul, Clement, Athanasius, and others—such an attitude was vehemently opposed, for example, by the heresiologists, including Irenaeus, and used in polemics against Valentinians and other so-called "heretics." Rather, virginity was a preferable choice that conferred elevated status.[59] Here, this story might subtly argue against such a lifestyle, claiming that God not only condones marriage but that, indeed, all of God's time is spent ensuring that marriages can continue in the most efficient and harmonious fashion possible.[60]

Regardless of the various possible apologetic or polemical undertones of the story (whether intended by the authors and tellers of this midrash or not), the narrative ultimately serves as a meditation on God's devotion to the well-being and reproduction of humanity. Unlike Matrona, who allots virtually no time or effort to matching up couples for marriage, God is willing to spend all the time necessary—indeed, all the hours since creation—on an activity that is wholly directed at upgrading humanity's quality of life.

This same ethos of divine care for humanity is conveyed in an alternative tradition about Matrona's question, also preserved in Leviticus Rabbah.[61] This second tradition records that Rabbi Yose ben Halafta did not tell Matrona that God spends all of God's hours making matches but rather that, ever since the world's creation, God "sits and makes ladders, by which He makes one go down and another go up."[62] Leviticus Rabbah explains that God is constantly elevating and downgrading people, probably in the context of judging them, as the midrash cites Psalm 75:8: "but it is God who executes judgment, putting down one and lifting up another." In this image, God devotes all the hours of the day to bridging the spheres of heaven and earth not only through time but also through space. This midrashic tradition, too, might implicitly connect God's time to the festival of Rosh Hashanah on which all human beings are judged.

God's Daily Schedule

The idea that God spends all or a portion of the day making matches in heaven also appears in a number of interrelated ancient Jewish sources that present a detailed schedule of God's entire day. The Palestinian targumic tradition on Deuteronomy 32:4 proposes that God spends a quarter of each day making matches in heaven.[63] Deuteronomy 32:4 states: "The Rock, his work is perfect, and all his ways are just; a faithful God, without deceit, just and upright is he." This biblical passage appears in a long chapter in the book of Deuteronomy devoted to "sin and punishment, divine favor and rejection, and . . . a description of certain qualities of God," and the Aramaic translations of this biblical chapter exhibit sophisticated theological stances.[64] In their reading of this particular passage, the targumim explicate what God's "perfect" (תמים) work entails on a daily—and even hourly—basis. The Fragment Targums, for example, explain that when Moses ascended Mount Sinai, he observed what

God does each day: "Moses the prophet said: When I ascended the mountain [of Sinai], I saw there the Lord of all the world divide the day into four parts: three hours occupied with Torah, three hours occupied with judgment, three hours providing for all the world, and three hours matching men and women [מזויג גבר לאיתתא]."[65] Similar versions appear in Targum Pseudo-Jonathan and Targum Neofiti, which recount the same schedule but flip the order of the third and fourth quarters, so that God makes matches in the third quarter and sustains the world in the fourth.[66] These varieties of God's schedule are based on the division of the day into twelve hours. Each set of three hours is then considered its own unit of time, creating four distinct segments of the day, a common organization of time mentioned frequently in both rabbinic and Roman sources. In all of the targum versions that contain God's schedule, God does the same set of four activities each day: God studies Torah, judges the world, makes matches, and provides sustenance or a livelihood for all of the world's creations. The first activity communicates the importance of Torah study: it is such a crucial task that God prioritizes it, starting each day with three hours of learning. The subsequent three activities represent care for humanity: providing food or financial resources for them, ensuring that they have companionship, and judging them.

This tradition about God's hourly schedule, preserved in the targumim, is related to the aforementioned tradition about Matrona questioning God's schedule. Though the answers differ slightly—in the Matrona story God spends all hours of the day matchmaking and in the targumim God only spends three hours each day matchmaking—it is clear that they allude to an underlying idea that a significant amount of God's time is occupied with pairing couples. In both traditions, God's ongoing matchmaking is linked with God's original pairing of Adam and Eve in the Garden of Eden.[67]

A late antique Palestinian Aramaic poem features the same divine schedule. The opening line of the poem refers to God as "Ancient of Days," establishing God as one who has existed since the beginning of time.[68] In the version of God's schedule that the poem describes, wisdom pervades the way in which God uses time: "God divides the day / wisely into four parts / for three hours God touches [i.e., engages with] the Torah / that preceded all creation / which is wisdom / that was gifted to the nation."[69] The reference to wisdom, made several times throughout the poem, likely alludes to Proverbs 8, in which God's companion Wisdom accompanies God during the period of the world's creation. The poem then describes God's three hours of judgment and three hours of providing sustenance to the inhabitants of the world, both of which are also described as being done "in wisdom."[70] The remaining focus of the poem, though, is on the time that God takes to pair up couples in marriage and the celebratory spirit with which God engages in this important task.

Though the purpose of the poem is unknown, it is reasonable to assume, as previous scholars have, based on its theme, style, tone, and rhetoric, that it could have been recited at a marriage celebration to commend a soon-to-be-wed or newlywed couple.[71] The poem describes how God makes perfect matches and how for three hours each day God binds together grooms with brides and adorns them with wedding crowns.[72] Just as God created the Torah before forming the rest of the world, so too God matches couples even before their births, when they are each in their mothers' wombs. The poem then addresses the groom directly, explaining that God weighed the man and woman to make sure that they balance each other out, creating the pair as one would a set of harmonious balances and then presenting them to the congregation. The poem continues by wishing the couple a good life ahead, that peace should dwell between them, and other blessings for good fortune, a continuous supply of wine, and a dozen sons.[73] The poem, though fragmentary, ends with a wish that the couple should mark the day with complete joy and imminent redemption, with all who have come to join them in celebration. This poem provides one example of a context in which the idea of God's daily schedule was not only discussed exegetically or polemically but also adapted for use in a ritual or liturgical context, in this case a wedding celebration.[74] The tradition that God spends hours each day matchmaking is evoked in this poem to argue that a divine bond links the celebrating couple to one another and that God will continue to watch over them in their subsequent life together. The couple is quite literally, the poem insists, a match made in heaven. This is a vivid example of the way in which God's heavenly time was imagined to have directly impacted earthly marriage on a special occasion for celebration—a wedding day.

A modified version of God's daily schedule appears in the opening pages of tractate *Avodah Zarah* in the Babylonian Talmud. Though this divine daily schedule is quite similar to the Palestinian traditions, it is embedded into a different literary context, appended to the end of a polemical story about all the nations of the world approaching God on the day of judgment at the end of time.[75] The broader homily asserts Israel's superiority over other peoples not only in the present world but also in the eschatological future. The narrative about God's time reads as follows:

> The day consists of twelve hours. During the first three [hours], the Holy One, blessed be He, sits and occupies Himself with the Torah. During the second three [hours], He sits and judges the whole world, and when He sees that the world is so guilty as to deserve destruction, He stands from the seat of Justice and sits on the seat of Mercy. During the third three [hours], He sits and feeds the whole world, from the horned buffalo to the brood of vermin. During the fourth [three hours], He sits and plays with Leviathan, as it says, "There is Leviathan, whom you formed to play there."[76]

In this text, God's day is also subdivided into four three-hour segments, but some of God's activities differ from the activities described in the targumim.

In both the Palestinian and the Babylonian texts, God spends the first quarter of the day studying Torah.[77] God's second task, judging the world, appears similar in the targumim and in the Babylonian Talmud. There is a key difference, however, inserted into the description of God's judgment. In the targumic traditions, God simply "deals with justice" or "sits in judgment." In the Babylonian Talmud, in contrast, God begins this segment of the day by sitting in the seat of judgment. The problem is that when God applies only strict justice to the world, the verdict is too harsh because, inevitably, humanity deserves to be completely eradicated (this sentiment resembles the gloomy ending to the Babylonian Talmud's account of the final hours of the sixth day of creation). Upon realizing that the world would be destroyed if justice is the only value used to judge it, God stands up, gains perspective, and considers the world through the lens of mercy. God plays "musical chairs," moving from the seat of justice and choosing the seat of mercy—a shift in perspective that allows the world to continue to exist.[78] In the Babylonian Talmud, as in the targumim, God then spends three hours feeding the creatures of the earth. Perhaps the activity of feeding all of the world's creations highlights God's supreme power.[79] Most significantly, however, whereas God creates matches between couples in all of the Palestinian targumic texts (sometimes in the third segment of the days, sometimes in the fourth) as well as in the Aramaic wedding poem, this dominant Palestinian motif is absent in the Babylonian Talmud's narrative of God's day. Instead, God spends three hours of each day laughing or playing with Leviathan (the verb used is שׂחק).[80] This last daily activity might relate to matchmaking more than appears at first glance.

Whereas the targumim anchor God's schedule to their interpretation of Deuteronomy 32:4, the Babylonian Talmud relates its conceptualization of God's time to a set of verses from Psalm 104.[81] Psalm 104:26, about the creation of Leviathan and its playing in the sea, is explicitly cited as a proof text for the role of Leviathan in God's day. A closer look at the text, however, suggests that the Psalm not only is evoked in relation to Leviathan but also offers a broader outline of God's creation of the world and how God has been spending time since then. The text from Psalms reads:

> He made the moon to mark the seasons; the sun knows its time for setting. You make darkness, and it is night, when all the animals of the forest come creeping out. The young lions roar for their prey, seeking their food from God. When the sun rises, they withdraw and lie down in their dens. People go out to their work and to their labor until evening. O Lord, how manifold are your works! In wisdom you have made them all; the earth is full of your creatures. Yonder is the sea, great and wide, creeping things innumerable are there, living things both small and great. There go the ships, and Leviathan that you formed to play in it. These all look to you to give them their food at their appropriate time

[לתת אכלם בעתו]; when you give to them, they gather it up; when you open your hand, they are filled with good things. When you hide your face, they are dismayed; when you take away their breath, they die and return to their dust. When you send forth your spirit, they are created; and you renew the face of the ground.[82]

This passage offers a biblical basis for what God does during each segment of the day: God feeds various animals, forms Leviathan to play in the waters, creates and takes away life. The text does not mention *when* God performs each activity, nor does it so neatly divide God's activities into distinct categories. The specific timing of God's acts, though, does have some basis in the proof text. The passage begins by referring to God's creation of the heavenly bodies, which "mark the seasons" along with the cycle of days. Night and day are described with the hustle and bustle of animals and people. Food is distributed "at the appropriate time." The narrative in the Babylonian Talmud assimilates these general time-related references, along with the activities the passage describes, into a daily schedule for the divine. Through a playful rereading of Psalm 104:26, in which Leviathan no longer frolics in the waters created *by* God but rather sports *with* God, the rabbinic passage also establishes Leviathan as a creature created specifically for divine play.

Why does God spend part of each day playing with Leviathan? Leviathan is associated in other ancient Jewish and rabbinic sources with the primordial past, the eschatological age, the World to Come, and the divine realm, and this narrative about God's daily schedule is embedded within a longer homily about the eschatological age.[83] This portion of God's day thus connects divine activity both with the world's creation (during which God created Leviathan, in some rabbinic traditions during the mysterious period of twilight in the transition between the sixth and seventh days, before the onset of the Sabbath when Israel is already required to cease from work but when God is permitted to continue the work of creation) and with the world's eschatological end (during which Leviathan's flesh serves as the main course of the eschatological heavenly banquet, and when Leviathan's skin will become a *sukkah*, a protective hut, for Israel).[84] God and Leviathan both find themselves in heaven during the period between the world's creation and the eschatological age. They are the only two beings without partners, and so they fill their time by keeping each other company between the beginning and the end of time.

God's playdate with Leviathan communicates God's superiority over this creature, as Debra Scoggins Ballentine notes about other biblical, Second Temple, and rabbinic Leviathan traditions: "These narrative details contribute to the texts' shared claim that Yahweh/*Theos* has universal dominion by implying the following: first, he is not threatened by any rival divine beings because he created everything, including Leviathan and Behemoth; and second, Yahweh/*Theos* has made preparations for the eschaton from the time of creation, which provides narrative proof that he controls the present."[85] Notwithstanding the assertion of God's power over Leviathan, by evoking Psalm 104, which depicts Leviathan as a plaything, the rabbinic text also presents Leviathan as God's partner. Job 40–41, too, presents Leviathan as a marvelous being created for God, interlacing the language of military conquest with that of romantic courting in its description of Leviathan (the word שחק, translated here as "to play," can have sexual connotations, as in "to frolic").[86] In the mythological background of the ancient Near East, from which the Leviathan motif derives, epic sea battles often unfolded between partner-adversaries, those simultaneously coupled and warring.[87] Perhaps unsurprisingly, Leviathan only appears in the Babylonian version of God's daily schedule, perhaps signaling long-standing local Mesopotamian traditions.[88] *B. Baba Batra* 74b preserves a tradition that God created two Leviathans, one male and one female, in language similar to the way in which God is said to create the first human as male and female:

> All that the Holy One, blessed be He, created in His world He created male and female. Even Leviathan, He created male and female, and lest they mate with one another they would have destroyed the whole world. What did the Holy One, blessed be He, do? He castrated the male and killed the female, preserving it in salt for the righteous in the future.[89]

In this passage, God destroys the female Leviathan and preserves her flesh in brine for the eschatological era, when Israel will feast on her body during the eschatological banquet. After God's slaying of the female Leviathan, a single castrated male Leviathan remains in the world. This surviving Leviathan and God are left as the only unpartnered entities in the world; the image of the two sporting together conveys the latter's dominance as well as enjoyment of the former's company. Rather than arranging human partnering during this quarter of the day, as the Palestinian traditions suggest, here God partners in play with Leviathan. The rabbinic text in *b. Avodah Zarah* 3b holds these two dimensions of Leviathan's identity—Leviathan as companion and as adversary—together in God's daily encounter with it.

The passage immediately following the description of God's daily playdate with Leviathan, however, has a rabbi objecting to the idea that God still plays or laughs with this creature. This rabbi recalls a competing rabbinic tradition that states that God has not laughed since the destruction of the temple: "Rav Aha said to Rav Nahman bar Isaac: Since the day of the destruction of the temple, there is no laughter for the Holy One, blessed be He."[90] The word שחק can mean both play and laughter, interrelated as they are. A slightly revised schedule is thus proposed to accommodate Rabbi Nahman bar Isaac's objection. The text explains that since the temple's destruction God spends the last quarter of each day instructing schoolchildren.[91] This tradition is itself based on a passage from Isaiah 28:9 that depicts God teaching children weaned from their mothers' milk. The talmudic text then asks who taught these children before the destruction of the temple and answers that either the angel Metatron did or, alternatively, God took care of this task even while the temple still stood, in addition to God's other responsibilities. Whereas God plays and laughs with Leviathan before the fall of Jerusalem, God does not play and laugh with these children after the temple's fall. Instead, God, in the role of a serious pedagogue, instructs them as their rabbi and teaches them as they grow.[92]

God's first activity of each day—the study of Torah—is absent from the Psalms passage, and it appears to be based on Palestinian rabbinic traditions unrelated to the biblical proof text (and is indeed found in targumic traditions).[93] Foregrounding Torah study comes as no surprise in a rabbinic text: God begins the day participating in the activity rabbis most esteem, a reflection of their own values, which they project onto God.[94] Immediately following this narrative, the pericope adds several passages praising those who devote their time to Torah study and outlining the punishment deserved by those who do not: "Anyone who ceases from [learning] words of the Torah and indulges in idle gossip will be fed glowing coals of juniper," "Anyone who engages in Torah at night, the Holy One, blessed be He, extends a thread of grace to him during the day," "Anyone who engages in the study of the Torah in this world, which resembles night, the Holy One, blessed be He, extends a thread of grace to him in the World to Come, which resembles the day."[95] A redactor might even have appended these passages here precisely because of their similar insistence that specific time each day be devoted to Torah study by those on earth just as it is by God in heaven.[96]

Eliyahu Rabbah, a later rabbinic midrash probably compiled in the region of Palestine, combines God's time during the creation of the world with the divine daily schedule thereafter. The midrash explains that God tells the People of Israel that God sat for 974 generations before the world's creation, and during this long period of time God expounded all of the words of the entire Torah. God then explains that "since the day when I created the world and I sat myself down on my throne of glory, a third of the day I read and study; a third of the day I mete out judgment to the whole world; and a third of the day I do charity [צדקה] and I feed and sustain the entire world and all that I created with my hands; and I only have a single hour of laughter [שחוק] each day!"[97] Unlike God's daily schedule in *b. Avodah Zarah* 3b, in this midrash, the divine day is divided into only three blocks of time. God engages in serious activities throughout the day and only manages a short time—an hour—at the end of the day for leisure. This midrash appears in a chapter devoted to the idea that a person should not waste too much time with שחוק; the midrash therefore expends much of its energy trying to define what שחוק entails. It offers different possibilities based on various biblical passages that use the terms שחק and צחק: gossip, inappropriate sexual activity, idolatrous worship, foolishness. The verb שחוק is also the word used to describe God's play or laughter with Leviathan for the last three hours of each day in *b. Avodah Zarah* 3b. In contrast to the tradition in the Babylonian Talmud, here God only laughs for a single hour (and the text does not specify that God spends that hour with Leviathan).

In this midrash, God's schedule explicitly serves a pedagogical function, modeling for people how to spend their daily hours and warning them not to waste too much time on leisure or pleasurable activities that do not have a higher or deeper purpose. The midrash ends by recounting a conversation that transpires between God and each person who has reached the end of life. God approaches each person and asks: "my son, why did you not learn from your father in heaven, who sits on his throne of glory, a third of the day he reads and studies, a third of the day he metes out judgment to the whole world, and a third of the day he engages in charity . . . and he only has a single hour of laughter [שחוק] each day?" Everyone is held accountable, in this conversation, for having applied their Torah studies to their actions or having wasted too much time on nonsensical activities.[98] God's daily schedule, the midrash explicitly argues, should be emulated in human organization and use of daily time.[99]

Other Divine Daily Activities

A number of other narratives in the Babylonian Talmud ascribe additional daily activities to God. In addition to the tradition that God spends a portion of each day playing or laughing with Leviathan, parallel passages found in *b. Sanhedrin* 105b, *b. Berakhot* 7a, and *b. Avodah Zarah* 4a explain that "God is angry every day." This opinion is based on a biblical verse, Psalm 7:11, that mentions God's daily fury: "God is a righteous judge, and a God who has indignation every day."[100] The rabbinic passage then inquires into the duration of God's wrath and answers that it lasts for only a moment each day.[101] *B. Berakhot* 7a and *b. Avodah Zarah* 4a both elaborate on this tradition by explaining that a moment (רגע) lasts for a tiny fraction of an hour—for example, "one fifty-eight thousand, eight hundred and eighty-eighth of an hour" or "one fifty-three thousand, eight hundred and forty-eighth of an hour."[102] *B. Avodah Zarah* 4b adds a second opinion about the length of a moment: "And how long does His wrath last? A moment. And how long is a moment? . . . As long as it takes to utter this word [that is, the word רגע]. And whence do we know that His wrath lasts a moment? As it is written, 'For His anger lasts a moment, His favor lasts a lifetime (Psalm 30:6).'"[103] Finally, the texts ask about the time of day when God is angry. The narratives explain that God is only angry "in the first three hours" of the day. *B. Avodah Zarah* 4b thus explains: "When is God wrathful? Abaye said: During the first three hours, when the comb of the cock is white. And is it not white at every hour? At all hours it has red streaks, but at that time there are none." *B. Berakhot* 7a expounds similarly, that God is angry sometime during the first three hours of the day, when the sun whitens the crest of the rooster and it stands on one leg. When a possible objection is raised that a rooster stands on a single leg "every hour" of the day, the objection is likewise resolved by explaining that God is only angry when there are no red streaks on the rooster's crest, which occurs only in the morning. In this set of traditions, the duration of God's anger is incredibly short, and even though God's wrath is predictable because it happens at the same time each day, its duration is so limited that humans cannot accurately anticipate when this anger will strike (that is, they have no control over God's anger). Finally, *b. Berakhot* 7a provides an explanation for why God's anger is a morning phenomenon: "At the hour when the sun shines, all of the kings of the east and the west put their crown on the ground and prostrate before the sun, immediately [God] grows angry."[104] According to this opinion, attributed to Rabbi Meir, God's momentary daily fit of anger is caused by earthly kings who worship the sun as it rises early each morning.[105] God, this tradition implies, throws a fleeting temper tantrum out of jealousy. God does so, moreover, at the very start of the day when the sun begins to rise—in fact, at precisely the time when one is permitted to begin reciting the morning Shema and morning prayers. The passage explains that God's daily prayers assist God in overcoming anger toward Israel for their transgressions and finding the mercy with which to judge them. This set of traditions, which reappears in various contexts in the Babylonian Talmud, depicts God as experiencing strong daily emotions similar to a human being but also presents divine anger as predictable, brief, and temporary.

These passages about God's anger also suggest that, despite God's rigid schedule, God remains available to respond spontaneously and in the moment to human beings. While God directs divine fury at those who do not worship correctly, God also reacts in gentler ways to those God cherishes, especially rabbinic figures. A story found in *b. Baba Metsia* 59b, known as the "Oven of Akhnai," narrates an extended debate between rabbis about an obscure purity regulation. At the end of the dramatic story—in which a tree moves, a river flows backward, a wall sways, a heavenly voice intervenes into the debate, and much interpersonal antics unfold—the Babylonian Talmud's redactor adds a follow-up: "Years later, Rabbi Nathan encountered Elijah. He [Rabbi Nathan] asked him: What did God do at this hour [שעתא]? He [Elijah] answered: He smiled and said: My children have defeated me, my children have defeated me!" At the time when this rabbinic debate ensues, God observes them from the heavens and reacts emotionally to them—in this case smiling and muttering in approval. Even as other rabbinic passages put God on a rigid schedule, this and other narratives also suggest that God is always present, keeping track of the world's inhabitants and their actions in real time, and able to intervene or comment at any hour of the day.

B. Berakhot 6a suggests that God also observes the paradigmatic positive time-bound commandment of wearing phylacteries every morning. By donning phylacteries, God marks the start of each day in the same way that rabbinic men who don phylacteries do. The parchment rolled into God's phylacteries, however, does not contain words of divine praise (the Shema, Deuteronomy 6:4), as Israel's do. They articulate, instead, God's love of Israel by quoting 1 Chronicles 17:21, "Who is like your people Israel, one nation on the earth whom God went to redeem to be his people."[106] Through these matching biblical verses, the narrative explains that while Israel's phylacteries express devotion to God, God's phylacteries reply with enthusiastic affirmations of God's devotion to Israel. This description of God's morning ritual (the quintessential positive time-bound commandment), alongside God's other daily activities, further cultivates a sense of divine-human reciprocity and focalizes God's care for humans—and for Israel in particular.[107] It also emphasizes, as so many sources do, that when God serves as an exemplar, it is primarily for rabbinic men, rather than for everyone.

Beyond the rabbinic corpus, God's participation in thrice-daily prayers appears in the mystical text Hekhalot Rabbati, a source roughly contemporaneous with the composition of the Babylonian Talmud and from the same geographical region.[108] In this text, God descends from the upper heaven to the seventh heaven three times each day as humans pray to God and as angels "recite hymns, play musical instruments, and dance."[109] Rather than receiving daily sacrifices in the temple, God accepts daily prayers as they are recited in heaven and on earth. Hekhalot Rabbati imagines God's time to be synchronized with both angelic and human prayer times. But God also prioritizes human prayer over angelic prayer in the way that God structures the day. The text explains that "each day, when dawn appears, the ministering angels request to recite songs. At first they surround the throne of glory like mountains ... the majestic King sits and blesses the Hayyot."[110] God blesses the heavenly beasts with these words: "May that hour [שעה] when I created you be blessed, may the planet under which I formed you be exalted, may the light of that day in which you occurred to the thoughts of My heart, shine."[111] At first, it seems as though God begins the day—at the hour of dawn, as the text emphasizes—by praising the heavenly beings. But then the text takes a surprising turn. God asks the heavenly creatures to quiet down so that God can listen to the prayers of God's children: "Be silent before Me, all creatures that I have made, that I may listen to the voice of the prayer of My children."[112] As Ithamar Gruenwald explains: "when the heavenly beings say their morning blessings, God asks them to be silent so as to enable Him to listen first to the prayers of His 'sons,' the People of Israel."[113] God listens first to humans praying and then pays attention to angelic prayer.

God's Nightlife

Whereas God's daily schedule accentuates God's connection to and care of the world and its inhabitants, God's nightly schedule more emphatically underscores divine difference, for, according to most sources, only created beings need sleep, whereas God does not—and therefore God needs to both stay busy and mark time in the heavens during the night (killing and keeping time, as it were) while those on earth get their rest.[114]

After describing God's daily schedule, the narrative in *b. Avodah Zarah* 3b turns to God's nightlife and offers a few alternatives for how God spends the evening hours.

> And at night, what does He do? If you like you may say, the kind of thing He does by day. Or if you like you may say that He rides a light cherub and floats and passes in the eighteen thousand worlds He created, as is written, "The chariots of God are myriads . . ." (Psalm 68:18) . . . Or if you like you may say that He sits and listens to singing from the mouths of the Hayyot, as is written, "By day the Lord will command His lovingkindness and at night a song shall be with me" (Psalm 42:9).

This passage is remarkably different in tone from the description of God's daytime that immediately precedes it in the text, for whereas the text presents with certainty God's daily schedule, it leaves ambiguous God's night by using more tentative language: God either travels through the heavens with a company of angels, enjoys a heavenly concert, or simply performs the same daytime tasks in an infinite loop. Such tentativeness adds an element of mystery about God's whereabouts and activities during the darkened hours. There are aspects of God's time, this passage implies, that remain unknown. Moreover, it places the angels, liminal beings, in the liminal time of night.

In antiquity and the medieval period, nighttime was not reserved exclusively for sleep. Nocturnal activities, especially prayer, worship, study, meditation, and reflection, were common, both because stars and planets made for an awe-inspiring celestial scene and because of the nighttime's silence.[115] Jeremy Penner, in an article about nighttime worship at Qumran, writes that, in a world without inexpensive artificial lighting, "the experiences with day and night stood in much greater contrast, as did the differences in the rhythms of work and sleep and the types of activities associated with daytime and nighttime. . . . Night was . . . a significant period of time for the religious person. . . . Human sleeping patterns helped foster an active nocturnal culture . . . nighttime was not just a hiatus from daily life, but rather an important part of it."[116] Sleeping patterns, as natural as they seem today, are culturally specific; in many ancient societies, nighttime sleep occurred in two periods, the first at the beginning of the evening (first sleep) and then later before the morning hours (second sleep).[117] In between, there was a period of time during which certain activities were performed. Whatever the specific rhythms of the night during this historical period and region and within rabbinic communities, God's active nightlife seems to have been imagined as corresponding to the kinds of practices associated with the darkened hours across the ancient Mediterranean world, including the connection between the night's starry sky and the heavenly angels in God's retinue. Additionally, the idea that God spends the nights singing and worshipping with the angels in the heavenly realm in "eighteen thousand worlds" resonates with other texts as well, including those in mystical traditions discussed earlier. They imagine God to reserve the evenings for the angels, leaving a free schedule with which to engage with humans during the day when they are awake.[118]

Synchronizing Heavenly and Earthly Time

Another narrative about God's nightly time-keeping appears within the Babylonian Talmud's discussion of the proper times for the recitation of the Shema prayer. The Mishnah states that the nighttime Shema may be recited anytime starting from the onset of dusk until the end of the first nighttime watch.[119] The later editors of the Babylonian Talmud were puzzled about why the Mishnah chooses to indicate the time of night by referencing nightly watches instead of hours (that is, why does it say "until the end of the first watch" rather than "until the third or fourth hour?") and subsequently wondered whether the night is divided into three or four watches (that is, is the night divided into three blocks of time, each of them four hours in length, or four blocks of time, each of them three hours in length?).[120] These are both technical questions about time-keeping as it relates to the performance of the ritual of the Shema. The anonymous voice of the Talmud responds to this practical halakhic question about ritual timing with a theologically inflected answer: "to teach us that there are watches in heaven as well as on earth."[121] The passage continues:

> The night has three watches, and at each watch the Holy One, blessed be He, sits and roars like a lion, as is written, "The Lord will roar [ישאג] from on high, and from His holy habitation utter His voice; he will roar mightily [שאג ישאג] against his fold" (Jeremiah 25:30).

Rather than providing a straightforward technical explanation for the division of the night into three units of time, the Talmud presents Rabbi Eliezer's opinion in vivid theological terms: the specific time-marker "watches" alludes to the idea that heavenly and earthly times are synchronized. Because the term "roar" (שאג) is used three times in Jeremiah 25:30, the Babylonian Talmud concludes that there are three nightly watches and that God marks the passage of each of these watches by roaring. One textual hook for Rabbi Eliezer's connection between this verse from Jeremiah and the recitation of the Shema might be the appearance of the phrase "these words [הדברים האלה]" in both

Jeremiah 25:30 and Deuteronomy 6:6, the biblical commandment upon which the Shema prayer is based. God's roars serve as time-markers signaling the transition between nightly watches, helpful for determining the correct ritual timing for the Shema prayer—for the recitation of "these words."[122]

The rabbinic passage continues by describing the details of this synchronization: when God roars, God's divine cries reverberate on earth as animal and human sounds: "The sign of the thing is: at the first watch, the donkey brays; at the second, the dogs bark; at the third, the child nurses from the breasts of his mother, and the woman talks with her husband."[123] As soon as the woman speaks, the man knows that it is the end of the third watch and therefore time for him to rise and recite the morning Shema, which can be recited as soon as the morning begins. Benovitz has argued that in the earliest strata of this passage, the animals represented constellations—Ursa Major, Hercules next to Ophiuchus, and Cassiopeia with Cepheus and Andromeda—and that the position of these constellations in the sky determined particular times of night.[124] By the period of the Babylonian Talmud's redaction, however, this original meaning seems to have been forgotten and the passage was understood more literally, as God roaring in heaven and God's cries reverberating on earth.

The text then raises a possible objection. Why would there need to be a heavenly sign for the end of the third watch, given that the dawn's rising sun already makes the transition between night and day obvious? The passage thus explains that it may be useful for determining the correct time for the morning recitation of the Shema "for a man who sleeps in a dark room and does not know when the time for the recitation arrives. When the woman talks with her husband and the child sucks from the breast of the mother, let him rise and recite [the Shema]."[125] In a dark room, where the sun does not shine, the baby's cries (which channel God's third heavenly roar) cause a ripple of events that concludes with the father's recitation of the morning Shema at its proper time.

This passage contains a cultural observation about the relationship between different kinds of heavenly and earthly times, as well as the ways in which various members of a community are portrayed as relating *differently* to the *same* time. On the one hand, God's time in heaven is completely in sync with the time of those who dwell on earth: the animals, children, women, and men. On the other hand, the synchronization is hardly straightforward. While each act of marking time is animated by all parties, through roaring, crying, nursing, and praying, morning-time itself entails a different set of rituals and signifies something distinct for each party involved. The woman marks her time by nursing and speaking, which are acts directed toward her family—her child, who feeds, and her husband, who listens. The man, upon hearing his wife's voice, realizes that morning has arrived and marks the first moment of the day by directing his actions to God, through rising up and reciting the words of the Shema, "Hear O Israel, the Lord our God the Lord is One," a declaration of faith in God and an articulation of devotion and love for God and God's commandments. More specifically, this text highlights the different ways that men, women, and children are described as marking their morning hours—it was only the men for whom the early signs of morning signaled the time to rise and praise God through the Shema. For the woman in this narrative, the morning was associated with the act of feeding a child and relating to her husband. For the child, the morning signaled the sensation of hunger and a desire for affection. The narrative stresses the contrast between God's time, men's time, women's time, children's time, and animal time (and others stress angelic time as well). These different entities each follow their own schedules and rituals. Indeed, the set of morning rituals each group performs constructs and defines their difference.

Divine and human temporal rituals and the time-markers around which they are anchored, then, were not only or even primarily functional. Rabbi Eliezer could just as easily have said "until four hours" rather than "until the end of the first watch" if he wanted to convey practical information about the Shema's timing. Instead, for the rabbinic authors of this passage, who try to decipher their predecessor's words, the time-marker "watches" deliberately evokes God and heavenly time. With the recitation of the Shema, the text comes full circle, back to God, who was the first to mark the moment. That it is God who marks the proper time to say the Shema in heaven is significant for the rabbis' understanding of the ways in which their liturgical time on earth relates to God's divine time in heaven.

One common feature of the two narratives in the Babylonian Talmud about God's nightly time is the merging of human and animal time in the earthly realm (men, women, children, donkeys, dogs, animals, buffalo, vermin) and the merging of God's time with that of other heavenly beings, including Leviathan, Metatron, the nighttime angels, and the Hayyot of the divine throne. The prominence of animals and angels in these narratives serves as a reminder of other forms of time and difference, such as human-animal and human-angelic difference, likewise important for understanding the use of time in rabbinic constructions of yet other forms of difference.[126] Perhaps these texts connect God so frequently to animals in these contexts because animals have a highly developed and surprisingly accurate sense of time. References to animals in these narratives also gesture toward the idea of the unity of cosmic time: God, the heavenly bodies, the angels, humans, and animals are all ultimately synchronized. This narrative insists that God, babies, women, and men all mark the same time for the recitation of the morning Shema in different ways. The answer to the opening words of the Mishnah—מאמתי, "from what time?" (the very passage with which this book began)—amplifies immeasurably when the full range of beings is considered.

God on Human Time, Humans on Divine Time

The texts analyzed in this chapter present God in strikingly anthropomorphic terms.[127] Over the course of the day, God studies, sits, worships, weeps, plays, cares for others, and engages in other activities performed by people. But even when God partakes in these seemingly human tasks, such activities stand in contrast to the activities of humans. Humans are able to match up couples for marriage, but only God does so with a perfect track record and on a mass scale. When God sits, it is in order to enact judgments on the world's inhabitants; when God plays, it is during God's daily playdate with Leviathan; when God worships, God does so in the heavenly sphere alongside the angels. That is not to say, however, that God's daily activities completely separate God from humanity. On the contrary: God spends each day's hours fulfilling tasks that affect humanity in direct and tangible ways, such as matrimonial interventions. Moreover, and equally important, God devotes time to looking after all of the world's creatures. The tasks that fill each hour of God's day insist on both similarity and difference.

Biblical and rabbinic sources describe God's body (image, hand, and finger of God), emotions (anger, mourning), and activities (creating, studying, feeding, judging, playing). In rabbinic narratives, however, God's very temporality is detailed in anthropomorphic terms. Perhaps imagining God in anthropomorphic fashion necessitated that God also be bound to a schedule or a structure of time just as humans are. After all, attempts to reconcile the tension between the nature of God's human form and God's incorruptibility (that is, the idea that God does not change and is therefore timeless) occupied church authorities and erupted in multiple theological controversies among Christian communities and figures in this very period.[128] Yet even while God is anthropomorphized to the point that the divine schedule resembles that of human beings in rabbinic sources, God is presented in these sources as more temporally precise than them.[129] And, unlike human beings, God wastes no time. Additionally, God has the power to add or remove hours to a day and is conceived as a divine being whose time is exponentially more expansive than human time. Several rabbinic sources engage, for example, with Psalm 90:4, "For a thousand years in your sight are like yesterday when it is past, or like a watch in the night."[130] Likewise, Pirqe de-Rabbi Eliezer 48 compares the Israelites' long enslavement in Egypt as a mere hour of God's day (שעה אחת מיומו של הקב״ה), and Pirqe de-Rabbi Eliezer 28:8 mentions that "the reign of the four kingdoms is but a day of all of God's days"—in both cases, the midrash emphasizes that Israel's seemingly long travails represent an almost insignificantly short amount of time for God.[131] Furthermore, God is depicted as a multitasker not bound by the limits of time in the way that humans are. Midrash Psalms and Exodus Rabbah make this point explicitly:

> Come and see that the ways of the Holy One, blessed be He, are not those of men. A mortal king cannot wage war and be a scribe and a teacher of little children, but God can [do all these things]. On the sea yesterday, [God] was like one waging war ... and today, at revelation, [God] descended to teach His children Torah.[132]

This midrash, part of the late antique collection of Tanhuma Yelamdenu traditions compiled within Exodus Rabbah, exegetically connects biblical passages about God's splitting of the sea and revelation at Sinai to explain that God can easily switch gears in a short span of time.[133] God can wage war and instruct humanity almost simultaneously. God's temporal flexibility and ability even to preempt human actions, another theme developed in rabbinic sources, captures the sentiment of Isaiah 65:24, "Before they call, I will answer; while they are yet speaking, I will hear."[134] All of the sources discussed in this chapter also take for granted that God does not sleep, even as some of them acknowledge that God rests on the Sabbath.[135]

A tradition in Pesiqta de-Rav Kahana highlights how tied God's divinity is to the divine use of time, and also points to its limits. The midrash explains that one of the roles of God's adversary (אנטידיקוס) is to disrupt the divine schedule. The adversary explains: "God's custom of ordering the world [מנהג סידורו של עולם] consists of twelve hours in the day and twelve hours at night, twelve months, twelve zodiacal signs, twelve tribes—I am able to cancel God's custom of ordering the world."[136] The phrase מנהג סידורו של עולם plays around with the multivalent meaning of the word עולם, which refers to God, the world, and eternity simultaneously. God has ordered the world and time—the division of daily and nightly time into twelve hours, the division of the year into twelve months, the division of Israel into twelve tribes—and the only entity that can overpower God is God's adversary. In fact, this entity's power consists precisely of the ability to disrupt God's ordering of hourly, yearly, and generational time.

Throughout these rabbinic sources, then, God remains temporally similar to and yet still temporally distinct from humans. Regarding narratives about God in rabbinic sources, Dov Weiss notes: "Assuming a humanlike body and emotions, the rabbinic God was not understood to be an unapproachable being, but a relational character who participates as a member in society, albeit a privileged one."[137] This observation aptly describes rabbinic sources about God's time as well and points to one of their functions, namely, to intimately connect humans with God while still maintaining God's difference from humanity. The texts about God's daily time also remain ambiguous about whether, in projecting human time and human activities onto God, they intend to suggest that God acts like humans, or whether humans—and rabbis in particular—act more like God.

In rabbinic narratives about God's schedule, God cares for human needs and empathizes with human loss, even when it appears as though God is absent at times of need or despite the fact that God also sometimes judges humans harshly. This theme appears in wide-ranging sources from both Palestine and Babylonia. There are a few activities during God's day, however, that mirror more closely human activities without a divine dimension that sets God categorically apart. While God's daily hours are devoted to maintaining cosmic order for all of the world's inhabitants regardless of differences among them, the only daily activities in which God participates alongside humans are those that are particular to Israel.[138] That is, God reserves key moments of each day for expressing devotion and appreciation for the People of Israel by performing the time-bound commandments of Torah study and donning phylacteries, incumbent (only) upon rabbinic men. It is during these times of day when God is imagined not only as a caretaker of the world but as empathetically mirroring or even participating in the daily activities of the People of Israel. Subtle regional and chronological trends emerge regarding these particular sources in which God acts as Israel does. Both Palestinian and Babylonian sources discuss God's daily study of Torah, highlighting the centrality of Torah study for the rabbis such that they consistently imagine God to begin each day with this activity. But whereas Palestinian sources about God's time tend to play up divine singularity, the Babylonian Talmud stresses God's human qualities and, through God's daily schedule, God's deep connection to the People of Israel, their past, and their daily rituals.[139] Not coincidentally, it is only in Babylonian sources that God spends time each night and day signaling the correct time for the recitation of the Shema and donning phylacteries that explicitly declare God's love for Israel. In these texts in particular, God not only organizes time into schedules of hours and watches but also spends these hours in ways that are similar to those of, and that express deep empathy for, God's people.

There are two narratives from the Babylonian Talmud in which the destruction of the temple plays a central role in God's daily and nightly schedule. They each describe God mourning the loss of Jerusalem at key moments of the day and night. In *b. Avodah Zarah* 3b, God no longer plays with Leviathan because God abstains from such joyous activities when the temple no longer stands. In *b. Berakhot* 3a, God's nightly roaring expresses God's anguished mourning over the temple's destruction: "The night has three watches and at each watch the Holy One, blessed be He, sits and roars like a lion . . . and says, 'Woe to me, that I destroyed my house and burnt my sanctuary and exiled my children among the nations of the world.'"[140] In this passage, attributed to Rabbi Isaac ben Samuel, God's roars are roars of mourning. The narrative cites Jeremiah 25:3 as the textual basis for God's three nightly roars.[141] In Jeremiah, however, God's roars are signs of anger toward and victory over the nations of the world, while in the rabbinic account God's roars transform into signs of divine pain over the defeat of Israel.[142] It is in such rabbinic sources that God's time is regularly marked by mourning and suffering. God's bitter cries in this passage stand in contrast to other rabbinic portrayals of God's silence in the face of destruction, in which silence is presented as a dimension of God's stoic strength.[143] The cries also juxtapose the silence of the night, echoing loudly.[144] God's silence becomes a sign of divine status, whereas God's suffering roars signal God's concern for and empathy with the People of Israel.

The topic of how God spends daily time gained new meaning when the destruction of the temple recaptured rabbinic imagination in the later amoraic and post-amoraic periods.[145] These later rabbis ask not only about God's *whereabouts* but also about God's *whenabouts* during this period without a temple. Where was God during the time of destruction? Where is God now? During the times of the temple, God was occupied with daily sacrifices and matters related to the temple cult, and before then, with creation. But what has God been doing to keep busy in the post-temple era? What is God's daily and nightly schedule now that divine time is no longer anchored in the rhythms of temple rituals? Without a temple, has God deserted Israel or does God keep busy caring for them on a daily basis? According to these two Babylonian rabbinic traditions, God spends at least part of each day and night mourning the loss of the temple.[146] In fact, at night, God marks time with divine cries. The contours of God's time are thus replete with divine mourning of the temple, destroyed so many centuries before. These particular narratives bring the reader full circle, back to the opening lines of the Mishnah that discuss the timing of the daily recitation of the Shema (marked first and foremost by "the time when the priests return to eat their *terumah* offering") and to the temporal void left by the destruction of the temple, which God fills with weeping. That these traditions appear in the Babylonian Talmud might also suggest that they participate in a long Babylonian Jewish exilic literary tradition, exemplified in texts such as Psalm 137, in which the trope of mourning for a destroyed city played a central role in constructing exilic identity and subjectivity, and in turn captures, in the rabbinic narratives, a sense of exilic time as well.

In addition to using time to construct human-divine similarity or divine exceptionalism, some rabbinic sources also suggest that to use one's time well is a way of getting closer *to* God as well as a strategy to become more divine. And in rabbinic sources, to use one's time well is, first and foremost, to devote one's time to the study of Torah. This sentiment is already found in the Mishnah, for example in a passage from tractate *Avot* that declares "if two sit together and no words of Torah [are exchanged] between them, there is the seat of the scornful . . . but if two sit together and occupy themselves with words of Torah, the Divine Presence rests between them."[147] It is embedded into the idea of "wasting the study house [ביטול בית המדרש]" and "wasting Torah [ביטול תורה]," defined as not devoting all possible time to Torah study—which therefore becomes synonymous with the later phrase "wasting time [ביטול זמן]."[148] The Babylonian Talmud quotes God as saying, "Better to me one day that you engage in Torah before me than one thousand sacrifices," communicating a clear preference for the study of Torah as a mechanism for human engagement with the divine over the sacrifices of old.[149] Another passage provides a study schedule for each day of a person's life to ensure that the proper subjects are covered: a third of the day ought to be spent studying *torah*, a third *mishnah*, and a third *talmud*.[150] The discussion also encompasses existential reckoning with the uncertainty of how much time one has to live: because people do not know how long they will live, each day's hours (rather than each day of the week, month of the year, or period of years) must be devoted to studying the correct proportion of subjects. One popular refrain in the redactorial layer of the Babylonian Talmud launches a critique against those who do not spend all of their time studying Torah; about these people it is said that "they forsake eternal life [lit. life of the world or life of the eternal] and busy themselves with temporal life [lit. life of the hour]."[151] In this formulation, the notion of eternal life is expressed with the word עולם, which denotes an expansive eternity in rabbinic sources as well as a notion of an eternal future and is associated with Torah study.[152] Eternal life is juxtaposed with temporary life, constructed as a more presentist notion of short-term duration with the word for "hour" (שעה), and is associated with activities other than Torah study (though rabbinic sources do not univocally condemn all other activities). These passages and many others similar to them argue that one's time is best spent studying God's Torah. The exercise of inquiring into God's time, outlining God's schedule, and determining God's daily activities through rabbinic Torah study thus becomes, itself, a way of getting closer to God. Using one's time as carefully as does God—which first entails determining God's schedule through careful exegesis of biblical sources and the examination of rabbinic traditions about God's time—is thus a way of bridging divine-human difference and becoming more similar to God. Nonetheless, there are certain aspects of Torah study that rabbinic sources limit or prohibit—for example, study of the creation of the world—precisely because they access too closely God's time and thus reveal too many secrets reserved for God and for those rabbinic authorities with sufficient knowledge to merit such intimate knowledge of the divine sphere.[153]

Conclusions

The set of stories analyzed in this chapter is playful and quirky and seems, at first glance, to address a niche topic. But below this whimsical surface lies surprising insight about the deepest of questions. Each narrative provides a theological portrait of God in time, in turn constructing, deconstructing, and complicating human-divine difference through detailing God's hours, watches, days, and nights. The question of what God does all day captures, fundamentally, a curiosity and concern about how the world operates: Is there a divinity keeping order and watching out for the world? It is a question about the world as much as, or even more than, about God. Strikingly, God spends each day's hours fulfilling tasks that affect the world and its inhabitants in direct and tangible ways.

Rabbinic narratives, as this chapter has argued, associate God particularly with hourly time. Doing so might have emphasized not only God's punctuality but also God's power and sovereignty. Within a Roman context, hourly time-keeping could function as a demonstration of Roman imperialism. Augustus erected a large monument, the Horologium Augusti, in the Campus Martius near his Mausoleum.[154] This monument associated the emperor with the idea not only of time-keeping in a general sense but of hourly time-keeping in particular. It contained a dedicatory inscription that began by declaring Augustus "Emperor Caesar, son of a *divus* [a god]."[155] Moreover, this time-keeping monument featured one pair of obelisks brought from Egypt; these obelisks signaled the recent defeat of Egypt and the imperialist and expansionist dimensions of Roman rule and Roman time (the inscription upon the Horologium obelisk makes this clear: "Egypt having been brought into the power of the Roman people, [Augustus] gave this gift to the sun").[156] Hours themselves had originated in ancient Egypt and there had been a long and vibrant local Egyptian tradition of hourly time-keeping before they became more widely used during the early Roman imperial era, as a direct result of Roman temporal colonization and imperialism. Notably, Roman emperors carefully fashioned themselves as accurate hourly time-keepers. Some emperors, including Augustus, time-stamped their correspondences to the hour, which was not a widespread practice beyond imperial military and postal records.[157] Suetonius, for example, recounts that not only did Augustus sign his dispatches and private letters with two seals (that of a sphinx as well as his own seal) but he also "always attached to all letters the exact hour, not only of the day, but even of the night, to indicate precisely when they were written."[158] Displaying access to technological tools and knowledge to mark time in this way projected elite status, power, and even divinity.[159] A sundial in Aphrodisias, too, honors the emperor Caracalla and his mother, Julia Domna, and another sundial, in Puteoli, was dedicated by an emperor (though certainly many sundials did not reference the emperor).[160] Galen, the second-century Roman physician, likewise appealed rhetorically to precise hourly time-keeping in his self-presentation as a sophisticated and expert doctor ahead of his time.[161] Others have argued that the earliest and crudest sundials were so inaccurate as to not be useful for coordinating human events and that they might have instead been used for divinatory practices because divinatory, apotropaic, and magical texts and artifacts often mention hours.[162] Rabbinic texts that describe God's time according to an hourly schedule might be engaging in a similar rhetorical move, associating hourly time-keeping with supreme power, expert knowledge, and divinatory and divine capabilities.

A focus on God's time down to the hour might also help further to contextualize the rabbinic preoccupation with determining precise times for prayer and other rituals. The opening lines of the Mishnah publicize that the evening Shema can be recited starting "at the hour" when the priests return home to eat the *terumah* offering, while other tannaitic sources suggest that it is at different "hours" of the evening when the Shema can be recited. Likewise, the latest time for the recitation of the morning Shema is capped at "the third hour." To be sure, additional time-markers are used in the Mishnah's discussion of the Shema, but it is notable that the unit of hours appears several times. Determining the correct hours for the recitation of the Shema—as well as for the periods of time for morning, afternoon, and evening daily prayers—was important precisely because of the desire to synchronize Israel's prayer times with God's times and, eventually, with God's well-known daily schedule. Rabbinic authors were worried about timing their rituals correctly not only because hours were a relatively new way of dividing time but also because they imagined God to be on a tight schedule. In addition, they regarded time as a mechanism through which to connect with God and to encourage continued divine attention in present times.

Rabbinic traditions about God's daily schedule advance a jolly, positive portrayal of divine time: God uses the day's hours to study like a learned rabbi, work as a successful matchmaker, traverse the heavens in song, and spend down time with a lonely fish. Such images stand in contrast to sources that associate divine time with discord and violence. In the Second Temple period, fierce calendar disputes, aimed at properly legislating and ritualizing the calendar in an attempt to synchronize human with heavenly time, ultimately tore communities into rival sects, and expectations of eschatological times and efforts to bring about time's end led to political movements and ideologies that ended in deadly, destructive wars. In contrast, the rabbinic narratives about God's time studied in this chapter calm and deactivate the fear of divine time as a political force by trivializing it and domesticating it: they offer an alternative perspective on divine time by associating God not with cosmic or eschatological time, with its attendant potential for inter- and intrapolitical conflicts, but with daily hours and thoroughly humane activities. Through these divine hours, the rabbis construct a different God, who cares for their well-being in each hour of the ongoing present and whose time—quotidian though it might be (and as Matrona naively assumes)—generally cultivates confidence in the present rather than fear of the future.

In rabbinic texts, God is anything but timeless. While rabbinic literature is often viewed as short on theological contemplation, when rabbinic texts did address the topic of God, they imagined their God in time. In fact, they portrayed God as having a daily and nightly routine and schedule defined by time as the rabbis knew it. Insofar as time distinguished God from humans, it was not because God existed free of time and timely concerns. Rather, the difference was that God was uniquely expert at telling the time and at using time. Extremely long periods of time (a thousand years) and periods of exceptionally short durations (such as a fleeting moment) are associated with God. Moreover, points in time—such as the silent passage between weekly profane time and the holiness of the Sabbath day, the exact time of midnight, or the mysterious moment of God's daily fit of fury—are only known by God. Furthermore, throughout rabbinic narratives, the unit of the hour is especially associated with God and God's time. The hourly division of daily time was not only a human temporal institution mapped onto the sun's daily natural path across the sky; it was a human institution that rabbinic sources assumed God could keep even more accurately than humans. It is thus the unit of time that epitomizes the intersection between human and divine. Linking God with hourly time also implied that not a single hour of God's time was wasted. If humans, in the time of the rabbis, had difficulty differentiating hours, God, in these rabbinic stories, had no trouble knowing the hour and using it well. If humans struggled with how to manage their time, God had figured out how to allot enough time to keep everyone fed, coupled, judged—and even forgiven. When needed, God could add hours to the day or expand the day to encompass a thousand years. At certain times, God even partook in the same daily activities as the rabbis. Time, in this way, united God with people and especially with the People of Israel; both existed on the same clock or sundial, as it were. God's clock, though, was more precise than that of humanity. God, after all, sat at the center of their synagogues, regulating annual, weekly, daily, and hourly time. The gnomon on God's sundial cast an exacting shadow at all hours of the day, while people most often needed to be satisfied with the imprecise shadow cast by the rays of the sun on earth and guess the time of day, imperfectly synchronizing their earthly time with that of God in heaven.

CONCLUSION

Temporal Legacies: What Difference Does Time Make?

RABBINIC SOURCES WERE PRODUCED BY ancient rabbis, whose voices and views are generally those articulated in the texts. That means that the texts analyzed in this book shed light on the perspectives of individuals who possessed—or those who perceived themselves as holding—various forms of communal authority. By conceptualizing and organizing time as they did, the rabbis also constructed inter- and intracommunal difference. Much like contemporaneous bishops, governors, military officials, and other figures who sought to exert power and influence over others, rabbis used their authority, including in matters of time-keeping, to impose boundaries between and thus forge identities within their (imagined) communities. Other ancient materials (e.g., inscriptions and graffiti on tombs and structures, letters and documentary sources on papyri and ostraca), produced by non-elites or by those who did not regard it as their role to order society or instruct others, remind us that many people in antiquity did not abide, in their lived lives, by the boundaries imposed by others. It was *because* so many Jews saw no problem celebrating Roman festivals (indeed, many probably happily did so), *because* some Christians joined Jews for Sabbath services, and *because* various Romans found the seven-day week a compelling way of organizing time that rabbis, bishops, and others insisted on temporal differences. Were this book to have analyzed the sources produced by such people, different dimensions of time-keeping would surely have emerged. The sources studied in this book were not composed by those border-crossers or by those who perceived no boundary in the first place. The texts analyzed here are rather those that were composed by the community of scholars who insisted on those boundaries—and their conceptions of time reflect, and are in fact part of, their broader efforts of community definition and boundary formation.

The main argument of this book has been that the conceptualization and legislation of time played significant discursive roles in rabbinic constructions and deconstructions of various forms of difference. Each chapter centered on the marking of annual, weekly, daily, or hourly times and on the ways that rabbinic laws and narratives created timescapes that both ordered and signified time, and that functioned to differentiate rabbinic from imperial subjects, Jews from Christians, men from women, and humans from God.

In her work on space and the construction of gendered, religious, and ethnic difference in rabbinic Judaism, Cynthia Baker writes:

> The built environment indeed participates in the creation, transmission, and contestation of knowledge about relation and difference. Yet rarely is such knowledge, and the power formations of which it is a part, encountered in the form of brute force or overt repression. . . . Instead, space becomes a part of subject and group identity in a far more subtle and pervasive fashion. Rather than locked doors, shuttered windows, and steadfast lines of demarcation . . . we are met in ancient Judaism with constructions of "womanhood" deeply embedded in the sociospatial discourses and practices of housing, dwelling, marriage, sexual purity and visibility/invisibility, while equally embodied in the discourses of the marketplace, of commercial interests and proprietary claims, of political accommodation and resistance . . . gender distinctions bear no simple correspondence to spaces or spatial practices, but rather manifest a range of locational possibilities. Furthermore, the spatialization of gender is hardly ever a matter of prohibition from, or admission to, particular spaces, but is instead carried out in terms of disciplines of the body associated with movement through, and occupation of, diverse spaces.[1]

Baker highlights the spatial discourses and practices in ancient Jewish sources that construct difference—rarely explicitly or forcefully but rather subtly, masking almost completely their own constructedness. By calling attention to the role that space plays in constructions of difference, however, Baker uncovers the architecture of those very constructions. The present book has pivoted, in turn, on the temporal discourses and practices that likewise permeate the rabbinic corpus and that constructed various forms of difference. As in Baker's study of space, these conceptions of time and constructions of difference are often woven delicately into the sources, creating timescapes that appear natural when they are not. This study has demonstrated how discourses of time within rabbinic sources can be analyzed, as discourses of space can be, to uncover the values and commitments that undergird and motivate them.

The various temporally constructed differences identified in this book are intertwined and bound together. Rabbinic-Roman difference was constructed not only through laws regarding the annual festival calendar but also through the deliberate abstention from work on the weekly Sabbath (and more generally the organization of time into weeks rather than nundinal cycles) and the daily acceptance of God's kingdom over that of any other ruling powers through the recitation of the Shema. Jewish-Christian difference emerged not only through debates about weekly worship, both on the Sabbath and on other days of the week, but also through the dates of the annual Jewish festivals, women's adherence to menstrual purity laws, and rabbinic conceptualizations of a God that was simultaneously hypertemporal and atemporal. Gendered time and divine-human time also crystallized rabbinic-Roman distinctions and Jewish-Christian difference, and the reverse. In short, the times and differences identified in this book were mutually reinforcing and created a complex timescape that cannot easily be separated out into discrete times and differences.

Notably, this constellation of times and differences was not confined to the classical rabbinic era. Rabbinic conceptions of time and difference persisted beyond antiquity and resonated in later generations. What was the effect of the rabbinic timescapes outlined in this book in subsequent historical periods? This conclusion examines the enduring legacy of these ancient times and differences.

The temporal framework—the calendar of months, weeks, and days—used in many parts of the world today is a blend of the Roman months, the Jewish weeks, and the Christian Lord's Day. What has become a unified and coherent system of time is actually the shared heritage of at least three once-competing ancient systems of time-keeping. The Roman Julian calendar is the basis of the Gregorian calendar, which remains the dominant civil calendar in many parts of the world. The nundinal cycle, the eight-day market cycle that was integral to the Roman calendar during antiquity, however, was eventually replaced by the seven-day weekly cycle. The seven-day week derives both from Jewish (and later Christian) traditions rooted in the Hebrew Bible and from the planetary week that originated during the Hellenistic period, possibly in Alexandrian astrological circles. The sanctioning of Sunday as a sacred day, on which many regular activities were banned, was officially adopted as a result of Emperor Constantine's incorporation of Christian time into Roman law. This harmonized system of times remains in use to this day.

During most of antiquity, these temporal frameworks—Roman, Jewish, and Christian—were at odds with one another. They defined different sets of communities that regarded their calendars as competing and mutually exclusive. This book examined rabbinic texts from the period prior to the merging of these systems, before time as we now know it. The first two chapters explored the challenges faced and the strategies employed by a group of people who had their own system of time, yet who lived within an empire and among other communities that had different ways of organizing their time. Analyzing various moments of contact between the Roman and rabbinic calendars as well as between the Jewish and Christian weeks and days illuminated what was at stake both in the differentiation of these times and in their synchronization.

The story does not end in antiquity, however. Despite the eventual merging of these temporal systems, Jews continued to contend with the challenge of living in contexts in which their own times conflicted with the times of others and served to differentiate them from others. This was the case both in regions that observed the Julian and Gregorian calendars and in regions that used other calendars. Once the Geonim regarded the Babylonian Talmud as the basis of Jewish law, talmudic precepts were considered binding (even if they were not always followed).[2] Medieval and modern rabbis and their adherents continued to interpret the rabbinic prohibition regarding "the festivals of gentiles" to determine which festivals were considered "idolatrous" and when to separate themselves from the majority culture, evoking lively debates that shifted from region to region. Rabbinic authorities likewise contended with the practical and philosophical challenges of abstaining from work each seventh day, a practice that continued to highlight difference in daily economic and social life. These temporal negotiations played an important role in continuing to forge, navigate, and complicate Jewish difference.

The beginning of Mishnah *Avodah Zarah* refers exclusively to Roman festivals in its list of days during which Jews ought to abstain from various interactions with gentiles. The Mishnah presents a comprehensive group of the prohibited festivals, limiting the category of "festivals of gentiles" to the particular Roman festivals listed. The Mishnah implies that these prohibitions do not apply to all other festivals, creating ample opportunities for encounters on other days of the year. While the Mishnah's concern with Roman festivals stems from a geographical and cultural context in which they were the most popular festivals observed in Roman Palestine, the religious and political landscape had changed dramatically by the time of the redaction of the Palestinian and Babylonian Talmuds. In the fourth century, Roman (pagan) festivals were still observed in the region, but rabbis must have also been concerned about the growing and increasingly influential Christian communities, which presented their own set of competing festivals and calendrical configurations that were at odds with, and often in direct opposition to, Jewish times and celebrations. Likewise, in the Babylonian context, Roman festivals were hardly a practical issue, while Zoroastrian and other festivals celebrated by those in the Sasanian Empire were of more immediate concern for Jews.

Rabbinic opinions preserved in the Palestinian and Babylonian Talmuds indicate that later rabbis were indeed not satisfied with the Mishnah's limited list of forbidden festivals. Both Talmuds transform the Mishnah's comprehensive list of Roman festivals into a set of *examples* of prohibited festivals, a catalogue that could be expanded based on new historical, geographical, and cultural circumstances. The Palestinian Talmud adds specific lists of Babylonian and Median festivals: "Rabbi Ba said in the name of Rav: [there are] three festivals in Babylon and three festivals in Media. Three festivals in Babylon: Mahuri, Kanauni, and Banauta. Three in Media: Nausardi, Tiriasqi, and Mahirkana [Nusardi, Triaski, and Moharneki]."[3] Rav Huna adds another festival, Nauruz. In the same vein, the Babylonian Talmud also stresses that the Mishnah's list is relevant to those living within the Roman Empire and explicitly asks which festivals apply within a Persian context: "Those are the Roman [festivals]. Which are the Persian ones?"[4] The pericope then adds Persian festivals and further expands the list, as the Palestinian Talmud does, to include Babylonian festivals as well: "These then are those of the Romans and Persians, which are the Babylonian ones? Muharnekai, Aknayata, Bahnani and the Tenth of Adar."[5] The implication of this new interpretive stance, exhibited in these brief talmudic passages, was to recast the Mishnah's exhaustive list of Roman festivals as an exemplary set of festivals from a particular historical and geographical context that must be applied to other non-Jewish festivals in subsequent periods and in new places. In these later rabbinic sources, the Mishnah's list became a template for all non-Jewish festivals that might be considered idolatrous, whenever and wherever Jews found themselves living.

The practice of applying these rabbinic prohibitions to other festivals not explicitly mentioned in the Mishnah continued in the medieval and early modern periods. While they originally targeted Roman festivals, they were eventually used to contend with Christian and Islamic ones. In Europe, for instance, some Jewish calendars listed Christian festivals, often in separate sections of calendrical documents.[6] These sections were added to Jewish calendars because Jews needed to be aware of the predominantly Christian temporal landscape in which they lived if they were to abstain from Christian festivals. A Christian calendar written in Hebrew, contained within the thirteenth-century *North French Hebrew Miscellany*, introduces a list of Christian Saints' Days with the words "These are the months of the gentiles and their abominations," an allusion to the language in Mishnah *Avodah Zarah* 1:3, "These are the festivals of the gentiles."[7] In place of Roman festivals there were now lists of Christian ones.

The appearance of side-by-side Jewish and Christian calendars in *sifrei evronot* and other Jewish manuscripts resembles the incorporation of the Roman calendar into the Jewish calendar through the Mishnah's laws and lists.[8] While the rabbis of the Mishnah and Talmuds did not produce written calendars, the detailed prohibitions against participating in activities before, during, and after Roman festivals effectively mapped the Roman calendar onto the Jewish one. As Carlebach writes in her study of early modern Jewish calendars, "the Christian religious calendar provided the primary framework for the rhythms of social life in premodern Europe.... For Jews living in Christian Europe, there was no refuge from this all-encompassing timescape."[9] In these later calendars that form the core of Carlebach's study, Jewish scribes produced lists of Christian festivals that functioned in much the same way as the Mishnah's list of Roman festivals and the later talmudic lists of Persian and Babylonian festivals. The subversive puns and hidden jabs used by Jewish scribes to denigrate Christian festivals in these calendars are likewise similar to the talmudic etiologies that cast the origins of Roman festivals in a disparaging light.[10]

Medieval Jews observed the talmudic prohibitions pertaining to non-Jewish sacred days in a variety of ways. Some, such as Rabbeinu Gershom Me'or Ha-Golah in late tenth-century Mainz, pointed out that the prohibitions could not be maintained effectively because "most of the days of the year are their holidays."[11] Unwilling to mandate the complete separation of Jews and Christians, which would have been necessary given the perceived frequency of Christian sacred days, this rabbi argued for maintaining halakhic leniency with regard to Christian festivals. Many medieval Jews in Ashkenaz had already abandoned these strictures, and the halakhists of the day attempted to justify such practices, by either declaring Christianity not idolatrous or circumscribing rabbinic laws.[12] In North Africa, in contrast, Maimonides considered Christianity idolatrous, primarily because of his understanding of the doctrine of the trinity, and argued that the rabbinic laws of *Avodah Zarah* ought to apply to Christian festivals. For much the same reason that rabbinic authorities in Europe chose not to characterize Christianity as idolatrous, though, Maimonides portrayed Islam as a monotheistic religion.[13] Maimonides thus argued that the talmudic prohibitions did not apply to Islamic festivals as they did to other "idolatrous" festivals and that Jews could maintain close financial ties with Muslims throughout the year.[14] Rabbis, then, could neutralize the festivals of the majority's religion to permit Jews to live comfortably among their neighbors. Different hermeneutical strategies were pursued at various historical and cultural moments in both Christian and Islamic contexts.

All these approaches regard calendrical time as an important mechanism through which to negotiate difference. Evolving rabbinic rules ensured that Jews both celebrated their own festivals and separated themselves from their non-Jewish neighbors precisely at the times of year when it most mattered. There were days and seasons of difference. There were times when Jewish difference was insisted upon and when Jews were thus more cognizant of their difference—and performed such difference by refraining from interactions with others. There were also seasons when such difference was downplayed and even elided.

A final example illustrates the continued significance of the Mishnah's prohibition regarding gentile festivals and of the sustained importance of calendrical time in the negotiation of difference. In a series of four responsa, the twentieth-century Modern Orthodox rabbinic authority Rav Moshe Feinstein dealt with the question of whether American Jews could celebrate their own festivities (e.g., weddings, bar mitzvahs, and so on) on the day of Thanksgiving, as well as whether Jews were permitted to celebrate the holiday of Thanksgiving itself.[15] Feinstein unequivocally permits Jews to hold their own celebrations on the day of Thanksgiving. He wavers, however, between forbidding and permitting Jews to celebrate the holiday of Thanksgiving: he forbids it in one responsum, permits it in another, and continues to struggle to articulate a definitive answer in a third. In all of Feinstein's writings on the topic, however, he makes the case that Thanksgiving is categorically different from other gentile festivals—which are obviously forbidden—because it is unrelated to pagan worship, and he builds his legal reasoning around this fundamental distinction.[16] By arguing that Thanksgiving is *not* an idolatrous festival, Feinstein opens up the possibility for the holiday to be celebrated and, intentionally or not, creates an opportunity for dismantling boundaries between Jews and other Americans. American Jews were, according to Feinstein, prohibited from permanently incorporating this American holiday into the Jewish calendar, but they could partake in the holiday on a year-to-year basis if they wished to do so. Feinstein's rulings end up carving out time within the American calendar year when Jews were permitted to be not only Jews but also Americans.[17] In other words, one of the ways that Jewish Americanness could be expressed was through the (informal, impermanent) incorporation of American holidays—and thus American time—into the Jewish year.

Imbedded in Feinstein's halakhic reasoning is a final ironic twist. Beth Berkowitz notes, in her discussion of Feinstein's first responsum on the topic, that the rabbi contrasts "the celebration of Thanksgiving with the celebration of other gentile festivals (*yeme ed shel ha-nokhrim*), when he prohibits Jews from scheduling their events. He groups Thanksgiving with New Year's Day (which he calls 'the first day of *their* year'), declaring both to be permitted, albeit not preferable, backdrops for Jewish weddings and bar mitzvahs and the like."[18] As Feinstein argues his case for not characterizing Thanksgiving as an idolatrous festival, he compares the holiday with New Year's Day, which, for Feinstein, represents the epitome of a "secular" or "civic" holiday. But—and here is the irony—New Year's Day is actually the Kalends of January, as it was celebrated in the Roman Empire, and thus the very first festival that the Mishnah explicitly lists in tractate *Avodah Zarah* as an idolatrous festival from which Jews ought to maintain temporal distance.[19] In Feinstein's responsum, the Mishnah's list of idolatrous festivals has come full circle. The very festival used in the Mishnah to define the category "idolatrous festival" is used by Feinstein, almost 1,800 years later, as the prime example of a civic festival that is, categorically, *not* an idolatrous festival. Feinstein's sustained efforts in contending with the question of Thanksgiving and the American New Year highlight the centrality of calendrical time and annual festivals in forging and negotiating difference, the surprising ways in which attitudes to particular festivals change over time, and the creativity with which rabbinic figures have met these changes.

The topic of Sabbath observance likewise continued to be a locus for managing Jewish-Muslim and Jewish-Christian difference in the medieval and modern eras, and various approaches to the Sabbath as a time of difference can be identified. Maimonides, for instance, discusses how Jews might forge business partnerships with Muslims, given the prohibition against earning money on the Sabbath.[20] If a Jew and a Muslim establish a store together, does Jewish law mandate that the store be closed on the Sabbath, or could the Muslim partner make sales and benefit from profits on that day without implicating her Jewish partner in Sabbath violations? Mark Cohen has identified the creative solutions that Maimonides, following halakhic discussions in the Babylonian Talmud and the writings of the Geonim, adopted to facilitate Jewish-Muslim collaboration.[21] Maimonides remained committed to the preservation of the Sabbath as a day of Jewish difference as well as to finding ways of permitting Jews to form close business relationships with their Muslim associates. The Sabbath was employed by Maimonides to negotiate difference in complex and sometimes counterintuitive ways. On the one hand, Maimonides' commitment to preserving prohibitions against work on the Sabbath maintained difference by highlighting the misaligned temporalities of Jews and those among whom they lived. Adherence to strict Sabbath laws guaranteed that Jews in such business arrangements would always be somewhat distinguished from their Muslim partners because on one day each week their partnership bonds dissolved. These Sabbath arrangements thus reinforced the fundamental differences between Jews and their partners. On the other hand, Maimonides allowed for a certain amount of temporal flexibility by constructing legal fictions whereby business ownership transferred to the non-Jewish partner one day each week in order to create the opportunity not only for occasional interaction and exchange but even for sustained partnerships. Time, in this example, constructed and maintained difference yet also facilitated long-term collaboration across religious and communal boundaries.

The problem of Jewish Sabbath observance figured centrally, as well, in debates about Jewish emancipation in the German lands in the latter half of the eighteenth century. Jewish time was cited as one of the main examples of Jewish difference, and, from the perspective of those lobbying against emancipation, Sabbath and festival observance posed an insurmountable obstacle for the integration of Jews into German society. Christian Wilhelm von Dohm, in advocating for Jewish emancipation, addressed critics who argued that "the most serious reason for asserting that the Jews cannot obtain equal rights with the rest of the citizens is the belief 'that the Jews are prohibited by their religion from serving in the army, because their Sabbath regulations forbid them to fight on the Sabbath, to make extended marches, and because they would not be able to fulfill their religious obligations and customs when in the army.'"[22] Emancipation opponents specifically cited Jewish Sabbath observance as the main hindrance for Jews to serve in the military and thus to become fully contributing citizens of the German nation-state.[23] In France, Monsieur de la Fare, in his arguments against Jewish emancipation, described the Jews as "a tribe that, in obeying both its own law and the national law, has 108 valueless days in the year."[24] According to de la Fare, the fact that Jews conceived of and used their time in ways divergent from the Christian majority disqualified them from becoming citizens. Here, again, difference was constructed through the organization and conception of time, though in this case not directly by rabbinic authorities but by those outside of the Jewish community who posited that Jewish time created too dramatic a difference for full integration and emancipation.

Von Dohm's response to his critics highlights the centrality of competing conceptions of time in the ongoing emancipation debates. He states that "there is not the slightest indication of [abstaining from military activity on the Sabbath] in the Mosaic law, and up to the destruction of the First Temple we do not find anywhere a remark that the Jews, in their numerous wars, refrained on the Sabbath from defense against their enemies or attack upon enemy armies."[25] Moses Mendelssohn likewise argued that Jews would find ways of fighting battles on the Sabbath despite their religious observances.[26] Both von Dohm and Mendelssohn strategically downplayed Jewish difference by accentuating Jewish flexibility with regard to the laws that pertained to the Sabbath and the activities from which Jews typically abstained on those days.

Two approaches emerge here. Maimonides proposed creative halakhic solutions for maintaining strict Sabbath observance in order to allow Jews to partner with non-Jews without violating any Sabbath prohibitions. Von Dohm, in contrast, minimized the practical differences between Jews and others by pointing to instances in Jewish history when Sabbath observance was suspended, such as during times of war, in order to make a case for Jewish emancipation despite the difficulties posed by a competing calendar. In other contexts, additional strategies were proposed to mitigate the significant difference that the Sabbath created between Jews and their neighbors.

Not long after these emancipation debates, some Jews began lobbying to change the day of the Jewish Sabbath so that it would conveniently coincide with the Christian Sunday. Initial proposals to celebrate the Sabbath on Sunday emerged precisely in the decades when Jews were becoming civilly and politically integrated into German life. In 1845, the Berlin Reform congregation introduced Sunday services along with those held on Saturdays, and by 1848 this congregation had abolished their Saturday services altogether.[27]

The debate about the timing of the Sabbath soon crossed the Atlantic. Sinai Temple in Hyde Park, Chicago, became the first American congregation to successfully institute Sunday services.[28] In 1873, the temple's rabbi, Kaufmann

Kohler, sent a letter to his congregation urging members to vote in favor of Sunday services. In this letter, the rabbi presented Sunday services as a mechanism for strengthening Jewish observance by facilitating his congregants' attendance at synagogue on the day of the week when it was most feasible for them to do so. He also argued that Sunday services would allow his congregants to continue to be integrated into American economic life, which necessitated that they work on Saturdays.[29] In other words, adding services on Sundays was the rabbi's strategy for maintaining Jewish difference (by drawing Jews to weekly synagogue services), while also an attempt to diminish Jewish difference (by providing a weekly Jewish service on the Christian day of worship for those who could not attend services on Saturdays). The rabbi presented his rationale for the solution of Sunday services, in part, in theological terms, even though he was largely motivated by economic factors: "We transfer all the blessings, and all the rich seed of moral and spiritual elevation, all our dear remembrances from the old historical Sabbath day to the public Sabbath, which we are in fact already celebrating, with our young, with our employees, with our fellow-citizens."[30] Those who opposed the change focused on the policy's likely effect of obliterating Jewish difference. They claimed, in Tobias Brinkman's words, that "Sunday services sidelined the Saturday Sabbath service, constituting a sacrifice of a powerful symbol of Jewish difference in an overwhelmingly Christian environment."[31] Brinkman adds that "indeed, Jewish critics wondered what would distinguish radical Reform Judaism from liberal Protestantism except for the recognition of Jesus as the Messiah. More than debates over the abolition of kosher butchering or the ritual of circumcision, this particular Sabbath reform stirred up strong Jewish emotions."[32] Here again, the politics of time played a central role in the construction of difference, especially in light of the prominent place of Jewish Sabbath observance in the long history of Jewish-Christian difference.[33] Aligning Jewish time with Christian time, even as the rabbi tried to present it as *American* time, was, according to the opposition, too high a price to pay for the integration of Jews into American life. Sinai Temple did hold Sabbath worship on Sunday for some time, but Sunday services did not become the norm in American Reform congregations.[34] Saturday remained the day for the Jewish Sabbath in most congregations across the denominational spectrum, and economic and social sacrifices made by Jews to maintain their observance became a trope of the hardships of Jewish American life.[35]

The introduction of Sunday services at Sinai Temple had class, gendered, and denominational dimensions as well. A Sunday Sabbath was presented by the temple's rabbi as a solution to an economic challenge precisely because so many of the congregants could not afford to take a day off or to lose their jobs as a result of their Sabbath observance. Similarly, but in a different context, Phillip Davis reflected in 1905 on his time as the organizer for the Ladies' Garment Workers. In his recollections, he lamented the lack of dedication "among the workers as a class" to the Sabbath and the synagogue: "After repeated visits to the greatest and smallest synagogues in New York, it was apparent that, as such, the synagogue everywhere has lost all its meaning to the American Jewish workingman. He hurries by it morning and night on his way to and from the factory without the slightest regard for its former sanctity." He quotes a colleague who notes that "During the Solemn Days, particularly the Day of Atonement, there is usually a burst of piety among them. Then they dress up, buy a seat and go to the synagogue. But even this rare visit is made in a perfunctory way. In most cases it is made to please an importunate mother or to appease a petulant wife."[36] Though Davis ultimately seeks to demonstrate that such lack of dedication to Judaism can be blamed on the Socialists and Anarchists, his particular focus on "workingmen," who run to and from the factory mornings and evenings without stopping in the synagogue for daily or Sabbath prayers, highlights that the issue not only was a religious or communal one but also hinged on economic and class dimensions. Likewise, Sinai Temple's women, many of whom did not work outside the home, continued attending Saturday services, as they did not need to be at a place of employment, while the congregation's men were unable to do so. Such gendered practices created a situation in which the congregation's men and women marked different sacred Sabbath days.[37] Finally, observing a Sunday Sabbath, while obscuring differences between Reform Jews and their Christian neighbors, in turn differentiated them from Jews of other denominations who continued to observe the Sabbath on Saturday. Orthodox polemics against the Reform movement, for example, often cited Reform violation of Sabbath practices as exemplary of their attitude to Jewish tradition more generally.[38] The dismantling of one dimension of difference often accentuates another.

Well into the twenty-first century, the idea of a uniquely Jewish day of rest and its centrality for the cultivation of Jewish identity and difference is actively promoted in both Israel and the United States. In January 2018, the Israeli Knesset passed the so-called "mini-market bill," concerning whether stores, especially grocery stores, can open on the Sabbath (the narrow majority approved the bill, which requires the Interior Ministry's approval for stores to open on the Sabbath, making it virtually impossible for them to do so).[39] The Knesset's official press release, in the wake of the bill's passage, presents the Sabbath as "the Jewish Day of Rest," and the Knesset's impassioned debates on the topic revolved, in large part, around the role of the Sabbath in a Jewish state (can the State of Israel be a Jewish state if it permits such extreme violation of Sabbath rest? the proponents of this bill asked). Discussions about the Sabbath in broader conversations about the character of a Jewish state persist, despite the bill's passage. In the 2019 Israeli elections, the ultra-orthodox Shas party ran a video ad that evoked the culture wars in which the Sabbath features prominently. In the ad, a man returns home from Friday night prayers, warmly greets his wife, and pours wine at a beautifully set Sabbath table. The camera then zooms out to reveal a table full of empty seats: only the man and his wife are home, while their children are all missing. Confused, the man turns to his wife and asks: "What is this, where are all the children?" The woman answers by listing the various places where their children have gone—shopping at the mall, renewing a passport at the Interior Ministry, working. Upset, the father responds: "At work?!? Today is the Sabbath day, for heaven's sake." Playing on the two meanings of the word לשמור—to observe and to protect—and a popular saying that "Jews observe [verb: שמר] the Sabbath and the Sabbath protects [verb: שמר] them," the ad then delivers its punchline: "This is what the Sabbath will look like with Lapid and Lieberman [leaders of rival secular political parties].... Only Shas will observe/protect the Sabbath and the Jewish State."[40] The ad's rhetoric works so effectively precisely because the weekly Sabbath represents, in these discussions, Jewish difference.

Employing traditions about the Sabbath to affirm Jewish distinctiveness is not confined to political realms; it features in contemporary cultural and educational projects as well. In 2012, the Jewish Federation of America, in collaboration with the Education Department of Israel, through its Sifriyat Pijama project (PJ Library, in America), republished a Hebrew children's book by Devorah Omer titled *The Missing Spice* for distribution among American Jews.[41] The illustrated book retells the story discussed in chapter 2 of Rabbi Judah the Patriarch hosting Emperor Antoninus for Sabbath lunch and the emperor's discovery that Sabbath food is more delicious than any other cuisine. The narrative celebrates the uniqueness of the Sabbath as a day with its own elevated character rather than a day of unnecessary, burdensome restrictions. It tries, in short, to get young children excited about Jewish temporal rhythms. Another, English adaptation of this rabbinic story, retold by Naomi Shulman in *The Missing Ingredient*, based on the same rabbinic story but featuring more relatable characters named Ruthie and Isaac rather than an ancient rabbi and emperor, was mailed by PJ Library in 2019, along with a children's apron, to encourage the next generation to observe the Sabbath through cooking and hospitality. The program of mailing children's books with Jewish themes to Jewish American children was designed with the explicit goal of teaching Jewish children of all denominations fundamental Jewish concepts and practices as well as instilling in them a love of Judaism and pride in their Jewish identities.[42] Not surprisingly, one prominent theme that appears in many of the books in the series relates to Jewish holidays and, especially, the Sabbath. Other classic Jewish children's books unrelated to this organization also convey the uniqueness of the Sabbath to readers: Mira Wasserman's 2004 *Too Much of a Good Thing* offers yet another retelling of the Rabbi-Antoninus tale, while Marilyn Hirsh's 1986 *Joseph Who Loved the Sabbath* illustrates a different rabbinic story about the Sabbath, also discussed in chapter 2.[43] These children's books highlight how classical rabbinic narratives about Jewish time and difference, originally composed in Roman Galilee and retold in Sasanian Babylonia, continue to be used as resources for grappling with similar temporal challenges faced by Jews living in contemporary contexts in which Jewish time competes with other temporal norms and values.[44]

The third chapter of this book explored two time-related sets of rabbinic innovations. The first included the marking of men's time through the obligation of reciting the Shema and other positive time-bound commandments, from which women were exempt, and the second encompassed the creation of an alternative women's time through increased emphasis on women's adherence to menstrual purity laws. As with the history of the Sabbath and festivals, the rabbinic legacies of these gendered constructions of time were likewise complicated. While it is difficult to surmise based on the largely prescriptive corpus of rabbinic sources how widely these rituals were practiced by late antique Jews, these gendered rituals and their times continued to impact medieval Jewish society. Rabbinic prescriptive writings as well as popular practices were, of course, not uniform throughout the medieval period. They differed from century to century, place to place, and community to community. Nevertheless, a few general trends related to the intersection of time and gendered difference can be identified.

The differentiation between men and women through time appears, for example, in the ethical will composed by the late thirteenth- and early fourteenth-century Eleazar of Mainz. Addressing his "sons and daughters," Eleazar outlines the practices he hopes that his children will observe throughout their lives.[45] He begins with rituals traditionally observed by Jewish men: "They should attend synagogue in the morning and in the evening, where they should be particularly attentive to the recitation of the standing prayer [the Amidah] and the Shema. Immediately following worship, they should spend a little time studying Torah or Psalms, or in charitable activities."[46] Thereafter, Eleazar details the practices he hopes his daughters will observe: "The women of my family must be exceedingly careful to examine themselves throughout their monthly cycles and to stay apart from their husbands during their unclean days."[47] In this document, men's daily recitation of the Shema and women's adherence to the daily examination of their bodies are presented as parallel, defining men's and women's times and differentiating between them.[48]

Medieval sources provide us with various stated reasons for why women were, at least theoretically, excluded from the practice of positive time-bound commandments.[49] Many of the explanations center on women's relationship with time in light of their domestic responsibilities and spiritual dispositions. Among the reasons offered by medieval rabbinic authorities were (1) the requirement for women to devote their time to their husbands' needs;[50] (2) the division of responsibilities to establish domestic harmony, such that a husband and wife did not need to perform the same rituals simultaneously but could divide their time among different tasks;[51] and (3) women's natural spiritual affinities to God, such that they do not require habitual time-bound rituals to reinforce their relationship with the divine.[52] Though these explanations do not indicate the origin or purpose of the category of rituals nor the exclusion of women from them in rabbinic sources, they do provide a window into the reception of this category of rituals and its evolution in the centuries following the rabbinic period. The sources that address the question of why women were not obligated to observe so many of the positive time-bound commandments attempt to resolve the discrepancy between men's and women's time that rabbinic law created and to offer explanations for it. While the normative force of this category in early rabbinic sources is debated by modern scholars, its application in the medieval and early modern periods appears to have generally been more widespread and accepted.

Even as the rabbinic strictures from antiquity concerning women's exemptions from positive time-bound commandments solidified, however, these norms and the time frames they imposed on men and women were challenged. Positive time-bound commandments were not uniformly practiced by men, for economic and social reasons.[53] Moreover, there is considerable evidence of pushback against these norms from both women and some medieval rabbinic authorities. In the second half of the eleventh century, Rabbi Isaac Halevi, who served as the head of the yeshiva in Worms at the time, ruled that "one does not prevent women from reciting the blessings over *lulav* and *sukkah*" because "if they wish to undertake the yoke of commandments they are permitted to do so, and one does not object."[54] In his study of women's piety in Germany and France during this period, Avraham Grossman notes that the language of this legal ruling indicates that it was women themselves who initiated the performance of these commandments and recited the corresponding blessings, and that sages such as Rabbi Isaac Halevi "'conceded' to reality" and to "a new norm."[55] Elisheva Baumgarten has further documented the evolution of halakhic rulings regarding women's observance of positive time-bound commandments, noting that eleventh- and twelfth-century Ashkenazi writings assume that a substantial number of women must have been practicing these rituals because rabbinic authorities wrestle with halakhic questions related to their participation.[56] In such cases, this set of rituals structured not only the time of men but also the time of the women who took it upon themselves to fulfill positive time-bound commandments. Acceptance of women's participation in these practives in Ashkenaz was relatively short-lived, however. By the thirteenth century, rabbinic authorities in the region expressed reservations about women's practices and began more deliberately banning them from full participation.[57] Moreover, throughout these centuries, most rabbinic figures in Spain, including Rabbi David Abudarham of Spain and the later Rabbi Elijah Capsali of Candia, objected to women's observance of these rituals and their recitation of the corresponding blessings.[58] In fifteenth-century Mainz, Jacob

Moelin, known as the Maharil, went so far as to conceptualize men and women as two distinct peoples precisely because of their different levels of obligation in positive time-bound commandments. Explaining that women "are not included in [the full obligation of] 613," the Maharil concludes: "they are a people unto themselves."[59]

In the Byzantine context, a late fourteenth- or early fifteenth-century pseudonymous treatise titled *Sefer HaKanah* (attributed to the first-century Palestinian rabbi Nehuniah ben HaKanah) preserves both sides of the debate over women's exemption from positive time-bound commandments in dialogue form. Resistance to women's exemption is articulated by a pupil in a series of critiques of the rule, while the voice of tradition is expressed by the teacher through primarily kabbalistic reasoning.[60] Specifically regarding the recitation of the Shema, the pupil presents his challenge directly to God:

> *Yihud* [the unification of God's Name, as done in the recitation of the Shema] is the foundation of all commandments, and You exempted women! They are left open to destruction, for if they do not unify God, they will worship the sun or moon! Eve's sin in the Garden was that she did not unify God, and her lot was one of pain. Do you wish to banish woman totally from the world-to-come?[61]

In her study of this text, Talya Fishman notes that the pupil in this dialogue invokes kabbalistic ideas that suggest that Eve's sin involved isolating the last divine hypostasis of the Creator. Given that the "fragmentation of God is ... part of woman's archetypal experience," Fishman explains, "*Sefer HaKanah*'s pupil argues, woman should hardly be exempted from the commandment to unify God's Name twice daily."[62] In *Sefer HaPeliah*, a different work composed by the same author, the pupil expresses exasperation about women's exclusion from an entire set of commandments, which he deems unfair because women thereby forfeit the reward they might have received had they been permitted to perform these rituals. The pupil declares: "Is there a greater injustice than this, that the woman is included in warnings about punishments, but is excluded from the reward of performing?!"[63] Rebuffing these types of claims that undermine the rationale for women's exemption from positive time-bound commandments, the teacher comes well equipped with kabbalistic rejoinders to the pupil's attacks. Fishman summarizes the teacher's rationale, which draws on a rich kabbalistic tradition: "As is not the case with laws that are applicable to all people or those which may be performed at all times, the gender-specificity and the temporal-specificity of these *mizvot* highlight the existence of boundaries within the Godhead: between the sacred and its nonsacred mirror image, between male and female, and between the timeless and the time-bound."[64] These laws, in other words, exemplified—and were intended to reify—secrets of the gendered dimensions of the divine through the way that they structured men's and women's ritual times, the teacher explains.

While women's participation in positive time-bound commandments fluctuated over the course of the medieval period, strict adherence to menstrual purity laws increasingly became, in some communal contexts, a marker of women's piety and in turn influenced the temporal rhythms of women's daily lives and monthly cycles.[65] The medieval text Baraita de-Niddah insists on ever-more-prolonged periods of menstrual impurity and progressively elaborate forms of marking times of purity and impurity in addition to a whole host of other stringencies concerning a menstruating woman's activities within her home and community.[66] Polemics were hurled against women who did not observe menstrual purity practices in the way deemed proper by rabbinic authorities, including failure properly to count the days of their menses or the seven clean days that followed.[67]

Not all communities of women adhered to laws of menstrual purity as they are outlined in rabbinic sources, however. As Eve Krakowski has shown, for centuries Jewish women in Fatimid and Ayyubid Egypt, and probably elsewhere in the region and beyond, did not immerse in ritual baths at the end of their period of impurity (they went, instead, to a bathhouse), nor did they adhere to rabbinic time frames of menstrual impurity, following the shorter biblical period of impurity.[68] It was only Maimonides' strict legal rulings—issued in part out of concern for his own authority at a time when he was relatively marginalized by his rabbinic peers—and the practical repercussions (forfeiting their dowers) that he put into place against women who violated these newly enforced rabbinic strictures that eventually coerced women to begin practicing menstrual purity laws in ways that aligned more directly with the talmudic practices and schedules developed centuries earlier, in the very texts examined in chapter 3.[69] Krakowski's work highlights not only the potential—and often very real—gap between normative texts and communal practices (thus cautioning against reading rabbinic sources as descriptive, even in periods when their authority has long been assumed to be well-established) but also the ways in which such prescriptive texts were redeployed in later periods to effect different consequences than those originally intended by their composers or redactors centuries earlier.

In other medieval texts, especially mystical literature, women symbolically existed in a state of constant impurity—they could not partake in mystical rituals because of fear of impurity.[70] Even while women could, theoretically, engage in mystical activities during the time of the month when they were not ritually impure, their potential for impurity at unpredictable times of the month prevented them from engaging in such activities altogether. Sharon Koren writes: "Women are susceptible to impurity at all times and are therefore continually barred from mystical practice—a legal construction that also accounts for the absence of post-menopausal women mystics."[71] According to such norms, not only was women's time segregated into periods of purity and impurity during which their behavior had to change but the entirety of their time was regarded as utterly distinct from men's time because of the potential for unexpected impurity. Thus, the laws that marked their bodies and constructed their time fundamentally changed their access to whole realms of spirituality that were predicated on predictable states of purity, which were defined as male.

The uncomfortable collision of men's and women's bodily and ritual times with those of God's temporal rhythms is movingly articulated in the much more recent diary of the Hebrew writer Hava Shapiro. In her personal journal dated October 21, 1941, Shapiro reflects on the exclusion of women from the rituals of sanctifying and blessing the new moon.[72] While the boys and men of her Ukrainian community marked the transition of months by gazing at the moon and reciting a blessing, the women, because of their potential for menstrual impurity, were ordered to abstain from sanctifying the new moon and the passage of time. Once she reached puberty, Shapiro was no longer allowed to tag along with her older brothers. She bemoaned her womanly fate: "And so the hour of the sanctification of the moon became a hidden torment: it seemed a terrible burden that we, the girls, were made to suffer. I could not be consoled, for it seemed to me a terrible decree."[73] Shapiro's words evoke the Babylonian Talmud's description of the sanctification of the moon as an act of "greeting the face of the Shekhinah," an expression of extreme spirituality and unity with the divine from which she was excluded by virtue of being a woman.[74] In fact, in his *Nishal David*, Rabbi David Oppenheim explicitly cites this talmudic passage about greeting the Shekhinah, along with women's menstrual impurity, as halakhic justification for not only women's *exemption* from sanctifying the new moon but even the *prohibition* against their participation in the ritual.[75] It was this sort of legal reasoning that kept Shapiro from blessing the moon alongside her brothers.

Shapiro's sadness, which eventually turns into anger and defiance in the story she recounts, seems to stem from being barred access to the holiness this ritual of marking monthly time cultivated in its practitioners. According to the rabbinic strictures observed in Shapiro's community, her body's temporal rhythms—specifically those of her monthly menses—necessarily replaced the cosmic rhythms of the moon's monthly cycles.[76] She could no longer partake in the ritual of observing and declaring a new moon because she was now obligated to observe her own bodily rhythms and declare the time of her impurity. Here, the legacy of the ancient rabbinic exclusion of women from positive time-bound rituals still echoes. On the one hand, the monthly cycles of the moon and of a woman's menses are placed in parallel. Yet on the other hand, it is their irreconcilability and incompatibility in the realm of ritual that dictates women's exclusion from the very timely declaration of the new month. Shapiro's brief journal entry captures the themes explored in the third and fourth chapters of this book: women's exclusion from a certain set of rituals that were deemed by the rabbis to constitute men's time, the emphasis on menstrual purity laws that in turn defined a corresponding women's time, and the messy intersection of male bodies, female bodies, and heavenly bodies in setting the times for worship of the divine.

Shapiro's confession was by no means the only twentieth-century reflection on the tense gendered intersection of monthly menstrual cycles, calendrical time, and the divine. An installation created by Helène Aylon, a New York–based Jewish American ecofeminist artist, features a poetic meditation on the temporal rhythms of Niddah.[77] Hung in large font on the wall, the poem begins as follows:

> Yes I counted in a system
> that followed the planets
> not even passing the salt at the table
> for fear that hands would touch.
>> I say the system was devised
>> by an ancient wife who lived
>> in a polygamous household
>> and it was she—it was she
>> who watched her monthly cycle
>> and brought other women
>> to bathe together
>> and watch their own cycles
>> in the fullness and waning of the moon.

The poem powerfully ends by reframing an imagined ancient woman's counting of the "clean" and "unclean" days of her cycle:

> "Unclean" was not the term that she would use
> as she counted her days
> Beneath the sun's rise and the light of its fall
> So that she could say when to enter waters
> On the last eve of her counting.
> This I know: the term "unclean"
> Came from those who do not bleed.

Aylon's poem stands alongside a series of video monitors screening images of Aylon's menstrual charts from November 24, 1949, until February 15, 1961, the years during which Aylon was married (her husband died the week of her thirtieth birthday, in 1961). The title of the installation, "My Clean Days," refers to the seven days following a woman's menstrual cycle that serve as a buffer between the days of menstrual impurity and the time of immersion in the ritual bath, after which a woman is considered pure and therefore able to engage in physical contact with her husband, a halakhic development first found in the Babylonian Talmud. Each projected image in this piece consists of a calendar of a single Jewish month, the corresponding Gregorian dates, and the weekly Torah portion read in synagogue during those weeks. Aylon has marked the days of her menstruation along with the seven clean days that followed by muting the dates until they almost disappeared on the calendar; the days of menstruation, in addition to being muted, also have Xs overlaid across them. The remaining days, during which a woman is considered pure, appear in regular dark font. It is as though she is only fully present—her time most visible—on her days of purity.

Each month appears in sequence, month after month and year after year, in which Aylon's days are divided between times of purity and impurity. In earlier iterations of this installation (paired alongside "My Marriage Bed," part of Aylon's "The G-D Project [1996–2017]"), the entire calendar, twenty-four feet long, covered the wall and was projected as well onto a marriage bed, itself covered with a blanket made out of seven sets of cloth napkins that women use to perform their morning and evening bodily examinations to determine their status of purity. A recording repeats the words "5 days of menstruation, 7 clean days" over and over in an infinite loop, to the rhythm of a heartbeat, as though to remind the viewer that Aylon's time relentlessly alternated in those years between her days of purity and impurity.

This installation provides a glimpse into the rhythmic daily pattern by which Aylon examined her body according to rabbinic tradition and "counted her days beneath the sun's rise and the light of its fall." The viewer experiences in an embodied sense the power of menstrual purity practices, on both daily and monthly cycles, to construct a particular temporality, as well as the gendered sense of self that these rituals and their temporalities cultivated for Aylon in particular. The piece displays how one woman, in a particular context, theorized her relationship to daily time, as she experienced life in a ritual system based on the rabbinic laws and norms developed within the very sources from antiquity that are at the heart of chapter 3. Aylon's meditation on time, and the ever-present entering and existing phases of impurity, clean days, and purity, as well as the daily examinations to determine her status of purity, highlight the temporal dimensions of these daily purity practices and their potential effects on the cultivation of an embodied, gendered self, even in contemporary times.

The fourth chapter of this book investigated rabbinic conceptions of divine time, and it suggested that rabbinic sources articulated many ideas about God's presence in and continual impact upon the world through imagining the divine daily schedule. The connection between the unit of the hour and divine time proved especially resonant in these rabbinic sources. God spends every hour caring for the created world, these texts insist. Insofar as people can imitate God and bridge the difference between humans and the divine, it is through the proper use of each hour of their day in activities that mirrored God's own use of time. These stories of God's hours spread far beyond rabbinic contexts of scholastic study, incorporated as they were in synagogue liturgies and songs sung during life-cycle celebrations.

Not all readers of these rabbinic stories understood them in the same way. These particular narratives, for example, served as fodder for significant anti-Jewish polemicizing in the medieval period.[78] Petrus Alphonsi, in the early twelfth century, mentions the story of God's roars in a longer discussion about divine mourning of the temple.[79] Alphonsi's main objections are the corporeal descriptions of God along with the assumption of God's weakness in crying instead of rehabilitating Israel's conditions. Peter the Venerable, in a chapter titled "On the Ridiculous and Very Foolish Fables of the Jews" in his *Against the Inveterate Obduracy of the Jews*, similarly argues against this narrative at great length.[80] The Christian account of the Disputation of Paris in 1240 notes that the first Jewish expert to speak during the disputation, Master Vivo, confessed that both rabbinic traditions, about God's nightly roars and God's daily activities, were found in the Talmud: "He said further that it is in the Talmud that God curses himself three times every night because he allowed the Temple to be destroyed and gave up the Jews to servitude. . . . He said further that it is in the Talmud that God exerts himself to teach children every day, and that he sits and plays with Leviathan."[81] The Christian disputant must have offered these accounts of God's schedule as examples of the absurdity of talmudic traditions, and thereafter Master Vivo affirmed that these stories are indeed included in the Talmud.

The discussion of these two narratives during the Disputation of Paris might have motivated Raymond Martí to offer rebuttals of these aggadot in his late thirteenth-century *Pugio Fidei* ("Dagger of Faith").[82] In this work, written for Christian missionizing preachers, the author uses close readings of Jewish sources from the Bible through medieval rabbinic commentaries to argue against Judaism and to prove Christian ideas from Jewish texts.[83] Talmudic sources form a large portion of Martí's discussion. In the final section of this 1,000-page treatise, Martí provides the full Hebrew and Aramaic texts along with Latin translations of both God's nightly schedule in *b. Berakhot* 3a and God's daily schedule in *b. Avodah Zarah* 3b.[84] Martí argues that God's nightly roars in Jeremiah were actually fulfilled by Jesus' roars on the cross and that the talmudic rabbis were mistaken to use this prophetic image to assert that God mourns the destruction of the Jewish temple. Rather, Jeremiah's image of nightly divine roars proved, according to Martí, that Jesus was the messiah and had fulfilled biblical prophecies about his coming. When Martí introduces God's hourly schedule from tractate *Avodah Zarah*, just two pages later, he notes the insanity (*insania*) of imagining God's time to be divided and used in this way, suggesting that this rabbinic tradition proves its own absurdity.

A century after Martí composed *Pugio Fidei*, Paul of Burgos, in a gloss on the book of Isaiah in his *Additio* to the *Postillae* of Nicholas de Lyre, pointed to these same two stories about how God spends time as prime examples of the foolishness of rabbinic texts and their view of God.[85] For Paul, as for Christian critics before and after him, these narratives were most problematic for associating human activities with God. These critics employed such texts and traditions to construct difference between Judaism and Christianity, with the double aim of disparaging rabbinic traditions about God and convincing Jews to convert to Christianity. This was in stark contrast to the rabbinic context of these stories in which they served as inspiring models of how humans ought to spend their time meaningfully or as celebrating God's close bond with Israel.

Rabbinic narratives about God's time continued to be reinterpreted in various contexts. The notion that God has a connection to temporality, and that people might find a worthy template in God's schedule, reappear in major works of modern Jewish thought. Time is a central theme of part III of Franz Rosenzweig's magnum opus, *The Star of Redemption*. Although it is beyond the scope of this discussion to offer a full consideration of time in Rosenzweig's discussions of Judaism and Christianity, and of his tripartite structure of God, the human being, and the world, it is instructive to consider his remarks on the relation between time and God. Rosenzweig writes: "Time and hour—only before God are they powerless ... any representation of a temporal becoming ... bounces off his eternity."[86] At first, echoing the temporal sentiments of Philo and Augustine, Rosenzweig associates temporality with people and eternity with God. But then Rosenzweig takes a surprising turn: "Not he himself for himself, but he, as Redeemer of world and man, needs time, and not because he needs it, but because man and world need it."[87] Rosenzweig explains that God does not need time for God's sake but that God orients toward time because of God's care for humanity. The notion of duration and future, explains Rosenzweig, provides an anticipatory orientation toward which people strive, through prayer—and through prayer, to redemption. And in prayer, timing is everything: "Over [the] empty idea of the 'right' content of prayer, faith elevates the idea of the right time."[88] Later in the work, Rosenzweig alludes to the rabbinic tradition in *b. Avodah Zarah* 3b, which suggests that God spends time each day studying Torah. He is critical of readings of rabbinic traditions that suggest God's time is constituted completely by Torah study, emphasizing instead that God's twelve-hour days consist of other activities as well: "the God who governs the world has more to do besides just learning the Law."[89] Though God's daily hours are not entirely consumed with study, God's learning is nonetheless a model for Rosenzweig: "Like God's life according to the legend, so, too, the pious man's life can now be consumed in more and more perfect 'learning' of the Law. His feeling collects into one the entire world, which grows towards Redemption."[90]

Like Rosenzweig, Emmanuel Levinas also emphasizes the significance of divine time in his Jewish philosophical writings. In contrast to Rosenzweig, however, Levinas connects the notion of God's hours not to prayer or study but to work. Rather than modeling human time on God's schedule, Levinas suggests that human hourly work schedules, when ordered justly with a view toward "the rights of the *other person*, even if this person finds himself in the inferior position," serve as a way of expressing love of God. "As little as I have ever understood the exact meaning of the expression 'the opening up of the soul in its love of God,'" Levinas writes, "I ask myself, nonetheless, whether there isn't a certain connection between the establishment of working hours and the love of God, with or without the opening up of the soul. I am even inclined to believe that there are not many other ways to love God than to establish these working hours correctly, no way that is more urgent."[91] Levinas refers here to tractate *Baba Metsia*, which outlines rules regarding the daily working hours of human beings, a text discussed at the end of chapter 3. Levinas suggests that the commitment to determining daily schedules in a way that takes the rights of those less powerful into account is the highest expression of love of the divine, comparable to praise of God when one encounters natural wonders such as the seashore, the mountains, and the starry sky. Levinas thus establishes a crucial link between human time and God.

The talmudic passage in *Baba Metsia* at the center of Levinas's essay cites Psalm 104:22–23. These verses describe how, as the sun rises each morning, wild animals retreat while "people go out to their work and to their labor until the evening."[92] The Babylonian Talmud cites this verse because it describes a human workday as beginning in the morning and ending in the evening. Levinas writes, however, that "we must . . . read Psalm 104 beyond verses 22–23." Levinas explains: "The psalm seems to place the work of men amid the successes of creation. In Resh Lakish's reference to Psalm 104, beyond the technical problem of the workday, from which we have mainly drawn a principle, we have an argument concerning the meaning of human work and thus a reason for the dignity of the worker; the rights of the worker are due to his function in the general economy of creation, to his ontological role."[93] The responsibility to treat workers properly—which includes limiting their work hours—emerges naturally and logically from conceiving of each creature as created by God and therefore deserving justice. It also evokes God's decision to balance work with rest by ceasing from creation on the seventh day. By insisting on a contextualized interpretation of verses 22–23 within their more expansive literary context in Psalm 104 and thus within the context of creation, Levinas also (whether deliberately or unwittingly) connects this pericope from the Babylonian Talmud about fair hourly working conditions, which cites Psalm 104:22–23, with the pericope about God's hourly schedule, which cites Psalm 104:26 as a proof text for God's daily encounter with Leviathan.[94] Psalm 104 is, according to Levinas, a "psalm of the perfected world." In ideal circumstances, then, human working hours ought to reflect divine values, while divine hours cultivate human well-being through continual creation, in both instances bridging the gap between heaven and earth through the division and organization of time.

***

The examples in this concluding chapter have pointed to the persistence of rabbinic times and differences long after antiquity, even when they appear in unexpected configurations. Among the legacies of rabbinic texts are the rhythms of time they dictated, which persisted (and persist): the annual calendar and its festivals, the week and its Sabbath, the day and its ritual schedule, the hour and its symbolism. Another legacy of rabbinic texts are the various configurations of difference—ethnic, communal, gendered, and theological—that their laws, rituals, and narratives constructed and cultivated. The central claim of this book has been that conceptions of time and practices of time-keeping can (and often do) function as mechanisms for constructing as well as challenging difference, even as, with the passage of time, such constructions of time and difference are reimagined. The examples and analyses presented in each chapter sought to demonstrate the various ways in which specific rabbinic times and differences were intertwined and mutually constitutive as well as to highlight the complexity of multiple times and the consequences of conflicting modes of time-keeping.

During the eighteenth century, in the context of philosophical debates about time, Johann Gottfried Herder argued that "no two worldly things have the same measure of time."[95] There are, he suggested, "(to be precise and audacious) at any one time in the Universe infinitely many times."[96] This book has explored the diversity of times not only in the universe but also within a single society or community and even in the lives of individuals, how enmeshed these times are with one another, and the many dimensions of difference that result from observing annual calendars, weekly cycles, daily rituals, and hourly schedules.

Drawing attention to time has exposed a dimension of the world that is usually rendered invisible even as it is inescapable—to grasp some of the tangible effects of the intangible quality of the human experience we call "time." In any given context, conceptions and structures of time are not only pervasive; they are also inordinately important for understanding the ways in which worlds, identities, and differences are created, navigated, and remembered.

ACKNOWLEDGMENTS

IN THE YEARS I SPENT writing this book, I joked that it's fitting for a book about time to take an eternity to complete. Here I thank the mentors, teachers, colleagues, students, friends, and family who accompanied me from beginning to end.

My interest in the ancient world sprouted in my first year of college and continued through my doctoral work at Princeton University. I am immensely grateful to those who guided me through my studies with unparalleled generosity. Peter Schäfer, my mentor, taught me to read closely, and his scholarship and instruction are evident on every page of this manuscript. It was from John Gager that I learned how to think critically and engage compassionately. Martha Himmelfarb trained me to be precise with my analyses and my words. Elaine Pagels encouraged me to take intellectual risks. AnneMarie Luijendijk served as a model scholar and advisor. Jeffrey Stout showed me how to learn from my students. Peter Brown, Denis Feeney, Harriet Flower, Michael Flower, and Anthony Grafton introduced me to adjacent fields. Moulie Vidas was a classmate, a coauthor, and then a reader. Naphtali Meshel was a helpful interlocutor. Wallace Best gave me the wisest advice: to read widely.

At Fordham University I found my scholarly voice, a debt I owe to my colleagues. Their model of rigorous, relevant, and accessible scholarship has inspired me; their confidence in me has empowered me. Thank you to Barbara Andolsen, Orit Avishai, Eva Badowska, Rufus Burnett, Mary Callaway, Charles Camosy, Bob Davis, George Demacopoulos, Benjamin Dunning, Ayala Fader, Emanuel Fiano, Jeannine Hill Fletcher, the late Stephen Freedman, Leo Guardado, Brad Hinze, Christine Firer Hinze, Anne Golomb Hoffman, Karina Martin Hogan, Elizabeth Johnson, Eve Keller, Judith Kubicki, Kathy Kueny, Michael Lee, Joe Lienhard, Tom Massaro, Bryan Massingale, Jim McCartin, Brenna Moore, Harry Nasuti, Telly Papanikolaou, Nick Paul, Michael Peppard, Kathryn Reklis, Nina Rowe, Pat Ryan, Josh Schapiro, Tom Scirghi, John Seitz, Daniel Soyer, the late Maureen Tilley, Terry Tilley, Beth Torres, Jennifer Udell, Larry Welborn, and Christiana Zenner—for conversation, advice, and friendship. Special thanks to Patrick Hornbeck, for being an exemplary department chair, and to Magda Teter, who has no parallel in both energy and insight. Lynne Bahr, Asher Harris, Claire Kim, Natalie Reynoso, and M Tong, students-turned-colleagues, deserve mention for fruitful discussions and collaborations. Joyce O'Leary, Sue Perciasepe, and Anne-Marie Sweeney have expertly managed the department. Erik Cuascut keeps the department in clean order.

[252] ACKNOWLEDGMENTS

Some of the early ideas in this book stem from courses I taught at the University of Toronto, the Jewish Theological Seminary, and Andover Newton Theological School, and from a semester I spent at Harvard University. I thank Shaye Cohen, Alan Cooper, Stephen Garfinkel, Sol Goldberg, Rachel Greenblatt, Richard Kalmin, Hindy Najman, David Novak, Jennifer Peace, Shuli Rubin Schwartz, and Rachel Zerin for welcoming me into their communities.

Elisheva Baumgarten and Laura Nasrallah have each served, over the years, as examples of kindness, creativity, and vision.

Parts of the book were written during my year as a fellow at the Israel Institute for Advanced Study (IIAS), where I participated in two research groups, the first about time and the second about conceptions of the self. The participants in these two groups became important daily interlocutors, teachers, and intellectual companions, and I thank them for reading chapters, debating texts, and helping me refine my writing: Albert Baumgarten, Eve-Marie Becker, Jonathan Ben-Dov, Alfons Fürst, Wayne Horowitz, Karen King, David Lambert, Tzvi Langermann, Joshua Levinson, Carlos Lévy, Maren Niehoff, Joachim Quack, Eshbal Ratzon, Gretchen Reydams-Schils, Ishay Rosen-Zvi, Janet Safford, Barbara Sattler, John Steele, Sacha Stern, Sarah Symons, Ed Watts, and Israel Yuval. Yossi Assulin, Iris Avivi, Smadar Bergman, Sarah Gabison, Michal Linial, Batia Matalov, Keren Rechnitzer, Efrat Shvily, and the rest of the IIAS staff created a nurturing community. At the final stages, I benefited from joining the Einstein Center Chronoi as a visiting fellow, and I thank Christoph Markschies and the Chronoi team for welcoming me to Berlin.

I am indebted to others who also read chapter drafts and offered helpful feedback: Clifford Ando, Mira Balberg, Katell Berthelot, Erez DeGolan, Maria Doerfler, Adam Gregerman, Ilana Kurshan, Mark Letteney, John Penniman, Naila Razzaq, Gila Rosen, Jeffrey Rubenstein, Paola Tartakoff, and Dov Weiss.

This book benefited from conversations with many additional colleagues: Elizabeth Shanks Alexander, Carol Bakhos, Arjen Bakker, Michal Bar-Asher Siegal, Mara Benjamin, AJ Berkowitz, Beth Berkowitz, Moshe Bernstein, Fannie Bialek, Noah Bickart, Mark Brettler, David Brezis, Menachem Butler, Elisheva Carlebach, Simeon Chavel, Graham Claytor, Naftali Cohn, Krista Dalton, Yaacov Deutsch, Natalie Dohrmann, Steven Exler, Zev Farber, Molly Farneth, Steven Fine, Steven Fraade, Yair Furstenberg, Gregg Gardner, Edward Greenstein, Jennie Grillo, Simcha Gross, Amit Gvaryahu, Jae Han, Christine Hayes, Matthias Henze, April Hughes, Lance Jenott, David Zvi Kalman, Ethan Katz, James Ker, Naomi Koltun-Fromm, Yedidah Koren, Eve Krakowski, Rena Lauer, Marjorie Lehman, Olivia Stewart Lester, Martin Lockshin, Ruth Lockshin, Jessica Marglin, Hanan Mazeh, Jason Mokhtarian, Judith Newman, Tzvi Novick, Derek Penslar, Yoni Pomeranz, Annette Yoshiko Reed, Adele Reinhartz, Joseph Riordan, Jordan Rosenblum, Aaron Rubin, Marina Rustow, Elias Sacks, Sara Schulman, Shai Secunda, Shuli

Shinnar, Yigal Sklarin, Olla Solomyak, David Stern, Dan Stolz, Loren Stuckenbruck, Josh Teplitsky, Ágnes Vetö, Tanya Zion Waldoks, Miriam-Simma Walfish, Gabriel Wasserman, Susan Weingarten, Alex Weisberg, Zeev Weiss, Steve Weitzman, Anja Wolkenhauer, Avraham Yoskovich, Holger Zellentin, Wendy Zierler, and Shlomo Zuckier. Eviatar Zerubavel and his scholarship on time continue to inspire me.

I thank as well those who invited me to share my work in various venues: David Biale, Mike Chin, Kathy Chow, Martin Goodman, Pratima Gopalakrishnan, Tim Harrison, Lucia Hulsether, John Kloppenborg, Ari Mermelstein, Yonatan Moss, Benjamin Porat, Seth Schwartz, Malka Simkovitch, and Anna Sternshis. I apologize to those whom I have unintentionally left out.

Many institutions have funded my scholarship, and I thank each for the resources they provided that in turn allowed me the time to learn, think, and write: Princeton University's Department of Religion, Program in Judaic Studies, Program in the Ancient World, Center for the Study of Religion, Laurance S. Rockefeller Graduate Prize, and the Center for Human Values; a Faculty Research Grant, a Faculty Fellowship, and a Manuscript and Book Publication Award from Fordham University; fellowships from the Wexner Foundation, the ACLS/Mellon, Josephine de Karman Fellowship Trust, Targum Shlishi, Harvard University, the Jewish Theological Seminary, the Israel Institute for Advanced Studies, Einstein Center Chronoi, and the National Endowment for the Humanities; a book subvention grant from the Association for Jewish Studies; and the Manfred Lautenschlaeger Award for Theological Promise from the University of Heidelberg. Without those who have so lovingly helped care for my children, I similarly would not have found the time to write; I thank Yeni, Gloria, Hadassah, Jackie, Constansa, and Maria.

Though parts of this book are based on articles and chapters I have published elsewhere, all of them have been substantially reworked into the present book. I thank Cambridge University Press, Mohr Siebeck, Routledge/Taylor & Francis Group, and Vandenhoeck & Ruprecht for permission to republish portions of the following publications, as well as the editors and peer reviewers of these pieces, whose advice continued to impact my thinking. Part of chapter 1 appeared in "A Matter of Time: Writing Jewish Memory into Roman History," *AJS Review* 40.1 (2016): 57–86; part of chapter 2 appeared in "Between Narrative and Polemic: The Sabbath in *Genesis Rabbah* and the Babylonian Talmud," in *Genesis Rabbah in Text and Context*, edited by Sarit Kattan Gribetz, David Grossberg, Martha Himmelfarb, and Peter Schäfer (Tübingen: Mohr Siebeck, 2016), 33–61; and parts of chapter 3 appeared in "The Shema in the Second Temple Period: a Reconsideration," *Journal of Ancient Judaism* 6.1 (2015): 58–84, and "Time, Gender and Ritual in Rabbinic Sources," in *Religious Studies and Rabbinics: A Conversation*, edited by Elizabeth Shanks Alexander and Beth A. Berkowitz (New York: Routledge, 2017), 139–57. Thanks as well to the institutions and individuals who permitted me to reproduce the images that appear in this book.

At Princeton University Press, I thank Fred Appel for his continued support and enthusiasm—not only for believing in this book but also for convincing me that it was worth sharing with others. Thanks as well to David Campbell, Laurie Schlesinger, and especially Ali Parrington and Jenny Tan for their work seeing this book to press. I am appreciative of the time that several anonymous readers took to meticulously review the manuscript at various stages from proposal to polished draft; their criticisms helped me to improve my arguments. Sara Tropper and Jenn Backer, copyeditors extraordinaire, offered assistance right in time, and Tobiah Waldron created the index. I take responsibility for all remaining errors and oversights.

I am honored that my book's cover features Jacqueline Nicholls's beautiful illustration of the opening page of the Babylonian Talmud, the first drawing from her *Draw Yomi* series and an inspiring interpretation of the very word—מאמתי, "from what time?"—with which this book begins. I was particularly drawn to this image because of the juxtaposition of the reciter of the Shema, who mysteriously peers at us through the night sky, and the eating utensils that refer to the time-marker used to indicate when the evening Shema may be recited. In the note beneath this drawing (unseen on the book's cover), Nicholls alludes to the discussion in Berakhot 2b: "when does the night begin? whose eating? the priests? the poor? or the ordinary?" These words remind us, as this book explores, that not everyone's time is the same.

Four colleagues' unparalleled friendships have sustained me through the publication process: Mika Ahuvia, Shira Billet, Lynn Kaye, and Avigail Manekin. I am better for knowing them; Jewish Studies is better for having them in it.

I am blessed with a large and loving family. I thank my father, Shlomo, and Miriam; my mother, Esther, and Robert; my in-laws, Rhonda and Michael; my siblings Gabi and Pavel, Seth and Orit, Eric and Carin, Etty and Josh, Lior and Jess, and their beautiful children—each of them has contributed, in their own way, to this project and I am extraordinarily grateful to them for this and so much more.

My children have shaped this book from its very beginning: my interest in the topic of time was sparked just as my temporal world was turned upside down, with the birth of premature twins, who left no time in my schedule for almost anything but caring for them. In the eleven years since, Sophie and Daniela have grown into sharp intellectual companions and incisive critics of the world around them. Their younger brother, Max, models curiosity and empathy in ways that leave me in awe. All three of them now yell "bingo!" every time they hear someone say the word "time," and they spot clocks and other time-keepers faster than anyone else I know. Each could easily write their own book about time already. I learn so much from them each day.

No words—or time—would be adequate to thank my partner, Jonathan, for his love, wisdom, warmth, and patience. I dedicate this book to him and to our children, with love.

NOTES

Prologue

1. On the political, legislative, economic, and ideological dimensions of European, American, and Middle Eastern times in the long nineteenth century, which account for some of the history embedded within these different temporal cultures, see Barak (2013); Ogle (2013; 2015). On the equality of such times, and the dark history of characterizing certain cultures as primitive and "past" in the disciplines of history and anthropology, see Nandy (1995); Chakrabarty (2000); McCarthy (2009); Nanni (2012); Fabian (2014); Brendese (2014); Birth (2016).

2. Hasidic Jews are famously flexible with prayer times, but there was no *minyan*, a quorum of ten men needed for communal prayer.

3. On which see, e.g., Cooper (2016). On punctuality in a Roman context, see Wolkenhauer (2019).

4. The phrase "temporal footprints" appears in Rifkin (1987:1), quoted and discussed in R. Levine (1997:xi, xvii).

Introduction

1. Augustine, *Confessions* XI.15; trans. Pine-Coffin (1961:263–64). On Augustine's philosophy of time and its legacy, see Flasch (1993).

2. Moses Maimonides, *The Guide of the Perplexed* II.13; trans. Rabin (1952:95).

3. V. Woolf (1928:72).

4. See, e.g., Lapham (2014); Fraser (1966) encourages scholars to study time interdisciplinarily.

5. In philosophy, see Sorabji (1984); Phillips (2017); McLure (2005); Dolev (2007); Tymieniecka (2007); Arstila and Lloyd (2014). On scientific dimensions of time, including physics, see Burdick (2017); D. Falk (2008); Carroll (2010); H. Price (1996); Hawking (1988). For theological reflections on time, see, e.g., Welker (1998:317ff.); Qu (2014). Other studies in various disciplines that have impacted my own work include E. Cohen (2018); Lightman (1992); Gould (1988); Du Bois (1903:esp. 204–17). These are only a handful of countless studies.

6. The sociological study of time was pioneered by Zerubavel (1979; 1981); B. Adam (1990). For a social-psychological perspective, see R. Levine (1997). For an overview of anthropological approaches, see Gell (2001). For a narrative approach, see Ricœur (1988). For a literary approach, see T. Stern (2015). For examples of historical studies of time in specific cultures, see Le Goff (1980); M. Smith (1997); W. Johnson (2000); Ekrich (2006); Feeney (2007); Ker (2009); Glennie and Thrift (2009); Rosenberg and Grafton (2010); McCrossen (2013); Barak (2013); Frumer (2014; 2018); Kaijian (2015); Wishnitzer (2015); Stolz (2015); Ogle (2015). On the history of time-reckoning, see Needham, Wang, and De Solla Price (1960, 1986); Aveni (1989, 2002); Dohrn-van Rossum (1996); Moosa (1998); Richards (2000); Pagani (2001); Holford-Strevens (2005). On time in antiquity, see Rosen (2004); Hannah (2005; 2009); Lehoux (2007); Jones (2016); Ben-Dov and Doering (2017); Miller and Symons (2019). In religious studies, see Kalupahana (1974); Schopen (2004); El

Guindi (2008). Each of these studies has been influential in my exploration of time in ancient Jewish culture.

7. For an overview of recent scholarship on time and temporality in ancient Judaism, rabbinic literature, and Jewish Studies, see Gribetz and Kaye (2019).

8. Here I am drawing on the evocative language of Koslofsky (2011:1).

9. E.g., Muilenburg (1961); von Rad (1968); Wilch (1969). Such scholarship is surveyed more extensively in Barr (1962); Momigliano (1966); Bundvard (2014). On time in biblical sources in a different vein, see De Vries (1975); Machinist (1995); Fox (1998); Peckham (1999); Bundvard (2015).

10. Momigliano (1966:6; 1990:5–28).

11. Momigliano (1966:6). S. Stern (2003) similarly observes that rabbinic sources, too, are most concerned with proper timing and accordingly develop detailed and sophisticated processes for time-reckoning.

12. As has been demonstrated most recently by Kaye (2018).

13. Ritual baths were often located near synagogues in late antiquity, on which see Spigel (2012:111).

14. The authority of the rabbis throughout late antiquity is a matter of considerable scholarly debate; see, e.g., S. J. D. Cohen (1981); Hezser (1993); Schwartz (2001; 2013); Goodblatt (2006); Lapin (2011).

15. Similar approaches to rabbinic discourse have been taken by Boyarin (1993); Fonrobert (2000); Rosen-Zvi (2012); Balberg (2014; 2017a).

16. I use the term "timescape" to refer to the many dimensions of time that operate simultaneously within any given society—similar to the use of "landscape" to describe the variety of natural and human dimensions of space in any given location. On analyzing texts written by elites as resources for thinking about the ordinary people they address, see Nasrallah (2017). Even in later chronological periods, adherence to rabbinic guidelines varied widely from region to region and law to law, on which see, e.g., Krakowski (2020).

17. I rely here on the legacies of Derrida (e.g., 1968); Deleuze (1968).

18. J. Z. Smith (1985:4).

19. In rabbinics and ancient Judaism, see Rosen-Zvi and Ophir (2011); Berkowitz (2012); Rosen-Zvi (2016a); Reed (2018).

20. Durkheim (2001:11).

21. Aristotle, *Physics* 4.10–14; Augustine, *Confessions* XI; Heidegger (1927, 1962); Ricœur (1988:esp. 104); Proust (1913–27, 2004); V. Woolf (1928); Coope (2005); J. Halberstam (2005); Freeman (2010); Dinshaw (2012:7–17). On "the potential queerness of time" in which "different time frames or temporal systems collid[e] in a single moment of *now*," see Dinshaw (2012:5). We might add the literature on cyclical and linear time, as well as sacred and profane time, distinctions that are at once useful and problematic; e.g., Eliade (1954; 1959:68–113); Steensgaard (1993); and critiques of these categories in Rubenstein (1997); Kaye (forthcoming a).

22. Ricœur (1988:104).

23. On the collectivity of sociotemporal order, see Zerubavel (1979:105–29); on the role of community in the formation of calendars, see S. Stern (2001).

24. I am informed here by the critique of Durkheim in Jay (1992:136), on which see Gribetz (2017b). On the Jewish lunar calendar as a marker of difference and also subversion within the Roman Empire, see S. Stern (2017).

25. This is especially true of the role of conflicting calendars in differentiating sects and defining sectarian identities. Social reality, though, is messier and more complicated than the temporal rift described in normative texts produced by such communities, on which see A. Baumgarten (2011).

26. Zerubavel (1985:22). For an interesting case of the development of "Jewish time," see Ratzon (2019).

27. *m. Rosh Hashanah* 1:1, MS Kaufmann; a later hand added "and" between "planting" and "vegetables," suggesting an alternative reading of "New Year for . . . planting and vegetables." Bet Hillel adds that the New Year for trees is on the 15th of Shevat. See also *b. Avodah Zarah* 10a.

28. On (multiple) New Years in the Hebrew Bible and other ancient cultures, see Fleming (2000:127–40).

29. *Mekhilta de-Rabbi Ishmael Pisha* 1 (ed. Horovitz and Rabin, 7; ed. Lauterbach, 13), with parallels in *t. Sukkah* 2:6; *b. Sukkah* 29a; *Pesiqta Rabbati* 15, on which see S. Stern (2017). See also Artemidorus, *Oneirokritikon*, in which the same dream means different things to those of varying social status, gender, ethnicity, and so on.

30. *Genesis Rabbah* 6:3 (ed. Theodor and Albeck, 42). In this midrash, Jacob represents Israel and Esau represents Rome and/or Christians. Edom becomes associated with Rome during the end of the tannaitic period and into the amoraic period, on which see Bakhos (2006:63–64, 79–80); G. Cohen (1967).

31. *Mekhilta de-Rabbi Ishmael Pisha* 1 (ed. Horovitz and Rabin, 7; ed. Lauterbach, 13).

32. *Mekhilta de-Rabbi Ishmael Bahodesh* 1 (ed. Horovitz and Rabin, 203–4; ed. Lauterbach, 290–92).

33. This midrash anticipates some of the arguments in Kosmin (2018).

34. I draw here on a helpful distinction between time as dynamic force or passive passage articulated by anthropologist Handelman (2018). S. Stern's (2003) distinction between "time" and "process" is likewise helpful—time not as abstract and passive but as concrete and dynamic. Even though the division and employment of time for particular ends are more prevalent in rabbinic texts than abstract philosophizing about time as a condition or dimension of the cosmos, we see here and elsewhere the ways in which time-keeping itself is based upon, and also affects, conceptual frameworks.

35. The impact of the temple's destruction continues to be debated, on which see, e.g., Schwartz and Weiss (2012); Balberg (2017a).

36. Even though Josephus, *Jewish War* 2.42–43, 515, 6.421–26 likely exaggerates the number of pilgrims in Jerusalem during festival times, his writings suggest that the city became crowded.

37. Balberg (2017a:5–6) explores the theme of the temple as a conceptual category.

38. On which see Trotter (2019).

39. On the Qumran calendar and calendrical debates in the Second Temple period, see Talmon (1958); VanderKam (1998); M. Kister (1999); S. Stern (2001); Elior (2004:82–164); J. M. Scott (2005); Talmon (2005; 2006); Rietz (2006); Dubs (2006); F. Schmidt (2006); Ben-Dov (2008; 2009; 2012); Jacobus (2015).

40. Other factors were also at play in the conceptualization of the timing of prayer at Qumran and elsewhere during the Second Temple period, on which see Penner (2012).

41. Newsom (1985). These hymns need not always have been used as substitutes for temple worship—they could also have accompanied temple rituals—but at Qumran they probably served as a replacement, on which see D. K. Falk (1998:137–38).

42. E.g., *Jubilees* 2:9, 6:32–38; Ben Sira 43:6–8; 1 Enoch 72–82. Calendrical texts from Qumran include 1QS 1.13–15; 4Q317; 4Q319; 4Q320–21, 4Q325, 4Q252; Ratzon and Ben-Dov (2017). Such calendrical texts do not preclude social interaction and collaboration with those who used a conflicting calendar, as argued in A. Baumgarten (2001).

43. *Pesher Habakkuk* 11:2–8.

44. D. K. Falk writes, e.g., that "even in the case of those works most likely to be connected with the Yahad, it is not a case of the creation of a new institution to replace the

sacrifices, but the desire to adapt and preserve liturgical patterns already associated with the Temple cult to a new setting" (1998:153). On the ways in which the Yahad's communal activities structured its sense of time and eternity, see Newman (2016).

45. 11QPsa; D. K. Falk (1998:125); Mroczek (2016:71–80). Even if the text is nonsectarian and preserves pre-Seleucid temple practices, as Falk argues, this scroll was preserved by the sect at Qumran, for whom the solar calendar was, by then, a defining sectarian feature.

46. VanderKam (1998:73); Beckwith (1996:79–92, 120–24); see, e.g., 4QCalendrical Document A; 4QMishmarot A.

47. Fraade (2009–10:167–68).

48. Philo, *De specialibus legibus* 2.41–223.

49. Niehoff (2018:162–65).

50. Gribetz (2018).

51. Gribetz (2018:361–62). That is not to say that the rhythms of Philo's days mirrored those in the temple, only that temple rhythms as they are described in biblical sources factored into Philo's conception of daily time.

52. 4 Ezra 3:1–4; Charlesworth (1983); M. Stone (1990).

53. Najman (2014:16).

54. On time in 4 Ezra, see Gribetz (2017c). Ezra's desire to know when the end will transpire is shared by the gospel writers, the author of the book of Revelation, and Paul.

55. 4 Ezra 4:33–43.

56. On the liminal time before active labor begins, see Studelska (2012).

57. On Josephus's use of hours, see Kalman (2019:44–45).

58. Kosmin (2018).

59. Zerubavel (1977); Shaw (2011); Perovic (2012).

60. Ruoff (2010:3).

61. Ogle (2015); Stolz (2015); Barak (2013); McCrossen (2000).

62. This is the case regardless of the precise effects of the destruction, on which see (variably) Schwartz (2001); Schremer (2008; 2010); Herr (2009); Schwartz and Weiss (2012).

63. These dilemmas are not unique to the period following the Second Temple's destruction. Texts such as the description of the heavenly temple in Ezekiel 40–42, the Priestly and Holiness Codes' detailed instructions for sacrificial worship, tabernacle construction, and purity practices, and Solomon's temple dedication address in 1 Kings 8 were also responses to the absence of a physical temple.

64. *m. Rosh Hashanah* 4:3 (משחרב בית המקדש); in tannaitic sources, the phrase is also used in *m. Rosh Hashanah* 4:1, 4; *m. Moed Katan* 3:6; *m. Menahot* 10:5; *m. Ma'aser Sheni* 5:2; *m. Sotah* 9:12–13; *m. Sukkah* 3:10; *t. Nedarim* 4:6; *t. Sotah* 13:3, 15:1; *t. Rosh Hashanah* 2:7, and it appears in the Palestinian and Babylonian Talmuds as well. The destruction of the temple is only one of several events used for purposes of periodization in rabbinic sources (e.g., the "end of prophecy" is another), on which see Gafni (1996). Other schemes of historical periodization based on the temple and its destruction are found in *Sifre Deuteronomy* 352 (ed. Finkelstein 410) and later rabbinic sources such as *Genesis Rabbah* 2:5, 28:17, 56:10, 65:23, explicated in Mazeh (forthcoming).

65. See, e.g., N. Cohn (2012).

66. *m. Rosh Hashanah* 4:3; MS Kaufmann seems to contain a mistake (it should state "in the land" not "in the temple" in the second half of the statement).

67. MS Kaufmann.

68. E.-M. Becker (2017:10–12). The Mishnah is explicit about this: "in memory of the temple."

69. See, e.g., Rosen-Zvi (2012:239–54); Balberg (2017a). We might also understand the continued treatment of temple-related rituals in the tannaitic corpus without acknowledgment of the temple's destruction as rabbinic denial, in which the world is still imagined to contain a standing temple. We alternatively might interpret this phenomenon as deliberate downplaying of the temple's destruction, in contrast to other groups that presented the temple's fall in apocalyptic or prophetic fashion.

70. N. Cohn (2012); Schumer (2017); Balberg (2017a).

71. *m. Berakhot* 1:1. On the continued observance of the *terumah* and other temple-related practices during the rabbinic period, see Rosen-Zvi (2012:246, 249; 2008:248n37); Zussman (1969). Aderet (1990:440–44) argues that such practices functioned as temple remnants during a temple-less time. Saiman (2018:48–50) notes as well the persistence of the temple's "ritual clock" in rabbinic sources.

72. As I have argued (Gribetz 2015), the Shema as it is described in *m. Berakhot* 1–2 is a rabbinic practice that, if it was performed prior to the rabbinic period, was likely limited to the liturgy of priests in the temple during the end of the Second Temple period. The only source that provides unequivocal evidence for the Shema's recitation during the Second Temple period is *m. Tamid* 5:1, itself a rabbinic text that probably reveals more about how tannaitic rabbis constructed the temple and its times in the period after its destruction than about temple practices.

73. Additional time-markers, unrelated to the temple, are also used in the Mishnah's discussions of the Shema's timing, reminding us that rabbinic conceptions of times were diverse.

74. E.g., *m. Yoma*.

75. *m. Avot* 1–2.

76. E.g., Josephus, *Jewish Antiquities* 17.271–84, 18.1–10; *Jewish War* 2.55–65; 1QM. Mézange (2006); Licht (1965); Funkenstein (1985); Gignoux (1990); R. Gray (1993); Steudel (1993); J. J. Collins (1997); Grabbe (2001); Werman (2009); Hamidović (2006; 2010); Dimant (2000; 2006; 2009); Henze (2011; 2018); Stuckenbruck (2015); Ben-Dov (2016).

77. 1 Corinthians 7:29–31 NRSV. Paul's apocalypticism and messianism have been explored in Gager (2000:59–76); Segal (2003); Henze (2011:324–30); Taubes (2003); Agamben (2005); Fredriksen (2009:71); Welborn (2015); Hogan (2017).

78. 1 Thessalonians 1–2 NRSV.

79. E.g., Mark 13; Luke 17:20–21; Bahr (2018); Schweitzer (1914, 1964); Dodd (1958:22–23); Allison (1960); J. Weiss (1971); Ehrman (1999). For a critique of scholarship that pits early Christian apocalyptic temporality as realized eschatology against ancient Jewish apocalyptic temporality as future-oriented eschatology, see Stuckenbruck (2016).

80. *t. Ta'anit* 4.8; Schäfer (1980; 2003); Oppenheimer (1983).

81. *m. Hagigah* 2:1; Furstenberg (2013); Schiffman (2006).

82. Irshai (2000; 2017).

83. *Avot de-Rabbi Natan* B31, discussed in Brezis (2015:78). See also the ambivalence about meeting the messiah in *b. Sanhedrin* 98b.

84. Adelman (2009a:quote on 4; 2009b); Himmelfarb (2017).

85. Yerushalmi (1982, 2002:17). Yerushalmi's observation about temporal flexibility in rabbinic historiography and the fluidity with which rabbinic texts treat time and conflate past, present, and future remains broadly accurate, even as scholars since Yerushalmi have added important nuance to his insights. For engagement with and revisions to Yerushalmi's work, see Funkenstein (1989; 1993); Myers (1992); Chazan (1994); Gafni (1996; 2007); the collection of essays in Myers (2007); Milgrom (1985); Neusner (1997; 2004a); Tropper (2004); Ben Shahar (2011). On historical consciousness in earlier Jewish antiquity, see Wacholder (1976); Neher (1976); Hughes (1990); Frölich (1996); Wise (1997).

86. Kaye (2018) has demonstrated that temporal flexibility and creativity underlie fundamental legal concepts, such as simultaneity and retroactivity, in rabbinic sources, not to the exclusion of rabbinic understandings of historical or natural time and time-keeping. Yerushalmi and Kaye both observe that sophisticated modes of temporal fluidity pervade not only rabbinic narratives of biblical events and figures and the legal architecture of rabbinic law but also rabbinic rituals and liturgy, a central purpose of which was to make the past repeatedly ever-present. The temporal dimensions of midrash have also been noted in Heinemann (1970); Bregman (1978); Fraenkel (1987; 1989a); Fraade (1991); Schlüter (2003a; 2003b); Adelman (2009a; 2009b). The idea of an "open" and "retrievable" past accessible through memory is the subject of Dolgopolski (2012).

87. In *m. Rosh Hashanah* 2:8–9, for example, Rabban Gamliel asserts rabbinic authority over the calendar—even in the face of false witnesses and inaccurate observations of the moon. The Mishnah fashions this narrative as a rabbinic attempt to stabilize time during a period of authorial and temporal instability.

88. Brezis (2015:71–95) argues similarly.

89. E.g., *m. Ma'aser Sheni* 5:7; the phrase is discussed in S. Stern (2003:29).

90. Schwartz (2006).

91. Schwartz (2006:25).

92. Schwartz (2006:28–29).

93. Schwartz (2006:26–27).

94. Schwartz (2001); L. Levine (1998); Dohrmann and Reed (2013).

95. On evolving notions of Romanness, see G. Woolf (1998).

96. Feeney (2010:882; 2007); see also Grafton and Swerdlow (1988); Rüpke (1995; 2006); Graf (1997; 2008); Beard (2003).

97. Salzman (1990:esp. 5–13; 1981); Hey (2018); Jones (2016); Divjak and Wischmeyers (2014); Kondoleon (1999); von Freeden (1983); H. Stern (1953).

98. Ker (2010); V. Johnson (1959).

99. E.g., at Sepphoris, Bet Alpha, Hamat Tiberias, Wadi Hamam, Naaran, Huqoq, Sisiya, Yaphia, and Huseifa, on which see Talgam (2010; 2014:esp. 257–332); Magness et al. (2018).

100. They often also labeled the months of the zodiac in Hebrew, discussed in Talgam (2014:273).

101. See, e.g., Heller (2014).

102. Feeney (2007:189).

103. Feeney (2007:210); see also Wallace-Hadrill (2005).

104. S. Stern (2002).

105. Friedheim (2000).

106. S. Stern (2012a:299; 2017). Stern points to similar developments in the transformations of the Gallic calendar under Roman influence as well as other "subcultural calendars" within the Roman Empire.

107. The ideas expressed in this paragraph are indebted to the collaborative research project "The Day Unit" in which I participated in the spring of 2018 at the Israel Institute for Advanced Study; specific contributions of the participants are detailed in the notes below.

108. Neugebauer (1975:560–61) notes that the twelve-hour division of the night was an Egyptian innovation. The word used for "hour" appears in the Pyramid texts (e.g., PT 269a [spell 251]; PT 515a [spell 320]) and Coffin texts (e.g., CT IV 268/269d [spell 335]; CT VII 25c [spell 824]; CT I 22c [spell 7]; CT VI 414z [spell 785]), compiled by Joachim Quack. Definitive divisions of the night into twelve hours, however, do not appear until the diagonal star clock found in the Osireion at Abydos, the later Ramesside star tables, the transit

star clock in the Book of Nut, and the coffin lids of Mesehti and those at Asyut, and a division of the day into twelve hours appears first in the Book of Day, all analyzed in Symons (2017; 2014; 2002a); Symons and Tasker (2015). On the hourly rituals detailed in the Book of the Dead, see Quack (2013). A second-millennium sundial was discovered in the Valley of the Kings, on which see Gautschy (2014); on other sundials and shadow clocks in Egypt, see Symons and Khurana (2016); Symons (2002b; 1998). See also Assmann (1999b). From the Hellenistic period, see the three water clocks that mention Alexander the Great, available at Symons et al. (2013); *Letter of Aristeas* 303 and 3 Maccabees 5:14, as well as the later writings of Philo, e.g., *De somniis* 2.257; *In Flaccum* 85, brought to my attention by Sacha Stern. On the use of hours in Ptolemaic and Roman Egypt, see Remijsen (2007).

109. See, e.g., Symons and Khurana (2016); Bonnin (2015); Winter (2013); A. J. Turner (2007); Gibbs (1976); Symons et al. (2013); Graßhoff (2011); Hannah (2016); M. Wright (2000). Delos and Rhodes were among the sites that produced sundials in the later Hellenistic period.

110. Hours are mentioned, e.g., in Polybius, *Histories* 9.8.4, 9.17.6, 10.12.1 and Strabo, *Geographica* 4.3.4, 4.5.2, 17.1.46, analyzed in S. Stern (2018). See also Hannah (2009:27-115); Wolkenhauer (2011:67-150; 2019); K. Miller (2017:1-15).

111. Pliny the Elder, *Historia naturalis* 7.214; Wolkenhauer (2019).

112. Julius Caesar, *de bello Gallico* 1.26.2; Cicero, *Epistulae ad Atticum* 2.10[12].4, 4.3.3.

113. Pliny the Elder, *Historia naturalis* 36.72, discussed in Heslin (2007); Hannah (2011; 2014).

114. Remijsen (2007:esp. 138-40). Clocks became symbols of status, e.g., Wiemer (1998).

115. Suetonius, *Vita divi Augusti* 50, discussed in Wolkenhauer (2018).

116. Pliny the Elder, *Historia naturalis* 7.212-15.

117. E.g., Pliny the Younger, *Epistula* 3.1; Josephus, *Jewish War* 2.129, 6.423, *Jewish Antiquities* 14.65, 16.162-65, and elsewhere in Josephus's writings; Mark 15:25, 33-34; Matthew 27:45-46; Luke 23:44-45; *m. Berakhot* 1:2; *m. Ketubot* 10:5; *m. Kelim* 12:5; *m. Eduyot* 3:8; *m. Sanhedrin* 5:1, 3; *m. Pesahim* 1:4, 5:1, discussed in Kaye (2018:56-85); S. Stern (2018). On sundials, see Ben-Dov (2011); Bonnin (2010; 2012a; 2012b); S. Adam (1997; 2002a; 2002b). On hourly time-keeping in Galen, see K. Miller (2017:10), who notes that even though sundials increased in popularity in the Roman period, attention to hourly precision declined. Seneca, *Apocolocyntosis* 2 notes the lack of synchrony between clocks.

118. The Romanness of the rabbis has also occupied recent scholarship, e.g., Lapin (2012); Dohrmann and Reed (2013); Furstenberg (2016b); Rosen-Zvi (2017a); Malka and Paz (2019).

119. E.g., Revelation of John.

120. Mark 13:1-37; Matthew 24:1-25:46; Luke 21:5-36. On the history and historiography of the "parting of the ways," see Burns (2016); Segal (1989); Becker and Reed (2003); Lapin (1998); Boyarin (2004); Schäfer (2012). On the role of the destruction in later Christian and rabbinic discourse, see Gregerman (2016).

121. Stökl Ben Ezra (2009).

122. Gager (2015:117-38). On Toledot Yeshu, see Meerson and Schäfer (2014); Schäfer, Meerson, and Deutsch (2011); Barbu and Deutsch (2020).

123. MS Strasbourg in Krauss (1902, 1994:48); trans. Stökl Ben Ezra (2009:487).

124. Similar negotiations occurred in early Islamic communities regarding Friday, on which see M. J. Kister (1989:324).

125. Galatians 4:10-11 NRSV. See also Colossians 2:16; Harker (2015).

126. Harker (2015).

127. *Didache* 8.1-2; trans. Lake (1912).

128. *Didache* 8.11 mandates prayer three times each day, as do rabbinic sources. While the Didache distinguishes between people based on fast days, the timing of daily prayer obscures those differences: the content of daily prayers differed, but their timing roughly aligned.

129. *Didascalia Apostolorum* 21:20. The identity of those behind the Didascalia is complicated, on which see Fonrobert (2001a); H. Weiss (2003). 5 Ezra 1:31 (2 Esdras 1:31), in a polemical passage against law-observing Jews, puts the following words into God's mouth: "When you offer oblations to me, I will turn my face from you; for I have rejected your festal days, and new moons, and circumcisions of the flesh" (NRSV). The Spanish recension adds "Sabbaths" to the list of rituals rejected by God; on 5 Ezra, see Hogan (2018).

130. John Chrysostom, *Homily against the Jews* 1:4:4, 7; trans. Harkins (1979:4). See also Hieronymus, *Adversus Jovinianum* 23, 290D, in which the apostle Peter is described as eating at the sixth hour rather than "waiting for the evening star like the Jews usually do."

131. Note that he disregards belief as a criterion of differentiation when one's temporal practices do not align with one's stated loyalties. On Chrysostom's construction of identity and difference, including through the celebration of Christian festivals, see Sandwell (2007:esp. 134–53). Hilarius, *De solstitiis* and Ambrose, *Letters* 23.4 likewise insist that Christians separate themselves from Roman "pagan" times, on which see Salzman (2004:193). In the sixth century, Caesarius bishop of Arles in Gaul (*Sermons* 13:5, 19:4, 52:2) and Martin bishop of Bracara Augusta in Galicia (*De correctione rusticorum*, 8–17) reprimanded those in their communities who celebrated the "pagan" Day of Jupiter (Thursday) as a day of rest instead of the Lord's Day (Sunday), and Martin also encouraged congregants to refrain from using weekday names that allude to the planetary gods, on which see Bultrighini (2018). Both Caesarius and Martin sought to forge Christian-pagan difference through such temporal regulations.

132. E.g., the Council of Nicaea and the Synod of Laodicea, on which see Hefele (1896:2.316), discussed in Zerubavel (1985:23). Dating Easter according to the Jewish calendar distinguished the Quatrodecimans from other Christians and caused considerable calendrical controversy, on which see Eusebius, *Ecclesiastical History* 5.23; Leonhard (2006). For a study of processes of differentiation between Jews and Christians through the celebration of Passover and Easter, see Yuval (2006:56–91). Whereas I generally refer to the "parting of the ways" between Jews and Christians as a mutual if complicated process of differentiation, with regard to calendrical matters in particular, including Sabbaths and festivals, it might more accurately be described as a process of distinguishing Christian festival dates from the dates of Jewish festivals (that is, Christian bishops consciously and deliberately tried to disentangle their festivals from the Jewish calendar) rather than a simultaneous process of calendrical differentiation. The Sabbath and festival rituals that developed among Jews and Christians, on the other hand, are indeed best regarded as continuously in dialogue with one another, evolving alongside and entangled with the other.

133. Socrates Scholasticus, *Ecclesiastical History* 1.9; trans. Zenos (1890).

134. Socrates Scholasticus, *Ecclesiastical History* 5.22; trans. Zenos (1890).

135. J. Shwartz (1987); Rouwhorst (2001a); Stökl Ben Ezra (2003); Horowitz (2006); Gribetz (2011). Calendrical difference also played an important role in defining difference among divergent groups of Christians, on which see Beckwith (1996:51–70).

136. When the empire itself Christianized, it began imposing revised rhythms of time, by then a hybrid of Roman and Christian time, on its Jewish inhabitants in yet new ways. See, e.g., *Theodosian Code* 2.8.1; *Justinian Code* 3.12.3, in S. Scott (1932, 1973:275); Eusebius, *Life of Constantine* 4.18–19; Salzman (2004).

137. These are now commonly known as the "Five Ws," on which see Copeland (1995:66–69).

138. In addition to the tractates detailed here, see also the beginning of tractates *Shevi'it, Pesahim, Shekalim, Yoma, Betzah, Rosh Hashanah, Ta'anit, Megillah, Moed Katan, Ketubot, Eduyot, Ohalot,* and *Zavim*; discussions of timing appear throughout the Mishnah and the rabbinic corpus.

139. On notions of sacredness or holiness in rabbinic sources, see N. Cohn (2018); Kaye (forthcoming a).

140. For an extensive discussion of previous scholarship, see Gribetz and Kaye (2019).

141. Kasher (1952); S. Safrai (1965); Tabory (1995); S. Stern (1996; 2001; 2002; 2012a; 2012b; 2019); Walfish (2001); Neusner (2004b); Schiffman (2012a); Bord (2006); Dimant (2000; 2009); Stern and Burnett (2014); Noam (2015); VanderKam (1998); Ben-Dov (2008); Ratzon (2019).

142. Barr (1962); S. Stern (2003:46–58); Brin (2001); Rubin (2008); S. Friedman (2008; 2014); Yoskovich (2014).

143. Yerushalmi (1982, 2002); Gafni (1996; 2007); Schlüter (2003a; 2003b; 2005); Tropper (2004); Ben Shahar (2011; 2015); N. Cohn (2012); Schumer (2017).

144. Heinemann (1970); Fraenkel (1989a; 1989b; 1989c); Adelman (2009a; 2009b); Ulmer (2009); Dolgopolski (2012); Vidas (2014). See also Bregman (1978); Talmon (1978); Robbins (1997); Rubenstein (1997); Steiner (2007); Gottlieb (2009); Wolfson (2003).

145. Strassfeld (2013).

146. Kaye (2018).

147. Carlebach (2011); E. Baumgarten (2015); Nothaft (2014); Nothaft and Isserles (2014).

148. Rudavsky (2000); Wolfson (2006); Krinis (2016).

149. Kalman (2019).

150. I use the term "identity" to refer primarily to forms of collective or social affiliation, while I use the term "subjectivity" to refer to individual or interior senses of self. I regard these analytical categories as unstable and complicated, not only in how they might have functioned in antiquity but also in how contemporary scholars employ them in their studies of such pasts, on which see, on identity: P. Gleason (1983); Wurgaft (1995); Brubaker and Cooper (2000); Kotrosits (2015); Berzon (2016); Reed (2018:389–435); on self and subjectivity: Foucault (1986:37–96); Sorabji (2006); Bartsch (2006); on identity, subjectivity, and difference in rabbinic sources, see Berkowitz (2012); Balberg (2014); Rosen-Zvi and Ophir (2011; 2018).

151. I do not, for example, attempt to discover or distill "the rabbinic conception of time," on which see also Goldberg (2000, 2004; 2000; 2011b; 2016); Kaye (2018).

152. There is necessarily overlap between these units of time in the various chapters, as they are interrelated and mutually informing (e.g., one cannot have hours without days, and calendars, though they organize annual time, consist of a series of individual days strung together).

153. Graf (1997).

154. Here, I invoke Merleau-Ponty (2002).

155. On the role of the Babylonian Talmud in geonic society, see Brody (1998). On the idea that exegetical debates often lie in the background of rabbinic discussions, see Alexander (2007); Kraemer (1996); Fonrobert (2000:40–67).

156. G. Woolf (1998).

157. *Digest* 1.5.17; P.Giss. 40, 1.1. See also Garnsey (2004); Mathisen (2006); Ando (2011).

158. Lapin (2012:1). See also G. Woolf (1998:206–9); Schwartz (2001).

159. Dohrmann and Reed (2013); Berthelot (2017; 2014).

160. Overlapping identities are not unique to the Roman imperial context. Consider, e.g., similar tensions between notions of German and Jewish identity in the nineteenth century, or "Americanness" and "Jewishness" in the twentieth and twenty-first.

161. On Roman polytheism and monotheism, see Athanassiadi and Frede (1999); Mitchell and Nuffelen (2010). On the derogatory employment of the term *paganus* by Christians in the Latin West, see Brown (1999).

162. On the history of these designations, see Barbu (2011; 2016); Ophir and Rosen-Zvi (2018).

163. E.g., Flusser (1988).

164. E.g., Segal (1989); Yuval (2006).

165. E.g., Becker and Reed (2003).

166. E.g., Boyarin (2004); Schäfer (2012).

167. E.g., Tong (2019). Also relevant is Weitzman (2017), who historicizes scholarly attempts to conceptualize Jewish origins.

168. E.g., Townsend (2008); Reed (2018).

169. E.g., Baker (2016); Boyarin (2018); Rosen-Zvi and Ophir (2011); Reinhartz (2014); Rosen-Zvi (2014; 2016a); Mason (2007; 2014); Schwartz (2011).

170. The categories "sex," "gender," and "sexual difference" are themselves overlapping and intertwined, on which see Dunning (2011:13–17); Butler (1990; 1993); J. W. Scott (1986).

171. E.g., *t. Bikurim* 2:3–3; Fonrobert (2006); Lev (2010); Strassfeld (2013); Kessler (2020). The rabbis also wrote within an ancient Roman context that conceived of gender and sexuality as a spectrum rather than a binary, on which see Holmes (2012); Hopkins and Wyke (2005); C. Williams (1999); F. Zeitlin (1995).

172. The rabbis also thought beyond binaries with regard to ethnicity, genealogy, and lineage, grappling with and developing numerous intermediary categories (e.g., Samaritans, *mamzerim*) even as they also constructed these binaries as stable categories, on which see Y. Koren (2014); Furstenberg (2017a; 2019); Lavee (2018).

Chapter 1

1. Katzoff and Schreiber (1998:106); S. Stern (2012a:331–32).

2. *CIJ* 777; Ameling (2004:414–22); translation and analysis in Harland (2006); Leonhard (2017:267–68).

3. Schwartz (2001) argues that participation of non-rabbinic Jews in Roman, and even specifically pagan, life was common at least until the late third or early fourth century. Whether or not the family was Jewish, however, the combination of Jewish and Roman festivals indicates that the two sets of festivals were integrated into the year.

4. *CIJ* i. no. 650; Noy (2005:187–92); S. Stern (2012a:340–41). The inscription also includes a reference to God's law and images of *menorot*.

5. Jews used Latin conventions of lunar reckoning to determine the times of Jewish festivals, on which see S. Stern (2012a:340–41).

6. Most extant Roman calendars and calendar fragments can be found in Degrassi (1963); Rüpke (1995); see in addition the *Feriale Duranum* as well as the codex calendars of Philocalus and Polemius Silvius. Literary sources about the Roman calendar include Ovid's *Fasti*, Plutarch's *Roman Questions*, M. Terentis Varro's *De lingua Latina*, fragments of M. Verrius Flaccus's *De verborum significatu*, Censorinus's *De die natali*, Macrobius's *Saturnalia*, John Lydus's *De mensibus*, and scattered comments throughout Latin litera-

ture, such as in Cicero's and Horace's writings, collected in A. Michels (1967:5–7). On the history of the republican and imperial Roman calendars, see Mommsen (1859); A. Michels (1967); Brind'Amour (1983); York (1986); Radke (1990); Salzman (1990); Rüpke (1995; 2006; 2011); Hannah (2005); Feeney (2007); Ker (2010); S. Stern (2012a:204–98).

7. Durkheim (2001:34–49).

8. Ricœur (1988:104); for a particular example, see Le Goff (2014).

9. Halbwachs (1992:223); Assmann (1995a).

10. Yerushalmi (1982, 2002:5). Other calendrical documents, such as *Megillat Ta'anit*, functioned in similar ways, on which see Noam (2003; 2006).

11. Graf (1997); Feeney (2007).

12. Throughout this chapter, I use the term "gentiles" to denote the Hebrew "גויים," as this is the term that is used in the rabbinic passages under discussion; in censored printed editions the term "עובדי כוכבים" or "עובדי עבודה זרה" is used in place of "גויים."

13. Seneca, *Epistulae morales* 18.2; trans. R. Campbell (1969:66).

14. The phenomenon of reading one's own past into the histories of a host culture is a common cultural practice. For ancient examples, see Josephus, *Jewish Antiquities* 12.225–27; 1 Maccabees 12:1–23, 14:16–23; *b. Tamid* 32a–b; for later examples, see Marcus (1990); Greenblatt (2014). On obsessions with origins, see Bloch (1992:24–31); Weitzman (2017).

15. On "counter-history," see Funkenstein (1989; 1993); on "competitive historiography," see J. J. Collins (1983:32–38).

16. Barak (2014); related notions of temporal resistance have been explored in J. Halberstam (2005:1–8); Carlebach (2011:115–40); Nothaft and Isserles (2014); Ogle (2015); Stolz (2017:207–70). The study of queer time highlights not only possibilities for diverse notions of temporality but also the ways in which communities and subcultures employ and embody such times as they engage different experiences and claim alternative values to those of heteronormative hegemonic society, on which see J. Halberstam (2005:1–21).

17. Much has been written about this, e.g., Halbertal (1998); Neis (2013:170–201).

18. This is especially noteworthy given that much scholarship on Roman religion has focused on the ritualization and sacralization of space; e.g., Beard, North, and Price (1998). Watts (2015:24–28, 32–35) outlines how Roman festivals throughout the Roman Empire would have affected not only those who participated in their celebration but also those who deliberately decided not to join in worship.

19. *m. Avodah Zarah* 1:1–2; critical edition in Rosenthal (1980:58–59); translation follows MS Kaufmann.

20. Perhaps the text assumes that its audience already knows that participation in such festivals was prohibited based on biblical prohibitions against idolatry and thus seeks to emphasize that related activities in the days before festivals are similarly prohibited. On earlier anxieties about participation in prohibited festivals, see *Jubilees* 6:34–35, 4QPHosea 2:15–17, 1 Maccabees 1:41–63, and Galatians 4:8–11, on which see M. J. Bernstein (1991); Talmon (1999:esp. 32).

21. Tertullian, *De idolatria*, also mentions financial aspects of participation in cultic worship.

22. On this topic, see also Friedheim (2006a).

23. See, e.g., Cicero, *Epistulae ad Atticum* 6.1.8 and *Pro Murena* 25; Livy, *Ab urbe condita* 9.46.5; Salzman (1990:6).

24. See the calendars in Degrassi (1963); Rüpke (1995).

25. A. Michels (1967:5); Feeney (2010:883) makes a similar observation about the imperial calendar. On medieval contexts, see Le Goff (1980:29–42); Carlebach (2011: 141–59).

26. L. Schmidt (1997; 2001).

27. Y. Cohn (2011:187).

28. E.g., *m. Avodah Zarah* 1:4 further restricts travel to and from cities associated with markets during festival times; see also *y. Avodah Zarah* 1.2, 39c–d. On markets, see Y. Cohn (2011); Z. Safrai (1984); de Ligt (1993); Kofsky (1998).

29. E.g., *m. Avodah Zarah* 1:5; *m. Avodah Zarah* 2:3–5 also prohibits acquiring other items from gentiles (e.g., wine, vinegar, certain types of earthenware, hides, and cheese) that are not directly related to festivals.

30. *y. Avodah Zarah* 1:2, 39c; Belayche (2004:12–14).

31. *y. Avodah Zarah* 1:4 39b. See also John Chrysostom, *Hom. de Se. Phil. PG* 48.747–52; Sozomen, *Historia ecclesiastica* 2.4; Sandwell (2007:135); Kofsky (1998:24).

32. Scullard (1981:43); Rüpke (2007:195). Libanius notes that teachers were paid on the Kalends (*Or.* 9.15).

33. P.Fay.119/P. Penn Museum inv. E02786; Abercrombie (1978); Hohlwein (1957).

34. British Museum 988,1005.237.

35. E.g., P. Oxy. 48.3406; P. Oxy. 14.1679; P. Oxy. 59.3991, published in Bagnall and Cribiore (2006).

36. Dio of Prusa, *Speech to Apamea Celaenae* 35:15, cited in S. Price (1984:107).

37. Ovid, *Fasti* 1.167–70; trans. Boyle and Woodard (2000:8).

38. Seneca, *Epistulae morales* 18.1; trans. R. Campbell in Seneca (1969:66).

39. This rabbinic passage is similar to Stoic notions of the joy of benefaction, on which see Seneca, *De beneficiis*; Graver (2019).

40. Halbertal (1998). See also *t. Avodah Zarah* 1:7.

41. *m. Avodah Zarah* 1:3; trans., with modification, I. Epstein (1935:36); *t. Avodah Zarah* 1:2 contains a similar list, which includes Kalends, Saturnalia, and Kratesis, but it confuses the meaning of these festivals, listing Saturnalia as the day on which Rome ascended to power and Kratesis as the *genousia* of emperors and so on.

42. On previous scholarship that analyzes these festivals as they appear in rabbinic sources, see the overview in Binder (2012:221–23); Gribetz (2016a); Neusner (2008:31–33, 126–29); Friedheim (2004; 2006b:307–82); Graf (2002; 2015:esp. 61–86); Schäfer (2002); Veltri (2000; 2015:64–96); Rosenthal (1980); Hadas-Lebel (1979; 2005:334–42, 358–60); Blidstein (1968); Urbach (1959); Krauss (1947); Elmslie (1911); Blaufuss (1909).

43. *y. Avodah Zarah* 1.3, 39c explicitly notes the Mishnah's categorization of public and private festivals: "עד כאן לציבור מיכן ואילך ליחיד" (Until here [the text refers to] public [festivals], from this point on, to private [ones]), on which see Graf (2002:439–40). *t. Avodah Zarah* 1:1 also differentiates between fixed and variable festivals.

44. Macrobius, *Saturnalia* 1.16.8; Veltri (2000:107; 2015:66–68).

45. Tertullian, *De idolatria* 14–16; see also Tertullian, *Apologeticus* 42.3 on the Saturnalia; text from Waszinik and Van Winden (1987:49, 51). On the relationship between Tertullian's *De idolatria* and the Mishnah, see Binder (2012); Fredriksen and Irshai (2015).

46. Nock (1952). On the *Feriale Osloenses* from Egypt, see Eitrem and Amundsen (1936:45–55); on other *ferialia*, see Degrassi (1963:277–93). Unlike the Mishnah's categorical organization, the *Feriale Duranum* lists the festivals according to their calendar dates.

47. *Theodosian Code* 2.8.19; Macrobius, *Saturnalia* 1.16.5–8 in Kaster (2011:188–91).

48. See, e.g., Scullard (1981); Rüpke (2007:186–201).

49. The name "Kalends" refers in the rabbinic text—as it did more generally in the Greek east—to the Kalends of January, on which see Graf (2015:132). Macrobius, *Saturnalia* 1.8.23–24 explains the interconnectedness of the two festivals.

50. On the Kalends of January and the Saturnalia, see Meslin (1970:51–93); Scullard (1981:51–58); Graf (2002:436–37, 440–43); Weinstock (1964); M. A. Bernstein (1987); Graf (1998); Bowersock, Brown, and Grabar (1999:532); Dolansky (2010).

51. Meslin (1970:51–93); Graf (1998); Bowersock, Brown, and Grabar (1999:532).

52. Isidore of Seville, *Etymologies* 5.33.3; Plutarch, *Moralia* 268. The nature and duration of the celebrations changed over the course of the republican and imperial periods, on which see Meslin (1970).

53. Graf (1997:24–25).

54. Graf (2015:239).

55. Urbach (1959); Bernett (2007); Eck (2007).

56. Feeney (2007); Argetsinger (1992:175).

57. S. Price (1984:105).

58. On the impact of the Roman army on popularizing Roman festivals in the east, see Friedheim (2000; 2004); Graf (2002:442–43, 446). On the imperial cult in the Greek east, see Peppard (2012b:91–93); Trummer (1983); S. Price (1984); Friesen (2001); Bernett (2007); Eck (2007); Gitler and Gambash (2017).

59. Sperber (1984:195–96); Graf (2002:437–38); Hadas-Lebel (2005:338); Veltri (2015:89–90); a summary of additional views can be found in Binder (2012:223).

60. Graf (2015:68–69).

61. E.g., P. Ryl. III 601; on the kratesis era, see Skeat (1994).

62. Dio Cassius, *Roman History* 51.19.6; trans. Snyder (1940:231). Aside from Dio Cassius's statement, the festival is not widely attested in ancient sources beyond Egypt.

63. Macrobius, *Saturnalia* 1.12.35; trans. Kaster (2011:152–53).

64. Graf (2002:438–40). On the celebration of birthdays of individuals, see Censorinus, *De die natali*, trans. H. Parker (2007); *I. Cret.* 4.300, discussed in Graf (2015:90–91).

65. Graf (2015:70); Binder (2012:224–25). Hadas-Lebel (2005:338) notes that "the expression ἡ γενεσιὰ ἡμέρα 'anniversary day' correspond[s] to the Latin *natalis dies*."

66. Feeney (2007:154).

67. S. Price (1984:105).

68. *IGR* 1 1509 = *I. Cret.* IV 333, no. 300; Graf (2015:71); S. Price (1984:104–6).

69. S. Price (1984:106–7). The Arval Acts and the *Feriale Duranum* record birthdays of imperial family members, including the birthday of Julia Maesa, the mother of two emperors (Graf [2015:70]). In Lapethos in Cyprus, a temple and statue of Tiberius were dedicated on the emperor's birthday, 16 November 29 CE; IRG III 933 = LBW 3.2773 = OGIS 2.583.

70. Rüpke (2006:81, 95).

71. Graf (2015:72). On practices of cultic cremation, especially in the context of the Roman military, see, e.g., Tertullian, *De corona* 11.3, which argues that Christians ought not participate in burning rituals after death.

72. Separating a festival's civic and cultic aspects might appear to impose modern categories onto an ancient society that did not dichotomize its practices in this way. Such distinctions, if not in these terms, however, were already made in antiquity, also by the rabbis. *m. Avodah Zarah* 3:4 regards the same object—a statue of a god—as having cultic significance in one setting (a temple, for instance) and having non-cultic significance in another (a bathhouse). In other words, this rabbinic text not only imagines the distinction between cultic and non-cultic but in fact relies on this distinction. Commerce was only prohibited when it served specifically idolatrous ends or was conducted before or during periods of worship. Rabbinic texts, not modern readers, draw these distinctions. It is also reasonable to think that many Jews would have been more comfortable participating in activities that deemphasized cultic rituals and that were geared toward civic engagement, even if other Jews wholeheartedly participated in all aspects of Roman cultic worship without similar qualms. On these distinctions in rabbinic sources, see Schwartz (1998; 2001:167–76); Yadin-Israel (2006).

73. Veltri (2000); Friedheim (2004); Z. Weiss (2014). The Kalends of January also increasingly incorporated imperial resonances, on which see Andrews and Flower (2015).

74. Graf (2002:441–42; 2015:74–75).

75. Brown (1995:85; 1993:50). Philocalus's codex calendar of 354 offers a vivid depiction of the blending of traditionally religious and civic devotion associated with the Kalends of January, on which see Salzman (1990:79).

76. The festivities could even be violent, e.g., Libanius, *Oratio* 1.230 [1.184] and Isaac of Antioch, *Homily on the Night Vigil*, line 17, on which see M. Gleason (1986); Belayche (2007); Brown (1992:87–88).

77. Origen, *Contra Celsum* 8.21.

78. m. *Avodah Zarah* 1:3; translated according to MS Kaufmann; the brackets represent a section of the text that was added later, on which see Hayes (1997:155–59).

79. Feeney (2007:148).

80. Macrobius, *Saturnalia* 1.16.8; Rawson (2005:134). See also Rowlandson (1998:296); Argetsinger (1992:176–79); Bowerman (1917:313).

81. Rawson (2005:134); Feeney (2007:158); Argetsinger (1992:180–81); Bowerman (1917).

82. Rawson (2005:134).

83. Rawson (2005:158–59).

84. Rawson (2005:134–35).

85. Rawson (2005:135).

86. Rawson (2005:135–37); see also Censorinus, *De die natali*, 29.

87. Dio Cassius, *Roman History* 62.19–20.

88. Pl. *Amph.* 462; Livy, *Ab urbe condita* 24.32.9, 30.45, 33.23; Seneca, *Epistulae morales* 47.18; Macrobius, *Saturnalia* 1.11.12; discussed in Olson (2017:80, 87). πῖλος in Greek.

89. Dixon (1992:135).

90. Gribetz (2017a).

91. Flower (2017); Lott (2004:34–35); Pollini (2008).

92. Hano (1986).

93. Muir (2011:44).

94. Staccioli (2003:30–31); van Straten (1981:144–45); Draycott (2017:155–60).

95. *InscItal* XI.1 (1932:27–38); Beard (1991).

96. See Hayes (1997:155–59) on the likelihood that this is a later addition based on a beraita in *b. Avodah Zarah* 14a. Nonetheless, similar banquets are mentioned in other tannaitic sources, e.g., *t. Avodah Zarah* 1:4, 1:21, as well as *y. Avodah Zarah* 1:3, 39c, discussed by Hayes.

97. Pliny, *Epistulae* 1.9.1–2; Dionysius of Halicarnassus, *Antiquitates Romanae* 4.15.5; Ovid, *Fasti* 3.787–88, discussed in Dolansky (2008).

98. On the development of these prohibitions, see Hayes (1997:esp. 127–43, 154–70).

99. *t. Avodah Zarah* 1:1; Carlebach (2011:149); Blidstein (1968:29–60).

100. Salzman (1990:236); Graf (2015:118), though agricultural work was still permitted.

101. *Theodosian Code* 16.10.3 (342); 16.10.8 (382); 16.10.17 (399); Markus (1990:107–9); Salzman (1999); Nothaft (2011:520); Fraschetti (1999:7–31). Later sources, e.g., Zosimus, *Historia nova*, portray Constantine as spurning traditional festivals and even blame the demise of the western empire on the failure to celebrate the *ludi saeculares*.

102. Salzman (1990).

103. Graf (2015:105–27).

104. Libanius, *Orationes* 9.4; Graf (2015:130).

105. Salzman (1990:240).

106. *Theodosian Code* 2.8.19; additional glosses were incorporated into the *Justinian Code*, the *Breviarium of Alaric*, and elsewhere, on which see Graf (2015:105–27).

107. In 395 CE, Theodosius's son Arcadius declared that "the regular superstitious days of the pagans should not be counted as legal holidays" (*Theodosian Code* 2.8.22), discussed in Graf (2015:122).

108. Graf (2015:118–19).

109. Salzman (1990:235–46).

110. Salzman (1990:236); Arcadius and Honorius removed these festivals from the calendar altogether.

111. Graf (2015:128–62).

112. Chrysostom, *On the Kalends*; Maxwell (2006a:154–57; 2006b:33–36); Sandwell (2007:146–48); Graf (2012).

113. Graf (2015:138–40). Graf (2015:144) also mentions prohibitions against participation in pagan festivals mandated by the Councils of Eliberi, Laodicea, and Carthage, as well as sermons by Petrus Chrysologus, bishop of Ravenna; Maximus, bishop of Turin; and a sermon misattributed to Ambrose of Milan, all of which similarly warn congregants against celebrating the Kalends in the late fourth and early fifth centuries.

114. Augustine, *Against the Pagans*, in I. Hill (1997:180–237).

115. On anxiety surrounding festival worship by bishops in Egypt, see Frankfurter (2018:114–25).

116. Bishops' opposition to such celebration continued for many centuries. At the Councils of Trullo (692) and Rome (743), the fact that Christians partook in the Kalends prompted the church synods again to forbid its celebration. See, e.g., Boniface Letter 40, in Emerton (1976, 2000:59–60). At a certain point, the Kalends came to be regarded as a Christian, rather than a pagan, festival. In some Toledot Yeshu manuscripts, Jesus instructs his followers to stop celebrating Hanukkah and instead to celebrate Kalends, implying that the text's author considered the Kalends an authentically Christian festival, on which see Stökl Ben Ezra (2009:487). Likewise, much to the chagrin of Christian clergy, when Muslims entered the cities of North Africa and the Levant and witnessed the celebration of the Kalends, they called it "a great feast of the Christians," on which see Brown (1995:86); Idri (1954).

117. On related notions surrounding the invention of "religion" and "Judaism" in this period, see Schwartz (2001:179–202); Boyarin (2008).

118. On Macrobius's identity and dates, see Cameron (1966).

119. Livy, *Ab urbe condita* I.1–13.

120. Livy, *Ab urbe condita* I.17–21.

121. Livy, *Ab urbe condita* Prologue; trans. Luce (2008).

122. On Ovid's *Fasti*, see Feeney (2007:138–211); Wallace-Hadrill (1987); Pasco-Pranger (2006).

123. Ovid, *Fasti* I.63–294.

124. Ovid, *Fasti* III.1–98; trans. Boyle and Woodard (2004:55).

125. Ovid, *Fasti* IV.806; Beard (2003).

126. Ovid, *Fasti* IV.857–58.

127. On the turn to pre-Roman history in late antiquity, see Ando (2015).

128. Beard (2003).

129. Ovid, *Ab urbe condita* Prologue; trans. Luce (2008).

130. J. C. Scott (1990). The hidden transcript is somewhat publicly shared through the rabbinic text, and yet the text's audience is still assumed to consist of rabbinic insiders.

131. J. C. Scott (1990:2).

132. J. C. Scott (1990:4).

133. Within Jewish communities, the rabbis were powerholders, but within the broader Roman context, especially during the period of the Palestinian Talmud's redaction, they were subordinates in relation to imperial figures of authority.

134. Kosmin (2018:186).

135. On the term's etymology, see Friedheim (2006a:274–82). Perhaps the term is also connected to the Latin *ides*, the middle of the month and itself a special day. On the etymology of *ides*, see Macrobius, *Saturnalia* 1.15.14–17.

136. NRSV.

137. NRSV.

138. A related midrash is attributed to Rabbi Yossi in *Sifre Deuteronomy Ha'azinu* 325 on Deuteronomy 32:35.

139. Rubenstein (1996) argues that the homily was likely delivered on Sukkot, juxtaposing Roman values with Jewish ones specifically in the context of the festival cycle. See also Wasserman (2017); Hayes (2020).

140. Ophir and Rosen-Zvi (2018:206–7).

141. *y. Avodah Zarah* 1:3, 39c; translated with modifications from Schäfer (2002:340). See the parallel in *y. Berakhot* 8:6, 12b; A. Gray (2005a:102–3).

142. NRSV, with modification. This midrashic tradition also appears in *Pirqe de-Rabbi Eliezer* 20.

143. Psalm 139:11–12 NRSV.

144. Schäfer (2002:339n13); this reading was first proposed by Lewy (1878:83). Lieberman (1962:10–11) offers an alternative interpretation of קלון דיאו, as a Greek proclamation (καλόν δύε) to the sun, "set well." Neusner (1982:20) suggests καλον deo.

145. It is unclear whether the text portrays Adam as specifically pagan, though his invention of the festival of Kalends in this story suggests that the rabbis did not necessarily regard him as Jewish. *b. Sanhedrin* 38b calls Adam a *min* and accuses him of practicing epispasm.

146. Schäfer (2002:340). Macrobius, too, mentions that some festivals, such as the Saturnalia, originated centuries before the founding of Rome, e.g., *Saturnalia* 1.8.36–37.

147. Ovid, *Fasti*,1.72, 161–64. See also Macrobius, *Saturnalia* 1.3.13. Plutarch, *Roman Questions*, 19 observes that the new year begins in January because the amount of light increases, bringing people closer to the divine.

148. In the Babylonian Talmud's version of this story, discussed below, it states explicitly that Adam made the day a *"yom tov."*

149. *y. Avodah Zarah* 1:3, 39c; translated with modifications and analysis in Schäfer (2002:340). The first half of the story is Hebrew, the second half is Aramaic.

150. See also Dio Cassius, *Roman History* 1.6.7.

151. John Lydos, *De mensibus* 4.2; Macrobius, *Saturnalia* 1.9.16; Veltri (2000:120–22); Schäfer (2002:340).

152. See also Philo, *De fuga* 184–85 and *Pesiqta de-Rav Kahana* 15:5, which connect the twelve tribes to the months of the years, constellations of the zodiac, and hours of day and night. On this passage, see also Berthelot (forthcoming:chap. 3).

153. Perhaps the text also alludes to the Greek καλεω, to call.

154. Graf (2002:438).

155. Isidore of Seville, *Etymologies* 5.33.3; Plutarch, *Moralia* 268; John Lydos, *De mensibus* 4.2.

156. Macrobius, *Saturnaia* 1.16.21–26; Schäfer (2002:340–41); Graf (2002:440). On the term, see Sokoloff (2002:50, 305); Jastrow (1943, 2005:51, 775). The days immediately following the named days (Kalends, Nones, Ides) were considered both days of rest (*dies nefasti*) and bad luck (*dies atri*); see, e.g., Varro, *De lingua Latina* 6:29.

NOTES TO CHAPTER 1 [273]

157. Ovid, *Fasti* 1.57–60 refers to these "black days" thusly: "The next day after these days will be black (watch you are not deceived!). The belief comes from a real event: for on those days Rome suffered sorrowful losses, with Mars not going their way"; see also Macrobius, *Saturnalia* 1.15.22; Ker (2010:381–82); Grafton and Swerdlow (1988:23–24).

158. On *dies aegyptiaci*, see Steele (1919); Neugebauer (1983:516); Skemer (2010). This term, *dies aegyptiacus*, was introduced during or after the reign of Constantine (though the term *dies ater* dates from the Augustan era) and appears in the writings of Ambrose, Augustine, and Marinus, as well as in later texts such as the Syriac Book of Medicine and Bede's hymns, among others. There are 25 such dates in Philocalus's calendar as well as in other similar calendars (2 per month, with an additional one in January), and scholars assume that the dates pertain to some sort of lunar phenomenon, which relates well to the centrality of the number twelve in the rabbinic story. The slippage between *dies atri* and *dies aegyptiacus* is attributed, in medieval manuscripts, to the idea that Egypt was associated with darkness in Greek, and in later texts it is January 1 rather than 2 listed as a *dies aegyptiaci*, on which see Skemer (2010:82, 100).

159. Schäfer (2002:340–41). On periods of good and bad luck in the Jewish calendar, see b. *Ta'anit* 29a–b. For further analysis of this narrative, see Berthelot (forthcoming).

160. y. *Avodah Zarah* 1.3, 39c.

161. NRSV.

162. y. *Avodah Zarah* 1.3, 39c, translated with modification from Schäfer (2002:341).

163. *Genesis Rabbah* 67:8 (ed. Theodor and Albeck, 763). See also y. *Hagigah* 1:7, 76c, on which see Berthelot (forthcoming).

164. Translated based on Freedman (1983:612), though I translate סנטרא as "centurion" or "guardsman" rather than "senate," as per Jastrow (1943, 2005:1006). For a reading of the phrase as "senate," see Bonesho (2020:167–69).

165. y. *Avodah Zarah* 1.3, 39c.

166. In tannaitic and early amoraic sources, Edom was associated with Rome; later, Edom was also sometimes associated with Christianity, on which see Bakhos (2006:47–64, 79–84); Berthelot (2016; 2017); Morgenstern (2016); Hadas-Lebel (1984; 2011); G. Cohen (1967).

167. Genesis 25:23 NRSV.

168. E.g., Pliny, *Epistula* 2.17.24; Lucian, *Saturnalia* 18; Horace, *Satires* 2; Seneca, *Epistulae Morales* 47.14; Plutarch, *Moralia* 272c, 1131c; Macrobius, *Saturnalia* 1.8; Historia Augusta, *Life of Verus* 7.5; discussed in Dolansky (2010).

169. Dolansky (2010).

170. Evans (1978); Sharland (2005).

171. Epictetus, *Discourses* 1.25.8, 4.1.58, discussed in Dolansky (2010:498–99).

172. Dolansky (2010:498–99).

173. John Lydos, *De mensibus* 4.2 mentions that Janus is called Saturn on the Kalends of January.

174. b. *Avodah Zarah* 8a; translation based on MS Paris 1337; see partial parallels in y. *Berakhot* 8:6, 12b; b. *Hullin* 60a; b. *Shabbat* 28b; *Avot de-Rabbi Natan* A1 (ed. Schechter, 4). The passage then retells the story as a tale about Adam's discovery of the start and end of the night on the sixth day of creation.

175. See, e.g., Rubenstein (1999).

176. On the festivals' length, see Macrobius, *Saturnalia* 1.10.2–6, 18, 23–24, 11.50. b. *Eruvin* 56a refers to the solstices as the longest and shortest days of the year, and discusses the equinoxes as well.

177. Benovitz (2003:26–27). y. *Avodah Zarah* 1:2, 39c mentions that Saturnalia begins eight days before the solstice and that the Kalends of January begins eight days thereafter.

In this textual reconstruction, Adam's observation of the decreasing and increasing sunlight is connected to the debate between Shammai and Hillel about whether Hanukkah candles ought to be lit in decreasing or increasing order. The text might also allude to the Roman nundinal cycle, which lasted eight days.

178. Herman (2014:263).

179. *b. Avodah Zarah* 8a; *b. Shabbat* 21b.

180. Benovitz (2003; 2007a).

181. BM 34035 1-8, from the Neo-Assyrian period, transcribed and translated in Livingstone (1986:255). The same is true before the summer solstice, when women go to Ezida, the "night temple" associated with the god of night, Nabu, "when the nights have become short . . . to lengthen the nights."

182. The solar calendar year began on the winter solstice during this period, while previously the solstice was celebrated as the midwinter festival (*Maidhyairya*), on which see Taqizadeh (1952); de Blois (1996:44); Boyce (1993:795).

183. Skeat (1994).

184. The festival thus evokes the Parilia, celebrated on April 21, associated in this period with Rome's *dies natalis*.

185. Ando (2015:207).

186. Here I follow Schäfer (2002).

187. Partial parallels containing significant manuscript variants appear in *Sifre Deuteronomy* 52 (MS London, Margoliot 341, Add 16,406 and Ed. princ., Venice 1545); *b. Shabbat* 56b; *b. Sanhedrin* 21a; *Song of Songs Rabbah* 42 on verse 1:6, on which see Terbuyken (1996); L. Feldman (1991); Naiweld (2016).

188. *y. Avodah Zarah* 1:2, 39c; translation with modifications from Neusner (1982:22-23). See the discussion in Schäfer (2002:342).

189. See also 1 Kings 7:8, 9:16 and 24; 2 Chronicles 8:11; Josephus, *Jewish Antiquities* 8.7.5; and later discussions in the *Testament of Solomon* 26:5-6; *Dialogue of Timothy and Aquila* 9:6-11; *b. Yevamot* 76a; *b. Shabbat* 56b; *b. Sanhedrin* 21b. 2 Kings 23:29 and 2 Chronicles 35:20-27 mention Pharaoh Necho II, but he lived at the time of King Josiah, several generations after King Solomon. Schäfer (2002:342) discusses an aggadah that connects the Pharaoh of 1 Kings 3:1 with Pharaoh Shishak, who is then identified as Pharaoh Necho.

190. In biblical texts, e.g., Exodus 34:15-17, the adoption of idolatrous practice rather than exogamy is presented as sinful, on which see S. J. D. Cohen (1999a:241-62).

191. Virgil, *Aeneid* 1.1-7.

192. Virgil, *Aeneid* 7.68.

193. Virgil, *Aeneid* 8.314-36.

194. Livy, *Ab urbe condita* 1.1.5-9.

195. *b. Sanhedrin* 21b and *b. Shabbat* 56b contain abridged versions of the story attributed to Rabbi Isaac and identify the angel as Gabriel rather than Michael. Solomon is also associated with the angel Michael in *Testament of Solomon* 1:6-7, where Michael gives Solomon a signet ring.

196. Mattingly et al. (1930a:187, no. 774), cited in B. Campbell (2012:13).

197. Sestertius, Bronze, Vespasian, Rome, 71 CE; RIC II.1 (rev. ed. XXX), no. 442, p. 69; British Museum: 1872,0709.477 (http://numismatics.org/ocre/id/ric.2_1(2).ves.108).

198. B. Campbell (2012:153), referring to Mattingly et al. (1930b:118, no. 707).

199. On the significance of coins in the Roman Empire, see Bond (1957); Levick (1982); Carradice (1982/83); Meshorer (1985); Harl (1987); Chancey (2004).

200. B. Campbell (2012:esp. 13-22, 153-57).

201. Baldi (2002:104-7).

202. Jastrow (1943, 2005:1587). The term שרטון is used in *b. Sanhedrin* 21b and *b. Shabbat* 56b to refer to "alluvial land" or "sandbank." See also *b. Eruvin* 8a; *b. Berakhot* 60a; *b. Bava Batra* 124a; Jastrow (1943, 2005:1629).

203. Jastrow (1943, 2005:440).

204. See, e.g., Heiken, Funiciello, and de Rita (2013:106–8, 197–99); Aldrete (2006).

205. Livy, *Ab urbe condita* 1.4. References to the founding of other cities out of muddy alluvium appear in Thucydides, *History of the Peloponnesian Wars* 2.102; Diodorus Siculus, *Bibliotheca historica* 3.3.2–3 and 1.34.1; Herodotus, *Histories* 2.10.

206. E.g., *Letter of Aristeas* 83–84; *Jubilees* 8:12–21; *b. Yoma* 54b. See also Vilnay (1973:5–10). On the portrayal of Rome as eternal and universal in Roman imperial propaganda and corresponding Jewish rejection of this idea, see also Berthelot (2017; forthcoming). On the history of Rome as eternal, see Pratt (1965).

207. E.g., *m. Yoma* 5:2; *t. Yoma* 2:12; *y. Yoma* 5:4, 42c; Palestinian Targum I to Exodus 28:30; *y. Sanhedrin* 10:2, 29a; *b. Sukkah* 53a–b; Koltun-Fromm (2013); Eliav (2005:esp. 224–27).

208. 1 Kings 12:25–33 (verse 32 accuses Jeroboam of instituting idolatrous festivals, which further connects him to the Mishnah's discussion about festival times). The reference to Jeroboam also works intertextually: Jeroboam's idolatrous sins are discussed earlier in the tractate, in *y. Avodah Zarah* 1:1, 39a, creating continuity on the redacted level of the text.

209. In *b. Shabbat* 56b, Jeroboam's erection of the two golden calves establishes "Greek Italy," i.e., Magna Graecia, the southern part of the Italian Peninsula, on which see Jastrow (1943, 2005:47).

210. 1 Kings 13:33–34 NRSV.

211. E.g., Livy, *Ab urbe condita* 1.4–10; Scullard (1935, 2014:42–50). Various versions of the myth circulated, including accounts in which both twins found the city together, discussed in Wiseman (1995), who considers the Remus myth relatively late; Ver Eecke (2008).

212. Neel (2014:119–74).

213. Belayche (2009:171–74).

214. This rabbinic source might be the earliest reference to this tradition, which reappears in medieval sources, on which see Geiger (2004).

215. 2 Kings 2:11 NRSV.

216. E.g., Livy, *Ab urbe condita* 1.17–20. See also Plutarch, *Life of Numa*. The figure of Numa is most developed in Greek literature from the east, rather than in Latin sources, on which see Deremetz (2013).

217. Plutarch, *Life of Numa* 2.1–2; trans. Perrin (1914:309). 2 Maccabees 2:4–8 connects Moses and Solomon with the Jerusalem temple via the imagery of a descending cloud.

218. Livy, *Ab urbe condita* 1.16.

219. E.g., Plutarch, *Life of Numa* 18.1–4; Macrobius, *Saturnalia* 1.13.1–3.

220. 2 Kings 2:11, 3:1–3.

221. See *y. Ta'anit* 1:1, 64a; *Pesiqta de-Rav Kahana* Piska 7 on Exodus 12:29, section 11 (ed. Mandelbaum, 134).

222. On which see Horn (2008).

223. Schäfer (2002:342).

224. Stories of origin were also popular during the era of the Antonines, especially in the Roman colonies, on which see Belayche (2009).

225. Gowing (2005); Dench (2005); Ando (2000); Zanker (1990); Wallace-Hadrill (1998).

226. Cooley (2011:256).

227. Geiger (2008); Cooley (2011:255–56).

228. E.g., RIC I (second edition) Augustus 390 (British Museum: R.3583), 391 and 392 (Münzkabinett Berlin), on which see A. Turner (2016); Deremetz (2013).

229. Belayche (2009).

230. *b. Avodah Zarah* 8b; a similar passage appears in *t. Avodah Zarah* 1:2.

231. The presence of the conjunction "and" (*vav*) in this *baraita* could originally have served an interpretive function, such that the clause "the day on which Rome extended her dominion" served to modify "Kratesis" (as in, "Kratesis, that is the day on which Rome extended her dominion"), just as Rav Judah understands it. The Babylonian Talmud's interpretation of this tradition takes for granted that the conjunction indicates two *different* festivals, and the text accuses Rav Judah of inappropriately conflating two festivals into one, the latter serving as an explanation of the former. That is, the Babylonian Talmud's interpretation of the *baraita* creates the contradiction with the Mishnah. On the interpretive *vav*, see N. Epstein (1948:1076–81).

232. This reference to victory in the days of Cleopatra is sometimes interpreted as the Battle of Actium in 31 BCE, but it likely refers to Augustus's victory in Alexandria the following year in 30 CE.

233. Rav Dimi is frequently associated with bringing traditions from Palestine. I treat it here as a source that reflects Babylonian rabbinic attitudes, as there are no Palestinian parallels and a Babylonian redactor chose to include it.

234. *b. Avodah Zarah* 8b; translation based on MS. Paris 1337 in consultation with I. Epstein (1935:39–40). The narrative switches from Aramaic to Hebrew, perhaps suggesting that two independent passages were combined. The comparison of the Torah to precious stones is reminiscent of Wisdom in Job 28; Proverbs 8; Ben Sira 24. See also *b. Megillah* 6b, in which 300 princes from Germanic tribes battle 365 chiefs from the Roman Empire, killing one each day so that neither side wins.

235. On the relationship between war and gods in Roman ideology, see Virgil, *Aeneid* 8.698–700; Ando (2008:122).

236. 1 Maccabees 8:1–31; Josephus, *Jewish Antiquities* 12.417–18, in contrast to the Palestinian Talmud, which does not refer to this alliance in its discussion of this festival; explored in Hadas-Lebel (2005:7–9). On the presence of similar historiographical traditions found in the Babylonian Talmud and Josephus, see Kalmin (2006:149–72); Ilan and Noam (2017).

237. *y. Avodah Zarah* 1.3, 39c.

238. Genesis 40:20.

239. *Mekhilta de-Rabbi Ishmael Vayehi Beshallah* 1 on Exodus 14:7 makes another association between Rome and Pharaoh, discussed in Berthelot (forthcoming).

240. *b. Avodah Zarah* 10a.

241. These stories and their incorporation into this section of the Babylonian Talmud are analyzed in A. Gray (2005b).

242. An early instance of what Yerushalmi (2002) explores.

243. See, e.g., Varro, *De Lingua Latina* 6.27–28; Isidore of Seville, *Etymologies* 5.33.13; Plutarch, *Roman Questions* 268–269D; *Fasti Praenestini*; a more detailed discussion is found in Gribetz (2013:96–100).

244. On which see, e.g., Boyarin (1994).

245. On the relationship between the two talmudic tractates, see A. Gray (2005a); Wasserman (2017:43–46).

246. On which see Rubenstein (1999); Hayes (1997).

247. Dolansky (2010:496) notes of Roman festivals that "the notion of the festival's origin lying in a mythical Golden Age persisted into Late Antiquity where we find the greatest

concentration of etiological interest in Macrobius' repository of ritual and literary lore. He records several traditions concerning the Saturnalia's establishment in Rome's remote past."

248. Even though Palestinian and Babylonian rabbis could be construed as "exilic," as they both lived under foreign rule in a multiethnic environment, I employ the term "diasporic" here to refer to Babylonian rabbis who lived outside the Roman province of Palestine and yet still choose to imagine themselves as contributing to that empire. On notions of diaspora and homeland in the rabbinic period, see Gafni (1997); S. Stern (2001:219–21); Hezser (2008); Boyarin (2015).

249. Philo, *Legatio ad Gaium* 143; Josephus, *Jewish Antiquities* 15.187–201, 16.160–73, 19.282–83; Josephus, *Against Apion* 2.61; Niehoff (2001:118, 128–33).

250. Philo's sentiments toward the Roman emperor are not identical to those expressed in the rabbinic source. Philo is more generous in his praise, focusing on Augustus's character and his respect for Jewish custom, while even the most positive rabbinic passage emphasizes the greatness of the Torah itself and its utility in Roman victory, rather than the Roman virtue of recognizing its power. The respective audience of each text also differed: Philo demonstrates the compatibility of Jewish and Roman values and customs to both diasporic Jews and Greek-speaking non-Jews, while the rabbinic author seeks to affirm the importance of the Torah in all realms of life, even those as far afield from the rabbinic study house as military battles between two foreign nations. Each text highlights the adoption of Jewish values and customs, but for different ends.

251. On which see Berthelot (2011).

252. On Artapanus, see Gruen (2004:201–12); Zellentin (2008); J. J. Collins (2010); Barclay (1996:127–32).

253. Artapanus, *Fragments* 27.4–6, discussed in Barclay (1996:130).

254. J. J. Collins (1983:33, 54n9).

255. The Jews of late antique Palestine also lived in a predominantly gentile context in which asserting their contribution to gentile society was important. And yet, the Babylonian Talmud's presentation of the Jews' place in Roman history is reminiscent of the writings of Philo and Artapanus in a way that those preserved in the Palestinian Talmud are not.

256. *Genesis Rabbah* 13:6 (ed. Theodor and Albeck, 116–17).

257. *Deuteronomy Rabbah* 7:7 (ed. Lieberman, 110–11). This version, which identifies the rabbi as Rabbi Yohanan ben Zakkai, evokes the Mishnah's list of Roman festivals and the prohibitions surrounding them. If the author viewed the Jewish festivals positively and the Roman festivals disparagingly, however, this aspect is not conveyed. This omission is understandable. *Deuteronomy Rabbah* dates to the end of the eighth century. Though the Kalends of January was still celebrated in certain regions in this period, Roman festivals were no longer overbearing seasonal symbols of Roman imperial rule, on which see Brown (1995:86).

258. Or, more simply: "when you celebrate, we do not celebrate, and when we celebrate, you do not celebrate."

259. On dialogues between rabbis and non-rabbinic figures in rabbinic sources, see Gribetz and Vidas (2012).

260. See, e.g., Bakhos (2016); Niehoff (2016); Himmelfarb (2016); Schäfer (2016).

261. *Lamentations Rabbah* 1.45.

262. Feeney (2007); Wallace-Hadrill (2005).

263. This is true as well of the New Testament and other texts composed within a Roman imperial context, e.g., Galatians 4:10; Origen, *Contra Celsum* 8.21; Chrysostom, *Homily against the Jews* 1:4:4, 7 and *On the Kalends*; Augustine, *Against the Pagans*.

264. On the Romanization of time in the province of Asia, see Heller (2014); on the rabbis as both thoroughly Roman and vehement critics of Roman "culture," see Schwartz (2010); for an additional example, see Berthelot (2018).

265. For later examples of similar phenomena, see Sarna (1996); Gitlitz (1996, 2002:54); de Madariaga (1940); Kayserling (1894); Rubinstein (2010); Koffman (2011); Wenger (2012:66–69); Hoberman (2011); Fingerhut (1967). For examples of competing etiologies about the Seleucid Empire, see Kosmin (2014:230–38).

266. Ando (2000:xi).

267. Ando (2000:xii).

268. Ando (2000:6).

269. Though not divinely ordained, as Josephus suggests in, e.g., *Jewish Antiquities* 10.275–76, but rather as a punishment for Israelite sin.

270. To cite a corollary in American history, Frederick Douglass (1955) delivered a speech on July 5, 1852, to the Rochester Ladies' Anti-Slavery Society in which he reflects on the meaning of the Fourth of July for enslaved and formerly enslaved Americans. In his remarks, he draws the distinction between what "American Independence Day" and the celebration of freedom means for white Americans and African Americans in ways that are similar to the contrasts drawn in the rabbinic narratives analyzed in this chapter about what Roman festivals mean for the Roman Empire and some of its oppressed subjects.

271. For a particular example of this shift, see Zellentin (2015); D. H. Weiss (2018).

Chapter 2

1. ἡμέρα σαβ(ά)τ . . . ἀγαθή.

2. This inscription, along with a review of previous scholarship about it, is found in Noy (2005:184–86). The inscription might note that the day of the Sabbath is a *yom tov* (lit. a "good day"), on which see van der Horst (2006:37).

3. Ker (2010); according to Roman inclusive counting, the nundinal cycles consisted of nine days.

4. E.g., Tacitus (*Historiae* V, 4:1–5:1) and Juvenal (*Saturae* XIV, 105) mention the sloth involved in abstaining from work on the Sabbath.

5. On this phenomenon, see, e.g., Seneca, *De superstitione*, cited in Augustine, *City of God* 6.11; Dio Cassius, *Roman History* 37.18. Josephus, *Against Apion* 2.282–83, in contrast, cites the popularity of the Sabbath as a mark of the worldliness and appeal of Judaism, on which see McKay (1994:101); Doering (1999:479–507). Roman awareness and adoption of the seven-day week began quite early, on which see Salzman (2004).

6. On the history of the seven-day week, see Salzman (2004); Zerubavel (1985); Pietri (1984); Heidel (1929:355–441); Colson (1926); Hehn (1907).

7. S. Stern (2017:252–53).

8. Goldenberg (1979).

9. I identified anti-Roman dimensions of several rabbinic texts about the Sabbath in an earlier work (Gribetz 2016b); here I amplify the anti-Christian dimension of some of these same texts.

10. It can be difficult to differentiate between responses to Christian and non-Christian polemics because the polemics themselves were often similar; rabbinic texts could respond to both simultaneously.

11. On observance of the Sabbath by Jews in the Roman Empire, see Clarysse, Remijsen, and Depauw (2010); on the ordering of the week around the Sabbath, see Katzoff and Schreiber (1998); on the participation of God-fearers in Jewish Sabbath practices, see

Reynolds and Tannenbaum (1987); Lieu (1995); and the extensive bibliographies in these studies.

12. On the Sabbath as a practice of idleness, see Juvenal, *Saturnae* XIV, 106; Augustine, *City of God* 6.11; Rutilius Namatianus, *De reditu suo* I, 391; Frontius, *Strategmata* II, 1:17; discussed in Schäfer (1997:87).

13. The oral dimension of these texts, revealed by their drastic manuscript variants, is the theme of Abate (2017).

14. The language here is deliberately vague, as each passage relates in its own way to this web of ideas and social practices. On the difficulty of properly recognizing allusions or "echoes" in ancient texts, see, e.g., Zevit (2017). Rosen-Zvi (2017b:175), in writing about rabbinic sources and Paul, also notes that rabbinic texts that engage with the ideas of others "may be interpreted as deliberate and polemical statements" but that one need not view them as either deliberate or polemical to acknowledge the impact that the ideas of others had on them: "it is sufficient to assume that the awareness of the Pauline ideas reshaped the manner in which they engaged with them. Old ideas are now heard through the sounding-board of Paul's objections and thus can no longer be stated straightforwardly or naïvely. Whether we adhere to the stronger reading or remain with the weaker one, I claim Paul's ideas are indispensable for a proper understanding."

15. On Origen's incorporation of Jewish ideas into his writings, see, e.g., de Lange (1976); S. Cohen (2010).

16. For overviews of these debates, see Sandmel (1962); Yuval (2010); Rosen-Zvi (2017b).

17. Himmelfarb (2008); Hirshman (1996); Yuval (2008); Rosen-Zvi (2016b; 2017b). I use the term "Christian" anachronistically here, to include texts that entered the New Testament canon even though many were actually ancient Jewish texts in the context of their composition and immediate reception.

18. Visotzky (2003); Niehoff (2006; 2016); Gregerman (2016); Brezis (2018:104–42); Mazeh (forthcoming).

19. Schäfer (2007; 2012); Kalmin (1994); Bar-Asher Siegal (2013; 2019).

20. E.g., S. J. D. Cohen (2010) examines Origen's interest in Jewish exegesis of the Sabbath in order to refute it.

21. Hirshman (1996:13).

22. Hirshman (1996:3).

23. This idea is developed further in Yuval (2011).

24. Hirshman (1996:12).

25. E.g., Stemberger (2000:287–88); M. Goodman (2000).

26. M. Goodman (2000:8–9).

27. M. Kister (2007; 2009); elsewhere, M. Kister (2013) argues for anti-Christian polemic in rabbinic literature.

28. Schremer (2009; 2010:101–19).

29. Schremer (2009); Schwartz (2001:179); Brown (1995).

30. Balberg (2017a:243).

31. Schremer (2009:357–58).

32. Ehrman (2018:160–77) conservatively estimates that there were 160,000 Christians (less than 1 percent of the empire's population) by 200 CE; 2–3 million Christians in the Roman Empire by 300 CE; and that by 400 CE a considerable percentage, perhaps as much as half (30 million people), of the population of the Roman Empire considered themselves Christian. About 50 communities are mentioned by name in extant texts prior to 100 CE, indicating that there must have been more (Ehrman guesses about 200). Ehrman also notes

that "Christianity grew at different rates in different cities and regions" and that it was more popular in the east than the west (168). Moreover, Christian communities were concentrated in urban centers rather than in rural contexts in the early centuries, similar to rabbinic communities. Tsafrir (1998:197) estimates that by 400 CE the majority of Palestine was Christian; even if Tsafrir overestimates, it is fair to assume that there were many Christians in the region of Palestine by then, even if they were not necessarily the overwhelming majority.

33. The presence of anti-Semitism or Islamophobia even in countries with small percentages of Jewish or Muslim residents is but one example of such a phenomenon. Additionally, perception of population growth, regardless of actual population size or percentage, can produce fear among others.

34. Rosen-Zvi (2017b:172); Rosen-Zvi (2017b:174) writes that "sometimes it is the penetration of new ideas, rather than changing political conditions, that triggers rabbinic re-engagement with traditions, making them into *issues* to be engaged with." Regarding the *Mekhilta*'s presentation of the Sabbath, it was probably both.

35. Ando (2012). The Roman lexicographer Sextus Pompeius Festus defines the term "municipalia sacra" in his *On the Meaning of Words* as those rites "that a people had from its origin, before receiving Roman citizenship, and which the *pontifices* wanted them to continue to observe and perform in the way in which they had been accustomed to perform them from antiquity" (s.v. *municipalia sacra* [146L], cited by Ando). Christians were the most famous exception to this policy, as were several eastern cults. The situation changed dramatically with the Christianization of the empire.

36. That the Sabbath was a widespread part of Judaism at the time is well attested, on which see S. J. D. Cohen (2008).

37. Josephus, *Jewish Antiquities* 14.185–267; 16.160–78; see also 12.125–46; Goldenberg (1979:416–18). Given other Roman sources on the matter, the status of the authenticity of these edicts cited by Josephus does not unsettle the larger argument; on the topic of their authenticity, see Moehring (1975).

38. Philo, *Legatio ad Gaium* 155–58. See also Josephus, *Jewish Antiquities* 19.282–83.

39. Goldenberg (1979:420–21).

40. Ovid, in a passage that otherwise does not polemicize against Jews, identifies the Sabbath as that which belongs to the "Syrian" or "foreign" Jews (*Remedia amoris* 219–20, cf. *Ars amatoria* 1.76). Cicero wrote generally of Jewish observances that "the practice of their sacred rites was at variance with the glory of our empire, the dignity of our name, and the customs of our ancestors" (*Pro Flacco* 28.69), cited in Gager (1985:56).

41. Agatharchides of Cnidus, cited in Josephus, *Against Apion* 1.209–11; Apion, *Aegyptiaca*, cited in Josephus, *Against Apion* 2.21; Seneca, *De superstitione*, cited in Augustine, *City of God* 6.11; Persius, *Saturae* 5.179–84; Tacitus, *Historiae* V, 4:1–5:1; Juvenal, *Saturae* XIV, 105; Martial, *Epigrammata* 4.4; Plutarch, *De superstitione* 3; Dio Cassius, *Historia Romana* XXXVII, 15:3–19:3, XLIX 22:4ff.; Rutilius Namatianus, *De reditu suo* I, 381–98. For analysis, see Michael (1924); Goldenberg (1979); Gilula (1986); Schäfer (1997:82–92).

42. Apion, cited in Josephus, *Against Apion* 2.20–27; Tacitus, *Historiae* 5.1; Persius, *Saturae* 5.179–84, trans. M. Stern (1974, 1:436); on this passage in Persius, see Gilula (1986:17–18).

43. Aristobulus, Fragment 5, cited in Eusebius, *Ecclesiastical History* 13.12.9–16. On this fragment and its authenticity, see Doering (1999:306–15; 2005).

44. Philo, *De specialibus legibus* II.15.60–64. See also Philo, *De opificio mundi* 128; *De Decalogo* 98; *De Abrahamo* 28–30; H. Weiss (2003:32–51); Niehoff (2001:107–8, 260–63); Boesenberg (2010); Gribetz (2018).

45. Gilula (1986), for instance, focuses on the comic and satirical writings of first- and

early second-century Roman authors Horace (first century BCE), Suetonius (late first and early second century CE), Persius (first century CE), Petronius (first century CE), Martial (first century CE), Plutarch (first and early second century CE), and Juvenal (late first and early second century CE). Gilula cites Macrobius but notes that he was an antiquarian who preserved an older source in his discussion of Jews. Schäfer (1997:82–92) too mainly cites sources from this early period; e.g., Schäfer (1997:88) quotes a passage by Rutilius Namatianus but notes that he is well-known for his allusions to classical Latin literature. Schäfer notes as well that Pliny the Elder, *Historia naturalis* 31.24 and Damascius, *Vita Isidori* mention the Sabbath without adding a polemical dimension.

46. Augustine, *City of God* 6.11.

47. S. J. D. Cohen (2012:32–33) notes: "while classical writers faulted the Jews for being idle on the Sabbath, Christian writers faulted the Jews not only for idleness but also for privileging the physical over the spiritual."

48. The Sabbath was one of several practices, such as circumcision and dietary laws, at the center of such texts. Various studies construct differing accounts of the history of the Sabbath and the Lord's Day in Christian communities; see, e.g., Gonzalez (1997); Rouwhorst (2001b); Bradshaw and Johnson (2011); Brattston (2014); Carson (1999); Bacchiocchi (1997); Rordorf (1968); Colson (1926).

49. Perhaps *Gospel of Thomas* 27; see also subsequent notes.

50. E.g., Hebrews 4:1–11; Justin Martyr, *Dialogue with Trypho* 12, 18, 21, 26; *Didascalia Apostolorum* 24; *Epistle of Barnabas* 15; Origen, *Homilies on Numbers* 23.4.2; Synod of Laodicea, canon 29. Specific aspects of biblical Sabbath prohibitions were critiqued, e.g., in Origen, *De principiis* 4.3.2., on which see, e.g., S. J. D. Cohen (2010).

51. See, e.g., Synod of Laodicea, canon 16; *Apostolic Constitutions* 2.36, 6.23, and 7.36. Distinctions between Jewish and Christian practices are noted in the writings of Augustine as well, e.g., *Epistle* 36.27–32, to Casulanus, on which see Strand (1965); *Enarrationes* on Psalm 91; *Enarrationes* on Psalm 92:2; *Iohannis evangelium* 3.19; *De decem chordis* sermon 9.3; discussed in S. J. D. Cohen (2012:38–39).

52. E.g., contrast Ignatius, *Letter to the Magnesians* with Pseudo-Ignatius, *Letter to the Magnesians*, on which see S. J. D. Cohen (2012); Tertullian, *De oratione* 23.1; *Didache* 14; *Didascalia Apostolorum* (Greek recension) in the Apostolic Constitutions II.59; Hippolytus, *Commentary on Daniel* 4:20; Timotheus bishop of Alexandria, *Responsa Canonica*; Epiphanius, *Exposition of the Faith* 24; discussed in Salzman (2004); Kraft (1965). A fragment of the mid-second-century text *Dialogue of Jason and Papiscus* offers a variety of reasons for the sanctity of Sunday in contrast to Saturday, on which see Bovon and Duffy (2012).

53. Revelation 1:10 contains the earliest extant reference to the phrase "the Lord's Day" ("τῇ κυριακῇ ἡμέρᾳ"), though it does not necessarily refer to Sunday; it appears as well in Ignatius's *Letter to the Magnesians* 9; *Didache* 14:1; *Gospel of Peter* 35, 50; these and others are studied in Bauckham (1999).

54. Jesus' resurrection is dated to the first day of the (Jewish) week in all four canonical Gospels (Matthew 28:1; Mark 16:2,9; Luke 24:1; John 20:1), and assemblies on Sundays are mentioned in Acts 20:7 and 1 Corinthians 16:2, on which see Zerubavel (1985; 146n58); Cotton (1933). These might be the traditions upon which Sunday gatherings were based. Revelation 1:10 similarly refers to the Lord's Day as the day on which the revelation of Christ occurred.

55. Zerubavel (1985:22); see also McCasland (1930).

56. Rordorf (1968); Rouwhorst (2001b:261–66); Salzman (2004).

57. See, e.g., John Chrysostom's sermons against such practices: *Against the Jews*, Homilies 1.8.1–2; 3.3.1–3, 3.5; 6.3.1–3.

58. *Justinian Code* 3.12.3, trans. S. P. Scott (1932, 1973:275).

59. *Theodosian Code* 2.8.1, trans. Pharr (1952:44).

60. *P.Oxy.* LIV 3759, on which see Llewelyn (2002:107–8). The Council of Nicaea does not mention a weekly Sunday as a day of regular worship, but its Easter decree moved the annual festival to Sunday.

61. Salzman (2004); Girardet (2006; 2008).

62. M. Goodman (2007:215); Salzman (2004); Girardet (2006; 2008). See also Justin Martyr, *Apologia maior* 67.8, which similarly uses the nomenclature the Day of Helios to refer to the day of Christian worship of Christ and creation; Tertullian, *Apologeticum* 16.9–11 draws a contrast between Christian and pagan celebration of Sunday; Jerome, *In die dominica paschae* 49–57 and Maximus of Turin, *De Pentecosten*, both allow Christians to call the Lord's Day the Day of Sol and connect Christ with the sun, discussed in Anderson (2019:137–38, 142–44). Anderson (2019:139) also notes that Sozomen, *Historia ecclesiastica* 1.18.11 edits Eusebius's account of Constantine, presenting Constantine as instituting a law about the Christian Lord's Day, with no mention whatsoever of the Day of Sol.

63. Salzman (2004:186).

64. Anderson (2019:140) notes that after Constantine, Greek sources no longer use the planetary weekday names but rather employ the by-then Christian weekday names instead.

65. Eusebius, *Life of Constantine* 4.18–20; trans. Cameron and Hall (1999).

66. See, e.g., *Theodosian Code* 11.7.10, 8.8.1.

67. Theodosius I's laws related to the Sabbath include *Theodosian Code* 11.7.13 (repeated in 2.8.18; 8.8.3); 15.5.2; 2.8.19; 2.8.20.

68. See, e.g., *Theodosian Code* 2.8.23; 9.3.7; 2.8.25; 15.5.5, from the late fourth through the fifth century CE.

69. E.g., *Theodosian Code* 11.7.10, 11.3.13, and 15.5.2 respectively. Though these laws applied throughout the empire, it is unclear whether or how they were enforced.

70. Laws of this period also became increasingly restrictive to the empire's Jewish inhabitants, on which see the sources in Linder (1988). On the status of spectacles and athletic games as religious or non-religious affairs in late antiquity, and on anti-paganism in late antiquity more generally, see Remijsen (2015:181–219).

71. See, e.g., Salzman (2004).

72. Zerubavel (1985:12–20); Colson (1926); Rüpke (1995:456–71); Bultrighini (2018).

73. Though the claim here is not one of causation. Zerubavel (1985:19) notes calendrical, epigraphic, papyrological, literary, and visual evidence for the adoption of the seven-day week in the first through third centuries CE; Bultrighini (2018) lists the earliest literary and epigraphic attestations of the planetary week in Tibullus, Ovid, Horace, and three *Fasti*: *Sabini*, *Nolani*, and *Foronovani*; additional sources, including parapegmata and inscriptions, are discussed in Salzman (2004).

74. E.g., Frontinus, *Stratagems* 2.1.17; Tacitus, *Histories* 5.4; Dio Cassius, *Roman History* 37.17–18; Juvenal, *Satires* 7.169; 14.96. Zerubavel (1985:17) notes that Jews even began calling the planet Saturn "Shabtai." The use and conflation of the Jewish and planetary weeks differed from region to region, on which see Bultrighini (2018) and Anderson (2019); on the use of weekdays in documentary sources, see Worp (1991).

75. Dio Cassius, *Roman History*, 37.17–18, discussed in Zerubavel (1985:19); Salzman (2004:189).

76. Salzman (2004). And perhaps Thursday as well, on which see Bultrighini (2018).

77. Salzman (1990).

78. Exodus 31:13–17 NRSV.

79. References to the Sabbath in the Hebrew Bible are found in Genesis 2:1–4; Exodus

16:21–30; 20:8–11; 23:10–13; 31:12–17; 34:21; 35:1–3; Leviticus 19:1–4; 24:5–9; 26:2; Numbers 15:32–36; 28:1–10; Deuteronomy 5:12–15; 2 Kings 4:22–23; 11:5–9; 16:18; Isaiah 1:12–14; 56:1–2, 6; 58:13–14; 66:22–23; Jeremiah 17:19–27; Ezekiel 20:8–26; 44:24; 46:4; 8:4–5; Lamentations 2:6; Amos 8:5; Nehemiah 9:13–14; 10:32–33; 13:14–22; 1 Chronicles 9:32. On the Sabbath in the Hebrew Bible, see Robinson (1988); on Second Temple practices and interpretations of these texts, see Doering (1999); Jassen (2014); Y. Miller (2019).

80. Exodus 20:8–11; Deuteronomy 5:12–15. On the significance of the decalogue in antiquity, see Lincicum (2010:43–44).

81. E.g., *Jubilees* 2:1, 9, 17–31, on which see Doering (1997); VanderKam (2013). *Jubilees* 1:9, 13 mentions the Sabbath twice in its list of Israel's transgressions. *Jubilees'* framing of the Sabbath as a sign in 2:1, 17, 21 directly references Exodus 31:13, 17, on which see Doering (1997:192).

82. *Jubilees* 2:19.

83. Doering (1997:189–91) emphasizes this point and contrasts *Jubilees'* exclusivist and particularist view of the Sabbath with the writings of Aristobulus (Fragment 5), Philo (*De opificio mundi* 89–128; *Vita Mosis* 2:21, 44), and Josephus (*Against Apion* 2:282), who all present the Sabbath in more universalist terms.

84. *Jubilees* 2:20.

85. On which see VanderKam (1995).

86. *Jubilees* 50:9.

87. Himmelfarb (2006:72). Doering (1997:201–2) notes that while *Jubilees'* Sabbath laws are "strict but not polemical," and its presentation of the Sabbath within the creation narrative is likely "priestly," the text's emphasis on the centrality of the Sabbath and its jabs against those who do not observe it properly can be attributed to its polemical stance. Doering attributes the distinction to different textual strata.

88. Schwarz (1982:180–81), discussed in Himmelfarb (2006:72).

89. The Sabbath as a marker of Jewishness appears in other Second Temple sources as well. In 2 Maccabees 5, e.g., Apollonius's victory over the Jews is attributed to his attacking the Jews while they observed the Sabbath. 2 Maccabees 6:6 explains that Antiochus prevented the Jews from observing the Sabbath and "the festivals of their ancestors, nor as much as confess themselves to be Jews," and 2 Maccabees 6:11 describes again that Jews decided to observe the Sabbath rather than desecrate it by fighting the Greek army in self-defense, leading to their defeat. In 1 Maccabees 1:39, 43, 45 sacrificing idols and profaning the Sabbath are the two activities used to describe how the Jews adopted gentile cults. Both texts associate the observance of sacred times, especially the Sabbath, with outward expressions of Jewish identity and difference while they frame the suppression of Sabbath observance as the denial of Jewish identity and difference. On these texts, see Borchardt (2015); Bonesho (2020).

90. Doering (1999); Shemesh (2012; 2013); Furstenberg (2017b:280–81).

91. *Mekhilta de-Rabbi Ishmael Shabbata* 1 on Exodus 31:12–17 (ed. Horovitz and Rabin, 341ff.; ed. Lauterbach 493ff.).

92. On rabbinic prohibitions regarding actions that are not considered restful, see Hidary (2015).

93. Whether or not the laws were derived from those passages. Saving a life on the Sabbath, for example, is discussed in *t. Shabbat* 15(16):16 (ed. Lieberman, 74) and throughout the rest of that chapter; on the history of this principle, see Shemesh (2012:501–5).

94. On the various layers of this text as well as manuscript variants, see Shemesh (2012:481–84).

95. This applies to the circumcision of males, but not others, on which see *m. Shabbat* 19:3–5, *t. Shabbat* 16:4.

96. The *Mekhilta* discusses this proof text in a later section as well (ed. Horovitz and Rabin, 8; ed. Lauterbach, 495). The second half of the verse commands that someone who violates the Sabbath be put to death, but this part of the biblical passage is not mentioned in the *Mekhilta*'s argument.

97. לכם שבת מסורה ואין אתם מסורין לשבת.

98. Even though the midrash proceeds according to the order of biblical passages, this editorial choice was not inevitable.

99. Shemesh (2013:271).

100. 1 Maccabees 2:29–41; *Jubilees* 50:10–13; 1QpHab XI:4–8; 4Q256; CD XI:13–17. Previous studies include Bear (1960); Herr (1961); Schiffman (1975:84–133); M. Kister (1984); Doering (1999:107–8, 201–4, 408–38, 566–68; 2010; 2015); Meier (2004); Shemesh (2012; 2013); Kiel and Skjærvø (2011); Boyarin (2012:59–70); N. Collins (2014).

101. On the various interpretations of these Qumranic passages, see Doering (1999); Jassen (2014); Shemesh (2012).

102. Mark 3:1–6; Matthew 12:9–14; Luke 6:6–11, 13:10–17, 14:1–6; John 5:2–18, 7:21–24, 9:1–7, on which see Back (2010), who surveys previous scholarship; N. Collins (2014).

103. NRSV.

104. Mark 2:23–3:6 NRSV; parallels in Matthew 12:1–14; Luke 6:1–11. See also John 5:1–18; 13:10–17. Notably, Luke includes wording that most resembles the phrase *piquah nefesh*, on which see M. Kister (1984). The last line should probably be read as "a human being is lord even of the Sabbath," rather than christologically, on which see A. Y. Collins (1996:149).

105. On the possibility that the gospel narrative is not about plucking grains but rubbing them, see M. Kister (1984); Pines (1967).

106. Matthew 1:1; Luke 3:31, on which see Daube (1956:67). M. Kister (1984) refers to later rabbinic traditions, e.g., *y. Yoma* 8:5, 45b, that discuss David's hunger as *bulmus*, a medical condition of extreme and sudden hunger, on which see also Shinnar (2019:160–66), though this does not seem to be what the gospel narratives have in mind.

107. A justification not entirely dissimilar from Rabbi Akiva's reasoning in the *Mekhilta*.

108. Mark 2:27: Τὸ σάββατον διὰ τὸν ἄνθρωπον ἐγένετο, καὶ οὐχ ὁ ἄνθρωπος διὰ τὸ σάββατον.

109. On which see, e.g., Flusser (1968:44–49); Sanders (1985); Doering (1999:445–50); Andrea J. Mayer-Haas (2003).

110. E.g., M. Kister (1984); Doering (1999; 2010; 2015); Shemesh (2012); Boyarin (2012:59–70).

111. See also *b. Yoma* 85b.

112. This interpretation is made twice, about Exodus 31:13 (ed. Horovitz and Rabin, 341) and Exodus 31:17 (ed. Horovitz and Rabin, 343).

113. The *Mekhilta* also explains that "the Sabbath adds holiness to Israel. . . . He thus bears witness to Him by whose word the world came into being that He created His world in six days and rested on the seventh" (ed. Horovitz and Rabin, 341; ed. Lauterbach, 495).

114. Justin Martyr, *Dialogue with Trypho* 21, 26; trans. Falls (2003).

115. Gregerman (2016:35–36).

116. Perhaps specifically to atone for the sin of the Golden Calf, which precedes the giving of the ten commandments in the desert. In *Dialogue with Trypho* 12, 18, Justin argues that one ought to lead an honorable life and remember God on all days of the week (thus observing a perpetual Sabbath) rather than singling out one day for special observance. Such tropes have a long history in antiquity; see, e.g., Eusebius, *Praeparatio evangelica* 7.6; *Ecclesiastical History* 1.4.8.

117. Justin Martyr, *Dialogue with Trypho* 23; trans. Falls (2003).

118. Tertullian, *An Answer to the Jews* 4, 6.

119. *Mekhilta de-Rabbi Ishmael Shabbata* 1 on Exodus 31:13 (ed. Horowitz and Rabin, 341; ed. Lauterbach, 494).

120. *Mekhilta de-Rabbi Ishmael Shabbata* 1 on Exodus 31:16 (ed. Horowitz and Rabin, 343; ed. Lauterbach, 498). Hirshman (1996:57) also notes the similarity between these texts.

121. Hebrews 4:1–11 NRSV. On the Sabbath in Hebrews, see Calaway (2013). Augustine thematizes a similar conception of rest in *Confessions* 13.35.50–36.51.

122. *Didascalia Apostolorum* 24; trans. Connolly (1929).

123. *Epistle of Barnabas* 15:4–9; translation with modifications from Lightfoot (1898).

124. Origen, *Homily 24 on Numbers* 28:1–29:39, 4.4; trans. Scheck (2009:143).

125. Doering (1997:194) notes that *Jubilees* does not connect the Sabbath with the eschaton. That the *Mekhilta* does, in contrast to Second Temple texts, is therefore significant.

126. *Mekhilta de-Rabbi Ishmael Shabbata* 1 on Exodus 31:13 (ed. Horowitz and Rabin, 341; ed. Lauterbach, 495); see also *b. Berakhot* 57b.

127. *Mekhilta de-Rabbi Ishmael Vayassa* 4 on Exodus 16:25 (ed. Horowitz and Rabin, 169; ed. Lauterbach, 245) also suggests that observance of the Sabbath will save a person from the three calamities of the end times: the battles of Gog and Magog, the messiah, and the final judgment. See also *b. Shabbat* 118a.

128. *Mekhilta de-Rabbi Ishmael Shabbata* 1 on Exodus 31:15 (ed. Horowitz and Rabin, 343; ed. Lauterbach, 497). See also *Pesiqta d-Rav Kahana* 5:13, in which God is likened to a father who bequeaths to his son a clock.

129. Zerubavel (1985:4) writes: "The week is the only major rhythm of human activity that is totally oblivious to nature, resting on mathematical regularity alone . . . its invention was one of the first major attempts by humans to break away from being prisoners of nature and create an artificial world of their own." In the *Mekhilta*, however, the week's independence from nature does not mark it as human but rather as divine. Zerubavel (1985:11) notes further that "the dissociation of the week from a natural cycle such as the waxing and waning of the moon can be seen as part of a general movement toward introducing a supranatural deity. Not being personified as any particular natural force, the Jewish god was to be regarded as untouched by nature in any way. Accordingly, the day dedicated to this god was to be regarded as part of a divine temporal pattern that transcends even nature itself. That obviously involved dissociating the week from nature and its rhythms. Only by being based on an entirely *artificial mathematical rhythm* could the Sabbath observance become totally independent of the lunar or any other natural cycle."

130. Ignatius, *Letter to the Magnesians* 9; trans. S. J. D. Cohen (2012:30); in *Codex Municeus Laurentius*: μηκέτι σαββατίζοντες αλλα κατα Κυριακης ζωντες; in *Codex Caiensis 395*: non amplius sabatizantes sed secundum Dominicam viventes; on which see Guy (1964).

131. *Didache* 14.

132. Justin Martyr, *Apology* 1:67. This text explains that the world's creation began on Sunday, an opinion that also appears in rabbinic sources (e.g., *Leviticus Rabbah* 29:1; *Pesiqta de-Rav Kahana* 23:1), discussed in chapter 4.

133. The manuscripts of the *Mekhilta* vary, but several note explicitly "שבת מסורה לייי," or a version thereof (ed. Horowitz and Rabin, 343). This passage stands in contrast to the opinion recalled earlier in the *Mekhilta*, that the Sabbath is מסורה to people rather than people to it. The phrase also indicates that the time of the Sabbath is up to God, i.e., that it is a divine tradition. In an ironic twist, both Christians and rabbis refer to their sacred weekly day as divine—followers of Christ called it the "Lord's Day," and rabbis insisted that it was "מסורה לייי."

134. E.g., Shemesh (2012).

135. Genesis 2:3.

136. *Genesis Rabbah* 11.2 (ed. Theodor and Albeck, 87). This midrash is based on *Mekhilta de-Rabbi Ishmael Bahodesh* 7, on which see Hirshman (1996:43–44).

137. E.g., Exodus 16:5, 22–30.

138. In addition to prohibiting the collection of manna on the Sabbath, biblical sources also ban the kindling of fire, associated primarily with cooking (Exodus 35:1–3; see also Exodus 12:16); berate residents of Jerusalem for selling and purchasing food on the Sabbath rather than abstaining from commercial activities (Nehemiah 13:15–22); and describe the preparation of the tabernacle's showbreads on the Sabbath (Leviticus 24:5–9; 1 Chronicles 9:32). Prohibitions against cooking and food preparation on the Sabbath also appear in the texts of the Dead Sea Scrolls, including *Jubilees* 2:17–21, 2:29, 50:9, CD-A X.22-XI.2, CD XI.7–11, and they feature in the gospel narratives discussed above (Mark 2:23–3:6; Matthew 12:1–14; Luke 6:1–11). The custom of eating elaborate meals on the Sabbath as part of Sabbath observance developed later than the biblical prohibitions against cooking and food collection but was already a widespread practice by the end of the first century CE. The earliest attestations to the celebration of the Sabbath through festive meals are *Jubilees* 2:17–21, 50:9 and Josephus, *Life* 54 (Isaiah 58:13–14 encourages the Sabbath to be marked as a time of delight but does not mention food). Only rabbinic sources (e.g., *m. Shabbat* 16:2; *b. Shabbat* 117b–118a), however, regard such meals as obligatory, on which see also S. J. D. Cohen (2012:36–38). On food in ancient Sabbath practice, see Gribetz (2019); on the cooking prohibition, see Zerubavel (1985:8); on the role of food in Jewish communal formation, see Kraemer (2007); Rosenblum (2010).

139. Rabbi Judah the Patriarch is a fifth-generation tanna. The name "Antoninus" refers to one of the Antonines, probably Antoninus Pius but possibly also Marcus Aurelius, Caracalla, or the Severan Elagabalus (Marcus Aurelius Anoninus Augustus). The precise historical figure referenced in the story is not crucial; the stock character represents imperial authority rather than a specific historical emperor.

140. This story is part of the Rabbi-Antoninus story cycle, which, according to Rubenstein (2002:163–68), might allude to a period of warm relations between imperial and rabbinic figures in the late second and early third centuries; the stories preserved in later sources could draw on such historical memories to comment on contemporary circumstances of later periods when relations between rabbis and imperial officials were not as comfortable. Rubenstein notes that the stories always affirm the wisdom of rabbinic beliefs and practices in light of competing ideas in their broader philosophical and cultural contexts. See also Naiweld (2014); Meir (1999:263–99; 1994); S. J. D. Cohen (1998); Jacobs (1995:125–52); Wallach (1940/41); Krauss (1910).

141. *Genesis Rabbah* 11:4 (ed. Theodor and Albeck, 90).

142. Several of the Antoninus stories involve food: radishes in *Genesis Rabbah* 67:5; berries, coriander, leeks, lettuces, wheat, cucumbers, and radishes in *b. Avodah Zarah* 10a–11a; figs in *b. Sanhedrin* 91a. On out-of-season artichokes and cucumbers as foods associated with both Roman and rabbinic aristocracy, including in the Antoninus-Rabbi story cycle, see Weingarten (2016).

143. Even warming food on the Sabbath presented a culinary challenge. The prohibition against cooking food on the Sabbath stems from Exodus 35:3, "You shall kindle no fire in all your dwellings on the Sabbath day." Without being able to kindle a fire, cooking and warming food were not activities permitted on the Sabbath.

144. On which see Weingarten (2018), who connects the pun to Jesus' criticism of the Pharisees tithing dill in Matthew 23:23. *b. Berakhot* 39a refers to a dill stalk giving its taste to a dish, on which see Jastrow (1943, 2005:1519).

145. *Jubilees* 2:17–21, 50:9; Josephus, *Life* 54.

146. Pseudo-Ignatius, *Letter to the Magnesians* 9, discussed in S. J. D. Cohen (2012:text and translation on pp. 31–32); Sperber (1965). John Chrysostom, *De Lazaro* PG 48.972, on the other hand, mentions that Jews feasted without commenting on the quality of the meal, discussed in S. J. D. Cohen (2012:33–34). Jerome, *Commentary on Isaiah* 56.2 also alludes in a derogatory aside to Jewish habits of feasting on the Sabbath, discussed in S. J. D. Cohen (2010:167). Cyril of Alexandria, in his sixth Festal Letter of 418 CE, section 9, probably drawing upon Origen, contrasts Jewish and Christian practices on the Sabbath and the Lord's Day. On other related texts, see Hidary (2015:16–19).

147. See also the reference to warm drinks on the Sabbath in Justin Martyr, *Dialogue with Trypho*, 29:3. *Leviticus Rabbah* Proem 17 presents a critique by a Roman mime about the difficulty of cooking on the Sabbath.

148. *Brevis Expositio in Vergilii Georgica* I.336, cited in Schäfer (1997:92).

149. Strabo of Amaseia, *Historia hypomnemata*, cited in Josephus, *Jewish Antiquities* 14.6; Pompeius Trogus, cited in Justinus, *Historiae Philippicae*, Libri 36 Epitoma 2:14; Lysimachus, *Aegyptiaca*, cited in Josephus, *Against Apion* 1.308; Tacitus, *Historiae* 5.4.3; Petronius, *Fragmenta* no. 37; Suetonius, *Vita divi Augusti* 76.2; *Jubilees* 50.12–13. See Schäfer (1997:89–90); M. Williams (2004; 2013:49–62). Rabbinic sources require eating by the sixth hour on the Sabbath to avoid the misconception that one is fasting, on which see Kalman (2019:64).

150. Gow and Page (1965:223 no. XXVI), and Rutilius Namatianus, *De reditu suo* I.389f, both cited in Schäfer (1997:92).

151. The relationship between the versions in *Genesis Rabbah* and the Babylonian Talmud is unclear; they probably both rely on a shared written or oral source, though neither story is similar enough in its wording to be based directly on the other. The Babylonian Talmud contains a fuller version of the story: the emperor asks for the special ingredient but is told that he cannot acquire it because he does not observe the Sabbath. The version in *Genesis Rabbah* only contains the line "Does then the royal pantry lack anything?" while the emperor's request for the mystery spice is missing; the *Genesis Rabbah* version is more comprehensible with the Babylonian Talmud version in mind.

152. *b. Shabbat* 118a, which builds on a tannaitic tradition preserved in *Mekhilta de-Rabbi Ishmael Beshalah* 4 on Exodus 16:25 (ed. Horovitz and Rabin, 169; ed. Lauterbach, 245).

153. *b. Shabbat* 119a. The compilers of the Babylonian Talmud were not reworking narratives as they are found in *Genesis Rabbah* but using versions of these stories not preserved in extant Palestinian sources. On the relationship between *Genesis Rabbah* and the Babylonian Talmud, see A. Gray (2005b:33–40); on *Genesis Rabbah* and the Palestinian Talmud, see Albeck (1965:66–84); Bokser (1979); H.-J. Becker (1999; 2000); Milikowsky (2002).

154. On the potency of smell as nourishment for the soul, see also *b. Berakhot* 43b. Scent is connected to taste, too, on which see D. Green (2011:7).

155. Martial, *Epigrammata* 4.4, in M. Stern (1974, 1:523–24). This source is considerably older than the Babylonian Talmud.

156. The two tales about the emperor and the rabbi also share a key narrative element—that what the royal pantry lacks is a spice (*tavlin*), the "Sabbath," that only the Jews possess. This characterization of the Sabbath might engage a cultural discourse in which certain salts and spices were associated with distant, foreign places, on which see, e.g., G. Parker (2002); Pollard (2009); Novick (2011); Fitzpatrick (2011); Nabhan (2014). That the Jews' food has its own flavors might have itself been a marker of Jews as ethnic others. Inverting this trope, this story claims that the spice at the center of the Jews' tastes and smells marks their uniqueness in a positive, rather than derisive, sense.

157. Suetonius, *Vita divi Augusti* 76; trans. Rolfe (1927).

158. *Genesis Rabbah* 11.4 (ed. Theodor and Albeck, 91); parallel in *b. Shabbat* 119a. The man is identified as being from Laodicea, where the Synod of Laodicea declared, in the 360s, that "Christians shall not Judaize and be idle on Saturday, but shall work on that day; but the Lord's day they shall especially honor, and, as being Christians, shall, if possible, do no work on that day. If, however, they are found Judaizing, they shall be shut out from Christ." Canon 29 in Hefele, *Councils*, vol. 2, b 6, reproduced in Andrews and Conradi (1912:409).

159. *b. Shabbat* 119a–b; see also Brezis (2018:104–42).

160. See Brezis (2018:108–16), who also cites additional rabbinic sources that develop this theme, e.g., *b. Beitzah* 15b; *b. Pesahim* 68:b, and highlights the development of *oneg Shabbat* as a key aspect of the rabbinic Sabbath.

161. Chrysostom, *De Lazaro* PG 48.972; trans. S. J. D. Cohen (2012:33–34).

162. Augustine, *Enarratio in Psalmos* 32, translation and discussion in S. J. D. Cohen (2012), along with other passages in which Augustine bemoans the Jews' luxurious Sabbath observance.

163. I follow the translation of Abate (2017:493); see the textual variants in Theodor and Albeck (1912–36, 1965:93) and MS Vatican 60.

164. Or, "are tortured," on which see Lieberman (1974:32–33).

165. *Genesis Rabbah* 11:5 (ed. Theodor and Albeck, 92–94). Different versions of this story appear in *b. Sanhedrin* 65b; *Pesiqta Rabbati* 23.8; *Tanhuma Ki Tissa* 33:5 on Exodus 34:27; *Exodus Rabbah* 30:9. On the possibility that this story originated in the tannaitic period, see Hirshman (1996:43–54); the story and the order of the different components of the conversation are significantly different in Vatican 60, on which see Hirshman (1996:47); Abate (2017).

166. Abate (2017:495) notes that Tinneus Rufus is associated, in other rabbinic sources, with "anti-Jewish measures enacted under Hadrian's reign, including the prohibition of Sabbath observance."

167. On which see Peppard (2012b).

168. Abate (2017:499) notes the paronomasy of the river's name as well as a pun in the construction of this exchange: "R. Akiva says in Hebrew, '*draws* stones,' and the antagonist protests, with an equivalent verb in Aramaic, 'Are you *drawing* me away?'"

169. It also alludes to a prohibition concerning necromancy mentioned in *t. Sanhedrin* 10:7.

170. Rabbinic texts do not distinguish between "natural" and "supernatural." I use the terms "natural" and "supernatural" heuristically.

171. This halakhah is discussed widely in earlier rabbinic sources, e.g., *m. Eruvin* and *m. Shabbat*.

172. A shorter parallel appears in *b. Sanhedrin* 65b, which centers on the ritual of conjuring up the dead. The text distinguishes between different methods of soothsaying and skull consultations, concluding that soothsaying is ineffective on the Sabbath while skull consultations work even on the Sabbath. To illustrate this point, the dialogue between Tinneus Rufus and Rabbi Akiva is retold. Whereas *Genesis Rabbah* treats Tinneus Rufus's inability to conjure up his father on the Sabbath as a single proof, the Babylonian Talmud uses the event to illustrate two aspects of the Sabbath: that certain practices in the category of *ba'al ob* do not work on the Sabbath and that the governor's father rests on the Sabbath (the governor does not suffer from the fires of purgatory on this day).

173. Pliny the Elder, *Historia naturalis* 31.24; trans. M. Stern (1974, 1:499).

174. Pliny the Elder, *Historia naturalis* 31.24. Josephus, *Jewish War* 7.96–99, 336–37 also records this legend, but Josephus claims that the river stays dry for six days and flows

only on the Sabbath, when it is blessed with an abundance of water. See also Plutarch, *The E of Delphi* 19, 392 E; Marcus Aurelius, *Meditations* 4.43. On the origin of this tradition, see Kokin (2013), who also reads the exchange between Tinneus Rufus and Rabbi Akiva in the context of Roman anti-Sabbath polemics (14–17); on later sources, see Reeves (2005:208–24). Pliny's reference is the oldest extant tradition associated with a river that does not flow on the Sabbath, but it could refer to an earlier pagan or Jewish tradition. Kokin argues that Pliny's reference is a product of broader anti-Sabbath sentiment in Roman culture and that Jewish sources, starting with Josephus, attempt to recast this legend to reflect favorably on the Jews and their customs. Other rabbinic references to the Sambatyon appear in *y. Sanhedrin* 10:5; *Tanhuma, Addition to par. Shelah* 6 (ed. Buber); *Lamentations Rabbah, par.* 2:4, to Lamentations 2:5 (ed. Buber, 112); *Tanhuma, Ki-Tissa 33*, to Exodus 34:27 (ed. Zondel, 126). The narrative employs a river to illustrate the alternative temporality of the Sabbath; the flowing of water often appears in philosophical contexts to describe the passage of time.

175. A similar point is made in Loewenthal (1990:657); Ben-Dor Benite (2009:80), both cited by Kokin (2013:14).

176. Pliny the Elder, *Naturalis historia* 31.24; trans. M. Stern (1974, 1:499).

177. For earlier evidence, see Plutarch, *De superstitione* 3; Josephus, *Against Apion* 2.282; perhaps also Tibullus, *Elegies* 1, 3.15–18; later sources include John Chrysostom and Augustine.

178. John Chrysostom, *Against the Jews*, Homilies 1.8.1–2; 3.3.1–3, 3.5; 6.3.1–3.

179. Augustine, *City of God* 6.11.

180. Augustine, *City of God* 6.11.

181. Seneca's statement about pagan ignorance might also bemoan the sense that Romans were forgetting their traditions, a common trope in literature of the time. See, e.g., Cicero, *Academica* 1.3. The line could also be read more critically: that some Romans *were* celebrating the Sabbath because they were drawn to the theological or communal dimensions of the day but that Seneca did not want to acknowledge this fact. Christians in later centuries were also accused of attraction to Sabbath practice for theological and communal reasons, e.g., John Chrysostom, *Against the Jews*, Homilies 1.8.1–2; 3.3.1–3, 3.5; 6.3.1–3.

182. Tertullian, *Ad nationes* 13.3–4 also comments on pagan attraction to the Sabbath, discussed in Schneider (1968); Salzman (2004:196–97).

183. Ambivalence about non-Jewish participation in the Sabbath appears in *b. Sanhedrin* 58b. In *b. Yevamot* 47a–b, conversion marks the moment at which full Sabbath observance is required and the punishment for Sabbath transgression applies. In both instances, Sabbath observance is constructed as a practice linked with Jewish communal identity and distinctions between Jews and others. To observe the Sabbath becomes a marker of Jewishness, obligatory for Jews from the moment they convert and forbidden to gentiles who have not converted.

184. A different version of this midrash is found in *Exodus Rabbah* 30:9. In that narrative, set in the city of Rome, a *min*, a figure often associated in rabbinic sources with Christian anti-Jewish exegetical positions, voices the objection that nature continues to operate on the Sabbath. On the role of *minim* in exegetical debates, see Bar-Asher Siegal (2019). Kugel (1998:123–25) reads *Jubilees* as responding to critiques that God must not rest on the Sabbath, and therefore *Jubilees* invents lower angels who are in charge of the weather. If Kugel's reading is correct, then these Christian critiques might stem from pre-Christian polemics against the Sabbath as well, though to my knowledge there are no extant critiques specifically about the weather in such sources.

185. In MS Vatican 60, this objection appears second, not last as in the Theodor and Albeck text, and it also contains a longer objection; I use the translation in Abate (2017:493)

here: "He makes the winds blow, the clouds soar, the rain fall, the dew drops. He makes plants grow, fruits ripen, the sun shine, responds to women giving birth, and all that He does on the profane time, He does on the Sabbath," and the rabbi responds with a more elaborate explanation of how an eruv works. Though the text differs significantly, the sentiment and argumentation remain similar. In fact, the longer objection fits even better with Origen's objection, cited below.

186. *Didascalia Apostolorum* 26; trans. Connolly (1929).

187. Justin Martyr, *Dialogue with Trypo* 23; on which see Hirshman (1996:39–40, 44–50), who identifies this argument as an originally non-Christian critique of the Sabbath that was adopted by Christian apologists and known to rabbinic authors.

188. Origen, *Homily 24 on Numbers 28:1–29:39*, 4.3; trans. Scheck (2009:143).

189. *Mekhilta de-Rabbi Ishmael Bahodesh* 7 on Exodus 20:10 can also be read in this context.

190. For a nuanced methodological approach to this question, see Schremer (2009); on heightened anti-imperial rhetoric in the fifth through seventh century, see Boustan (2009).

191. On the general intersection between Babylonian rabbis and ideas from the Roman east, see Kalmin (2014). The *History of Abda Damshikha* mentions the Sabbath, on which see Butts and Gross (2017).

192. E.g., Aphrahat, *De Sabbato* (*Demonstrations* 13). Scholarship on Jewish-Christian relations in this region is vast; see, e.g., Koltun-Fromm (1996; 1997).

193. Butts and Gross (2017:116–21, 184–89).

194. *The History of the Slave of Christ*, 10; trans. Butts and Gross (2017:118–21).

195. Hayes (1998); Gribetz and Vidas (2012).

196. Tractate *Kutim*, which lists halakhic matters for which Samaritan-Jewish difference mattered, also does not mention the Sabbath. Josephus, *Jewish Antiquities* 11.346 mentions that when someone from Jerusalem was accused of eating unclean food or violating the Sabbath, they would flee to the Samaritan community and claim unjust expulsion (Josephus does not comment on Samaritan Sabbath observance in the passage but indicates that Sabbath violation prompted Jews to join Samaritans). In *Jewish Antiquities* 12.257–61, Josephus accuses Samaritans of disavowing their connection to the Sabbath. They try to convince Antiochus Epiphanes that they are not Jews but people of other ethnic origins, to gain his favor and preserve their community at a time when Jews were being persecuted. In the process of this exchange with Antiochus, the Samaritans explain to the king that Sabbath observance was not an originally Samaritan practice. Rather, it became their community's custom to observe the Sabbath following a drought, when the Samaritans' forefathers adopted the Jewish Sabbath in the hope that it would help them overcome their desperate circumstances. In this passage, Josephus suggests that the Samaritans tried to distance themselves from Jews by explaining that Samaritans only inadvertently observe the Jewish Sabbath and that the Sabbath is not an original Samaritan ancestral practice. On the topic of the Samaritan Sabbath in Josephus, see Montgomery (1907, 1968); Bickerman (2007); Schalit (1970–71); Coggins (1987); L. Feldman (1992); H. Weiss (1994; 2003:52–64); Pummer (2009). Sabbath observance also plays a role in scholarship on Samaritans origins, e.g., Nodet (1997:12) argues that the Samaritans were the original Israelites and that "the material in the Hexateuch should generally be attributed to them [Samaritans], with the conspicuous exception of the weekly Sabbath," which was brought by Jews from Babylon and later adopted by the Samaritans.

197. Rabbinic sources that discuss Samaritan status, often in the context of marriage, include *m. Berakhot* 7:1; *m. Qiddushin* 4:3; *m. Ketubbot* 3:1; *m. Sheqalim* 1:5; *m. Demai* 3:4, 5:9; *t. Qiddushin* 5:1; *t. Ketubbot* 3:1, 5; *t. Demai* 4:24–27, 5:21–24; *t. Terumot* 4:12, 14; *t. Gittin* 1:5; *t. Hullin* 1:1; *t. peah* 4:1; *t. Pesahim* 2:3; *y. Qiddushin* 1:4, 65b; *y. Berakhot* 11b;

NOTES TO CHAPTER 3 [291]

y. Gittin 1:5, 43c; *y. Avodah Zarah* 5:4, 44d; *y. Pesahim* 1:1, 27b; *b. Qiddushinn* 75a–76b; *b. Yevamot* 24b; *b. Avodah Zarah* 31a–b; *b. Hullin* 3b–4a, 5b–6a, 17a; *b. Moed Katan* 12a; *b. Berakhot* 47b. On Samaritans in rabbinic sources, see Taglicht (1888); Montgomery (1907, 1968:165–96); Hershkovitz (1940); Gafni (1969); Alon (1977:354–73); Schiffman (1985; 2012b); Oppenheimer (1981); van der Horst (2006:134–50); Lavee (2010); Chalmers (2017; 2019).

198. Other rabbinic sources comment on this difference as well, e.g., *Genesis Rabbah* 81:3.

199. On *m. Nedarim* 3:11 in the context of Jewish-Christian difference, see Tong (2019); Rosen-Zvi (2017b); Y. Koren (2014).

200. *Kutim* 1:1.

201. *t. Terumot* 4:12, 14; translation and discussion in Schiffman (1985:326).

202. In *m. Rosh Hashanah* 2:2 and *t. Rosh Hashanah* 1(2):17, discussed in Schiffman (1985:345–46).

203. Schiffman (1985:346–49).

204. *b. Avodah Zarah* 21b–22a.

205. Schiffman (1985; 2012b).

206. Origen, *De Principiis* 4.3.2; on which see H. Weiss (1994); S. J. D. Cohen (2010). Origen's text does not imply that these two positions were necessarily held by all rabbinic Jews or Samaritans. On Dositheus's identity, see S. J. D. Cohen (2010:175).

207. *m. Eruvin* 4:3; *m. Sotah* 5:3; cf. Acts 1:12, which mentions the Sabbath limit but not an exact distance.

208. H. Weiss (1994:273) notes that Samaritans "remained in full dialogue with the cacophony of halakic voices within Judaism." Memar Marqah (II.10, 138), a later text, builds upon Genesis 2 and connects the Sabbath to the world's creation, listing the Sabbath among seven special creations, defending Sabbath observance, and arguing that those who observe the Sabbath will be blessed by God. On Memar Marqah, see H. Weiss (1994:265–73); MacDonald (1963); Ben-Hayyim (1998).

209. On which see, e.g., Watts (2015); on shifting religious affiliations in a later period, see Tannous (2018:403), including on days of worship distinguishing Muslims from Jews and Christians.

210. S. J. D. Cohen (2012).

Chapter 3

1. On the history of the start of the day in ancient Jewish sources, see J. Baumgarten (1958); S. Zeitlin (1959); Talmon (1994); Ben-Dov (2018).

2. By the rabbinic construction of men's and women's time, I mean just that: how the rabbis, through their laws, constructed a system of time for men and women. This does not assume that men and women followed these rules or that those who did experienced time in the way devised by the system, even if they followed the rabbinic rulings to the letter. On women not following rabbinic purity laws in medieval Egypt, see Krakowski (2020). The discussion in this chapter, as in the others in this book, addresses rabbinic texts and discourse, not the lives of real people, though their lives were surely impacted in various ways by these texts.

3. Though times for prayer (Tefillah) are more flexible and less exacting, splitting the day into morning, afternoon, and evening rather than delineate exact times, e.g., *m. Berakhot* 4:1, *t. Berakhot* 3:1–2.

4. See, e.g., Rackman (1958:16–17); Lamm (1966, 1987:68–78).

5. Foster (1996) notes various ways that the "menstrual cycle" is divided into periods or

stages of time in modern medical contexts and how such discourses have attempted to standardize an inherently unstandardizable bodily phenomenon for cultural and scientific purposes. On the cultural gendering of cyclical bodily rhythms, see Delaney, Lupton, and Toth (1976:267–73). On other intersections between biological and social rhythms, see Roenneberg (2012); Lefebvre (2004).

6. Cosmological and bodily times are intertwined: plant, animal, and human bodies are profoundly affected by and synchronized with the rising and setting of the sun and in turn also by the seasons, on which see Bargiello, Jackson, and Young (1984); Hardin, Hall, and Rosbash (1990); Meuti and Denlinger (2013).

7. Alexander (2013:155–77); Neis (2018).

8. Milgrom (1991:745); Meacham (1999a:23); Fonrobert (2000:16–19); L. Feinstein (2014:181–83). On dimensions of menstrual separation in the Babylonian Talmud, see Secunda (2020:chap. 6).

9. Both sets of practices are also connected to temple practices and thus to the historical past.

10. My approach to ritual is informed by J. Z. Smith (1987); Bell (1992); Rosen-Zvi (2012); Balberg (2017b).

11. Balberg (2017b:74).

12. Balberg (2017b:74).

13. Bell (1992:xv).

14. Balberg (2017b:74), following the work of Humphrey and Laidlow (1994).

15. Bell (1992).

16. Balberg (2017b:75) notes that rabbinic texts ritualize almost all aspects of life.

17. A related conceptual idea is articulated in J. Halberstam (2005:7).

18. Scholarship on time and gender has focused on the gendered orientation of conventional historical periodization, the way women used their time in different periods and places, the timeliness of feminism, and reconceptions of temporality from the perspective of feminist theory. See, e.g., Kristeva (1981); Kelly Gadol (1977); Davies (1990); Felski (2000); Hjorthol (2001); Griffiths (2004:134–54); Grosz (2005); Radstone (2007); R. Hill (2008); Baraitser (2008; 2017); Schües, Olkowski, and Fielding (2011); A. Stone (2012:128–47); Larson (2012); Wajcman (2015:esp. 111–36); B. Smith (2016); Ortega (2016:78–86); Beynon-Jones (2017); Burke (2018); Pursley (2019). One pioneering study of time and gender can be found in Jahoda, Lazarsfeld, and Zeisel (1960); most recently, see Eidinow and Maurizio (2020). On time and gender in Judaism more specifically, see C. Safrai (1995); Wolfson (2006); Goldberg (2011a); Strassfeld (2013:94–138); Pedaya (2015).

19. Barak (2014:18). In Barak's account, men also exist at the center of the temporal discourse and women's time must be teased out from the boundaries. On the use of times of prayer to construct gender roles in another Egyptian context, see Rock-Singer (2016; 2018:106–31).

20. *m. Berakhot* 1:1–3:6; *t. Berakhot* 1:1–5.

21. Numbers 15 seems to have been added later than the passages from Deuteronomy. A number of blessings were appended before and after the Shema prayer; the enveloping blessings differed depending on the time of their recitation. An emended version of Psalm 72:19, a blessing formula discussed in tannaitic and amoraic sources, was inserted between the recitation of Deuteronomy 6:4 and 6:5. The first full text of the Shema and its blessings survives in Amram Gaon's ninth-century *Order of Prayers* as well as in Geniza fragments. On the historical development of the Shema prayer, see Kimelman (1987; 2001); Reif (1993:83–85; 2006); J. Katz (1998); Wyse (2005); Fleischer (2007); Tabory (2006); Penner (2012:73–100); Alexander (2013:138–77).

22. It is not clear exactly when the order of the mishnaic tractates was set, but it hap-

pened fairly early, on which see Strack and Stemberger (1992:119-21); Frankel (1923:254); J. Epstein (1965:980-83); Kahana (2006).

23. A fuller treatment of this question appears in Gribetz (2015; 2013:73-100); Alexander (2013:137-77); Kimelman (2006).

24. NJPSV. For a study of the passage's textual variants in Second Temple sources, see Lange and Weigold (2012).

25. The practices of donning phylacteries and fixing mezuzot formed in the Hellenistic period, e.g., *Letter of Aristeas* 159; Philo, *De specialibus legibus* 141-42; Josephus, *Jewish Antiquities* 4:213; Matthew 23:5. Archaeological evidence from Qumran, Wadi Murabba'at, Nahal Se'elim, and Nahal Hever attests to the wide use of phylacteries and mezuzot during and after the Second Temple period, on which see Stegemann and Becker (1961). Tannaitic sources do not cover these two rituals systematically (i.e., there is no tractate or subsection devoted to systematically detailing laws about them), but sources mention them in passing numerous times, e.g., *m. Shevi'it* 3:8, 11; *m. Berakhot* 3:3; *m. Kelim* 17:16; *m. Avodah Zarah* 2:4; *Mekhilta de-Rabbi Ishmael Bo* 17; *Sifre Deuteronomy* 35. For a detailed study of the history of phylacteries in antiquity, see Y. Cohn (2008).

26. Kimelman (2001:18n35). The same construct of "lying down and getting up" appears in Genesis 19:33, 35, about Lot and his daughters. There, too, the phrase בשכבה ובקומה functions as a merism, i.e., that Lot did not recognize his daughters during the entire duration of the encounter, from beginning to end, and thus is absolved of sin.

27. Proverbs 6:20-22 NRSV.

28. The word *tamid* alludes to a sense of permanence, though the precise temporal conception is difficult to discern. There is a subtle distinction between "always" and "at all times": the former implies continuity and the latter implies an ongoing sequence of individual moments. See also 2 Kings 23:3, in which the temporal dimension is missing; Joshua 1:8, in which "day and night" is more continuous, implying "always"; *b. Menahot* 99b, which implies constancy.

29. 1QS 10.13-14; translation based on García Martínez and Tigchelaar (1998:95). Schiffman (1995:293-95); D. K. Falk (1998:112-16); Weinfeld (1992); Bradshaw (2002:40) regard this passage as a reference to the recitation of the Shema. In *Jubilees* 25:2, Rebecca tells Jacob that she loves him at every moment of the day and night.

30. 1QS 10.16. See also 4Q417 1 I 6-13 *par* 4Q418 43-45 I 1-10; 1QHa XXII 36; 1QHa XX 7-14; 1QS 6.6-7 *par* 4QSd II 10, which connect the idea of devoting one's self fully to God with the practice of doing so at all times (*tamid*), through either prayer or study. On these and related texts, see Bakker (2016; 2017); Newman (2018).

31. In 1QS 10.10, the narrator proclaims that "with the arrival of day and night, I shall enter the covenant of God, and with the departure of evening and morning, I shall repeat his laws [חוקיו]." The terminology of "entering the covenant of God" (אבואה בברית אל) mirrors the terms used in the text to describe the act of entering into the covenant of the sect, "and all those who enter the Yahad will pass into a covenant with God" (וכל הבאים בסרך היחד יעבורו בברית אל). D. K. Falk (1998:114) suggests that members of the community marked sunrise and sunset by "commemorat[ing] their initial entry into the covenant and their annual renewal." On whether this passage refers to Deuteronomy 6, see the differing opinions in Sarason (2000); Talmon (1960); Schiffman (1995:293-95); D. K. Falk (1998:112-16); Weinfeld (1992:242-43).

32. Philo, *De specialibus legibus* 136-40.

33. Philo, *De specialibus legibus* 141-42; trans. Colson (1939, 1999:96-97); on which see N. Cohen (1995:129-77); Mendelson (1994).

34. E.g., Philo mentions morning and evening prayers in *De vita contemplativa* 27. The Dead Sea Scrolls preserve a number of prayers and references to prayers, e.g., Daily Prayers

(4Q503), the *Songs of the Sabbath Sacrifice* (4Q400–407, 11Q17), the *Hodayot* (1QHa–b), Psalms collections (1QPsalmsa), Festival Prayers (1Q34), the *Words of the Luminaries* (4Q504–6), on which see Sarason (2000); Chazon (1998). Morning and evening prayers were common in the Greek world (e.g., Hesiod, *Opera et dies* 338–39; Plato, *Leges* 887e; Xenophon, *Republica Lacedaemoniorum* 13.3) and perhaps also among Jews, on which see Jonquière (2007:48); Pulleyn (1997:157); Penner (2012:104).

35. A similar tension between constancy and regularity occurs in the development of Christian prayer. Regular prayer at various hours of the day, discussed, e.g., in the *Didascalia Apostolorum* (fol. 11a–b) and the *Pilgrimage of Egeria* (45–90), builds upon Psalm 119:164, "Seven times a day do I praise you, because of your righteous ordinances," as a command to pray seven times a day—that is, regularly. The Desert Fathers and the Churches of the East, in contrast, advocated continual prayer, in light of Paul's call to "rejoice always, pray continually, give thanks in all circumstances" in 1 Thessalonians 5:16–18 (the Didascalia also presents its command to pray seven times each day as an enactment of Paul's instructions). See, e.g., Aphrahat, *Demonstrations* 6. On the development of the Benedictine liturgy, see Dohrn-van Rossum (1996:29–43); Zerubavel (1981:31–69). The Didascalia is often regarded as a Jewish-Christian text, e.g., Fonrobert (2001a), but on the matter of prayer times it follows the trajectory of Christian practice. On temporal regularity and fixed practice in rabbinic sources, including the daily recitation of the Shema, see Kaye (2018:86–109).

36. An analogous literalization occurs with the phrase "heaven and earth," e.g., Genesis 1:1 and 2:4. In its biblical context, the two words function as a merism to mean "the whole world," while rabbinic sources sometimes suggest that the heavens and the earth are two separate spheres. Thus in *Genesis Rabbah* 1:15, the House of Shammai and the House of Hillel debate whether heaven or earth was created first.

37. *Letter of Aristeas* 159–60; translation based on Shutt (1985:23) and Charles (1913:109). For analyses of this passage, especially its use of the Septuagint, see Penner (2012:73–100); B. Wright (2008).

38. The *Letter of Aristeas* uses identical forms as the Septuagint to refer to the timing of the ritual—καὶ κοιταζομένους καὶ διανισταμένους—but the author of the letter implies two specific moments of the day (sleeping and waking).

39. The phrase "works of God" (τὰς τοῦ θεοῦ κατασκευάς) references Genesis 1:2 in its Greek form in the Septuagint, ἡ δὲ γῆ ἦν ἀόρατος καὶ ἀκατασκεύαστος (God transforms what is uncreated into creations), about the creation of the world out of nothingness, the creation of light, and the distinction between day and night on the first day of creation.

40. Josephus, *Jewish Antiquities* 4.212; trans. Feldman (1999:406–7). The language in the *Letter of Aristeas* is more ambiguous, "*when* lying down and rising up."

41. Naeh and Shemesh (1995) argue that Josephus refers to the daily manna and quail delivered each morning and evening (e.g., Exodus 16:8–12). Penner (2012:126) observes that Josephus connects Moses' prayer of thanks for these divine gifts with the custom of daily prayer. *Wisdom of Solomon* 16:27–28 links the gift of manna with prayer, using the same term, εὐχαριστία, as Josephus, on which see Penner (2012:106, 108). *t. Sotah* 11:8 refers to the manna, the pillar of cloud, and the well provided by God in the desert specifically as "gifts" (מתנות); *Mekhilta de-Rabbi Shimon bar Yohai* on Exodus 16:4 explains that God's daily sustenance to the Israelites through the manna and quail was designed to elicit their daily worship of God each morning and evening.

42. Ancient Jews ate two main meals a day, on which see Eager (1939); Noy (1998). Other Romans, in contrast, usually ate three or four meals, on which see D. Smith (2004:20–22).

43. *m. Tamid* 5:1; translation based on Neusner (1991:869). See also Hammer (1991).

NOTES TO CHAPTER 3 [295]

On the dating of the tractate, see Ginzberg (1919); Neusner (1980). I suspect that both positions are partially correct: the tractate might preserve earlier material than most other mishnaic tractates and yet, like other texts in the Mishnah, underwent significant editing and updating. My analysis takes both of these assessments into account. On the relationship between rabbinic texts and temple practices, see N. Cohn (2012); Balberg (2017a). On the antiquity of the tannaitic debates about the Shema, see Kahana (2002:160–62).

44. The Nash Papyrus (second century BCE) preserves the Decalogue (Exodus 20:2ff.), immediately followed by the text of Deuteronomy 6:4 and the first half of 6:5. The form of the text suggests that it was related to the use of phylacteries. On the pairing of the Decalogue and the Shema, see Kimelman (1987:74); Oppenheimer (2011).

45. *m. Berakhot* 1:1–2, MS Kaufmann.

46. *m. Berakhot* 1:3, on which see Kahana (2002:149–52).

47. *m. Berakhot* 1:3; *t. Berakhot* 1:6; see also *Leviticus Rabbah* 27.6. Yadin-Israel (2009:210–11) highlights the shift in meaning of this mishnaic passage.

48. *Sifre Deuteronomy* 34–35.

49. On the end time for the evening Shema, see also 1QS 6.7–8 (ed. Qimron, 220), in which the first third of the night is devoted to prayer.

50. *t. Berakhot* 1:1–2; *Sifre Zuta Deuteronomy* 11:19 (ed. Kahana, 160).

51. Kahana (2002:160, discussion on 149–52, 161–63). Kahana explains that this debate between the Houses of Shammai and Hillel is not mentioned in the Mishnah or Tosefta. The House of Shammai's answer, about the time of the purification of the priests, seems to be a different version of the answer proposed by the Mishnah (the priests are able to go home to eat their offering once they are purified), perhaps based on Leviticus 22:7. The two versions (Mishnah and *Sifre Zuta*) are then combined in Rabbi Joshua's statement about the Shema's timing in *b. Berakhot* 2a ("from the hour when the priests are purified in order to eat the *terumah*"). The Mishnah thus seems to rule according to the House of Shammai rather than the House of Hillel, whose opinion ("when it gets dark [in the evening]") is not replicated in other sources, though the time of the priests entering to eat the *terumah* is considered to be the same as the time for the appearance of stars in the night sky according to the Palestinian Talmud.

52. On these time-markers, see Yoskovich (2014); Martin (2001). See also *m. Tamid* 1:2, which mentions the time of the crowing of the cock but also indicates some temporal flexibility.

53. On the relationship between the Shema's timing and the temple sacrifices, see Perkins (1994).

54. *t. Berakhot* 1:1 includes a broader explanation about time and its division, including a debate between Rabbi and Rabbi Nathan about the proper division of time and an explanation of time-units: an *'onah* is 1/24th of a *sha'ah*, an *'et* is 1/24th of an *'onah*, a *reg'a* is 1/24th of an *'et*.

55. *m. Berakhot* 1:7, MS Kaufmann. In *b. Berakhot* 10b, a person can even recite the benedictions before and after the Shema as usual. On the ways in which the recitation of these Shema verses functions as a specialized form of Torah study, see Alexander (2013:531–79). The term הפסיד ("has not lost") connotes suffering loss or being at a disadvantage, meaning that someone who recites the Shema verses at the improper time "loses nothing" because the act now constitutes reading Torah passages, on which see Jastrow (1943, 2005:1192). Other mishnaic instances use the longer phrase לא הפסיד כלום (*m. Demai* 7:7; *m. Nazir* 2:10; *m. Qinnim* 2:3, 5). Here, the word כלום does not appear, perhaps indicating that while one has not lost everything, one has still lost something by not reciting the Shema in its proper time.

56. A similar concept relates to discussions of proper sacrificial times, as certain sacri-

fices are only efficacious if they are performed at the correct time (see, e.g., *m. Zevahim* 2:3, 14:3; *t. Pesahim* 3:7), on which see S. Stern (2003:46–58).

57. Or, alternatively, there is flexibility for certain rituals even when they have fixed times; e.g., *m. Pesahim* 1:3.

58. *m. Megillah* 2:6. This "general principle" follows a list of rituals that ought to be performed during the day (e.g., reading the *megillah*, reciting *hallel*, sounding the shofar, waving the *lulav*, a series of sacrificial acts, and so on) and at night (e.g., cutting wheat for the *omer*, offering up fats and sacrificial parts), on which see Novick (2010:44n9), who notes that *m. Berakhot* 1:1 applies to the end point of the acceptable time range, while *m. Megillah* 2:6 refers to a commandment that ought to be performed simply "at night," not at a specific time of night (or day). The timely performance of commandments is praised in *Sifra Hova* 10:3 (25a): "Rabbi Yehudah says: Beloved is a commandment in its time"; *b. Qiddushin* 33a; *b. Hullin* 54a, 133a; on which see Novick (2010:170–73), who writes that "the sense of the maxim is: one who fulfills a commandment in its time manifests love toward it" (170).

59. E.g., *m. Zevahim* 2:3, 14:3; *t. Pesahim* 3:7; S. Stern (2003:46–58). Timing is also a factor in magical practices, as words are most efficacious when they are said at correct times, on which see Edmonds (2003:236–38); Isbell (1975:25, 28, 32–33); Shaked (2010).

60. *m. Pesahim* 5:3. *t. Pesahim* 9:6 adds that an animal must be designated to serve as a Passover offering before midday. There are cases in which a "failed" sacrifice is still valid as a different sacrifice, e.g., *m. Terumah* 4:3, in which a sin offering is redesignated a freewill offering if it is purchased with money that was meant for the former but not used in time; the sacrifice does not satisfy the owner's obligation but is still considered valid as a sacrifice of a different sort, a case analogous to the Shema. See Kaye (2012:184–87) on the function of time in the Passover sacrifice.

61. Novick (2010:164–75) identifies two sets of temporal categories in rabbinic literature: (1) timeliness, which presumes an ideal time for an action and a spectrum of better to worse depending on the action's proximity to the ideal time; and (2) the deontological frame, wherein there is a right time for an action and all other times are wrong. Novick identifies instances in which the norm of timeliness is applied to deontological time to instill a sense of immediacy—that it is best to perform a commandment as soon as possible rather than at any point during its appropriate time—to create an internal differentiation within the appropriate period of ritual performance. The analysis of the Shema in this chapter suggests that, in certain instances, there was also a third rabbinic approach to time in law, which defines the same act differently depending on the time in which it is performed.

62. Deuteronomy 6:4–9 and 11:13–21 were also appealed to for their healing and protective powers, e.g., the Halbturn amulet contains a transliteration of the opening line from the Shema into Greek, on which see Eshel, Eshel, and Lange (2010); Doneus and Lange (2010); and Bowl No. 11:6–7 in Naveh and Shaked (1987:184–87); Levene (2003). Geniza fragments attest to the continued use of Deuteronomy 6:4–9 in magical spells; see T-S K 1.147, fol. 1e, lines 1–16 in Schäfer and Shaked (1994:223); T-S K 1.95 in Shaked (1988:228, 230). *b. Berakhot* 6a assures that the recitation of the Shema before sleep keeps the nighttime demons away; see also *y. Peah* 15d and *Genesis Rabbah* 35:3.

63. *m. Berakhot* 2:3, translated according to the text in MS Kaufmann fol. 2r; MS Parma 3173 (De Rossi 138) fol. 1v; and Geniza fragments (e.g., T-S E2.4). Printed editions add the term "yoke" to the "kingdom of heaven" as well; this was an attempt to create uniformity between the two halves of the passage ("yoke of the kingdom of heaven and yoke of the commandments").

64. *m. Berakhot* 1:5.

65. *m. Berakhot* 2:1; *t. Berakhot* 2:2, 7; Neis (2018).

66. Other ancient sources also regard the Shema verses as singularly important. In the Synoptic Gospels, Jesus answers the question "which commandment is first of all?" by quoting a variant of Deuteronomy 6:4–6: "the first is, 'Hear, O Israel! The Lord is our God, the Lord is One; you shall love the Lord your God with all your heart, and with all your soul, and with all your mind, and with all your strength'" (Mark 12:28–34; parallels: Matthew 22:34–40; Luke 10:25–28; see also *Didache* 1).

67. *m. Tamid* 5:1.

68. Alexander (2013:178–234).

69. *m. Berakhot* 2:5.

70. The following passage (*m. Berakhot* 2:6) mentions that Rabban Gamliel also did not follow the proper rules of mourning after his wife's death, again presenting his actions in a gendered framework.

71. *b. Berakhot* 21a highlights the Shema's continued importance when it states that if one is in doubt about whether one has recited the Shema, one should recite it again, but if one is in doubt regarding the Amidah, one should not recite the Amidah a second time, implying that the Shema is of greater importance and thus the stakes of ensuring its daily recitation are higher. In later midrashim, the daily recitation of the Shema is compared to the daily sacrifices, both of which were also offered in the evenings and mornings and served to mark those times with the acceptance of God (e.g., *Deuteronomy Rabbah* on Deuteronomy 6:4; *Yalkut Shimoni* 247).

72. *m. Berakhot* 3:3, MS Kaufmann. The verb פטר is used to describe women's exemption (חיב is used to describe men's obligation in the Mishnah); I understand the idea of "exemption" (פטורין) to effectively be a form of exclusion. See Alexander (2013:237–39); Neusner (1987:71–73); Hauptman (1998:233–34). This term is used here of women's exemption from both the obligation to recite the Shema and the entire set of positive time-bound commandments.

73. Josephus, *Jewish Antiquities* 4.8.12; translated with modifications by Thackeray and Marcus (1930:100–103).

74. Philo might read the passage to imply men, as he mentions the instruction of "young men" in *De specialibus legibus* 4.141, but presents twice-daily prayer as a practice among the Therapeutae in *De vita contemplativa* 27.

75. I use the term "justify" in its doubled meaning: the midrash explains the connection between rabbinic traditions and biblical scripture, and also provides a justification for the exclusion of women. *y. Berakhot* 3:3, 6b continues this line of exegesis, on which see Alexander (2013:107–8).

76. *Sifre Zuta* on Deuteronomy 6:6–7; ed. Kahana, 149. Kahana notes that this interpretation is unique to *Sifre Zuta* and is perhaps based on its reading of Deuteronomy 4:9, "make them known to your children and your children's children" (והודעתם לבניך ולבני בניך), which uses the same language; *b. Qiddushin* 30a connects these two verses and derives exclusion of women from them as well. The midrash provides an exegetical rather than a logical explanation: it does not explain *why* sons are obligated but daughters are not, other than that the Torah uses the word בנים in its limited meaning ("sons") rather than its expansive meaning ("children"). Had this interpretation of the verse been obvious, the rabbinic interpretation would not have needed so adamantly to make its case. That the text raises the possible interpretation that the verse includes women, only to refute it, suggests that some readers might have understood it otherwise. The Septuagint uses the word *tekna* (i.e., gender neutral) in Deuteronomy 11:19 but *uious* (i.e., gendered male) in Deuteronomy 6:7, suggesting no single stable understanding of the implied gender of the Hebrew term (בניך), on which see Alexander (2013:184–85, esp. nn. 16–17). *Sifre Deuteronomy* (ed. Kahana, 150) provides a different interpretation of Deuteronomy 6:7, stating that the verse indicates that

those you teach are called "sons," and therefore students are like children. See also *Sifre Deuteronomy* on Deuteronomy 11:19 (ed. Finkelstein, 104), which limits the verse to sons and commands a father to speak Hebrew and teach his sons Torah; see also *y. Berakhot* 3:3, 6b. A similar interpretation of Deuteronomy 21:19 appears in *t. Sanhedrin* 11:6 and *b. Sanhedrin* 69a in reference to the rebellious son, on which see Hayes (2015:259).

77. Alexander (2013:176).

78. On which see Boyarin (1993:134–225); Alexander (2013:178–210); Satlow (2013); Weiss and Stav (2018); and the sources cited in these works (e.g., *t. Qiddushin* 1:11; *b. Kettubot* 62b–63a). The idea that Torah study should occupy all of one's time is anchored in rabbinic readings of biblical passages such as Joshua 1:8; Psalms 1:2, 63:7, 119:97.

79. On which see Boyarin (1993:134–66).

80. E.g., *m. Sotah* 3:4; see also interpretations of this *mishnah* in *y. Sotah* 3:4, 19a; *b. Sotah* 21b.

81. *m. Avot* 1:5, MS Kaufmann.

82. *b. Berakhot* 20b; this text also expresses surprise that women are exempt from such a central religious obligation.

83. The exclusion of women from this category was itself a matter of dispute in the tannaitic period, on which see Ginzberg (1971:159–63); M. Katz (2003:189–93).

84. *m. Qiddushin* 1:7; the first half of this *mishnah* offers a different categorization of commandments (women are exempt from commandments incumbent on fathers to their sons but obligated to fulfill those incumbent on sons to their parents), implying that time is not the only dimension on which gendered difference is constructed in this text. *t. Qiddushin* 1:10 also assumes that women are not obligated in this category: "Rabbi Shimon exempts the women from [the ritual of *tzitzit*] because it is a positive commandment that is time-bound." In both texts, the verb פטר describes women's exemption (חיב describes men's obligation in the Mishnah, and the Tosefta takes for granted men's obligation and does not use the term explicitly). Other rabbinic sources discuss this category as well: *Mekhilta de-Rabbi Ishmael Pisha* 17 on Exodus 13:9 (ed. Horovitz and Rabin, 68); *Mekhilta de-Rabbi Shimon bar Yohai* on Exodus 13:9 (ed. Epstein and Melamed, 41); *Sifre Numbers Shelah* 115 (ed. Horowitz, 124); *t. Sotah* 2:8; *y. Qiddushin* 1:7, 61c; *y. Berakhot* 2:3, 4c; *y. Berakhot* 3:3, 6b; *b. Qiddushin* 33b–35a; *b. Eruvin* 96a–b; and *b. Sukkah* 28a–b. The *Mekhilta de-Rabbi Shimon bar Yohai* derives women's exemption from the entire category from their exemption specifically of phylacteries: "Just as women are exempt [from the commandment to wear] phylacteries, [which is] a particular positive, time-bound commandment, likewise are women exempt from all positive, time-bound commandments." *Mekhilta de-Rabbi Shimon bar Yohai* on Exodus 13:9, trans. Nelson (2006:73), discussed in Alexander (2013:37–40).

85. There are other categorizations offered for the commandments, e.g., *m. Qiddushin* 1:9; *t. Qiddushin* 1:10.

86. Hauptman (1998:222–33); S. Safrai (1995); Baskin (1985:esp. 5–6); Yalon (1989); Biale (1984:10–17); Wegner (1992:145–56); Zohar (1993); L. Hoffman (1996:164–70); Margalit (2004).

87. See, e.g., S. J. D. Cohen (2005:115–20); Israeli (2012; 2015).

88. As described in *y. Berakhot* 3:3, 6b and *b. Qiddushin* 34a–b. Alexander (2007; 2013:1–42) argues that the category derived from exegetical considerations unrelated to matters of gender and that questions of gender are not part of the categorization's initial formulation but rather of its transmission. See also Weiss-Goldman (1999); Labovitz (2015). Benovitz (2007b:67–82) proposes that the category of rituals served primarily as an entry point for Torah study, and because women are not obligated in that practice, they are also exempt from the category of positive time-bound commandments. It is far from obvi-

ous, however, that the exclusion of women from Torah study ought to extend to other obligations derived from Deuteronomy 6, though it is the explanation given in *Sifre Deuteronomy* on Deuteronomy 11:19; *Sifre Zuta* on Deuteronomy 6:7; *y. Berakhot* 3:3, 4c; *b. Qiddushin* 30a.

89. Hauptman (1998:226) argues that "the Talmud mentions the phrase 'positive time-bound' or 'non-time-bound' mitzvoth *only* in connection with women." She adds: "this distinction was created solely for the purpose of distinguishing between a woman's ritual obligations and her exemptions. It was not a category that had any other use. For men, who are obligated to perform all positive mitzvoth, there is no significance to this distinction." Rhein (2016) also argues that one of the motivations behind this categorization was to create a gendered ritual hierarchy.

90. Alexander (2013:108–10) notes that in *y. Berakhot* 3:3, 6b women are exempt because they are not obligated in Torah study and enslaved people are exempt because they are not free and cannot therefore wholeheartedly accept the "kingdom of heaven." On the shared status of women and enslaved people, see Hezser (1998).

91. *Sifre Shellah*, piska 115 (ed. Horovitz, 124) extends the applicability of the category of positive time-bound commandments to other categories of "unqualified people," probably enslaved people, on which see Ginzberg (1971:63n47); Alexander (2013:37).

92. *y. Pesahim* 1:4, 27c, discussed in Kaye (2018:61–68, esp. 66); on *y. Pesahim* 1:1, 27b, see Moscovitz (2006).

93. This is similar to the characterization of women as not punctual, discussed in Barak (2014).

94. The Mishnah offers a near-absolute categorization but does not provide examples of each category. The Tosefta provides examples of the category of positive time-bound and non-time-bound commandments, but the Shema is not included in the list of examples even though it is considered to be part of it elsewhere. The rituals from which tannaitic and amoraic sources exempt women because the rituals are considered positive and time-bound include phylacteries (*m. Berakhot* 3:3, *t. Qiddushin* 1:10, *y. Qiddushin* 1:7, 61c, *b. Qiddushin* 33b–34a), *tzitzit* (*b. Qiddushin* 33b), *shofar* (*t. Rosh HaShanah* 2:4, *y. Qiddushin* 1:7, 61c, *b. Qiddushin* 33b), *lulav* (*t. Qiddushin* 1:10, *y. Qiddushin* 1:7, 61c, *b. Qiddushin* 33b), and *sukkah* (*t. Qiddushin* 1:10, *y. Qiddushin* 1:7, 61c, *b. Qiddushin* 33b–34b); some sources also include the paschal sacrifice (e.g., *t. Pesahim* 2:22, 8:10, *y. Pesahim* 8:1, 35d, *b. Pesahim* 91b), on which see Benovitz (2007b:49–50, 67). There are other rituals that fit the criteria of "positive" and "time-bound" that sources do not mention. The category's exclusion of women is not absolute, however; exceptions include eating matzah, hearing the Torah reading during *haqhel*, bringing a *simha* offering during the pilgrimage festivals, hearing *kiddush* on the Sabbath, lighting Hanukkah candles, fasting on Yom Kippur, and hearing the *megillah*. See Lehman (2006:314–15); Alexander (2013:120–33).

95. *b. Berakhot* 20b. I am indebted here to the insights of Alexander (2013:107–19). On the Babylonian Talmud, see Rovner (1994); Kraemer (1996:86–108); Benovitz (2007b: 71–79).

96. That phylacteries became the paradigmatic time-bound commandment is interesting, given that phylacteries were worn continuously in some Second Temple contexts, e.g., at Qumran. Like the Shema, this practice underwent a temporal shift from continuous to periodic.

97. *b. Berakhot* 47b; In amoraic sources, the term *am ha-aretz* refers to non-rabbinic male Jews, though the term is used as a broader category of Jewish "other" in earlier tannaitic sources, usually defined as those who do not comply with a certain standard of ritual observance, on which see Pomeranz (2016a; 2016b). The story of Rabbi Akiva's martyrdom during which he recites the Shema (*b. Berakhot* 61b) exemplifies the way that the Shema is

used to affirm identity and piety; the story builds upon the tannaitic sources at the core of the story, *m. Berakhot* 9:5 and *t. Berakhot* 6:11: אפילו הוא נוטל את נפשך. See Urbach (1987:19); Segal (1977:152).

98. A distinction between the categories of "women" and "*amei ha-aretz*" must be made, however: whereas *amei ha-aretz* are construed as actively neglecting their obligation, women are not obligated in the first place and thus are not transgressing the law—they are simply exempt from it. Neither group, however, participates.

99. On the association of gender, and specifically femininity, with the category of *'am ha-aretz*, see Jaffee (2006).

100. *m. Berakhot* 3:1–2.

101. *m. Niddah* 1:1.

102. In *m. Shabbat* 2:6–7, women are obligated in two additional rituals (lighting Sabbath candles and removing part of the dough when preparing Sabbath bread). The text declares that women die in childbirth as a result of neglecting to fulfill these three rituals.

103. For a summary of these categories, see Himmelfarb (2001); for analyses of the biblical, Second Temple, and rabbinic sources, see Büchler (1928); Douglas (1966, 2002); Alon (1977); Milgrom (1991:641–1008, esp. 902–1008); Neusner (1977); Klawans (2000); Hayes (2002); Himmelfarb (2004); Philip (2006); Ruane (2007); S. Fishbane (2007:42–66); Noam (2010); C. Halberstam (2010:17–41); Balberg (2014); Furstenberg (2016a). On purity and impurity in ancient Near Eastern cultures, see Wilson (1994); on the related concept of "miasma" (pollution) in Greek religious culture, see R. Parker (1996); Lennon (2014); on laws of ritual impurity in Islamic texts, see M. H. Katz (2002). For cross-cultural studies of menstruation and menstrual purity, see Delaney, Lupton, and Toth (1976); Buckley and Gottlieb (1988); Allen (1992:46–47); De Troyer et al. (2003); Stein and Kim (2006); Tsoffar (2006); Freidenfelds (2009); Bobel (2010).

104. On tractate *Niddah*, see Meacham (1989; 1999a).

105. Balberg (2014:148–79); Vetö (2015); Furstenberg (2016b); Hoffmann Libson (2018:64–97). The abundance of ritual baths from areas beyond Jerusalem and centuries after the temple's destruction also provide clues about the importance of purity within Jewish communities, on which see Y. Adler (2011; 2017); S. Miller (2015), though Jews did not necessarily follow specifically rabbinic purity laws.

106. Destro (1996:125).

107. In addition to the time frames outlined in biblical texts, temporal language is used to describe states of impurity. Leviticus 14:54–57 states: "Such is the law for every eruptive affection—for scalls, for an eruption on a cloth or a house, for swellings, for rashes, for discolorations—to determine when they are impure and when they are pure [lit. the day of impurity and the day of purity, ביום הטמא וביום הטהר]. Such is the law concerning eruptions." The times of a woman's impurity after childbirth are referred to as "her days of impurity" (כימי נדת דותה) and "her days of purity" (ימי טהרה). These laws describe the framework in which one enters and exits periods of purity and impurity based on the state of one's body or contact with one's surroundings. Most explicit is the way in which a menstruating woman's state of impurity is described in Leviticus 15:19: "she will be in her impurity seven days" (שבעת ימים תהיה בנדתה).

108. E.g., Leviticus 13:4–6, 21, 26, 31–34.

109. Numbers 19.

110. Foster (1996:539–40) comments on the notion of "abnormal" in such contexts: "The strangeness of ovulating twice a cycle, or the dangers of 'intermenstrual bleeding' is better understood in terms of 'temporal anomalies' (Zerubavel, 1981:21–30). Here, certain events become problematic not because there is anything inevitably perilous or even pecu-

liar about them but because they transpire at times other than those prescribed by convention. Such 'anomalies' are cognitively disturbing precisely because they are reminders that the temporal rhythms that groups depend on so readily to ensure the smooth functioning of day-to-day living, such as the weekly cycle or the rotation of work shifts, are not inevitable patterns but ones that collectives have themselves produced ... the sense of strangeness is a result of an event located outside of the conventional temporal framework, not from anything particularly abnormal about the activity itself. Similarly, what is so often disturbing about 'menstrual anomalies' like 'spotting' is that such events unmask collective attempts to standardize what are otherwise highly variable rhythmic patterns. Much of this so-called problematic cycling is in many cases not a threat to a woman's health, but rather a threat to collective notions of temporal regularity, an alarm that some event has occurred outside of the bounds determined via sociotemporal maps."

111. Leviticus 12:1–5.

112. In Leviticus 15, one key difference is that women do not immerse in water, on which see Ruane (2007:23–39).

113. Vetö (2015:viii, 21–38).

114. Meacham (1999a:26) explains similarly: "The difference between the *niddah* and the *zava* is the time factor. Normal menstruation is considered to end within seven days, which may reflect either the choice of a significant number (as found in other rituals) or the fact that nearly all women complete their periods within seven days. Abnormal uterine bleeding is that which comes at a time other than the menstrual period or exceeds the seven days allotted to menstruation by several days."

115. Leviticus 15:25.

116. Meacham (1999a:26). In contrast, Milgrom (1991:953) cites statistics of onset and cessation of menses as well as duration of nursing in antiquity to argue that women in antiquity rarely menstruated because they were often pregnant or nursing during their menstruating years; Meacham (1999a) argues that so many laws of menstrual purity would not have been required had women rarely menstruated.

117. *m. Zavim* 1:1–2. The debate hinges on comparisons with other male and female forms of impurity, discussed in Vetö (2015:47–51). The debate also appears in *m. Eduyot* 1:1; *m. Eduyot* 1:4–6 reflects on the debate.

118. Vetö (2015:59–62) notes that the time-unit used in the Mishnah for distinguishing between occurrences of flux is the time it takes for a man to immerse himself in a ritual bath and dry himself off, which is a most fitting time-unit for this set of purity laws.

119. E.g., *m. Zavim* 2:3, which uses units of days and hours for durations of impurity.

120. According to Meacham (1999a:30), eleven days was the minimum time that the rabbis assumed could pass between two menstrual flows. For a woman to become a *zavah*, she would need to bleed for three consecutive days within these eleven non-menstruating days.

121. Consider, e.g., the language of *m. Niddah* 4:7; trans. Danby (1933:749): "Throughout the eleven days she can be presumed clean; and if she sat herself down and had not examined herself, or did aught in error, or through constraint, or wantonly, and had not examined herself, she may be deemed unclean. But if the time of her fixed period had come [הגיע שעת וסתה] and she had not examined herself, she is deemed unclean. ... But during the [seven clean] days [that must be taken count of] by the man or the woman that has a flux, or [the one day of cleanness to be taken count of] by her that awaits day against day, [during such time] they must be presumed to be unclean."

122. Additional permutations about the timing of menstrual impurity—the onset of impurity, the timing of a woman's bodily examinations, the timing of her rituals of purification, the categories of women who do and do not follow these guidelines, and so on—occupy

the remainder of the tractate, emphasizing that proper timing is essential to the fulfillment of this complex commandment.

123. Leviticus 15:19 NRSV: ואשה כי תהיה זבה דם יהיה זבה בבשרה שבעת ימים תהיה בנדתה וכל הנגע בה יטמא עד הערב.

124. On other distinctions between biblical and rabbinic adjudications of purity, see C. Halberstam (2010:17–41).

125. *Sifra Metzora Zavim* 4:1; *m. Niddah* 5:1; Meacham (1999b:257).

126. For discussion about retroactivity in tractate *Niddah*, see Fonrobert (2000:68-102). On the role of retroactivity and "conjunctive" time in other rabbinic contexts, see Kaye (2012:231–97). *b. Niddah* 9a states explicitly that retroactive impurity is a rabbinic enactment.

127. *t. Niddah* 1:1.

128. *m. Niddah* 1:1, a *veset*.

129. *m. Niddah* 9:9, MS Kaufmann.

130. *m. Niddah* 9:8-10 elaborates upon these rules; *b. Niddah* 11a.

131. *m. Niddah* 1:3–5, with additional clarifications in 1:6.

132. *t. Niddah* 1:1, MS Kaufmann. *y. Niddah* 1.1, 7d explains that impurity need not be imposed retroactively because doing so would go against the principle that one cannot legislate based on two matters of doubt—in this case the sex of the subject and the potential for retroactive impurity. Therefore, impurity is assumed only from the sight of blood and not beforehand, which is usually done in case of prior impurity.

133. *m. Zavim* 2:1.

134. *m. Niddah* 4:7; *m. Zavim* 1:1, discussed in Fonrobert (2018).

135. *m. Niddah* 1:7. On this practice, see Hauptman (1998:150–53); Meacham (1999b:256–57).

136. *m. Niddah* 1:7–2:4. Women were also required to examine themselves in preparation for sexual intercourse, and those from priestly castes were expected to examine themselves before eating the heave offering in order to avoid eating the offering in a state of impurity, which was prohibited. A leniency for such examinations is added in *m. Niddah* 4:7. On precoital examinations, see Rosenberg (2011:142–227).

137. *m. Niddah* 2:2. Etymologically, the term stems from the root עוד, which means both "time/anniversary" and "witness/testimony." The literal translation of the term is either "the cloth of her time" (that is, the time of her menstruation/impurity) or "the cloth that serves as witness" (to her menstruation/impurity). The Mishnah uses the term to refer to a "cloth for checking," a test rag. The term might also relate to Isaiah 64:5.

138. See Rosenberg (2011:144–45), also on the range of terms used for such examinations; I use Rosenberg's translation here for clarity, with modifications. Precoital examinations are discussed a few lines later.

139. On the Mishnah's allusion to women's ritual innovation in matters of menstrual purity, including daily examinations, see Ahuvia and Gribetz (2018).

140. See, e.g., *y. Niddah* 1:7, 49c; 2:1, 49d; 2:4, 50a; *b. Niddah* 9a–16a.

141. *y. Niddah* 2:3, 5a; *b. Niddah* 11b–12b, 16b; Hauptman (1998:151–52); Hayes (2015:240–43).

142. Secunda (2020); see also Rosenberg (2011:142–227).

143. The debates are recorded in *b. Niddah* 9a; *b. Niddah* 16a.

144. *m. Niddah* 2.1. *m. Niddah* 10:3 mentions examination by both men and women.

145. E.g., *b. Niddah* 13a.

146. *b. Niddah* 13a determines that while men are not obligated to examine themselves, they are permitted to do so if they use proper equipment. Permission for men to perform

NOTES TO CHAPTER 3 [303]

this practice without the obligation to do so mirrors the same permission that women receive to recite the Shema without being obligated.

147. *t. Niddah* 2:6 and *m. Niddah* 10:3; *y. Niddah* 2.1, 49d extends praise to men who examine themselves for abnormal flows.

148. Elsewhere, e.g., *m. Zavim* 5:7; *m. Makkot* 6:6; *t. Zavim* 2:1; *t. Niddah* 9:14; *Sifra Zavim* 1:1; *b. Niddah* 34a, 69b; *b. Shabbat* 17b; *b. Avodah Zarah* 36b, rabbinic sources also proclaim, contrary to biblical law, that gentiles defile like *zavim*, thus associating gentile impurity with the category of *zavim*, on which see Hayes (2002:122–31).

149. Balberg (2011:230–34). Furstenberg (2014) explains that male *zav* impurity in rabbinic sources was modeled according to female *zavah* impurity.

150. Balberg (2011:230–31).

151. Balberg (2011:232–33) discusses *t. Zavim* 2.4's characterizations of abnormal discharges coming from "dead flesh" and seminal emissions coming from "living flesh" in light of a passage from the first-century Greek physician Aretaeus of Cappadocia's *De causis et signis diuturnorum morborum* II.5 about the "living seed" of men defining their masculinity. Balberg writes: "the Mishnah does not suggest that men with genital discharge are *actually* transformed into women, but merely asserts that their natural analogue in terms of impurity is women" (233–34). See also *b. Niddah* 13a. On similar trends in Greek and Roman medical sources, see Flemming (2000); Dean-Jones (1996). The association between menstruation and other bodily flows with men is taken further in medieval Christian sources, in which attributing menstrual flows to (Jewish) men was a polemical strategy to emasculate them, on which see S. Koren (2009:45–47).

152. *m. Niddah* 1:7, MS Kaufmann.

153. *m. Berakhot* 1:1-2, MS Kaufmann.

154. Jastrow (1943, 2005:1551–52). On the related term עמוד השחר, including biblical and Akkadian references to שחר, see Yoskovich (2014:39–59). עמוד השחר is often understood as referring to dawn, the earliest period of morning when light appears but the sun has not yet risen over the horizon, but there are alternative understandings as well. Yoskovich (2014:44) concludes that שחר and שחרית both refer to morning (in opposition to night) in tannaitic sources, while the term עמוד השחר refers specifically to the earliest part of the morning; it also signals the moment at which the night ends and the day begins, which is why Rabban Gamliel allows for the recitation of the evening Shema until then, discussed explicitly in *t. Berakhot* 1:1.

155. שחרים is the plural form of שחר, while שחרית is a noun derived from שחר. These different endings reflect dialectical preferences. שחרית is used in the printed edition of the Mishnah, whereas שחרים is used in MS Kaufmann and MS Parma 3173. שחרים is also used in MS Vienna of *t. Berakhot* 1:2, but שחרין is used in MS Erfort and שחרית in the first printed edition. שחרין is used in *b. Berakhot* 9b in MS Oxford and MS Paris, in the quotation of the Mishnah; other manuscripts omit the full quotation of the Mishnah. The terms ערבים/ערבין/ערבית are similarly used interchangeably in the manuscripts.

156. See also *y. Berakhot* 1:2, 2b; *b. Shabbat* 34b–35b. On twilight in rabbinic sources, see Friedman (2005:496–500), who also suggests that the original meaning of the term indicated the entire period of night, between the setting of the sun and its rising the next morning, and later came to mean the very beginning of the period of night; this is an example of a temporal term first indicating a duration and later indicating a point in time or border of that duration (other examples include חודש, which can mean both "month" and the first day of the month, and שבת, which means both "week" and the day of the week named "Sabbath").

157. Though the "time when the priests return home" has been variably interpreted.

158. Moreover, the times for both rituals do not denote the all-encompassing units of "day" and "night" but rather "morning" and either "twilight" or "evening," that is, the beginning periods of day and night. When the texts use שחרית or its variants they mean "morning" (the first portion of the day) as opposed to "all day" *and* "nighttime," and when they use ערבית or its variants they likewise mean "evening" (the first portion of the night) as opposed to "all night" *and* "daytime."

159. *y. Niddah* 1.7, 49c.

160. *y. Berakhot* 4:1, 7a and *Genesis Rabbah* 68:9 use the same phrase to describe the timing of daily prayers but mention the *three* times of day when the day changes. A parallel between daily prayer and daily bodily inspection is also established through the similarities in the way their timing is described.

161. *b. Niddah* 4b; the manuscripts consistently use שחרית וערבית; there is further discussion of when and which types of women ought to perform these daily examinations in *b. Niddah* 11b. Secunda (2020:chap. 7) argues that daily examinations are abolished in the Babylonian Talmud.

162. *t. Yadaim* 2:20.

163. *y. Berakhot* 3:4, 6c. Kiperwasser (2012) notes that the following pericope in the Palestinian Talmud assumes that both men and women immerse daily; in the passage analyzed here, however, those immersing seem to be men, given that they are told to quit the practice in favor of studying. Other halakhic authorities in these sources (e.g., Rabbi Joshua ben Levi), however, defend the practice, suggesting that it was a disputed topic.

164. But not necessarily limited to women, because men who checked their bodies are, in rabbinic sources, described as feminine.

165. This suggestion accords with Klawans's conclusions (2000:93) that tannaitic sources generally regard bodily impurity as ritual impurity, whereas later rabbinic sources occasionally add a moral dimension to some forms of bodily impurity.

166. The trajectory can also be the opposite or, most likely, multidirectional.

167. *Genesis Rabbah* 17:8 (ed. Theodor and Albeck, 160). These sources are analyzed in Baskin (2002:65–87; 2006); Fonrobert (2000:30–33).

168. *m. Shabbat* 2:6–7.

169. *Avot de-Rabbi Natan* B9. See also *Avot de-Rabbi Natan* B42, which refers to *m. Shabbat* 2:6–7.

170. *b. Eruvin* 100b. Marienberg (2003) details additional traditions that cast menstruation, and especially transgressing menstrual purity laws, in a negative light.

171. *y. Niddah* 2.1, 49d. See also the parallel in *b. Niddah* 6a.

172. *b. Niddah* 6b; see also a similar story about Rabban Gamliel's servant who checked herself after kneading each loaf of bread for the *terumah* in the same pericope.

173. E.g., in the Temple Scroll, a man with a normal flow remains impure for three days, rather than one, on which see Himmelfarb (1999). This extension of male impurity is justified by likening this form of impurity to that of a woman's normal menstrual flows, calling it "their *niddah*-like uncleanness [נדת טמאתמה]" (11Q19 45:7–10); Himmelfarb (1999:18); trans. Yadin (1983:192). Perhaps because of its new association with female impurity, the period of impurity is lengthened to align more closely to the time a woman waits. A similar extension is imposed on men with seminal emissions as a result of sexual intercourse (45:11–12), demonstrating that in the Qumran community male impurity was characterized more similarly to female impurity than in the biblical texts on which these laws are based. Men with normal flows were commanded to wait a longer period of time (several days, instead of until evening of the first day), similar to the duration of a woman's menstruation. The prolonged time of impurity might also evoke Exodus 19:10–11 and 19:15, passages that implore the Israelites to stay pure and be ready for the "third day" (Himmelfarb [1999:19]).

The laws of purity and purification became more stringent in the texts of the Dead Sea Scrolls in other regards as well, e.g., the command to leave the camp or the city of the sanctuary. On purity at Qumran in relation to rabbinic sources, see Furstenberg (2010:chaps. 3–4; 2016b).

174. Leviticus 15:19, 25, 28.

175. *b. Berakhot* 31a; *b. Niddah* 66a, 67b; *b. Megillah* 28b. On whether *y. Berakhot* 5:1, 8d also refers to this practice, see Secunda (2020); Meacham (1999c:255).

176. See *b. Niddah* 57b, 69a.

177. *b. Niddah* 67b (Vatican 111: כולהי זבות; T-S F2 (1) 173: כולהו ספק זבות; Soncino: כולהו ספק זכות; Vilna: כולהו ספק זבות); translation and discussion in Hauptman (1998:159). On the transformation of *niddah* into *ziva*, see also Meacham (1999a:29–33; 1999c).

178. So too in aggadic sources, e.g., *b. Shabbat* 13a–b. The time of impurity is extended even further in *Baraita de-Niddah*, according to which a woman remains impure for 14 days from the onset of menstruation (rather than the talmudic 10–12, and twice as long as the period of impurity mandated in Leviticus) and must consider herself impure two days prior (rather than one). This text's attitude to menstrual purity laws is more extreme than those found even in the Babylonian Talmud and regards menstruating women as both impure and dangerous. Whether and to what extent these laws were observed are matters of debate, on which see Milgrom (1991:948). On *Baraita de-Niddah*, see Marienberg (2003:chap. 6; 2012a); S. J. D. Cohen (1992:108–9).

179. *b. Niddah* 66a.

180. Elman (2007a); on the Zoroastrian context for the increasingly stringent rabbinic attitude toward menstrual purity, see Elman (2007b); Secunda (2009; 2020). Though Hauptman (1998:156–60, 174n42) leaves open the possibility that the tendency toward stringency in later amoraic sources is related to Zoroastrian practice, she argues that women's requirement to add seven "clean" days is attributed to rabbinic (and thus male) conflation of the categories of *niddah* and *zavah* rather than popular female practice. Emanuel (2007) traces the restrictions of these seven clean days into the medieval period.

181. V 16:8–10; Secunda (2007:210) concludes that "since ancient times, Zoroastrian law does not permit women to purify themselves immediately upon the cessation of menstruation, but requires an extra day spent in the *daštānistān*."

182. Secunda (2020) points to similar terminology in the Rabbinic Hebrew and Middle Persian phrases "to sit in cleanness/clean days."

183. *b. Berakhot* 31a, consistent in the manuscripts. The phrase "the daughters of Israel" appears several times, e.g., *m. Niddah* 2:1; *t. Niddah* 5:4, 6:12; *b. Niddah* 5a, 10d, often in contexts in which women served as ritual innovators, on which see Ahuvia and Gribetz (2018).

184. See also *b. Niddah* 12b, in which Rabbi Kahana asks a group of women if the rabbis require them to perform examinations after returning from the schoolhouse, and they answer that the rabbis do not. The anonymous layer of the text then asks why Rav Kahana asked the women, rather than asking the rabbis directly, about the appropriate rules, and the text answers "because it is possible that they [the women] imposed additional restrictions upon themselves." The sources do not provide sufficient evidence to determine whether these stringencies originated with women or rabbis, nor whether they had empowering or disempowering effects on the women who sought to follow such laws (they likely had many different effects depending on individual women, their social status, personality, and communities), on which see Ahuvia and Gribetz (2018:12–15); Secunda (2020). More broadly on the (im)possibility of women's ritual innovation and empowerment within patriarchal systems and texts, see R. Adler (1976; 2007); Fonrobert (1999); Avishai (2008a; 2008b); Mahmoud (2005); Griffith (2000); M. H. Katz (2015).

185. I do not suppose that the historical Hillel or Shammai had this debate, nor that the redactors of the Mishnah had these opinions in mind when they compiled the Mishnah, but rather that those behind this passage in the Babylonian Talmud chose to highlight the impact of different attitudes to menstrual time in this way.

186. *b. Niddah* 3b.

187. Balberg (2014:148–79) uses the term "self-examination" in a more all-encompassing sense than I do here. I use the phrase more narrowly to denote women's physical examination of their bodily interiors, a practice men were not obligated typically/regularly to perform.

188. Hauptman (1998:149–50); similarly in R. Adler (2007). Noam (2008) deciphers two competing trends in rabbinic sources about purity: on the one hand, exegetical sources limit biblical purity to the sacred realm and make it irrelevant for contemporary life, while on the other hand rabbinic texts acknowledge and embrace practical adherence to strict purity laws even though they never present such practices as being based on biblical sources. It seems as though women's impurity is the only or one of the only forms of purity in which exegesis of biblical sources is used in rabbinic texts to justify more expansive contemporary practices of purity.

189. Hauptman (1998:149–50). Stewart (2008) argues that Leviticus 11–15 ought to be read as a women's text, dealing with domestic issues, such as cooking, childbirth, scale disease on the body and house, menstruation, and hypermenorrhea; the topics of concern to men, such as seminal emissions, discharges, and baldness, were placed in the same section "by attraction." He writes: "This is not to say that the Purity Code is fully an example of écriture feminine, but rather that here there are matters from women's experience—pregnancy, mothering, health, menses, domestic work, and marriage" (65). While the chapters in Leviticus pay much attention to impurity affecting men as well, Stewart's observation highlights the increased stringency on women's impurity, also noted by Vetö (2015:150–51); Stewart's thesis might fit even more comfortably with rabbinic sources.

190. Balberg (2014:172); though this perspective seems to shift in post-mishnaic sources, as explored earlier. M. H. Katz (2015) notes similar trends in Islamic laws of menstrual purity.

191. Secunda (2020).

192. E.g., *m. Zavim* 1:1, 2:2, 2:3, *Sifre Deuteronomy* 256, *b. Niddah* 86a. See also Vetö (2015:124–28).

193. Furstenberg (2014). See also J. Baumgarten (1994).

194. *m. Zavim* 2:2, MS Kaufmann, discussed in J. Baumgarten (1994:274), who adds: "Those Tannaim who did not go as far as R. Akiba in practically abolishing *zab* impurity nonetheless mitigated its effect on religious performance."

195. Hauptman (1998:149–50); Fonrobert (2000:20–22).

196. On which see Rosenberg (2014).

197. Douglas (1966, 2002:5). We might also point to various forms of rejection or embrace of bodily purity practices in early Christian and Jewish-Christian sources, e.g., Didascalia Apostolorum and the *Clementine Homilies* as a counterpoint to rabbinic texts, on which see Fonrobert (2000:160–209); S. J. D. Cohen (1991); Marienberg (2012b:273–75); Larin (2008); Zellentin (2013:90–95). In some early Christian and Jewish-Christian sources, menstrual purity practices persisted far longer (some to this day) than did practices of male impurity, which were abandoned earlier.

198. This emphasis continues into the medieval period, but is also complicated, on which see E. Baumgarten (2014:21–50); Fishman (1992); Krakowski (2020).

199. Alexander (2013:1).

200. A similar gendering of spatiality has been studied by Fonrobert (2000); Baker (2002).

201. *m. Berakhot* 3:4–6; the Mishnah also discusses a man's obligations to recite the blessings before and after a meal as well as the Tefillah. See also *m. Terumot* 1:6.

202. *t. Berakhot* 2:11, 13.

203. Tooth whitening, orthodontal work, and so on also function as symbols of class and status.

204. On additional dimensions of gender as they are mapped onto interiority and exteriority, see Fonrobert (2000:40–67); Baker (2002).

205. Rosen-Zvi (2010) similarly notes the ways in which rabbinic sources conceptualize certain commandments (e.g., *tefillin, mezuzah*, circumcision) as men's adornments to serve God, while women, enslaved people, and children are associated with adornments that direct their attention to serving men rather than God.

206. Balberg's work is part of a broader effort to understand rabbinic notions of the self and subjectivity, including Hoffmann Libson (2018); Rosen-Zvi (2015); Levinson (2012).

207. Balberg (2014:180).

208. On the role of embodied liturgical practices in cultivating conceptions of self and subjectivity in Second Temple sources, see, e.g., Newman (2018).

209. Other aspects of purity and immersion rituals likewise constructed gendered difference, as demonstrated in Ruane (2007; 2013). On the role of ritual in constructing social inequality in biblical texts, see Olyan (2011).

210. *y. Berakhot* 3:3, 6b.

211. *m. Berakhot* 1:2. Kalman (2019:60–61) identifies the third hour as the time when the day is in "full swing" and discusses a midrash in *Mekhilta de-Rabbi Ishmael* Bo 17 and *Mekhilta de-Rabbi Shimon bar Yohai* on Exodus 14:22 in which a king asks two of his sons to wake him up at two different hours of the morning.

212. *b. Berakhot* 2b.

213. *m. Niddah* 1:7; *b. Niddah* 11a; the same is true for priests, who needed to be more vigilant about purity than other men.

214. On which see Fonrobert (2001b; 2008); Hayes (2002:127–31); Ilan (2006:103–5); Boyarin (2004:60–63). On the use of purity legislation to construct communal and religious difference in later contexts, see Zellentin (2013:90–95); Mazuz (2012).

215. E.g., *t. Zavim* 2:1, the topic of Hayes (2002:esp. 122–31).

216. See Fonrobert (2000:160–209), who also cites Christian sources that mandate separation of women during menstruation.

217. *Didascalia Apostolorum*, 242, lines 11–15; trans. Connolly (1929). Among the Didascalia's target audiences are those who, despite having joined the community, continued observing the Jewish laws of purity and impurity. Whether they observed rabbinic laws of menstrual purity or adhered to the biblical laws is unclear. It seems that certain members of the community abstained from prayers and other activities during periods of impurity, a practice with which the author of the Didascalia disagrees. There is no indication that Jewish women refrained from attending the synagogue during this period, though in earlier periods those with all forms of impurity were prohibited from entering sacred spaces for fear of defilement and in later centuries the separation of men and women in synagogue seating might have developed as a result of more stringent attitudes toward ritual purity; Levine (2005:517); Z. Safrai (1989:78–79); S. J. D. Cohen (1991; 1992).

218. *Didascalia Apostolorum*, 242, lines 15–19; trans. Connolly (1929). The text continues in 244, lines 3–8, 29–30: "For if you think, woman, that in the seven days of your flux you are void of the Holy Spirit, if you die in those days, you will depart empty and without

hope. But if the Holy Spirit is always in you, without (just) impediment do you keep yourself from prayer and from the Scriptures and from the Eucharist.... For the Holy Spirit continues ever with those who possess Him; but from whom He departs, to him an unclean spirit joins himself."

219. *m. Peah* 4:5.
220. *m. Pesahim* 4:1.
221. *m. Pesahim* 4:5.
222. *m. Pesahim* 4:6.
223. *b. Baba Metsia* 83a, which also discusses the time of the commute to and from work. This pericope is the subject of Levinas (1990:94–119).
224. *b. Baba Metsia* 83b.
225. Trans. Soncino.
226. *b. Pesahim* 12b.
227. *b. Shabbat* 10a.
228. *m. Berakhot* 2:5. Here, the term שעה is used in both its senses, as a precise unit of time as well as an unspecified but sufficient period of time to denote duration; on similar ambiguities in the Greek term ὥρα, see Sattler (2019).
229. Schües (2011:8).
230. Saiman (2018:105).
231. *m. Niddah* 1:7–2:1.
232. Rhein (2016).
233. E.g., *m. Tamid* 5.
234. Zerubavel (1985:2).
235. On notions of the "everyday," see de Certeau (1984); Highmore (2001); on conceptions of quotidian time in ancient Roman literature, see Ker (forthcoming).
236. From Elden's introduction to Lefebvre (2004:viii). See also Lefebvre (1947, 1961). Daily rituals of care and their embodied dimensions are also explored in Benjamin (2018).

Chapter 4

1. On hours and hourly time-keeping in rabbinic sources, see S. Stern (2003:48–53); Kaye (2018:57–61).
2. Sissa and Detienne (2000:119–20).
3. Radice (2009:131–35). Philo puzzled over the discrepancy between Genesis's opening verse, which describes God's creation as a singular and simultaneous act, and the remainder of the creation narrative, in which distinct aspects of the physical world are said to have been created incrementally over the course of six days. Philo also notes that the first day of creation is called "day one," in contrast to the other days, which are described with ordinal numbers. Philo explains that prior to the world's creation there was no time and that God must have created the whole world in a single instant. This all-encompassing instantaneous creation, however, was not the creation of the material world but rather of the immaterial cosmos. Genesis's subsequent verses about a step-by-step creation of the world over the course of six days represent, for Philo, a logical (atemporal) order of creation rather than a chronological (temporal) order. Once the immaterial cosmos had been conceived by God, the material world could then be created incrementally.
4. On God's time in 4 Ezra, see Henze (2018:27–32); in other eschatological contexts, see Hultgård and Norin (2009).
5. Augustine, *Confessions* 11; Sorabji (1984:29–32); Flasch (1993); Knuuttila (2001). Alternate conceptualizations of God that challenge divine unchangeability have also been proposed; see, e.g., Coleman (2008).

6. Sorabji (1984:32).

7. This discrepancy presents a challenge for accessing the divine across this temporal/atemporal divide, on which see Augustine, *Confessions* 11.7.9. Ancient Jews and Christians conceived of God's temporality in diverse ways. I cite Augustine not as a representative of "the Christian" perspective on God's time but rather as a later thinker whose notion of God's time corresponds well to Philo's.

8. Rabbinic texts are not unique in synchronizing heavenly and earthly time. In *Jubilees* 2:8, God observes the Sabbath in the heavens with the angels, while human Sabbath observance imitates God's time. John 5:17 insists that God works even on the Sabbath: when Jesus heals a man on the Sabbath, Jesus answers his critics by explaining that, on the Sabbath, "My Father is still working, and I also am working." *Mekhilta de-Rabbi Ishmael Bahodesh* 7 on Exodus 20:10 (ed. Horovitz and Rabin, 230; ed. Lauterbach, 2:330–31) interprets God's Sabbath rest in figurative terms, insisting that God does not need six days to create the world nor a seventh to rest. Several texts from the Second Temple period, including texts among the Dead Sea Scrolls, present the calendar as a means of not only coordinating personal with communal time but also synchronizing earthly and heavenly time, on which see VanderKam (1998:71–74); Fraade (2009–10). Early rabbinic approaches to the calendar, e.g., *m. Rosh HaShanah* 2:8–9, place emphasis on calendrical uniformity rather than synchronization with heaven, even at the expense of celebrating festivals on (astronomically—that is, divinely) incorrect days.

9. That these texts all appear in amoraic and post-amoraic sources corresponds well with the conclusions of D. Weiss (2016:16).

10. On the circulation of other rabbinic mythological traditions in late antiquity, including in synagogue settings, see M. Fishbane (2003:esp. 1998); Münz-Manor (2013).

11. Scholarship demonstrating that rabbinic sources were interested in theology includes M. Fishbane (2003); Schofer (2010); Fisher (2010); Alexander (2015); D. Weiss (2016).

12. They also evoked other motifs, such as the twelve tribes, that featured in the piyyutim that would have been recited alongside them, on which see Mirsky (1990:93–101); Yahalom (1986).

13. On synagogue zodiac mosaics and their depiction of Helios, see, e.g., Talgam (2014:268–81, 285–87); M. Goodman (2007:205–17), on the mosaic depicting the God of the Jews; Magness (2005), who suggests that the central figure might be associated with the angel Metatron. The dates of these zodiac mosaics correspond to the dates of rabbinic sources about God's hourly schedule. These synagogue mosaics are found on the floor, in contrast to mosaics of gods in churches and temples (e.g., *Justinian Code* 1.8, which forbade images of the divine on the floor). On correspondences between ideas and images in ancient spaces of worship, see Maguire (1987).

14. On sundials in the Roman world, see Gibbs (1976); S. Adam (1997; 2002a; 2002b); Bonnin (2010; 2012a; 2012b); Hannah (2016); Schaldach (2016).

15. For a related thesis, see M. Goodman (2007:205–17).

16. On vision, light, sacred spaces, and knowledge of the divine in antiquity, see Nasrallah (2018; 2019b); Watts (2019); Pentcheva (2011); Cain (2016). An interesting integration of human vision and hourly time-keeping within a third- or fourth-century Roman mosaic is explored in Schaldach (2009).

17. Talbert (2017; 2019).

18. Kaye (2018:56–85; forthcoming a).

19. E.g., Exodus 11:4.

20. *Mekhilta de-Rabbi Ishmael Pisha* 12 on Exodus 12:29 (ed. Horovitz, 42; ed. Lauterbach, 67). *Mekhilta de-Rabbi Shimon Bar Yohai* 15:1 on Exodus 12:29 (ed. Epstein and

Melamed, 27–28) provides a similar tradition about the discrepancy between the approximate temporal language used in Exodus 11:4 and 12:29; this exegetical tradition appears as well in *b. Avodah Zarah* 4a. See also *Mekhilta de-Rabbi Shimon Bar Yohai* on Exodus 12:42, in which redemption occurs precisely at the correct preordained moment, a time so precise that only God can act thusly.

21. *Genesis Rabbah* 10:9 (ed. Theodor and Albeck, 85).

22. Genesis 2:2. The Septuagint alters the text so that God stops creation on the sixth day and rests on the seventh.

23. Rabbinic Sabbath laws added extra time to the start of the Sabbath so as to ensure that the Sabbath is not violated (a clear example can be found in *b. Yoma* 81b though it appears in earlier sources as well); the practice originated with the Day of Atonement and was then extended to the Sabbath. This is the legal principle to which *Genesis Rabbah* refers. See also *y. Berakhot* 1:2, 1a–b, about dividing precisely between days at twilight, in the context of the end of the Sabbath, which is similarly deemed an impossible task for human beings but simple for God. Perhaps it is for this reason that the time of twilight between the sixth and seventh days of the first week of creation is the time, in several rabbinic sources, when God forms special creations (e.g., *m. Avot* 5:6; *b. Pesahim* 54a; *Pirqe de-Rabbi Eliezer* 19; *Avot de-Rabbi Nathan* B42). It is not only a liminal time between days (literally "between the two suns") but also a unique time when only God can create, while Israel must already begin observing the Sabbath. On Sabbath start times, see Ta-Shma (2004).

24. See also *m. Berakhot* 1:1, on temporal leniency to account for human procrastination.

25. Kaye (2018:61–71) analyzes legal passages that highlight rabbinic skepticism about human abilities to reliably determine hours (e.g., *y. Pesahim* 1:4, 27c; *b. Pesahim* 11b–12b). Rabbinic texts assume that, in contrast to God, humans lack the ability to tell time precisely and therefore cannot be held accountable for certain hourly inaccuracies when providing testimony of an event as legal witnesses.

26. *Leviticus Rabbah* 29:1; *Pesiqta de-Rav Kahana* 23:1; *Avot de-Rabbi Natan* B42; *Pesiqta Rabbati* 46; *Deuteronomy Rabbah* 13 (ed. Lieberman); *Tanhuma* (ed. Buber) Bereshit 25, Shemini 13; the manuscripts vary in wording and in which events are associated with each hour, especially in the hours during which God forms Adam's body and soul. Only the variants that affect the analysis are noted. *Genesis Rabbah* 18:6 also incorporates the hours of the first day of creation.

27. Such midrashim appear, e.g., in *Genesis Rabbah* 8:4–5, which interprets the plural verbs in Genesis 1:26–27. On this tradition and other rabbinic views of angels, see Marmorstein (1927; 1937; 1968); Urbach (1987:135–83); Schäfer (1975:esp. 75–107; 2012:165–78); Ahuvia (2014).

28. On which see, e.g., Trible (1973).

29. NRSV.

30. *m. Rosh Hashanah* 1:1 lists several different rabbinic New Years.

31. *Pesiqta de-Rav Kahana* was likely the original context of this midrash. *Pesiqta de-Rav Kahana* and *Leviticus Rabbah* both connect Leviticus 23:24 with Psalm 119:89.

32. Connections between the creation of the world and Rosh Hashanah, and between the Sabbath and Rosh Hashanah, appear in piyyutim as well, on which see Elizur (2013:128–29, 140–43). Several piyyutim of Qalir draw on the midrashic tradition found in *Pesiqta de-Rav Kahana* 23:1 and its parallels, found in Elizur (2013:261–62, 294–95, 434).

33. *Pesiqta de-Rav Kahana* 23:1 (ed. Mendelbaum, 333–34); trans. Braude and Kapstein (1975:352–53).

34. On *Pesiqta de-Rav Kahana*, see Anisfeld (2009).

35. Qalir also connects the Sabbath and Rosh Hashanah because the former is the sev-

NOTES TO CHAPTER 4 [311]

enth day and the latter is at the beginning of the seventh month, on which see Elizur (2013:142–43).

36. Text and translation with slight modification from Lieber (2010a:314).

37. On this liturgical genre, see Elizur (2019).

38. *b. Sanhedrin* 38b; trans. Soncino, with modifications; the narrative in *Pirqe de-Rabbi Eliezer* 11 is a close parallel and appears in a chapter that contains other midrashim that accompany the narrative in the Babylonian Talmud as well. Parallels also appear in *Avot de-Rabbi Natan* A1.8.

39. On this text, including its relationship with Jewish traditions, see Minov (2013); on its date, see Minov (2017). The thematization of the twelve hours of Adam's creation also appears at the beginning of the *Testament of Adam*.

40. *Cave of Treasures* fol. 4b, col. 1; trans. Budge (2018:32).

41. *Cave of Treasures* fol. 7a, col. 2; trans. Budge (2018:39).

42. Matthew 27:45–46; Mark 15:25, 33–34; Luke 23:44–45; John 19:14 all mention specific hours associated with the passion, on which see Minov (2013:70).

43. *Cave of Treasures* fol. 9a, col. 1; trans. Budge (2018:42).

44. *Cave of Treasures* fol. 44a, col. 1; trans. Budge (2018:114).

45. *Cave of Treasures* fol. 44a, col. 2–fol. 44b, col. 2; trans. Budge (2018:115).

46. *Cave of Treasures* fol. 44b, col. 2; trans. Budge (2018:42). On the Adam-Christ typology in related texts (e.g., Philoxenus of Mabbug's *Commentary on Matthew* and a heortological tractate attributed to Basil of Caesarea), see Minov (2013:70–74).

47. Minov (2013:71) also notes a set of seventh-century liturgical texts (*Sedrā for the Three Hours of the Friday* and *Sedrā for the Nine Hours of the Good Friday*) that build upon this tradition.

48. מכאן ואילך is used in most manuscripts, though the phrase ומאותה שעה עד עכשיו appears in Cambridge, T-S C2.52 and the printed edition.

49. Or לשעה קלה in some manuscripts. The term appears elsewhere in rabbinic texts, e.g., *m. Berakhot* 5:1; *m. Sotah* 1:9; *m. Avot* 4:17; *b. Shabbat* 10a; on the range of meanings of the term שעה in rabbinic sources, see Kalman (2019:51–55).

50. *Leviticus Rabbah* 8:1. Parallels to this text are found in *Genesis Rabbah* 68:4, as a marginal note in MS Vatican 30, and *Pesiqta de-Rav Kahana* 2:4; see also *y. Qiddushin* 3:12. The dialogues between Matrona and Rabbi Yose are analyzed in Ilan (1994); Gershonzon and Slomovic (1985); Böhl (1975); Herr (1971).

51. NRSV.

52. קשטה ככלה והביאה לו (ed. Theodor and Albeck, 161); on God braiding Eve's hair: *Genesis Rabbah* 8:13; *b. Berakhot* 61a; *b. Shabbat* 95a; *b. Niddah* 45b; *b. Eruvin* 18a; *Midrash Psalms* 68:4 (ed. Buber); *Tanhuma Hayei Sarah* 2 (ed. Buber).

53. Sedley (2009); Kugel (1998) notes counterpolemics in Aristobulus and Philo as well. This story can also be read as an attempt to convince its audience that male figures should be in charge of marital affairs, while women should stay out of them: Matrona, a woman, is incapable of acting as an effective matchmaker, while God, usually gendered masculine, succeeds. In rabbinic sources, matchmaking is assumed to be a father's task (or a husband's choice), though mothers and potential wives seem to have taken part in the process as well, as suggested in Satlow (2001:101–32, esp. 111–16).

54. In Plato's *Timaeus*, the demiurge also maintains cosmic order.

55. On procreation as a form of creation, see Kessler (2013).

56. Such ideas are read back into 1 Corinthians 7, e.g., in the Acts of Thecla; Brown (2008).

57. E.g., Clement of Alexandria; *Excerpts from Theodotus*; *Gospel of Philip* 65, 67, 69–72, 74, 76, 82, 84–86; Pagels (1991); Strathearn (2004).

58. *Apologia Ad Constantium* 33; trans. Atkinson and Robertson (1892:252).

59. E.g., Clement of Alexandria, *Stromata* 3.49.

60. On asceticism in rabbinic literature, see Fraade (1986); Bar-Asher Siegel (2013:133–69).

61. See also *Pesiqta de-Rav Kahana* 23.

62. *Leviticus Rabbah* 8:1, with reference to Psalm 75:8. On ladders, including ladders between heaven and earth, in Hekhalot literature, see Gruenwald (1980, 2014:155).

63. Neofiti, Fragment Targum P, Fragment Targum V, and Pseudo-Jonathan on Deuteronomy 32:4; Targum Onqelos does not include this tradition. See also Klein (2011:49–50). The passage into which this midrash is inserted is part of a longer meditation on Deuteronomy 32:1–4, about God's relationship with humans and the earthly sphere.

64. M. J. Bernstein (2002:31, 38–39).

65. Translation based on the text in FTP; FTV is similar.

66. Targum Pseudo-Jonathan and Neofiti add an extra phrase (מברזג בין גבר לאיתא וגזר למרומם ומאיך in Pseudo-Jonathan and מזווג זוגין בין גבר לאתתה ומרים וממך in Neofiti). Two similar versions of this tradition seem to have circulated.

67. The verb מברזג is used again in Pseudo-Jonathan's translation of Deuteronomy 34:6, in reference to God's pairing of Adam and Eve, though this tradition is unique to Pseudo-Jonathan.

68. Yahalom and Sokoloff (1999:47:2–5, pp. 272–73); trans. Lieber (2018a:169–17).

69. Yahalom and Sokoloff (1999:47:2–5); my translation.

70. Yahalom and Sokoloff (1999:47:8–9); my translation.

71. On the liturgical and performative context of the recitation of such poems, see Lieber (2010b; 2014a; 2018b); Novick (2018).

72. On wedding crowns and other wedding rituals, see Lieber (2014b).

73. The idea of peace (*shalom*) between husband and wife is a rabbinic innovation (e.g., *Sifra Ahare Mot* 8.3, 92d; *Sifre Numbers* 42), perhaps indebted to Roman notions of concordia, on which see Wilfand (2019).

74. For additional examples of wedding poems, see Lieber (2014b).

75. On which see Rubenstein (1999:212–42).

76. *b. Avodah Zarah* 3b; translation based on MS New York JTS Rab. 15. This passage was inserted into the story about the end of time because of the theme of laughter, and is largely unrelated to it. See also *b. Pesahim* 12b, on the hours of the day when different people eat their meals, and *b. Megillah* 30b, on the schedule of the day during fasts, which mirrors God's schedule in some ways.

77. For other texts about God's study of Torah, see *Pesiqta de-Rav Kahana* 4, 12:21. On the division of human time according to the study of Torah, see *b. Qiddushin* 30a.

78. For additional narratives about God balancing between justice and mercy, see *Genesis Rabbah* 12:15 and *b. Berakhot* 7a.

79. Earlier rabbinic traditions juxtapose God's ability to feed all of the world's creations with a human king's difficulty feeding a single army, e.g., *Mekhilta de-Rabbi Ishmael Shirata* 4 (ed. Horovitz and Rabin, 130–31; ed. Lauterbach, 190); *Mekhilta de-Rabbi Shimon bar Yokhai* 15:3 (ed. Epstein and Melamed, 82), discussed in Berthelot (forthcoming).

80. Jastrow (1943, 2005:1150) translates the term as both to "laugh" and to "play"; the term is synonymous with צחק. Hayes (2020) connects God's laughter, in the homily that immediately precedes God's daily schedule, with laughter associated with Roman tyrants as well as those who subvert them, on which see also Beard (2015). At least one Aramaic incantation bowl associates Leviathan with a particular time of day, on which see MS 2053/159:1–9 from the Schøyen Collection, discussed in Shaked (2010:229–30).

81. This is the same Psalm around which the narrative about "the fourth hour" is built in *b. Baba Metsia* 83b, discussed in the previous chapter.

82. Psalm 104:19–30 NRSV. See also Psalm 74:14, about how Leviathan is feasted upon in the wilderness; Job 40–41, about God taming Leviathan.

83. E.g., Psalm 74:13–14; Isaiah 27:1; Job 3:8; 1 Enoch 60:7–25; 2 Baruch 29:4; 4 Ezra 6:47–52; *Leviticus Rabbah* 8.3, 13.3; *b. Baba Batra* 73a–75b; *Pirqe de-Rabbi Eliezer* 9. On the figure of Leviathan and its association with the eschaton, see Ballentine (2015:esp. 150–65); Kiperwasser and Shapira (2012); Whitney (2006); M. Fishbane (2003:esp. 95–252); Gutmann (1968); on *Pirqe de-Rabbi Eliezer* 9, see Adelman (2009a:243–47). The association of Leviathan with messianic redemption and eschatology in rabbinic texts contrasts with contemporaneous Christian interpretations of Leviathan as associated with evil and Satan, on which see Seow (2019). The description of God laughing with Leviathan also evokes the image of Christ laughing in heaven during the earthly crucifixion, on which see Stroumsa (2004).

84. For traditions about God's creations during twilight at the start of the seventh day, see *m. Avot* 5:6; *b. Pesahim* 54a; *Pirqe de-Rabbi Eliezer* 19; *Avot de-Rabbi Nathan* B42. The tradition of Leviathan's skin used to form a *sukkah* derives from Job 40:31 and might also relate to the narrative about God's schedule in *b. Avodah Zarah* 3b, about the celebration of the festival of Sukkot.

85. Ballentine (2015:150–51), a theme developed, e.g., in Psalm 74:13–14.

86. E.g., "Will it make many supplications to you? Will it speak soft words to you? Will it make a covenant with you to be taken as your servant forever? Will you play with it as with a bird, or will you put it on a leash for your girls? . . . Who can strip off its outer garment? Who can penetrate its double coat of mail? . . . On earth it has no equal, a creature without fear. It surveys everything that is lofty; it is king over all that are proud" (Job 40–41). Leviathan as God's companion also vaguely evokes Proverbs 8:22, in which wisdom is God's primordial companion.

87. On which see M. Fishbane (2003); Ballentine (2015).

88. On this phenomenon also in Palestinian midrashim, see Houtman (2016).

89. Translation based on MS Oxford Opp. 249 (369); in MS Vatican 115, the two Leviathans are differentiated as follows: לויתן נחש בריח ולויתן נחש עקלתון.

90. *b. Avodah Zarah* 3b.

91. E.g., MS New York JTS Rab. 15: תינוקות של בית רבן.

92. In Theodoret of Cyrus, *Life of Simeon the Stylite* 26, Simeon devotes the first nine hours of the day to prayer, and the final three hours to instructing others and settling disputes, after which he converses with God.

93. Martial, *Epigram* 4.8, constructs the daily schedule of an elite person, while Pliny the Younger, *Epistula* 9.36.1–5, describes Pliny's personal schedule. This rabbinic story depicts God as having a schedule that resembles an elite Roman man's schedule—except that it adds Torah study to the day's activities. Pliny even ends his day on a walk with his companions, similar to God's final hours with Leviathan as companion. On a typical day in Roman cities, see Laurence (1994:154–66), which focuses on the differing schedules of elites and non-elites.

94. God is also said to study Torah in other sources, e.g., *b. Mava Metzia* 86a, and to engage in related activities, e.g., *b. Menahot* 29a. On the value on Torah study in Babylonian rabbinic culture, see Boyarin (1993:134–66); Rubenstein (2003); Hirshman (2006:920); Rawidowicz (1974); Marmorstein (1937, 1968:133–57). The emphasis on devoting one's time to Torah study should not be taken for granted, however. In Hekhalot Rabbati (§§281–98), the mystery of the Sar ha-Torah's name allows the one who conjures it to memorize and

retain Torah study without devoting time to this task—that is, rather than promoting regular or constant study, this text imagines a miracle in which retention of Torah is instantaneous, on which see Vidas (2014:167–202); Swartz (1996:53–152). See also Merkavah Rabbah §675, which instructs the recitation of the mystery every morning and uses the language of Deuteronomy 6:7 in its instruction, suggesting that if one repeats the mystery each day and devotes one's entire being to this task, God will be with that person at all times of the day. The temporal dimension of this instruction is radically different from the temporality that rabbinic texts associate with the task of Torah study.

95. *b. Avodah Zarah* 3b. In *Avot de-Rabbi Natan* 21.1, the first hours of the morning are also associated with Torah study, on which see McAlpine (1987:110).

96. God's daytime schedule is slightly modified in *b. Avodah Zarah* 4b, which warns against reciting the additional prayer for the first day of the New Year during the first three hours of the day, because that is when God judges without mercy.

97. *Tanna Debei Eliyahu Rabbah* 13. The midrash then tries to identify the particular hour when God engages in שחוק: when the idolatrous nations of the world try to wage war on God.

98. An alternative idea is offered in Midrash Proverbs, cited in Scholem (1995:71): "If there comes before Him one who is learned in the Talmud, the Holy One, blessed be He, says to him: 'My son, since you have studied the Talmud, why have you not also studied the Merkabah and perceived my splendor? For none of the pleasures I have in My creation is equal to that which is given to me in the hour when the scholars sit and study the Torah and, looking beyond it, see and behold and meditate these questions.'"

99. At least by those (rabbinic men) obligated to study Torah.

100. NRSV. On God's anger in biblical sources, see Grant (2014).

101. *b. Sanhedrin* 105b cites Psalm 30:5 and Isaiah 26:20 to prove that God's anger is fleeting.

102. The text notes that only Balaam succeeded in determining the precise moment of God's anger.

103. Other discussions of the duration of a רגע appear in *t. Berakhot* 1:1; *b. Nazir* 20b–21a; *b. Makkot* 6a; *b. Baba Batra* 129b–130a; *b. Baba Kama* 73a–b; *b. Nedarim* 87a–b, discussed in Kalman (2019:50, 85–88, 99).

104. Translation according to MS Paris 671; Oxford Opp. Add. fol. 23 and several other MSS do not include the reference to the sun shining and describe the kings putting their crowns on their heads rather than on the ground.

105. Among those who seem to have prayed to the sun are some Christians and Manicheans, e.g., Clement of Alexandria, *Stromata* 7.7; Tertullian, *Apology* 16; *Song of the Bema* CCXLL, lines 7–8.

106. NRSV.

107. *b. Berakhot* 6a also imagines that God is present in the synagogue when men arrive for daily prayers, in a gathering of judges, or among those who study Torah, even if just a single individual studies on his own. The idea is that when a person engages the divine, the divine presence is ever-present.

108. Hekhalot Rabbati §§100–102.

109. Gruenwald (1980, 2014:32–33).

110. Hekhalot Rabbati §173; ed. Schäfer (1981); translated with modifications from M. Smith (1943–47, 2009).

111. Hekhalot Rabbati §173; ed. Schäfer (1981); translated with modifications from M. Smith (1995).

112. Hekhalot Rabbati §173; ed. Schäfer (1981); translated with modifications from M. Smith (1995).

113. Gruenwald (1980, 2014:188), referring to Hekhalot Rabbati §§173–79.

114. McAlpine (1987:181–99).

115. E.g., Joshua 1:8 ("this book of the law shall not depart out of your mouth, you shall meditate on it day and night"); Psalm 1:2 ("on his law they meditate day and night"); Psalm 6:7 ("every night I flood my bed with tears"); Psalm 63:7 ("when I think of you upon my bed, and meditate on you in the watches of the night"). See also McAlpine (1987); Ekirch (2005). On nighttime watches and a threefold night office, see Isidore of Seville, *De officiis ecclesiasticis* 1.22, on Luke 12:38, discussed in Taft (1986:120).

116. Penner (2014); see also Koslofsky (2011); Ker (2004).

117. Holladay (2007).

118. See also *b. Sanhedrin* 39b. *Apocalypse of Abraham* 10.9 describes Iaoel teaching others in the heavenly retinue songs at night, discussed in Gruenwald (1980, 2014:93–94).

119. In rabbinic sources, the night is divided into "watches." The term "watches" refers to the priestly watches in the Jerusalem temple but relates to biblical divisions of the night into three watches (אשמורות) and to the Roman division of nightly hours into four watches (*vigiliae*). On whether there are three or four nightly watches, see *t. Berakhot* 1:1. Rabbi states that there are four watches, and Rabbi Nathan, citing Judges 7:19, claims that the night has only three watches. This might be an argument over whether the night ought to be divided according to biblical watches, which divided the night into three, or Roman watches, which divided the night into four, rather than displaying ignorance by rabbis of how many watches each night has. On rabbinic time-keeping, see S. Stern (2003:47–53); Kalman (2019:50–51); on Roman hours, see Aldrete (2004:241); on nighttime watches, see Taft (1986:120); Holford-Strevens (2005:3–5).

120. Practically, the answer to this second question makes a difference of a full astronomical hour.

121. *b. Berakhot* 3a.

122. Jeremiah 25:30 makes no reference to *when* God roars, but the rabbinic passage references specific times of God's roars.

123. Rabbi Eliezer conjures up these specific ways in which God "makes His voice heard from His holy dwelling" in heaven by those on earth. While Jeremiah 25:30 only vaguely refers to this idea, Rabbi Eliezer depicts in detail the associated animal sounds.

124. Benovitz (2006:iv).

125. *b. Berakhot* 3a.

126. On animals in the Babylonian Talmud, see Berkowitz (2018); on angelic-human time, especially at Qumran and in Hekhalot literature, see Ahuvia (2014:216–30).

127. On anthropomorphism, see Shah (2012); Chavel (2012); Costa (2010; 2012); Hamori (2010); H. Shwartz (2010); Halbertal (2000); Amiet (1997); D. Stern (1992; 1994:97–101; 1996:76); Goshen-Gottstein (1994).

128. On the Arian controversy, see Alexander's *Letter to Alexander of Byzantium*, esp. sections 11, 22–29, 46–47, in Theodoret, *Church History* 1.4. Depicting God as human or human-like while also assuming God's timelessness was a more difficult philosophical and theological position to defend than admitting, as rabbinic texts do, that if God resembles humans in some way then God is also bound by time as humans are—even if God's anthropomorphization was regarded primarily in a metaphorical sense in rabbinic texts. Nonetheless, the notion of unchangeability itself can—and was—figured as dynamic rather than static in ancient Christian theology, on which see Peppard (2012a).

129. Kaye (2018:56–85).

130. NRSV. See, e.g., *Genesis Rabbah* 8:2; *b. Sanhedrin* 97a; *Pesiqta Rabbati* 1:1, 40:1; *Midrash Psalms* 90:7; *Song of Songs Rabbah* 5:11:1.

131. On these passages, see McDowell (2017:193–94).

132. *Exodus Rabbah* 28:5; *Midrash Psalms* 133:8.

133. By citing the splitting of the sea, perhaps this midrash references the Matrona tradition (*Leviticus Rabbah* 8:1).

134. NRSV.

135. Though cf. *Mekhilta de-Rabbi Ishmael Bahodesh* 7 on Exodus 20:11, which insists that God does not rest. Perhaps this is the case because certain biblical verses, e.g., Psalm 121:3-4, describe God as not needing sleep. Other passages, however, assume that God does sometimes sleep, e.g., 1 Kings 18:27, Psalms 44:24-25, 59:5-6, 78:65. On divine sleep in the Hebrew Bible, see McAlpine (1987:181-99).

136. *Pesiqta de-Rav Kahana* 16:5 (ed. Mandelbaum). On the association of the tribes with the zodiac and/or daily hours, see, e.g., Philo, *De somniis* 2.113, *Vita Moses* 2.123-24, *De fuga* 184; *Pesiqta Rabbati* 4:1; *Genesis Rabbah* 100:9, on which see Marshall (2005).

137. D. Weiss (2016:16).

138. The two rituals God performs—Torah study and phylacteries—are characterized in rabbinic sources as men's rituals.

139. This distinction is subtle, but it maps onto the Babylonian Talmud's greater tendency to anthropomorphize God, outlined in Neusner (1988, 2001).

140. God's lament appears again a few lines later, as words recited by the *bat qol* at the ruins of Jerusalem, but in that lament the heavenly voice cries out "woe to the children." Elijah explains to Rabbi Yose that the divine voice recites this line three times each day, as well as whenever Israelites say "May His great name be blessed!" in synagogues and schoolhouses. On the reception of this passage, see Saperstein (1980:1-20).

141. In Jeremiah 25:31, God's roaring signals the destruction of the nations. This explanation therefore continues the exegesis of the Jeremiah passage that preceded it in the rabbinic pericope.

142. D. Weiss (2016:150); M. Fishbane (2003:14-15). The conception of God as mourning develops especially around the idea of the *shekhina*, on which see E. Johnson (1992:82-86); Schäfer (2004:98-102).

143. E.g., *Mekhilta de-Rabbi Ishmael Beshallah* 8 (ed. Horovitz and Rabin, 142; ed. Lauterbach, 204); *y. Berakhot* 7:4, 11c; *y. Megillah* 3:8, 74c, discussed at length in Berthelot (forthcoming).

144. On which see *Lamentations Rabbah* 1:24. In the same talmudic pericope (*b. Berakhot* 3b), God miraculously wakes David at midnight by sending a wind to play his lyre, another example of a divine sound breaking the night's silence.

145. On reasons for this shift, see Hasan-Rokem (2000).

146. In *y. Berakhot* 9:2, 13c, God also mourns the destruction by roaring, but that passage does not present it in the context of God's daily schedule.

147. *m. Avot* 3.3, MS Kaufmann; translated with modification from Danby (1933:450).

148. Kaye (forthcoming b) is writing a history of the concept of *bittul*, from antiquity to contemporary discourse, especially as it relates to time and Torah study.

149. *b. Menahot* 10a; translation and discussion in Rubenstein (2003:31).

150. *b. Qiddushin* 30a. A three-part division of the day, including for study, also appears in Manichaean and Zoroastrian sources, discussed in Colditz (2009:esp. 86-93).

151. שמניחין חיי עולם הבא ועוסקין בחיי שעה; e.g., *b. Ta'anit* 21a; *b. Shabbat* 10a, 33b-34a; *b. Betzah* 15b; this phrase is discussed in Rubenstein (2003:32-33).

152. On the term עולם, see, e.g., S. Friedman (2008; 2014:1-116).

153. E.g., *m. Hagigah* 2:1, on which see Furstenberg (2013).

154. Pliny the Elder, *Historia naturalis* 36.72-73. Augustus erected a monument commemorating his intercalary reform to the Julian calendar as well. Pliny also discusses earlier sundials in Rome, emphasizing their inaccuracy.

155. Nasrallah (2019a:205).

156. Nasrallah (2019a:179–223, at 206); Sorek (2010).

157. Pliny the Younger, *Epistula* 2.7, discussed in Wolkenhauer (2018); Remijsen (2007). Josephus, too, mentions hours in the context of military activity, on which see Kalman (2019:45).

158. Suetonius, *Vita divi Augusti* 50.

159. Wolkenhauer (2018).

160. Both discussed in Talbert (2017:5).

161. K. Miller (2017; 2018); Arnaldi and Schaldach (1997).

162. Graßhoff (2018); Ehrlich (2012). The notion of hourly time-keeping as a feature of the divine contrasts with other notions of hours that regarded them as the most human of time-units. According to Sattler (2019), Plato's corpus contains only one reference to hours as a subdivision of the day, and there it regards hours as human-made divisions of time. In ancient Egyptian sources, hours were associated with work shifts and burial practices, in which embalming rituals were performed at different hours of the night.

Conclusion

1. Baker (2002:5).

2. This did not necessarily mean that there was strict or uniform adherence to rabbinic laws but rather that communities and individuals applied and contended with such laws in new ways, on which see, e.g., Brody (1998); Simonsohn (2011); Krakowski (2017).

3. *y. Avodah Zarah* 1.2, 4c; see also *y. Avodah Zarah* 1.3, 39c. I have adapted the names of the festivals based on Kohut (1898); Taqizadeh (1940:637–39); Bokser (1975); Neusner (1976:141–43).

4. *b. Avodah Zarah* 11b; trans. Soncino.

5. *b. Avodah Zarah* 11b; trans. Soncino.

6. Carlebach (2011:115–59).

7. *British Library Add. MS* 11639, fol. 542v; Schonfield (2003a and b); E. Baumgarten (2015).

8. Visually, it also evokes Philocalus's codex calendar of 354, with its side-by-side lists of festivals and cycles.

9. Carlebach (2011:142).

10. Carlebach (2011:125–32).

11. Carlebach (2011:120).

12. E.g., see Tosafot on *b. Avodah Zarah* 2a, which redefines Christian offerings to icons as solely for the upkeep of the clergy and not a form of idolatry, discussed in M. Cohen (2017:62–64). The thirteenth-century *Sefer Amudei HaGolah* (passages #60–68) similarly maintains a narrow definition of idolatry so as to exclude Christian festivals, discussed in E. Baumgarten (2015:267–68). On this broader trend, see Carlebach (2011:120–21); J. Katz (1961:32–34); Halbertal and Margalit (1992:210–13); Ta-Shma (1996:241–50).

13. M. Cohen (2017:63–64).

14. See Maimonides, *Laws of Idolatry* 9:4; *Commentary on the Mishnah, Avodah Zarah* 1:3; *Mishneh Torah*, *Hilkhot Ma'akhalot Asurot* 11:7 and 13:11; responsum #448 to Rabbi Obadiah the Proselyte; Kreisel (1999:39–40); Novak (1986).

15. On Feinstein's responsa, see Berkowitz (2012:219–27).

16. The possible prohibition against celebrating Thanksgiving rests, in Feinstein's view, on the interpretation of Leviticus 18:3, which prohibits following the "laws" of gentiles, rather than on the prohibition against participating in pagan festivals, on which see Berkowitz (2012:219–27).

17. This overlap of Jewish and American time is given full expression in the term *Thanksgivukkah*, used to refer to the time when Hanukkah and Thanksgiving overlap. See also Ashton (2013).

18. Berkowitz (2012:220); for Feinstein's responsa, see *Igrot Moshe*, Heleq Even ha-Ezer 2 Siman 13; Heleq Oreh Hayyim 5 Siman 20; Heleq Yoreh Deah 4 Siman 11.

19. Similar assumptions about the civic character of the New Year in January appear in early modern responsa from Europe, on which see Carlebach (2011:115).

20. M. Cohen (2017:61–67).

21. *b. Avodah Zarah* 22a; Maimonides, *Laws of the Sabbath* 6:17. M. Cohen (2017:64) observes that Maimonides moves the discussion of partnerships from the tractate on idolatry, where it is located in the Babylonian Talmud, to his section on the Sabbath.

22. von Dohm (1781), in Mendes-Flohr and Reinharz (1980, 1995:35); see also Penslar (2013:30–50).

23. This critique of Sabbath observance appears in responses to von Dohm as well, such as that of Johann David Michaelis, found in Mendes-Flohr and Reinharz (1980, 1995:43).

24. Mendes-Flohr and Reinharz (1980, 1995:115).

25. Mendes-Flohr and Reinharz (1980, 1995:35). There were wide-ranging debates about whether military activity violated Sabbath law already in antiquity, on which see, e.g., 1 Maccabees 2:29–41; *Jubilees* 50:12–13; Josephus, *Against Apion* 1.209–12; *Jewish War* 2.391–94; *Antiquities* 14.63–68; Dio Cassius, *Historia Romana* 37.15:3–19:3, 49.22:4–5; Plutarch, *De Superstitione* 8; Frontinus, *Strategemata* 2.1:17; Gribetz (2016b:51–57).

26. Mendelssohn ([1783] 1980, 1995), in Mendes-Flohr and Reinharz (1980, 1995:48–49).

27. Brinkman (2012:93); Olitzky (1982). In Hamburg, the first Reform congregation noted the celebration of a Saturday Sabbath in their constitution of 1817, on which see Mendes-Flohr and Reinharz (1980, 1995:161).

28. Brinkman (2012:79–99); Temkin (1971:12–13, 37, 112). The Hebrew Reformed Association in Baltimore introduced Sunday services in 1854, but the organization did not last long. The 1870s were precisely a time when the identity of the American Sunday, too, was contested and changing, on which see McCrossen (2000).

29. Brinkman (2012:99) explains that the necessity for Sunday services was, primarily, an economic problem. The rabbi thus instituted an additional day for worship that would correspond to the Christian Sunday, already a day on which people did not generally work. See also A. Goodman (1951); S. Rabin (2017:26–27).

30. Brinkman (2012:94).

31. Brinkman (2012:93).

32. Brinkman (2012:93).

33. This might also be the reason that Friday night services, introduced in 1869 as an alternative to Saturday services, became more mainstream than Sunday services in American Reform congregations, on which see Brinkman (2012:97).

34. See, e.g., the Columbus platform, adopted by the American Reform movement in 1937, which states that "Judaism as a way of life requires in addition to its moral and spiritual demands, the preservation of the Sabbath, festivals and Holy Days," in Mendes-Flohr and Reinharz (1980, 1995:518). For an alternative view advocating for a temporally flexible Sabbath, see Reines (1987).

35. On which see S. Rabin (2017:36–39).

36. Davis (1905), in T. Michels (2012:170–71).

37. Brinkman (2012:96–97).

38. On which see, e.g., Mendes-Flohr and Reinharz (1980, 1995:169–72).

39. Harkov (2018).

40. Ahad Ha'am wrote, e.g., that "one can say without any exaggeration that more than the Jewish people has kept the Sabbath, the Sabbath has kept [the Jewish people]," found in Batnitzky (2009:294).

41. Omer (2012), originally published in 1978 with an Israeli readership in mind.

42. On PJ Library, see Gross (2017).

43. Wasserman (2003); Hirsh (1986).

44. Consider as well recent movements such as the Sabbath Manifesto (sabbathmanifesto.org); Shabbat Across America and Canada (http://njop.org/programs/shabbat/shabbat-across-america-canada/); One Table: A New Way to Friday (https://onetable.org).

45. Baskin (2001:140–41).

46. Baskin (2001:140–41).

47. Baskin (2001:140–41).

48. Despite the fact that the twelfth and thirteenth centuries are considered exceptional for the degree to which Jewish women participated in men's rituals, on which see E. Baumgarten (2014:143).

49. Even though there were exceptions to this rule and the principle was not considered to carry prescriptive value in the Babylonian Talmud (e.g., *b. Qiddushin* 34a) and by later authorities such as Maimonides (e.g., *Commentary on the Mishnah, Qiddushin* 1:7, *Mishneh Torah*, Hil. Akum 12:3), the general principle was nonetheless upheld and explanations for its purpose were offered, on which see Goren (1965); Fishman (1992:209); Benovitz (2007b:47–60).

50. As suggested by Jacob Anatoli (thirteenth-century Provence or Italy), *Malmad HaTalmidim*, Parashat Lekh Lekha, Lik. Ed., no. 15, cited in Fishman (1992:209); Joseph of Orléans (Joseph Bekhor Shor), *Perushei* 226–227, discussed in E. Baumgarten (2014:163); and *Sefer Hasidim* #1011, which states: "A woman should serve her husband so he can study Torah. This is why men were given dominance. [Moreover] whoever serves [one master] day and night cannot set time aside for another; therefore women are exempt from positive time-bound commandments"; translation and discussion in E. Baumgarten (2014:163).

51. As suggested by David ben Joshua Abudarham (fourteenth-century Spain), *Sefer Abudarham*, Sha'ar 3, Birkat HaMizvot, cited in Fishman (1992:209). Benovitz (2007b:47–50) suggests that the modern adaptation of this explanation is that women were too occupied with household duties and did not have time for other rituals.

52. The Marahal of Prague offers this opinion; Meiselman (1978:43–44); Alexander (2013:3). See also Hirsch (1971, 3:711–12) on Leviticus 23:43, cited in Benovitz (2007b:58–59). Women's impurity was often used to justify women's exemption from donning phylacteries but was not usually extended as the reason for their exemption from the entire category of positive time-bound commandments; Moses ben Menahem of Zurich states, for example, that "women should not put on tefillin because they do not know how to maintain [their] purity," discussed in E. Baumgarten (2014:159–64, quote at 162).

53. Kanarfogel (1992); Grossman (2004:178–80, 309–12); E. Baumgarten (2014:138–71).

54. *Mahzor Vitry* (ed. Hurwitz, 413–14), cited in Grossman (2004:178); E. Baumgarten (2014:144); Fishman (1992:210–15, esp. 210nn49–56).

55. Grossman (2004:178–79). Grossman also cites the writings of Rabbi Eliezer ben Nathan (*Mordekhai, Shabbat §286*) and Rabbenu Tam (Tosafot at *b. Eruvin* 96a), both of which suggest women's initiation of this trend, and the later Rabbi Yitzhak ben Samuel, whose rulings indicate that such practices persisted at least until the late twelfth century.

56. E. Baumgarten (2014:143–46).

57. On the increasing discomfort with women's participation in positive time-bound

commandments in the thirteenth century, see E. Baumgarten (2004:88; 2014:143–49); Fishman (1992).

58. Grossman (2004:180).

59. E. Baumgarten (2014:164).

60. Fishman (1992:215–33).

61. *Sefer HaKanah* (Crawkow 1894 edition, repr. Jerusalem, 1973), p. 15a, cited and discussed in Fishman (1992:218–19).

62. Fishman (1992:219).

63. *Sefer HaPeliah* (Przemysl 1883), pt. II, p. 20a, cited and discussed in Fishman (1992:217).

64. Fishman (1992:228).

65. A late medieval medical manual titled *Sefer Ahavat Nashim* provides suggestions for therapeutic measures women could perform on the day that they immersed in the ritual bath, on which see Caballero-Navas (2004:92). Women's observance of Niddah as a practice of piety continued through the medieval and modern periods, on which see E. Baumgarten (2014:21–50); Weissler (1999:66–75).

66. S. Koren (2011:28–42); Marienberg (2012a:17–73).

67. S. J. D. Cohen (1999b); Dinari (1979–80); M. Friedman (1990); Baskin (2001).

68. Krakowski (2020); see also Dinari (1979–80), S. J. D. Cohen (1999b) for additional examples from other regions.

69. Krakowski (2020); see also Emanuel (2007). Even so, Krakowski points to evidence that many women continued to ignore Maimonides' stricter menstrual purity laws, at least for some time after his rulings—though eventually Maimonides' rulings were more widely adopted.

70. S. Koren (2009; 2011).

71. S. Koren (2011:10–11).

72. On Shapiro, see Zierler (2012; 2008).

73. Shapiro (2008:89–92).

74. *b. Sanhedrin* 42a. For a feminist analysis and reclaiming of this ritual, see Ner-David (2014:184–87).

75. Oppenheim, *Nishal David*, 3.8.

76. While women were barred from observing and sanctifying the moon, the first of the month was considered to be a woman's festival; e.g., *y. Ta'anit* 1.6, 64c and *Pirqe de-Rabbi Eliezer* 45, discussed in R. Feldman (2001; 2012); Rosen and Rosen (2000).

77. On Aylon's work, see Aylon (2012); Sperber (2011; 2019). I viewed this installation at the Museum on the Seam's 2018 exhibit "Thou Shalt Not" in Jerusalem in 2018.

78. Merchavia (1965:118n11) provides a long list.

79. Petrus Alfonsi, *Dialogue against the Jews*, Titulus 1; trans. Resnick (2006:68–71).

80. Peter the Venerable, *Against the Inveterate Obduracy of the Jews*, 5; trans. Resnick (2013:211, 245–46).

81. Maccoby (1993:165–66).

82. R. Chazan (1989:115–36); Merchavia (1965:118n11).

83. On *Pugio Fidei*, see Bonfil (1971); J. Cohen (1982:129–69; 1999:343–63); R. Chazan (1989:115–36); Bobichon (2015); Hasselhoff and Fidora (2017).

84. *Pugio Fidei* 928, 930–31.

85. Merchavia (1965:118) suggests in notes 9–11 that Paul of Burgos might have found these references in *Pugio Fidei*, though they also appear in many earlier anti-Jewish treatises; Hacohen (2019:136) also notes that Paul of Burgos relied on "the Christian compendium of Talmudic blasphemies, prepared for the 1240 Talmud Trial."

86. Rosenzweig (2005:290); on eternity and cyclical rhythms in Rosenzweig's philosophy, see Breiterman (2002).

87. Rosenzweig (2005:290); Rosenzweig (306–7) also describes each person as an hour in the history of the world.

88. Rosenzweig (2005:291); on Rosenzweig's idea of prayer, Yaffe (1979:225) writes: "Whereas the fanatic's prayer is too early (since the object of his wish has already been granted willy-nilly), proper prayer is said to occur, in the psalmist's expression, 'at an acceptable time' (Psalm 69:14). According to Rosenzweig, this is possible only if the believer relates his wish not merely to temporal objects in the world, but also to a God Who—as author of the miracles of past creation, present revelation and future redemption—is eternal.... Ritual prayer is regular prayer—having occurred with remembered regularity in the past, and about to occur with anticipated regularity in the future, as well as occurring regularly at the present moment. It occurs at regular hours. Its regular 'hour'—or day or week or month or year—is at once a particular moment in time and a permanent moment timelessly set for past and present and future repetition." Rosenzweig focuses his analytic energy on the prayers and rituals of Yom Kippur.

89. Rosenzweig (2005:428).

90. Rosenzweig (2005:428–29).

91. Levinas (1990:97, 103). On Levinas as a reader of the Talmud, see Moyn (2003).

92. NRSV.

93. Levinas (1990:104).

94. On reading talmudic pericopes intertextually, see Septimus (2009).

95. Herder (1799, 1955:68), quoted in Koselleck (2004:2).

96. Herder (1799, 1955:68).

BIBLIOGRAPHY

Abate, Elisabetta. 2017. "Sabbath in the Netherworld (Genesis Rabba 11:5)." In *Reading the Way to the Netherworld: Education and the Representations of the Beyond in Later Antiquity*, edited by Ilinca Tanaseanu-Döbler, Anna Lefteratou, Gabriela Ryser, and Konstantinos Stamatopoulos, 489–507. Göttingen: Vandenhoeck & Ruprecht.

Abercrombie, John R. 1978. "The University Museum's Collection of Papyri and Related Materials." *Expedition* 20.2:32–37.

Adam, Barbara. 1990. *Time and Social Theory*. Cambridge: Polity Press.

Adam, Shaul. 1997. "Sundials in Israel." *Bulletin of the British Sundial Society* 97:3–7.

———. 2002a. "Ancient Sundials of Israel Part I: Sundials Found in Jerusalem." *British Sundial Society Journal* 14.2:52–57.

———. 2002b. "Ancient Sundials of Israel Part II: Sundials Found outside Jerusalem." *British Sundial Society Journal* 14.3:109–15.

Adelman, Rachel. 2009a. *The Return of the Repressed: Pirqe de-Rabbi Eliezer and the Pseudepigrapha*. Leiden: Brill.

———. 2009b. "Midrash, Myth, and Bakhtin's Chronotope: The Itinerant Well and the Foundation Stone in *Pirqe de-Rabbi Eliezer*." *Journal of Jewish Thought and Philosophy* 17.2:143–76.

Aderet, Avraham. 1990. *From Destruction to Rebirth: The Role of Yavneh in the Rehabilitation of the Nation*. Jerusalem: Magnes Press.

Adler, Rachel. 1976. "*Tum'ah* and *Taharah*: Ends and Beginnings." In *The Jewish Woman: New Perspectives*, edited by Elizabeth Koltun, 63–71. New York: Schocken Books.

———. 2007. "In Your Blood, Live: Re-visions of a Theology of Purity." In *Tikkun Reader: 20th Anniversary*, edited by Michael Lerner, 157–63. Lanham, MD: Rowman & Littlefield.

Adler, Yonatan. 2011. "Archaeological Evidence for the Observance of Ritual Purity in Erez-Israel from the Hasmonean Period until the End of the Talmudic Era (164 BCE–400 CE)." Ph.D. diss., Bar Ilan University.

———. 2017. "The Decline of Jewish Ritual Purity Observance in Roman Palaestina: An Archaeological Perspective on Chronology and Historical Context." In *Expressions of Cult in the Southern Levant in the Greco-Roman Period*, edited by Oren Tal and Zeev Weiss, 269–84. Turnhout: Brepols.

Agamben, Giorgio. 2005. *The Time That Remains: A Commentary on the Letter to the Romans*. Stanford: Stanford University Press.

Ahuvia, Mika. 2014. "'Israel among the Angels': A Study of Angels in Jewish Texts from the Fourth to Eighth Century C.E." Ph.D. diss., Princeton University.

Ahuvia, Mika, and Sarit Kattan Gribetz. 2018. "'The Daughters of Israel': An Analysis of the Term in Late Ancient Jewish Sources." *Jewish Quarterly Review* 108.1:1–27.

Albeck, Chanoch. 1965. "Einleitung und Register zum Bereshit Rabba." In *Midrash Bereshit Rabba mit kritischem Apparat und Kommentar*, vol. 3. Jerusalem: Wahrmann Books.

Aldrete, Gregory S. 2004. *Daily Life in the Roman City: Rome, Pompeii and Ostia*. Westport, CT: Greenwood.

———. 2006. *Floods of the Tiber in Ancient Rome*. Baltimore: Johns Hopkins University Press.

Alexander, Elizabeth Shanks. 2007. "From Whence the Phrase 'Timebound, Positive Commandments'?" *Jewish Quarterly Review* 97.3:317–46.

———. 2013. *Gender and Timebound Commandments in Judaism*. Cambridge: Cambridge University Press.

———. 2015. "When the Dead Want to Primp: Talmudic Gender as Theological Prompt: BT Berakhot 18b." *Nashim: A Journal of Jewish Women's Studies & Gender Issues* 28:120–33.

Allen, Paula Gunn. 1992. *The Sacred Hoop: Recovering the Feminine in American Indian Traditions*. Boston: Beacon Press.

Allison, Dale C. 1960. *Jesus of Nazareth: Millenarian Prophet*. Minneapolis: Fortress Press.

Alon, Gedaliah. 1977. *Jews, Judaism and the Classical World: Studies in Jewish History in the Time of the Second Temple and Talmud*. Jerusalem: Magnes Press.

Ameling, Walter, ed. 2004. *Inscriptiones Judaicae Orientis II Kleinasien*. Tübingen: Mohr Siebeck.

Amiet, Pierre. 1997. "Anthropomorphisme et aniconisme dans l'antiquité orientale." *Revue Biblique* 104.3:321–37.

Anderson, Mark. 2019. "Christianizing the Planetary Week and Globalizing the Seven-Day Cycle." *Studies in Late Antiquity* 3.2:128–91.

Ando, Clifford. 2000. *Imperial Ideology and Provincial Loyalty in the Roman Empire*. Berkeley: University of California Press.

———. 2008. *The Matter of the Gods: Religion and the Roman Empire*. Berkeley: University of California Press.

———. 2011. *Law, Language, and Empire in the Roman Tradition*. Philadelphia: University of Pennsylvania Press.

———. 2012. "Die Riten der Anderen." *Mediterraneo Antico* 15.1–2:31–50.

———. 2015. "Mythistory: The Pre-Roman Past in Latin Late Antiquity." In *Antike Mythologie in Christlichen Kontexten Der Spätantike*, edited by Hartmut Leppin, 205–18. Berlin: de Gruyter.

Andrews, John Nevins, and Louis Richard Conradi. 1912. *History of the Sabbath and the First Day of the Week*. 4th ed. Washington, DC: Review & Herald Publishing Association.

Andrews, Margaret M., and Harriet I. Flower. 2015. "Mercury on the Esquiline: A Reconsideration of a Local Shrine Restored by Augustus." *American Journal of Archaeology* 119.1:47–67.

Anisfeld, Rachel. 2009. *Sustain Me with Raisin Cakes: Pesikta deRav Kahana and the Popularization of Rabbinic Judaism*. Leiden: Brill.

Argetsinger, Kathryn. 1992. "Birthday Rituals: Friends and Patrons in Roman Poetry and Cult." *Classical Antiquity* 11.2:175–93.

Arnaldi, Mario, and Karlheinz Schaldach. 1997. "A Roman Cylinder Dial: Witness to a Forgotten Tradition." *Journal for the History of Astronomy* 28:107–31.

Arstila, Valtteri, and Dan Lloyd, eds. 2014. *Subjective Time: The Philosophy, Psychology and Neuroscience of Temporality*. Cambridge, MA: MIT Press.

Ashton, Dianne. 2013. *Hanukkah in America: A History*. New York: New York University Press.

Assmann, Jan. 1995a. "Collective Memory and Cultural Identity." *New German Critique* 65:125–33.

———. 1995b. *Egyptian Solar Religion in the New Kingdom: Re, Amun and the Crisis of Polytheism*. London: Kegan Paul International.

Athanassiadi, Polymnia, and Michael Frede. 1999. *Pagan Monotheism in Late Antiquity*. Oxford: Oxford University Press.

Atkinson, M., and Archibald Robertson, trans. 1892. "Apologia Ad Constantium." In *Nicene and Post-Nicene Fathers, Second Series*, edited by Philip Schaff and Henry Wace. Buffalo: Christian Publishing.

Aveni, Anthony. 1989, 2002. *Empires of Time: Calendars, Clocks, and Cultures*. Boulder: University Press of Colorado.

Avishai, Orit. 2008a. "Doing Religion in a Secular World: Women in Conservative Religions and the Question of Agency." *Gender and Society* 22.4:409–33.

———. 2008b. "Halakhic *Niddah* Consultants and the Orthodox Women's Movement: Evaluating the Story of Enlightened Progress." *Journal of Modern Jewish Studies* 7.2:195–216.

Aylon, Helène. 2012. *Whatever Is Contained Must Be Released: My Jewish Orthodox Girlhood, My Life as a Feminist Artist*. New York: Feminist Press at CUNY.

Bacchiocchi, Samuele. 1977. *From Sabbath to Sunday: A Historical Investigation of the Rise of Sunday Observance in Early Christianity*. Rome: Pontifical Gregorian University Press.

Back, Sven-Olav. 2010. "Jesus and the Sabbath." In *Handbook for the Study of the Historical Jesus*, edited by Tom Holmén and Stanley E. Porter, 2597–2633. Leiden: Brill.

Bagnall, Roger S., and Raffaella Cribiore. 2006. *Women's Letters from Ancient Egypt, 300 BC–AD 800*. Ann Arbor: University of Michigan Press.

Bahr, Lynne Moss. 2018. *"The Time Is Fulfilled": Jesus' Apocalypticism in the Context of Continental Philosophy*. New York: T&T Clark.

Baker, Cynthia. 2002. *Rebuilding the House of Israel: Architectures of Gender in Jewish Antiquity*. Philadelphia: University of Pennsylvania Press.

———. 2016. *Jew*. New Brunswick, NJ: Rutgers University Press.

Bakhos, Carol. 2006. *Ishmael on the Border: Rabbinic Portrayals of the First Arab*. Albany: State University of New York Press.

———. 2016. "The Family of Abraham in *Genesis Rabbah*." In *Genesis Rabbah in Text and Context*, edited by Sarit Kattan Gribetz, David Grossberg, Martha Himmelfarb, and Peter Schäfer, 115–27. Tübingen: Mohr Siebeck.

Bakker, Arjen. 2016. "Sages and Saints: Continuous Study and Transformation in *Musar le-Mevin* and *Serek ha-Yahad*." In *Tracing Sapiential Traditions in Ancient Judaism*, edited by Hindy Najman, Jean-Sébastien Rey, and Eibert J. C. Tigchelaar, 106–18. Leiden: Brill.

———. 2017. "Praise of the Luminaries in *The Book of the Similitudes* and Its Parallels at Qumran." *Meghillot* 13:171–84. [Hebrew]

Balberg, Mira. 2011. "Recomposed Corporealities: Purity, Body and Self in the Mishnah." Ph.D. diss., Stanford University.

———. 2014. *Purity, Body, and Self in Early Rabbinic Literature*. Berkeley: University of California Press.

———. 2017a. *Blood for Thought: The Reinvention of Sacrifice in Early Rabbinic Literature*. Berkeley: University of California Press.

———. 2017b. "Ritual Studies and the Study of Rabbinic Literature." *Currents in Biblical Research* 16.1:71–98.

Baldi, Philip. 2002. *The Foundations of Latin*. Berlin: de Gruyter.

Ballentine, Debra Scoggins. 2015. *The Conflict Myth and the Biblical Tradition*. Oxford: Oxford University Press.

Bar Ilan University Responsa Project. https://www.responsa.co.il/home.en-US.aspx.

Bar-Asher Siegel, Michal. 2013. *Early Christian Monastic Literature and the Babylonian Talmud*. New York: Cambridge University Press.

Bar-Asher Siegel, Michal. 2019. *Jewish-Christian Dialogues on Scripture in Late Antiquity: Heretic Narratives of the Babylonian Talmud*. Cambridge: Cambridge University Press.
Baraitser, Lisa. 2008. *Maternal Encounters: The Ethics of Interruption*. London: Routledge.
———. 2017. *Enduring Time*. London: Bloomsbury Academic.
Barak, On. 2013. *On Time: Technology and Temporality in Modern Egypt*. Berkeley: University of California Press.
———. 2014. "Times of *Tamaddun*: Gender, Urbanity, and Temporality in Colonial Egypt." In *Women and the City, Women in the City: A Gendered Perspective on Ottoman Urban History*, edited by Nazan Maksudyan. Oxford: Berghahn Books.
Barbu, Daniel. 2011. "Idole, idolâtre, idolâtrie." In *Les representations des dieux des autres*, edited by Corinne Bonnet, Amandine Declercq, and Iwo Slobodzianeck, 31–49. Caltanissetta: Salvatore Sciascia Editore.
———. 2016. *Naissance de l'idolâtrie: Image, identité, religion*. Paris: Presses Universitaires de Liège.
Barbu, Daniel, and Yaacov Deutsch, eds. 2020. *Toledot Yeshu in Context*. Tübingen: Mohr Siebeck.
Barclay, John M. G. 1996. *Jews in the Mediterranean Diaspora: From Alexander to Trajan 323 B.C.E.–117 C.E.* Edinburgh: T&T Clark.
Bargiello, Thaddeus A., Fannie R. Jackson, and Michael W. Young. 1984. "Restoration of Circadian Behavioural Rhythms by Gene Transfer in Drosophila." *Nature* 312:752–54.
Barr, James. 1962. *Biblical Words for Time*. London: SCM Press.
Bartsch, Shadi. 2006. *The Mirror of the Self*. Chicago: University of Chicago Press.
Baskin, Judith R. 1985. "The Separation of Women in Rabbinic Judaism." In *Women, Religion, and Social Change*, edited by Yvonne Yazbeck Haddad and Ellison Banks Findly, 3–18. Albany: State University of New York Press.
———. 2001. "Women and Ritual Immersion in Medieval Ashkenaz: The Sexual Politics of Piety." In *Judaism in Practice: From the Middle Ages through the Early Modern Period*, edited by Lawrence Fine, 131–42. Princeton: Princeton University Press.
———. 2002. *Midrashic Woman: Formations of the Feminine in Rabbinic Literature*. Hanover, NH: Brandeis University Press.
———. 2006. "'She Extinguished the Light of the World': Justifications for Women's Disabilities in *Avot de-Rabbi Nathan* B." In *Current Trends in the Study of Midrash*, edited by Carol Bakhos, 277–97. Leiden: Brill.
Batnitzky, Leora. 2009. "From Resurrection to Immortality: Theological and Political Implications in Modern Jewish Thought." *Harvard Theological Review* 102.3:279–96.
Bauckham, R. J. 1999. "The Lord's Day." In *From Sabbath to Lord's Day: A Biblical, Historical, and Theological Investigation*, edited by D. A. Carson, 221–50. Eugene: Wipf and Stock.
Baumgarten, Albert I. 2011. "Karaites, Qumran, the Calendar, and Beyond: At the Beginning of the Twenty-First Century." In *The Dead Sea Scrolls and Contemporary Culture*, edited by Adolfo D. Roitman, Lawrence H. Schiffman, and Shani Tzoref, 601–20. Leiden: Brill.
Baumgarten, Elisheva. 2004. *Mothers and Children: Jewish Family Life in Medieval Europe*. Princeton: Princeton University Press.
———. 2014. *Practicing Piety in Medieval Ashkenaz: Men, Women, and Everyday Religious Observance*. Philadelphia: University of Pennsylvania Press.
———. 2015. "Calendars Shared and Contested: Jews and the Christian Ritual Calendar in the Late Thirteenth Century." *Viator* 46.2:253–76.
Baumgarten, Joseph M. 1958. "The Beginning of the Day in the Calendar of Jubilees." *Journal of Biblical Literature* 77:355–60.

———. 1994. "Zab Impurity in Qumran and Rabbinic Law." *Journal of Jewish Studies* 45:273-77.
Bear, F. W. 1960. "'The Sabbath Was Made for Man?'" *Journal of Biblical Literature* 79.2:130-36.
Beard, Mary. 1991. "Writing and Religion: *Ancient Literacy* and the Function of the Written Word in Roman Religion." In *Literacy in the Roman World*, edited by J. H. Humphrey, 35-58. Ann Arbor: Journal of Roman Archaeology.
———. 2003. "A Complex of Times: No More Sheep on Romulus' Birthday." In *Roman Religion*, edited by Clifford Ando, 273-88. Edinburgh: Edinburgh University Press.
———. 2015. *Laughter in Ancient Rome: On Joking, Tickling, and Cracking Up*. Berkeley: University of California Press.
Beard, Mary, John North, and Simon Price, eds. 1998. *Religions of Rome: Volume 1: A History*. Cambridge: Cambridge University Press.
Becker, Adam H., and Annette Yoshiko Reed, eds. 2003. *The Ways That Never Parted: Jews and Christians in Late Antiquity and the Early Middle Ages*. Tübingen: Mohr Siebeck.
Becker, Eve-Marie. 2017. *The Birth of Christian History*. New Haven: Yale University Press.
Becker, Hans-Jürgen. 1999. *Die großen rabbinischen Sammelwerke Palastinas: Zur literarischen Genese von Talmud Yerushalmi und Midrash Bereshit Rabba*. Tübingen: Mohr Siebeck.
———. 2000. "Texts and History: The Dynamic Relationship between Talmud Yerushalmi and Genesis Rabbah." In *The Synoptic Problem in Rabbinic Literature*, edited by Shaye J. D. Cohen, 145-58. Providence: Brown Judaic Studies.
Beckwith, Roger T. 1996. *Calendar and Chronology, Jewish and Christian: Biblical, Intertestamental and Patristic Studies*. Leiden: Brill.
Belayche, Nicole. 2001. *Iudaea-Palaestina: The Pagan Cults in Roman Palestine (Second to Fourth Century)*. Tübingen: Mohr Siebeck.
———. 2004. "Pagan Festivals in Fourth-Century Gaza." In *Christian Gaza in Late Antiquity*, edited by Brouria Bitton-Ashkelony and Arieh Kofsky, 5-21. Leiden: Brill.
———. 2007. "Des lieux pour le 'profane' dans l'Empire tardo-antique? Les fêtes entre koinônia sociale et espaces de rivalités religieuses." *Antiquité tardive* 15:35-46.
———. 2009. "Foundation Myths in Roman Palestine: Traditions and Reworkings." In *Ethnic Constructs in Antiquity: The Role of Power and Tradition*, edited by Ton Derks and Nico Roymans, 167-88. Amsterdam: Archaeological Studies.
Bell, Catherine. 1992. *Ritual Theory, Ritual Practice*. Oxford: Oxford University Press.
Ben Shahar, Meir. 2011. "Biblical and Post-Biblical History in Rabbinic Literature." Ph.D. diss., Hebrew University of Jerusalem.
———. 2015. "When Was the Second Temple Destroyed? Chronology and Ideology in Josephus and in Rabbinic Literature." *Journal for the Study of Judaism* 46:547-73.
Ben-Dov, Jonathan. 2008. *Head of All Years: Astronomy and Calendars at Qumran in Their Ancient Context*. Leiden: Brill.
———. 2009. "The 364-Day Year at Qumran and in the Pseudepigrapha." In *The Qumran Scrolls and Their World*, edited by Menahem Kister, 435-76. Jerusalem: Yad Ben-Zvi.
———. 2011. "The Qumran Dial: Artifact, Text, and Context." In *Qumran und die Archaeologie*, edited by J. Frey, C. Claussen, and N. Kessler, 211-37. Tübingen: Mohr Siebeck.
———. 2012. "Lunar Calendars a Qumran? A Comparative and Ideological Study." In *Living the Lunar Calendar*, edited by Jonathan Ben-Dov, Wayne Horowitz, and John M. Steele, 173-90. Oxford: Oxbow Books.
———. 2016. "Apocalyptic Temporality: The Force of the Here and Now." *Hebrew Bible and Ancient Israel* 5:17-31.

Ben-Dov, Jonathan. 2018. "The Beginning of the Day." Lecture at the Israel Institute for Advanced Study, Jerusalem.

Ben-Dov, Jonathan, and Lutz Doering, eds. 2017. *The Construction of Time in Antiquity: Ritual, Art and Identity*. Cambridge: Cambridge University Press.

Ben-Dor Benite, Zev. 2009. *The Ten Lost Tribes: A World History*. Oxford: Oxford University Press.

Ben-Hayyim, Ze'ev. 1998. *Tibat Marqe: A Collection of Samaritan Midrashim*. Jerusalem: Israel Academy of Sciences and Humanities.

Benjamin, Mara H. 2018. *The Obligated Self: Maternal Subjectivity and Jewish Thought*. Bloomington: Indiana University Press.

Benovitz, Moshe. 2003. "Herod and Hanukkah." *Zion* 68:5–40.

———. 2006. *BT Berakhot Chapter 1 with Comprehensive Commentary*. Jerusalem: Society for the Interpretation of the Talmud. [Hebrew]

———. 2007a. "'Until the Feet of the Tarmoda'I Are Gone': The Hanukkah Light in Palestine during the Tannaitic and Amoraic Periods." In *Torah Lishma: Essays in Jewish Studies in Honor of Professor Shamma Friedman*, edited by Daniel Sperber, David Golinkin, Menachem Shmelzer, Mordechai Akiva Friedman, and Moshe Benovitz, 39–78. Jerusalem: Schechter Institute, Bar Ilan University Press.

———. 2007b. "Time-Triggered Positive Commandments as Conversation Pieces." *Hebrew Union College Annual* 78:45–90.

Berkowitz, Beth. 2012. *Defining Jewish Difference: From Antiquity to the Present*. Cambridge: Cambridge University Press.

———. 2018. *Animals and Animality in the Babylonian Talmud*. Cambridge: Cambridge University Press.

Bernett, Monika. 2007. "Roman Imperial Cult in the Galilee: Structures, Functions, and Dynamics." In *Religion, Ethnicity, and Identity in Ancient Galilee: A Region in Transition*, edited by Jürgen Zangenberg, Harold W. Attridge, and Dale B. Martin, 337–56. Tübingen: Mohr Siebeck.

Bernstein, Michael André. 1987. "'O Totiens Servus': Saturnalia and Servitude in Augustan Rome." *Critical Inquiry* 13.3:450–74.

Bernstein, Moshe J. 1991. "'Walking in the Festivals of the Gentiles': 4Qphosea a 2.15–17 and Jubilees 6.34–38." *Journal for the Study of the Pseudepigrapha* 5.21:21–34.

———. 2002. "The Aramaic Versions of Deuteronomy 32: Comparative Targumic Theology." In *Targum and Scripture: Studies in Aramaic Translations and Interpretation in Memory of Ernest G. Clarke*, edited by Paul V. M. Flesher, 29–52. Leiden: Brill.

Berthelot, Katell. 2011. "Philo's Perception of the Roman Empire." *Journal for the Study of Judaism* 42.2:166–87.

———, ed. 2014. "Judaism and Rome: Re-thinking Judaism's Encounter with the Roman Empire." http://judaism-and-rome.cnrs.fr/erc-project-judaism-and-rome.

———. 2016. "*The Rabbis Write Back!* L'enjeu de la 'parenté' entre Israël et Rome-Ésaü-Édom." *Revue de l'histoire des religions* 233.2:165–92.

———. 2017. "The Paradoxical Similarities between the Jews and the Roman Other." In *Perceiving the Other in Ancient Judaism and Early Christianity*, edited by Michal Bar-Asher Siegal, Wolfgang Grünstäudl, and Matthew Thiessen, 95–109. Tübingen: Mohr Siebeck.

———. 2018. "Rabbinic Universalism Reconsidered: The Roman Context of Some Rabbinic Traditions Pertaining to the Revelation of the Torah in Different Languages." *Jewish Quarterly Review* 108.4:393–421.

———. Forthcoming. *Jews and Their Roman Rivals: Pagan Rome's Challenge to Israel*. Princeton: Princeton University Press.

Berzon, Todd. 2016. "Identity, a Way Forward (Perhaps)." *Ancient Jew Review*. http://www.ancientjewreview.com/articles/2016/8/16/identity-a-way-forward-perhaps.
Beynon-Jones, Siân M. 2017. "Gestating Times: Women's Accounts of the Temporalities of Pregnancies That End in Abortion in England." *Sociology of Health & Illness* 39.6: 832–46.
Biale, Rachel. 1984. *Women and Jewish Law: An Exploration of Women's Issues in Halakhic Sources*. New York: Schocken Books.
Bickerman, Elias J. 2007. "A Document Concerning the Persecution by Antiochus IV Epiphanes." In *Studies in Jewish and Christian History*, edited by Amram D. Tropper, 376–407. Leiden: Brill.
Binder, Stéphanie E. 2012. *Tertullian, On Idolatry and Mishnah Avodah Zarah: Questioning the Parting of the Ways between Christians and Jews*. Leiden: Brill.
Birth, Kevin K. 2016. *Time Blind: Problems in Perceiving Other Temporalities*. London: Palgrave Macmillan.
Blaufuss, Hans. 1909. *Römische Feste und Feiertage nach den Tractaten über fremden Dienst*. Nürnberg: Stich.
Blidstein, Gerald. 1968. "Rabbinic Legislation on Idolatry: Tractate Abodah Zarah, Chapter 1." Ph.D. diss., Yeshiva University.
Bloch, Marc. 1992. *The Historian's Craft*. Manchester: Manchester University Press.
Bobel, Chris. 2010. *New Blood: Third-Wave Feminism and the Politics of Menstruation*. New Brunswick, NJ: Rutgers University Press.
Bobichon, Philippe. 2015. "Quotations, Translations, and Uses of Jewish Texts in Ramon Martí's *Pugio Fidei*." In *The Late Medieval Hebrew Book in the Western Mediterranean: Hebrew Manuscripts and Incunabula in Context*, edited by Javier del Barco, 266–94.
Boesenberg, Dulcinea. 2010. "Philo's Descriptions of Jewish Sabbath Practice." *Studia Philonica Annual* 22:143–63.
Böhl, Felix. 1975. "Die Matronenfrage im Midrasch." *Frankfurter judaistische Beiträge* 3:29–64.
Bokser, Baruch Micah. 1975. "Talmudic Names of the Iranian Festivals." *Journal of the American Oriental Society* 95.2:261–62.
———. 1979. "A Minor for 'Zimmun' (Y. Ber. 7:2, 11c) and Recensions of Yerushalmi." *Association for Jewish Studies Review* 4:1–25.
Bond, Shelagh M. 1957. "The Coinage of the Early Roman Empire." *Greece & Rome* 4.2:149–59.
Bonesho, Catherine. 2020. "The Terror of Time: The Festival of Dionysus and Saturnalia in Jewish Responses to Foreign Rule." *Journal for the Study of Judaism* 51:151–78.
Bonfil, Robert. 1971. "The Nature of Judaism in Raymundus Martini's *Pugio fidei*." *Tarbiz* 40:360–75.
Bonnin, Jérôme. 2010. "Les *Horologia Romana* dans les provinces hispaniques, mobilier, histoire et réalités archéologiques." *Archivo Español de Archeología* 83:183–98.
———. 2012a. "Horologia Romana: Cadrans et instrument à eau." *Les Dossiers d'Archéologie* 354:18–25.
———. 2012b. "Les horloges au quotidian dans l'Antiquité romaine." *Les Dossiers d'Archéologie* 354:70–75.
———. 2015. *La mesure du temps dans l'Antiquité*. Paris: Les Belles Lettres.
Bord, Licien-Jean. 2006. "L'adoption du calendrier babylonien au moment de l'Exil." In *Le Temps et les Temps dans les literatures juives et chrétiennes au tournant de notre ère*, edited by Christian Grappe and Jean-Claude Ingelaere, 21–36. Leiden: Brill.
Borchardt, Francis. 2015. "Sabbath Observance, Sabbath Innovation: The Hasmoneans and Their Legacy as Interpreters of the Law." *Journal for the Study of Judaism* 46:159–81.

Boustan, Ra'anan S. 2009. "Immolating Emperors: Spectacles of Imperial Suffering and the Making of a Jewish Minority Culture in Late Antiquity." *Biblical Interpretation* 17:207–38.

Bovon, François, and John M. Duffy. 2012. "A New Greek Fragment from Ariston of Pella's 'Dialogue of Jason and Papiscus.'" *Harvard Theological Review* 105.4:457–65.

Bowerman, Helen C. 1917. "The Birthday as a Commonplace of Roman Elegy." *Classical Journal* 21.5:310–18.

Bowersock, Glen Warren, Peter Brown, and Oleg Grabar, eds. 1999. *Late Antiquity: A Guide to the Postclassical*. Cambridge, MA: Harvard University Press.

Boyarin, Daniel. 1993. *Carnal Israel: Reading Sex in Talmudic Culture*. Berkeley: University of California Press.

———. 1994. *Intertextuality and the Reading of Midrash*. Bloomington: Indiana University Press.

———. 2004. *Border Lines: The Partition of Judaeo-Christianity*. Philadelphia: University of Pennsylvania Press.

———. 2008. "The Christian Invention of Judaism: The Theodosian Empire and the Rabbinic Refusal of Religion." In *Religion: Beyond a Concept*, edited by Hent de Vries, 150–77. New York: Fordham University Press.

———. 2012. *The Jewish Gospels: The Story of the Jewish Christ*. New York: The New Press.

———. 2015. *A Traveling Homeland: The Babylonian Talmud as Diaspora*. Philadelphia: University of Pennsylvania Press.

———. 2018. *Judaism: The Genealogy of a Modern Notion*. New Brunswick, NJ: Rutgers University Press.

Boyce, Mary. 1993. "Iranian Festivals." In *The Cambridge History of Iran*. Vol. 3: *The Seleucid, Parthian and Sasanian Periods*, edited by Ehsan Yarshater, 792–816. Cambridge: Cambridge University Press.

Boyle, A. J., and E. D. Woodard, trans. 2000. *Ovid: Fasti*. London: Penguin Books.

Bradshaw, Paul F. 2002. *The Search for the Origins of Christian Worship: Sources and Methods for the Study of Early Liturgy*. Oxford: Oxford University Press.

Bradshaw, Paul F., and Maxwell E. Johnson. 2011. *The Origins of Feasts, Fasts and Seasons in Early Christianity*. Collegeville, MN: Pueblo Books.

Brattston, David W. T. 2014. *Sabbath and Sunday among the Earliest Christians: When Was the Day of Public Worship?* Eugene, OR: Wipf and Stock.

Braude, William G., and Israel J. Kapstein. 1975. *Pesikta d-Rab Kahana: R. Kahana's Compilation of Discourses for Sabbaths and Festal Days*. Philadelphia: Jewish Publication Society.

Bregman, Marc. 1978. "Past and Present in Midrashic Literature." *Hebrew Annual Review* 2:45–59.

Breiterman, Zachary. 2002. "Cyclical Motions and the Force of Repetition in the Thought of Franz Rosenzweig." In *Beginning a Reading/Reading Beginnings: Towards a Hermeneutic of Jewish Texts*, edited by Aryeh Cohen and Shaul Magid, 215–38. New York: Seven Bridges Press.

Brendese, P. J. 2014. "Black Noise in White Time: Segregated Temporality and Mass Incarceration." In *Radical Future Pasts: Untimely Political Theory*, edited by Romand Coles, Mark Reinhardt, and George Shulman, 81–111. Lexington: University Press of Kentucky.

Brezis, David. 2015. *Between Zealotry and Grace: Anti-zealotic Trends in Rabbinic Thought*. Ramat Gan: Bar-Ilan University Press.

———. 2018. *The Sages and Their Hidden Debate with Christianity*. Jerusalem: Magnes Press.

Brin, Gershon. 2001. *The Concept of Time in the Bible and the Dead Sea Scrolls*. Leiden: Brill.
Brind'Amour, Pierre. 1983. *Le Calendrier romain: Recherches chronologiques*. Ottawa: Éditions de l'Université d'Ottawa.
Brinkman, Tobias. 2012. *Sundays at Sinai: A Jewish Congregation in Chicago*. Chicago: University of Chicago Press.
Brody, Robert. 1998. *The Geonim of Babylonia and the Shaping of Medieval Jewish Culture*. New Haven: Yale University Press.
Brown, Peter. 1992. *Power and Persuasion in Late Antiquity: Towards a Christian Empire*. Madison: University of Wisconsin Press.
——. 1993. *The Making of Late Antiquity*. Cambridge, MA: Harvard University Press.
——. 1995. *The Rise of Western Christendom: Triumph and Diversity 200–1000 AD*. Oxford: Blackwell.
——. 1999. "Pagan." In *Late Antiquity: A Guide to the Postclassical World*, edited by Glen W. Bowersock, Peter Brown, and Oleg Grabar, 625. Cambridge, MA: Belknap Press of Harvard University Press.
——. 2008. *The Body and Society: Men, Women, and Sexual Renunciation in Early Christianity*. 2nd ed. New York: Columbia University Press.
Brubaker, Rogers, and Frederick Cooper. 2000. "Beyond 'Identity.'" *Theory and Society* 29.1:1–47.
Buber, Solomon. 1883. *Midrash Tanhuma*. Vilna.
Büchler, Adolf. 1928. *Studies in Sin and Atonement in the Rabbinic Literature of the First Century*. Oxford: Oxford University Press.
Buckley, Thomas, and Alma Gottlieb. 1988. *Blood Magic: The Anthropology of Menstruation*. Berkeley: University of California Press.
Budge, E. A. Wallis, trans. 2018. *The Book of the Cave of Treasures*. London: Aziloth Books.
Bultrighini, Ilaria. 2018. "Thursday (dies Iovis) in the Later Roman Empire." *Papers of the British School at Rome* 86:61–84.
Bundvard, Mette. 2014. "Defending the Concept of Time in the Hebrew Bible." *Scandinavian Journal of the Old Testament* 28.2:280–97.
——. 2015. *Time in the Book of Ecclesiastes*. Oxford: Oxford University Press.
Burdick, Alan. 2017. *Why Time Flies: A Mostly Scientific Investigation*. New York: Simon & Schuster.
Burke, Megan M. 2018. "Gender as Lived Time: Reading *The Second Sex* for a Feminist Phenomenology of Temporality." *Hypatia* 33.1:111–27.
Burns, Joshua Ezra. 2016. *The Christian Schism in Jewish History and Jewish Memory*. Cambridge: Cambridge University Press.
Butler, Judith. 1990. *Gender Trouble: Feminism and the Subversion of Identity*. New York: Routledge.
——. 1993. *Bodies That Matter: On the Discursive Limits of "Sex."* New York: Routledge.
Butts, Aaron Michael, and Simcha Gross. 2017. *The History of the "Slave of Christ": From Jewish Child to Christian Martyr*. Piscataway, NJ: Gorgias Press.
Caballero-Navas, Carmen. 2004. *The Book of Women's Love and Jewish Medieval Medical Literature on Women: Sefer Ahavat Nashim*. London: Kegan Paul.
Cain, Emily. 2016. "Through a Mirror Darkly: Mystical Metaphors of Sight from Paul to Gregory of Nyssa and Augustine of Hippo." Ph.D. diss., Fordham University.
Calaway, Jared C. 2013. *The Sabbath and the Sanctuary: Access to God in the Letter to the Hebrews and Its Priestly Context*. Tübingen: Mohr Siebeck.
Cameron, Alan. 1966. "The Date and Identity of Macrobius." *Journal of Roman Studies* 56.1–2:25–38.

Cameron, Averil, and Stuart G. Hall. 1999. *Eusebius' Life of Constantine: Introduction, Translation and Commentary.* Oxford: Oxford University Press.

Campbell, Brian. 2012. *Rivers and the Power of Ancient Rome.* Chapel Hill: University of North Carolina Press.

Campbell, Robin. 1969. *Letters from a Stoic: Epistulae Morales ad Lucilium.* London: Penguin.

Carlebach, Elisheva. 2011. *Palaces of Time: Jewish Calendar and Culture in Early Modern Europe.* Cambridge, MA: Harvard University Press.

Carradice, Ian. 1982/83. "Coinage in Judaea in the Flavian Period, AD 70–96." *Israel Numismatics Journal* 6/7:14–21.

Carroll, Sean. 2010. *From Eternity to Here: The Quest for the Ultimate Theory of Time.* New York: Dutton.

Carson, D. A., ed. 1999. *From Sabbath to Lord's Day: A Biblical, Historical, and Theological Investigation.* Eugene, OR: Wipf and Stock.

Cary, Earnest, and Herbert B. Foster, trans. 1914. *Dio Cassius: Roman History.* Cambridge, MA: Harvard University Press.

Chakrabarty, Dipesh. 2000. *Provincializing Europe: Postcolonial Thought and Historical Difference.* Princeton: Princeton University Press.

Chalmers, Matthew. 2017. "Thinking with Samaritans and Cynthia Baker's *Jew*." *Marginalia.* https://marginalia.lareviewofbooks.org/thinking-samaritans-cynthia-bakers-jew/.

———. 2019. "Representations of Samaritans in Late Antique Jewish and Christian Texts." Ph.D. diss., University of Pennsylvania.

Chancey, Mark A. 2004. "City Coins and Roman Power in Palestine: From Pompey to the Great Revolt." In *Religion and Society in Roman Palestine: Old Questions, New Approaches*, edited by Douglas R. Edwards, 103–12. New York: Routledge.

Charles, R. H. 1913. *The Apocrypha and Pseudepigrapha of the Old Testament in English.* Vol. 2. Oxford: Clarendon Press.

Charlesworth, James H. 1983. *The Old Testament Pseudepigrapha.* Vol. 1. New York: Doubleday.

Chavel, Simeon. 2012. "The Face of God and the Etiquette of Eye-Contact: Visitation, Pilgrimage, and Prophetic Vision in Ancient Israelite and Early Jewish Imagination." *Jewish Studies Quarterly* 19.1:1–55.

Chazan, Robert. 1989. *Daggers of Faith: Thirteenth-Century Christian Missionizing and Jewish Response.* Berkeley: University of California Press.

———. 1994. "The Timebound and the Timeless: Medieval Jewish Narration of Events." *History and Memory* 6.1:5–34.

Chazon, Esther G. 1998. "Hymns and Prayers in the Dead Sea Scrolls." In *The Dead Sea Scrolls after Fifty Years: A Comprehensive Assessment*, vol. 1, edited by James C. VanderKam and Peter W. Flint, 244–70. Leiden: Brill.

Clarysse, Willy, Sofie Remijsen, and Mark Depauw. 2010. "Observing the Sabbath in the Roman Empire: A Case Study." *Scripta Classica Israelica* 29:51–57.

Coggins, R. J. 1987. "Samaritans in Post-biblical Literature." In *Josephus, Judaism, and Christianity*, edited by Louis H. Feldman and Gohei Hata, 257–73. Detroit: Wayne State University Press.

Cohen, Elizabeth. 2018. *The Political Value of Time: Citizenship, Duration, and Democratic Justice.* Cambridge: Cambridge University Press.

Cohen, Gerson. 1967. "Esau as Symbol in Early Medieval Thought." In *Jewish Medieval and Renaissance Studies*, edited by Alexander Altmann, 19–48. Cambridge, MA: Harvard University Press.

Cohen, Jeremy. 1982. *The Friars and the Jews: The Evolution of Medieval Anti-Judaism.* Ithaca, NY: Cornell University Press.

———. 1999. *Living Letters of the Law: Ideas of the Jew in Medieval Christianity.* Berkeley: University of California Press.

Cohen, Mark R. 2017. *Maimonides and the Merchants: Jewish Law and Society in the Medieval Islamic World.* Philadelphia: University of Pennsylvania Press.

Cohen, Naomi G. 1995. *Philo Judaeus: His Universe of Discourse.* Frankfurt am Main: Peter Lang.

Cohen, Shaye J. D. 1981. "Epigraphical Rabbis." *Jewish Quarterly Review* 72:1–17.

———. 1991. "Menstruants and the Sacred in Judaism and Christianity." In *Women's History and Ancient History*, edited by Sarah B. Pomeroy, 273–99. Chapel Hill: University of North Carolina Press.

———. 1992. "Purity and Piety: The Separation of Menstruants from the Sancta." In *Daughters of the King: Women and the Synagogue*, edited by Susan Grossman and Rivka Haut, 103–15. Philadelphia: Jewish Publication Society.

———. 1998. "The Conversion of Antoninus." In *The Talmud Yerushalmi and Graeco-Roman Culture I*, edited by Peter Schäfer, 141–72. Tübingen: Mohr Siebeck.

———. 1999a. *The Beginnings of Jewishness: Boundaries, Varieties, Uncertainties.* Berkeley: University of California Press.

———. 1999b. "Purity, Piety, and Polemic: Medieval Rabbinic Denunciations of 'Incorrect' Purification Practices." In *Women and Water: Menstruation in Jewish Life and Law*, edited by Rahel R. Wasserfall, 82–100. Hanover, NH: Brandeis University Press.

———. 2005. *Why Aren't Jewish Women Circumcised?: Gender and Covenant in Judaism.* Berkeley: University of California Press.

———. 2008. "Common Judaism in Greek and Latin Authors." In *Redefining First-Century Jewish and Christian Identities: Essays in Honor of Ed Parish Sanders*, edited by Fabian E. Udoh, 69–87. Notre Dame, IN: University of Notre Dame Press.

———. 2010. "Sabbath Law and Mishnah Shabbat in Origen De Principiis." *Jewish Quarterly Review* 17.2:160–89.

———. 2012. "Dancing, Clapping, Meditating: Jewish and Christian Observance of the Sabbath in Pseudo-Ignatius." In *Judaea-Palaestina, Babylon and Rome: Jews in Antiquity*, edited by Benjamin Isaac and Yuval Shahar, 29–51. Tübingen: Mohr Siebeck.

Cohn, Naftali S. 2012. *The Memory of the Temple and the Making of the Rabbis.* Philadelphia: University of Pennsylvania Press.

———. 2018. "Sacred Space in the Mishnah: From Temple to Synagogue and . . . City." In *La Question de la "Sacerdotalisation" dans le Judaïsm Synagogal, le Christianisme et le Rabbinisme*, edited by Simon C. Mimouni and Louis Painchaud, 85–121. Turnhout: Brepols.

Cohn, Yehudah B. 2008. *Tangled Up in Text: Tefillin and the Ancient World.* Atlanta: Society of Biblical Literature.

———. 2011. "The Graeco-Roman Trade Fair and the Rabbis." *Journal of the American Oriental Society* 131.2:187–93.

Colditz, Iris. 2009. "Manichaean Time-Management: Laymen between Religious and Secular Duties." In *New Light on Manichaeism: Papers from the Sixth International Congress on Manichaeism*, edited by Jason BeDuhn, 73–99. Leiden: Brill.

Coleman, Monica A. 2008. *Making a Way Out of No Way: A Womanist Theology.* Minneapolis: Fortress Press.

Collins, Adela Yarbro. 1996. *Cosmology and Eschatology in Jewish and Christian Apocalypticism.* Leiden: Brill.

Collins, John J. 1983. *Between Athens and Jerusalem: Jewish Identity in the Hellenistic Diaspora.* New York: Crossroad.

———. 1997. "The Expectation of the End in the Dead Sea Scrolls." In *Eschatology, Messianism, and the Dead Sea Scrolls*, edited by Craig A. Evans and Peter W. Flint, 74–90. Grand Rapids, MI: Eerdmans.

———. 2010. "Artapanus Revisited." In *From Judaism to Christianity: Tradition and Transition: A Festschrift for Thomas H. Tobin, S.J., On the Occasion of His Sixty-fifth Birthday*, edited by Patricia Walters, 59–68. Leiden: Brill.

Collins, Nina L. 2014. *Jesus, the Sabbath and the Jewish Debate: Healing on the Sabbath in the 1st and 2nd Centuries.* London: Bloomsbury.

Colson, Francis H. 1926. *The Week: An Essay on the Development of the Seven-Day Cycle.* Cambridge: Cambridge University Press.

———. 1939, 1999. *Philo.* Cambridge, MA: Harvard University Press.

Connolly, R. Hugh. 1929. *Didascalia Apostolorum.* Oxford: Clarendon Press.

Cooley, Alison E. 2011. "History and Inscriptions, Rome." In *The Oxford History of Historical Writing: Volume I: Beginnings to AD 600*, edited by Andrew Feldherr and Grant Hardy, 244–64. Oxford: Oxford University Press.

Coope, Ursula. 2005. *Time for Aristotle.* Oxford: Oxford University Press.

Cooper, Brittney. 2016. "The Racial Politics of Time." TEDWomen Video, 12:30. https://www.ted.com/talks/brittney_cooper_the_racial_politics_of_time?language=en #t-6509.

Copeland, Rita. 1995. *Rhetoric, Hermeneutics, and Translation in the Middle Ages: Academic Traditions and Vernacular Texts.* Cambridge: Cambridge University Press.

Costa, C. D. N., trans. 1997. *Seneca: On the Shortness of Life.* New York: Penguin Books.

Costa, José. 2010. "Le corps de Dieu dans le judaïsme rabbinique ancien: Problèmes d'interprétation." *Revue de l'Histoire des Religions* 227.3:286–316.

———. 2012. "La représentation anthropomorphique du divin chez les rabbins de l'Antiquité." In *Dieux et déesses d'Arabie*, edited by Isabell Sachet, 149–77. Paris: De Boccard.

Cotton, Paul. 1993. *From Sabbath to Sunday: A Study in Early Christianity.* Bethlehem: Times Publishing.

Danby, Herbert. 1933. *The Mishnah.* Oxford: Clarendon Press.

Daube, David. 1956. *The New Testament and Rabbinic Judaism.* London: Athlone Press.

Davies, Karen. 1990. *Women, Time and the Weaving of the Strands of Everyday Life.* Aldershot: Avebury.

Davis, Phillip. 1905. "Making Americans of Russian Jews." *Outlook* (July 8):631–35.

de Blois, François. 1996. "The Persian Calendar." *Iran* 34.1:39–54.

de Certeau, Michel. 1984. *The Practice of Everyday Life.* Translated by Steven Rendall. Berkeley: University of California Press.

de Lange, Nicholas Robert Michael. 1976. *Origen and the Jews: Studies in Jewish-Christian Relations in Third-Century Palestine.* Cambridge: Cambridge University Press.

de Ligt, Lukas. 1993. *Fairs and Markets in the Roman Empire: Economic and Social Aspects of Periodic Trade in a Pre-Industrial Society.* Amsterdam: J. C. Gieben.

de Madariaga, Salvador. 1940. *Christopher Columbus: Being the Life of the Very Magnificent Lord Don Cristóbal Cólon.* New York: Macmillan.

De Troyer, Kristin, Judith A. Herbert, Judith Ann Johnson, and Anne-Marie Korte, eds. 2003. *Wholly Woman, Holy Blood: A Feminist Critique of Purity and Impurity.* Harrisburg, PA: Trinity Press International.

de Vries, S. J. 1975. *Yesterday, Today and Tomorrow: Time and History in the Old Testament.* Grand Rapids, MI: Eerdmans.

Dean-Jones, Lesley. 1996. *Women's Bodies in Classical Greek Science*. Oxford: Clarendon Press.
Degrassi, Atilius. 1937. *Inscriptiones Italiae, Volume 13: Fasti et Elogia*. Fasc. 1, *Fasti Consulares et Triumphales*. Rome: Libreria dello Stato.
———. 1963. *Inscriptiones Italiae, Volume 13: Fasti et Elogia*. Fasc. 2, *Fasti Anni Numani et Iuliani*. Rome: Libreria dello Stato.
Delaney, Janice, Mary Jane Lupton, and Emily Toth. 1976. *The Curse: A Cultural History of Menstruation*. New York: Dutton.
Deleuze, Gilles. 1968. *Différence and Repetition*. Paris: Presses Universitaires de France.
Dench, Emma. 2005. *Romulus' Asylum: Roman Identities from the Age of Alexander to the Age of Hadrian*. Oxford: Oxford University Press.
Deremetz, Alain. 2013. "Numa in Augustan Poetry." In *Augustan Poetry and the Roman Republic*, edited by Joseph Farrell and Damien P. Nelis. Oxford: Oxford University Press.
Derrida, Jacques. 1968. "Différance." *Bulletin de la Société française de philosophie* 62.3:73–101.
Destro, Adriana. 1996. "The Witness of Times: An Anthropological Reading of *Niddah*." In *Reading Leviticus: A Conversation with Mary Douglas*, edited by John F. A. Sawyer, 124–38. Sheffield: Sheffield Academic Press.
Dimant, Devorah. 2000. "Resurrection, Restoration, and Time-Curtailing in Qumran, Early Judaism, and Christianity." *Revue de Qumran* 19.4:527–48.
———. 2006. "Temps, Torah et prophétie à Qoumrân." In *Le Temps et les Temps dans les literatures juives et chrétiennes au tournant de notre ère*, edited by Christian Grappe and Jean-Claude Ingelaere, 147–67. Leiden: Brill.
———. 2009. "Exegesis and Time in the Pesharim from Qumran." *Revue des Études Juives* 168.3–4:373–93.
Dinari, Yedidyah. 1979–80. "The Customs of Menstrual Impurity: Their Origin and Development." *Tarbiz* 49:302–24. [Hebrew]
Dinshaw, Carolyn. 2012. *How Soon Is Now? Medieval Texts, Amateur Readers, and the Queerness of Time*. Durham, NC: Duke University Press.
Divjak, Johannes, and Wolfgang Wischmeyers, eds. 2014. *Das Kalenderhandbuch von 354: Der Chronograph des Filocalus*. 2 vols. Vienna: Holzhausen.
Dixon, Suzanne. 1992. *The Roman Family*. Baltimore: Johns Hopkins University Press.
Dodd, C. H. 1958. *Parables of the Kingdom*. Welwyn: James Nisbet and Company.
Doering, Lutz. 1997. "The Concept of the Sabbath in the Book of Jubilees." In *Studies in the Book of Jubilees*, edited by Matthias Albani, Jörg Frey, and Armin Lange, 179–205. Tübingen: Mohr Siebeck.
———. 1999. *Schabbat: Sabbathalacha und-praxis im Früjudentum*. Tübingen: Mohr Siebeck.
———. 2005. "Excerpted Texts in Second Temple Judaism: A Survey of the Evidence." In *Beiträge zur Technik des Sammelns und Kompilierens griechischer Texte von der Antike bis zum Humanismus*, edited by Rosa Maria Piccione and Matthias Perkams, 4–15. Alessandria: Edizioni dell'Orso.
———. 2010. "Sabbath Laws in the New Testament Gospels." In *The New Testament and Rabbinic Literature*, edited by Reimund Bieringer, Florentino García Martínez, Didier Pollefeyt, and Peter J. Tomson, 207–53. Leiden: Brill.
———. 2015. "Jesus und der Sabbat im Licht der Qumrantexte." In *Jesus, Paulus und die Texte von Qumran*, edited Jörg Frey and Enno Edzard Popkes, 33–61. Tübingen: Mohr Siebeck.
Dohrmann, Natalie B., and Annette Yoshiko Reed, eds. 2013. *Jews, Christians, and the*

Roman Empire: The Poetics of Power in Late Antiquity. Philadelphia: University of Pennsylvania Press.

Dohrn-van Rossum, Gerhard. 1996. *History of the Hour: Clocks and Modern Temporal Orders*. Chicago: University of Chicago Press.

Dolansky, Fanny. 2008. "*Togam Virilem Sumere*: Coming of Age in the Roman World." In *Roman Dress and the Fabrics of Roman Culture*, edited by Jonathan Edmondson and Alison Keith, 47–70. Toronto: University of Toronto Press.

———. 2010. "Celebrating the Saturnalia: Religious Ritual and Roman Domestic Life." In *Companion to Families in the Greek and Roman Worlds*, edited by Beryl Rawson, 488–503. Hoboken, NJ: Wiley.

Dolev, Yuval. 2007. *Time and Realism: Metaphysical and Antimetaphysical Perspectives*. Cambridge, MA: MIT Press.

Dolgopolski, Sergey. 2012. *The Open Past: Subjectivity and Remembering in the Talmud*. New York: Fordham University Press.

Doneus, Nives, and Armin Lange, eds. 2010. "Golden Words: An Ancient Jewish Amulet from Austria and the Jewish Presence in Roman Pannonia." *Journal of Ancient Judaism* 1.2:141–277.

Douglas, Mary. 1966, 2002. *Purity and Danger: An Analysis of Concepts of Pollution and Taboo*. London: Routledge Classics.

Douglass, Frederick. 1855. *My Bondage and My Freedom*. London: Partridge and Oakley.

Draycott, Jane. 2017. *Bodies of Evidence: Ancient Anatomical Votives Past, Present and Future*. London: Routledge.

Du Bois, W. E. B. 1903. *The Souls of Black Folk*. New York: Penguin.

Dubs, Jean-Claude. 2006. "4Q317 et le role de l'observation de la Pleine Lune pour la determination du temps à Qoumrân." In *Le Temps et les Temps dans les literatures juives et chrétiennes au tournant de notre ère*, edited by Christian Grappe and Jean-Claude Ingelaere, 37–54. Leiden: Brill.

Dunning, Benjamin H. 2011. *Specters of Paul: Sexual Difference in Early Christian Thought*. Philadelphia: University of Pennsylvania Press.

Durkheim, Émile. 2001. *The Elementary Forms of Religious Life*. Translated by Carol Cosman. Oxford: Oxford University Press.

Eager, George B. 1939. "Meals, Meal-time." In *The International Standard Bible Encyclopedia*, edited by James Orr. Grand Rapids, MI: Eerdmans.

Eck, Werner. 2007. *Rom und Judaea: Fünf Vorträge zur Römischen Herrschaft in Palaestina*. Tübingen: Mohr Siebeck.

Edmonds, Radcliffe G. III. 2003. "At the Seizure of the Moon: The Absence of the Moon in the Mithras Liturgy." In *Prayer, Magic, and the Stars in the Ancient and Late Antique World*, edited by Scott B. Noegel, Joel Thomas Walker, and Brannon M. Wheeler, 223–39. University Park: Pennsylvania State University Press.

Ehrlich, Simeon D. 2012. "'Horae' in Roman Funerary Inscriptions." Ph.D. diss., University of Western Ontario.

Ehrman, Bart D. 1999. *Jesus: Apocalyptic Prophet of the New Millennium*. Oxford: Oxford University Press.

———. 2018. *The Triumph of Christianity: How a Forbidden Religion Swept the World*. New York: Simon and Schuster.

Eidinow, Esther, and Lisa Maurizio, eds. 2020. *Narrative Constructions of Gender and Time in the Greco-Roman Mediterranean*. Abington: Taylor & Francis.

Eitrem, S., and L. Amundsen. 1936. *Papyri Osloense III*. Oslo: Dybwad.

Ekirch, A. Roger. 2005. *At Day's Close: Night in Times Past*. New York: W. W. Norton.

Eliade, Mircea. 1954. *Cosmos and History: The Myth of Eternal Return.* Translated by Willard R. Trask. New York: Harper Torchbooks.

———. 1959. *The Sacred and Profane: The Nature of Religion.* Translated by Willard R. Trask. Orlando: Harcourt.

Eliav, Yaron. 2005. *God's Mountain: The Temple Mount in Time, Place and Memory.* Baltimore: Johns Hopkins University Press.

Elior, Rachel. 2004. *The Three Temples: On the Emergence of Jewish Mysticism.* Oxford: Littman Library of Jewish Civilization.

Elizur, Shulamit. 2019. *Sod MeShalshei Qodesh: The Qedushta from Its Origins until the Era of Rabbi Elazar be-Rabbi Qalir.* Jerusalem: Magnes Press. [Hebrew]

Elizur, Shulamit, and Michael Rand. 2013. *Rabbi Elazar bi-Rabbi Qalir: Piyyutim for Rosh HaShanah.* Jerusalem: International Association for Jewish Studies. [Hebrew]

Elman, Yaakov. 2007a. "Middle Persian Culture and Babylonian Sages: Accommodation and Resistance in the Shaping of Rabbinic Legal Tradition." In *The Cambridge Companion to the Talmud and Rabbinic Literature,* edited by Charlotte Elisheva Fonrobert and Martin S. Jaffee, 165–97. New York: Cambridge University Press.

———. 2007b. "'He in His Cloak and She in Her Cloak': Conflicting Images of Sexuality in Sasanian Mesopotamia." In *Discussing Cultural Differences: Text, Context, and Non-Text in Rabbinic Judaism,* edited by Rivka Ulmer, 129–63. Lanham, MD: University Press of America.

Elmslie, W. A. L. 1911. *The Mishnah on Idolatry, 'Aboda Zara.* Cambridge: Cambridge University Press.

Emanuel, Simcha. 2007. "The Seven Clean Days: A Chapter in the History of the Halakhah." *Tarbiz* 76.1–2:233–54.

Emerton, Ephraim, trans. 1976, 2000. *The Letters of Saint Boniface.* New York: Columbia University Press.

Epstein, Isidore, trans. 1935. *The Babylonian Talmud: Seder Nezikin.* London: Soncino.

Epstein, Jacob Nahum. 1965. *Mavo le-nusah ha-Mishnah.* Jerusalem: Magnes Press.

Epstein, Jacob Nahum, and Ezra Zion Melamed. 1959. *Mekhilta de-Rabbi Shimon ben Yohai.* Jerusalem: Meqitze Nirdamim.

Epstein, Nahum Yaacov Halevi. 1948. *Introduction to the Mishnaic Text.* Jerusalem: Magnes Press.

Eshel, Esther, Hanan Eshel, and Armin Lange. 2010. "'Hear, O Israel' in Gold: An Ancient Amulet from Halbturn in Austria." *Journal of Ancient Judaism* 1.1:43–64.

Eskenazi, Tamara C., Daniel J. Harrington, William H. Shea. 1991. *The Sabbath in Jewish and Christian Traditions.* New York: Crossroads.

Evans, Harry B. 1978. "Horace, Satires 2.7: Saturnalia and Satire." *Classical Journal* 73.4:307–12.

Fabian, Johannes. 2014. *Time and the Other: How Anthropology Makes Its Object.* 2nd ed. New York: Columbia University Press.

Falk, Dan. 2008. *In Search of Time: The History, Physics, and Philosophy of Time.* New York: Thomas Dunne Books.

Falk, Daniel K. 1998. *Daily, Sabbath, and Festival Prayers in the Dead Sea Scrolls.* Leiden: Brill.

Feeney, Denis. 2007. *Caesar's Calendar: Ancient Time and the Beginnings of History.* Berkeley: University of California Press.

———. 2010. "Time and Calendar." In *The Oxford Handbook of Roman Studies,* edited by Alessandro Barchiesi and Walter Scheidel, 882–94. Oxford: Oxford University Press.

Feinstein, Levavi. 2014. *Sexual Pollution in the Hebrew Bible.* Oxford: Oxford University Press.

Feinstein, Moshe. 2012. *Sefer Igrot Moshe*. New York: Beth Medrash L'Torah V'Horaah.
Feldman, Louis. 1991. "Abba Kolon and the Founding of Rome." *Jewish Quarterly Review* 81.3/4:239–66.
———. 1992. "Josephus' Attitude toward the Samaritans: A Study in Ambivalence." In *Jewish Sects, Religious Movements, and Political Parties*, edited by Menachem Mor, 23–45. Omaha: Creighton University Press.
———. 1999. *Flavian Josephus: Translation and Commentary, Judean Antiquities 1–4*. Leiden: Brill.
Feldman, Ron H. 2001. "'On Your New Moons': The Feminist Transformation of the Jewish New Moon Festival." *Journal of Women and Religion* 19:25–51.
———. 2012. "Tame and Wild Time in the Qumran and Rabbinic Calendars." In *Living the Lunar Calendar*, edited by Jonathan Ben-Dov, Wayne Horowitz, and John M. Steele, 191–210. Oxford: Oxbow Books.
Felski, Rita. 2000. *Doing Time: Feminist Theory and Postmodern Culture*. New York: New York University Press.
Fingerhut, Eugene R. 1967. "Were the Massachusetts Puritans Hebraic?" *New England Quarterly* 40:521–31.
Finkelstein, Louis, ed. 1939, 2001. *Sifre on Deuteronomy*. New York: Jewish Theological Seminary.
Fishbane, Michael. 2003. *Biblical Myth and Rabbinic Mythmaking*. Oxford: Oxford University Press.
Fishbane, Simcha. 2007. *Deviancy in Early Rabbinic Literature: A Collection of Socio-Anthropological Essays*. Leiden: Brill.
Fisher, Cass. 2010. "Beyond the Homiletical: Rabbinic Theology as Discursive and Reflective Practice." *Journal of Religion* 90.2:199–236.
Fishman, Talya. 1992. "A Kabbalistic Perspective on Gender-Specific Commandments: On the Interplay of Symbols and Society." *Association for Jewish Studies Review* 17:199–245.
Fitzpatrick, Matthew P. 2011. "Provincializing Rome: The Indian Ocean Trade Network and Roman Imperialism." *Journal of World History* 22.1:27–54.
Flasch, Kurt. 1993. *Was ist Zeit? Augustinus von Hippo, Das XI. Buch der Confessiones: Historisch-philosophische Studie*. Frankfurt: Klostermann.
Fleischer, Ezra. 2007. "The Recitation of the Evening Shema as a Custom from the Land of Israel: Between Ancient *Halakhah* and Later Custom." In *Torah LiShma: Research in Jewish Studies in Honor of Professor Shamma Yehudah Friedman*, edited by David Golinkin, Moshe Benovitz, Mordechai Akiva Friedman, Menachem Schmelzer, and Daniel Sperber. 268–302. Jerusalem: JTS Press. [Hebrew]
Fleming, Daniel E. 2000. *Time at Emar: The Cultic Calendar and the Rituals from the Diviner's Archive*. Winona Lake, IN: Eisenbrauns.
Flemming, Rebecca. 2000. *Medicine and the Making of Roman Women: Gender, Nature, and Authority from Celsus to Galen*. Oxford: Oxford University Press.
Flower, Harriet I. 2017. *The Dancing Lares and the Serpent in the Garden*. Princeton: Princeton University Press.
Flusser, David. 1968. *Jesus in Selbstzeugnissen und Bilddokumenten*. Reinbeck bei Hamburg: Rowohlt.
———. 1988. *Judaism and the Origins of Christianity*. Jerusalem: Magnes Press.
Fonrobert, Charlotte Elisheva. 1999. "Yalta's Ruse: Resistance against Rabbinic Menstrual Authority in Talmudic Literature." In *Women and Water: Menstruation in Jewish Life and Law*, edited by Rahel R. Wasserfall, 60–81. Hanover, NH: Brandeis University Press.

———. 2000. *Menstrual Purity: Rabbinic and Christian Reconstructions of Biblical Gender*. Stanford: Stanford University Press.

———. 2001a. "The Didascalia Apostolorum: A Mishnah for the Disciples of Jesus." *Journal of Early Christian Studies* 9.4:483–511.

———. 2001b. "When Women Walk in the Way of Their Fathers: On Gendering the Rabbinic Claim for Authority." *Journal of the History of Sexuality* 10.3–4:398–415.

———. 2006. "The Semiotics of the Sexed Body in Early Halakhic Discourse." In *How Should Rabbinic Literature Be Read in the Modern World?*, edited by Matthew Kraus, 79–108. Piscataway, NJ: Gorgias Press.

———. 2008. "Blood and Law: Uterine Fluids and Rabbinic Maps of Identity." *Henoch* 30.2:243–66.

———. 2018. "Menstruant as *Zavah*: How the Laws of Niddah Developed." thetorah.com: https://thetorah.com/menstruant-as-zavah-how-the-laws-of-niddah-developed/.

Foster, Johanna. 1996. "Menstrual Time: The Sociocognitive Mapping of 'The Menstrual Cycle.'" *Sociological Forum* 11.3:523–47.

Foucault, Michel. 1986. *The Care of the Self*. Translated by Robert Hurley. New York: Pantheon Books.

Fox, Michael V. 1998. "Time in Qohelet's 'Catalogue of Times.'" *Journal of Northwest Semitic Languages* 24:25–39.

Fraade, Steven D. 1986. "Ascetical Aspects of Ancient Judaism." In *Jewish Spirituality: From the Bible through the Middle Ages*, edited by Arthur Green, 253–88. New York: Crossroad Press.

———. 1991. *From Tradition to Commentary: Torah and Its Interpretation in the Midrash Sifre to Deuteronomy*. Albany: State University of New York Press.

———. 2009–10. "Theory, Practice, and Polemic in Ancient Jewish Calendars." *Diné Israel: Studies in Halakhah and Jewish Law* 26/27:147–81.

Fraenkel, Jonah. 1987. *Time and Its Role in the Aggadic Story*. Jerusalem: International Center for University Teaching of Jewish Civilization.

———. 1989a. "Time and Its Role the Aggadic Story." *Binah* 2:31–56.

———. 1989b. *Studies in Jewish Thought*. Edited by Joseph Dan. New York: Praeger.

———. 1989c. "Time and Its Role in Aggadic Narrative." In *Studies in Jewish Thought*, edited by Joseph Dan, 31–56. New York: Praeger.

Frankel, Zacharias. 1923. *Darkhe ha-Mishnah*. Warsaw: Tsailingold.

Frankfurter, David. 2018. *Christianizing Egypt: Syncretism and Local Worlds in Late Antiquity*. Princeton: Princeton University Press.

Fraschetti, Augusto. 1999. *La Conversione: Da Roma Pagana a Roma Cristiana*. Rome: Laterza.

Fraser, J. T. 1966. *The Voices of Time: A Cooperative Survey of Man's Views of Time as Expressed by the Sciences and by the Humanities*. New York: George Braziller.

Fredriksen, Paula. 2009. "Historical Integrity, Interpretive Freedom: The Philosopher's Paul and the Problem of Anachronism." In *St. Paul and the Philosophers*, edited by John D. Caputo and Linda Martin Alcoff, 61–73. Bloomington: Indiana University Press.

Fredriksen, Paula, and Oded Irshai. 2015. "Include Me Out: Tertullian, the Rabbis, and the Graeco-Roman City." In *Identité à travers l'éthique: Nouvelles perspectives sur la formation des identités collectives dans le monde gréco-romain*, edited by Katell Berthelot, Ron Naiwald, and Daniel Stökl ben Ezra, 117–32. Turnhout: Brepols.

Freedman, Harry. 1983. *Midrash Rabbah: Genesis*. Vols. 1–2. London: Soncino Press.

Freeman, Elizabeth. 2010. *Time Binds: Queer Temporalities, Queer Histories*. Durham, NC: Duke University Press.

Freidenfelds, Lara. 2009. *The Modern Period: Menstruation in Twentieth Century America.* Baltimore: Johns Hopkins University Press.

Friedheim, Emmanuel. 2000. "On the Question of the Role of the Roman Army in the Spread of Roman Cults in Judea and Samaria after the Destruction of the Second Temple." *Meḥkerei yehudah veshomron* 9:201–18. [Hebrew]

———. 2004. "Public Festivals in Mishnah Avodah Zarah 1:2 and the Cultural Reality in Palestine and Its Surroundings in the Time of the Mishnah and the Talmud." *Bekhol Derakhekha' Da'ehu* 14:47–72. [Hebrew]

———. 2006a. "A New Study of Historical Realia in the First *Mishnah* of the Chapter 'Before Their Festivals.'" *Zion* 71.3:273–300.

———. 2006b. *Rabbinisme et Paganisme en Palestine romaine: Étude historique des Realia talmudiques (Ier–IVème siècles).* Leiden: Brill.

Friedman, Mordechai A. 1990. "Menstrual Impurity and Sectarianism in the Writings of the Geonim and of Moses and Abraham Maimonides." In *Maimonidean Studies*, vol. 1, edited by Arthur Hyman, 1–21. New York: Yeshiva University Press.

Friedman, Shamma. 2005. "The Language of the Festivals: Light on the Fourteenth." In *Studies in Talmud and Midrash: Memory Volume for Tirzah Lifshitz*, edited by Meir Bar-Asher et al., 475–519. Jerusalem: Bialik.

———. 2008. "*Meolam ve-ad Olam.*" *Leshonenu* 70:77–97. [Hebrew]

———. 2014. *Studies in the Language and Terminology of Talmudic Literature.* Jerusalem: Academy of Hebrew Language.

Friesen, Steven J. 2001. *Imperial Cults and the Apocalypse of John: Reading Revelation in the Ruins.* Oxford: Oxford University Press.

Frölich, Ida. 1996. *Time and Times and Half a Time: Historical Consciousness in the Jewish Literature of the Persian and Hellenistic Eras.* Sheffield: Sheffield Academic Press.

Frumer, Yulia. 2014. "Translating Time: Habits of Western Style Timekeeping in Late Tokugawa Japan." *Technology and Culture* 55.4:785–820.

———. 2018. *Making Time: Astronomical Time Measurement in Tokugawa Japan.* Chicago: University of Chicago Press.

Funkenstein, Amos. 1985. "A Schedule for the End of the World: The Origins and Persistence of the Apocalyptic Mentality." In *Visions of Apocalypse*, edited by Saul Friedlander, 44–60. New York: Holmes & Meier.

———. 1989. "Collective Memory and Historical Consciousness." *History and Memory* 1.1:5–26.

———. 1993. *Perceptions of Jewish History.* Berkeley: University of California Press.

Furstenberg, Yair. 2010. "Eating in a State of Purity in the Tannaitic Period: Tractate *Tohorot* and Its Historical and Cultural Contexts." Ph.D. diss., Hebrew University of Jerusalem.

———. 2013. "The Rabbinic Ban on Maaseh Bereshit: Sources, Contexts and Concerns." In *Jewish and Christian Cosmogony in Late Antiquity*, edited by Sarit Kattan Gribetz and Lance Jenott, 39–63. Tübingen: Mohr Siebeck.

———. 2014. "Genital Discharge: Judaism." In *Encyclopedia of the Bible and Its Reception 9*, edited Dale C. Allison Jr., 1199–1204. Berlin: de Gruyter.

———, ed. 2016a. *Jewish and Christian Communal Identities in the Roman World.* Leiden: Brill.

———. 2016b. *Purity and Community in Antiquity: Traditions of the Law from Second Temple Judaism to the Mishnah.* Jerusalem: Magnes Press.

———. 2017a. "The Status of the Samaritans in Tannaitic Halakhah in Light of the Roman Concept of Citizenship." *Zion* 82:157–92. [Hebrew]

———. 2017b. "Sabbath Laws at Qumran: Between Biblical Language and Traditions of Halakhah." *Megillot* 13:271–81.

———. 2019. "The Rabbis and the Roman Citizenship Model: The Case of the Samaritans." In *In the Crucible of Empire: The Impact of Roman Citizenship upon Greeks, Jews and Christians*, edited by Katell Berthelot and Jonathan Price, 181–216. Leuven: Peeters.

Gafni, Isaiah M. 1969. "Hayyahasim ben hayyehudim vehashomronim bitqufat hammishnah vehattalmud." Master's thesis, Hebrew University of Jerusalem.

———. 1996. "Concepts of Periodization and Causality in Talmudic Literature." *Jewish History* 10.1:21–38.

———. 1997. *Land, Center and Diaspora: Jewish Constructs in Late Antiquity*. Sheffield: Sheffield Academic Press.

———. 2007. "Rabbinic Historiography and Representations of the Past." In *The Cambridge Companion to the Talmud and Rabbinic Literature*, edited by Charlotte Elisheva Fonrobert and Martin S. Jaffee, 295–312. New York: Cambridge University Press.

Gager, John G. 1985. *The Origins of Anti-Semitism: Attitudes toward Judaism in Pagan and Christian Antiquity*. New York: Oxford University Press.

———. 2000. *Reinventing Paul*. Oxford: Oxford University Press.

———. 2015. *Who Made Early Christianity? The Jewish Lives of the Apostle Paul*. New York: Columbia University Press.

García Martínez, Florentino, and Eibert Tigchelaar. 1998. *The Dead Sea Scrolls Study Edition*. Grand Rapids, MI: Eerdmans.

Garnsey, Peter. 2004. "Roman Citizenship and Roman Law in the Late Empire." In *Approaching Late Antiquity: The Transformation from Early to Late Empire*, edited by Simon Swain and Mark Edwards, 133–55. Oxford: Oxford University Press.

Gautschy, Rita. 2014. "A Ramesside Sundial in the Valley of the Kings." *Zeitschrift für Ägyptische Sprache und Altertumskunde* 141.1:3–14.

Geiger, Joseph. 2004. "The Tombs of Remus and Romulus: An Overlooked Source." *Athenaeum: Studi di letteratura e Storia dell/antichità* 92:245–54.

———. 2008. *The First Hall of Fame*. Leiden: Brill.

Gell, Alfred. 2001. *The Anthropology of Time: Cultural Constructions of Temporal Maps and Images*. Oxford: Berg Publishers.

Gershonzon, Rosalie, and Elieser Slomovic. 1985. "A Second Century Jewish-Gnostic Debate: Rabbi Jose ben Halafta and the Matrona." *Journal for the Study of Judaism* 16:1–41.

Gibbs, Sharon. 1976. *Greek and Roman Sundials*. New Haven: Yale University Press.

Gignoux, Philippe. 1990. "Hexaéméron et millénarisme: Quelques motifs de comparaison entre Mazdéisme et Judaïsme." *Irano-Judaica* 2:72–84.

Gilula, Dwora. 1986. "Facetious References to Jews in Roman Literature." *Jerusalem Studies in Jewish Folklore* 9:7–37. [Hebrew]

Ginzberg, Louis. 1919. "Tamid: The Oldest Treatise of the Mishnah." *Journal of Jewish Lore and Philosophy* 1:33–44.

———. 1971. *A Commentary on the Palestinian Talmud: A Study of the Development of Halakhah and Haggadah in Palestine and Babylonia*. New York: Ktav.

Girardet, Klaus Martin. 2006. "Vom Sonnentag zum Sonntag: Die *dies solis* in Gezetzgebung und Politik Konstanins." *Zeitschrift für antikes Christentum* 11:279–310.

———. 2008. "L'invention du dimanche: Du jour de soleil au dimanche: Les *dies solis* dans la legislation et la politique de Constantin le Grand." In *Empire chrétien et église aux IVe et Ve siècles: Intégration ou concordat? Le témoignage du Code Théodosien*, edited by Jean-Noël Guinot and François Richard, 341–70. Paris: Editions du Cerf.

Gitler, Haim, and Gil Gambash, eds. 2017. *Faces of Power: Roman Gold Coins from the Victor A. Adda Collection*. Jerusalem: Israel Museum.

Gitlitz, David Martin. 1996, 2002. *Secrecy and Deceit: The Religion of the Crypto-Jews*. Philadelphia: Jewish Publication Society; repr. Albuquerque: New Mexico University Press.

Gleason, Maud W. 1986. "Festive Satire: Julian's *Misopogon* and the New Year at Antioch." *Journal of Roman Studies* 76:106–19.

Gleason, Philip. 1983. "Identifying Identity: A Semantic History." *Journal of American History* 69:910–31.

Glennie, Paul, and Nigel Thrift. 2009. *Shaping the Day: A History of Timekeeping in England and Wales, 1300–1800*. Oxford: Oxford University Press.

Goldberg, Sylvie Anne. 2000, 2004. *La Clepsydre*. Paris: Albin Michel.

———. 2000. "Questions of Time: Conflicting Time Scales in Historical Perspective." *Jewish History* 14.3:267–86.

———. 2011a. "Is Time a Gendered Affair? Category and Concept—'Women' and 'Mitzvah.'" In *Tov Elem—Memory, Community and Gender in Medieval and Early Modern Jewish Societies: Essays in Honor of Robert Bonfil*, edited by Elisheva Baumgarten, Amnon Raz-Krakotzkin, and Roni Weinstein, 15–28. Jerusalem: Bialik.

———. 2011b. "In the Path of Our Fathers: On Tradition and Time from Jerusalem to Babylonia and Beyond." In *Jewish Studies at the Crossroads of Anthropology and History: Authority, Diaspora, Tradition*, edited by Ra'anan S. Boustan, Oren Kosansky, and Marina Rustow, 238–49. Philadelphia: University of Pennsylvania Press.

———. 2016. *Clepsydra: Essays on the Plurality of Time in Judaism*. Translated by Benjamin Ivry. Stanford: Stanford University Press.

Goldenberg, Robert. 1979. "The Jewish Sabbath in the Roman World up to the Time of Constantine the Great." *Aufstieg und Niedergang der Römischen Welt II* 19.2:414–47.

Gonzalez, Justo L. 2017. *A Brief History of Sunday: From the New Testament to the New Creation*. Grand Rapids, MI: Eerdmans.

Goodblatt, David. 2006. "The Political and Social History of the Jewish Community of Palestine c. 235–638." In *The Cambridge History of Judaism IV*, edited by Steven T. Katz, 404–30. Cambridge: Cambridge University Press.

Goodman, Abraham Vossen. 1951. "A Jewish Peddler's Diary, 1842–1843." *American Jewish Archives* 4:81–111.

Goodman, Martin. 2000. "Palestinian Rabbis and the Conversion of Constantine to Christianity." In *The Talmud Yerushalmi and Graeco-Roman Culture II*, edited by Peter Schäfer and Catherine Hezser, 1–9. Tübingen: Mohr Siebeck.

———. 2007. *Judaism in the Roman World: Collected Essays*. Leiden: Brill.

Goren, Shlomo. 1965. "Women as Regards Timebound, Positive Commandments." *Mahanayim* 98:10–16. [Hebrew]

Goshen-Gottstein, Alon. 1994. "The Body as Image of God in Rabbinic Literature." *Harvard Theological Review* 87.2:171–95.

Gottlieb, Y. B. 2009. *Order in the Bible (Yesh Seder La-Mikra): The Arrangement of the Torah in Rabbinic and Medieval Jewish Commentary*. Jerusalem: Bar Ilan University Press and Magnes Press.

Gould, Stephen Jay. 1988. *Time's Arrow, Time's Cycle: Myth and Metaphor in the Discovery of Geological Time*. Cambridge, MA: Harvard University Press.

Gow, A. S. F., and D. L. Page, eds. 1965. *The Greek Anthology: Hellenistic Epigrams*. Vol. 1. Cambridge: Cambridge University Press.

Gowing, Alain. 2005. *Empire and Memory: The Representation of the Roman Republic in Imperial Culture*. Cambridge: Cambridge University Press.

Grabbe, Lester L. 2001. "Eschatology in Philo and Josephus." In *Judaism in Late Antiquity*

III, edited by Jacob Neusner, Alan J. Avery-Peck, and Bruce Chilton, 163–85. Leiden: Brill.

Graf, Fritz. 1997. *Der Lauf des rollenden Jahres: Zeit und Kalender in Rom*. Stuttgart: Teubner.

———. 1998. "Kalendae Ianuariae." In *Ansichten griechischer Rituale: Geburtstagssymposium für Walter Burkert*, edited by Fritz Graf, 199–216. Stuttgart: Teubner.

———. 2002. "Roman Festivals in Syria Palaestina." In *The Talmud Yerushalmi and Graeco-Roman Culture III*, edited by Peter Schäfer, 435–51. Tübingen: Mohr Siebeck.

———. 2008. "Feste und Fehden: Städtische Feste und der Konflikt der Religionen im spätantiken römischen Reich." In *Chrysostomosbilder in 1600 Jahren: Facetten der Wirkungsgeschichte eines Kirchenvaters*, edited by Martin Wallraff and Rudolf Brändle, 3–22. Berlin: de Gruyter.

———. 2012. "Fights about Festivals: Libanius and John Chrysostom on the Kalendae Ianuariae in Antioch." *Archiv für Religionsgeschichte* 13.1:175–86.

———. 2015. *Roman Festivals in the Greek East: From the Early Empire to the Middle Byzantine Era*. Cambridge: Cambridge University Press.

Grafton, Anthony T., and Noel M. Swerdlow. 1988. "Calendar Dates and Ominous Days in Ancient Historiography." *Journal of the Warburg and Courtauld Institutes* 51:14–42.

Grant, Deena E. 2014. *Divine Anger in the Hebrew Bible*. Washington, DC: Catholic Biblical Association of America.

Graßhoff, Gerd. 2011. *Topoi Sundial Database*. https://www.topoi.org/project/d-5-6/.

———. 2018. "The Hour as Divine Sign: Ancient Sundials for Reading Time." Paper presented at "The Day Unit in Antiquity and the Middle Ages" conference. Jerusalem: Israel Institute for Advanced Study.

Graver, Margaret. 2019. "An Ethics of Positive Aid: Beneficence, Intention, Gratitude." In *Self, Self-Fashioning and Individuality in Late Antiquity*, edited by Maren Niehoff and Joshua Levinson. Tübingen: Mohr Siebeck.

Gray, Alyssa M. 2005a. *A Talmud in Exile: The Influence of Yerushalmi Avodah Zarah on the Formation of Bavli Avodah Zarah*. Providence: Brown Judaic Studies.

———. 2005b. "The Power Conferred by Distance from Power: Redaction and Meaning in b. A.Z. 10a–11a." In *Creation and Composition: The Contribution of the Bavli Redactors (Stammaim) to the Aggada*, edited by Jeffrey L. Rubenstein, 23–69. Tübingen: Mohr Siebeck.

Gray, Rebecca. 1993. *Prophetic Figures in Late Second Temple Judaism: The Evidence from Josephus*. New York: Oxford University Press.

Green, Deborah A. 2011. *The Aroma of Righteousness: Scent and Seduction in Rabbinic Life and Literature*. University Park: Pennsylvania State University Press.

Green, William H., trans. 1963. *Augustine: The City of God against the Pagans*. Cambridge, MA: Harvard University Press.

Greenblatt, Rachel. 2014. *To Tell Their Children: Jewish Communal Memory in Early Modern Prague*. Stanford: Stanford University Press.

Gregerman, Adam. 2016. *Building on the Ruins of the Temple: Apologetics and Polemics in Early Christianity and Rabbinic Judaism*. Tübingen: Mohr Siebeck.

Gribetz, Sarit Kattan. 2011. "Hanged and Crucified: The Book of Esther and *Toledot Yeshu*." In *Toledot Yeshu Reconsidered*, edited by Peter Schäfer, Michael Meerson, and Yaacov Deutsch, 159–80. Tübingen: Mohr Siebeck.

———. 2013. "Conceptions of Time and Rhythms of Daily Life in Rabbinic Literature, 200–600 C.E." Ph.D. diss., Princeton University.

———. 2015. "The Shema in the Second Temple Period: A Reconsideration." *Journal of Ancient Judaism* 6.1:58–84.

Gribetz, Sarit Kattan. 2016a. "A Matter of Time: Writing Jewish Memory into Roman History." *Association for Jewish Studies Review* 40.1:57–86.

———. 2016b. "Between Narrative and Polemic: The Sabbath in *Genesis Rabbah* and the Babylonian Talmud." In *Genesis Rabbah in Text and Context*, edited by Sarit Kattan Gribetz, David Grossberg, Martha Himmelfarb, and Peter Schäfer, 33–61. Tübingen: Mohr Siebeck.

———. 2017a. "'Lead Me Forth in Peace': The Wayfarer's Prayer and Rabbinic Rituals of Travel in the Roman World." In *Journeys in the Roman East: Imagined and Real*, edited by Maren Niehoff, 297–327. Tübingen: Mohr Siebeck.

———. 2017b. "Time, Gender and Ritual in Rabbinic Sources." In *Religious Studies and Rabbinics: A Conversation*, edited by Elizabeth Shanks Alexander and Beth A. Berkowitz, 139–57. New York: Routledge.

———. 2017c. "Women's Bodies as Metaphors for Time in Biblical, Second Temple, and Rabbinic Literature." In *The Construction of Time in Antiquity: Ritual, Art and Identity*, edited by Jonathan Ben-Dov and Lutz Doering, 173–204. Cambridge: Cambridge University Press.

———. 2018. "The Festival of Every Day: Philo and Seneca on Quotidian Time." *Harvard Theological Review* 11.3:357–81.

———. 2019. "Shabbat with Food: From Biblical Prohibitions to Rabbinic Feasts." *thetorah.com*. https://thetorah.com/shabbat-with-food-from-biblical-prohibitions-to-rabbinic-feasts/.

Gribetz, Sarit Kattan, David Grossberg, Martha Himmelfarb, and Peter Schäfer, eds. 2016. *Genesis Rabbah in Text and Context*. Tübingen: Mohr Siebeck.

Gribetz, Sarit Kattan, and Lynn Kaye. 2019. "The Temporal Turn in Ancient Judaism and Jewish Studies." *Currents for Biblical Research* 17.3:332–95.

Gribetz, Sarit Kattan, and Moulie Vidas. 2012. "Rabbis and Others in Conversation." *Jewish Studies Quarterly* 19.2:91–103.

Griffith, Marie. 2000. *God's Daughters: Evangelical Women and the Power of Submission*. Berkeley: University of California Press.

Griffiths, Jay. 2004. *A Sideways Look at Time*. New York: Penguin.

Gross, Rachel. 2017. "People of the Picture Book: PJ Library and American Jewish Religion." In *Religion and Popular Culture in America*, 3rd ed., edited by Bruce David Forbes and Jeffrey H. Mahan, 177–94. Oakland: University of California Press.

Grossman, Avraham. 2004. *Pious and Rebellious: Jewish Women in Medieval Europe*. Translated by Jonathan Chipman. Waltham, MA: Brandeis University Press.

Grosz, Elizabeth. 2005. *Time Travels: Feminism, Nature, Power*. Durham, NC: Duke University Press.

Gruen, Erich S. 2004. *Diaspora: Jews amidst Greeks and Romans*. Cambridge, MA: Harvard University Press.

Gruenwald, Ithamar. 1980, 2014. *Apocalyptic and Merkavah Mysticism*. 2nd ed. Leiden: Brill.

Guindi, Fadqa El. 2008. *By Noon Prayer: The Rhythm of Islam*. Oxford: Berg.

Gutmann, Joseph. 1968. "Leviathan, Behemoth and Ziz: Jewish Messianic Symbols in Art." *Hebrew Union College Annual* 39:219–30.

Guy, Fritz. 1964. "'The Lord's Day' in the Letter of Ignatius to the Magnesians." *Andrews University Seminary Studies* 2:1–17.

Hacohen, Malachi Haim. 2019. *Jacob & Esau: Jewish European History between Nation and Empire*. Cambridge: Cambridge University Press.

Hadas-Lebel, Mireille. 1979. "Le paganism à travers les sources rabbiniques des IIe et IIIe siècles." *Aufstieg und Niedergang der Römischen Welt* II 19.2:397–485.

———. 1984. "Jacob et Ésaü, ou Israël-Édom, dans le Talmud et le Midrash." *Revue de l'Histoire des Religions* 201.4:369–92.

———. 2005. *Jerusalem against Rome*. Leuven: Peeters, 2005.

———. 2011. "Le thème des frères ennemis: Jacob et Ésaü ou Israël-Édom, de la Bible au Midrash." *Sens* 63.3:195–202.

Halberstam, Chaya T. 2010. *Law and Truth in Biblical and Rabbinic Literature*. Bloomington: Indiana University Press.

Halberstam, J. 2005. *In a Queer Time and Place: Transgender Bodies, Subcultural Lives*. New York: New York University Press.

Halbertal, Moshe. 1998. "Coexisting with the Enemy: Jews and Pagans in the Mishnah." In *Tolerance and Intolerance in Early Judaism and Christianity*, edited by Graham N. Stanton and Guy G. Stroumsa, 159–72. Cambridge: Cambridge University Press.

———. 2000. "If the Text Had Not Been Written, It Could Not Be Said." *Tarbiz* 68.1:39–59. [Hebrew]

———. 2009. "If the Text Had Not Been Written, It Could Not Be Said." In *Scriptural Exegesis—The Shapes of Culture and Religious Imagination, Essays in Honour of Michael Fishbane*, edited by Deborah A. Green and Laura S. Lieber, 146–61. Oxford: Oxford University Press.

Halbertal, Moshe, and Avishai Margalit. 1992. *Idolatry*. Translated by Naomi Goldblum. Cambridge, MA: Harvard University Press.

Halbwachs, Maurice. 1992. *On Collective Memory*. Edited by Lewis A. Coser. Chicago: University of Chicago Press.

Hamidović, David. 2006. "*Les repartitions des temps*, titre du *Livre des Jubilés* dans les manuscrits de Qoumrân." In *Le Temps et les Temps dans les literatures juives et chrétiennes au tournant de notre ère*, edited by Christian Grappe and Jean-Claude Ingelaere, 137–46. Leiden: Brill.

———. 2010. "L'eschatologie essénienne dans la littérature apocalyptique: Temporalités et limites chronologiques." *Revue des Etudes Juives* 169.1–2:37–55.

Hammer, Reuven. 1991. "What Did They Bless? A Study of Mishnah Tamid 5.1." *JQR* 8.3/4:305–24.

Hamori, Esther J. 2010. "Divine Embodiment in the Hebrew Bible and Some Implications for Jewish and Christian Incarnational Theologies." In *Bodies, Embodiment, and Theology of the Hebrew Bible*, edited by S. Tamar Kamionkowski and Wonil Kim, 161–83. New York: T&T Clark.

Handelman, Don. 2018. "Is Time a Dynamic Force? A Passive Passage?" Lecture at the Annual Multidisciplinary Sciences and Humanities Meeting at the Israel Academy of Sciences and Humanities, Jerusalem.

Hannah, Robert. 2005. *Greek and Roman Calendars: Constructions of Time in the Classical World*. London: Duckworth.

———. 2009. *Time in Antiquity*. London: Routledge.

———. 2011. "The Horologium of Augustus as a Sundial." *Journal of Roman Archaeology* 24:41–49.

———. 2014. "The Horologium of Augustus as a Sundial: Addendum." In *The Horologium of Augustus: Debate and Context*, edited by Lothar Haselberger. Portsmouth: Journal of Roman Archaeology.

———. 2016. "Time-telling Devices." In *A Companion to Science, Technology, and Medicine in Ancient Greece and Rome*, edited by Georgia L. Irby, 923–40. Hoboken, NJ: Wiley Blackwell.

Hano, Michel. 1986. "A l'origine du culte impérial: Les autels des Lares Augusti; Recherches sur les thèmes iconographiques et leur signification." *Aufstief und Niedergang der Römischen Welt* 2.16.3:2333–81.

Hardin, Paul E., Jeffrey C. Hall, and Michael Rosbash. 1990. "Feedback of the Drosophila Period Gene Product on Circadian Cycling of Its Messenger RNA Levels." *Nature* 343:536–40.

Harker, Christina Clair. 2015. "Paul, Empire, Calendar, & Galatia: A Postcolonial Analysis of Galatians and Its Modern Interpretation." Ph.D. diss., Yale University.

Harkov, Lahav. 2018. "Knesset Passes Contentious Shabbat Law by One Vote after All-Nighter." *Jerusalem Post*. January 9.

Harl, Kenneth W. 1987. *Civic Coins and Civic Politics in the Roman East AD 180–275*. Berkeley: University of California Press.

Harland, Peter A. 2006. "Acculturation and Identity in the Diaspora: A Jewish Family and 'Pagan' Guilds at Hierapolis." *JJS* 57:222–44.

Harrington, Daniel J. "Sabbath Tensions: Matthew 12:1–14 and Other New Testament Texts." In *The Sabbath in Jewish and Christian Traditions*, edited by Tamar Eskenazi, Daniel J. Harrington, and William H. Shea, 45–56. New York: Crossroad.

Hasan-Rokem, Galit. 2000. *Web of Life: Folklore and Midrash in Rabbinic Literature*. Stanford: Stanford University Press.

Hasselhoff, Görge K., and Alexander Fidora. 2017. *Ramon Martí's* Pugio Fidei*: Studies and Texts*. Santa Coloma de Queralt: Obrado Edèndum.

Hauptman, Judith. 1998. *Rereading the Rabbis: A Woman's Voice*. Boulder, CO: Westview Press.

Hawking, Stephen. 1988. *A Brief History of Time: From the Big Bang to Black Holes*. New York: Bantam Books.

Hayes, Christine. 1997. *Between the Palestinian and Babylonian Talmuds: Accounting for Halakhic Difference in Selected Sugyot from Tractate Avodah Zarah*. Oxford: Oxford University Press.

———. 1998. "Displaced Self-Perceptions: The Deployment of Minim and Romans in Bavli Sanhedrin 90b–91a." In *Religious and Ethnic Communities in Later Roman Palestine*, edited by Hayim Lapin, 249–89. Bethesda: University Press of Maryland.

———. 2002. *Gentile Impurities and Jewish Identities: Intermarriage and Conversion from the Bible to the Talmud*. Oxford: Oxford University Press.

———. 2015. *What's Divine about Divine Law?* Princeton: Princeton University Press.

———. 2020. "Roman Power through Rabbinic Eyes: Tragedy or Comedy." In *Reconsidering Roman Power: Roman, Greek, Jewish and Christian Perceptions and Reactions*, edited by Katell Berthelot. Rome: Publications de l'École française de Rome. http://books.openedition.org/efr/5283.

Hefele, Charles J. 1896. *A History of the Councils of the Church*. Edinburgh: T&T Clark.

Hehn, Johannes. 1907. *Siebenzahl und Sabbat bei den Babyloniern und im Alten Testament: Eine religionsgeschichtliche Studie*. Leipzig: Hinrichs.

Heidegger, Martin. 1927, 1962. *Being and Time*. Translated by John Macquarrie and Edward Robinson. New York: Harper Perennial.

Heidel, William A. 1929. *The Day of Yahweh: A Study of Sacred Days and Ritual Norms in the Ancient Near East*. New York: American Historical Association.

Heiken, Grank, Renato Funiciello, and Donatella de Rita, eds. 2013. *The Seven Hills of Rome: A Geological Tour of the Eternal City*. Princeton: Princeton University Press.

Heinemann, Isaac. 1970. *Darkhe Ha-Aggadah*. 3rd ed. Jerusalem: Magnes Press.

Heller, Anna. 2014. "Domination subie, domination choisie: Les cités d'Asie Mineure face au pouvoir romain, de la République à l'Empire." *Pallas* 96:217–32.

Henze, Matthias. 2011. *Jewish Apocalypticism in Late First Century Israel: Reading Second Baruch in Context*. Tübingen: Mohr Siebeck.
———. 2018. "Dimensions of Time in Jewish Apocalyptic Thought: The Case of 4 Ezra." In *Figures of Ezra*, edited by Jan N. Bremmer, Veronika Hirschberger, and Tobias Nicklas, 13–34. Leuven: Peeters.
Herder, Johann Gottfried. 1799, 1955. *Metakritik zur Kritik der reinen Vernunft*. Berlin: Aufbau-Verlag.
Herman, Geoffrey. 2014. "Religious Transformation between East and West: Hanukkah in the Babylonian Talmud and Zoroastrianism." In *Religion and Trade: Religious Formation, Transformation and Cross-Cultural Exchange between East and West*, edited by Peter Wick and Volker Rabens, 261–81. Leiden: Brill.
Herr, Moshe David. 1961. "The Laws of War on the Sabbath in the Second Temple and Talmudic Periods." *Tarbiz* 30:242–56. [Hebrew]
———. 1971. "Dialogues between Sages and Roman Dignitaries." *Scripta Hierosolymitana* 22:145–49.
———. 2009. "The Identity of the Jewish People before and after the Destruction of the Second Temple: Continuity or Change?" In *Jewish Identities in Antiquity*, edited by Lee Levine and Daniel Schwartz, 211–36. Tübingen: Mohr Siebeck.
Hershkovitz, Yehudah. 1940. "The Samaritans in Tannaitic Words." *Yavneh* 2:71–105.
Heslin, Peter. 2007. "Augustus, Domitian and the So-called Horologium Augusti." *Journal of Roman Studies* 97:1–20.
Hey, J. D. 2018. "On an Ancient Sundial Unearthed at Pompeii." *Transactions of the Royal Society of South Africa* 73.1:56–72.
Hezser, Catherine. 1993. "Social Fragmentation, Plurality of Opinion, and Nonobservance of Halakhah: Rabbis and Community in Late Roman Palestine." *Jewish Studies Quarterly* 1.3:234–51.
———. 1998. "The Social Status of Slaves in the Talmud Yerushalmi and in Graeco-Roman Society." In *The Talmud Yerushalmi and Graeco-Roman Culture III*, edited by Peter Schäfer and Catherine Hezser, 91–137. Tübingen: Mohr Siebeck.
———. 2008. "Diaspora and Rabbinic Judaism." In *The Oxford Handbook of Biblical Studies*, edited by Judith M. Lieu and J. W. Rogerson, 120–32. Oxford: Oxford University Press.
Hidary, Richard. 2015. "'One May Come to Repair Musical Instruments': Rabbinic Authority and the History of the *Shevut* Laws." *JSIS* 13:1–26.
Highmore, Ben. 2001. *The Everyday Life Reader*. London: Routledge.
Hill, I. E. 1997. *The Complete Works of Saint Augustine: A Translation for the 21st Century. Sermons III/11: Newly Discovered Sermons*. Hyde Park, NY: City Press.
Hill, Rebecca. 2008. "Interval, Sexual Difference: Luce Irigaray and Henri Bergson." *Hypatia* 23.1:119–31.
Himmelfarb, Martha. 1999. "Sexual Relations and Purity in the Temple Scroll and the Book of Jubilees." *Dead Sea Discoveries* 6.1:11–36.
———. 2001. "Impurity and Sin in 4QD, 1QS, and 4Q512." *Dead Sea Discoveries* 8.1:9–37.
———. 2004. "The Purity Laws of 4QD: Exegesis and Sectarianism." In *Things Revealed: Studies in Early Jewish and Christian Literature in Honor of Michael E. Stone*, edited by Esther G. Chazon, David Satran, and Ruth A. Clements, 155–69. Leiden: Brill.
———. 2006. *A Kingdom of Priests: Ancestry and Merit in Ancient Judaism*. Philadelphia: University of Pennsylvania Press.
———. 2008. "The Ordeals of Abraham: Circumcision and the *Aqedah* in Origen, the *Mekhilta*, and *Genesis Rabbah*." *Henoch* 30:289–310.
———. 2016. "Abraham and the Messianism of *Genesis Rabbah*." In *Genesis Rabbah in Text*

and Context, edited by Sarit Kattan Gribetz, David Grossberg, Martha Himmelfarb, and Peter Schäfer, 99–114. Tübingen: Mohr Siebeck.

Himmelfarb, Martha. 2017. *Jewish Messiahs in a Christian Empire: A History of the Book of Zerubbabel*. Cambridge, MA: Harvard University Press.

Hirsch, Samson R. 1971. *The Pentateuch*. Translated by Isaac Levy. 2nd ed. 5 vols. New York: Judaica Press.

Hirsh, Marilyn. 1986. *Joseph Who Loved the Sabbath*. Illustrated by Devis Grebu. New York: Viking Juvenile.

Hirshman, Marc. 1996. *A Rivalry of Genius: Jewish and Christian Biblical Interpretation in Late Antiquity*. Translated by Batya Stein. Albany: State University of New York Press.

———. 2006. "Torah in Rabbinic Thought: The Theology of Learning." In *The Cambridge History of Judaism IV: The Late Roman-Rabbinic Periods*, edited by Steven T. Katz, 899–924. Cambridge: Cambridge University Press.

Hjorthol, Randi. 2001. "Gendered Aspects of Time Related to Everyday Journeys." *Acta Sociologica* 44.1:37–49.

Hoberman, Michael. 2011. *New Israel/New England: Jews and Puritans in Early America*. Amherst: University of Massachusetts Press.

Hoffman, David, ed. 1908. *Midrasch Tannaim zum Deuteronomium*. Berlin: H. Itzkowiski.

Hoffman, Lawrence. 1996. *Covenant of Blood: Circumcision and Gender in Rabbinic Judaism*. Chicago: University of Chicago Press.

Hoffmann Libson, Ayelet. 2018. *Law and Self-Knowledge in the Talmud*. Cambridge: Cambridge University Press.

Hogan, Karina Martin. 2017. "The Apocalyptic Eschatology of Romans: Creation, Judgment, Resurrection, and Glory." In *Jewish Apocalyptic Tradition and the Shaping of New Testament Thought*, edited by Benjamin Reynolds and Loren Stuckenbruck, 205–31. Minneapolis: Fortress Press.

———. 2018. "Christian Appropriation of Zion in *5 Ezra*." Paper delivered at the "Appropriation in and of the Premodern World" conference. New York: Fordham University.

Hohlwein, Nicolas. 1957. "Le veteran Lucius Ballienus Gemellus: Gentleman-farmer au Fayoum." *Etudes de Papyrologie* 8:69–91.

Holford-Strevens, Leofranc. 2005. *The History of Time: A Very Short Introduction*. Oxford: Oxford University Press.

Holladay, William. 2007. "Indications of Segmented Sleep in the Bible." *Catholic Biblical Quarterly* 69:215–21.

Holmes, Brooke. 2012. *Gender: Antiquity and Its Legacy*. Oxford: Oxford University Press.

Hopkins, Andrew, and Maria Wyke, eds. 2005. *Roman Bodies: Antiquity to the Eighteenth Century*. London: British School at Rome.

Horn, Dara. 2008. "The Eicha Problem." In *Arguing the Modern Jewish Canon: Essays on Literature and Culture in Honor of Ruth R. Wisse*, edited by Justin Daniel Cammy, Dara Horn, Alyssa Quint, and Rachel Rubinstein, 687–700. Cambridge, MA: Harvard University.

Horovitz, Hayim Saul, ed. 1917, 1992. *Sifre Numbers*. Jerusalem: Shalem.

———. 1917, 1992. *Sifre Zuta*. Jerusalem: Shalem.

Horovitz, Hayim Saul, and Israel Rabin, eds. 1970. *Mekhilta de-Rabbi Ishmael*. Jerusalem: Wahrmann.

Horowitz, Elliott. 2006. *Reckless Rites: Purim and the Legacy of Jewish Violence*. Princeton: Princeton University Press.

Houtman, Alberdina. 2016. "The Development of the Adamic Myth in Genesis Rabbah." In

Religion Stories in Transformation: Conflict, Revision and Reception, edited by Alberdina Houtman, Tamar Kadari, Marcel Poorthuis, and Vered Tohar, 36–51. Leiden: Brill.

Hughes, Jeremy. 1990. *Secrets of the Times: Myth and History in Biblical Chronology*. Sheffield: JSOT Press.

Hultgård, Anders, and Stig Norin, eds. 2009. *Le Jour De Dieu—Der Tag Gottes*. Tübingen: Mohr Siebeck.

Humphrey, Caroline, and James Laidlow. 1994. *Things: Religion and the Question of Materiality*. New York: Fordham University Press.

Hurwitz, Simeon, ed. 1893. *Mahzor Vitry*. Berlin.

Idri, H. R. 1954. "Fêtes chrétiennes en Ifriqiya à l'époque ziride." *Revue africaine* 98: 261–76.

Ilan, Tal. 1994. "Matrona and Rabbi Jose: An Alternative Interpretation." *Journal for the Study of Judaism* 25:18–51.

———. 2006. *Jewish Women in Greco-Roman Palestine: An Inquiry into Image and Status*. Tübingen: Mohr Siebeck.

Ilan, Tal, and Vered Noam. 2017. *Josephus and the Rabbis*. Jerusalem: Yad Ben-Zvi.

Irshai, Oded. 2000. "Dating the Eschaton: Jewish and Christian Apocalyptic Calculations in Late Antiquity." In *Apocalyptic Time*, edited by Albert Baumgarten, 113–53. Leiden: Brill.

———. 2017. "'If You See Kingdoms Preparing for War with One Another, Expect the Footsteps of the Messiah': Chronography and Apocalypticism in Late Antiquity." In Yehuda Ibn Shmuel, *Midrash ha-Geulah*, i–li. Jerusalem: Carmel. [Hebrew]

Isbell, Charles D. 1975. *Corpus of Aramaic Incantation Bowls: Aramaic Incantations of Late Antiquity*. Missoula: Society of Biblical Literature and Scholars Press.

Ish-Shalom, Meir, ed. 1880. *Pesiqta Rabbati*. Vienna.

Israeli, Anat. 2012. "In Those Days and during This Time: Thoughts of Women, Judaism and Time." *D'varim* 4:47–52. [Hebrew]

———. 2015. "Jewish Women and Positive Time-bound Commandments: Reconsidering the Rabbinic Texts." *Women in Judaism: A Multidisciplinary Journal* 12.1:1–27.

Jacobs, Martin. 1995. *Die Institution des Jüdischen Patriarchen*. Tübingen: Mohr Siebeck.

Jacobus, Helen R. 2015. *Zodiac Calendars in the Dead Sea Scrolls and Their Reception: Ancient Astronomy and Astrology in Early Judaism*. Leiden: Brill.

Jaffee, Martin S. 2006. "Gender and Otherness in Rabbinic Oral Culture: On Gentiles, Undisciplined Jews, and Their Women." In *Performing the Gospel: Orality, Memory, and Mark*, edited by Richard A. Horsley, Jonathan A. Draper, John Miles Foley, and Werner H. Kelber, 31–43. Minneapolis: Fortress Press.

Jahoda, Marie, Paul F. Lazarsfeld, and Hans Zeisel. 1960. *Die Arbeitslosen von Marienthal: Ein soziographischer Versuch mit einem Anhang zur Geschichte der Soziographie*. 2nd ed. Allensbach–Bonn: Verlag für Demoskopie.

Jassen, Alex. 2014. *Scripture and Law in the Dead Sea Scrolls*. Cambridge: Cambridge University Press.

Jastrow, Marcus. 1943, 2005. *Dictionary of the Targumim, the Talmud Babli, and Yerushalmi, and the Midrashic Literature*. Peabody, MA: Hendrickson Publishers.

Jay, Nancy. 1992. *Throughout Your Generations Forever: Sacrifice, Religion, and Paternity*. Chicago: University of Chicago Press.

John Chrysostom. 1979. *Discourses against Judaizing Christians*. Translated by Paul W. Harkins. Washington, DC: Catholic University of America Press.

Johnson, Elizabeth. 1992. *She Who Is: The Mystery of God in Feminist Theological Discourse*. New York: Crossroad.

Johnson, Van L. 1959. "The Superstitions about the Nundinae." *American Journal of Philology* 80.2:133–49.
Johnson, Walter. 2000. "Possible Pasts: Some Speculations on Time, Temporality, and the History of Atlantic Slavery." *Amerikastudien/American Studies* 45.4:485–99.
Jones, Alexander R., ed. 2016. *Time and Cosmos in Greco-Roman Antiquity*. Princeton: Princeton University Press.
Jonquière, Tessel Marina. 2007. *Prayer in Josephus*. Leiden: Brill.
Justin Martyr. 2003. *Dialogue with Trypho*. Translated by Thomas B. Falls. Washington, DC: Catholic University of America Press.
Kahana, Menahem I. 2002. *Sifre Zuta on Deuteronomy: Citations from a New Tannaitic Midrash*. Jerusalem: Magnes Press.
———. 2006. "'Golden Apples in Silver Settings': The Mishnah and the Order of Its Tractates." *Tarbiz* 76:29–40. [Hebrew]
Kaijian, Tang. 2015. *Setting Off for Macau: Essays on Jesuit History during the Ming and Qing Dynasties*. New York: Brill.
Kalman, David Zvi. 2019. "Unequal Hours: The Jewish Reception of Timekeeping Technology from the Bible to the Twentieth Century." Ph.D. diss., University of Pennsylvania.
Kalmin, Richard. 1994. "Christians and Heretics in Rabbinic Literature of Late Antiquity." *Harvard Theological Review* 87.2:155–69.
———. 2006. *Jewish Babylonia between Persia and Roman Palestine*. Oxford: Oxford University Press.
———. 2014. *Migrating Tales: The Talmud's Narratives and Their Historical Context*. Berkeley: University of California Press.
Kalupahana, David. 1974. "The Buddhist Conception of Time and Temporality." *Philosophy East and West* 24:181–91.
Kanarfogel, Ephraim. 1992. "Rabbinic Attitudes toward Observance and Non-Observance in the Medieval Period." In *Jewish Tradition and the Non-traditional Jews*, edited by Jacob J. Schacter, 3–35. Montvale, NJ: Jason Aronson.
Kasher, Menachem. 1952. "The Concept of Time in Scripture and the Early Rabbis." *Talpiot* 5:799–827.
Kaster, Robert A., trans. 2011. *Macrobius: Saturnalia*. 3 vols. Cambridge, MA: Harvard University Press.
Katz, Jacob. 1961. *Exclusiveness and Tolerance: Studies in Jewish-Gentile Relations in Medieval and Modern Times*. Springfield, NJ: Behrman House/Oxford University Press.
———. 1998. *Divine Law in Human Hands: Case Studies in Halakhic Flexibility*. Jerusalem: Magnes Press.
Katz, Marion Holmes. 2002. *Body of Text: The Emergence of the Sunni Law of Ritual Purity*. Albany: State University of New York Press.
———. 2015. "Scholarly versus Women's Authority in the Islamic Law of Menstrual Purity." In *Gender in Judaism and Islam: Common Lives, Uncommon Heritage*, edited by Firoozeh Kashani-Sabet and Beth S. Wenger, 73–105. New York: New York University Press.
Katz, Menachem. 2003. "The First Chapter of Tractate Qiddushin of the Talmud Yerushalmi: Text, Commentary and Studies in the Editorial Process." Ph.D. diss., Bar Ilan University.
Katzoff, Ranon, and Bertram M. Schreiber. 1998. "Week and Sabbath in Judaean Desert Documents." *Scripta Classica Israelica* 17:102–14.
Kaye, Lynn. 2012. "Law and Temporality in Bavli *Mo'ed*." Ph.D. diss., New York University.
———. 2018. *Time in the Babylonian Talmud*. Cambridge: Cambridge University Press.
———. Forthcoming a. "Sacred Time and Rabbinic Literature: New Directions for an Old Question." *Journal of the American Academy of Religion*.

———. Forthcoming b. *Negating Time: Rabbinic Ideologies of Time-Wasting and Sacred Occupation.*
Kayserling, Meyer. 1894. *Christopher Columbus and the Participation of the Jews in the Spanish and Portuguese Discoveries.* Translated by Charles Gross. New York: Longmans, Green.
Kelly Gadol, Joan. 1977. "Did Women Have a Renaissance?" In *Becoming Visible: Women in European History*, edited by Renate Bridenthal and Claudia Koonz, 137–64. Boston: Houghton Mifflin.
Ker, James. 2004. "Nocturnal Writers in Imperial Rome: The Culture of *Lucubratio*." *Classical Philology* 99.3:209–42.
———. 2009. "Drinking from the Water-Clock: Time and Speech in Imperial Rome." *Arethusa* 42.3:279–302.
———. 2010. "*Nundinae*: The Culture of the Roman Week." *Phoenix* 64.3/4:360–85.
———. Forthcoming. *The Ordered Day: Quotidian Time and Forms of Life in Ancient Rome.*
Kessler, Gwynn. 2013. "Constant Creation: (Pro)Creation in Palestinian Rabbinic Midrashim." In *Jewish and Christian Cosmogony in Late Antiquity*, edited by Lance Jenott and Sarit Kattan Gribetz, 126–38. Tübingen: Mohr Siebeck.
———. 2020. "Rabbinic Gender: Beyond Male and Female." In *A Companion to Late Ancient Jews and Judaism, Third Century BCE to Seventh Century CE*, edited by Naomi Koltun-Fromm and Gwynn Kessler, 353–70. Hoboken, NJ: Wiley.
Kiel, Yishai, and Prods Oktor Skjærvø. 2011. "'The Sabbath Was Made for Humankind': A Rabbinic and Christian Principle in Its Iranian Context." *Bulletin of the Asia Institute* 25:1–18.
Kimelman, Reuven. 1987. "The *Shema* and Its Blessings: The Realization of God's Kingship." In *The Synagogue in Late Antiquity*, edited by Lee I. Levine, 73–86. Philadelphia: American Schools of Oriental Research.
———. 2001. "The Shema' Liturgy: From Covenant to Coronation." In *Kenishta: Studies of the Synagogue World*, edited by Joseph Tabory, 9–105. Ramat Gan: Bar Ilan University Press.
———. 2006. "Rabbinic Prayer in Late Antiquity." In *The Cambridge History of Judaism*, vol. 4, edited by S. T. Katz, 573–611. Cambridge: Cambridge University Press.
Kiperwasser, Reuven. 2012. "The Immersion of *Baallei Qerain*." *Jewish Studies Quarterly* 19:311–38.
Kiperwasser, Reuven, and Dan D. Y. Shapira. 2012. "Irano-Talmudica II: Leviathan, Behemoth and the 'Domestication' of Iranian Mythological Creatures in Eschatological Narratives of the Babylonian Talmud." In *Shoshannat Yaakov: Jewish and Iranian Studies in Honor of Yaakov Elman*, edited by Shai Secunda and Steven Fine, 203–35. Leiden: Brill, 2012.
Kister, Meir J. 1989. "'Do Not Assimilate Yourselves... *Lā tashabbahū.*'" *Jerusalem Studies in Arabic and Islam* 12:231–370.
Kister, Menahem. 1984. "Plucking on the Sabbath and Christian-Jewish Polemic." *Jerusalem Studies in Jewish Thought* 3.3:349–66. [Hebrew]
———. 1999. "Studies in 4QMMT and Its World: Law, Theology, Language and Calendar." *Tarbiz* 68:360–64. [Hebrew]
———. 2007. "Romans 5:12–21 against the Background of Torah-Theology and Hebrew Usage." *Harvard Theological Review* 100.1:391–424.
———. 2009. "'First Adam' and 'Second Adam' in 1 Cor 15:45–49 in Light of Midrashic Exegesis and Hebrew Usage." In *The New Testament and Rabbinic Literature*, edited by Reimund Bieringer, Florentino García Martínez, Didier Pollefeyt, and Peter Tomson, 351–65. Leiden: Brill.

Kister, Menahem. 2013. "The Manifestations of God in the Midrashic Literature in Light of Christian Texts." *Tarbiz* 81:103–42. [Hebrew]

Klawans, Jonathan. 2000. *Impurity and Sin in Ancient Judaism*. Oxford: Oxford University Press.

Klein, Michael. 2011. "Palestinian Targum and Synagogue Mosaics." In *Michael Klein on the Targums: Collected Essays, 1972–2002*, edited by Michael L. Klein and Rimon Kasher, 49–58. Leiden: Brill.

Knuuttila, Simo. 2001. "Time and Creation in Augustine." In *The Cambridge Companion to Augustine*, edited by Eleonore Stump and Norman Kretzmann, 103–15. Cambridge: Cambridge University Press.

Koffman, David S. 2011. "The Jews' Indian: Native Americans in the Jewish Imagination and Experience, 1850–1950." Ph.D. diss., New York University.

Kofsky, Aryeh. 1998. "Mamre: A Case of a Regional Cult?" In *Sharing the Sacred: Religious Contacts and Conflicts in the Holy Land*, edited by Aryeh Kofsky and Guy G. Stroumsa, 19–30. Jerusalem: Yad Izhak Ben Zvi.

Kohut, Alexander. 1898. "The Talmudic Records of Persian and Babylonian Festivals Critically Illustrated." *American Journal of Semitic Languages and Literatures* 14.3:183–94.

Kokin, Daniel Stein. 2013. "Toward the Source of the Sambatyon: Shabbat Discourse and the Origins of the Sabbatical River Legend." *Association for Jewish Studies Review* 37:1–28.

Koltun-Fromm, Naomi. 1996. "A Jewish-Christian Conversation in Fourth-Century Persian Mesopotamia." *Journal of Jewish Studies* 47.1:45–63.

———. 1997. "Aphrahat and Rabbis on Noah's Righteousness in Light of the Jewish-Christian Polemic." In *The Book of Genesis in Jewish and Oriental Christian Interpretation*, edited by Judith Frishman and Lucas Van Rompey, 57–71. Leuven: Peeters.

———. 2013. "Rock over Water: Historic Rocks and Primordial Waters from Creation to Salvation in Jerusalem." In *Jewish and Christian Cosmogony in Late Antiquity*, edited by Lance Jenott and Sarit Kattan Gribetz, 239–54. Tübingen: Mohr Siebeck.

Kondoleon, Christine. 1999. "Timing Spectacles: Roman Domestic Art and Performance." *Studies in the History of Art* 56:320–41.

Koren, Sharon Faye. 2009. "The Menstruant as 'Other' in Medieval Judaism and Christianity." *Nashim: A Journal of Jewish Women's Studies and Gender Issues* 17:33–59.

———. 2011. *Forsaken: The Menstruant in Medieval Jewish Mysticism*. Waltham, MA/Hanover, NH: Brandeis University Press/University Press of New England.

Koren, Yedidah. 2014. "The Foreskin and the 'Foreskinned' in Ancient Jewish Literature and the Creation of the 'Foreskinned Jew.'" Master's thesis, Tel Aviv University.

Koselleck, Reinhart. 2004. *Futures Past: On the Semantics of Historical Time*. Translated by Keith Tribe. New York: Columbia University Press.

Koslofsky, Craig. 2011. *Evening's Empire: The History of the Night in Early Modern Europe*. Cambridge: Cambridge University Press.

Kosmin, Paul. 2014. *The Land of the Elephant Kings*. Cambridge, MA: Harvard University Press.

———. 2018. *Time and Its Adversaries in the Seleucid Empire*. Cambridge, MA: Harvard University Press.

Kotrosits, Maia. 2015. *Rethinking Early Christian Identity: Affect, Violence, and Belonging*. Minneapolis: Fortress Press.

Kraemer, David. 1996. *Reading the Rabbis: The Talmud as Literature*. Oxford: Oxford University Press.

———. 2007. *Jewish Eating and Identity through the Ages*. New York: Routledge.

Kraft, Robert. 1965. "Some Notes on Sabbath Observance in Early Christianity." *Andrews University Seminary Studies* 31.1:18–33.
Krakowski, Eve. 2017. *Coming of Age in Medieval Egypt: Female Adolescence, Jewish Law, and Ordinary Culture*. Princeton: Princeton University Press.
———. 2020. "Maimonides' Menstrual Reform in Egypt." *Jewish Quarterly Review* 110.2:245–89.
Krauss, Samuel. 1902, 1994. *Das Leben Jesu nach jüdischen Quellen*. Berlin: S. Cavalry/Hildesheim: Olms.
———. 1910. *Antoninus und Rabbi*. Vienna: Verlag der Israelitisch-Theologische Lehranstalt.
———. 1947. *Persia and Rome in the Talmud and the Midrashim*. Jerusalem: Bialik.
Kreisel, Howard T. 1999. *Maimonides' Political Thought: Studies in Ethics, Law, and the Human Ideal*. Albany: State University of New York Press.
Krinis, Ehud. 2016. "Cyclical Time in the Ismāʿīlī Circle of Ikhwān al-safā' (Tenth Century) and in Early Jewish Kabbalistic Circles (Thirteenth and Fourteenth Centuries)." *Studia Islamica* 111:20–108.
Kristeva, Julia. 1981. "Women's Time." Translated by Alice Jardine and Harry Blake. *Signs* 7.1:13–35.
Kugel, James. 1998. "4Q369 'Prayer of Enosh' and Ancient Biblical Interpretation." *Dead Sea Discoveries* 5.2:119–48.
La Regina, Adriano, ed. 1998. *Palazzo Massimo Alle Terme*. Milan: Electa.
Labovitz, Gail. 2015. "A Man Spinning on His Thigh: Gender, Positive Time-Bound Commandments and Ritual Fringes, Mishnah Moʻed Katan 3:4." *Nashim: A Journal of Jewish Women's Studies & Gender Issues* 28:75–87.
Lake, Kirsopp, trans. 1912. *Didascalia*. Cambridge, MA: Harvard University Press.
Lamm, Norman. 1966, 1987. *A Hedge of Roses*. New York: Feldheim.
Landes, David S. 2000. *Revolution in Time: Clocks and the Making of the Modern World*. 2nd ed. Cambridge, MA: Harvard University Press.
Lange, Armin, and Matthias Weigold. 2012. "The Text of the Shema Yisrael in Qumran Literature and Elsewhere." In *Textual Criticism and Dead Sea Scrolls Studies in Honour of Julio Trebolle Barrera: Florilegium Complutense*, edited by A. Piquer Otero and P. Torijano Morales, 147–77. Leiden: Brill.
Langer, Ruth. 2011. *Cursing the Christians? A History of the Birkat Haminim*. Oxford: Oxford University Press.
Lapham, Lewis, ed. 2014. "Time." *Lapham's Quarterly* 7.4.
Lapin, Hayim, ed. 1998. *Religious and Ethnic Communities in Later Roman Palestine*. Bethesda: University of Maryland Press.
———. 2011. "Epigraphical Rabbis: A Reconsideration." *Jewish Quarterly Review* 101:311–46.
———. 2012. *Rabbis as Romans: The Rabbinic Movement in Palestine, 100–400 CE*. New York: Oxford University Press.
Larin, Vassa. 2008. "What Is 'Ritual Im/Purity' and Why?" *St. Vladimir's Theological Quarterly* 52.3-4:275–92.
Larson, Satyel. 2012. "Bearing Knowledge: Law, Reproduction and the Female Body in Modern Morocco, 1912–Present." Ph.D. diss., University of California, Berkeley.
Laurence, Ray. 1994. *Roman Pompeii: Space and Society*. London: Routledge.
Lauterbach, Jacob Z. 2004. *Mekhilta de-Rabbi Ishmael*. Philadelphia: Jewish Publication Society.
Lavee, Moshe. 2010. "The Samaritan May Be Included: Another Look at the Samaritan in

Talmudic Literature." In *Samaritans: Past and Present*, edited by Menachem Mor and Friedrich V. Reiterer, 147–74. Berlin: de Gruyter.

Lavee, Moshe. 2018. "Either Jews or Gentiles, Men or Women: The Talmudic Move from Legal to Essentialist Polarization of Identities." *Jewish Studies Quarterly* 25.4:345–67.

Lefebvre, Henri. 1947, 1961. *Critique de la vie quotidienne I–II*. Paris: Grasset/Paris: l'Arche, 1961.

———. 2004. *Rhythmanalysis: Space, Time and Everyday Life*. Translated by Stuart Elden and Gerald Moore. London: Continuum.

Le Goff, Jacques. 1980. *Time, Work, and Culture in the Middle Ages*. Chicago: University of Chicago Press.

———. 2014. *In Search of Sacred Time: Jacobus de Voragine and The Golden Legend*. Princeton: Princeton University Press.

Lehman, Marjorie. 2006. "The Gendered Rhetoric of Sukkah Observance." *Jewish Quarterly Review* 96.3:309–35.

Lehoux, Daryn. 2007. *Astronomy, Weather, and Calendars in the Ancient World: Parapegmata and Related Texts in Classical and Near Eastern Societies*. New York: Cambridge University Press.

Lennon, Jack L. 2014. *Pollution and Religion in Ancient Rome*. New York: Cambridge University Press.

Leonhard, Clemens. 2006. *The Jewish Pesach and the Origins of the Christian Easter: Open Questions in Current Research*. Berlin: de Gruyter.

———. 2017. "Celebrations and the Abstention from Celebrations of Sacred Time in Early Christianity." In *The Construction of Time in Antiquity: Ritual, Art and Identity*, edited by Jonathan Ben-Dov and Lutz Doering, 267–68. Cambridge: Cambridge University Press.

Lev, Sarra. 2010. "They Treat Him as a Man and See Him as a Woman: The Tannaitic Understanding of the Congenital Eunuch." *Jewish Studies Quarterly* 17.3:213–43.

Levene, Dan. 2003. "Hear O' Israel: A Pair of Duplicate Magic Bowls from the Pergamon Museum in Berlin." *Journal of Jewish Studies* 54:104–21.

Levick, Barbara. 1982. "Propaganda and the Imperial Coinage." *Antichthon* 16:104–16.

Levinas, Emmanuel. 1990. *Nine Talmudic Readings*. Translated by Annette Aronowicz. Bloomington: Indiana University Press.

Levine, Lee I. 1998. *Judaism and Hellenism in Antiquity: Conflict or Confluence?* Seattle: University of Washington Press.

———. 2005. *The Ancient Synagogue: The First Thousand Years*. 2nd ed. New Haven: Yale University Press.

Levine, Robert. 1997. *A Geography of Time: The Temporal Misadventures of a Social Psychologist; or, How Every Culture Keeps Time Just a Little Bit Differently*. New York: Basic Books.

Levinson, Joshua. 2012. "From Narrative Practice to Cultural Poetics: Literary Anthropology and the Rabbinic Sense of Self." In *Homer and the Bible in the Eyes of Ancient Interpreters*, edited by Maren R. Niehoff, 345–67. Leiden: Brill.

Lewy, Israel. 1878. "Über die Spuren des griechischen und römischen Alterhums im talmudischen Schrifttum." *Verhandlungen des Versammlung Deutscher Philologen und Schulmänner* 33:77–88.

Licht, Jacob. 1965. "Time and Eschatology in Apocalyptic Literature and in Qumran." *JJS* 16:173–82.

Liddell, Henry George, and Robert Scott. 1889. *An Intermediate Greek-English Lexicon*. 7th ed. Oxford: Clarendon Press.

Lieber, Laura S. 2010a. *Yannai on Genesis: An Invitation to Piyyut*. Cincinnati: Hebrew Union College Press.
———. 2010b. "The Rhetoric of Participation: The Experiential Elements of Early Hebrew Liturgical Poetry." *Journal of Religion* 90:119–47.
———. 2014a. "Setting the Stage: The Theatricality of Jewish Aramaic Poetry from Late Antiquity." *Jewish Quarterly Review* 104:537–72.
———. 2014b. "The *Piyyutim le-Hatan* of Qallir and Amittai: Jewish Marriage Customs in Early Byzantium." In *Talmuda de-Erez Yisrael: Archaeology and the Rabbis in Late Ancient Palestine*, edited by Steven Fine and Aaron Koller, 275–99. Berlin: de Gruyter.
———. 2018a. *Jewish Aramaic Poetry from Late Antiquity: Translations and Commentary*. Leiden: Brill.
———. 2018b. "Daru in the Winehouse: Dancing and Performance in the Jewish East in Late Antiquity." *Journal of Religion* 98.1:90–113.
Lieberman, Saul. 1955, 1992. *The Tosefta According to Codex Vienna*. 4 vols. New York: Jewish Theological Seminary of America.
———. 1962. *Hellenism in Jewish Palestine: Studies in the Literary Transmission, Beliefs and Manners of Palestine in the I Century B.C.E.–IV Century C.E.* New York: Jewish Theological Seminary.
———. 1964. *Midrash Devarim Rabbah*. Jerusalem: Wharmann.
———. 1974. *Texts and Studies*. New York: Ktav.
Lieberman Talmud Databank. https://www-lieberman-institute-com.
Lieu, Judith M. 1995. "The Race of the God-Fearers." *Journal of Theological Studies* 46.2:483–501.
Lightfoot, J. B., trans. 1898. *The Apostolic Fathers*. New York: Macmillan Company.
Lightman, Alan. 1992. *Einstein's Dreams: A Novel*. New York: Vintage.
Lincicum, David. 2010. *Paul and the Early Jewish Encounter with Deuteronomy*. Tübingen: Mohr Siebeck.
Linder, Amnon. 1988. *The Jews in Roman Imperial Legislation*. Detroit: Wayne State University Press.
Livingstone, Alasdair. 1986. *Mystical and Mythological Explanatory Works of Assyrian and Babylonian Scholars*. Winona Lake, IN: Eisenbrauns.
Llewelyn, Stephen. 2002. *New Documents Illustrating Early Christianity*. Vol. 9: *A Review of the Greek Inscriptions and Papyri Published in 1986–87*. Grand Rapids, MI: Eerdmans.
Loewenthal, Elena. 1990. "La storia del fiume Sambation: Alcune note sulla tradizione ebraica antica e medieval." In *Biblische und Judaistische Studien: Festschrift für Paolo Sacchi*, edited by Paolo Sacchi and Angelo Vivian, 651–63. Frankfurt am Main: Peter Lang.
Lott, John Bert. 2004. *The Neighborhoods of Augustan Rome*. Cambridge: Cambridge University Press.
Luce, T. J. 2008. *Livy: The Rise of Rome, Books 1–5*. Oxford: Oxford University Press.
Maccoby, Hyam. 1993. *Judaism on Trial: Jewish-Christian Disputations in the Middle Ages*. Oxford: Littman Library of Jewish Civilization.
MacDonald, John. 1963. *Memar Marqah: The Teaching of Marqah*. Berlin: de Gruyter.
Machinist, Peter. 1995. "Fate, 'Miqreh,' and Reason: Some Reflections on Qohelet and Biblical Thought." In *Solving Riddles and Untying Knots: Biblical, Epigraphic, and Semitic Studies in Honor of Jonas C. Greenfield*, edited by Ziony Zevit, Seymour Gitin, and Michael Sokoloff, 159–75. Winona Lake, IN: Eisenbrauns.
Magness, Jodi. 2005. "Heaven on Earth: Helios and the Zodiac Cycle in Ancient Palestinian Synagogues." *Dumbarton Oaks Papers* 59:1–52.

Magness, Jodi, et al. 2018. "The Huqoq Excavation Project 2014–2017 Interim Report." *Bulletin of the American Schools of Oriental Research* 380:106–11.

Maguire, Henry. 1987. *Earth and Ocean: The Terrestrial World in Early Byzantine Art.* University Park: Pennsylvania State University Press.

Mahmoud, Saba. 2005. *Politics of Piety: The Islamic Revival and the Feminist Subject.* Princeton: Princeton University Press.

Malka, Orit, and Yakir Paz. 2019. "*Ab hostibus captus et a latronibus captus*: The Impact of the Roman Model of Citizenship on Rabbinic Law." *Jewish Quarterly Review* 109.2:141–72.

Marcus, Ivan G. 1990. "History, Story and Collective Memory: Narrativity in Early Ashkenazic Culture." *Prooftexts* 10:365–88.

Margalit, Natan. 2004. "Priestly Men and Invisible Women: Male Appropriation of the Feminine and the Exemption of Women from Positive Time-Bound Commandments." *Association for Jewish Studies Review* 28.2:297–316.

Margulies, Mordechai, ed. 1953–60. *Midrash Wayyikra Rabba: A Critical Edition Based on Manuscripts and Genizah Fragments with Variants and Notes.* New York: Jewish Theological Seminary.

Marienberg, Evyatar. 2003. *Niddah: Lorsque les juifs conceptualisent la menstruation.* Paris: Les Belles Lettres.

———. 2012a. *La Baraïta de-Niddah: Un texte juif pseudo-talmudique sur les lois religieuses relatives à la menstruation.* Brepols: Turnhout.

———. 2012b. "*Qui coierit cum muliere in fluxo menstruo . . . interficientur ambo* (Lev. 20:18): The Biblical Prohibition of Sexual Relations with a Menstruant in the Eyes of Some Medieval Christian Theologians." In *Shoshannat Yaakov: Jewish and Iranian Studies in Honor of Yaakov Elman*, edited by Shai Secunda and Steven Fine, 271–84. Leiden: Brill.

Markus, Robert. 1990. *The End of Ancient Christianity.* Cambridge: Cambridge University Press.

Marmorstein, Arthur. 1927. "Anges et Hommes dans l'Agada." *Revue des études juive* 84:37–50, 138–40.

———. 1937, 1968. *The Old Rabbinic Doctrine of God: Essays in Anthropomorphism.* Oxford: Oxford University Press.

Marshall, John W. 2005. "The Patriarchs and the Zodiac: Revelation 12." In *Religious Rivalries and the Struggle for Success in Sardis and Smyrna*, edited by Richard S. Ascough, 186–213. Waterloo: Wilfrid Laurier University Press.

Martin, Troy W. 2001. "Watch during the Watches (Mark 13:35)." *Journal of Biblical Literature* 120:685–701.

Mason, Steve, ed. 1999–2016. *Flavius Josephus: Translation and Commentary.* Leiden: Brill.

———. 2007. "Jews, Judaeans, Judaizing, Judaism: Problems of Categorization in Ancient History." *Journal for the Study of Judaism* 38:457–512.

———. 2014. "Jew and Judean: A Forum on Politics and Historiography in the Translation of Ancient Texts." *Marginalia Review of Books.* http://marginalia.lareviewofbooks.org/jew-judean-forum/.

Mathisen, Ralph W. 2006. "*Peregrini, Barbari*, and *Cives Romani*: Concepts of Citizenship and the Legal Identity of Barbarians in the Later Roman Empire." *American Historical Review* 111:1011–40.

Mattingly, Harold, et al., eds. 1930a. *Coins of the Roman Empire in the British Museum.* Vol. 2: *Vespasian to Domitian.* London: By Order of the Trustees of the British Museum.

———. 1930b. *The Roman Imperial Coinage*. Vol. 3: *Antoninus Pius to Commodus*. London: Spink & Son.
Maxwell, Jaclyn L. 2006a. *Christianization and Communication in Late Antiquity: John Chrysostom and His Congregation in Antioch*. Cambridge: Cambridge University Press.
———. 2006b. "Lay Piety in the Sermons of John Chrysostom." In *Byzantine Christianity*, edited by Derek Krueger, 19–38. Minneapolis: Fortress Press.
Mayer-Haas, Andrea J. 2003. *"Geschenk aus Gottes Schatzkammer" (bSchab 10b): Jesus und der Sabbat in Speigel der neutestamentlichen Schriften*. Münster: Aschendorff.
Mazeh, Hanan. Forthcoming. "Built, Destroyed, and Built Again: Temple and History in *Genesis Rabba* in Light of Christian Sources." *Jewish Quarterly Review*.
Mazuz, Haggai. 2012. "Menstruation and Differentiation: How Muslims Differentiated Themselves from Jews Regarding the Laws of Menstruation." *Der Islam* 87.1–2:204–23.
McAlpine, Thomas. 1987. *Sleep, Divine and Human, in the Old Testament*. Sheffield: Sheffield Academic Press.
McCarthy, Thomas. 2009. *Race, Empire, and the Idea of Human Development*. Cambridge: Cambridge University Press.
McCasland, S. V. 1930. "The Origin of the Lord's Day." *Journal of Biblical Literature* 49:65–82.
McCrossen, Alexis. 2000. *Holy Day, Holiday: The American Sunday*. Ithaca, NY: Cornell University Press.
———. 2013. *Marking Modern Times: A History of Clocks, Watches, and Other Timekeepers in American Life*. Chicago: University of Chicago Press.
McDowell, Gavin. 2017. "The Sacred History in Late Antiquity: Pirqe de-Rabbi Eliezer and Its Relationship to the Book of Jubilees and the Cave of Treasures." Ph.D. diss., PSL Research University.
McKay, Heather A. 1994. *Sabbath and Synagogue: The Question of Sabbath Worship in Ancient Judaism*. Leiden: Brill.
McKenzie, Judith S., et al. 2013–. Manar al-Athar Photo-Archive. Oxford. http://www.manar-al-athar.ox.ac.uk.
McLure, Roger. 2005. *The Philosophy of Time: Time before Times*. London: Routledge.
Meacham, Tirzah Zechura. 1989. "Mishnah Tractate Niddah with Introduction: Editions with Notes on Variants, Commentary, Redaction and Chapters in Legal History and Realia." Ph.D. diss., Hebrew University of Jerusalem.
———. 1999a. "An Abbreviated History of the Development of the Jewish Menstrual Laws." In *Women and Water: Menstruation in Jewish Life and Law*, edited by Rahel R. Wasserfall, 23–39. Hanover, NH: Brandeis University Press.
———. 1999b. "Retroactive and Internal Impurity and the Varieties of Blood." In *Women and Water: Menstruation in Jewish Life and Law*, edited by Rahel R. Wasserfall, 256–61. Hanover, NH: Brandeis University Press.
———. 1999c. "The Elimination of *Niddah* in favor of *Ziva*." In *Women and Water: Menstruation in Jewish Life and Law*, edited by Rahel R. Wasserfall, 255–56. Hanover, NH: Brandeis University Press.
Meerson, Michael, and Peter Schäfer. 2014. *Toledot Yeshu: The Life Story of Jesus*. Tübingen: Mohr Siebeck.
Meier, John Paul. 2004. "The Historical Jesus and the Plucking of the Grain on the Sabbath." *Catholic Biblical Quarterly* 66:561–81.
Meir, Ofra. 1994. "The Historical Contribution of the Jewish Sage Aggadot in Light of the Rabbi-Antoninus Tales." *Mahanaim* 7:8–25. [Hebrew]

Meir, Ofra. 1999. *Rabbi Judah the Patriarch: Palestinian and Babylonian Portraits of a Leader*. Tel Aviv: Hakibbutz Hameuchad. [Hebrew]

Meiselman, Moshe. 1978. *The Jewish Woman in Jewish Law*. New York: Ktav.

Mendelbaum, Bernard, ed. 1987. *Pesiqta de Rav Kahana According to an Oxford Manuscript*. 2 vols. 2nd ed. New York: Jewish Theological Seminary.

Mendelson, Alan. 1994. "'Did Philo Say the Shema?' and Other Reflections on E. P. Sanders' *Judaism: Practice and Believe*." *Studia Philonica Annual* 6.160–70.

Mendelssohn, Moses. (1783) 1980, 1995. "Remarks Concerning Michaelis' Response to Dohm (1783)." In *The Jew in the Modern World: A Documentary History*, 2nd ed., edited by Paul Mendes-Flohr and Judah Reinharz, 48–49. New York: Oxford University Press.

Mendes-Flohr, Paul, and Judah Reinharz, eds. 1980, 1995. *The Jew in the Modern World: A Documentary History*. 2nd ed. New York: Oxford University Press.

Merchavia, Chenmelech. 1965. "The Talmud in the Additiones of Paul of Burgos." *Journal of Jewish Studies* 16:115–34.

Merleau-Ponty, Maurice. 2002. *Phenomenology of Perception*. New York: Routledge.

Meshorer, Ya'akov. 1985. *City-Coins of Eretz-Israel and the Decapolis in the Roman Period*. Jerusalem: Israel Museum.

Meslin, Michel. 1970. *La fête des kalendes de janvier dans l'empire romain*. Brussels: Latmos.

Meuti, Megan E., and David L. Denlinger. 2013. "Evolutionary Links between Circadian Clocks and Photoperiodic Diapause in Insects." *Integrative and Comparative Biology* 53:131–43.

Mézange, Christophe. 2006. "Josèphe et la fin des temps." In *Le Temps et les Temps dans les littératures juives et chrétiennes au tournant de notre ère*, edited by Christian Grappe and Jean-Claude Ingelaere, 209–30. Leiden: Brill.

Michael, J. Hugh. 1924. "The Jewish Sabbath in the Latin Classical Writers." *American Journal of Semitic Languages and Literatures* 40.2:117–24.

Michels, Agnes Kirsopp. 1967. *The Calendar of the Roman Republic*. Princeton: Princeton University Press.

Michels, Tony. 2012. *Jewish Radicals: A Documentary Reader*. New York: New York University Press.

Milgrom, Jacob. 1985. "*Seder Olam* and Jewish Chronography in the Hellenistic and Roman Periods." *Proceedings of the American Academy for Jewish Research* 52:115–39.

———. 1991. *Leviticus 1–16: A New Translation with Introduction and Commentary*. Vol. 3. New York: Doubleday.

Milikowsky, Chaim. 2002. "On the Formation and Transmission of Bereshit Rabba and the Yerushalmi: Questions of Redaction, Text-Criticism and Literary Relationships." *Jewish Quarterly Review* 92.3/4:521–67.

Miller, Kassandra Jackson. 2017. "A Doctor on the Clock: Hourly Timekeeping and Galen's Scientific Method." Ph.D. diss., University of Chicago.

———. 2018. "From Critical Days to Critical Hours: Galenic Refinements of Hippocratic Models." *TAPA* 148.1:111–38.

Miller, Kassandra J., and Sarah L. Symons. 2019. *Down to the Hour: Short Time in the Ancient Mediterranean and Near East*. Leiden: Brill.

Miller, Stuart S. 2015. *At the Intersection of Texts and Material Finds: Stepped Pools, Stone Vessels and Ritual Purity among the Jews of Roman Galilee*. Göttingen: Vandenhoeck & Ruprecht.

Miller, Yonatan S. 2019. "Sabbath-Temple-Eden: Purity Rituals at the Intersection of Sacred Time and Space." *Journal of Ancient Judaism* 9:46–74.

Minov, Sergey. 2013. "Syriac Christian Identity in Late Sasanian Mesopotamia: The *Cave of Treasures* in Context." Ph.D. diss., Hebrew University of Jerusalem.

———. 2017. "Date and Provenance of the Syriac *Cave of Treasures*: A Reappraisal." *Hygoye: Journal of Syriac Studies* 20.1:129–229.

Mirsky, Aaron. 1990. *The Piyyut: The Development of Post-Biblical Poetry in Eretz Israel and the Diaspora*. Jerusalem: Magnes Press. [Hebrew]

Mitchell, Stephen, and Peter van Nuffelen. 2010. *One God: Pagan Monotheism in the Roman Empire*. Cambridge: Cambridge University Press.

Moehring, Horst R. 1975. "The *Acta pro Judaeis* in the *Antiquities* of Flavius Josephus." In *Christianity, Judaism and Other Greco-Roman Cults*, edited by Jacob Neusner, 124–58. Leiden: Brill.

Momigliano, Arnaldo. 1966. "Time in Ancient Historiography." *History and Theory* 6:1–23.

———. 1990. *The Classical Foundations of Modern Historiography*. Berkeley: University of California Press.

Mommsen, Theodor. 1859. *Die römische Chronologie bis auf Caesar*. Berlin: Weidmann.

Montgomery, James Alan. 1907, 1968. *The Samaritans: The Earliest Jewish Sect*. New York: Ktav.

Moosa, Ebrahim. 1998. "Shaykh Aḥmad Shākir and the Adoption of a Scientifically-Based Lunar Calendar." *Islamic Law and Society* 5.1:57–89.

Morgenstern, Matthias. 2016. "The Image of Edom in *Midrash Bereshit Rabbah*." *Revue de l'histoire des religions* 233.2:193–222.

Moscovitz, Leib. 2006. "'Women Are (Not) Trustworthy': Towards the Resolution of a Talmudic Crux." In *Studies in Josephus and the Varieties of Ancient Judaism: Louis H. Feldman Jubilee Volume*, edited by Shaye J. D. Cohen and Joshua J. Schwartz, 127–40. Leiden: Brill.

Moyn, Samuel. 2003. "Emmanuel Levinas's Talmudic Readings: Between Tradition and Invention." *Prooftexts* 23.3:338–64.

Mroczek, Eva. 2016. *The Literary Imagination in Jewish Antiquity*. Oxford: Oxford University Press.

Muilenburg, James. 1961. "The Biblical View of Time." *Harvard Theological Review* 54:225–52.

Muir, Steven. 2011. "Religion on the Road in Ancient Greece and Rome." In *Travel and Religion in Antiquity*, edited by Philip A. Harland, 29–47. Waterloo: Wilfrid Laurier University Press.

Münz-Manor, Ophir. 2013. "The Ritualization of Creation in Jewish and Christian Liturgical Texts from Late Antiquity." In *Jewish and Christian Cosmogony in Late Antiquity*, edited by Sarit Kattan Gribetz and Lance Jenott, 271–86. Tübingen: Mohr Siebeck.

Murgatroyd, Paul. 1980. *Tibullus I: A Commentary on the First Book of the Elegies of Albius Tibullus*. Pietermaritzburg: University of Natal Press.

Myers, David N. 1992. "Remembering *Zakhor*: A Super-Commentary." *History and Memory* 4.2:129–46.

———. 2007. "Recalling Zakhor: A Quarter-Century's Perspective." *Jewish Quarterly Review* 97.4:487–90.

Nabhan, Gary Paul. 2014. *Cumin, Camels, and Caravans: A Spice Odyssey*. Berkeley: University of California Press.

Naeh, Shlomo, and Aharon Shemesh. 1995. "The Manna Story and the Time of Morning Prayer." *Tarbiz* 64.3:335–40. [Hebrew]

Naiweld, Ron. 2014. "There Is Only One Other: The Fabrication of Antoninus in a Multilayered Talmudic Dialogue." *Jewish Quarterly Review* 104.1:81–104.

Naiweld, Ron. 2016. "The Use of Rabbinic Traditions about Rome in the Babylonian Talmud." *Revue de l'histoire des religions* 233.2:272–85.
Najman, Hindy. 2014. *Losing the Temple and Recovering the Future*. Cambridge: Cambridge University Press.
Nandy, Ashis. 1995. "History's Forgotten Doubles." *History and Theory* 34.2:44–66.
Nanni, Giorodano. 2012. *The Colonization of Time: Ritual, Routine, and Resistance in the British Empire*. Manchester: Manchester University Press.
Nasrallah, Laura S. 2017. "Imposing Travelers: An Inscription from Galatia and the Journeys of the Earliest Christians." In *Journeys in the Roman East: Imagined and Real*, edited by Maren R. Niehoff, 273–98. Tübingen: Mohr Siebeck.
———. 2018. "Ezekiel's Vision in Late Antiquity: The Case of the Mosaic of Moni Latomou, Thessaloniki." In *The Mosaics of Thessaloniki Revisited*, edited by Antony Eastmond and Myrto Hadzaki, 76–89. Athens/Oxford: Kapon Editions/Oxbow Books.
———. 2019a. *Archaeology and the Letters of Paul*. Oxford: Oxford University Press.
———. 2019b. "The Worshipping Self, the Self in Light." In *Self, Self-Fashioning and Individuality in Late Antiquity*, edited by Maren R. Niehoff and Joshua Levinson. Tübingen: Mohr Siebeck.
Naveh, Joseph, and Shaul Shaked. 1987. *Amulets and Magic Bowls: Aramaic Incantations of Late Antiquity*. Jerusalem: Magnes Press.
Needham, Joseph, Ling Wang, and Derek J. De Solla Price. 1960, 1986. *Heavenly Clockwork: The Great Astronomical Clocks of Medieval China*. Cambridge: Cambridge University Press.
Neel, Jaclyn. 2014. *Legendary Rivals: Collegiality and Ambition in the Tales of Early Rome*. Leiden: Brill.
Neher, André. 1976. "The View of Time and History in Jewish Culture." In *Cultures and Time*, edited by Louis Gardet, 149–68. Paris: Unesco Press.
Neis, Rachel. 2013. *The Sense of Sight in Rabbinic Culture*. Cambridge: Cambridge University Press.
———. 2018. "Directing the Heart: Corporeal Language and the Anatomy of Ritual Space." In *Placing Ancient Texts*, edited by Mika Ahuvia and Alex Kocar, 131–66. Tübingen: Mohr Siebeck.
Nelson, W. David. 2006. *Mekhilta de-Rabbi Shimon bar Yohai*. Philadelphia: Jewish Publication Society.
Ner-David, Haviva. 2014. *Chanah's Voice: A Rabbi Wrestles with Gender, Commandment, and the Women's Rituals of Baking, Bathing, and Brightening*. Teaneck, NJ: Ben Yehuda Press.
Neugebauer, Otto E. 1975. *A History of Ancient Mathematical Astronomy*. Berlin: Springer.
———. 1983. *Astronomy and History: Selected Essays*. New York: Springer.
Neusner, Jacob. 1976. *Talmudic Judaism in Sasanian Babylonia: Essays and Studies*. Vol. 1. Leiden: Brill.
———. 1977. *A History of the Mishnaic Laws of Purities: Niddah*. Leiden: Brill.
———. 1980. "Dating a Mishnah-Tractate: The Case of Tamid." In *History, Religion, and Spiritual Democracy: Essays in Honor of Joseph L. Blau*, edited by M. Wohlgelernter, 97–112. New York: Columbia University Press.
———. 1982. *The Talmud of the Land of Israel: A Preliminary Translation and Explanation*. Vol. 33. Chicago: University of Chicago Press.
———. 1987. *Oral Tradition in Judaism: The Case of the Mishnah*. New York: Garland Publishing.
———. 1988, 2001. *The Incarnation of God: The Character of Divinity in Formative Judaism*. Binghamton: Global Publications, Binghamton University.

———. 1991. *The Mishnah: A New Translation*. New Haven: Yale University Press.
———. 1997. "Paradigmatic versus Historical Thinking: The Case of Rabbinic Judaism." *History and Theory* 36:353–77.
———. 2004a. *The Idea of History in Rabbinic Judaism*. Leiden: Brill.
———. 2004b. "Telling Time in Rabbinic Judaism: Correlating the Lunar-Solar Calendar with the Lectionary Cycle." *Miscelánea de Estudios Árabes y Hebraicos* 53:231–48.
———. 2008. *Persia and Rome in Classical Judaism*. Lanham, MD: Rowman and Littlefield.
Newman, Judith H. 2016. "Accessing Eternity: The Transformation of Time through Speech and Blessing." Paper delivered at the "It's About Time! Rethinking Temporality in Early Judaism" conference. University of Toronto.
———. 2018. *Before the Bible: The Liturgical Body and the Formation of Scriptures in Early Judaism*. Oxford: Oxford University Press.
Newsom, Carol A. 1985. *Songs of the Sabbath Sacrifice: A Critical Edition*. Atlanta: Scholars Press.
———. 2018. *The Self as Symbolic Space: Constructing Identity and Community at Qumran*. Leiden: Brill.
Niehoff, Maren. 2001. *Philo on Jewish Identity and Culture*. Tübingen: Mohr Siebeck.
———. 2006. "*Creatio ex Nihilo* Theology in *Genesis Rabbah* in Light of Christian Exegesis." *Harvard Theological Review* 99.1:37–64.
———. 2016. "Origen's *Commentary on Genesis* as a Key to *Genesis Rabbah*." In *Genesis Rabbah in Text and Context*, edited by Sarit Kattan Gribetz, David Grossberg, Martha Himmelfarb, and Peter Schäfer, 129–53. Tübingen: Mohr Siebeck.
———. 2018. *Philo of Alexandria: An Intellectual Biography*. New Haven: Yale University Press.
Noam, Vered. 2003. *Megillat Ta'anit: Versions, Interpretation, History*. Jerusalem: Yad Ben-Zvi Press. [Hebrew]
———. 2006. "Megillat Taanit: The Scroll of Fasting." In *The Literature of the Sages II*, edited by Shmuel Safrai, Zeev Safrai, Joshua Schwartz, and Peter J. Tomso, 339–62. Minneapolis: Fortress Press.
———. 2008. "The Dual Strategy of Rabbinic Purity Legislation." *JSJ* 39:471–512.
———. 2010. *From Qumran to the Rabbinic Revolution: Conceptions of Impurity*. Jerusalem: Yad Ben Zvi. [Hebrew]
———. 2015. "Essentialism, Freedom of Choice, and the Calendar: Contradictory Trends in Rabbinic Halakhah." *Dine Israel* 30:121–37.
Nock, Arthur Darby. 1952. "The Roman Army and the Roman Religious Year." *Harvard Theological Review* 45.4:187–252.
Nodet, Etienne. 1997. *A Search for the Origins of Judaism: From Joshua to the Mishnah*. Translated by Ed Crowley. Sheffield: Sheffield Academic Press.
Nothaft, Carl Philipp Emanuel. 2011. "From Sukkot to Saturnalia: The Attack on Christmas in Sixteenth-Century Chronological Scholarship." *Journal of the History of Ideas* 74.4:503–22.
———. 2014. *Medieval Latin Christian Texts on the Jewish Calendar: A Study with Five Editions and Translations*. Leiden: Brill.
Nothaft, Carl Philipp Emanuel, and Justine Isserles. 2014. "Calendars beyond Border: Exchange of Calendrical Knowledge between Jews and Christians in Medieval Europe (12th–15th Century)." *Medieval Encounters* 20:1–37.
Novak, David. 1986. "The Treatment of Islam and Muslims in the Legal Writings of Maimonides." In *Studies in Islamic and Judaic Traditions*, edited by William M. Brinner and Stephen D. Ricks, 233–50. Atlanta: Scholars Press. Reprinted in 2008. *Tradition*

in the Public Square: A David Novak Reader, edited by Randi L. Rashkover and Martin Kavka, 231–50. Grand Rapids, MI: Eerdmans.

Novick, Tzvi. 2010. *What Is Good, and What God Demands*. Leiden: Brill.

———. 2011. "Peddling Scents: Merchandise and Meaning in 2 Corinthians 2:14–17." *Journal of Biblical Literature* 130.3:543–49.

———. 2018. *Piyyut and Midrash: Form, Genre, and History*. Göttingen: Vandenhoeck & Ruprecht.

Noy, David. 1998. "The Sixth Hour Is the Mealtime for Scholars: Jewish Meals in the Roman World." In *Meals in a Social Context: Aspects of the Communal Meal in the Hellenistic and Roman World*, edited by Hanne Sigismund Nielson and Inge Nielson, 134–44. Aarhus: Aarhus University Press.

———. 2005. *Jewish Inscriptions of Western Europe*. Vol. 1: *Italy (excluding the City of Rome), Spain and Gaul*. Cambridge: Cambridge University Press.

Ogle, Vanessa. 2013. "Whose Time Is It? The Pluralization of Time and the Global Condition, 1870s–1940s." *American Historical Review* 118:1376–1402.

———. 2015. *The Global Transformation of Time: 1870–1950*. Cambridge, MA: Harvard University Press.

Olitzky, Kerry M. 1982. "The Sunday-Sabbath Movement in American Reform Judaism: Strategy or Evolution?" *American Jewish Archives* 34:75–88.

Olson, Kelly. 2017. *Masculinity and Dress in Roman Antiquity*. London: Routledge.

Olyan, Saul M. 2011. *Social Inequality in the World of the Text: The Significance of Ritual and Social Distinctions in the Hebrew Bible*. Göttingen: Vandenhoeck & Ruprecht.

Omer, Devora. 2012. *The Missing Spice, According to Rabbinic Narrative*. Illustrated by Yael Albert. Ben Shemen: Modan. [Hebrew]

Ophir, Adi, and Ishay Rosen-Zvi. 2018. *Goy: Israel's Multiple Others and the Birth of the Gentile*. Oxford: Oxford University Press.

Oppenheimer, Aharon. 1981. "The View of the Sages Regarding the Samaritans." A. B. *The Samaritans News* 274, 275:3–5, 4–8.

———. 1983. "The Messianism of Bar Kokhba." In *Messianism and Eschatology: A Collection of Essays*, edited by Z. Baras, 153–65. Jerusalem: Merkaz Shazar. [Hebrew]

———. 2011. "Removing the Decalogue from the 'Shema' and Phylacteries: The Historical Implications." In *The Decalogue in Jewish and Christian Tradition*, edited by Henning Graf Reventlow and Yair Hoffman, 97–105. New York: Continuum.

Origen. 2009. *Homilies on Numbers*. Translated by Thomas P. Scheck. Edited by Christopher A. Hall. Westmont, IL: InterVarsity Press.

Ortega, Mariana. 2016. *In-Between: Latina Feminist Phenomenology, Multiplicity, and the Self*. Albany: State University of New York Press.

Pagani, Catherine Mary. 2001. *Eastern Magnificence and European Ingenuity: Clocks of Late Imperial China*. Ann Arbor: University of Michigan Press.

Pagels, Elaine. 1991. "The 'Mystery of Marriage' in the *Gospel of Philip* Revisited." In *The Future of Early Christianity*, edited by Birger A. Pearson, 442–54. Minneapolis: Fortress Press.

Parker, Grant. 2002. "*Ex Oriente Luxuria*: Indian Commodities and Roman Experience." *Journal of the Economic and Social History of the Orient* 45.1:40–95.

Parker, Holt N., trans. 2007. *Censorinus: The Birthday Book*. Chicago: University of Chicago Press.

Parker, Robert. 1996. *Miasma: Pollution and Purification in Early Greek Religion*. Oxford: Oxford University Press.

Pasco-Pranger, Molly. 2006. *Founding the Year: Ovid's* Fasti *and the Poetics of the Roman Calendar*. Leiden: Brill.

Peckham, Brian. 1999. "History and Time." In *Ki Baruch Hu: B. A. Levine Jubilee Volume*, edited by Robert Chazan, W. W. Hallo, and Lawrence H. Schiffman, 295–314. Winona Lake, IN: Eisenbrauns.

Pedaya, Haviva. 2015. "Circular Time and Linear Time: The Big Mother and the Small Mother, the *Shekhina*: Between Nahmonidean Circles and Zoharic Circles." In *Fields in the Wind: A Tribute to Avraham Shapira*, edited by Aviyahu Zakkai, Paul Mandel-Fleur, and Zeev Griss, 332–37. Jerusalem: Carmel. [Hebrew]

Penner, Jeremy. 2012. *Patterns of Daily Prayer in Second Temple Period Judaism*. Leiden: Brill.

———. 2014. "Nocturnal Worship in the Dead Sea Scrolls." *Studia Liturgica*. https://www.academia.edu/4917243/Nocturnal_Worship_in_the_Dead_Sea_Scrolls.

Penslar, Derek J. 2013. *Jews and the Military: A History*. Princeton: Princeton University Press.

Pentcheva, Bissera V. 2011. "Hagia Sophia and Multisensory Aesthetics." *Gesta* 50.2:93–111.

Peppard, Michael. 2012a. "Archived Portraits of Jesus: Unorthodox Christological Images from John and Athanasius." In *Portraits of Jesus: Studies in Christology*, edited by Susan E. Myers, 1–16. Tübingen: Mohr Siebeck.

———. 2012b. *The Son of God in the Roman World: Divine Sonship in Its Social and Political Context*. Oxford: Oxford University Press.

Perkins, Carl M. 1994. "The Evening *Shema*: A Study in Rabbinic Consolation." *Judaism* 43.1:27–28.

Perovic, Sanja. 2012. *The Calendar in Revolutionary France: Perceptions of Time in Literature, Culture, Politics*. Cambridge: Cambridge University Press.

Pharr, Clyde. 1952. *The Theodosian Code and Novels, and the Sirmondian Constitutions: A Translation, with Commentary, Glossary, and Bibliography*. Princeton: Princeton University Press.

Philip, Tarja S. 2006. *Menstruation and Childbirth in the Bible: Fertility and Impurity*. New York: Peter Lang.

Phillips, Ian, ed. 2017. *The Routledge Handbook of Philosophy of Temporal Experience*. London: Routledge.

Pietersma, Albert, and Benjamin G. Wright, eds. 2007. *A New English Translation of the Septuagint*. Oxford: Oxford University Press.

Pietri, Charles. 1984. "Le Temps de la Semaine à Rome et dans L'Italie Chrétienne (IV–VIe S.)." In *Le temps Chrétien de la Fin de l'Antiquité au Moyen-Age (II–XIIIe s.)*, edited by Jean-Marie Leroux, 63–98. Paris: Editions du Centre national de la Recherché Scientifique.

Pine-Coffin, R. S., trans. 1961. *Augustine: Confessions*. London: Penguin Books.

Pines, Shlomo. 1967. "Judaeo-Christian Materials in an Arabic Jewish Treatise." *Proceedings of the American Academy for Jewish Research* 35:187–217.

Plutarch. 1914. *Life of Numa*. Translated by Bernadotte Perrin. Cambridge, MA: Harvard University Press.

Pollard, Elizabeth Ann. 2009. "Pliny's Natural History and the Flavian Templum Pacis: Roman Imperialism in First-Century C.E. Rome." *Journal of World History* 20.3:309–38.

Pollini, John. 2008. "A New Bronze Lar and the Role of the Lares in the Domestic and Civic Religion of the Romans." *Latomus* 67/2:391–98.

Pomeranz, Yoni. 2016a. "Ordinary Jews in the Babylonian Talmud: Rabbinic Representations and Historical Interpretation." Ph.D. diss., Yale University.

Pomeranz, Yoni. 2016b. "Did the Babylonian Sages Regard the Ammei-ha'Aretz as Subhuman?" *Hebrew Union College Annual* 87:115–43.

Prack, Norbert. 1996. *Der römische Kalendar (264–168 v. Chr.): Verlauf und Synchronisation*. Sinzheim: Pro Universitate Verlag.

Pratt, Kenneth J. 1965. "Rome as Eternal." *Journal of the History of Ideas* 26.1:25–44.

Price, Huw. 1996. *Time's Arrow and Archimedes' Point*. Oxford: Oxford University Press.

Price, Simon R. F. 1984. *Rituals and Power: The Roman Imperial Cult in Asia Minor*. Cambridge: Cambridge University Press.

Proust, Marcel. 1913–27, 2004. *In Search of Lost Time*. Translated by Lydia Davis. New York: Penguin.

Pulleyn, Simon. 1997. *Prayer in Greek Religion*. Oxford: Oxford University Press.

Pummer, Reinhard. 2009. *The Samaritans in Flavius Josephus*. Tübingen: Mohr Siebeck.

Pursley, Sara. 2019. *Familiar Futures: Time, Selfhood, and Sovereignty in Iraq*. Stanford: Stanford University Press.

Qu, Lu. 2014. *Concrete Time and Concrete Eternity: Karl Barth's Doctrine of Time and Eternity and Its Trinitarian Background*. Carlisle: Langham Monographs.

Quack, Joachim Freidrich. 2013. "Conceptions of Purity in Egyptian Religion." In *Purity and the Forming of Religious Traditions in the Ancient Mediterranean World and Ancient Judaism*, edited by Christian Fevel and Christophe Nihan, 115–58. Leiden: Brill.

Qimron, Elisha. 1996. *The Temple Scroll: A Critical Edition with Extensive Reconstructions*. Beer Sheva and Jerusalem: Ben Gurion University of the Negev Press and Israel Exploration Society.

Rabin, Chaim, trans. 1952. *Maimonides, Moses: The Guide of the Perplexed*. London: East and West Library.

Rabin, Shari. 2017. *Jews on the Frontier*. New York: New York University Press.

Rackman, Emanuel. 1958. "Arrogance or Humility in Prayer." *Tradition* 1.1:13–26.

Radice, Roberto. 2009. "Philo's Theology and Theory of Creation." In *The Cambridge Companion to Philo*, edited by Adam Kamesar, 124–45. Cambridge: Cambridge University Press.

Radke, Gerhard. 1990. *Fasti Romani: Betrachtungen zur Frühgeschichte des römischen Kalenders*. Münster: Aschendorff.

Radstone, Susannah. 2007. *The Sexual Politics of Time: Confession, Nostalgia, Memory*. New York: Routledge.

Ratzon, Eshbal. 2019. "Jewish Time: First Stages of Seasonal Hours in Judea." *Studies in History and Philosophy of Science* 75:23–33.

Ratzon, Eshbal, and Jonathan Ben-Dov. 2017. "A Newly Reconstructed Calendrical Scroll from Qumran in Cryptic Script." *Journal of Biblical Literature* 136.4:905–36.

Rawidowicz, Simon. 1974. *Studies in Jewish Thought*. Philadelphia: Jewish Publication Society of America.

Rawson, Beryl. 2005. *Children and Childhood in Roman Italy*. Oxford: Oxford University Press.

Reed, Annette Yoshiko. 2018. *Jewish-Christianity and the History of Judaism*. Tübingen: Mohr Siebeck.

Reeves, John C. 2005. *Trajectories in Near Eastern Apocalyptic: A Postrabbinic Jewish Apocalypse Reader*. Atlanta: Society of Biblical Literature.

Reif, Stephan. 1993. *Judaism and Hebrew Prayer: New Perspectives on Jewish Liturgical History*. Cambridge: Cambridge University Press.

———. 2006. *Problems with Prayers: Studies in the Textual History of Early Rabbinic Liturgy*. Berlin: de Gruyter.

Reines, Alvin Jay. 1987. "Two Concepts of Shabbat: The State of Being Shabbat and the Seventh Day Shabbat." *Journal of Reform Judaism* 34.3:13-28.
Reinhartz, Adele. 2014. "The Vanishing Jews of Antiquity." *Marginalia*. https://marginalia.lareviewofbooks.org/vanishing-jews-antiquity-adele-reinhartz/.
Remijsen, Sofie. 2007. "The Postal Service and the Hour as a Unit of Time in Antiquity." *Historia: Zeitschrift für Alte Geschichte* 56.2:127-40.
———. 2015. *The End of Greek Athletics in Late Antiquity*. Cambridge: Cambridge University Press.
Resnick, Irven M. 2006. *Petrus Alfonsi: Dialogue against the Jews*. Washington, DC: Catholic University of America Press.
Reynolds, Joyce Maire, and Robert F. Tannenbaum. 1987. *Jews and God-Fearers at Aphrodisias: Greek Inscriptions with Commentary*. Cambridge: Cambridge Philological Society.
Rhein, Valérie. 2016. "In den Fußstapfen des Priesters: Betrachtungen zu Gesetz und Gender in Tora und rabbinischer Literatur am Beispiel der Befreiung der Frau von zeitgebundenen Geboten." *Chilufim: Zeitschrift für Jüdische Kulturgeschichte* 21:5-74.
Richards, Edward Graham. 2000. *Mapping Time: The Calendar and Its History*. Oxford: Oxford University Press.
Ricœur, Paul. 1988. *Time and Narrative*. Vol. 3. Chicago: University of Chicago Press.
Rietz, Henry W. Morisada. 2006. "The Qumran Concept of Time." In *The Bible and the Dead Sea Scrolls*. Vol. 2, edited by James H. Charlesworth, 203-34. Waco: Baylor University Press.
Rifkin, Jeremy. 1987. *Time Wars: The Primary Conflict in Human History*. New York: Henry Hold.
Robbins, Ellen. 1997. "Time-telling in Ritual and Myth." *Journal of Jewish Thought and Philosophy* 6:71-88.
Robertson, Archibald. 1892. "Select Writings and Letters of Athanasius, Bishop of Alexandria." In *Nicene and Post-Nicene Fathers*, edited by Philip Schaff and Henry Wace. Buffalo: Christian Literature.
Robinson, Gnana. 1988. *The Origin and Development of the Old Testament Sabbath: A Comprehensive Exegetical Approach*. Frankfurt am Main: Peter Lang.
Rock-Singer, Aaron. 2016. "Prayer and the Islamic Revival: A Timely Challenge." *International Journal of Middle East Studies* 48.293-213.
———. 2018. *Practicing Islam in Egypt: Print Media and the Islamic Revival*. Cambridge: Cambridge University Press.
Roenneberg, Till. 2012. *Internal Time: Chronotypes, Social Jet Lag, and Why You're So Tired*. Cambridge, MA: Harvard University Press.
Rolfe, J. C., trans. 1927. *Suetonius: Vita Divi Augusti*. Oxford: Clarendon Press.
Rordorf, Willy. 1968. *Sunday: The History of the Day of Rest and Worship in the Earliest Centuries of the Christian Church*. Translated by A. A. K. Graham. Philadelphia: Westminster Press.
Rosen, David M., and Victoria P. Rosen. 2000. "New Myths and Meanings in Jewish New Moon Rituals." *Ethnology* 39.3:263-77.
Rosen, Ralph M., ed. 2004. *Time and Temporality in the Ancient World*. Philadelphia: University of Pennsylvania Museum of Archaeology and Anthropology.
Rosen-Zvi, Ishay. 2008. *The Rite that Was Not: Temple, Midrash, and Gender in Tractate Sotah*. Jerusalem: Magnes Press. [Hebrew]
———. 2010. "Male Adornments, Female Adornments: A New View on Women's Religious Standing in the Sages' *Mishnah*." *Reshit* 2:1-25. [Hebrew]
———. 2012. *The Mishnaic Sotah Ritual: Temple, Gender and Midrash*. Leiden: Brill.

Rosen-Zvi, Ishay. 2014. "*Huledet ha-goy be-siferut hazal.*" *Te'uda* 26:361–438.
———. 2015. "The Mishnaic Mental Revolution: A Reassessment." *Journal of Jewish Studies* 66.1:36–58.
———. 2016a. "What If We Got Rid of the Goy? Rereading Ancient Jewish Distinctions." *Journal for the Study of Judaism* 47:1–34.
———. 2016b. "Like a Priest Exposing His Own Wayward Mother: Jeremiah in Rabbinic Literature." In *Jeremiah's Scriptures: Production, Reception, Interaction, Transformation*, edited by Konrad Schmidt and Hindy Najman, 570–90. Leiden: Brill.
———. 2017a. "Rabbis and Romanization: A Review Essay." In *Jewish Cultural Encounters in the Ancient Mediterranean and Near Eastern World*, edited by Mladen Popović, Myles Schoonover, and Marijn Vandenberghe, 218–45. Leiden: Brill.
———. 2017b. "Pauline Traditions and the Rabbis: Three Case Studies." *Harvard Theological Review* 110.2:169–94.
Rosen-Zvi, Ishay, and Adi Ophir. 2011. "Goy: Towards a Genealogy." *Dine Israel* 28:69–122.
———. 2018. *Goy: Israel's Others and the Birth of the Gentile*. Oxford: Oxford University Press.
Rosenberg, Daniel, and Anthony Grafton. 2010. *Cartographies of Time: A History of the Timeline*. Princeton: Princeton Architectural Press.
Rosenberg, Michael. 2011. "'I Am Impure'/'I Am Forbidden': Purity and Prohibition as Distinct Formal Categories in the Laws of Niddah." Ph.D. diss., Jewish Theological Seminary of America.
———. 2014. "The Conflation of Purity and Prohibition: An Interpretation of Leviticus 18:19." *Harvard Theological Review* 107.4:447–69.
Rosenblum, Jordan. 2010. *Food and Identity in Early Rabbinic Judaism*. New York: Cambridge University Press.
Rosenthal, David. 1980. "Mishnah Avodah Zarah: A Critical Edition and Introduction." Ph.D. diss., Hebrew University of Jerusalem.
Rosenzweig, Franz. 2005. *The Star of Redemption*. Translated by Barbara E. Galli. Madison: University of Wisconsin Press.
Rouwhorst, Gerard. 2001a. "The Origins and Evolution of Early Christian Pentecost." *Studia Patristica* 35:309–22.
———. 2001b. "The Reception of the Jewish Sabbath in Early Christianity." In *Christian Feast and Festival: The Dynamics of Western Liturgy and Culture*, edited by P. Post et al. Leuven: Peeters.
Rovner, Jay. 1994. "Rhetorical Strategy and Dialectical Necessity in the Babylonian Talmud: The Case of Kiddushin 34a–35a." *Hebrew Union College Annual* 65:177–231.
Rowlandson, Jane. 1998. *Women and Society in Greek and Roman Egypt*. Cambridge: Cambridge University Press.
Ruane, Nicole J. 2007. "Bathing, Status and Gender in Priestly Ritual." In *A Question of Sex? Gender and Difference in the Hebrew Bible and Beyond*, edited by Deborah W. Rooke, 66–81. Sheffield: Sheffield Phoenix Press.
———. 2013. *Sacrifice and Gender in Biblical Law*. Cambridge: Cambridge University Press.
Rubenstein, Jeffrey L. 1996. "An Eschatological Drama: Bavli Avodah Zarah 2a–3b." *Association for Jewish Studies Review* 21.1:1–37.
———. 1997. "Mythic Time and the Festival Cycle." *Journal of Jewish Thought and Philosophy* 6:157–83.
———. 1999. *Talmudic Stories: Narrative Art, Composition, and Culture*. Baltimore: Johns Hopkins University Press.
———. 2002. *Rabbinic Stories*. New York: Paulist Press.

———. 2003. *The Culture of the Babylonian Talmud*. Baltimore: Johns Hopkins University Press.
Rubin, Nissan. 2008. *Time and Life Cycle in Talmud and Midrash: Socio-Anthropological Perspectives*. Brighton: Academic Studies Press.
Rubinstein, Rachel. 2010. *Members of the Tribe: Native America in the Jewish Imagination*. Detroit: Wayne State University Press.
Rudavsky, Tamar. 2000. *Time Matters: Time, Creation, and Cosmology in Medieval Jewish Philosophy*. Albany: State University of New York Press.
Ruoff, Kenneth J. 2010. *Imperial Japan at Its Zenith: The Wartime Celebration of the Empire's 2,600th Anniversary*. Ithaca, NY: Cornell University Press.
Rüpke, Jörg. 1995. *Kalender und Öffentlichkeit: Die Geschichte der Repräsentation und religiösen Qualifikation von Zeit in Rom*. Berlin: de Gruyter.
———. 2006. *Zeit und Fest: Eine Kulturgeschichte des Kalenders*. Munich: C. H. Beck.
———. 2007. *Religion of the Romans*. Translated by Richard Gordon. Malden, MA: Polity Press.
———. 2011. *The Roman Calendar from Numa to Constantine: Time, History, and the Fasti*. Translated by David M. B. Richardson. Malden, MA: Wiley-Blackwell.
Safrai, Chana. 1995. "Women and Processes of Change in the Temple in Jerusalem." In *A View into the Lives of Women in Jewish Societies*, edited by Yael Azmon, 63–76. Jerusalem: Zalman Shazar.
Safrai, Shmuel. 1965. "The Localities of the Sanctification of Lunar Months and the Intercalations of Years in Palestine after 70 CE." *Tarbiz* 35:27–38. [Hebrew]
———. 1995. "The Mitzva Obligation of Women in Tannaitic Thought." *Bar Ilan: Studies in Judaica and the Humanities* 26–27:227–36. [Hebrew]
Safrai, Zeev. 1984. "Fairs in the Land of Israel in the Mishnaic and Talmudic Period." *Zion* 49:139–58. [Hebrew]
———. 1989. "Dukhan, Aron and Teva: How Was the Ancient Synagogue Furnished?" In *Ancient Synagogues in Israel*, edited by Rachel Hachlili, 69–84. Oxford: Bar International Series.
Saiman, Chaim N. 2018. *Halakhah: The Rabbinic Idea of Law*. Princeton: Princeton University Press.
Salzman, Michele Renee. 1981. "New Evidence for the Dating of the Calendar at Santa Maria Maggiore in Rome." *Transactions of the American Philological Association* 111:215–27.
———. 1990. *On Roman Time: The Codex-Calendar of 354 and the Rhythms of Urban Life in Late Antiquity*. Berkeley: University of California Press.
———. 1999. "The Christianization of Sacred Time and Sacred Space." *Journal of Roman Archaeology*, Supplementary Series 33:124–27.
———. 2004. "Pagan and Christian Notions of the Week in the 4th Century CE Western Roman Empire." In *Time and Temporality in the Ancient World*, edited by Ralph Mark Rosen, 185–212. Philadelphia: University of Pennsylvania Museum of Archaeology and Anthropology.
Sanders, Ed P. 1985. *Jesus and Judaism*. London: SCM.
Sandmel, Samuel. 1962. "Parallelomania." *Journal of Biblical Literature* 81:1–13.
Sandwell, Isabella. 2007. *Religious Identity in Late Antiquity: Greeks, Jews and Christians in Antioch*. Cambridge: Cambridge University Press.
Saperstein, Marc. 1980. *Decoding the Rabbis: A Thirteenth-Century Commentary on the Aggadah*. Cambridge, MA: Harvard University Press.
Sarason, Richard S. 2000. "Communal Prayer at Qumran and among the Rabbis: Certainties

and Uncertainties." In *Liturgical Perspectives: Prayer and Poetry in Light of the Dead Sea Scrolls*, edited by Esther G. Chazon, 152–72. Leiden: Brill.

Sarna, Jonathan. 1996. "The Mythical Jewish Columbus and the History of America's Jews." In *Religion in the Age of Exploration: The Case of Spain and New Spain*, edited by Bryan F. Le Beau and Menachem Mor, 81–95. Omaha: Creighton University Press.

Satlow, Michael L. 2001. *Jewish Marriage in Antiquity*. Princeton: Princeton University Press.

———. 2013. "From Salve to Weapon: Torah Study, Masculinity, and the Babylonian Talmud." In *Religious Men and Masculine Identity in the Middle Ages*, edited by P. H. Cullum and Katherine J. Lewis, 16–27. Woodbridge: Boydell & Brewer Ltd.

Sattler, Barbara. 2019. "Cosmology and Ideal Society: The Division of the Day into Hours in Plato's *Laws*." In *Down to the Hour: Short Time in the Ancient Mediterranean and Near East*, edited by Kassandra Jackson Miller and Sarah Symons. Leiden: Brill.

Schäfer, Peter. 1975. *Rivalität zwischen Engeln und Menschen: Untersuchungen zur Rabbinischen Engelvorstellung*. Berlin: de Gruyter.

———. 1980. "Rabbi Aqiva and Bar Kokhba." In *Approaches to Ancient Judaism*. Vol. 2, edited by William Scott Green, 113–30. Chico: Scholars Press.

———. 1997. *Judeophobia: Attitudes toward the Jews in the Ancient World*. Cambridge, MA: Harvard University Press.

———. 2002. "Jews and Gentiles in Yerushalmi Avodah Zarah." In *The Talmud Yerushalmi and Graeco-Roman Culture III*, edited by Peter Schäfer, 336–52. Tübingen: Mohr Siebeck.

———, ed. 2003. *The Bar Kokhba War Reconsidered: New Perspectives on the Second Jewish Revolt against Rome*. Tübingen: Mohr Siebeck.

———. 2004. *Mirror of His Beauty: Feminine Images of God from the Bible to the Early Kabbalah*. Princeton: Princeton University Press.

———. 2007. *Jesus in the Talmud*. Princeton: Princeton University Press.

———. 2012. *The Jewish Jesus: How Judaism and Christianity Shaped Each Other*. Princeton: Princeton University Press.

———. 2016. "*Genesis Rabbah*'s Enoch." In *Genesis Rabbah in Text and Context*, edited by Sarit Kattan Gribetz, David Grossberg, Martha Himmelfarb, and Peter Schäfer, 63–80. Tübingen: Mohr Siebeck.

Schäfer, Peter, and Hans-Jürgen Becker, eds. 1991–2001. *Synopse zum Talmud Yerushalmi*. Tübingen: Mohr Siebeck.

Schäfer, Peter, Michael Meerson, and Yaacov Deutsch, eds. 2011. *Toledot Yeshu ("The Life Story of Jesus") Revisited: A Princeton Conference*. Tübingen: Mohr Siebeck.

Schäfer, Peter, in collaboration with Margarete Schlüter and Hans Georg von Mutius. 1981. *Synopse zur Hekhalot-Literatur*. Tübingen: Mohr Siebeck.

Schäfer, Peter, and Shaul Shaked. 1994. *Magische Texte aus der Kairoer Genizah*. Tübingen: Mohr Siebeck.

Schaldach, Karlheinz. 2009. "Ein Mosaik: Ein Auge und eine Sonnenuhr." *Gnomonica Italiana* 18:44–52.

———. 2016. "Measuring the Hours: Sundials, Water Clocks, and Portable Sundials." In *Time and Cosmos in Greco-Roman Antiquity*, edited by Alexander Jones, 63–94. Princeton: Princeton University Press.

Schalit, Abraham. 1970–71. "Die Denkschrift der Samaritaner an König Antiochus Epiphanes zu Beginn der großen Verfolgung der jüdischen Religion im Jahre 167 v. Chr. (*Josephus, AJ, XII, §§258-264*)." *Annual of the Swedish Theological Institute* 8:130–83.

Schechter, Shneur Zalman, ed. 1967, 1997. *Avot de-Rabbi Natan*. New York: Jewish Theological Seminary.

Schiffman, Lawrence H. 1975. *The Halakhah at Qumran*. Leiden: Brill.

———. 1985. "The Samaritans in Tannaitic Halakhah." *Jewish Quarterly Review* 75:323–50.

———. 1995. *Reclaiming the Dead Sea Scrolls: Their True Meaning for Judaism and Christianity*. New York: Doubleday.

———. 2006. "Messianism and Apocalypticism in Rabbinic Literature." In *The Cambridge History of Judaism IV*, edited by Steven T. Katz, 1053–72. Cambridge: Cambridge University Press.

———. 2012a. "From Observation to Calculation: The Development of the Rabbinic Lunar Calendar." In *Living the Lunar Calendar*, edited by Jonathan Ben-Dov, Wayne Horowitz, and John M. Steele, 231–44. Oxford: Oxbow Books.

———. 2012b. "The Samaritans in Amoraic Halakhah." In *Shoshannat Yaakov: Jewish and Iranian Studies in Honor of Yaakov Elman*, edited by Shai Secunda and Steven Fine, 371–89. Leiden: Brill.

Schlüter, Margarete. 2003a. "Kein 'früher' und 'später' in der Tora? Polemische Aspekte eines rabbinischen Prinzip." *Frankfurter Judaistiche Beiträge* 30:1–38.

———. 2003b. "'Es gibt kein früher und später in der Tora': Zur Verwendung eines tannaitischen Prinzips im Talmud Yerushalmi." In *Jewish Studies between the Disciplines: Papers in Honor of Peter Schäfer*, edited by Klaus Herrmann, Margarete Schlüter, and Giuseppe Veltri, 73–92. Leiden: Brill.

———. 2005. "The Creative Force of a Hermeneutic Rule: The Principle 'There Is No Earlier and Later in the Torah' in Midrashic and Talmudic Literature." In *Creation and Re-Creation in Jewish Thought: Festschrift in Honor of Joseph Dan*, edited by Rachel Elior and Peter Schäfer, 59–84. Tübingen: Mohr Siebeck.

Schmidt, Francis. 2006. "Le calendrier liturgique des Prières quotidiennes (4Q503)." In *Le Temps et les Temps dans les literatures juives et chrétiennes au tournant de notre ère*, edited by Christian Grappe and Jean-Claude Ingelaere, 37–87. Leiden: Brill.

Schmidt, Leigh Eric. 1997. *Consumer Rites: The Buying and Selling of American Holidays*. Princeton: Princeton University Press.

———. 2001. *Holy Fairs: Scotland and the Making of American Revivalism*. 2nd ed. Princeton: Princeton University Press.

Schneider, André. 1968. *Le premier livre Ad nationes de Tertullien: Introduction, texte, traduction et commentoire*. Rome: Institut Suisse.

Schofer, Jonathan Wyn. 2010. *Confronting Vulnerability: The Body and the Divine in Rabbinic Ethics*. Chicago: University of Chicago Press.

Scholem, Gershom. 1995. *Major Trends in Jewish Mysticism*. New York: Schocken.

Schonfield, Jeremy, ed. 2003a. *Companion Volume to Edited Manuscript from Thirteenth Century France in Facsimile*. London: Facsimile Editions.

———. 2003b. *The North French Hebrew Miscellany: British Library Add. MS 11639*. London: Facsimile Editions.

Schopen, Gregory. 2004. *Buddhist Monks and Business Matters: Still More Papers on Monastic Buddhism in India*. Honolulu: University of Hawaii Press.

Schremer, Adiel. 2008. "'The Lord Has Forsaken the Lord': Radical Explanations of the Military and Political Defeat of the Jews in Tannaitic Literature." *Journal of Jewish Studies* 59.2:183–200.

———. 2009. "The Christianization of the Roman Empire and Rabbinic Literature." In *Jewish Identities in Antiquity: Studies in Memory of Menahem Stern*, edited by Lee I. Levine and Daniel R. Schwartz, 349–66. Tübingen: Mohr Siebeck.

Schremer, Adiel. 2010. *Brothers Estranged: Heresy, Christianity, and Jewish Identity in Late Antiquity.* Oxford: Oxford University Press.

Schües, Christina. 2011. "Introduction: Toward a Feminist Phenomenology of Time." In *Time in Feminist Phenomenology*, edited by Christina Schües, Dorothea Olkowski, and Helen Fielding, 1–17. Bloomington: Indiana University Press.

Schües, Christina, Dorothea Olkowski, and Helen Fielding, eds. 2011. *Time in Feminist Phenomenology.* Bloomington: Indiana University Press.

Schumer, Nathan. 2017. "The Memory of the Temple in Palestinian Rabbinic Literature." Ph.D. diss., Columbia University.

Schwartz, Daniel R., and Zeev Weiss, eds. 2012. *Was 70 CE a Watershed in Jewish History? On Jews and Judaism before and after the Destruction of the Second Temple.* Leiden: Brill.

Schwartz, Seth. 1998. "Gamaliel in Aphrodite's Bath: Palestinian Judaism and Urban Culture in the Third and Fourth Centuries." In *The Talmud Yerushalmi and Graeco-Roman Culture III*, edited by Peter Schäfer, 203–17. Tübingen: Mohr Siebeck.

———. 2001. *Imperialism and Jewish Society, 200 B.C.E. to 640 C.E.* Princeton: Princeton University Press.

———. 2006. "Political, Social, and Economic Life in the Land of Israel, 66–c. 235." In *The Cambridge History of Judaism IV*, edited by Steven T. Katz, 23–52. Cambridge: Cambridge University Press.

———. 2010. "'Rabbinic Culture' and Roman Culture." In *Rabbinic Texts and the History of Late-Roman Palestine*, edited by Martin Goodman and Philippe Alexander, 283–99. Oxford: Oxford University Press.

———. 2011. "How Many Judaisms Were There? A Critique of Neusner and Smith on Definition and Mason and Boyarin on Categorization." *Journal of Ancient Judaism* 2.2:208–38.

———. 2013. "Was There a 'Common Judaism' after the Destruction?" In *Envisioning Judaism: Studies in Honor of Peter Schäfer on the Occasion of His Seventieth Birthday*, edited by Ra'anan S. Boustan, Klaus Herrmann, Reimund Leicht, Annette Yoshiko Reed, and Giuseppe Veltri, 1:3–21. Tübingen: Mohr Siebeck.

Schwarz, Eberhard. 1982. *Identität durch Abgrenzung: Abgrenzungsprozesse in Israel im 2. vorchristlichen Jahrhundert und ihre traditionsgeschichtlichen Voraussetzungen: Zugleich ein Beitrag zur Erforschung des Juiläenbuches.* Frankfurt: Peter Lang.

Schweitzer, Albert. 1914, 1964. *The Mystery of the Kingdom of God: The Secret of Jesus' Messiahship and Passion.* New York: Schocken Books.

Scott, James C. 1990. *Domination and the Arts of Resistance: Hidden Transcripts.* New Haven: Yale University Press.

Scott, James M. 2005. *On Earth as in Heaven: The Restoration of Sacred Time and Sacred Space in the Book of Jubilees.* Leiden: Brill.

Scott, Joan W. 1986. "Gender: A Useful Category of Historical Analysis." *American Historical Review* 91.5:1053–75.

Scott, Samuel Parsons. 1932, 1973. *The Civil Code.* Vol. 12. Cincinnati: Central Trust Co./ New York: AMS Press.

Scullard, H. H. 1935, 2014. *A History of the Roman World, 753–146 BC.* New York: Routledge.

———. 1981. *Festivals and Ceremonies of the Roman Republic.* Ithaca, NY: Cornell University Press.

Secunda, Shai. 2007. "'Dashtana—ki derekh nashim li': A Study of the Babylonian Rabbinic Laws of Menstruation in Relation to Corresponding Zoroastrian Texts." Ph.D. diss., Yeshiva University.

——. 2009. "Talmudic Text and Iranian Contexts: On the Development of Two Talmudic Narratives." *Association for Jewish Studies Review* 33:45–69.
——. 2020. *The Talmud's Red Fence: Menstrual Impurity and Difference in Babylonian Judaism and Its Sasanian Context*. Oxford: Oxford University Press.
Sedley, David. 2009. *Creationism and Its Critics in Antiquity*. Berkeley: University of California Press.
Segal, Alan F. 1977. *Two Powers in Heaven: Early Rabbinic Reports about Christianity and Gnosticism*. Leiden: Brill.
——. 1989. *Rebecca's Children: Judaism and Christianity in the Roman World*. Cambridge, MA: Harvard University Press.
——. 2003. "Paul's Jewish Presuppositions." In *The Cambridge Companion to St. Paul*, edited by James D. G. Dunn, 159–72. Cambridge: Cambridge University Press.
Seow, Choon-Leong. 2019. "Imaginations of Leviathan." Lectured delivered at Fordham University, April 15.
Septimus, Tzvi. 2009. "Trigger Words and Simultexts: The Experience of Reading the Bavli." In *Wisdom of Bat Sheva, in Memory of Beth Samuels*, edited by Barry S. Wimpfheimer, 163–85. Jersey City: Ktav.
Shah, Zulfiqar Ali. 2012. *Anthropomorphic Depictions of God: The Concept of God in Judaic, Christian and Islamic Traditions, Representing the Unrepresentable*. Herndon: International Institute of Islamic Thought.
Shaked, Shaul. 1998. "An Early Geniza Fragment in an Unknown Iranian Dialect." *Acta Iranica* 28:219–35.
——. 2010. "Time Designations and Other Recurrent Themes in Aramaic Incantation Bowls." In *Gazing on the Deep: Ancient Near Eastern and Other Studies in Honor of Tzvi Abusch*, edited by Jeffrey Stackert, Barbara Nevling Porter, and David P. Wright, 221–34. Bethesda, MD: Eisenbrauns.
Shapiro, Hava. 2008. *In My Entering Now*. Edited by Carole B. Balin and Wendy Zierler. Tel Aviv: Resling. [Hebrew]
Sharland, Suzanne. 2005. "Saturnalian Satire: Proto-Carnivalesque Reversals and Inversions in Horace, 'Satire' 2.7." *Acta Classica* 48:103–20.
Shaw, Matthew. 2011. *Time and the French Revolution: The Republican Calendar, 1789–Year XIV*. Suffolk: Boydell & Brewer Ltd.
Shemesh, Aharon. 2012. "*Piquah Nefesh* Supersedes the Sabbath: *Piquah Nefesh* and Other Matters That Supersede the Sabbath." *Tarbiz* 80.4:481–505. [Hebrew]
——. 2013. "Sabbath, Circumcision and Circumcision on Shabbat in Jubilees and the Dead Sea Scrolls." In *Rewriting and Interpreting the Hebrew Bible: The Biblical Patriarchs in the Light of the Dead Sea Scrolls*, edited by Devorah Dimant and Reinhard G. Kratz, 163–287. Berlin: de Gruyter.
Shinan, Avigdor, ed. 1984. *Midrash Shemot Rabbah, Chapters 1–14*. Jerusalem: Dvir.
Shinnar, Shulamit. 2019. "'The Best Doctors Go to Hell': Rabbinic Medical Culture in Late Antiquity (200–600 C.E.)." Ph.D. diss., Columbia University.
Shulman, Naomi. 2019. *The Missing Ingredient: A Jewish Folktale*. Illustrated by Barb Bastian. Newton, MA: Harold Grinspoon Foundation.
Shutt, R. J. H. 1985. "Letter of Aristeas." In *The Old Testament Pseudepigrapha*, edited by James H. Charles. Vol. 2. New York: Doubleday.
Shwartz, Howard. 2010. "Does God Have a Body?: The Problem of Metaphor and Literal Language in Biblical Interpretation." In *Bodies, Embodiment, and Theology of the Hebrew Bible*, edited by S. Tamar Kamionkowski and Wonil Kim, 201–37. New York: T&T Clark.

Shwartz, Joshua. 1987. "The Encaenia of the Church of the Holy Sepulchre, the Temple of Solomon and the Jews." *Theologishce Zeitschrift* 43:265–81.

Simonsohn, Uriel I. 2011. *A Common Justice: The Legal Allegiances of Christians and Jews under Early Islam.* Philadelphia: University of Pennsylvania Press.

Sissa, Giulia, and Marcel Detienne. 2000. *The Daily Life of the Greek Gods.* Translated by Janet Lloyd. Stanford: Stanford University Press.

Skeat, T. C. 1994. "The Beginning and the End of the Καίσαρας κράτησις Era in Egypt." *Chronique d'Egypte* 69.138:308–12.

Skemer, Don. 2010. "*Armis Gunfe*: Remembering Egyptian Days." *Traditio* 65:75–106.

Smith, Bonnie G. 2016. "Temporality." In *The Oxford Handbook of Feminist Theory*, edited by Lisa Disch and Mary Hawkesworth, 973–90. Oxford: Oxford University Press.

Smith, Dennis Edwin. 2004. *From Symposium to Eucharist: The Banquet in the Early Christian World.* Minneapolis: Fortress Press.

Smith, Jonathan Z. 1985. "What a Difference a Difference Makes." In *"To See Ourselves as Others See Us": Christians, Jews, "Others" in Late Antiquity*, edited by Jacob Neusner and Ernest S. Frerichs, 3–48. Chico, CA: Scholars Press.

———. 1987. *To Take Place: Toward Theory in Ritual.* Chicago: University of Chicago Press.

Smith, Mark M. 1997. *Mastered by the Clock: Time, Slavery and Freedom in the American South.* Chapel Hill: University of North Carolina Press.

Smith, Morton, trans. 1943–47, 2009. *Hekhalot Rabbati.* Corrections by Gershom Scholem, edited by Don Karr. http://www.digital-brilliance.com/kab/karr/HekRab/HekRab.pdf.

Snyder, Walter F. 1940. "Public Anniversaries in the Roman Empire: The Epigraphical Evidence for Their Observance during the First Three Centuries." *Yale Classical Studies* 7:223–317.

Sokoloff, Michael. 2002. *A Dictionary of Jewish Palestinian Aramaic.* 2nd ed. Ramat Gan: Bar Ilan University Press; Baltimore: Johns Hopkins University Press.

Sorabji, Richard. 1984. *Time, Creation and the Continuum.* London: Bloomsbury.

———. 2006. *Self: Ancient and Modern Insights about Individuality, Life, and Death.* Chicago: University of Chicago Press.

Sorek, Susan. 2010. *The Emperors' Needles: Egyptian Obelisks and Rome.* Exeter: Bristol Phoenix Press.

Sperber, Daniel. 1965. "Dancing on the Sabbath." *Sinai* 57:122–26.

———. 1984. *Dictionary of Greek and Latin Legal Terms in Rabbinic Literature.* Ramat Gan: Bar Ilan University Press.

Sperber, David. 2011. "The Abject: The Menstruant, Impurity and Purity in Feminist-Jewish Art." *History and Theory (Bezalel Journal)* 22:193–225. [Hebrew]

———. 2019. "The Liberation of G-D: Helène Aylon's Jewish Feminist Art." *Images* 12.1:122–33.

Spigel, Chad S. 2012. *Ancient Synagogue Seating Capacities: Methodology, Analysis and Limits.* Tübingen: Mohr Siebeck.

Staccioli, Romolo Augusto. 2003. *The Roads of the Romans.* Los Angeles: Getty.

Steele, Robert. 1919. "Dies Aegyptiaci." *Proceedings of the Royal Society of Medicine* 12:108–21.

Steensgaard, P. 1993. "Time in Judaism." In *Religion and Time*, edited by Aninditia Niyogi Balslev and J. N. Mohanty, 63–108. Leiden: Brill.

Stegemann, Hartmut, and Jürgen Becker. 1961. "Zum Text von Fragment 5 aus Wadi Murabba'at." *RevQ* 3.11:443–48.

Stein, Elissa, and Susan Kim. 2006. *Flow: The Cultural Story of Menstruation.* New York: St. Martin's Press.

Steiner, R. C. 2007. "Muqdam U-Me'uhar and Muqaddam Wa-Mu'ahhar: On the History of Some Hebrew and Arabic Terms for Hysteron Proteron and Anastrophe." *JNES* 66:33–46.

Stemberger, Günter. 2000. *Jews and Christians in the Holy Land: Palestine in the Fourth Century*. Edinburgh: T&T Clark.

Stern, David. 1992. "Imitatio Hominis: Anthropomorphism and the Character(s) of God in Rabbinic Literature." *Prooftexts* 12.2:151–74.

———. 1994. *Parables in Midrash: Narrative and Exegesis in Rabbinic Literature*. Cambridge, MA: Harvard University Press.

———. 1996. *Midrash and Theory: Ancient Jewish Exegesis and Contemporary Literary Studies*. Evanston, IL: Northwestern University Press.

Stern, Henri. 1953. *Le calendrier de 354*. Paris: Institut français d'archéologie de Beyrouth, Bibliothèque archéologique et historique.

Stern, Menachem. 1974. *Greek and Latin Authors on Jews and Judaism*. 2 vols. Jerusalem: Israel Academy of Sciences and Humanities.

Stern, Sacha. 1996. "Fictitious Calendars: Early Rabbinic Notions of Time, Astronomy, and Reality." *Jewish Quarterly Review* 87.1–2:103–29.

———. 2001. *Calendar and Community: A History of the Jewish Calendar, Second Century BCE–Tenth Century CE*. Oxford: Oxford University Press.

———. 2002. "Jewish Calendar Reckoning in the Graeco-Roman Cities." In *Jews in the Hellenistic and Roman Cities*, edited by John R. Bartlett, 107–16. New York: Routledge.

———. 2003. *Time and Process in Ancient Judaism*. Oxford: Littman Library of Jewish Civilization.

———. 2012a. *Calendars in Antiquity: Empires, States, and Societies*. Oxford: Oxford University Press.

———. 2012b. "From Observation to Calculation: Context and Significance." In *Living the Lunar Calendar*, edited by Jonathan Ben-Dov, Wayne Horowitz, and John M. Steele, 211–30. Oxford: Oxbow Books.

———. 2017. "Subversion and Subculture: Jewish Time-Keeping in the Roman Empire." In *Jewish Cultural Encounters in the Ancient Mediterranean and Near Eastern Worlds*, edited by Mladen Popović, Mylse Schoonover, and Marjin Vandenberghe, 246–64. Leiden: Brill.

———. 2018. "The Twelve-Hour Division in First-Century CE Jewish Literature." Paper delivered at the Israel Institute for Advanced Study.

———. 2019. *The Jewish Calendar Controversy of 921/2 CE*. Leiden: Brill.

Stern, Sacha, and Charles Burnett, eds. 2014. *Time, Astronomy, and Calendars in the Jewish Tradition*. Leiden: Brill.

Stern, Tiffany. 2015. "'The Two Hours' Traffic of Our Stage': Time for Shakespeare." *Journal of the British Academy* 3:1–33.

Steudel, Annette. 1993. "*'Aharit hayyamim* in the Texts from Qumran." *Revue de Qumran* 16.2:225–46.

Stewart, David Tabb. 2008. "Does the Priestly Purity Code Domesticate Women?" In *Perspectives on Purity and Purification in the Bible*, edited by Naphtali S. Meshel, Jeffrey Stackert, and David P. Wright, 65–83. New York: Continuum.

Stökl Ben Ezra, Daniel. 2003. *The Impact of Yom Kippur on Early Christianity: The Day of Atonement in Second Temple Judaism to the Fifth Century*. Tübingen: Mohr Siebeck.

———. 2009. "An Ancient List of Christian Festivals in *Toledot Yeshu*: Polemics as Indication for Interaction." *Harvard Theological Review* 102.4:481–96.

Stolz, Daniel A. 2015. "Positioning the Watch Hand: 'Ulama' and the Practice of Mechanical

Timekeeping in Cairo, 1737–1874." *International Journal of Middle East Studies* 47:489–510.

Stolz, Daniel A. 2017. *The Observatory and the Lighthouse: Islam, Science, and Empire in Late Ottoman Egypt*. Cambridge: Cambridge University Press.

Stone, Alison. 2012. *Feminism, Psychoanalysis, and Maternal Subjectivity*. London: Routledge.

Stone, Michael Edward. 1990. *A Commentary on the Book of Fourth Ezra*. Minneapolis: Fortress Press.

Strack, Hermann L., and Günter Stemberger. 1992. *Introduction to the Talmud and Midrash*. Minneapolis: Fortress Press.

Strand, Kenneth A. 1965. "Some Notes on the Sabbath Fast in Early Christianity." *Andrews University Seminary Studies* 3.1:167–74.

Strassfeld, Max K. 2013. "Classically Queer: Eunuchs and Androgynes in Rabbinic Literature." Ph.D. diss., Stanford University Press.

Strathearn, Gaye. 2004. "The Valentinian Bridal Chamber." Ph.D. diss., Claremont Graduate University.

Stroumsa, Guy G. 2004. "Christ's Laughter: Docetic Origins Reconsidered." *Journal of Early Christian Studies* 12.3:267–88.

Stuckenbruck, Loren L. 2015. "Eschatologie und Zeit im 1 Henoch." In *Q in Context I: The Separation between the Just and the Unjust in Early Judaism and in the Sayings Source*, edited by Markus Tiwald, 43–60. Göttingen: Vandenhoeck & Ruprecht.

———. 2016. "Jesus and Eschatology: The Notion of God's Presence in the Second Temple Period." Paper delivered at the "It's About Time! Rethinking Temporality in Early Judaism" conference. University of Toronto.

Studelska, Jana. 2012. "The Last Days of Pregnancy: A Place of In-Between." *Mothering Blog*. http://www.mothering.com/community/a/the-last-days-of-pregnancy-a-place-of-in- between.

Sussman, Yaacov, ed. 2001. *Talmud Yerushalmi According to Ms. Or. 4720 (Scal. 3) of the Leiden University Library with Restorations and Corrections*. Jerusalem: Academy of the Hebrew Language.

Swartz, Michael. 1996. *Scholastic Magic: Ritual and Revelation in Ancient Judaism*. Princeton: Princeton University Press.

Symons, Sarah. 1998. "Egyptian Shadow Clocks and Sloping Sundials." *Bulletin of the British Sundial Society* 98.3:30–36.

———. 2002a. "The 'Transit Star Clock' from the Book of Nut." In *Under One Sky: Astronomy and Mathematics in the Ancient Near East*, edited by John Steele and Annette Imhausen, 429–46. Münster: Ugarit Verlag.

———. 2002b. "Egyptian Shadow Clocks." In *Proceedings of the XXth International Congress of History of Science Vol. XVI*, edited by M. Dorikens, 3–20. Turnhout: Brepols.

———. 2014. "Egyptian 'Star Clocks.'" In *Handbook of Archaeoastronomy and Ethnoastronomy*, edited by Clive L. N. Ruggles, 1495–1500. New York: Springer.

———. 2017. "A Survey of Astronomical Tables on Middle Kingdom Coffin Lids." In *Proceedings of the 11th International Congress of Egyptologists*, edited by M. Christina Guidotti and Gloria Rosati, 608–12. Oxford: Archaeopress.

Symons, Sarah, R. Cockcroft, J. Bettencourt, and C. Koykka. 2013. *Ancient Egyptian Astronomy* (online database). http://aea.physics.mcmaster.ca/ (ID WCO 3, 4, and 5).

Symons, Sarah, and Himanshi Khurana. 2016. "A Catalogue of Ancient Egyptian Sundials." *Journal for the History of Astronomy* 47.4:375–85.

Symons, Sarah, and Elizabeth Tasker. 2015. "Stars of the Dead." *Scientific American* 313.4:70–75.

Ta-Shma, Israel M. 1996. *Ritual, Custom and Reality in Franco-Germany, 1000–1350*. Jerusalem: Magnes Press. [Hebrew]

———. 2004. "Times of the Start and End of the Sabbath." In *Sabbath: Idea, History, Reality*, edited by Gerald Blidstein, 9–17. Beer Sheva: Ben Gurion University Press. [Hebrew]

Tabory, Joseph. 1995. *Festivals in the Time of the Mishnah and Talmud*. Jerusalem: Magnes Press.

———. 2006. "Prayers and Berakhot." In *The Literature of the Sages II*, edited by Shmuel Safrai, Zeev Safrai, Joshua Schwartz, and Peter J. Tomson, 281–326. Minneapolis: Fortress Press.

Taft, Robert F. 1986. *The Liturgy of the Hours in the East and West: The Origins of the Divine Office*. Collegeville: The Order of St. Benedict.

Taglicht, Israel. 1888. *Die Kuthäer als Beobachter des Gesetzes nach talmudischen Quellen*. Berlin: Feiertag.

Talbert, Richard J. A. 2017. *Roman Portable Sundials: The Empire in Your Hand*. Oxford: Oxford University Press.

———. 2019. "A Lost Sundial Found, and the Role of the Hour in Roman Daily Life." *Indo-European Linguistics and Classical Philology* 23:971–88.

Talgam, Rina. 2010. "The Zodiac and Helios in the Synagogue: Between Paganism and Christianity." In *"Follow the Wise": Studies in Jewish History and Culture in Honor of Lee I. Levine*, edited by Oded Irshai, Jodi Magness, Seth Schwartz, and Zeev Weiss, 63–80. New York: Jewish Theological Seminary. [Hebrew]

———. 2014. *Mosaics of Faith: Floors of Pagans, Jews, Samaritans, Christians, and Muslims in the Holy Land*. Jerusalem: Yad Ben-Zvi Institute; University Park: Pennsylvania State University Press.

Talmon, Shemaryahu. 1958. "The Calendar Reckoning of the Sect from the Judean Desert." *Scripta Hierosolymitana* 4:162–99.

———. 1960. "The 'Manual of Benedictions' of the Sect of the Judaean Desert." *RevQ* 2.4:475–500.

———. 1978. "The Presentation of Synchroneity and Simultaneity in Biblical Narrative." In *Studies in Hebrew Narrative Art throughout the Ages*, edited by Joseph Heinemann and Samuel Werses, 9–26. Jerusalem: Magnes Press.

———. 1994. "The Reckoning of the Day in the Biblical and Early Post-Biblical Periods: From the Morning or From the Evening?" In *Sara Kamin Memorial Volume*, edited by Sara Japhet, 109–29. Jerusalem: Magnes Press. [Hebrew]

———. 1999. "Anti-Lunar-Calendar Polemics in Covenanters' Writings." In *Das Ende der Tage und die Gegenwart des Heils: Begegnungen mit dem Neuen Testament und seiner Umwelt, Festschrift für Heinz-Wolfgang Kuhn zum 65 Geburtstag*, edited by Michael Becker and Wolfgang Fenske, 29–40. Leiden: Brill.

———. 2005. "The Polemics against the Lunar Calendar Year in the Writings of the Community of the Renewed Covenant of Qumran." *Meghillot* 3:69–84. [Hebrew]

———. 2006. "What's in a Calendar? Calendar Conformity and Calendar Controversy in Ancient Judaism: The Case of the 'Community of the Renewed Covenant.'" In *The Bible and the Dead Sea Scrolls*. Vol. 2, edited James H. Charlesworth, 25–58. Waco: Baylor University Press.

Tanakh: The Holy Scriptures, The New JPS Translation According to the Traditional Hebrew Text. 1985. Philadelphia: Jewish Publication Society.

Tannous, Jack. 2018. *The Making of the Medieval Middle East: Religion, Society, and Simple Believers*. Princeton: Princeton University Press.

Taqizadeh, S. H. 1940. "The Iranian Festivals Adopted by the Christians and Condemned by the Jews." *Bulletin of the School of Oriental and African Studies* 10.2:632–53.

Taqizadeh, S. H. 1952. "The Old Iranian Calendars Again." *Bulletin of the School of Oriental and African Studies* 14.3:603–5.

Taubes, Jacob. 2003. *The Political Theology of Paul*. Translated by Dana Hollander. Stanford: Stanford University Press.

Temkin, Sefton D. 1971. *The New World of Reform*. London: Leo Baeck College.

Terbuyken, Peri. 1996. "Rom in der rabbinischen Hermeneutik: Die Kompositionstechnik von *j'Abodah Zarah* 1,2 und *Cant. Rabbah* 1,35/42." *JEC* 39:116–27.

Thackeray, H. St. J., and Ralph Marcus, trans. 1930. *Josephus: Jewish Antiquities, Books 4–6*. Cambridge, MA: Harvard University Press.

Theodor, Julius, and Chanoch Albeck. 1912–36, 1965. *Midrash Bereshit Rabba: Critical Edition with Notes and Commentary*. 3 vols., 2nd printing. Jerusalem: Wahrmann Books.

Tong, M. 2019. " 'Given as a Sign': Circumcision and Bodily Discourse in Late Antique Judaism and Christianity." Ph.D. diss., Fordham University.

Townsend, Philippa. 2008. "Who Were the First Christians? Jews, Gentiles and the *Christianoi*." In *Heresy and Identity in Late Antiquity*, edited by Eduard Iricinschi and Holger M. Zellentin, 212–30. Tübingen: Mohr Siebeck.

Trible, Phyllis. 1973. "Eve and Adam: Genesis 2–3 Reread." *Andover Newton Quarterly* 13:251–58.

Tropper, Amram. 2004. "The Fate of Jewish Historiography after the Bible: A New Interpretation." *History and Theory* 43.2:179–97.

Trotter, Jonathan R. 2019. *The Jerusalem Temple in Diaspora Jewish Practice and Thought during the Second Temple Period*. Leiden: Brill.

Trummer, Regina. 1983. "Josephus Flavius und der Kaiserkult im Heiligen Land." In *Meqor Hayyim*, edited by Irmtraut Seybold, 387–408. Graz: Akademische Druck und Verlagsanstalt.

Tsafrir, Yoram. 1998. "The Fate of Pagan Cult Places in Palestine: The Archaeological Evidence with Emphasis on Beth Shean." In *Religious and Ethnic Communities in Later Roman Palestine*, edited by Hayim Lapin, 197–218. Bethesda, MD: University of Maryland Press.

Tsoffar, Ruth. 2006. *The Stains of Culture: An Ethno-reading of Karaite Jewish Women*. Detroit: Wayne State University Press.

Turner, Aimee. 2016. "The Importance of Numa Pompilius: A Reconsideration of Augustan Coins." *Open Library of Humanities* 2.1. http://doi.org/10.16995/olh.58.

Turner, Anthony J. 2007. *Catalogue of Sundials, Nocturnals and Related Instruments*. Florence: Giunti.

Tymieniecka, Anna-Teresa, ed. 2007. *Timing and Temporality in Islamic Philosophy and Phenomenology of Life*. Dordrecht: Springer.

Ulmer, Rivka. 2009. *Egyptian Cultural Icons in Midrash*. Berlin: de Gruyter.

Urbach, Ephraim E. 1959. "The Rabbinical Laws of Idolatry in the Second and Third Centuries in the Light of Archaeological and Historical Facts." *Israel Exploration Journal* 9.4:239–41.

———. 1987. *The Sages: Their Concepts and Beliefs*. Jerusalem: Magnes Press.

van der Horst, Pieter W. 2006. *Jews and Christians in Their Graeco-Roman Context*. Tübingen: Mohr Siebeck.

van Straten, F. T. 1981. "Gifts for the Gods." In *Faith, Hope and Worship: Aspects of Religious Mentality in the Ancient World*, edited by H. S. Versnel, 65–151. Leiden: Brill.

VanderKam, James C., ed. and trans. 1989. *The Book of Jubilees: A Critical Text*. Leuven: Peeters.

———. 1995. "Das chronologische Konzept des Jubiläenbuches." *ZAW* 107:80–100.

———. 1998. *Calendars in the Dead Sea Scrolls: Measuring Time*. London: Routledge.

———. 2013. "Made to Order: Creation in *Jubilees*." In *Jewish and Christian Cosmogony in Late Antiquity*, edited by Sarit Kattan Gribetz and Lance Jenott, 23–38. Tübingen: Mohr Siebeck.

Veltri, Guiseppe. 2000. "Romische Religion an Der Peripherie Des Reiches: Ein Kapitel Rabbinischer Rhetorik." In *The Talmud Yerushalmi and Graeco-Roman Culture II*, edited by Peter Schäfer and Catherine Heszer, 81–138. Tübingen: Mohr Siebeck.

———. 2015. *A Mirror of Rabbinic Hermeneutics: Studies in Religion, Magic, and Language Theory in Ancient Judaism*. Berlin: de Gruyter.

Ver Eecke, Marie. 2008. *La République et le roi: Le mythe de Romulus à la fin de la République romaine: De l'archéologie à l'histoire*. Paris: De Boccard.

Vetö, Ágnes. 2015. "Rabbinic Conceptualization of the Male Body as Reflected in the Halakhic System of Male Genital Emissions." Ph.D. diss., New York University.

Vidas, Moulie. 2014. *Tradition and the Formation of the Talmud*. Princeton: Princeton University Press.

Vilnay, Zev. 1973. *Legends of Jerusalem, The Sacred Land*. Philadelphia: Jewish Publication Society of America.

Visotzky, Burton L. 2003. *Golden Bells and Pomegranates: Studies in Midrash Leviticus Rabbah*. Tübingen: Mohr Siebeck.

von Dohm, Christian Wilhelm. 1781. "On the Civil Improvement of the Jews." In *The Jew in the Modern World: A Documentary History*, 2nd ed., edited by Paul Mendes-Flohr and Judah Reinharz, 28–36. New York: Oxford University Press, 1980, 1995.

von Freeden, Joachim. 1983. *ΟΙΚΙΑ ΚΥΡΡΗΣΤΟΥ: Studien zum sogenannten Turm der Winde in Athen*. Rome: Giorgio Bretschneider.

von Rad, Gerhard. 1968. *Theologie des Alten Testaments*. Vol. 2. Munich: C. Kaiser.

Vööbus, Arthur, ed. 1979. *The Didascalia Apostolorum in Syriac*. Leuven: Secrétariat du Corpus SCO.

Wacholder, Ben Zion. 1976. *Essays in Jewish Chronology and Chronography*. New York: Ktav.

Wajcman, Judy. 2015. *Pressed for Time: The Acceleration of Life in Digital Capitalism*. Chicago: University of Chicago Press.

Walfish, Avraham. 2001. "Literary Method of Redaction in Mishnah Based on Tractate Rosh Hashanah." Ph.D. diss., Hebrew University of Jerusalem. [Hebrew]

Wallace-Hadrill, Andrew. 1987. "Time for Augustus: Ovid, Augustus, and the *Fasti*." In *Homo Viator: Classical Essays for John Bramble*, edited by Michael Whitby, Philip R. Hardie, and Mary Whitby, 221–30. Bristol: Bristol Classical Press.

———. 1998. *Augustan Rome*. Bristol: Bristol Classical Press.

———. 2005. "*Mutatas Formas*: The Augustan Transformation of Roman Knowledge." In *The Cambridge Companion to the Age of Augustus*, edited by Karl Galinsky, 55–84. Cambridge: Cambridge University Press.

Wallach, Luitpold. 1940/41. "The Colloquy of Marcus Aurelius with the Patriarch Judah I." *Jewish Quarterly Review* 31:259–86.

Wasserman, Mira. 2004. *Too Much of a Good Thing*. Illustrated by Christine Mannone Corlan. Minneapolis: Kar-Ben Publishing.

———. 2017. *Jews, Gentiles, and Other Animals: The Talmud after the Humanities*. Philadelphia: University of Pennsylvania Press.

Waszinik, J. H., and J. C. M. Van Winden. 1987. *Tertullianus, De Idolatria: Critical Text, Translation and Commentary*. Leiden: Brill.

Watts, Edwards J. 2015. *The Final Pagan Generation*. Berkeley: University of California Press.

Watts, Edwards J. 2019. "The Senses, the Self, and the Christian Roman Imperial Subject: Hagia Sophia as a Space of Directed Interiority." In *Self, Self-Fashioning and Individuality in Late Antiquity*, edited by Maren R. Niehoff and Joshua Levinson. Tübingen: Mohr Siebeck.

Wegner, Judith Romney. 1992. *Chattel or Person?: The Status of Women in the Mishnah*. Oxford: Oxford University Press.

Weinfeld, Moshe. 1992. "Prayer and Liturgical Practice in the Qumran Sect." In *The Dead Sea Scrolls: Forty Years of Research*, edited by Devorah Dimant and Uriel Rappaport, 241–58. Leiden: Brill.

Weingarten, Susan. 2016. "The Rabbis and the Emperors: Artichokes and Cucumbers as Symbols of Status in Talmudic Literature." In *When West Met East: The Encounter of Greece and Rome with the Jews, Egyptians and Others: Studies Presented to Ranon Katzoff in Honor of His 75th Birthday*, edited by David M. Schaps, Uri Yiftach, and Daniela Dueck. Trieste: Edizioni Università di Trieste.

———. 2018. "Food in the Context of First-Century Galilee: The Mishnah and the so-called 'Jesus Diet.'" In *Food and Landscape: Proceedings of the Oxford Symposium on Food and Cookery*, edited by Mark McWilliams. London: Prospect Books.

Weinstock, Stephan. 1964. "Saturnalien und Neujahrsfest in den Märtyrerakten." In *Mullus: Festschrift Theodor Klauser*, edited by Alfred Stuiber, 391–406. Münster: Aschendorff.

Weiss, Daniel H. 2018. "The Christianization of Rome and the Edomization of Christianity: *Avodah Zarah* and Political Power." *Jewish Studies Quarterly* 25:394–422.

Weiss, Dov. 2016. *Pious Irreverence: Confronting God in Rabbinic Judaism*. Philadelphia: University of Pennsylvania Press.

Weiss, Haim, and Shira Stav. 2018. *The Return of the Missing Father: A New Reading of a Chain of Stories from the Babylonian Talmud*. Jerusalem: Bialik.

Weiss, Harold. 1994. "The Sabbath among the Samaritans." *Journal for the Study of Judaism* 25.2:252–73.

———. 2003. *A Day of Gladness: The Sabbath among Jews and Christians in Antiquity*. Columbia: University of South Carolina Press.

Weiss, I. H., ed. 1862. *Sifra: Commentar zu Leviticus*. Vienna: Schlossberg.

Weiss, Johannes. 1971. *Jesus' Proclamation of the Kingdom of God*. Minneapolis: Fortress Press.

Weiss, Zeev. 2014. *Public Spectacles in Roman and Late Antique Palestine*. Cambridge, MA: Harvard University Press.

Weiss-Goldman, Ruhama. 1999. "'I Want to Wrap You in Phylacteries': Women Performing Male Commandments." In *Blessed Is He Who Made Me a Woman? Women in Judaism from the Bible until Modern Times*, edited by David Yoel Ariel, Maya Leibovich, and Yoram Mazor, 105–20. Tel Aviv: Yediyot Ahronot. [Hebrew]

Weissler, Chava. 1999. *Voices of the Matriarchs: Listening to the Prayers of Early Modern Jewish Women*. Boston: Beacon Press.

Weitzman, Steven P. 2017. *The Origin of the Jews: The Quest for Roots in a Rootless Age*. Princeton: Princeton University Press.

Welborn, Larry L. 2015. *Paul's Summons to Messianic Life*. New York: Columbia University Press.

Welker, Michael. 1998. "God's Eternity, God's Temporality, and Trinitarian Theology." *Theology Today* 55.3:317–28.

Wenger, Beth S. 2012. *History Lessons: The Creation of American Jewish Heritage*. Princeton: Princeton University Press.

Werman, Cana. 2009. "Eschatology in the Dead Sea Scrolls." In *The Qumran Scrolls and*

Their World, edited by Menahem Kister, 529–49. Jerusalem: Yad ben Zvi, 2009. [Hebrew]

Whitney, William K. 2006. *Two Strange Beasts: Leviathan and Behemoth in Second Temple and Early Rabbinic Judaism*. Winona Lake, IN: Eisenbrauns.

Wiemer, H.-U. 1998. "Zwei Epigramme und eine Sonnenuhr im kaiserzeitlichen Sillyon." *Epigraphica Anatolic* 30:149–52.

Wilch, John R. 1969. *Time and Event: An Exegetical Study of the Ese of 'eth in the Old Testament in Comparison to Other Temporal Expressions in Clarification of the Concept of Time*. Leiden: Brill.

Wilfand, Yael. 2019. "'How Great Is Peace': Tannaitic Thinking on Shalom and the *Pax Romana*." *Journal for the Study of Judaism* 50:223–51.

Williams, Craig A. 1999. *Roman Homosexuality: Ideologies of Masculinity in Classical Antiquity*. Oxford: Oxford University Press.

Williams, Margaret H. 2004. "Being a Jew in Rome: Sabbath Fasting as an Expression of Romano-Jewish Identity." In *Negotiating Diaspora: Jewish Strategies in the Roman Empire*, edited by John M. G. Barclay, 8–18. London: T&T Clark.

———. 2013. *Jews in a Greco-Roman Environment*. Tübingen: Mohr Siebeck, 2013.

Wilson, Jan. 1994. *"Holiness" and "Purity" in Mesopotamia*. Kevelaer: Butzon & Bercker.

Winter, Eva. 2013. *Zeitzeichen: Zur Entwicklung und Verwendung antiker Zeitmesser*. 2 vols. Berlin: de Gruyter.

Wise, Michael O. 1997. "The Time and the Seasons: A Study of the Aramaic Chronograph 4Q559." *Journal for the Study of the Pseudepigrapha* 8.3:3–51.

Wiseman, T. P. 1995. *Remus: A Roman Myth*. Cambridge: Cambridge University Press.

Wishnitzer, Avner. 2015. *Reading Clocks, Alla Turca: Time and Society in the Late Ottoman Empire*. Chicago: University of Chicago Press.

Wolfson, Elliot R. 2003. "Zoharic Literature and Midrashic Temporality." In *Midrash Unbound: Transformations and Innovations*, edited by Michael Fishbane and Joanna Weinberg, 321–43. Oxford: Littman Library of Jewish Civilization.

———. 2006. *Alef, Mem, Tau: Kabbalistic Musings on Time, Truth, and Death*. Berkeley: University of California Press.

Wolkenhauer, Anja. 2011. *Sonne und Mond, Kalender und Uhr: Studien zur Darstellung und poetischen Reflexion der Zeitordnung in der römischen Literatur*. Berlin: de Gruyter.

———. 2018. "Dividio diei: The Hour in Latin Letters 100 BCE–500 CE." Paper presented at "The Day Unit in Antiquity and the Middle Ages" conference at the Israel Institute for Advanced Study, Jerusalem.

———. 2019. "Time, Punctuality, and Chronotopes: Concepts and Attitudes Concerning Short Time in Ancient Rome." In *Down to the Hour: Short Time in the Ancient Mediterranean and Near East*, edited by Kassandra J. Miller and Sarah L. Symons. Leiden: Brill.

Woolf, Greg. 1998. *Becoming Roman: The Origins of Provincial Civilization in Gaul*. Cambridge: Cambridge University Press.

Woolf, Virginia. 1928. *Orlando: A Biography*. New York: Houghton Mifflin.

Worp, Klaas. 1991. "Remarks on Weekdays in Late Antiquity Occurring in Documentary Sources." *Tyche* 6:221–30.

Wright, Benjamin G. 2008. *Praise Israel for Wisdom and Instruction: Essays on Ben Sira and Wisdom, the Letter of Aristeas and the Septuagint*. Leiden: Brill.

Wright, M. T. 2000. "Greek and Roman Portable Sundials: An Ancient Essay in Approximation." *Archive for History of Exact Sciences* 55:177–87.

Wurgaft, Lewis D. 1995. "Identity in World History: A Postmodern Perspective." *HT* 34:67–85.
Wyse, Jackie A. 2005. "Loving God as an Act of Obedience: The Shema in Context." In *Take This Word to Heart: The Shema in Torah and Gospel*, edited by P. B. Yoder, 11–51. Elkhart, IN: Institute of Mennonite Studies.
Yadin, Yigael. 1983. *The Temple Scroll*. Vol. 2. Jerusalem: Israel Exploration Society.
Yadin-Israel, Azzan. 2006. "Rabban Gamliel, Aphrodite's Bath, and the Question of Pagan Monotheism." *Jewish Quarterly Review* 96:149–79.
———. 2009. "Engaging Rabbinic Literature: Four Texts." In *Why Study Talmud in the Twenty-first Century? The Relevance of the Ancient Jewish Text to Our World*, edited by Paul Socken, 207–19. Lanham, MD: Rowman & Littlefield.
Yaffe, Martin D. 1979. "Liturgy and Ethics: Hermann Cohen and Franz Rosenzweig on the Day of Atonement." *Journal of Religious Ethics* 7.2:215–28.
Yahalom, Joseph. 1986. "Zodiac Signs in the Palestinian Piyyut." *Jerusalem Studies in Hebrew Literature* 9:313–22. [Hebrew]
Yahalom, Joseph, and Michael Sokoloff. 1999. *Shirat benei maarava: Shirim aramiyim shel yehudei erez yisrael betekufa habizantit*. Jerusalem: National Israel Academy of Science.
Yalon, Shevah. 1989. "'Women Are Exempted from All Positive Ordinances That Are Bound Up with a Stated Time': A Study in Tannaitic and Amoraic Sources." Ph.D. diss., Bar Ilan University.
Yerushalmi, Yosef Hayim. 1982, 2002. *Zakhor: Jewish History and Jewish Memory*. Seattle: University of Washington Press.
———. 2002. "'Servants of Kings, Not Servants of Servants': Some Aspects of the Jewish Political History." *Raisons Politiques* 7:19–52.
Yonge, C. D. 2006. *The Works of Philo Judaeus: The Contemporary of Josephus*. Vol. 3. Whitefish, MT: Kessinger Publishing.
York, Michael. 1986. *The Roman Festival Calendar of Numa Pompilius*. New York: Peter Lang.
Yoskovich, Avraham. 2014. "Time Markers in Tannaitic Literature: Cock Crow, Dawn, Sunrise, and the Eastern Light." Master's thesis, Hebrew University of Jerusalem.
Yuval, Israel. 2006. *Two Nations in Your Womb: Perceptions of Jews and Christians in Late Antiquity*. Berkeley: University of California Press.
———. 2008. "All Israel Have a Portion in the World to Come." In *First Century Jewish and Christian Identities: Essays in Honor of Ed Parish Sanders*, edited by Fabian E. Edoh et al., 114–38. Notre Dame, IN: University of Notre Dame Press.
———. 2010. "Christianity in the Talmud and Midrash: Parallelomania or Parallelophobia?" In *Transforming Relations: Essays on Jews and Christians throughout History in Honor of Michael A. Signer*, 50–74. Notre Dame, IN: University of Notre Dame Press.
———. 2011. "The Orality of Jewish Oral Law: From Pedagogy to Ideology." In *Judaism, Christianity, and Islam in the Course of History: Exchange and Conflicts*, edited by Lothar Gall and Dietmar Willoweit, 237–60. Munich: Oldenbourg Wissenchaftsverlag.
Zanker, Paul. 1990. *The Power of Images in the Age of Augustus*. Ann Arbor: University of Michigan Press.
Zeitlin, Froma I. 1995. *Playing the Other: Gender and Society in Classical Greek Literature*. Chicago: University of Chicago Press.
Zeitlin, Shlomo. 1959. "The Beginning of the Day in the Calendar of Jubilees." *Journal of Biblical Literature* 78:153–56.
Zellentin, Holger M. 2008. "The End of Jewish Egypt: Artapanus and the Second Exodus."

In *Antiquity in Antiquity: Jewish and Christian Pasts in the Greco-Roman World*, edited by Gregg Gardner and Kevin Osterloh, 27–73. Tübingen: Mohr Siebeck.

———. 2013. *The Qur'ān's Legal Culture: The* Didascalia Apostolorum *as a Point of Departure*. Tübingen: Mohr Siebeck.

———. 2015. "The Rabbis on (the Christianization of) the Imperial Cult: Mishnah and Yerushalmi Avodah Zarah 3:1 (42b, 54–42c, 61)." In *Jewish Art in Its Late Antique Context*, edited by Catherine Hezser, 319–55. Tübingen: Mohr Siebeck.

Zenos, A. C. 1890. "Socrates Scholasticus, *Church History.*" In *Nicene and Post-Nicene Fathers, Second Series*, edited by Philip Schaff and Henry Wace. Buffalo: Christian Literature.

Zerubavel, Eviatar. 1977. "The French Republican Calendar: A Case Study in the Sociology of Time." *American Sociological Review* 42:868–77.

———. 1979. *Patterns of Time in Hospital Life: A Sociological Perspective*. Chicago: University of Chicago Press.

———. 1981. *Hidden Rhythms: Schedules and Calendars in Social Life*. Berkeley: University of California Press.

———. 1985. *The Seven Day Circle: The History and Meaning of the Week*. New York: Free Press.

Zevit, Ziony, ed. 2017. *Subtle Citation, Allusion, and Translation in the Hebrew Bible*. Sheffield: Equinox.

Zierler, Wendy. 2008. "Hava Shapiro's Letters to Reuven Brainin." *Nashim: A Journal of Jewish Women's Studies and Gender Issues* 16.2:67–97.

———. 2012. "'My Own Special Corner, Sacred, Beloved': The Hebrew Diary of Hava Shapiro (1878–1943)." *Hebrew Studies* 53:231–55.

Zohar, Noam J. 1993. "Women, Men and Religious Status: Deciphering a Chapter in Mishnah." *Approaches to Ancient Judaism* 5:33–51.

Zondel ben Joseph, Enoch. 1875. *Midrash Tanhuma*. Warsaw: Visberg.

Zussman, Yaakov. 1969. "Babylonian *Sugiyot* to the Order *Zeraim* and *Taharot*." Ph.D. diss., Hebrew University of Jerusalem. [Hebrew]

INDEX

Abaye, 181, 214
Abraham, 113
Abudarham, David, 241
Adam, 27, 56, 59–67, 83–84, 89, 171, 196–204, 207, 272n145, 272n148, 273n174, 273n177, 310n26, 311n39
Aeneas, 55, 69–70, 77–79
Agatharchides of Cnidus, 99
Aha (R.), 211
Akiva (R.), 16, 108–9, 124–28, 176, 183, 284n107, 288n172, 288n174, 299n97
Alexander the Great, 262n108
Alphonsi, Petrus, 247
Alternate Side Parking Suspension Calendar, xi
ʿam ha-aretz, 159, 299n97, 300n98, 300n99
angels, 2, 10–11, 29, 68–71, 106, 115, 196–97, 201, 205, 212, 215–20, 274n195, 289n184, 309n8, 309n13, 310n27, 315n126
animals, 3, 6, 9, 39, 123, 127, 151–52, 198, 200, 202, 204–5, 209–10, 218–19, 249, 292n6, 296n60, 315n123, 315n126
Antoninus, 45, 70–71, 81, 83, 120–25, 129, 239, 286n139, 286n140, 286n142
Apamea Celaenea, 42
Aphrahat, 100, 129, 290n192, 294n35
Apion, 99
Apollo, 48
Apollonius, 283n89
Aretaeus of Cappadocia, 303n151
Aristobulus, 100, 280n43, 283n83, 311n53
Artapanus, 84, 277n255
Athanasius of Alexandria, 205–6
Augustine, 3, 54, 100, 123, 126–27, 189, 248, 278n5, 285n121, 288n162, 308n5, 309n7
Augustus, 19, 47–48, 51, 68, 77–80, 83–84, 87, 99, 122–23, 225, 276n232, 277n250, 316n154
Avesta/Avestan, 173
Avot de-Rabbi Natan, 16
Aylon, Hélène, 245

Ba (R.), 231–32
Banias, 47
Baraita de-Niddah, 243
Bar Kokhba revolt, 14, 16, 99
Behemoth, 210
birthdays, 42, 47–53, 81, 245, 269n64, 269n69
bishops, 22, 33, 49, 54, 93, 96, 121, 228, 264n131, 264n132, 271n113, 271n116, 281n52
Brevis Expositio in Vergilii Georgica, 121

Caesarea, 47, 49, 72, 79, 100, 102
calendars, 1, 4–13, 17–28, 31, 35–58, 62–68, 75, 77, 80–93, 95, 103, 105, 118, 135, 187, 228–35, 245–46, 250, 258n24, 260n45, 264n131, 264n132, 266n6, 267n25, 271n116, 273n159, 274n182, 316n154, 317n12
Campus Martius, 19–20, 126, 225, 280n45, 288n174, 313n93, 316n154
Candidus, 42
Capsali, Elijah, 241
Caracalla, 45, 225, 286n139
Cave of Treasures, 201–2
celibacy, 182–83
Censorinus, 50
Christmas, xi, 42
Chrysostom, John, 21, 54, 100–101, 123, 126–27, 264n130, 264n131, 281n57, 287n146, 289n177, 289n181
Cicero, 19, 188, 266n6, 280n40, 289n181
circumcision, 94, 108, 110, 112–13, 264n129, 281n48, 283n95, 307n205
Clement of Alexandria, 206
Cleopatra, 80, 276n232
clocks, 3, 12–13, 18–20, 139, 143, 181, 185, 227, 254, 261n71, 262n108, 263n114, 285n128
commerce, 40–43, 50, 269n72
Constantine, 54, 98, 101–4, 230, 270n101, 273n158, 282n62, 282n64
Constantius II, 205
Council of Nicaea, 264n132

[383]

Council of Trullo, 271n116
creation of the world, 59–61, 67, 70, 72, 105–6, 116–17, 123, 147, 188–90, 194–212, 223–24, 229, 240, 246, 249–50, 273n174, 282n62, 283n87, 285n132, 291n208, 294n39, 308n3, 310n22, 310n23, 310n26, 310n31, 311n39, 312n79, 313n84, 321n88

David, 10, 110, 284n106, 316n144
Day of Jupiter, 264n131
Dead Sea Scrolls, 9–10, 16, 24, 94, 109, 111, 118, 146–48, 172, 286n138, 293n34, 304n173, 309n8
Decalogue, 148, 283n80, 295n44
de la Fare, Monsieur, 236
de Lyre, Nicholas, 247–48
Deuteronomy Rabbah, 85, 210n26, 277n257, 297n71
Diaspora, 9, 52, 84, 277n248
Didascalia Apostolorum, 21, 94, 107, 114, 127–29, 182, 264n129, 294n35, 306n197, 307n217, 307n218
Dimi (R.), 80, 276n233
Dio Cassius, 47, 50, 99–100, 104, 269n62
Dionysius of Halicarnassus, 56
Dio of Prusa, 42
Disputation of Paris, 247
Douglass, Frederick, 278n270

Easter, 21–22, 46, 53, 257, 264n132, 282n60
Edom, 69, 75, 259n30, 273n166
Egypt, 7, 9, 19, 38, 42, 47–48, 61–63, 68–69, 78, 81–84, 89, 99, 102–5, 143, 147–48, 153, 194–95, 220, 225, 243, 262n108, 263n108, 268n46, 269n62, 271n115, 273n158, 274n189, 276n239, 291n2, 292n19, 317n162
Eleazar (R.), 184–85
Eleazar ben Azariah (R.), 108
Eleazar of Mainz, 240
Eliezer (R.), 16, 183, 315n123
Elijah, 20, 69, 74–75, 76, 89, 214, 316n140
Elisha, 74
emperor cult, 45–48, 53–54, 67
Ephesus, 48
Ephrem, 129
Epistle of Barnabas, 94, 107, 114–15
Erine, Lasia, 35

Esau, 7, 63–65, 82–83, 89, 259n30
Eucharist, 182, 307n218
Eusebius, 96, 100, 102–3, 264n132, 282n62
Eve, 60, 140–41, 171, 197–204, 207, 242, 311n52
Exodus Rabbah, 220–21, 288n165, 289n184

Feinstein, Moshe, 233–34, 317n16
Festus, Sextus Pompeius, 280n35
First Punic War, 19
food, 27–28, 39, 42, 51, 95, 110, 112, 119–124, 129–30, 134, 137, 160, 166, 170, 176, 184, 186, 201, 207, 209–10, 239, 286n138, 286n142, 286n143, 287n156, 290n196
forbidden fruit, 201–2
Fragment Targums, 206–7
French Revolution, 12

Gabriel (angel), 274n195
Galen, 225, 263n117
Garden of Eden, 60, 197, 200–202, 207
Gemellus, Lucius Bellenus, 42
Genesis Rabbah, 7, 64, 85–87, 99, 119–129, 134, 171, 195, 200, 204, 259n30, 260n64, 287n150, 287n151, 287n153, 288n172, 304n160, 310n23, 310n27, 320n26
Genousia, 45–46, 48, 81–85, 89, 268n41
Geonim, 231, 235
God, 23, 28, 67, 70, 72, 102–6, 116–19, 123, 135–36, 140, 144–49, 153–54, 179, 188–227, 242, 244, 247–249, 291n208, 293n30, 294n39, 294n41, 297n66, 308n3, 310n22, 310n23, 310n26, 312n76, 312n79, 312n80, 313n84, 313n92, 314n96, 321n88
Gospels, 16, 33, 94, 107–11, 260n54, 281n54, 284n105, 284n106, 286n138, 297n66
Gregorian calendar, 12, 230–31, 245
Gytheum, 48

Hadrian, 74, 288n166
Halevi, Isaac, 241
Hanukkah, 21, 66, 83, 87, 271n116, 273n177, 299n94, 318n17
Hayyot, 215–16, 219

Hekhalot literature, 215, 312n62, 313n94, 314nn110-12, 315n126
Helena, Queen of Adiabene, 181
Helios, 18, 60-61, 67, 192, 274n181, 282n62, 309n13
Herder, Johann Gottfried, 250
Herod, 47
Hesiod, 100
Hierapolis, 35
History of the Slave of Christ, 130
Holy Spirit, 182, 307n218
Homer, 100
Horace, 280n45
Horologium Augusti, 225
hours, 1-6, 9-13, 16-20, 25-26, 29, 54, 60-61, 75, 123, 149-53, 158, 160, 163-64, 180-209, 212-27, 229, 244-50, 260n57, 262n108, 263n109, 263n110, 263n117, 264n130, 265n152, 272n152, 287n149, 294n35, 295n51, 301n119, 307n211, 308n1, 309n13, 309n16, 310n25, 310n26, 311n39, 311n42, 311n47, 312n76, 313n81, 313n92, 313n93, 314nn95-98, 315n119, 315n120, 316n136, 317n157, 317n162, 321n87, 321n88
House of Hillel, 150-51, 162, 174, 182, 294n36, 295n51, 306n185
House of Shammai, 150-51, 162, 164, 174, 182, 295n51, 306n185
Huna (R.), 232

idolatry, 27, 32, 38-45, 49, 54-59, 65-77, 81-90, 103, 188, 231-34, 267n20, 268n45, 269n72, 274n190, 275n208, 283n89, 284n116, 317n12
impurity, 15, 23, 28-30, 33, 136-43, 160-82, 186, 230, 240, 243-46, 265n138, 300n103, 300n107, 301nn116-19, 301n122, 302n126, 302n132, 302n137, 302n139, 303n148, 303n151, 304n165, 304n170, 304n173, 305n178, 305n180, 306n189, 306n190, 306n194, 307n217, 319n52, 320n69
Isaac, 18, 64

Jacob, 7, 62-65, 83, 89, 106, 112, 259n30, 293n29
Januarius, 61-63, 68
Janus, 43, 46, 51, 55-56, 62, 89, 273n173

Jeroboam, 69, 72, 74, 76, 89, 275n208, 275n209
Jerusalem, xi-xii, 8-20, 30, 64, 72, 87-88, 124, 131, 154, 181, 212, 222, 275n217, 286n138, 290n196, 300n105, 315n119
Jesus, 16, 20-21, 33, 93-94, 97, 101-4, 107-13, 116-18, 122, 129, 134, 201-2, 230, 237, 247, 260n54, 264n131, 281n48, 281n53, 281n54, 282n62, 284n105, 284n106, 285n133, 286n138, 286n144, 287n146, 297n66, 309n8
Joseph, 84, 123
Joseph (R.), 79-80
Josephus, 16, 80, 99, 121, 148, 260n57, 263n117, 288n174, 293n25, 294n41; *Against Apion* and, 278n5, 280n41, 280n42, 283n83, 287n149, 289n177, 318n25; *Antiquities of the Jews* and, 12, 147, 154, 276n236, 280n37, 290n196; *Jewish Wars* and, 12; *Life* and, 286n138
Joshua, 15
Joshua ben Karha (R.), 85, 150, 152, 295n51, 304n163
Jubilees, 7, 9, 105-9, 113, 121, 283n83, 283n87, 286n138, 289n184, 309n8
Judah (R.), 43-44, 79, 81, 120, 155, 170, 239, 276n31, 286n139
judgment, 125-26, 130, 197-99, 202, 206-9, 212-13, 220, 285n127
Julia Domna, 225
Julian calendar, 19, 35, 47, 93, 230-31, 316n154
Julius Caesar, 13, 19, 47, 50, 87, 103, 225
Jupiter Capitolinus, 18, 47
Jupiter Poeninus, 51
Justinian Code, 101-2
Justin Martyr, 94, 100, 107, 112-13, 116, 128, 284n116, 285n132, 290n187
Juvenal, 99, 104, 278n4, 280n45
Juvenalia, 50

Kalends, 21, 27, 35, 42-48, 51-68, 82-85, 89, 234, 268n41, 268n49, 268n50, 270n73, 270n75, 272n145, 273n173, 273n177, 277n257, 277n263
Kohler, Kaufmann, 236-37
Kratesis, 27, 45-47, 55, 64, 68-85, 89, 268n41, 276n231

Lamentations Rabbah, 87, 316n144
Letter of Aristeas, 147–48, 154, 294n38
Levi (R.), 68–70, 77–78
Leviathan, 210–11, 247
Levinas, Emmanuel, 248–50
Leviticus Rabbah, 196–203, 206, 310n31, 311n50, 312n62
Libanius, 54, 268n32
light, 60–61, 66–67, 87, 100, 102, 139–40, 149–52, 168–71, 181, 210, 215–16, 245–46, 272n147, 273n177, 294n39, 299n94, 300n102, 303n154, 303n156, 304n158, 309n16, 310n23
Livy, 55–57, 70–72, 75, 77
Lord's Day, 20, 93–94, 101–4, 107, 116–17, 129, 134, 230, 264n131, 281n48, 281n53, 281n54, 282n62, 285n133, 287n146, 288n158
Lucian, 188
Lydos, John, 62

Maccabees, 80, 109, 262n108, 267n14, 267n20, 275n217, 276n236, 283n89, 284n100, 318n25
Macrobius, 45–47, 54–56, 75, 266, 272n146, 276n247, 280n45
Maimonides, 3, 233, 235–36, 243, 318n21, 319n49, 320n69
manna, 105, 119, 148, 286n138, 294n41
Marahal of Prague, 319n52
Marcus Aurelius, 45, 48, 286n139, 288n174
market days, 40–41, 230
marriage, 69–70, 107, 132, 153, 182, 185, 203–8, 220, 229, 246, 290n197, 306n189
Martí, Raymond, 247
Martial, 99, 122, 280n45, 313n93
Matrona, 203–7, 226, 311n50, 311n53, 316n133
medical literature, 168, 273n158, 303n151, 320n65
Meir (R.), 45, 151, 214
Mendelssohn, Moses, 236
menstruation, 2, 6, 18, 23, 28–30, 33, 49, 94–95, 100, 102, 107, 112, 115, 118, 121, 123–24, 127, 129, 134–43, 156, 160–77, 181–82, 186, 205, 220, 230, 240, 243–48, 264n131, 265n138, 285n133, 289n184, 300n103, 300n107, 301n114, 301n116, 301n117, 301n119, 301n122, 302n126, 302n132, 302n136, 302n137, 303n148, 303n151, 304n170, 304n173, 305n178, 305n180, 306n187, 306n189, 306n190, 306n194, 307n217, 309n7, 313n83, 315n128, 320n69
messiah, 16, 122, 237, 247, 261n83, 285n127
mezuzot, 145, 293n25
Michael (angel), 68–71, 274n195
military, 13, 17–19, 44–48, 56, 61–64, 68, 78, 80, 84, 89, 99, 102–3, 211, 225, 228, 235–36, 269n58, 269n71, 277n250, 283n89, 312n79, 317n157, 318n25
Mithras, 102
Moelin, Jacob (Maharil), 241–42
mosaics, 18, 72, 73, 111, 192–93, 236, 309n13, 309n16
Moses, 15, 84, 105, 113, 130, 148, 206–7, 236, 275n127, 294n41
Mount Gerizim, 131

Nahman bar Isaac (R.), 211
Nathan (R.), 109, 214
Nehuniah ben HaKanah (R.), 242
Nero, 50
New Years, 7, 43, 46, 54, 56, 61, 67, 199, 234, 259n27, 259n28, 310n30, 314n96, 318n19
night watches, 9, 30, 149, 151, 189, 217–24, 315n115, 315n119
North French Hebrew Miscellany, 232
Numa, 55, 62, 74–79, 275n216
nundinal cycle, 18, 41, 53, 92, 103–5, 230, 273n177, 278n3

omens, 7, 62–63, 82, 126
Oppenheim, David, 244
Origen, 49, 96, 115, 128, 132–33, 279n15, 279n20, 287n146, 291n206
"Oven of Akhnai," 214
Ovid, 19, 42–43, 55–56, 60, 77, 89, 266n6, 280n40, 282n73

Palatine Hill, 55
Parilia, 55
Passover, 11, 21–22, 35, 57, 81, 85, 90, 132, 152, 158, 183, 264n132, 296n60
Paul (Apostle), 16, 20–21, 33, 97–98, 206, 260n54, 261n77, 279n14, 294n35

Paul of Burgos, 247–48, 320n85
Pentecost, 11, 21–22, 35, 57, 85
Persius, 99, 280n45
Pesiqta de-Rav Kahana, 196–202, 221, 305n184
Peter the Venerable, 247
Petronius, 280n45
Pharaoh, 68–69, 81–82, 89, 274n189, 276n239
Pharisees, 110, 286n144
Philocalus, 53, 63, 104–5, 266n6, 273n158, 277n75, 317n8
Philo of Alexandria, 9–11, 84, 99–100, 146–48, 189, 195, 248, 260n51, 277n250, 277n255, 283n83, 293n34, 297n74, 308n3, 309n7, 311n53
phylacteries, 29, 145, 155, 159, 215, 222, 293n25, 295n44, 298n84, 299n94, 299n96, 316n138, 319n52
pilgrims, 9, 72, 131, 259n36, 299n94
Pirqe de-Rabbi Eliezer, 16, 196, 199–200, 202, 220, 311n38, 313n83, 313n84
piyyut, 202, 309n12, 310n32
Plato, 11, 311n54, 317n162
Pliny the Elder, 19–20, 126, 280n45, 288n174, 316n154
Pliny the Younger, 263n117, 313n93, 317n157
Plutarch, 56, 72, 74–75, 99, 266n6, 269n52, 272n147, 280n45
poetry, 50, 121, 191, 199, 207–9, 245, 312n71
prayer, 5, 9–10, 15, 23, 28, 30, 50, 102–3, 135–39, 143–60, 168–70, 179–82, 186, 197, 214–19, 226, 238–40, 248–49, 254, 257n2, 264n128, 291n3, 292n19, 292n21, 293n30, 293n34, 294n35, 294n41, 294n49, 295n51, 297n71, 297n74, 303n154, 304n160, 307n217, 313n92, 314n107, 321n88
pregnancy, 11, 64, 164, 174, 301n116, 306n189
Priestly Blessing, 148
priests, 9–10, 15, 55, 72, 109–10, 144, 148–54, 161, 166, 169, 181, 186–87, 223, 226, 254, 260–61, 283n87, 295n51, 302n136, 303n157, 307n213, 315n119
Pseudo-Ignatius, 121, 129, 281n52, 287n146

punctuality, ix–x, 3, 19, 158, 194, 196, 225, 257n3, 299n93
purity, 5, 9, 23, 28–29, 33, 132, 135–43, 160–66, 171–82, 186, 230, 240, 243–46, 258n13, 260n63, 291n2, 300n103, 300n105, 300n107, 301n116, 301n118, 301n122, 302n126, 302n132, 302n136, 302n137, 302n139, 303n148, 303n151, 304n170, 304n173, 305n178, 305n180, 306n189, 306n190, 307n217, 320n65, 320n69
Pyramid of Cestius, 74

Qumran, 9, 16, 107, 148, 216, 259nn39–42, 260n45, 284n101, 293n25, 299n96, 299n98, 304n173

Rabbeinu Gershom, 233
Rav, 52, 58–63, 65, 67
Rebecca, 64, 293n29
redemption, 11, 16, 90, 202, 208, 248, 309n20, 313n83, 321n88
Rehoboam, 72
Remus, 55, 69–74, 77, 275n211
Resh Lakish, 184, 249
Rhea Silvia, 55
ritual baths, 5, 139, 172, 178, 243, 245, 258n13, 300n105, 301n118, 320n65
Romans, 1–8, 13–105, 118–35, 188, 192, 194, 204, 225, 228–34, 240, 263n108, 264n131, 264n136, 266n3, 266n6, 266n161, 267n18, 268n41, 268n43, 268n45, 268n50, 269n58, 269n71, 269n72, 272n133, 272n139, 272n146, 273n177, 276n231, 276n232, 276n234, 276n247, 277n250, 277n255, 277n257, 277n263, 278n270, 278n9, 279n32, 280n35, 289n181, 303n151, 313n93, 316n154
Rome, 9, 12–13, 17–20, 27, 35–38, 46, 48, 53–90, 97, 153, 218, 259n30, 268n41, 271n116, 272n146, 273n157, 273n166, 274n184, 275n206, 276n231, 276n239, 276n247, 289n184, 316n154
Romulus, 55, 69–79
Rosenzweig, Franz, 248, 321nn86–90
Rosh Hashanah, 7, 11, 14, 21–22, 67, 132, 197–99, 202, 206, 260n64, 310n32, 310n35
Rutilius Namatianus, 99, 121

INDEX

Sabbath, 9–10, 21–23, 27–30, 92–135, 171, 181, 186, 188, 191, 195–202, 210, 221, 227–30, 235–40, 249–50, 253, 264n129, 264n132, 278n2, 278n4, 278n5, 278n9, 278n11, 279n12, 279n20, 280n34, 280n36, 280n40, 280n45, 281n47, 281n48, 281n50, 282n67, 282n79, 283n81, 283n83, 283n87, 283n89, 283n93, 284n96, 284n104, 284n113, 284n116, 285n121, 285n125, 285n127, 285n129, 285n133, 286n138, 286n143, 287n146, 287n147, 287n149, 287n152, 287n156, 288n160, 288n162, 288n166, 288n172, 288n174, 289nn181–85, 290n187, 290n191, 290n196, 291n207, 291n208, 299n94, 300n102, 303n156, 309n8, 310n23, 310n32, 310n35, 313n84, 318n21, 318n23, 318n25, 318n27, 318n34, 319n40, 319n44
Sabbatical years, 7, 106, 113, 154
sacrifices, 7–18, 39, 46–53, 62, 69, 74–75, 103, 113, 130–33, 149–52, 159, 161, 166, 181, 186, 215, 223–26, 237, 259n44, 260n63, 261n71, 283n89, 290n196, 291n208, 295n51, 295n53, 295n56, 296n58, 296n60, 299n94, 304n172
Sadducees, 109, 182
Samaritans, 130–33, 182, 266n172, 290n196, 291n208
Samuel, Aurelius, 35
Samuel, Isaac ben, 222
Samuel, Yitzhak ben, 319n55
Sasanian Empire, 8, 66–67, 91, 133, 194, 231, 240
Saturnalia, 36–37, 42–48, 53–54, 58–68, 75, 82–85, 89, 266n6, 268n41, 268n45, 268n49, 268n50, 272n146, 273n177, 276n247
Second Temple, 8–19, 24, 27, 69, 94, 105–20, 135–36, 144–48, 154, 165, 175, 185, 210, 226, 259n39, 259n49, 260n63, 261n72, 261n79, 293n25, 299n96, 300n103, 309n8
Seleucid Empire, 12, 79, 278n265
Seneca, 36–37, 43, 99–100, 127, 188, 263n117, 289n181
Sepphoris, 49, 191–92, *193*, 262n99
Septuagint, 11, 294nn37–39, 297n76, 310n22

serpent, 60
Seutonius, 280n45
seven-day week, 53, 92–93, 101–5, 134, 136, 189, 228, 278n5, 278n6, 282n73
Severus, 42, 45
Shavuot, 21–22, 90
Shekhinah, 244
Shema, 5, 15, 23, 28–29, 135–60, 166–71, 177–88, 214–23, 226, 230, 240, 242, 254, 261nn71–73, 292n21, 294n43, 295n44, 295n49, 295n51, 296n62, 297n66, 297n71, 297n72, 299n94, 299n97, 300n98, 300n99, 302n146, 303n154, 304n172
Sifre Deuteronomy, 150, 260n64, 272n138, 296n76
Sifre Zuta, 151, 155, 295n51, 297n76, 298n88
Simeon ben Gamliel (R.), 132, 149, 153–54, 172, 185, 203, 262n87, 297n70, 303n154, 304n172
Simon ben Menasiah (R.), 109
Sinai, 105, 206–7, 221, 236
slavery, 42, 46, 50, 65, 81, 102, 105, 128, 130, 135, 154–55, 157, 180, 187, 203–4, 220, 278n270, 299n90, 299n91, 307n205
sleep, 12, 138–40, 145–51, 158, 204, 216, 218, 221, 294n38, 296n62, 316n135
Sol Invictus, 18
Solomon, 68–70, 74, 76, 89, 260n63, 274n189, 274n195, 275n217
solstices, 60–67, 273n176, 273n177, 274n181, 274n182
Suetonius, 19, 123, 225, 280n45, 287n149
Sukkot, 9, 11, 14, 22, 90, 156, 272n139, 313n84
sundials, 18, 192, 194, 225, 227, 262n108, 263n109, 263n117, 309n14, 316n154
synagogues, 5, 18, 99, 101, 126, 181, 191–94, 197, 199, 227, 237–40, 246–47, 258n13, 307n217, 309n13, 314n107, 316n140
Synod of Laodicea, 264n132, 281n51, 281n52, 288n158
Syria, 48, 121, 129–30, 201, 273n158, 280n40

tabernacle, 9, 11, 260n63, 286n138
Tacitus, 99–100, 104
Targum Neofiti, 207, 312n63, 312n66

Targum Pseudo-Jonathan, 207, 312n66, 312n67

temple, Jewish, 7–24, 27–30, 38, 51, 64, 69, 81, 88, 94, 105–20, 135–37, 144–48, 151–54, 159–60, 165, 175, 181, 185–87, 191, 210–12, 215, 222–23, 226, 236–38, 247, 253, 259n35, 259n37, 259nn39–41, 259n44, 260n45, 260n51, 260n63, 260n64, 260n66, 261n69, 261nn71–73, 275n217, 282n79, 283n89, 285n125, 293n24, 293n25, 294n43, 295n53, 299n96, 300n103, 300n105, 307n208, 309n8, 315n119

Temple of Mars the Avenger, 77

Tenth Legion Frentesis, 18

Tenth of Adar, 232

Tertullian, 45, 49, 113, 268n45, 282n62

terumah offering, 15, 149, 151, 166, 181, 186, 223, 226, 261n71, 295n51, 304n172

Thanksgiving, 44–45, 49, 51, 87, 116, 146, 148–49, 234, 317n16, 318n17

Theodosian Code, 54, 101–3

Theodosius I, 45, 53–54, 103, 271n107, 282n67

Tiberias, 49, 191–92, 262n99

Tiberius, 123, 269n69

time-bound commandments, 28–30, 136–41, 156–59, 177, 179, 188, 222, 240–43, 297n72, 298n84, 299n91, 299n94, 319n50, 319n52

Tinneus Rufus, 124–28, 288n166, 288n172, 288n174

tithing, 7, 132, 159, 286n144

Trajan, 45, 87

Trebonianus Gallus, 72

Valentinians, 206

Verus, 45

Vidēvdād, 173

Virgil, 69–70, 77–78

Virgin Mary, 113

Vivo, Master, 247

von Dohm, Wilhelm, 235–36, 318n23

Woolf, Virginia, 3

World to Come, 59, 114–15, 117, 127, 210, 212, 242

Yahad, 259n44, 293n31

Yannai, 199, 202

Yehoshua ben Hananiah (R.), 121–22

yeshiva, 241

Yohanan ben Zakkai (R.) 14, 52, 59, 61–63, 68, 277n257

Yom Kippur, xi, 10, 21–22, 238, 299n94, 310n23, 321n88

Yose bar Judah, (R.), 184

Yose ben Halafta (R.), 64, 109, 158, 203–4, 206, 311n50, 316n140

Yose ben Rabbi Bun (R.), 169

zodiac, 18, 192, *193*, 221, 262n100, 272n152, 309n13, 316n136

Zoroaster, 67, 91, 173, 231, 305n180, 316n150

FIGURE CREDITS

1. Fasti Antiates Maiores (reconstruction). Museo Nazionale Romano, Rome, Italy. Mandadori Portfolio/Electa/Sergio Anelli/Bridgeman Images.
2. Fasti Praenestini. Fragment of 6–15 January. Degrassi 1963, 112.
3. Sestertius issued by Antoninus Pius. Personified Tiber River holding a reed in water. British Museum R.13490. © The Trustees of the British Museum.
4. Sestertius issued by Vespasian. She-wolf suckling twins alongside Tiber River. British Museum 1872,0709.477. © The Trustees of the British Museum.
5. Frikya floor mosaic. She-wolf suckling Remus and Romulus. Maarat an-Numan Museum. Sean Leatherbury/Manar al-Athar (http://www.manar-al-athar.ox.ac.uk).
6. Wall painting from Dura-Europos synagogue. Elijah on Mt. Carmel (Panel SC 4, colorized scan). Yale University Art Gallery/Dura-Europos Collection.
7. Coin with depiction of Augustus and Numa Pompilius, 16–15 BCE. British Museum R.3583. © The Trustees of the British Museum.
8. Wall painting fragment from Royal Room at Herodium. Nautical scene featuring ships in battle. The Israel Museum, Jerusalem/Meidad Suchowolski.
9. Codex Vaticanus Barberini latinus 2154. Saturday and Sunday in Philocalus's codex calendar. Public domain.
10. Hamat Tiberias synagogue mosaic. Helios. Photograph by author.
11. Sepphoris synagogue mosaic. Zodiac. Drawing by Pnina Arad, courtesy of Prof. Zeev Weiss. The Sepphoris Excavations/The Hebrew University of Jerusalem.

A NOTE ON THE TYPE

THIS BOOK has been composed in Miller, a Scotch Roman typeface designed by Matthew Carter and first released by Font Bureau in 1997. It resembles Monticello, the typeface developed for The Papers of Thomas Jefferson in the 1940s by C. H. Griffith and P. J. Conkwright and reinterpreted in digital form by Carter in 2003.

Pleasant Jefferson ("P. J.") Conkwright (1905–1986) was Typographer at Princeton University Press from 1939 to 1970. He was an acclaimed book designer and AIGA Medalist.

The ornament used throughout this book was designed by Pierre Simon Fournier (1712–1768) and was a favorite of Conkwright's, used in his design of the *Princeton University Library Chronicle*.

GPSR Authorized Representative: Easy Access System Europe - Mustamäe tee
50, 10621 Tallinn, Estonia, gpsr.requests@easproject.com